How to use your Connected Casebook

Step 1: Go to **www.CasebookConnect.com** and redeem your access code to get started.

Access Code: 

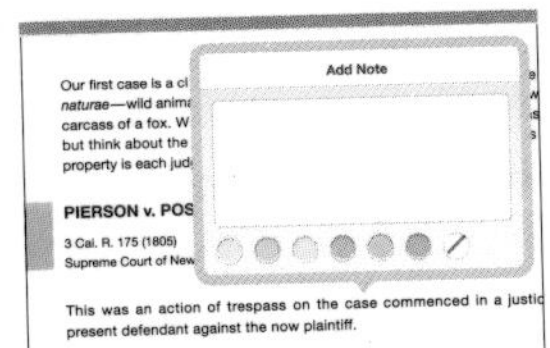

Step 2: Go to your **BOOKSHELF** and select your Connected Casebook to start reading, highlighting, and taking notes in the margins of your e-book.

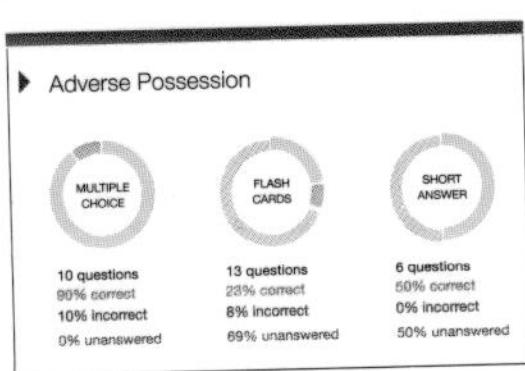

Step 3: Select the **STUDY** tab in your toolbar to access a variety of practice materials designed to help you master the course material. These materials may include explanations, videos, multiple-choice questions, flashcards, short answer, essays, and issue spotting.

Step 4: Select the **OUTLINE** tab in your toolbar to access chapter outlines that automatically incorporate your highlights and annotations from the e-book. Use the My Notes area for copying, pasting, and editing your book notes or creating new notes.

Step 5: If your professor has enrolled your class, you can select the **CLASS INSIGHTS** tab and compare your own study center results against the average of your classmates.

Is this a used casebook? Access code already scratched off?

You can purchase the Digital Version and still access all of the powerful tools listed above. Please visit CasebookConnect.com and select Catalog to learn more.

PIN: 9111149703

76872

WILLS, TRUSTS, AND ESTATES

THE ESSENTIALS

ASPEN CASEBOOK SERIES

WILLS, TRUSTS, AND ESTATES

THE ESSENTIALS

Reid Kress Weisbord
Vice Dean, Professor of Law, and Judge Norma L. Shapiro Scholar
Rutgers Law School

David Horton
Professor of Law
University of California, Davis School of Law

Stephen K. Urice
Professor of Law
University of Miami School of Law

Published by Wolters Kluwer in New York.

Wolters Kluwer Legal & Regulatory U.S. serves customers worldwide with CCH, Aspen Publishers, and Kluwer Law International products. (www.WKLegaledu.com)

To contact Customer Service, e-mail customer.service@wolterskluwer.com, call 1-800-234-1660, fax 1-800-901-9075, or mail correspondence to:

Wolters Kluwer
Attn: Order Department
PO Box 990
Frederick, MD 21705

Printed in the United States of America.

1 2 3 4 5 6 7 8 9 0

ISBN 978-1-4548-5609-2

Library of Congress Cataloging-in-Publication Data

Names: Weisbord, Reid Kress, author. | Horton, David (Law teacher), author. | Urice, Stephen K., 1950- author.
Title: Wills, trusts, and estates: the essentials / Reid Kress Weisbord, Vice Dean, Professor of Law, and Judge Norma L. Shapiro Scholar, Rutgers Law School; David Horton, Professor of Law, University of California, Davis School of Law; Stephen K. Urice, Professor of Law, University of Miami School of Law.
Description: New York: Wolters Kluwer, [2018] | Series: Aspen casebook series
Identifiers: LCCN 2017055869 | ISBN 9781454856092
Subjects: LCSH: Wills — United States. | Trusts and trustees — United States. | Estate planning — United States. | LCGFT: Casebooks.
Classification: LCC KF755.W45 2018 | DDC 346.7305 — dc23
LC record available at https://lccn.loc.gov/2017055869

About Wolters Kluwer Legal & Regulatory U.S.

Wolters Kluwer Legal & Regulatory U.S. delivers expert content and solutions in the areas of law, corporate compliance, health compliance, reimbursement, and legal education. Its practical solutions help customers successfully navigate the demands of a changing environment to drive their daily activities, enhance decision quality and inspire confident outcomes.

Serving customers worldwide, its legal and regulatory portfolio includes products under the Aspen Publishers, CCH Incorporated, Kluwer Law International, ftwilliam.com and MediRegs names. They are regarded as exceptional and trusted resources for general legal and practice-specific knowledge, compliance and risk management, dynamic workflow solutions, and expert commentary.

About Wolters Kluwer Legal & Regulatory U.S.

For my parents, Richard and Karen, who personify the law as a noble profession; for my sister, Rory, an accomplished and published author in her own right; and for Michael Alden, whose unwavering enthusiasm made this publication possible. RKW

For my dad, who taught me to love the law, and for my mom, who taught me to love to teach. DH

For Jesse Dukeminier, who recruited me to the teaching of law; for Bruce Mann, who first suggested I teach a course in wills, trusts, and estates; for David Abraham, Mary Coombs, and Mary Doyle, who helped make the University of Miami School of Law my academic home; and for Sam Small. SKU

Summary of Contents

Contents		xi
Preface		xix
A Note About the Diagrams		xxi
Acknowledgments		xxiii
1	Overview	1
2	Intestacy—Statutory Distribution	43
3	Wills: Protecting Testamentary Intent	77
4	Wills: Formalities	113
5	Wills: Components and Provisions	191
6	Will Drafting Principles and Default Rules	241
7	Family Status and Family Protection	307
8	Trust Formation and Elements	343
9	Trust Distributions and Modification; Implied Trusts	389
10	Nonprobate Transfers at Death and Will Substitutes	447
11	Fiduciary Duties	493
12	Federal Transfer Taxes: An Introduction	537
Table of Cases		617
Table of Authorities		621
Table of Authors		629
Index		631

Summary of Contents

Contents

PREFACE xix
A NOTE ABOUT THE DIAGRAMS xxi
ACKNOWLEDGMENTS xxiii

1 OVERVIEW 1

1.1 Introduction 1
1.2 Testamentary Freedom 2
1.2.1 State Law 3
Eyerman v. Mercantile Trust Co. 6
1.2.2 Constitutional Law 9
Hodel v. Irving 10
1.3 Sources of Law, Probate Courts, and Probate Administration 13
1.3.1 State Probate Courts 14
1.3.2 Probate 14
1.3.3 Probate and Nonprobate Property 16
1.4 Preliminary Topics on Death and Dying 18
1.4.1 Determination of Death 18
1.4.2 Incapacity and Planning for Death 20
1.4.3 Digital Assets 23
1.4.4 Disposition of Final Remains 25
Cohen v. Guardianship of Cohen 27
1.4.5 The Slayer Rule 30
Castro v. Ballesteros-Suarez 32
1.4.6 Disclaimers 36
In re Estate of Gardner 38
1.4.7 Professional Responsibility 40

2 INTESTACY—STATUTORY DISTRIBUTION 43

2.1 Intestate Estates—Introduction 43
Weisbord, Wills for Everyone: Helping Individuals Opt Out of Intestacy 44

2.2 **Who Gets (Takers) and How Much (Shares)?** 48
2.3 **Modes of Distribution: Representation** 55
2.3.1 English Per Stirpes 57
2.3.2 Modern Per Stirpes (UPC 1969) 58
2.3.3 Per Capita at Each Generation (UPC 1990) 59
Estate of Mebust *60*
2.4 **Half-Blood** 65
In re Estate of Thiemann *66*
2.5 **Adoption** 70
2.6 **Advancements** 75

3 WILLS: PROTECTING TESTAMENTARY INTENT 77

3.1 **Introduction** 77
3.2 **Protective Doctrines: Internal Factors** 79
3.2.1 Testamentary Intent 79
Estate of Hand *80*
3.2.2 Testamentary Capacity 82
Estate of Nalaschi *86*
3.2.3 Lucid Intervals 89
3.2.4 Insane Delusion 93
Estate of Zielinski *94*
3.3 **Protective Doctrines: External Factors** 97
3.3.1 Undue Influence 98
In re Estate of Kurrle *100*
3.3.2 Duress 104
In re Estate of Rosasco *105*
3.3.3 Fraud 110

4 WILLS: FORMALITIES 113

4.1 **Formalities — Introduction** 113
4.1.1 Attested Wills 115
In re Estate of Henneghan *116*
4.1.1.1 Witness Competency and "Purging" Statutes 122
4.1.1.2 Attestation Clauses and Self-Proving Affidavits 123
Estate of Griffith *126*
4.1.1.3 Safeguarding the Will 136
4.1.1.4 Acts of Independent Significance 136
4.1.2 Holographic Wills 138
In re Will of Morris *140*
4.1.3 Curative Doctrines 146
4.1.3.1 Substantial Compliance 146

4.1.3.2 Harmless Error 149
Estate of Ehrlich *150*
4.2 Will Amendment and Revocation 156
4.2.1 Codicils 157
4.2.2 Revocation by Subsequent Writing 160
4.2.3 Revocation by Physical Act 162
Estate of Gushwa *162*
4.2.3.1 Lost Wills 172
In re Estate of Conley *172*
4.2.3.2 Partial Revocation by Physical Act 176
In re Estate of Schumacher *177*
4.2.4 Revocation by Operation of Law 181
4.2.5 Dependent Relative Revocation (Doctrine of Ineffective Revocation) 183
4.3 Revival of Revoked Wills 186
Mellinkoff, Using the Language of the Law 187
4.4 Contracts Concerning Testamentary Succession 188

5 WILLS: COMPONENTS AND PROVISIONS 191

5.1 Introduction 191
5.2 Components of Wills 191
5.2.1 Integration: Staple Rule 191
5.2.2 Incorporation by Reference 192
Gifford v. Gifford *193*
5.2.3 Lists of Tangible Personal Property 196
In re Last Will and Testament and Trust Agreement of Moor *197*
5.3 Dispositive Provisions 201
5.3.1 Classification of Devises 201
Aldrich v. Basile *201*
5.3.2 Powers of Appointment: General and Special 205
5.3.2.1 Definitions 206
In re Estate of Muchemore *207*
5.3.2.2 Exercise of a Power of Appointment 211
Hargrove v. Rich *212*
5.4 Administrative Provisions 215
5.4.1 Appointment of Fiduciaries 215
In re Estate of Jones *216*
5.4.2 Personal Representative Powers 219
5.4.3 Bond 220
5.5 Other Provisions 220
5.5.1 In Terrorem or No Contest Clauses 220
In re Estate of Shumway *222*

5.5.2 Minor Children 226
In re R.M.S. *227*
5.5.3 "Just Debts" 232
In re Estate of Vincent *233*
5.6 Negative Wills: The Right to Exclude Intestate Heirs 236
Cook v. Estate of Seeman *237*

6 WILL DRAFTING PRINCIPLES AND DEFAULT RULES 241

6.1 Introduction 241
6.2 Failure to Survive — Lapse 242
Carpenter v. Miller *244*
6.3 Simultaneous Death 249
In re Leete Estate *252*
6.4 Antilapse 257
Lorenzo v. Medina *260*
In re Edwards *262*
6.5 Class Gifts 266
Waggoner, What's in the Third and Final Volume of the New Restatement of Property That Estate Planners Should Know About 266
6.6 Discrepancies Between Dispositive Provisions and the Probate Estate 267
6.6.1 Ademption by Extinction 269
In re Estate of Sagel *270*
6.6.2 Ademption by Satisfaction 275
Estate of Condon *276*
6.6.3 Abatement 279
6.6.4 Accession 281
Polson v. Craig *282*
6.7 Limitations of Language: Rules of Construction and Extrinsic Evidence 286
6.7.1 Common Law Rules of Construction 287
6.7.2 Ambiguities 288
6.7.2.1 Patent Ambiguities 289
6.7.2.2 Latent Ambiguities 290
6.7.2.3 Resolving Ambiguities: The Introduction of Extrinsic Evidence 291
University of Southern Indiana Foundation v. Baker *292*
6.7.3 Mistake 298
6.7.3.1 Reformation to Correct Mistakes 299
Estate of Herceg *300*
6.7.3.2 Probable Intent 304

7 FAMILY STATUS AND FAMILY PROTECTION 307

7.1 Introduction 307
7.2 Changes in Family Status 307
Lincoln Benefit Life Co. v. Guerrero *308*
7.3 Family Protection 315
7.3.1 The Elective Share 317
7.3.2 The 1969 UPC 317
7.3.3 The 1990 UPC 320
7.3.4 Community Property 324
Benavides v. Mathis *325*
7.3.5 Additional Protections 329
7.4 Protection Against Accidental Omission 330
7.4.1 Omitted Spouse 331
Bell v. Estate of Bell *332*
7.4.2 Omitted Children 337
Estate of Maher v. Iglikova *339*

8 TRUST FORMATION AND ELEMENTS 343

8.1 Trusts: Introduction 343
8.2 The Distinction Between Gifts and Trusts 345
Peterson v. Peck *348*
8.3 Elements of Private Trusts 352
8.3.1 Trust Settlor's Capacity and Intent 354
In re Estate of Mannara *357*
8.3.2 Trust Property 361
Cate-Schweyen v. Cate *362*
8.3.3 Deeds and Declarations of Trusts 369
8.3.4 Trust Beneficiaries 370
8.3.5 Trustees 372
In re Estate of Rauschenberg *373*
8.4 Types of Private Trusts 381
8.4.1 Inter Vivos and Testamentary Trusts 382
8.4.2 Revocable and Irrevocable Trusts 382
8.4.3 Perpetual Trusts 383
8.5 Charitable Trusts 384
8.5.1 Charitable Beneficiaries 384
8.5.2 Charitable Purposes 385
8.5.3 Duration and Modification of Charitable Trusts 386
8.5.4 Enforcement of Charitable Trusts 387

9 TRUST DISTRIBUTIONS AND MODIFICATION; IMPLIED TRUSTS 389

9.1 Distributions: Rights of Beneficiaries and Creditors in Private Trusts 389
9.1.1 Beneficiaries 389
In re JP Morgan Chase Bank, N.A. *392*
9.1.2 Creditors 403
9.1.2.1 Effect of Discretionary Standard 404
9.1.2.2 Effect of Support Standard 406
9.1.2.3 Spendthrift Trusts 406
Scheffel v. Krueger *410*
9.1.2.4 Self-Settled Asset Protection Trusts 416
In re Mortensen *418*
9.1.3 Special Needs Trusts for Disabled Beneficiaries 424
9.2 Modification and Termination of Private Trusts 427
Claflin v. Claflin *428*
9.3 Implied Trusts and "Non-Trusts" 435
9.3.1 Resulting Trusts 435
9.3.2 Constructive Trusts 439
9.3.3 Secret and Semi-Secret Trusts 442
9.3.4 Honorary Trusts 444

10 NONPROBATE TRANSFERS AT DEATH AND WILL SUBSTITUTES 447

10.1 Introduction 447
10.2 Will Substitutes 447
10.2.1 Revocable Trusts as Will Substitutes and Pour-Over Wills 450
10.3 Joint Tenancies 452
10.3.1 Joint Tenancies — Real Property 452
10.3.2 Joint Tenancies in Tangible Personal Property 454
Robinson v. Robinson *456*
10.3.3 Joint Tenancies — Intangible Personal Property: Multiple-Party Accounts 461
Robinson v. Delfino *462*
10.4 Payable-on-Death Accounts 470
Newman v. Thomas *470*
10.5 Pension Plans and Retirement Accounts 476
Emmert v. Prade *480*
10.6 Life Insurance 485
Richmond, Drugs, Sex, and Accidental Death Insurance 486
10.7 "Superwills" 491

11 FIDUCIARY DUTIES 493

11.1 Introduction 493
11.2 Duty of Loyalty 494
In re Blumenstyk *497*
Stegemeier v. Magness *503*
11.3 Duty of Prudence 512
In re Will of Crabtree *513*
In re HSBC Bank USA (formerly Marine Midland Bank) (Ely) *525*
11.4 Subsidiary Duties 531
11.4.1 Impartiality 531
11.4.2 Duty to Inform and Report 533
11.5 Remedies for Breach and Exculpatory Clauses 535

12 FEDERAL TRANSFER TAXES: AN INTRODUCTION 537
By Jay A. Soled, Contributing Author

12.1 Introduction 537
12.2 The Basics of Federal Wealth Transfer Taxation 538
12.3 Gift Tax 539
12.3.1 What Is a "Taxable Gift"? 539
12.3.2 Valuation of a Gift 541
12.3.3 Deductions and Exclusions 542
12.3.3.1 The Marital Deduction 542
12.3.3.2 The Gift Tax Charitable Deduction 544
12.3.3.3 The Annual Exclusion 545
12.3.3.4 Medical and Education Exclusions 546
12.3.4 Computation of the Gift Tax 547
12.3.5 Trusts in Contemporary Gift Tax Practice 549
12.3.5.1 Crummey Trust 550
Crummey v. Commissioner *550*
12.3.5.2 Grantor Retained Annuity Trust 556
12.3.5.3 Qualified Personal Residence Trust 559
12.4 Estate Tax 560
12.4.1 Estate Tax Fundamentals 560
12.4.1.1 Items Included in the Decedent's Gross Estate 561
12.4.1.2 Items Deducted from the Gross Estate 565
12.4.1.3 Computation of the Estate Tax and Preparation of the Estate Tax Return 567
12.4.2 Estate Tax Application 569
12.4.2.1 Bypass Trusts 570
12.4.2.2 QTIP Trusts 571
12.4.2.3 Minors' Trust 573

12.5	**Generation-Skipping Transfer Tax**	**574**
	12.5.1 Generation-Skipping Transfer Tax Fundamentals	575
	12.5.1.1 Determination of a GST Taxable Event	575
	12.5.1.2 Computation of the GST Tax	576
	12.5.1.2.1 Taxable Amount	576
	12.5.1.2.2 Applicable Rate	577
	12.5.2 Generation-Skipping Transfer Tax Application	579
	12.5.2.1 Inter Vivos Dynasty Trusts	579
	12.5.2.2 Testamentary Dynasty Trusts	580
	12.5.2.3 Grandchildren Trusts with General Power of Appointment	581
12.6	**Conclusion**	**582**
	Appendix 1 Life Insurance Trust	583
	Appendix 2 Sample GRAT	596
	Appendix 3 Sample QPRT with Subsequent Grantor Trust	603
	Appendix 4 Sample Testamentary Minor's Trust	615

TABLE OF CASES 617
TABLE OF AUTHORITIES 621
TABLE OF AUTHORS 629
INDEX 631

Preface

In *Wills, Trusts, and Estates: The Essentials* ("*Essentials*"), we present a "sleek and slender" treatment of the law for an introductory law school course that emphasizes problem-solving and interactive classroom discussion. *Essentials* provides a comprehensive yet concise coverage of key topics in an innovative pedagogical format designed to facilitate efficient learning and maximum comprehension of core legal principles. *Essentials* is flexible enough to accommodate a range of teaching styles and is easily adaptable for two, three, and four academic credit survey courses.

The format is straightforward and incorporates the following features:

1. We introduce each legal doctrine with a plain-English summary of the law. Whereas the traditional casebook format relies primarily on judicial opinions to explain legal doctrine, this book lays out the basics of each topic with an introductory précis to establish baseline knowledge. These succinct explanations of the law emphasize the prevailing rule adopted in a majority of states and, where applicable, call attention to rule variations followed in a minority of jurisdictions.
2. We illustrate each legal doctrine with a recent, clearly written, and well-reasoned judicial opinion and, for most cases, we provide a block diagram visually depicting the relationships between and among relevant parties. To facilitate student comprehension, we provide a series of analytical questions accompanied by narrative answers following each case. We believe that this Q&A case analysis format, replacing string citations to external references in traditional casebooks, allows students to grapple with doctrinal material more effectively prior to class without leaving the four corners of the textbook.
3. We apply each legal doctrine in problem sets throughout each chapter. We designed the problems to stimulate creative legal analysis by inviting students to apply newly-learned doctrines to realistic fact patterns that expand upon examples presented in the cases. To simulate problems encountered by trusts and estates practitioners, a majority of the problems are based on actual cases.

As authors, we are excited to publish a textbook that reflects our shared pedagogical philosophy and strong enthusiasm for classroom teaching. We hope to learn from the insight of others and therefore gladly welcome feedback from students and professors willing to share their experiences in learning and teaching with these materials.

Reid Kress Weisbord
David Horton
Stephen K. Urice

January 2018

A Note About the Diagrams

Block diagrams illustrate the relationships between and among relevant parties described in most judicial opinion excerpts featured in this textbook. The block diagrams use the following formatting conventions to describe various relationships and statuses:

- A circle represents an individual party mentioned in the case.
- A circle with a name that appears in bold type represents the party whose estate generated the litigation.
- An "X" superimposed on a circle represents the status of the party as deceased.
- A double line connecting two circles represents a marital relationship between the two connected parties.
- A single dashed line with a superimposed "D" represents a former marital relationship terminated by divorce or dissolution.
- Square brackets represent a party identified by family relationship to the decedent rather than by name.

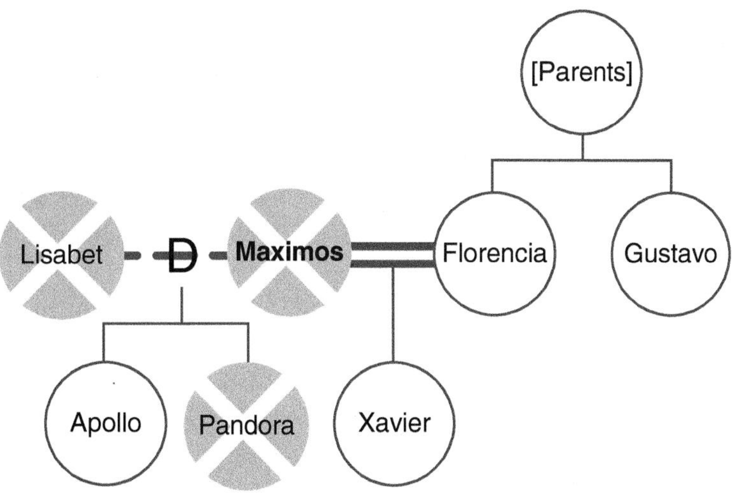

For example, the diagram above illustrates Maximos's familial relationships at the time of his death. Maximos was previously married to Lisabet, but that marriage ended in divorce. Maximos and Lisabet had two children, Apollo and Pandora. Both Lisabet and Pandora predeceased Maximos. Maximos was married to Florencia at the time of his death; they had a son, Xavier. Florencia has a brother, Gustavo.

Acknowledgments

This book has benefited from the assistance of many hands. Although we retain all responsibility for errors and omissions, we thank those who have helped us. We benefited from the remarkable professionalism of Troy Froebe, Yannick Grant, Tom Daughhetee, Geoffrey Lokke, and their colleagues at The Froebe Group, whose astute observations and ideas, expertise, and patience transformed our manuscript into a handsome book. At Wolters Kluwer, we thank John Devins, Richard Mixtner, Anton Yakovlev, and Carol McGeehan (now at Carolina Academic Press). We are especially grateful to Jay A. Soled, Professor and Director of Master of Accountancy in Taxation at Rutgers Business School, for contributing Chapter 12, "Federal Transfer Taxes: An Introduction." Three of Professor Urice's research assistants at the University of Miami School of Law proved essential in bringing this book from idea to publication, and we thank them: Brian Stewart, Esq., John Fogleman, JD (expected 2018), and Katherine Brennan, Esq. Professors Urice and Weisbord are grateful to their students who were assigned chapters of this book in early drafts and suggested many improvements. We thank O'Conor G. Ashby, Alexander Boni-Saenz, Felix Chang, Steve Clowney, Andrew Gilden, and Mark Glover. Finally, Professor Horton thanks Dylan Burns, Sam Ting, and Blaine Yamauchi, research assistants at the University of California, Davis School of Law; and Professor Urice thanks Dean Patricia White, University of Miami School of Law, for her support of his work on this book and other projects.

The authors gratefully acknowledge the permissions granted to reproduce the following materials:

American Law Institute. Restatement (Third) of Property (Wills and Other Donative Transfers) §§1.1, 2.7, 3.2 & com a, 3.5, 3.8, 3.8, 4.3, 5.1, 5.2(c), 5.3, 5.4, 6.1, 8.1 & coms c, m, j, s, 8.3, 11.1, 11.2, 12.1, 13.1, 17.1, 19.1. Copyright © 1999, 2003, 2011 by the American Law Institute. Reproduced by permission. All rights reserved.

American Law Institute. Restatement (Third) of Restitution and Unjust Enrichment §55. Copyright © 2011 by the American Law Institute. Reproduced by permission. All rights reserved.

American Law Institute. Restatement (Third) of Trusts §§10, 11, 13 & com d, 17, 18, 19 & com a, 20, 40, 41, 44, 47, 50, 77, 78, 79. Copyright © 2003, 2007 by the American Law Institute. Reproduced by permission. All rights reserved.

Autumn Leaves, c. 1955 by Alexander Calder. Copyright © by Calder Foundation, New York / Artists Rights Society (ARS), New York, NY. Reproduced by permission. All rights reserved.

Canyon, 1959 by Robert Rauschenberg. Combine: oil, pencil, paper, fabric, metal, cardboard box, printed paper, printed reproductions, photograph, wood, paint tube, and mirror on canvas with oil on bald eagle, string, and pillow. 81 3/4 x 70 x 24 inches (207.6 x 177.8 x 61 cm). The Museum of Modern Art, New York. Copyright © by Robert Rauschenberg Foundation / Licensed by VAGA, New York, NY. Reprinted by permission. All rights reserved.

Carrie Fisher. Courtesy of Riccardo Ghilardi / Wikimedia Commons.

Debbie Reynolds. Courtesy of Allan Warren / Wikimedia Commons.

Essex Courthouse in Newark, NJ. Courtesy of Jim Henderson / Wikimedia Commons.

Farrah Fawcett. Copyright © by Glasshouse Images / Alamy. Reproduced by permission. All rights reserved.

Heath Ledger. Copyright © 2005 by Allstar Picture Library / Alamy. Reproduced by permission. All rights reserved.

Hooters, Morrisville, NC. Courtesy of Ildar Sagdejev / Wikimedia Commons.

John Goodman in King Ralph (1991). Copyright © by Photo 12 / Alamy. Reproduced by permission. All rights reserved.

King Louis XVI, 1874 by Louis-Marie Sicardi. Courtesy of the American Philosophical Society. Gift of the Richard Bache Duane Family of New York, 2014. Reproduced by permission. All rights reserved.

Kingsbury Place, St. Louis, MO. Courtesy of Reading Tom / Flickr.

LaLaurie Mansion, New Orleans, LA. Courtesy of Reading Tom / Flickr.

Prince. Copyright © by Patrick Baldwin / Alamy. Reprinted by permission. All rights reserved.

Tom Cruise in Rain Man (1988). Copyright © by RGR Collection / Alamy. Reproduced by permission. All rights reserved.

"Yes, our investments are diversified: 20% out the window, 65% down the drain, and 15% gone with the wind." by Randy Glasbergen. Copyright © by Randy Glasbergen. Reproduced by permission. All rights reserved.

Zurawner Society Gate, Mt. Zion Cemetery, Brooklyn, NY. Courtesy of Scott Kraft / Flickr.

WILLS, TRUSTS, AND ESTATES

THE ESSENTIALS

1 | Overview

1.1 INTRODUCTION

Welcome to *Wills, Trusts, and Estates*! In this class, we will learn how society regulates the transmission of property from the dead to the living. Our main goal in this textbook is to teach you these rules in a sleek and straightforward fashion.

But we also hope to convey why we love this area of law. Trusts and estates is unique for several reasons. First, it is one of the few legal niches that impacts everyone. During your life, you may never be faced with a question of securities, antitrust, or (we hope) tort or criminal law. But it is nearly inevitable that you will confront a trusts and estates matter. To paraphrase Benjamin Franklin, "[i]n this world nothing can be said to be certain, except death and taxes." Because trusts and estates is woven into the fabric of life, the knowledge you gain in this class will serve you well in the future. Even if you are planning to specialize in a different area, we can assure you that some new acquaintance, upon learning that you are an attorney, will ask you questions about her estate plan. And if you are still making up your mind about what you want to do, we hope you will seriously consider becoming a trusts and estates lawyer. It is a wonderful practice area that usually involves performing a valuable service for everyday people.

A second quality that makes trusts and estates unique is that it provides a window into both the best and the worst aspects of human nature. Estate planning choices (or the choice not to make an estate plan) can profoundly affect a person's friends and family. The pecuniary and emotional stakes are high. The cases are shot through with elements that belong in a soap opera: greed, lust, friendship, betrayal, and love.

Finally, trusts and estates is fascinating because it is torn between the past and the present. Its roots trace back to the Middle Ages, and much of its key vocabulary — for instance, "intestate," "settlor," "executor" — sounds like an ancient foreign language. Nevertheless, the field faces constant pressure to evolve. Should the law apply principles that arose during an era when people valued land above all other possessions now that wealth consists primarily of paper assets, like stocks? How should the law keep pace as concepts like "family" and "marriage" acquire new dimensions? See Nancy F. Cott, Public Vows (2000). Are email, text messaging, and social media accounts "property" that can be inherited by a decedent's family? As you learn how judges, policymakers, and scholars have answered these questions, you will see why this very old field is also as contemporary as the world we inhabit.

We look forward to embarking on this journey with you.

1.2 TESTAMENTARY FREEDOM

When we are alive, we have nearly unlimited control over our property. We can sell it, give it away, abandon it, or consume it. Should we enjoy the same vast power when we die? Generally, the American law of trusts and estates answers that question in the affirmative. Indeed, the field's first principle is freedom of testamentary disposition: that *testators* (people who make wills) and *settlors* (people who make trusts) enjoy "the nearly unrestricted right to dispose of their property as they please." Restatement (Third) of Property: Wills & Other Donative Transfers §10.1, comment a.

There has been a long and lively debate about whether this regime is good policy. See, e.g., Adam J. Hirsch & William K.S. Wang, A Qualitative Theory of the Dead Hand, 68 Ind. L.J. 1 (1992). One common rationale for testamentary freedom is that it encourages people to work hard and save. Arguably, individuals accumulate property, in part, because they derive satisfaction from knowing they will be able to give it to whom they like after death. Thus, by adding another stick to the bundle of property rights, freedom of testamentary disposition creates incentives for creativity, diligence, and thrift.

But whether testamentary freedom actually creates an incentive to work or save, and whether such incentives lead to economic growth, are contestable empirical questions. People probably seek prosperity for a variety of reasons having nothing to do with a desire to transfer wealth at death (for example, in order to live comfortably or to impress others during life). It is not clear that restrictions on testamentary freedom would dampen these impulses.

Another popular justification for testamentary freedom is that it binds loved ones together. As people age, they often become dependent on family members or friends for various forms of care. Testamentary freedom allows testators and settlors to reward these caretakers for their time and effort. See, e.g., Joshua C. Tate, Caregiving and the Case for Testamentary Freedom, 42 U.C. Davis L. Rev. 129 (2008).

Then again, to the extent that testamentary freedom keeps property within families, it leads to unsavory results. As assets accumulate and pass down from one generation to the next, wealth tends to concentrate in the hands of families who benefit from riches they did not earn. The fact that some individuals are born with such exceptional advantages strikes many people as unfair.

Finally, in any discussion of testamentary freedom, it is important to distinguish between the power to transfer assets at death and the right to inherit. In civil law countries, such as France, Italy, and Germany, the power to direct who receives property is sharply limited by the rights of family members to inherit and receive support from the decedent's estate. For example, children are assured a "forced share" of their parents' property at death. Conversely, American trusts and estates grants an almost unlimited right to distribute property at death to anyone in any amount. We now take a closer look at this issue.

1.2.1 State Law

Testamentary freedom consists of two components. The first is "dispositional control": the privilege of saying *who* gets your property and *how much* they get. In the United States, there are very few restrictions on dispositional control.[1] Indeed, testators and settlors may make dispositions that are completely arbitrary.[2] As a comment to §10.1 of the Restatement (Third) of Property: Wills & Other Donative Transfers puts it:

> American law does not grant courts any general authority to question the wisdom, fairness, or reasonableness of the donor's decisions . . . . The main function of the law . . . is to facilitate rather than regulate . . . . American law curtails freedom of [testamentary] disposition only to the extent that the donor attempts to make a disposition or achieve a purpose that is prohibited or restricted by an overriding rule of law . . . .

Subject to a handful of rules that protect creditors and surviving spouses — which we will discuss later in Chapter 7 — decedents may make dispositions that are "unreasonable, unjust, injudicious, or cruel." In re Raynolds' Estate, 27 A.2d 226, 236 (N.J. Prerog. Ct. 1942).

Second, owners sometimes try to exercise "dead hand control" and impose terms and conditions on their estates that affect their beneficiaries or that last long after their death. See Ray D. Madoff, Immortality and the Law: The Rising Power of the American Dead Hand (2010). Some states regulate dead hand control by imposing limitations on the duration of donor-imposed restrictions. For instance, the Rule Against Perpetuities — an ancient common law principle of property law — prevents settlors from creating interests that remain contingent for too long in the future.[3]

In addition, courts occasionally reject attempts to exert dead hand control on the ground that it violates public policy. For example, decedents might try to condition a beneficiary's inheritance on his or her marrying a person who meets certain criteria. When the beneficiary has not been married before, courts generally uphold these clauses as long as they are "reasonable."

---

1. This deferential approach is uniquely American. Countries like England and New Zealand have family maintenance statutes, which allow a decedent's spouse or relatives to file a lawsuit alleging that the decedent should have provided for them. See, e.g., Inheritance (Provisions for Family and Dependents) Act, 1975, ch. 63, §1(1) (Eng.).

2. For anecdotes that illustrate this point, see Karen Houppert, A Room of Her Own, Wash. Post, Nov. 1, 2009 (describing a professor who left $75,000 to a former student to whom she had not spoken for over twenty years); Cranky Patron Leaves $50,000, Car to Waitress, Cin. Post, Dec. 29, 2007 (the headline says it all, although, according to the waitress, the customer was "kind of mean"); A Richer Bronson, Cin. Post, Feb. 25, 1999 (mentioning a woman who left $300,000 to 1970s action star Charles Bronson, whom she had never met).

3. Most states, however, have jettisoned or significantly weakened the Rule Against Perpetuities, thereby yielding to a seemingly voracious appetite among donors for long-term posthumous control.

Consider Shapira v. Union National Bank, 315 N.E.2d 825 (Ohio C.P. 1974). David Shapira, a doctor, had three adult children: a daughter, Ruth, who lived in Tel Aviv, and two sons, Daniel and Mark, who resided in the United States. David left his property equally to his three children, but conditioned Daniel's and Mark's devise on their marrying "a Jewish girl whose both parents were Jewish" within seven years of their father's death. If the sons failed to do so, their share of the estate would pass to the State of Israel. Daniel, then a 21-year-old college student, sued the executor and alleged that the condition violated public policy. The court disagreed, reasoning that Daniel had ample time to decide whether to satisfy the condition and find a suitable spouse. The court also relied on the provision in David's will directing the sons' shares to the State of Israel if either or both failed to meet the condition. In upholding the condition, the court observed:

> [This "gift-over" provision] demonstrates the depth of the testator's conviction. His purpose was not merely a negative one designed to punish his son for not carrying out his wishes. His unmistakable testamentary plan was that his possessions be used to encourage the preservation of the Jewish faith and blood, hopefully through his sons, but, if not, then through the State of Israel.

PROBLEM I

Max, a wealthy dentist, is the son of immigrants who fled anti-Semitism in Russia. As a result, he has always been proud of his religious heritage. His wife, Erla, describes him as a "traditionalist": a conservative investor who wears a coat and tie to the office even on weekends. But as Max has gotten older, he has become preoccupied with the high rate of intermarriage among young Jews. He decides that he wants to encourage his own children, Michael and Leila, to marry within the faith.

A. Michael marries a Jewish woman, but Leila marries a non-Jewish man. As a result, Max executes a will that leaves his entire estate to Michael. Could a court conclude that Max's will violates public policy and decline to enforce the condition on that basis? Why or why not?

B. Neither Michael nor Leila is married when Max makes his will. Knowing that Erla will disinherit any of their children who do not marry within the faith, Max's will leaves all of his property to Erla. Could a court conclude that Max's will violates public policy and decline to enforce the condition on that basis? Why or why not?

C. Neither Michael nor Leila is married when Max makes his will. Max inserts a clause into the document that says: "I leave my property to my children, Michael and Leila, in equal shares. However, to inherit their share, my children must marry a Jew who lives in the city of Jerusalem within one year of my death." When Max dies, Michael is 19 and Leila is 17. On what basis might a court conclude that the condition violates public policy?

Decedents sometimes instruct their executor or trustee to burn, shred, or annihilate an asset of the estate.[4] For example, Pulitzer Prize–winning playwright Edward Albee (*Who's Afraid of Virginia Woolf?*) asked his executors "to destroy [his] incomplete manuscripts" and Beastie Boy Adam Yauch added a clause to his will prohibiting the use of his music in advertising.[5] Our next case grapples with a similar testamentary instruction involving a house located within a "private place," a type of community developed in the 1860s by planner Julius Pitzman. This particular enclave, Kingsbury Place, still retains its elaborate front gate:

Kingsbury Place, St. Louis, Missouri.

4. See, e.g., Lior Jacob Strahilevitz, The Right to Destroy, 114 Yale L.J. 781 (2005), with an extensive review of case law. For the particularly difficult issue of the destruction of cultural property, see Joseph L. Sax, Playing Darts with a Rembrandt: Public and Private Rights in Cultural Treasures (2001). For an interesting account of celebrities who have asked to be buried with unusual objects, see Greg Daughtery, Nine Famous People and What They're Buried With, Smithsonian.com (Oct. 29, 2014), at http://www.smithsonianmag.com/arts-culture/nine-famous-people-and-what-theyre-buried-180953186 (noting, among other things, that Frank Sinatra requested that his body be placed in a casket with "a bottle of Jack Daniel's whiskey, a pack of Camel cigarettes, a Zippo lighter, and a dollar's worth of dimes . . . in case he needed to use a pay phone").

5. See Michael Paulson, Edward Albee's Final Wish: Destroy My Unfinished Work, N.Y. Times, July 4, 2017, at https://www.nytimes.com/2017/07/04/theater/edward-albees-final-wish-destroy-my-unfinishedwork.html.

Eyerman v. Mercantile Trust Co.
524 S.W.2d 210 (Mo. Ct. App. 1975)

Plaintiffs appeal from denial of their petition seeking [an] injunction to prevent demolition of a house at #4 Kingsbury Place in the City of St. Louis. The action is brought by individual neighboring property owners and certain trustees for the Kingsbury Place Subdivision. We reverse.

Louise Woodruff Johnston, owner of the property in question, died January 14, 1973, and by her will directed the executor ". . . to cause our home at 4 Kingsbury Place . . . to be razed and to sell the land upon which it is located . . . and to transfer the proceeds of the sale . . . to the residue of my estate." Plaintiffs assert that razing the home will adversely affect their property rights . . . and is contrary to public policy.

. . .

Demolition of the dwelling will result in an unwarranted loss to this estate, the plaintiffs and the public. The uncontradicted testimony was that the current value of the house and land is $40,000.00; yet the estate could expect no more than $5,000.00 for the empty lot, less the cost of demolition at $4,350.00, making a grand loss of $39,350.33 if the unexplained and capricious direction to the executor is effected. Only $650.00 of the $40,000.00 asset would remain.

Kingsbury Place is an area of high architectural significance, representing excellence in urban space utilization. Razing the home will depreciate adjoining property values by an estimated $10,000.00 and effect corresponding losses for other neighborhood homes. The cost of constructing a house of comparable size and architectural exquisiteness would approach $200,000.00.

The importance of this house to its neighborhood and the community is reflected in the action of the St. Louis Commission on Landmarks and Urban Design designating Kingsbury Place as a landmark of the City of St. Louis. This designation, under consideration prior to the institution of this suit, points up the aesthetic and historical qualities of the area and assists in stabilizing Central West End St. Louis. It was testified by the Landmarks Commission chairman that the private place concept, once unique to St. Louis, fosters higher home maintenance standards and is among the most effective methods for stabilizing otherwise deteriorating neighborhoods. The executive director of Heritage St. Louis, an organization operating to preserve the architecture of the city, testified to the importance of preserving Kingsbury Place intact:

> The reasons (sic) for making Kingsbury Place a landmark is that it is a definite piece of urban design and architecture. It starts out with monumental gates on Union. There is a long corridor of space, furnished with a parkway in the center, with houses on either side of the street. . . . The existence of this piece of architecture depends on the continuity of thc (sic) both sides. Breaks in this continuity would be as holes in this wall, and would detract from the urban design qualities of the streets. And the richness of the street is this belt of green lot on either side, with rich tapestry of the individual houses along the sides. Many of these houses are landmarks in themselves, but they add up to much

> more. . . . I would say Kingsbury Place, as a whole, with its design, with its important houses . . . is a most significant piece of urban design by any standard.

To remove #4 Kingsbury from the street was described as having the effect of a missing front tooth. The space created would permit direct access to Kingsbury Place from the adjacent alley, increasing the likelihood the lot will be subject to uses detrimental to the health, safety and beauty of the neighborhood. The mere possibility that a future owner might build a new home with the inherent architectural significance of the present dwelling offers little support to sustain the condition for destruction.

. . . It becomes apparent that no individual, group of individuals nor the community generally benefits from the senseless destruction of the house; instead, all are harmed and only the caprice of the dead testatrix is served. Destruction of the house harms the neighbors, detrimentally affects the community, causes monetary loss in excess of $39,000.00 to the estate and is without benefit to the dead woman. No reason, good or bad, is suggested by the will or record for the eccentric condition. This is not a living person who seeks to exercise a right to reshape or dispose of her property; instead, it is an attempt by will to confer the power to destroy upon an executor who is given no other interest in the property. To allow an executor to exercise such power stemming from apparent whim and caprice of the testatrix contravenes public policy.

. . . While living, a person may manage, use or dispose of his money or property with fewer restraints than a decedent by will. One is generally restrained from wasteful expenditure or destructive inclinations by the natural desire to enjoy his property or to accumulate it during his lifetime. Such considerations however have not tempered the extravagance or eccentricity of the testamentary disposition here on which there is no check except the courts.

. . .

The term "public policy" cannot be comprehensively defined in specific terms but the phrase "against public policy" has been characterized as that which conflicts with the morals of the time and contravenes any established interest of society. . . . Although public policy may evade precise, objective definition, it is evident from the authorities cited that this senseless destruction serving no apparent good purpose is to be held in disfavor. A well-ordered society cannot tolerate the waste and destruction of resources when such acts directly affect important interests of other members of that society. . . .

CLEMENS, Judge (dissenting).

I dissent.

. . .

The simple issue in this case is whether the trial court erred by refusing to enjoin a[n executor] from carrying out an explicit testamentary directive. In an emotional opinion, the majority assumes a phychic (sic) knowledge of the testatrix' reasons for directing her home be razed; her testamentary disposition is characterized as "capricious," "unwarranted," "senseless," and "eccentric." But the record is utterly silent as to her motives.

The majority's reversal of the trial court here spawns bizarre and legally untenable results. By its decision, the court officiously confers a "benefit" upon testamentary beneficiaries who have never litigated or protested against the razing. The majority opinion further proclaims that public policy demands we enjoin the razing of this private residence in order to prevent land misuse in the City of St. Louis. But the City, like the beneficiaries, is not a party to this lawsuit. The fact is the majority's holding is based upon wispy, self-proclaimed public policy grounds that were only vaguely pleaded, were not in evidence, and were only sketchily briefed by the plaintiffs.

. . .

As much as our aesthetic sympathies might lie with neighbors near a house to be razed, those sympathies should not so interfere with our considered legal judgment as to create a questionable legal precedent. Mrs. Johnston had the right during her lifetime to have her house razed, and I find nothing which precludes her right to order her executor to raze the house upon her death. . . .

QUESTIONS

1. Both the majority and the dissent seem to assume that Louise could have ordered her house to be torn down when she was alive. Why should she not enjoy the same privilege after she dies?

   ANSWER. The fear seems to be that people are more likely to make rash decisions in their estate plans because they will not personally experience the consequences of those decisions.

2. Arguably, the parties who stand to lose the most from the disputed condition are the beneficiaries of Louise's will. Although the neighbors' homes will decline in value by $10,000 if the court upholds the clause, the estate will forfeit more than $39,000. What is unusual about the beneficiaries' role in the litigation?

   ANSWER. They did not participate. Apparently, they never filed a formal legal complaint to try to prevent the executor from carrying out Louise's wishes.

3. The record is silent about what Louise hoped to accomplish. Would your view of the outcome change if Louise had articulated a reason for wanting to raze the property? Would it matter if her motivation was good, bad, or bizarre? Suppose she had contracted a rare disease and believed that it had been caused by the structure? Suppose her ex-husband, whom she hated, had built it with his two hands? Suppose she thought it was haunted?

   ANSWER. It is not clear how Louise's reasons for wanting to raze the house might impact the court's analysis. Perhaps the strongest argument that her motivations might be relevant stems from the passage in the *Shapira* case: Maybe courts should be more respectful of eccentric testamentary commands when they stem from a "de[ep] . . . conviction."

PROBLEM II

While suffering from the tuberculosis that would end his life, Franz Kafka (1883-1924), author of the novel *The Trial* (1925) and the short story *The Metamorphosis* (1915), wrote to the close friend whom Kafka had named as the executor of his estate and instructed him to immediately destroy all of Kafka's unpublished manuscripts. At the time, most of Kafka's work had not yet been published. During his lifetime, Maurice Sendak (1928-2012), author and illustrator of *Where the Wild Things Are* (1964), signed a will with this provision: "I direct my executors to destroy, immediately following my death, all of my personal letters, journals and diaries. I have informed my executors of the location of these articles in my residence located at [address]."

A. What, if any, difference is there between Kafka's and Sendak's instructions?

B. If you were Kafka's friend who received his letter directing you to destroy all of his unpublished manuscripts, what would you do?

C. If you had been appointed the executor of Sendak's will, what would you do?

D. How do Kafka's and Sendak's instructions differ from those included in the will of Louise Woodruff Johnston in the case above?

E. What result if Sendak had directed his executor to re-purpose his country residence into a charitable nonprofit museum, with specific instructions to leave all furnishings and decorations in place permanently and never to alter the physical structure?

1.2.2 Constitutional Law

In the early and mid-twentieth century, the freedom of disposition was not generally viewed as a constitutional right. During that period, the Supreme Court suggested that the U.S. Constitution did not prevent the state or federal government from regulating testation by adding or subtracting rights from the power to transmit property at death. For instance, the federal estate tax effectively limits testamentary freedom by redirecting a portion of a decedent's estate to the government. Thus, the Supreme Court held that the estate tax is constitutional in New York Trust Co. v. Eisner, 256 U.S. 345 (1921), even though the estate tax impaired the freedom of disposition. Similarly, as we will see in Chapter 7, some states protect the rights of a decedent's surviving spouse through a mechanism called the elective share, which also restricts the decedent's autonomy to transmit property at death to beneficiaries other than the surviving spouse. In Irving Trust Co. v. Day, 314 U.S. 556 (1942), the Court reiterated the constitutionality of regulating testamentary disposition by rejecting an argument that New York's elective share statute violated the Contract Clause of Article I and the Due Process Clause of the Fourteenth Amendment. Justice Jackson's majority opinion declared that "[n]othing in the Federal Constitution forbids the legislature of a state to limit, condition, or even abolish the power of testamentary disposition over property within its jurisdiction." *Id.* at 562. For decades, scholars generally agreed with this assessment. See, e.g., Daniel J. Kornstein, Inheritance: A Constitutional Right?, 36 Rutgers L. Rev. 741 (1984). Forty-five years later, however, the Court muddied the waters.

Hodel v. Irving
481 U.S. 704 (1987)

The question presented is whether . . . the "escheat" provision of the Indian Land Consolidation Act of 1983, Pub. L. 97-459, Tit. II, 96 Stat. 2519, effected a "taking" of appellees' decedents' property without just compensation.

I

Towards the end of the 19th century, Congress enacted a series of land Acts which divided the communal reservations of Indian tribes into individual allotments for Indians. . . . Two years after the enactment of the General Allotment Act of 1887, Congress adopted a specific statute authorizing the division of the Great Reservation of the Sioux Nation into separate reservations and the allotment of specific tracts of reservation land to individual Indians. . . . Under the Act, each male Sioux head of household took 320 acres of land and most other individuals 160 acres. . . . Until 1910, the lands of deceased allottees passed to their heirs "according to the laws of the State or Territory" where the land was located, and after 1910, allottees were permitted to dispose of their interests by will in accordance with regulations promulgated by the Secretary of the Interior. Those regulations generally served to protect Indian ownership of the allotted lands.

[However,] the policy of allotment of Indian lands quickly proved disastrous for the Indians. Cash generated by land sales to whites was quickly dissipated, and the Indians, rather than farming the land themselves, evolved into petty landlords, leasing their allotted lands to white ranchers and farmers and living off the meager rentals. . . . The failure of the allotment program became even clearer as successive generations came to hold the allotted lands. Thus 40-, 80-, and 160-acre parcels became splintered into multiple undivided interests in land, with some parcels having hundreds, and many parcels having dozens, of owners.

. . .

In 1934, in response to arguments such as these, the Congress acknowledged the failure of its policy and ended further allotment of Indian lands.

But the end of future allotment by itself could not prevent the further compounding of the existing problem caused by the passage of time. Ownership continued to fragment as succeeding generations came to hold the property, since, in the order of things, each property owner was apt to have more than one heir.

Section 207 of the Indian Land Consolidation Act — the escheat provision at issue in this case — provided:

> No undivided fractional interest in any tract of . . . restricted land within a tribe's reservation or otherwise subjected to a tribe's jurisdiction shall descedent [sic] by intestacy or devise but shall escheat to that tribe if such interest represents 2 per centum or less of the total acreage in such tract and has earned to its owner less than $100 in the preceding year before it is due to escheat.

Congress made no provision for the payment of compensation to the owners of the interests covered by §207. The statute was signed into law on January 12, 1983, and became effective immediately.

The three appellees — Mary Irving, Patrick Pumpkin Seed, and Eileen Bissonette — are enrolled members of the Oglala Sioux Tribe. They are, or represent, heirs or devisees of members of the Tribe who died in March, April, and June 1983. Eileen Bissonette's decedent, Mary Poor Bear-Little Hoop Cross, purported to will all her property, including property subject to §207, to her five minor children in whose name Bissonette claims the property. Chester Irving, Charles Leroy Pumpkin Seed, and Edgar Pumpkin Seed all died intestate. At the time of their deaths, the four decedents owned 41 fractional interests subject to the provisions of §207. . . . But for §207, this property would have passed, in the ordinary course, to appellees or those they represent.

Appellees filed suit in the United States District Court for the District of South Dakota, claiming that §207 resulted in a taking of property without just compensation in violation of the Fifth Amendment. . . .

III

The Congress, acting pursuant to its broad authority to regulate the descent and devise of Indian trust lands, . . . enacted §207 as a means of ameliorating, over time, the problem of extreme fractionation of certain Indian lands. By forbidding the passing on at death of small, undivided interests in Indian lands, Congress hoped that future generations of Indians would be able to make more productive use of the Indians' ancestral lands. We agree with the Government that encouraging the consolidation of Indian lands is a public purpose of high order. The fractionation problem on Indian reservations is extraordinary and may call for dramatic action to encourage consolidation. . . .

This Court has held that the Government has considerable latitude in regulating property rights in ways that may adversely affect the owners. . . . The framework for examining the question whether a regulation of property amounts to a taking requiring just compensation is firmly established and has been regularly and recently reaffirmed. . . . As the Chief Justice has written:

> [T]his Court has generally "been unable to develop any 'set formula' for determining when 'justice and fairness' require that economic injuries caused by public action be compensated by the government, rather than remain disproportionately concentrated on a few persons." Rather, it has examined the "taking" question by engaging in

> essentially ad hoc, factual inquiries that have identified several factors — such as the economic impact of the regulation, its interference with reasonable investment backed expectations, and the character of the governmental action — that have particular significance.

There is no question that the relative economic impact of §207 upon the owners of these property rights can be substantial. Section 207 provides for the escheat of small undivided property interests that are unproductive during the year preceding the owner's death. Even if we accept the Government's assertion that the income generated by such parcels may be properly thought of as de minimis, their value may not be. While the Irving estate lost two interests whose value together was only approximately $100, the Bureau of Indian Affairs placed total values of approximately $2,700 and $1,816 on the escheatable interests in the Cross and Pumpkin Seed estates. . . . Of course, the whole of appellees' decedents' property interests were not taken by §207. Appellees' decedents retained full beneficial use of the property during their lifetimes as well as the right to convey it inter vivos. There is no question, however, that the right to pass on valuable property to one's heirs is itself a valuable right. . . .

The extent to which any of appellees' decedents had "investment-backed expectations" in passing on the property is dubious. None of the appellees here can point to any specific investment-backed expectations. . . .

If we were to stop our analysis at this point, we might well find §207 constitutional. But the character of the Government regulation here is extraordinary. In Kaiser Aetna v. United States, [444 U.S. 164, 176 (1979)], we emphasized that the regulation destroyed "one of the most essential sticks in the bundle of rights that are commonly characterized as property — the right to exclude others." Similarly, the regulation here amounts to virtually the abrogation of the right to pass on a certain type of property — the small undivided interest — to one's heirs. In one form or another, the right to pass on property — to one's family in particular — has been part of the Anglo-American legal system since feudal times. . . . The fact that it may be possible for the owners of these interests to effectively control disposition upon death through complex inter vivos transactions such as revocable trusts is simply not an adequate substitute for the rights taken, given the nature of the property. Even the United States concedes that total abrogation of the right to pass property [at death] is unprecedented and likely unconstitutional. . . .

In holding that complete abolition of both the descent and devise of a particular class of property may be a taking, we reaffirm the continuing vitality of the long line of cases recognizing the States', and where appropriate, the United States', broad authority to adjust the rules governing the descent and devise of property without implicating the guarantees of the Just Compensation Clause. See, e.g., Irving Trust Co. v. Day, 314 U.S. 556, 562 (1942). . . . The difference in this case is the fact that both descent and devise are completely abolished. . . .

QUESTIONS

4. Takings cases involve an alleged government confiscation of property. Did the government confiscate property here? Did §207 prohibit the original owners — Mary Poor Bear-Little Hoop Cross, Chester Irving, Charles Leroy Pumpkin Seed, and Edgar Pumpkin Seed — from using, selling, or giving away their fractionated interests in land?

   ANSWER. No. Section 207 only prevented the owners from transmitting their interests in the land by will or intestate succession. Otherwise, they were free to treat the property as their own. Importantly, they could have given away or sold the property during their lifetime.

5. As we have discussed briefly above and will see again in Chapter 9, people sometimes transmit property after death through trusts. Very roughly, a trust arises when an owner, called a settlor, transfers property to a trustee, who manages it for the benefit of the trust beneficiaries. Trusts and other nonprobate transfers have become the dominant method of posthumous wealth transmission in contemporary society. Would §207 have prohibited the decedents in *Hodel* from placing their landholdings in trust for the benefit of their relatives?

   ANSWER. No. Section 207 would not have prohibited the decedents from placing their land in trust because the statute only applies to "intestacy and devise." As *Hodel* acknowledged, it does not prevent tribe members from passing small interests in land through trusts.

PROBLEM III

Suppose that Congress decides to amend §207 of the Indian Land Consolidation Act. The revamped provision states:

> No undivided fractional interest in any tract of restricted land within a tribe's reservation or otherwise subjected to a tribe's jurisdiction shall be passed by will, trust, or intestacy, but shall escheat to that tribe if such interest represents 1 percent or less of the total acreage in such tract and has earned to its owner less than $10 in each of the preceding ten years before it is due to escheat. However, this rule shall not apply if the heir or beneficiary of the decedent's fractional interest also owns a share of the same tract of land.

Again, Congress does not offer to pay the landowners for this interference with their rights. Does the amended statute violate the Takings Clause of the Fifth Amendment, entitling the landowners to receive "just compensation"?

1.3 SOURCES OF LAW, PROBATE COURTS, AND PROBATE ADMINISTRATION

Trusts and estates laws arise almost entirely under state law and vary from one jurisdiction to the next. T&E practitioners,[6] of course, must familiarize themselves with the

6. Practitioners commonly refer to Trusts and Estates with the shorthand abbreviation, "T&E." We will use this abbreviation on occasion throughout the book.

governing laws applicable to their client matters. At the national level, notable law reform projects have sought to promote uniformity across the jurisdictions in many areas of T&E law. The most significant of these projects include the Uniform Probate Code (UPC) and Uniform Trust Code (UTC) promulgated by the National Conference of Commissioners on Uniform State Laws (also known as the "Uniform Law Commission"). A sizable minority of U.S. states has enacted significant portions of the UPC. A majority of U.S. states has enacted significant portions of the UTC. This text, therefore, focuses largely on T&E law as codified by these uniform codes. On occasion, we will also refer to complementary law reform projects published by the American Law Institute: the Restatement (Third) of Property: Wills & Other Donative Transfers, and the Restatement (Third) of Trusts. T&E practitioners also often rely on authoritative jurisdiction-specific commentaries, formbooks, and practice manuals for local rules and guidance. See, e.g., Margaret V. Turano, McKinney's Laws of New York, Estates Powers & Trusts Law (six volumes).

1.3.1 State Probate Courts

Among the local variations of T&E laws across the states is the name and jurisdictional reach of state courts empowered to oversee the administration of decedents' estates. In general, these courts are known as *probate courts*, but other monikers include *surrogate's court*, *orphans' court*, and *prerogative court*. Some states, such as Florida, have no separate probate courts; rather, probate matters are handled by Florida's circuit courts.

Regardless of the name used, probate courts (as we will refer to them) are courts of limited jurisdiction. The degree of limitation varies by jurisdiction. Generally, a probate court is empowered to determine the validity of a decedent's will (or the absence of a will, i.e., an intestacy), to appoint a *personal representative* (the person who is in charge of administering an estate),[7] to settle some disputes, and to accept a final report from the personal representative when that process ends. In some jurisdictions, probate courts have authority to hear a broad range of litigated matters; in others, conflict must be resolved in another court altogether.

Probate judges are typically elected. In a few jurisdictions, they are appointed by the governor. Not all states require a probate judge to be admitted to the bar. Some require that probate judges hold a law degree, but others do not.

1.3.2 Probate

Probate is the traditional process for administrating a decedent's property after death. Property passes through probate by direction of the decedent's will or pursuant to the intestacy statutes. The probate system ensures that a decedent's *heirs* (who take through *intestacy*) or beneficiaries (who inherit under the terms of a will) hold marketable title to property received from the decedent's estate. The probate system also serves to protect

7. The personal representative is called an "executor" for estates with a will and an "administrator" for intestate estates.

the decedent's creditors (including local, state, and federal taxing authorities). Finally, probate provides for an orderly distribution of the decedent's possessions to the heirs and beneficiaries.

Restatement (Third) of Property: Wills & Other Donative Transfers
§1.1 Probate Estate

(a) A decedent's "probate estate" is the estate subject to administration under applicable laws relating to decedents' estates. The probate estate consists of property owned by the decedent at death and property acquired by the decedent's estate at or after the decedent's death.

(b) The "net probate estate" is the probate estate after deduction for family, exempt property, and homestead allowances, claims against the estate (including funeral expenses and expenses of administration), and taxes for which the estate is liable. Subject to overriding claims and rights provided by applicable law, such as the right of the decedent's surviving spouse to take an elective share or to elect other marital rights, the decedent's net probate estate passes to the decedent's heirs or devisees by intestate or testate succession.

UPC Article III addresses Probate of Wills and Administration [of Estates]. Probate may take one of two basic forms: informal and formal. Today, *informal probate* is the default process in most jurisdictions, especially if the value of the estate is small or moderate and there are a limited number of heirs or beneficiaries.

In informal probate involving *testacies* (decedents who made wills), the *executor* (the personal representative in a testate estate) first petitions the probate court to admit the decedent's will. This filing must list the names and addresses of any spouse, children, heirs, and devisees (including ages of any minors) of the decedent. If the court deems the will to be valid, it grants *letters testamentary* to the executor. With *intestacies* (where there is no will), the court will appoint a personal representative called an *administrator* and issues *letters of administration*. Letters testamentary and letters of administration verify the personal representative's authority to act on behalf of the decedent's estate when interacting with beneficiaries and third parties, such as banks, account custodians, and creditors. After the court grants letters, the executor or administrator has thirty days to notify any interested party of the appointment.

As long as no one objects to informal probate, personal representatives perform their duties without court supervision. An interested party, however, may file a petition for formal probate or a supervised proceeding at any time, subject to time limits on proceedings initiated more than three years after the decedent's death. UPC §§3-108(a); 3-401; 3-502. If there is a will contest or a dispute about the management of the decedent's property, the case must go through *formal probate*.

In formal probate, the probate court supervises the administration of the estate. Court approval may be required before an executor can sell estate assets (especially real property), borrow, lease, or mortgage estate property, pay debts and attorneys' fees, or collect commissions as personal representative. The larger the estate and the greater the number of interested parties, the greater the chances are that a dispute will lead to formal probate. Obviously, the cost of formal probate is higher than an informal proceeding.

The estate must be probated in the jurisdiction where the decedent was domiciled at death, also known as primary or domiciliary jurisdiction. All personal property, regardless of where it is located, will be administered through the probate court in the primary jurisdiction. Any real property outside of that jurisdiction must be administered in the jurisdiction where it is located, a process known as ancillary administration. Real property subject to ancillary administration will be handled according to the laws of that state, even if it conflicts with the law in the primary jurisdiction.

The personal representative has four primary duties: to collect and protect the decedent's probate estate, to satisfy the decedent's creditors, to pay all transfer taxes imposed on the estate, and to distribute the estate in accordance with the decedent's will or under applicable intestacy laws. Collecting and identifying a decedent's property is usually not difficult but requires the personal representative to conduct an appropriate search and, in some cases, prepare an inventory.

Creditors must file claims against the decedent's estate within a designated period of time established by the applicable nonclaim statute. Nonclaim statutes start to run when the personal representative provides notice of the decedent's death. Under the UPC, the personal representative must give actual notice to known or reasonably ascertainable creditors. See Tulsa Prof'l Collection Servs. v. Pope, 485 U.S. 478 (1988). In addition, to reach unknown creditors, the personal representative can publish notice of the decedent's death in a newspaper once a week for three successive weeks. Nonclaim statutes tend to be very short — they usually require creditors to file claims within four months of the first published notice — to further the public policy of settling a decedent's affairs as quickly as possible. See UPC §3-801. Finally, nonclaim statutes also place a limit on the length of time creditors have to bring claims even if probate proceedings have not commenced. Under UPC §3-803, this period is one year from the decedent's death; in other jurisdictions, the period may extend to five years.

If the decedent left no will, if the will does not name an executor, or if the executor named in the will refuses to serve, the probate court will name an administrator. The court selects the administrator based on a priority list starting with the decedent's spouse or domestic partner, then any adult children, parents, siblings, or other family members. An administrator has the same duties and responsibilities as an executor, serving in a fiduciary capacity for the estate.

1.3.3 Probate and Nonprobate Property

People own property in many forms and in many places. They may have real property, including homes or investment properties in different states; tangible personal property, such as clothing, furniture, works of art, and jewelry; money in bank accounts; certificates of deposit; or cash currency stashed in safe deposit boxes (or under mattresses). They may have investments in securities, individual retirement accounts (IRAs), annuities, and pension plans. They may have life insurance policies. And they may have retirement accounts or pension plans.

Because of the perception that probate is slow and expensive, people often try to hold title to property in forms that will avoid the necessity of probate proceedings when they die. Thus, a couple will generally take title to their house as joint tenants with right of survivorship (or, for married couples if permitted under state law, as tenants by the entirety)[8] and register their bank and investment accounts also as joint tenants with right of survivorship. Individuals often hold bank accounts titled in their own name but with a payable-on-death (POD) provision designating the person who will succeed to the account when the individual dies. They may also take title to real property under a transfer-on-death (TOD) deed that will effect a transfer of the property to the beneficiary named on the deed when the original owner dies. And, generally, people designate beneficiaries who will receive proceeds of their retirement and pension plans and life insurance policies rather than having the proceeds payable to an individual's estate (which is the default recipient if there is no designated beneficiary).

The joint tenancy is the most common means by which individuals attempt to avoid a probate proceeding. Joint tenancies are especially appropriate for married couples and individuals in other long-term relationships. Such couples typically hold title to their house, cars, and bank and investment accounts in joint tenancy. By operation of law, when one member of the couple dies, the survivor becomes the sole owner of the joint tenancy property and the interest of the decedent vanishes (at least, according to the legal fiction of property law).[9]

A key purpose of probate is to create a clear record of the transfer of the decedent's title in property to his or her successors in interest. In the case of real property held in a joint tenancy, a clear chain of title is generally established simply by filing with the register of deeds a certified copy of the deceased joint tenant's death certificate. Banks and investment houses will usually accept a death certificate as sufficient proof that a joint tenancy account has become property owned entirely by the surviving joint tenant.

Joint tenancy is sometimes described as a "poor person's will" because it costs much less than a will and provides a simple way of conveying the primary residence, which, for poorer decedents, is likely to be the most valuable asset in the estate. "Poor person's will," however, is a misnomer: Most middle-class and even wealthy couples rely on joint tenancies to transfer some, if not most, of their property on death. If a couple has been deliberate and careful in completing all relevant beneficiary designation forms to their life insurance policies, pension accounts, and other accounts that transfer on death pursuant to a contractual provision permitting designation of a beneficiary, they can avoid probate entirely.

Over the last four decades, the widespread popularity of nonprobate transfer techniques has shifted the center of gravity away from the process of probate administration to privatized alternatives. Professor John Langbein famously described this sea change as the "nonprobate revolution." John H. Langbein, The Nonprobate Revolution and the Future of the Law of Succession, 97 Harv. L. Rev. 108 (1984). Although the costs, delays, and complications of the probate process are often overstated,[10] the "nonprobate revolution" has shaped — and will continue to shape — the ways people transfer property at death. For many individuals, even those of modest means, avoiding probate is a hallmark of good planning. For individuals of wealth or fame, avoiding probate has

8. For purposes here, a joint tenancy with right of survivorship (sometimes referred to by the abbreviations "JTWROS") is generally referred to simply as a "joint tenancy." The term joint tenancy includes, unless otherwise stated, property held by married couples in a tenancy by the entirety.

9. For estate tax purposes, however, the decedent's interest in a joint tenancy with right of survivorship is treated as a transfer of property.

10. See generally David Horton, In Partial Defense of Probate: Evidence from Alameda County, California, 103 Geo. L.J. 605 (2015).

an additional advantage: Probate creates a public record, which is why wills of the "rich and famous" are so easily available. Most nonprobate transfers fly under the radar. Accordingly, individuals often structure ownership of their assets to minimize the prospect of a probate proceeding.

1.4 PRELIMINARY TOPICS ON DEATH AND DYING

This section examines a selection of preliminary but poignant topics concerning death and the process of dying. By nature, death pervades nearly every area of inheritance law. We acknowledge at the outset that grief is an intensely personal process and that everyone internalizes the death of a loved one differently. The academic treatment of death in this text, therefore, reflects our deep respect for the intensity of grief and gravity of human loss. See Elisabeth Kübler-Ross, On Death and Dying (1969). To focus analytically on the *law*, our discussion seeks to maintain a tone of dispassion rather than emotion.

Before wading into the mechanics of inheritance law and the disposition of property at death, we introduce five selected topics concerning the death itself and the process of dying. The first topic is the determination of death, which refers to the definitional question of how to determine whether a person is legally dead. The second is incapacity and planning for death, considerations that concern important end-of-life decisions and the delegation of control to third parties. The third is the emerging issue of the inheritability of so-called digital assets, such as emails and social media accounts. The fourth is the slayer rule, which precludes a decedent's killer from inheriting from the decedent's estate under certain circumstances. The fifth is disclaimer: an heir or beneficiary's voluntary decision not to accept inherited property.

1.4.1 Determination of Death

What does it mean to die? As a general rule, a person is declared dead as a matter of law upon sustaining irreversible cessation of all circulatory and respiratory functions. Thus, when the lungs stop breathing air and the heart stops pumping blood — and those critical life functions cannot be restored — a person is no longer alive.[11]

In some cases, a person's circulatory and respiratory functions can be maintained by artificial means, such as a life support machine in a hospital intensive care unit. In circumstances where the person is unlikely to recover, a doctor may declare death based on neurological criteria, which means that the person "has sustained irreversible cessation of all functions of the entire brain, including the brain stem."[12] Perhaps the

---

11. See, e.g., N.J. Stat. §26:6A-2 (declaration of death based on cardio-respiratory criteria). But as a practical matter, rather than a legal one, the answer is not always so clear. See Sherwin B. Nuland, How We Die 42 (1993) (noting that the experience of dying "does not belong to the heart alone," and describing how the law must define death with "with appropriate blurriness").

12. See, e.g., N.J. Stat. §26:6A-3 (declaration of death based on neurological criteria).

most high profile example of this type of declaration occurred in the case of Terry Schiavo, who suffered a catastrophic heart attack in 1990 but remained comatose on life support for fifteen years until her death in 2005. Terry's family fought bitterly over whether to remove her feeding tubes in a heartrending public dispute that wound its way through all three branches of government.[13]

Although rarely invoked, the law also provides for the presumptive declaration of death following a prolonged absence (typically five years) or exposure to a catastrophic event.[14] This definition of death was invoked in the tragic case of teenager Natalee Holloway, as reported by CNN in January 2012:[15]

> An Alabama judge signed an order Thursday declaring Natalee Holloway legally dead, attorneys for her family said.
>
> Probate Judge Alan King signed the order after an afternoon hearing in Jefferson County court in Birmingham.
>
> Holloway was 18 when she was last seen in the early hours of May 30, 2005, leaving a nightclub on the Caribbean island of Aruba with Joran van der Sloot and two other men. No one was charged in her disappearance, and her body has never been found.
>
> On Wednesday, van der Sloot—who was detained twice in connection with Holloway's disappearance but never charged—confessed in a Lima court to murdering a 21-year-old Peruvian woman five years after Holloway went missing.
>
> Natalee's father, Dave Holloway, filed a petition to declare his daughter dead in June, six years after she went to the Caribbean island with 100 classmates to celebrate their graduation from Mountain Brook High School in suburban Birmingham.
>
> He was present at Thursday's hearing, as was his ex-wife, Beth Holloway. She opposed the move to declare Natalee dead, pointing to a lack of evidence indicating her daughter is

---

13. In 2005, Congress took the extraordinary act of passing a private bill, signed by President George W. Bush, that created federal jurisdiction specifically for the Schiavo litigation, which had wound its way through the Florida state courts:

> SECTION 1. RELIEF OF THE PARENTS OF THERESA MARIE SCHIAVO.
>
> The United States District Court for the Middle District of Florida shall have jurisdiction to hear, determine, and render judgment on a suit or claim by or on behalf of Theresa Marie Schiavo for the alleged violation of any right of Theresa Marie Schiavo under the Constitution or laws of the United States relating to the withholding or withdrawal of food, fluids, or medical treatment necessary to sustain her life.
>
> SEC. 2. PROCEDURE.
>
> Any parent of Theresa Marie Schiavo shall have standing to bring a suit under this Act. The suit may be brought against any other person who was a party to State court proceedings relating to the withholding or withdrawal of food, fluids, or medical treatment necessary to sustain the life of Theresa Marie Schiavo, or who may act pursuant to a State court order authorizing or directing the withholding or withdrawal of food, fluids, or medical treatment necessary to sustain her life. In such a suit, the District Court shall determine de novo any claim of a violation of any right of Theresa Marie Schiavo within the scope of this Act, notwithstanding any prior State court determination and regardless of whether such a claim has previously been raised, considered, or decided in State court proceedings. The District Court shall entertain and determine the suit without any delay or abstention in favor of State court proceedings, and regardless of whether remedies available in the State courts have been exhausted.
>
> Pub. L. No. 109-3, Mar. 21, 2005, 119 Stat. 15.

14. See, e.g., N.J. STAT. §3B:27-1(a) (death presumed after five years' absence or exposure to specific catastrophic event).

15. Natalee Holloway Declared Legally Dead, CNN Wire Staff (Jan. 12, 2012), at http://www.cnn.com/2012/01/12/justice/alabama-natalee-holloway/.

deceased and saying in a September statement that she "will always hope and pray for Natalee's safe return."

On Thursday, she told reporters while leaving the courtroom that she was upset by the judge's decision.

"Natalee's father wanted to see this through, and of course it makes me very sad," said Beth Holloway, who now works with groups and families of missing children.

Dave Holloway acknowledged Thursday that the ruling is "tough," though he said he's considered it a possibility ever since the FBI told him 10 days after his daughter went missing that they were approaching her case as a homicide.

"We've been dealing with this death for the last six and a half years," he told reporters Thursday. "Hopefully, this meeting today will (provide) some closure."

1.4.2 Incapacity and Planning for Death

Planning for one's own incapacity or death can be highly effective in preventing stressful family conflict, but such planning often requires an uncomfortably vivid contemplation of one's own mortality. Prudent planning must anticipate the possibility of incapacitation and, in particular, how to make decisions about (1) medical care, and (2) management of property.

As a general rule, individuals have a right to make decisions about their own medical care, including the right to decline treatment necessary for survival.[16] In most circumstances, individuals exercise that right by communicating directly with their medical provider.[17] Incapacitation, however, can interfere with a person's ability to make his own medical decisions or communicate such decisions to his doctor. Planning for incapacitation, therefore, often includes execution of an advance medical directive. Professor Rebecca Dressler explains:

> The person completing an advance directive seeks to commit her future impaired self, and the family, physicians, and others confronting that self, to a particular treatment approach. She believes that she is in a better position now, than others will be in the future, to make decisions about the treatment she receives as an incompetent patient.
>
> There are two types of advance treatment directives: instruction and proxy directives. Living wills and other instruction directives are statements indicating the sorts of life-sustaining treatment that would be acceptable and unacceptable in various compromised conditions. People making proxy directives designate a specific individual as their preferred treatment decisionmaker in the event of incapacity. People seeking control over future

16. See, e.g., Quill v. Koppell, 870 F. Supp. 78, 84 (S.D.N.Y. 1994) ("It is established under New York law that a competent person may refuse medical treatment, even if the withdrawal of such treatment will result in death."). This right, however, does not guarantee access to physician-assisted suicide. Vacco v. Quill, 521 U.S. 793 (1997) (upholding constitutionality of a New York state law prohibition on aiding another in the commission of a suicide).

17. Indeed, federal law requires covered hospitals and medical providers to notify patients in writing of their "rights under State law (whether statutory or as recognized by the courts of the State) to make decisions concerning such medical care, including the right to accept or refuse medical or surgical treatment and the right to formulate advance directives." 42 U.S.C. §1395cc(f)(1)(A)(i).

> treatment may complete each type of directive, choosing someone they trust to make decisions and instructing that person to make certain sorts of choices.

Rebecca Dresser, Precommitment: A Misguided Strategy for Securing Death with Dignity, 81 Tex. L. Rev. 1823, 1825-26 (2003).

Absent a proxy directive, medical decisions (not otherwise addressed in an instruction directive) are made by a surrogate. Under the Uniform Health Care Decisions Act, for example, the following members of the patient's family are authorized to act as a surrogate in descending order of priority: (1) the spouse, unless legally separated; (2) an adult child; (3) a parent; or (4) an adult brother or sister. UNIFORM HEALTH CARE DECISIONS ACT §5(b). Individuals with contrary preferences to this default order of priority in selecting a surrogate to make medical decisions should memorialize their intent in writing by completing an advance medical directive.

A related, thought-provoking question is whether one's planning for incapacity should include prospective consent to sex. To this, Professor Alexander Boni-Saenz offers the following proposal:

> [T]he law should recognize *sexual advance directives* for people with persistent acquired incapacity living in long-term care institutions. In other words, people facing chronic conditions that threaten their sexual-consent capacity, such as Alzheimer's Disease, should be able to engage in sexual advance planning to preserve the possibility of a sexual life while in residential care, such as nursing homes. . . .
>
> To ensure that prospective consent is authentic, the sexual advance directive must be executed with the heightened level of formalities typically required of wills — a writing, signature, and attestation of two witnesses. . . . To ensure that contemporaneous consent is voluntary, the individual must verbally or nonverbally express consent to sexual contact. In other words, silence or inaction should not be taken to constitute consent, as it risks being the product of a cognitive or communicative impairment instead. . . . Finally, to protect the individual with cognitive impairments against harmful consequences of sexual activity, long-term care institutions and agents acting under a sexual advance directive must comply with a duty of care, taking reasonable steps to shield the person with cognitive impairments from objective welfare threats stemming from the sexual activity.

Alexander A. Boni-Saenz, Sexual Advance Directives, 68 Ala. L. Rev. 1, 4-5 (2016).

Planning for the management of property during a period of incapacitation involves similar considerations of control delegation. There are three primary ways of managing property on behalf of an incapacitated person: (1) conservatorships; (2) durable powers of attorney; (3) trusts.

A *conservatorship* is the default mechanism for managing property of an incapacitated person. Upon adjudication of incapacitation, a conservatorship authorizes a court-appointed conservator to manage the disabled person's property under the court's supervision. In a widely known although quite unusual application, 1990s pop star Britney Spears has lived under the control of a conservatorship since 2008, when it was revealed that she had suffered from undisclosed mental illness and substance abuse conditions. The *New York Times* reported on the Spears conservatorship in 2016:

> According to the [conservatorship] arrangement, which is typically used to protect the old, the mentally disabled or the extremely ill, Ms. Spears cannot make key decisions, personal or financial, without the approval of her conservators: her father, Jamie Spears, and a

> lawyer, Andrew M. Wallet. Her most mundane purchases, from a drink at Starbucks to a song on iTunes, are tracked in court documents as part of the plan to safeguard the great fortune she has earned but does not ultimately control.
>
> While the conservators are widely credited with rescuing Ms. Spears's career — and her life — her apparent stability and success could belie the need for continuing restrictions.
>
> There are recent signs, in fact, that the conservators are now acknowledging the great progress she has made. After successfully fighting to keep her from testifying in at least three prior lawsuits — (a probate judge had previously agreed that doing so could cause her "irreparable harm") — Ms. Spears's conservators allowed her to testify on Monday in a case filed against her by a former self-described manager. They agreed that "giving such testimony is not likely to cause harm to her," according to court papers.
>
> Could this be the start of a major unfastening of the strictures she lives under?

Serge F. Kovaleski & Joe Coscarelli, Is Britney Spears Ready to Stand on Her Own?, N.Y. Times, May 4, 2016.

Individuals who prefer to avoid a court-imposed conservatorship in the event of incapacitation can plan for incapacity in two ways that, absent a litigated conflict, do not involve any court supervision.

First, individuals can plan for incapacity through a durable power of attorney. A *durable power of attorney* provides for the appointment of an agent to transact legally on a person's behalf during any period of incapacity. Unlike a traditional power of attorney, which terminates automatically upon the principal's incapacity, a durable power of attorney survives the principal's incapacitation and can be drawn as narrowly or broadly as the principal desires.[18] By default, the power generally confers the agent with authority to buy, sell, exchange, and deal in property on the principal's behalf. Under the Uniform Power of Attorney Act (2008), however, an agent may make donative transfers on the principal's behalf "only if the power of attorney expressly grants the agent the authority."[19]

Second, an individual can plan for incapacity through a trust. Specifically, a person may transfer property into a *trust* to be managed by third-party trustees during any period of incapacitation. In addition to providing for third-party management of property by a trustee,[20] the trust can establish procedures for determining whether the settlor has become incapacitated (such as by majority vote of a committee consisting of the settlor's family and primary care physician). Such a provision was recently invoked in the Sterling Family Trust, which owned the Los Angeles Clippers professional basketball team. Donald Sterling and his wife Rochelle had placed their ownership interests in the team into a family trust in 1998. See Sterling v. Sterling, 242 Cal. App. 4th 185, 189 (2015) ("In addition to owning the Clippers, the trust owned real property worth approximately $2.5 billion and subject to approximately $480 million in debt. The assets included 150 apartment buildings, 15 residential properties, land, and a hotel. The apartment buildings housed approximately 20,000 tenants."). In 2014, however, Donald's mistress secretly taped him making statements that were "deeply offensive, demeaning, and discriminatory . . . toward African Americans,

---

18. Under the Uniform Power of Attorney Act (2008), "[a] power of attorney . . . is durable unless it expressly provides that it is terminated by the incapacity of the principal." Section 104.

19. *Id.* §201(a).

20. We examine trusts in detail in Chapters 8 and 9.

Latinos, and 'minorities' in general." *Id.* In the wake of the scandal, Rochelle, as co-trustee, sought to sell the Clippers over Donald's objection and successfully sought Donald's removal as co-trustee:

> [T]he trust provided for removal of a trustee due to incapacity. Specifically, the trust provided: "Any individual who is deemed incapacitated, as defined in Paragraph 10.24., shall cease to serve as a Trustee of all trusts administered under this document." Paragraph 10.24. in turn provided: "'Incapacity' and derivations thereof mean incapable of managing an individual's affairs under the criteria set forth in California Probate Code §810 et seq. An individual shall be deemed to be incapacitated if . . . two licensed physicians who, as a regular part of their practice are called upon to determine the capacity of others, and neither of whom is related by blood or marriage to any Trustee or beneficiary, examine the individual and certify in writing that the individual is incapacitated. . . ."

Id. at 188-89.

Two of Donald's doctors concluded that he lacked mental capacity to continue serving as trustee of the family trust:

> Dr. Platzer testified Donald was unable to spell the word "world" backwards. When asked to subtract seven from 100, he could not perform the calculation past 93 (100 – 7 = 93); he could not subtract seven from 93 (93 – 7 = 86). Dr. Platzer testified that Donald's PET (positron-emission tomography) scan indicated he suffered from Alzheimer's disease. She concluded he suffered from Alzheimer's disease for at least three years and more likely five years. She further testified that she considered Probate Code section 811 in reaching her conclusion that Donald was unable to serve as trustee.
>
> Dr. James Spar, a geriatric psychiatrist regularly called upon to determine capacity, also evaluated Donald. Dr. Spar concluded that Donald's performance on a battery of tests was consistent with early Alzheimer's disease or other brain disease. According to Dr. Spar: "Because of his cognitive impairment, Mr. Sterling is at risk of making potentially serious errors of judgment, impulse control, and recall in the management of his finances and his trust. Accordingly, in my opinion he is substantially unable to manage his finances and resist fraud and undue influence, and is no longer competent to act as trustee of his trust."

Id. at 872.

1.4.3 Digital Assets

Americans spend an average of twenty-three hours per week texting or on the web. Each minute, users add 600 videos to YouTube, create 320 Twitter handles, and post 6,600 images to Flickr. With Snapchat, Instagram, Shutterfly, and Tumblr replacing the family photo album, and Facebook attracting a rising number of senior citizens, there has been rising interest in what happens to online accounts after their owner's death.

The law in this area is unsettled and evolving. Traditionally, Internet search and social media platforms such as Google and Facebook have rejected requests from surviving family members to access a decedent's electronic accounts. Some Internet firms, such as Yahoo!, have invoked clauses in their terms-of-service agreements with their customers that state that accounts are "non-transferable" and "will be cancelled upon your death."[21] Because customers tend to ignore the fine print in these contracts, commentators have been critical of this practice. See, e.g., Natalie M. Banta, Inherit the Cloud: The Role of Private Contracts in Distributing or Deleting Digital Assets at Death, 83 Fordham L. Rev. 799 (2014).

In addition, Internet search and social media platforms are worried about violating a thirty-year-old federal statute called the Stored Communications Act (SCA). See Electronic Communications Privacy Act of 1986, Pub. L. No. 99-508, 100 Stat. 1848. Congress passed the SCA in 1986 to extend Fourth Amendment–style protections from the physical world into cyberspace. Section 2702 of the statute imposes civil liability on firms that share the contents of a customer's electronic communications—in other words, the actual text of a message—with third parties. 18 U.S.C. §2702(a)(1). However, §2702 also carves out an exception when a user has given her "lawful consent" to disclosure. *Id.* §2702(b)(3).

What does "lawful consent" mean? Recently, the Uniform Law Commission has attempted to provide an answer by promulgating the Revised Uniform Fiduciary Access to Digital Assets Act (RUFADAA). As of 2017, about twenty states have adopted the model law.[22] The RUFADAA allows people to express their consent to disclose the contents of their electronic accounts through an "online tool." Features like Google's Inactive Accounts Manager and Facebook's Legacy Contact allow users to specify that someone else should be able to access their media after a set period of inactivity, and the RUFADAA ratifies these choices. Alternatively, the RUFADAA states that users can make their desires known in several ways: "a will, trust . . . or other record." *Id.* §4(a). The statute defines "record" expansively, to include "information that . . . is stored in an electronic or other medium and is retrievable in a perceivable form." *Id.* §2(22). Finally, the RUFADAA is hostile to non-inheritability clauses, stating that a user's use of an online tool or express directive in a will, trust, or record "overrides a contrary provision in a terms-of-service agreement." *Id.* §4(c).

Revised Uniform Fiduciary Access to Digital Assets Act
§4 User Direction for Disclosure of Digital Assets

(a) A user may use an online tool to direct the custodian to disclose to a designated recipient or not to disclose some or all of the user's digital assets, including the content of electronic communications. If the online tool allows the user to modify or delete a direction at all times, a direction regarding disclosure using an online tool overrides a contrary direction by the user in a will, trust, . . . or other record.

(b) If a user has not used an online tool to give direction under subsection (a) or if the custodian has not provided an online tool, the user may allow or prohibit in a will, trust . . . or other record, disclosure to a fiduciary of some or all of the user's digital assets, including the content of electronic communications sent or received by the user.

(c) A user's direction under subsection (a) or (b) overrides a contrary provision in a terms-of-service agreement that does not require the user to act affirmatively and distinctly from the user's assent to the terms of service.

---

21. Yahoo!, Yahoo! Terms of Service, https://policies.yahoo.com/ie/en/yahoo/terms/utos/.

22. See Uniform Law Comm'n, Fiduciary Access to Digital Assets Act, Revised (2015), at http://www.uniformlaws.org/Act.aspx?title=Fiduciary%20Access%20to%20Digital%20Assets%20Act,%20Revised%20 (2015).

QUESTIONS

6. Suppose you die without using an "online tool" or making a will or trust. What happens to your digital assets under the RUFADAA?

   ANSWER. Under the RUFADAA, you can only transmit digital assets by engaging in some voluntary act: using an online tool or making a will, trust, or "record." If you do not do one of these things, you do not consent to allowing someone else to access your electronic accounts after you die.

7. Would the answer to Question 6 change if you wrote an email to your cousin in which you explained that you wanted her to receive your email account after you die?

   ANSWER. The RUFADAA allows users to consent to disclosure through a "record," which the statute defines as information that is "stored in an electronic . . . medium." Thus, the email should suffice, even though (as we will see) it falls far short of the formalities required to make a valid will.

1.4.4 Disposition of Final Remains

At common law, a written instruction concerning the disposal of one's final remains was not legally enforceable. Professor Ray Madoff explains:

> The most important rule regarding controlling bodies after death was one that the United States inherited from the common law of England, that is, the rule that a person does not have a property interest in his or her own body after death. The principle of common law is "corpus nullius in bonis," the body belongs to no one.
>
> The decision most often cited for this proposition is the English case, *Williams v. Williams*[, 20 Ch. Div. 659 (1882)]. In that case, a man by the name of Henry Crookenden — an early advocate of cremation — provided in his will that on his death, his body was to be given to his friend Eliza Williams "to be dealt with in the manner provided for in a letter to her." In this letter, he laid out his wishes with specificity: he wanted his body burned under a pile of wood and the remains stored in a particular Wedgwood vase that Crookenden had conveniently provided to Williams through his will.
>
> When Crookenden died, rather than following the wishes laid out in his will, his family buried him with the rites of the Roman Catholic Church. Eliza Williams tried to enforce the provisions of the will. In refusing her request, however, the court ruled that "there can be no property in a dead body": "[A] man cannot by will dispose of his dead body. If there be no property in a dead body it is impossible that by will or any other instrument the body can be disposed of."

Ray D. Madoff, Immortality and the Law: The Rising Power of the American Dead Hand 16-17 (2010).

Today, by contrast, the law is more likely to enforce a decedent's preferences concerning the disposition of final remains. Some people express the desire to be buried in a specific place, or to be cremated, or to have their organs used for transplantation or donated to science. These directives are usually binding,[23] although scholars have criticized courts and funeral directors for occasionally neglecting decedents' wishes and yielding to conflicting demands from the decedent's spouse or kin. See, e.g., Tanya K. Hernandez, The Property of Death, 60 U. Pitt. L. Rev. 971, 973 (1999).

When disputes arise over decedents' remains, they raise a range of fascinating issues. Is the body property? If so, to whom does it belong? What happens when decedents change their mind after making their will? Our next case addresses some of these complexities.

Mt. Zion Cemetery, Brooklyn, New York

23. In fact, courts sometimes honor decedents' wishes even if they are not memorialized in a formal testamentary instrument. See, e.g., ARIZ. REV. STAT. ANN. §32-1365.01 (West 2016) ("A legally competent adult may prepare a written statement directing the cremation or other lawful disposition of the legally competent adult's own remains. . . . The written statement may but need not be part of the legally competent adult's will."); see also Frances H. Foster, Individualized Justice in Disputes over Dead Bodies, 61 Vand. L. Rev. 1351 (2008). If there is no evidence of a decedent's intent, many states have statutes that allocate decision-making authority to the decedent's spouse, followed by their children. See, e.g., CAL. HEALTH & SAFETY CODE §7100 (West 2016).

Cohen v. Guardianship of Cohen
896 So. 2d 950 (Fla. Dist. Ct. App. 2005)

WARNER, J.

The brother and sister of the deceased, Hilliard Cohen, appeal the probate court's order requiring the burial of the deceased in a Florida cemetery, where he could be buried next to his wife of forty years, instead of the family cemetery plot in New York. Hilliard's 1992 will contained a request to be buried in the family plot, but his wife and others testified that he wished to be buried in Florida where his wife could also be buried. Because we conclude that the provisions of the will are not conclusive, we affirm the court's refusal to enforce the burial instructions in the will under the evidence presented in this case.

Hilliard and Margaret Cohen were married for forty years at the time of his death. They had four children together, and she had two from a previous marriage. Hilliard was Jewish and Margaret was not. They celebrated some religious holidays with the family, but they did not belong to a temple, nor did the children regularly attend services. Hilliard never had a bar mitzvah ceremony. The Cohen family had a family plot in Mount Hebron Cemetery, a Jewish cemetery in New York, purchased by Hilliard's grandfather. All of Hilliard's family and their spouses were buried there. Hilliard and Margaret lived in New York until 1998 when they moved to Florida.

After relocating to Florida, Hilliard began to have health problems. Around 1999, Hilliard told Margaret that he wanted to be buried in his family plot in Mount Hebron with her. However, in May of 2001, when Hilliard went into the hospital, he and Margaret first discussed being buried together in Florida.

Hilliard's brother and sister, Ivan and Cressie, were close to him, but they did not have a good relationship with Margaret. As a result, Hilliard would visit with them in Arizona and New York after he moved to Florida. . . .

In May of 2003, Margaret filed a petition to determine Hilliard's incapacity, alleging that Hilliard suffered from various diseases, including dementia and Alzheimer's. . . . A physician who examined Hilliard testified that during the examination Hilliard expressed the sentiment that he wished to be buried in Florida with his wife. . . .

Shortly before Hilliard's death, Ivan produced a will that Hilliard had apparently executed in 1992 in New York, in which he directed that he be buried in "a traditional Jewish burial in our family plot in Mount Hebron Cemetery, Flushing, Queens, N.Y." In that will, he appointed Ivan as executor. The will also left only the statutory minimum to Margaret. . . .

After Hilliard's death, Margaret planned to have Hilliard cremated, as they had discussed before his death. They chose cremation due to financial considerations and because Hilliard was angry with his brother. Prior to the cremation, Ivan sought a court order to enforce the burial provisions of the will. During a hearing to prevent the cremation, Margaret changed her mind after hearing a rabbi testify that it was against Jewish law. She then wanted a burial in Florida as they had discussed, where she could be by his side like she "ha[d] been the last forty years."

The trial court held two evidentiary hearings regarding the disposition and burial of the deceased. In addition to the testimony of Margaret, Ivan, and Cressie, a rabbi testified as to Jewish burial customs. He explained that: a) Cremation is prohibited under Jewish law and would not be considered a traditional Jewish burial; b) Jewish tradition is that husbands and wives are buried together as long as the wife is Jewish; c) Some Jewish cemeteries allow a non-Jew to be buried but not in the confined Jewish cemetery area; and d) More recent traditions allow Jews who are married to non-Jewish spouses to be buried in the same cemetery but not in the exclusive restricted area. The family plot in Mount Hebron was in the Jewish restricted area; therefore, Margaret could not be buried there. Finally, Hilliard's daughter testified that he had expressed a desire to be buried with his wife in Florida.

The trial court determined that the will was ambiguous as to Hilliard's intent because it stated that Hilliard wanted a "traditional Jewish burial," yet his wife could not be buried in Mount Hebron with him. Because the will was ambiguous, the court considered the extrinsic evidence and determined that Hilliard's true intent was to be buried alongside Margaret. The court therefore ordered Hilliard to be buried in the Florida cemetery.

This case presents an issue of first impression in Florida. The question presented is whether a deceased's testamentary burial instructions are binding upon the court or may be disregarded when the testator has made a subsequent oral statement of desire as to his final resting arrangements. The parties and the trial court considered the issue as though it was necessary to find an ambiguity in the will in order to vary its terms by the oral statements of the deceased. We instead affirm the trial court's ruling, adopting the majority view that provisions in a will regarding burial instructions are not conclusive of a testator's intent, and the trial court may take evidence that the testator changed his or her mind regarding disposition of his body.

The common law recognized no property right in the body of a deceased. In the absence of a testamentary disposition, the spouse of the deceased or the next of kin has the right to the possession of the body for burial or other lawful disposition.

Where the testator has expressed his exclusive intention through the will, the testator's wishes should be honored. . . . [However, l]ooking to decisions of other states, whether to enforce the will provisions regarding disposition of the testator's body depends upon the circumstances of the case.

> Having recognized certain property rights in dead bodies, many courts have announced the rule that a person has the right to dispose of his own body by will. However, courts, while paying lip service to the doctrine of testamentary disposal, have in certain instances permitted the wishes of the decedent's spouse or next of kin to prevail over those of the testator. In other instances, courts have accepted and acted upon evidence that indicated that the decedent's wishes concerning the disposition of his body had changed since the execution of his will.

B.C. Ricketts, Annotation, Validity and Effect of Testamentary Direction as to Disposition of Testator's Body, 7 A.L.R.3d 747 §1[b] (1966) (footnotes omitted).

Courts have held that a will provision directing the disposition of the testator's body may be altered or cancelled informally. For instance, in Nelson v. Schoonover, 89 Kan. 779, 132 P. 1183 (1913), overruled on other grounds, Daum v. Inheritance Tax Commission of Kansas, 135 Kan. 210, 9 P.2d 992 (1932), the testatrix specified her burial location in her will, yet the court refused to enforce the provision because her husband stated that she had expressed a different desire. The court said:

> Courts have sometimes been called upon to settle disagreements between relatives as to the place in which an interment shall be made. In each of these cases such decision has been made as seemed most equitable under all the circumstances. Ordinarily the choice of a surviving spouse will prevail over that of the next of kin. . . . The statement in a will is practically conclusive evidence of the wish of the testator in this regard at the time of its execution, but should not control over a different desire, afterwards expressed, although shown only by oral evidence.

132 P. at 1185. . . .

We have found no cases in Florida or across the country in which a testamentary disposition has been upheld even though credible evidence has been introduced to show that the testator changed his or her mind as to the disposition of his/her body. In Florida, . . . a will is construed to pass all property that the testator owns at death. See §732.6005(2), Fla. Stat. As set forth above, the testator's body is not considered property. Therefore, . . . a directive in a will regarding the disposition of a body does not have the same force and effect as do provisions directing the disposition of property. We therefore conclude that a testamentary disposition is not conclusive of the decedent's intent if it can be shown by clear and convincing evidence that he intended another disposition for his body. . . .

Our current society is exceedingly mobile. One might live in several states during a lifetime. A provision made in a will that is not revisited for many years may not reflect the intent of the testator as to the disposition of his or her remains. A direction for the disposition of one's body should not be conclusive when contrary and convincing oral or written evidence of a change in intent is present.

In this case, the deceased executed a will in 1992 requesting burial in his family's plot in New York. However, six years later he and his wife moved to Florida. He spoke of burial plans with his wife, as well as his daughter, and expressed a desire to be buried with his wife. At first, he wished to be buried with her in New York. Later, he agreed to burial with her in Florida. Hilliard's desire was also expressed to a doctor who examined him. Although his statement to the doctor may be discounted because he was being examined for competency, it was consistent with his prior statements that he wished to be buried with his wife. In all of his verbal expressions on this matter, Hilliard expressed a desire for burial in a place where his wife of forty years could also rest upon her death. This could not occur if he were buried in the family plot in Mount Hebron. . . .

It is a sorrowful matter to have relatives disputing in court over the remains of the deceased. In this case in particular, there is no solution that will bring peace to all parties. We express our sympathies to both sides in their loss, which must be magnified by these proceedings. Cases such as this require the most sensitive exercise of the equitable powers of the trial courts. We are confident that the experienced trial judge exercised his power with due regard for the serious and emotional issues presented. We find no abuse of the discretion afforded to the trial court.

Affirmed.

QUESTIONS

8. In most trusts and estates litigation, the parties are fighting about money. That is not the case here. What do you think is motivating Margaret, Ivan, and Cressie?

   ANSWER. They seem to be placing tremendous emotional or symbolic weight on where Hillard is buried, as though it is a proxy for who he loved more.

9. How does the body's status as "quasi-property" affect the outcome?

   ANSWER. The court reasons that because Hillard does not possess a full-fledged property right in his body, his will is less authoritative than it would be if some more mundane possession were at issue. As a result, in sharp contrast to most other contexts in the law of wills, Hillard's oral statements are treated as equally probative of his intent as his will.

10. Could Crookenden have phrased his wishes in a way that might make them more likely to be enforceable?

    ANSWER. Crookenden could have provided for Eliza to receive the vase that contained his ashes, recognizing both his love of the vase and their friendship. The court might be less likely to characterize a devise of tangible property as an instruction for the disposal of his remains.

1.4.5 The Slayer Rule

Every state seeks to prevent killers from inheriting from their victims. Many accomplish this goal through "slayer" statutes, although some have adopted the principle through the common law. The rationale for these rules is that no one should profit from a wrongful act. Thus, a killer should not receive a benefit from slaying the decedent even if the killer's action was not motivated by financial gain from the estate. See, e.g., Restatement (Third) of Restitution and Unjust Enrichment §45; Restatement (Third) of Property: Wills & Other Donative Transfers §8.4.

Generally, a slayer must forfeit all benefits he or she might derive from the victim under a will, trust, intestacy, or nonprobate instrument. See UPC §2-803(b). Similarly, the slayer loses any right of survivorship in joint tenancies held with the victim and cannot serve in a fiduciary capacity on behalf of the victim. See UPC §2-803(c)(1)-(2).

Uniform Probate Code
§2-803 Effect of Homicide on Intestate Succession, Wills, Trusts, Joint Assets, Life Insurance, and Beneficiary Designations

(a) [Definitions.] [Omitted]

(b) [Forfeiture of Statutory Benefits.] An individual who feloniously and intentionally kills the decedent forfeits all benefits under this [article] with respect to the decedent's estate, including an intestate share, an elective share, an omitted spouse's or child's share, a homestead allowance, exempt property,

> and a family allowance. If the decedent died intestate, the decedent's intestate estate passes as if the killer disclaimed his [or her] intestate share.
>
> (c) [Revocation of Benefits Under Governing Instruments.] The felonious and intentional killing of the decedent: (1) revokes any revocable (i) disposition or appointment of property made by the decedent to the killer in a governing instrument, (ii) provision in a governing instrument conferring a general or nongeneral power of appointment on the killer, and (iii) nomination of the killer in a governing instrument, nominating or appointing the killer to serve in any fiduciary or representative capacity, including a personal representative, executor, trustee, or agent; and (2) severs the interests of the decedent and killer in property held by them at the time of the killing as joint tenants with the right of survivorship [or as community property with the right of survivorship], transforming the interests of the decedent and killer into equal tenancies in common. . . .

When does causing a decedent's death make an heir or beneficiary a disqualified "slayer"? The UPC and many jurisdictions predicate "slayer" status on a "felonious and intentional killing." As a result, the slayer rule usually does not apply if the heir or beneficiary is guilty merely of negligent homicide or involuntary manslaughter. See Carla Spivack, Killers Shouldn't Inherit from Their Victims — Or Should They?, 48 Ga. L. Rev. 145, 158 (2013).

A common complication stems from the fact that probate courts often deal with slayer issues after the criminal case against the heir or beneficiary. Under the UPC, a person who has been found guilty of feloniously and intentionally killing the decedent and exhausted all appellate rights is conclusively a "slayer." UPC §2-803(g). Yet the converse is not true: A person who has been found *not guilty* in the criminal trial is not conclusively eligible to inherit and may *still* be barred in probate. Because criminal cases require proof of guilt beyond a reasonable doubt, but probate cases employ the lesser preponderance of the evidence standard, it is entirely possible to be exonerated in criminal court and nevertheless be stripped of inheritance rights.[24]

Finally, some jurisdictions disinherit not only the slayer, but anyone else who would unduly profit from the crime. Suppose the victim's will left property to the slayer, but if the slayer died first, to the slayer's children from another marriage. A few courts have extended the slayer rule to these "indirect beneficiaries," holding that it would be unfair to allow the slayer's actions to enrich his or her kin (at least where the slayer's kin are not also the victim's kin). See, e.g., Swain v. Estate of Tyre ex rel. Reilly, 57 A.3d 283 (R.I. 2012); In re Estate of Mueller, 655 N.E.2d 1040 (Ill. Ct. App. 1994). But see Diep v. Rivas, 745 A.2d 1098 (Md. 2000); In re Estate of Covert, 761 N.E.2d 751 (N.Y. 2001).

24. This difference in evidentiary standards also appears in the related context of civil wrongful death proceedings: A prosecutor may not be able to prove a slayer's guilt beyond a reasonable doubt on criminal charges of murder or manslaughter, but the slayer may be found liable in a civil wrongful death action under the preponderance standard.

Castro v. Ballesteros-Suarez
213 P.3d 197 (Ariz. Ct. App. 2009)

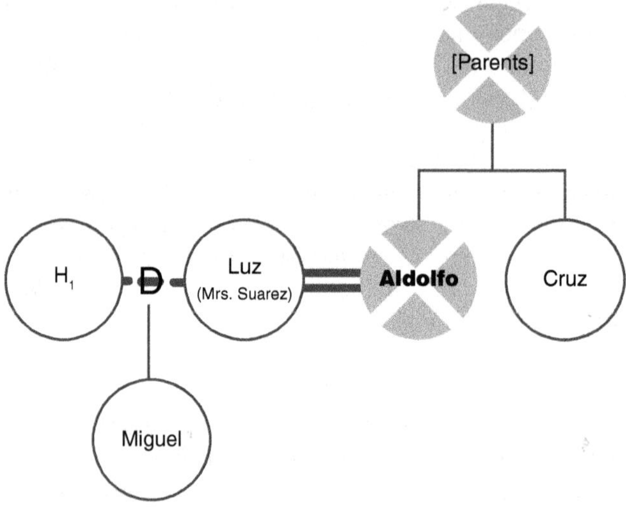

PORTLEY, Judge.

We are asked to determine whether the slayer statute, Arizona Revised Statutes ("A.R.S.") section 14-2803 (2005), can preclude the decedent's widow from collecting all or part of the proceeds from two life insurance policies. Because the slayer statute prohibits a person who is found to have feloniously and intentionally killed another from profiting by that act, we affirm.

FACTS AND PROCEDURAL BACKGROUND

[On November 29, 2004, Adolfo F. Suarez was shot to death in his home. The police never arrested anyone for the murder. However, Adolfo's widow, Luz Ballesteros-Suarez, was a suspect. Mrs. Suarez was also the beneficiary under Adolfo's two life insurance policies. In a civil trial over who should receive the proceeds of these policies, Cruz Antonia Suarez Castro, Adolfo's sister, testified that Mrs. Suarez had offered her money to help her cash in on Adolfo's life insurance. Mrs. Suarez and her adult son, Miguel Carrasco, also took the witness stand, but invoked their Fifth Amendment right to remain silent.]

The [trial] court . . . found that:

> [Mrs. Suarez's] invocation of her privilege against self-incrimination gives rise to an inference that she was involved in and is responsible in whole or in part for the murder of Adolfo Suarez as a matter of fact.
>
> [Ms.] Castro's un-rebutted testimony that [Mrs. Suarez] offered her money if she would help [her sister-in-law] go against [Ms.] Castro's family and not oppose her attempt to obtain the insurance proceeds on [the Decedent's] life buttresses the allowable inference that [Mrs. Suarez] was involved in the murder of her husband. . . .

The Court finds that, because of the allowable inferences the Court can make from [Mrs. Suarez's] taking the Fifth Amendment when questioned about the murder of Adolfo Francisco Suarez . . . the preponderance of the evidence in this civil case is that Defendant, Luz Ballesteros-Suarez would be found guilty of the intentional and felonious killing of Adolfo Francisco Suarez.

DISCUSSION

Mrs. Suarez argues that the slayer statute is inapplicable. We disagree.

To determine whether the statute applies, we review its plain language to find and give effect to the legislative intent. The slayer statute, in relevant part, provides that:

> A. A person who feloniously and intentionally kills the decedent forfeits all benefits under this chapter with respect to the decedent's estate, including an intestate share, an elective share, an omitted spouse's or child's share, a homestead allowance, exempt property and a family allowance. . . .
>
> B. The felonious and intentional killing of the decedent:
>
> 1. Revokes any revocable:
>
> (a) Disposition or appointment of property made by the decedent to the killer in a governing instrument. . . .

A.R.S. §14-2803.

The plain language of A.R.S. §14-2803 demonstrates that the Arizona Legislature intended to prevent a person who feloniously and intentionally kills another from receiving any property belonging to his victim. Any doubt about the legislative intent was resolved in the 1994 statutory amendments, which provided that "the principle [is] that a killer cannot profit from that person's wrong." A.R.S. §14-2803(E).

Here, the slayer statute was raised at the outset of the action after the insurance companies learned that Mrs. Suarez was a suspect in her husband's murder. Ms. Castro subsequently petitioned the court to find that Mrs. Suarez was responsible for the Decedent's death. As a result, the trial focused on whether Mrs. Suarez was responsible for her husband's murder.

During the trial, Detective Hawkins of the Glendale Police Department testified that the investigation led him to believe that Mrs. Suarez committed first-degree murder and other crimes against her husband to collect the insurance proceeds. Specifically, the detective testified that the investigation revealed that the Decedent and Mrs. Suarez's son had been in the home earlier that evening; that the son took the Decedent out drinking and they later returned home; that someone entered the house without force; that person shot and killed another man before shooting Decedent twice with a shotgun; that the house was not ransacked nor was anything removed; and that the blinds to Mrs. Suarez's room were open as if someone had looked out. Additionally, he testified that, in his opinion, based on the phone records, she called her son earlier in the evening, called the house at approximately 11:25 P.M. and had a short conversation; called again at 11:30 P.M., had another brief conversation and then came home. The 9-1-1 operator was called at 11:47 P.M. He also testified that in the days following the murders, Mrs. Suarez called Ms. Castro numerous times and after each conversation would immediately call her son.

The trial court also noted that a witness or party in a civil case can invoke their Fifth Amendment privilege against self-incrimination, but the trier of fact is free to infer the truth of the charged misconduct. Mrs. Suarez does not dispute the inference that she committed the crime. Instead, she challenges the sufficiency of the inferences to establish the applicability of the slayer statute.

Although there was no direct evidence that Mrs. Suarez killed her husband, there was circumstantial evidence that she was responsible for his death; namely, the detective's testimony . . . and Mrs. Suarez's attempt to convince Ms. Castro not to challenge her efforts to recover the insurance proceeds. Circumstantial evidence has the same probative value as direct evidence. Consequently, based on all of the trial evidence, there was substantial evidence to support the trial court's conclusion by a preponderance of the evidence that Mrs. Suarez was criminally accountable for the intentional and felonious death of her husband.

. . .

Mrs. Suarez also contends that she cannot be held responsible for her husband's murder because there was no probable cause to arrest her.

The slayer statute's provisions may be invoked without having probable cause to arrest. In the absence of a criminal conviction for feloniously and intentionally killing another that has been sustained on appeal, the slayer statute can be invoked if the trier of fact finds by a preponderance of the evidence that "the person would be found criminally accountable for the felonious and intentional killing of the decedent." A.R.S. §14-2803(F).

Although the Glendale Police Department did not believe it had sufficient probable cause to arrest Mrs. Suarez, the trial court found that Ms. Castro demonstrated by a preponderance of the evidence that Decedent's widow was responsible for his death. She met her burden of proof. Consequently, when the court found that the evidence established that Mrs. Suarez was criminally accountable for Decedent's felonious and intentional death by a preponderance of the evidence, it did not err.

CONCLUSION

Because there is substantial evidence to support the trial court's determination that Mrs. Suarez was responsible for the felonious and intentional murder of her husband, she is not entitled to any portion of his life insurance proceeds. Accordingly, we affirm the trial court's judgment.

QUESTIONS

11. How can Mrs. Suarez be a "slayer" if the police determined that they did not even have probable cause to arrest her?

    ANSWER. "[T]he showing required for probable cause is lower than . . . the preponderance of the evidence standard." United States v. Mustapher, 459 F. Supp. 2d 752, 756 (N.D. Ill. 2006). But as a strictly legal matter, the fact that the police decided that they did not have enough evidence to charge Mrs. Suarez does not have preclusive effect on a subsequent civil trial. And on a pragmatic level, the trial court heard testimony that the police did not.

12. Suppose Mrs. Suarez had been arrested, charged, and found guilty of voluntary manslaughter. Would that automatically bar her from taking her husband's life insurance proceeds? What result if Mrs. Suarez had been convicted of involuntary manslaughter?

    ANSWER. Yes. Voluntary manslaughter is an intentional and felonious killing, and thus satisfies the elements of most slayer statutes. See, e.g., In re Nale Estate, 803 N.W.2d 907, 911 (Mich. Ct. App. 2010); In re Estate of Bartolovich, 616 A.2d 1043, 1044 (Pa. Super. Ct. 1992).

PROBLEM IV

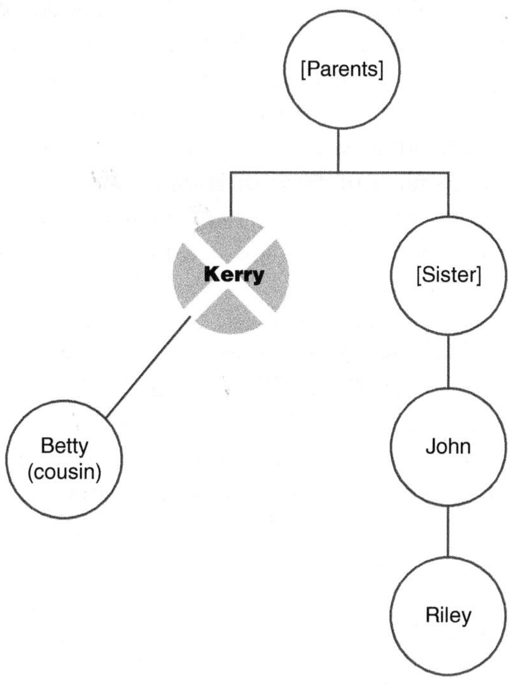

Kerry is a 65-year-old widow with no children. She is close to her sister's son John, who has a long history of paranoid schizophrenia. Kerry's will leaves all of her property to John, or, if John dies first, to John's daughter, Riley. Kerry's will also provides that if both John and Riley predecease Kerry, Kerry's cousin Betty will inherit all of Kerry's estate. Finally, Kerry's will names John as executor and Betty as successor executor.

One day, John is driving Kerry to an appointment, when he begins to have severe hallucinations. He lets go of the steering wheel and waves his hands wildly. The car veers across a double yellow line and strikes an oncoming big rig. Kerry is killed instantly, but John survives.

John is charged with involuntary manslaughter. However, John's symptoms have worsened since the accident, and the court rules that he is mentally incompetent to stand trial. He is sent to a mental institution for treatment.

Betty files a motion in probate court asking to be named as Kerry's executor and arguing that she should inherit all of Kerry's property. How should a court rule?

1.4.6 Disclaimers

An heir or beneficiary can refuse to inherit by executing what is sometimes called a "renunciation," or, more commonly, a "disclaimer."[25] A person who disclaims (the "disclaimant") is treated as having predeceased the decedent for purposes of distributing the decedent's estate. See UPC §2-1106(b)(3). A disclaimer may be of the entire property or only a part. Under a legal fiction known as the "relation-back doctrine," a valid disclaimer "relates back" to immediately before the decedent's death, meaning that the disclaimant never gained possession of the disclaimed property.[26] The relation-back doctrine is important because, if the disclaimant were treated as possessing the property before giving it away, the disclaimant may have to pay a gift tax on the gift or the property could be seized by the disclaimant's creditors.

Importantly, a disclaimant may not select alternate takers for the disclaimed property. Instead, the property passes to the next eligible taker under the decedent's will or by priority established in the intestacy statutes. Generally, however, a disclaimant knows who the next eligible takers are, and that knowledge is often a key factor in deciding whether to disclaim.

Individuals can disclaim more than assets: They can also disclaim rights of survivorship, powers of appointment, and fiduciary duties (topics we discuss later in Chapters 5, 10, and 11, respectively). UPC §§2-1107 through 2-1111. Once an individual makes a valid disclaimer, the disclaimer becomes irrevocable. UPC §2-1105(e).

Why would anyone choose *not* to receive some valuable property or right? The most common reasons are to avoid taxes or creditors. For example, suppose Donna is unmarried and has one child, Albert. Albert, a wealthy lawyer, also has one child,

25. "'Disclaimer' means the refusal to accept an interest in or power over property." UPC §2-1102(3).

26. The relation-back doctrine is required by the fundamental rule that devises and inheritances devolve to beneficiaries and heirs upon the decedent's death. UPC §3-101. By treating a disclaimant as having predeceased the decedent, the disclaimed property never devolves to the disclaimant but, instead, devolves to the alternate beneficiary or heir.

Xavier, who is a struggling artist. If Donna dies intestate, her property will pass to Albert, who values it less than Xavier would. Although Albert could accept Donna's assets and then either leave them to Xavier in his estate plan or give them to Xavier during his life, Albert runs the risk of having to pay estate or gift taxes on these transfers. Instead, if Albert disclaims, he can effectively funnel Donna's estate directly to Xavier without incurring an additional level wealth transfer taxation. Alternatively, suppose that Albert negligently injured a third party, Lotta, in a car accident. Lotta has filed a personal injury claim against Albert and is likely to recover a large judgment. If Albert disclaims his interest in Donna's estate, Xavier — rather than Lotta — will inherit Donna's funds, thereby shielding them from being paid over to Lotta.

Disclaimers are not always effective. For example, a disclaimer by an insolvent heir or beneficiary might be considered a fraudulent transfer. UPC §2-1113, comment. Some jurisdictions prohibit disclaimers that are used to ensure that the heir or beneficiary qualifies for Medicaid or other forms of public assistance. Finally, many states (and the Internal Revenue Code for gift tax purposes) require disclaimers to be made within nine months of the decedent's death. Although the UPC does not impose a time limit on disclaimers, it does provide that an heir or beneficiary forfeits the right to disclaim by *accepting* property from a decedent's estate or trust. Under the federal gift tax, a disclaimer is "qualified" and, therefore, not treated as a taxable gift from the disclaimant to the next eligible taker if, among other criteria, the disclaimer is made within nine months of the transfer or the disclaimant's twenty-first birthday. 26 U.S.C. §2518.[27]

Uniform Probate Code
§2-1105 Power to Disclaim . . .

(a) A person may disclaim, in whole or part, any interest in or power over property. . . . A person may disclaim the interest . . . even if its creator imposed a . . . restriction on transfer or a restriction or limitation on the right to disclaim.

. . .

(c) To be effective, a disclaimer must be in a writing or other record, declare the disclaimer, describe the interest or power disclaimed, be signed by the person making the disclaimer, and be delivered [to the decedent's trustee or personal representative] or filed [with the court]. . . .

§2-1113 When Disclaimer Barred or Limited

(a) A disclaimer is barred by a written waiver of the right to disclaim.

(b) A disclaimer of an interest in property is barred if any of the following events occur before the disclaimer becomes effective: (1) the disclaimant accepts the interest sought to be disclaimed [or] (2) the disclaimant voluntarily assigns, conveys, encumbers, pledges, or transfers the interest sought to be disclaimed or contracts to do so. . . .

27. For more on the background and applicability of disclaimers, see William P. LaPiana, Some Property Law Issues in the Law of Disclaimers, 38 Real Prop. Prob. & Tr. J. 207 (2003); Adam J. Hirsch, Revisions in Need of Revising: The Uniform Disclaimer of Property Interests Act, 29 Fla. St. U. L. Rev. 109 (2001); Adam J. Hirsch, Disclaimer Law and UDPIA's Unintended Consequences, 36 Est. Plan. 34 (2009).

In re Estate of Gardner
283 P.3d 676 (Ariz. Ct. App. 2012)

GOULD, Judge.

This is an appeal taken from the trial court's order determining that Appellant, Marlene Richardson, was responsible for payment of the mortgage interest and all other expenses associated with the life estate interest she received in Decedent J. Scott Gardner's Prescott house ("the Property"). Richardson challenges the court's finding that her disclaimer was barred under Arizona Revised Statutes ("A.R.S.") section 14-10013(B)(1). Based on Richardson's conduct in continuing to occupy the Property to the exclusion of others, her knowledge of her liability for expenses related to the Property, and her belated attempt to disclaim her life estate interest, we affirm the trial court's determination her disclaimer was ineffective.

FACTS AND PROCEDURAL BACKGROUND

Upon Decedent's death, Richardson was granted a life estate interest in the Property. Under the terms of Decedent's Amended Trust, at the termination of Richardson's life estate, the Property would pass to Decedent's two children ("Remaindermen"). The life estate provisions directed Richardson to maintain the Property as if it was her own; to pay all taxes, utilities, homeowners association fees and insurance on the property; and to be responsible for "[a]ny other reasonable and customary fees that would normally accompany a property."

At Decedent's death, the Property was subject to a $205,330 mortgage ("the Mortgage"). From the time of Decedent's death, the Trust paid the principal and interest expenses on the Mortgage. Wayne Gardner, the successor trustee of Decedent's Trust, petitioned the court for instructions to determine who, between Richardson and Remaindermen, would be responsible for paying the interest and the principal of the Mortgage. In August 2009, the court found that Richardson, in exchange for her life estate, was required under the terms of the Trust to pay "reasonable interest" on the Mortgage, and that the current interest on the mortgage payment of 6% "is a reasonable rate."

On May 21, 2010, Richardson mailed Gardner a letter seeking to disclaim her interest in the Property effective September 23, 2008. In August 2010, Gardner sought "a declaration from the Court stating that Richardson is responsible to pay (i) all Mortgage interest paid by the Trust from the date of Decedent's death until current and (ii) all other expenses associated with the Property as set forth in the First Amendment [to Decedent's Trust]." Gardner argued Richardson's acceptance of the life estate, as evidenced by emails Gardner received from her spanning October 2008 to February 2009, barred Richardson's later attempt to disclaim. Gardner further argued that Richardson's disclaimer was untimely. Gardner asserted Richardson did not disclaim her interest until May 21, 2010—over nine months after the court issued instructions that Richardson was required to pay interest on the Mortgage—and two months after Gardner sent Richardson a form of renunciation, which purportedly provided Richardson an opportunity to renounce her interest in the life estate.

The court concluded Richardson had accepted the life estate "by asserting her right to exclusive possession" to the exclusion of Remaindermen and "their agents," and thus, any later disclaimer was "irrevocably barred."

DISCUSSION

Both parties agree that the sole issue on appeal is whether Richardson's disclaimer is barred by her prior acceptance of the subject life estate. "[D]isclaimer of an interest in property is barred if . . . [t]he disclaimant accepts the interest sought to be disclaimed." A.R.S. §14-10013(B)(1). "Disclaimer" is defined as "the refusal to accept an interest in or power over property." A.R.S. §14-10002(3). The statute, however, does not define "accept" or "acceptance."

In the absence of a statutory definition for "acceptance," we will examine the facts of the case to determine whether Richardson's conduct constitutes acceptance of the life estate. When a devisee takes possession and exercises control over the devised property, without contemporaneously and objectively manifesting any intent to disclaim, the acts of possession and control constitute conclusive evidence of acceptance. The conclusion that such actions represent acceptance is further evidenced by a devisee's failure to exercise her opportunity to renounce or disclaim her interest within a reasonable time period.

The undisputed facts show that Richardson accepted her life estate interest in the Property prior to any attempts at disclaimer. Richardson physically occupied the property in the same manner she had prior to Decedent's death. Richardson arranged to pay the utilities and taxes on the Property as required by the life estate agreement. Finally Richardson made repeated and affirmative statements to Gardner asserting her present right to "enjoy the benefits of ownership during [her] lifetime."

> Please pass along my[] reply and remind [Remaindermen] that they do not have the right to enter the house at will. Nor do their agents.
>
> [Decedent] bought the house for me. There's no way I would even consider giving it up.

Richardson's statements also indicate her understanding that as life tenant she would be financially responsible for a portion of the Mortgage — a "reasonable and customary fee[ ] that would normally accompany a property." Richardson sent Gardner two emails that evidence her awareness of the financial encumbrances of the Property. In an email sent on January 30, 2009 she said:

> I'm content with the way Scott left things. He had planned to leave me the Prescott house with a $100,000 mortgage. Since he refinanced, unbeknownst to me, he ended up with a mortgage of $208,000. So that explains why he left me the odd amount of $108,000.

We reject Richardson's argument that these statements merely expressed her desire to accept the life estate before she learned of her responsibility to pay the interest portion of the Mortgage. This claim is unsupported by the record, and it does not overcome Richardson's burden of proving she effectively disclaimed the interest prior to accepting it. Although Richardson may have concluded that the Mortgage rendered her life estate interest in the Property an onerous, rather than beneficial gift, her failure to act on this conclusion before she exercised her interest barred any later attempts to disclaim. Accordingly, Richardson's disclaimer is ineffective.

QUESTIONS

13. Suppose Richardson neither occupied the house nor sent any of the emails to the trustee that asserted her right to live there. However, in the winter of 2008, she had rented the property to tenants for a six-month term. Then, in the spring of 2009, she had tried to disclaim. Would the analysis or outcome change?

    ANSWER. One way an heir or beneficiary can accept an inheritance is if she does not disclaim within a reasonable time. In the case, Richardson waited more than a year and a half; conversely, in this hypo, Richardson would have tried to reject the property within a matter of months, which seems more reasonable. Nevertheless, the outcome would probably be the same. Renting property is an act of ownership and control that constitutes an acceptance.

1.4.7 Professional Responsibility

Two ethical issues are particularly relevant to trusts and estates attorneys. The first is malpractice liability. Estate planning is an extremely rewarding niche, in which you perform a valuable service for individuals and their loved ones. But one of its few downsides is that potentially dire consequences flow from mistakes during the drafting process. One typo or oversight can distort a decedent's wishes, increase the estate's tax liability, or even invalidate an attempt to create a will or trust.

Traditionally, estate planners were shielded from lawsuits brought by their client's intended beneficiaries. Professionals only owed a duty of reasonable care to people to whom they were in privity (bound by contract). Although estate planners are in privity with their clients, they are not in privity with a client's intended beneficiaries. In addition, estate planning blunders usually do not surface until the client has died. For these reasons, under orthodox tort law—and even today in several states—estate planners were rarely liable for drafting errors. See, e.g., Baker v. Wood, Ris & Hames, Prof'l Corp., 364 P.3d 872 (Colo. 2016).

Yet in the last few decades, the law has changed. Most jurisdictions have carved out exceptions to the privity requirement in the estate planning context. The rationale behind this shift is that it is obvious to all of the parties that the client has hired the lawyer primarily to confer a benefit upon the beneficiaries of his or her estate plan. See, e.g., Restatement (Third) of Law Governing Lawyers §51(3)(a) (2000). Thus, many courts have allowed beneficiaries or would-be beneficiaries to sue for malpractice when a lawyer botches a decedent's express directives. See, e.g., Paul v. Patton, 185 Cal. Rptr. 3d 830 (Ct. App. 2015).

A second set of ethical rules that impact probate practice are those that govern client communications and conflicts of interest. Estate planners often jointly represent multiple members of the same family, such as married couples. Joint representation can be an efficient way to harmonize a family's estate plan. Yet it also is a minefield. Even in functional relationships, each person's wishes may diverge from his or her partner's. For example, individuals may want to favor their children over their stepchildren, or have warring views about a potential beneficiary's maturity or financial responsibility. In addition, the estate planner may learn confidential information about one spouse that affects the other. This creates serious tension between the lawyer's duty to keep his client's secrets and to keep his clients reasonably informed. For these reasons, it is critically important that an estate planner explain these nuances and secure a written waiver of conflicts of interest before agreeing to any joint representation.

American Bar Association Model Rules of Professional Conduct Rule 1.6 Confidentiality of Information

(a) A lawyer shall not reveal information relating to the representation of a client unless the client gives informed consent, the disclosure is impliedly authorized in order to carry out the representation or the disclosure is permitted by paragraph (b).

(b) A lawyer may reveal information relating to the representation of a client to the extent the lawyer reasonably believes necessary:

(1) to prevent reasonably certain death or substantial bodily harm;

. . .

(3) to prevent, mitigate or rectify substantial injury to the financial interests or property of another that is reasonably certain to result or has resulted from the client's commission of a crime or fraud in furtherance of which the client has used the lawyer's services;

. . .

(c) A lawyer shall make reasonable efforts to prevent the inadvertent or unauthorized disclosure of, or unauthorized access to, information relating to the representation of a client.

American Bar Association Model Rules of Professional Conduct Rule 1.7 Conflict of Interest, Current Clients

(a) Except as provided in paragraph (b), a lawyer shall not represent a client if the representation involves a concurrent conflict of interest. A concurrent conflict of interest exists if:

(1) the representation of one client will be directly adverse to another client; or

(2) there is a significant risk that the representation of one or more clients will be materially limited by the lawyer's responsibilities to another client, a former client or a third person or by a personal interest of the lawyer.

(b) Notwithstanding the existence of a concurrent conflict of interest under paragraph (a), a lawyer may represent a client if:

(1) the lawyer reasonably believes that the lawyer will be able provide competent and diligent representation to each affected client;

. . .

(3) the representation does not involve the assertion of a claim by one client against another client represented by the lawyer in the same litigation or other proceeding before a tribunal; and

(4) each affected client gives informed consent, confirmed in writing.

PROBLEM V

Paul is married to Tawny. Unbeknownst to Tawny, Paul has recently fathered a child with another woman, Janet.

In January 2015, Paul and Tawny hire Wallace & Bingham, a fifty-lawyer firm, to draft their wills. Paul and Tawny sign an engagement letter, which has a paragraph entitled "Waiver of Conflict of Interest." It explains that information that one spouse provides to Wallace & Bingham may be disclosed to the other spouse. It does not, however, contain an explicit waiver of client confidentiality.

In March 2015, before Paul and Tawny sign their wills, Janet hires Wallace & Bingham to pursue a paternity claim against Paul. Janet's engagement letter does not contain a waiver of conflicts of interest. Due to a clerical error, Wallace & Bingham does not realize that it is currently representing Paul. DNA testing in the paternity case reveals that Paul is indeed the father of Janet's child. Paul does not inform Wallace & Bingham of this fact.

In April 2015, Paul and Tawny sign the wills that Wallace & Bingham has prepared. They each leave their property to each other, and then to their own biological children. As a result, if Tawny dies before Paul, her property might ultimately pass via Paul's will to Paul's child with Janet.

In November 2015, Wallace & Bingham discovers that it is representing Paul and Tawny for the purposes of estate planning and Janet for the purposes of her paternity claim against Paul. Should the firm withdraw from representing Janet in the paternity action? Can it inform Tawny of Paul's child with Janet?

2 | Intestacy — Statutory Distribution

2.1 INTESTATE ESTATES — INTRODUCTION

Most Americans die *intestate*, that is, without a valid will. In an intestate estate, the decedent's probate property passes to *heirs* determined by statutory rules that, in effect, comprise a default estate plan. Those rules, historically codified as *statutes of descent and distribution*,[1] are now usually referred to simply as *intestacy statutes*.

This chapter addresses the inheritance of property by intestacy, including the composition of the intestate estate, the frequency of intestacies, the determination of intestate heirs, and the division of the intestate estate among intestate heirs. Intestacy statutes vary across the states, so we will focus on the intestacy system codified in the UPC.[2]

The Uniform Probate Code succinctly defines the intestate estate by establishing those parts of a decedent's estate that pass by intestacy.

Uniform Probate Code
§2-101 Intestate Estate

> (a) Any part of a decedent's estate not effectively disposed of by will passes by intestate succession to the decedent's heirs as prescribed in this Code, except as modified by the decedent's will.

Individuals may die completely intestate. They may never have made a will; they may have made a will but later revoked it entirely without making a new one; they may have tried to write their own will but failed to execute it properly. In those situations, the decedent's probate property is distributed entirely by intestacy.

---

1. Historically, statutes of descent governed the disposition of real property whereas statutes of distribution governed the disposition of personal property.

2. As of 2017, the following states have enacted or substantially enacted the intestacy provisions of the UPC: Alaska, Arizona, Colorado, Hawaii, Idaho, Maine, Massachusetts, Michigan, Minnesota, Montana, Nebraska, New Jersey, New Mexico, North Dakota, South Carolina, South Dakota, Utah, and the United States Virgin Islands. As noted in Chapter 1, a decedent's personal property wherever located and real property located within the domicile state is subject to the domicile state's intestacy laws. A decedent's real property located in another state is subject to the intestacy laws of the state where that property is located.

Intestacies can also be *partial.* For example, an individual may die having executed a valid will that contains one or more provisions that are unenforceable or cannot be administered. Alternatively, the will may dispose of only part of the decedent's property. In those situations, a partial intestacy occurs: To the extent the provisions of the will are enforceable and can be administered, the decedent's intent is given effect as stated in the will. Probate property that does not pass under the will passes to the decedent's heirs by intestacy.[3]

Most individuals intend to make a will, but die without making one. In the following article, Professor Weisbord describes the high rate of intestacy in the United States and the disadvantages of dying intestate.

Wills for Everyone: Helping Individuals Opt Out of Intestacy

Reid Kress Weisbord
53 B.C. L. Rev. 877 (2012)

WIDESPREAD INTESTACY: A PERVASIVE, UNINTENDED LAPSE OF TESTAMENTARY FREEDOM

[Although most Americans support the freedom of testamentary disposition], decades of empirical studies have repeatedly confirmed that most Americans do not have a will. Although no nationwide study has ever quantified the number of intestate decedents, scholars agree that a high rate of intestacy has persisted throughout most of American history. In the eighteenth and nineteenth centuries, wills were uncommon except among the wealthy. [More] recently, a 2009 publication estimated that sixty-five percent of Americans do not have a will. A 2006 nationwide survey found that sixty-eight percent of respondents lacked a will. Both estimates corroborate older studies reporting similar findings. Scholars believe that most individuals who lack a will never obtain one and die having allowed the right of testamentary freedom to lapse.

The question of why so many Americans do not have a will is difficult to answer, but empirical and anecdotal evidence suggests that procrastination is, by far, the most plausible explanation for intestacy. In a 1977 intestacy study, 63.6% of respondents who lacked a will cited "laziness" as the reason. In a 1978 survey of randomly selected Iowa citizens, 57% of respondents who lacked a will said they "ha[d] not gotten around to making a will." . . .

Procrastination, the most frequently cited reason, does not manifest an intent to die intestate. To the contrary, procrastination implies that such individuals want to avoid intestacy and hope to obtain a will. If most individuals who lack a will want to

3. Recall from Chapter 1 that "[t]he probate estate consists of property owned by the decedent at death and property acquired by the decedent's estate at or after the decedent's death." Restatement (Third) of Property: Wills & Other Donative Transfers §1.1(a) (1999).

obtain one, then what is preventing them? In both the 1977 and 1978 intestacy studies, procrastination appear[ed] to serve as a catchall response, but unfortunately, empirical studies have not inquired further into why so many individuals procrastinate in making a will. The high rate of intestacy [does not appear to be] the result of widespread agreement with or reliance on the default rules of heirship. Although in theory, agreement with the default rules could reduce the need for a will, both the 1977 and 1978 intestacy studies concluded that individuals lacking a will did not intentionally rely on the default rules. . . . Taken together, these studies suggest that Americans value testamentary freedom and want to exercise that right by executing a will, but for various reasons (largely procrastination), they do not. This is troubling because most individuals do not understand even the most basic consequences of dying intestate. The fact that most individuals cannot correctly identify their intestate heirs means that, for many individuals who do not currently have a will, the need to obtain one might be far more important than they realize.

DISADVANTAGES OF INTESTACY

Intestacy statutes govern the disposition of property owned at death and not disposed of by will. In most states, with minor variation, the intestate estate is distributed to heirs in the following order: surviving spouse, descendants, parents, descendants of parents, grandparents, descendants of grandparents, and (in some states) stepchildren and descendants of stepchildren. This priority reflects a legislative presumption that most individuals prefer that property pass to surviving family members, generally defined as the surviving spouse and blood relatives, to the exclusion of friends, cohabitants, favorite charities, or anyone else. Scholars argue that principles of testamentary freedom mandate agreement between heirship rules and probable intent because to do otherwise would create a trap for the uninformed.

Although there are notable exceptions, intestacy statutes tend to reflect the probable intent of most individuals.

But even when intestacy statutes correctly capture majoritarian preferences, dying intestate remains disadvantageous in a significant number of cases. Intestacy is unsuitable for all individuals whose preferences differ from the statutory rules of heirship, but it is acutely unsuitable for a large and growing population of nontraditional families, which include relationships other than those defined by consanguinity, marriage (as legally defined within the decedent's state), or legal adoption. Intestacy is structurally unsuitable for nontraditional families because the legislature cannot (or will not) make presumptions about probable intent when the decedent's relationship to intended beneficiaries is not clearly defined by traditionally accepted indicia of familial status.

For example, unmarried cohabitants living in a marriage-like arrangement may intend mutual inheritance rights for each other, but without an outward, objective manifestation regarding the status of their relationship, it is difficult to make legislative presumptions about their probable intent. When unmarried cohabitants have the right to marry but choose not to, cohabitation does not serve as a reliable

> proxy for testamentary intent. Some cohabitants maintain committed relationships but choose not to marry for financial reasons [(e.g., tax treatment, eligibility for certain entitlements)] and other cohabitants live together because they are not yet sure if they are ready to marry; many nontraditional families probably fall somewhere in between. Without a factual inquiry, it is impossible to know whether cohabitants live together because their relationship operates like a family or for some other reason, and post-mortem factual inquiries tend to be unreliable because the best evidence, the decedent's testimony, is not available. Intestacy statutes therefore are especially unsuitable for committed, same-sex partners [who did not marry following the national legalization of same-sex marriage in 2015]. The structural unsuitability of intestacy for nontraditional families is a salient problem because of the growing trend of unmarried cohabitation and same-sex partnerships. In 2010, there were 16.3 million Americans living in unmarried cohabitation households.
>
> Even when intestacy statutes correctly anticipate the decedent's intended beneficiaries, dying intestate can lead to undesirable, costly, and acrimonious guardianship and administration contests, which could otherwise be avoided by executing a will. Guardianship issues are an especially important consideration for individuals with minor children. [Upon the death of a parent with a minor child, a court must appoint a responsible adult, known as a "guardian of the person," to care for the surviving child left without a legal guardian. During life, the parent may nominate a guardian of the person by will, but failure to nominate forces the court to select from a statutory hierarchy of possible guardians to care for the child without direction from the decedent parent. Further, if an unmarried single parent dies intestate, all or most of the estate passes to the decedent's children, but a court proceeding may be necessary to appoint a "guardian of the estate" or conservator of the child's property. During life, it is advantageous for the minor child's parent to nominate the guardian of the estate or conservator; such nominations are typically made by will.]
>
> All individuals should be concerned about conflicts regarding the selection of a personal representative to administer their estates. Absent testamentary appointment of an executor, a court must appoint a personal representative without express direction from the decedent. The personal representative plays a critical role in the estate administration process because she is typically given authority and discretion to decide whether and how to liquidate property in the estate to satisfy creditor claims and general bequests. Disagreement among beneficiaries regarding selection of the personal representative can lead to expensive and contentious proceedings that dissipate the decedent's estate. The testator can resolve such disagreements in advance by designating an executor in the will.

The disadvantages of dying intestate can also compound over time as property, particularly the decedent's primary residence, descends from one generation of relatives to the next. Professor Palma Strand explains in the following hypothetical:

> The widow/mother/grandmother [inherits the family home from a predeceased spouse and] dies intestate. Several children and perhaps several grandchildren, if at least one

child predeceased her, are heirs by representation as tenants in common so that each heir has a fractional interest in the whole property—which leads to the designation "heirs' property." . . .

The value of the house (likely located in a low-value neighborhood) may not be substantial, and the house may already have been neglected somewhat as the husband aged or after he died. This in conjunction with each heir having a small interest leads to the heirs not claiming their economic share of the home's value. Or they may regard it as the family homestead with a history worth preserving. All heirs, at least all those present, agree not to sell the home to extract its economic value, and the estate is never probated. This failure to probate can occur even if the wife has a will.

In conjunction with the decision not to sell the home, the heirs agree that the family member or members who were living in the house before the wife's death can continue to live there. He or she pays property taxes in the original owners' or owner's name. This may continue for a substantial period of time or into additional generations. By operation of intestacy law, as time passes, ownership becomes more and more fractionated until a number of people, perhaps even a dozen or more, have very small ownership interests while at the same time having experienced little connection with the home or even a complete lack of awareness that they have an interest in it.

At some point, this arrangement, with the house still titled to the original owner(s) but with legal ownership as heirs' property spread far and wide, hits a brick wall. Often, the problem is the payment of property taxes. Perhaps the occupant cannot pay, or he or she seeks contributions from the other owners, who cannot or see no reason to invest in a property from which they receive no benefit. Or low-cost loans are available to fix or improve the home, or a reverse mortgage to support the occupant is indicated, but a lack of clear title precludes eligibility. Or the area in which the home is located is being redeveloped and the developer wants to purchase the home. Or disaster hits, and disaster relief is conditioned on proof of title.

Depending on the economic incentives, the current occupant—usually but not always a part owner—may or may not be able to secure the legal assistance necessary to open probate, locate all the heirs, and clear title. While conceptually straightforward, this action is often a logistical nightmare: people move away, lose touch, have and adopt children, remarry and have more children, have children out of wedlock, go to prison, and die in faraway places without their families knowing. When the economic benefits are relatively low (saving a modest home from being lost due to property tax liens), legal assistance with estate administration is often unavailable. These cases demand many hours, and the rewards appear minimal—though they may constitute a significant part of the overall wealth holdings of the family. When the economic benefits are high (clearing title to sell the home for a redevelopment project, for example), legal assistance may be forthcoming, but legal fees may take a substantial percentage of the proceeds from the sale.

The final step may be eviction of or abandonment by the occupant, repossession for tax liens by the local government, and razing the property if deterioration is too far along. Blighted neighborhoods are one result. Another is loss to the family of the wealth earned by a prior generation.

Palma Joy Strand, Inheriting Inequality: Wealth, Race, and the Laws of Succession, 89 Or. L. Rev. 453, 493-95 (2010).

President Abraham Lincoln, assassinated April 14, 1865, was survived by his wife, Mary, and two children, Robert and Thomas. President Lincoln did not make a will and left an estate of $85,000.

2.2 WHO GETS (TAKERS) AND HOW MUCH (SHARES)?

Intestacy statutes establish the default rules that determine who inherits from the decedent and how much. These default rules are, by definition, optional in that they apply only in the absence of an expressed preference by the decedent (that is, a valid, enforceable will). The policy rationale underlying intestacy is to implement the probable preferences of a typical decedent. Ascertaining those preferences, however, presents an empirical challenge. As Professor Adam Hirsch explains, "[t]he mind of a decedent is the ultimate sanctum sanctorum. It refuses to yield itself to view." Adam J. Hirsch, Default Rules in Inheritance Law: A Problem in Search of Its Context, 73 Fordham L. Rev. 1031, 1069 (2004). Thus, at bottom, intestacy statutes reflect well-informed, although perhaps imperfect, presumptions by the legislature about the probable intent of intestate decedents.

In determining who inherits from an intestate estate, the first step is to determine the decedent's *heirs*. Heirs, also known as heirs-at-law, are the surviving members of the decedent's family who are entitled, by statute, to inherit a portion of the probate estate not disposed of by will. A brief comment about the word *heir*. The common law Latin expression *nemo est haeres viventis* remains the law today: No living person has heirs. A living person has *heirs apparent*: those who *might* take by intestacy. Heirs apparent have absolutely no property interest in the estate of a living person; they have only a mere *expectancy*. That expectancy is easily, swiftly, and often unexpectedly destroyed. The heir apparent may fail to survive the decedent; the decedent may have made a valid will and have given nothing to the heir apparent; or the decedent may have made a negative will disinheriting a particular heir apparent or a group of heirs apparent.

The possibilities include a *surviving spouse*; *descendants* — that is, children, grandchildren, great-grandchildren, etc.; *ancestors* — parents, grandparents, great-grandparents etc.; and *collateral relatives* — siblings, aunts/uncles, and cousins (that is, the decedent's family members who are neither descendants nor ancestors). The following Table of Consanguinity illustrates these familial relationships.

TABLE OF CONSANGUINITY

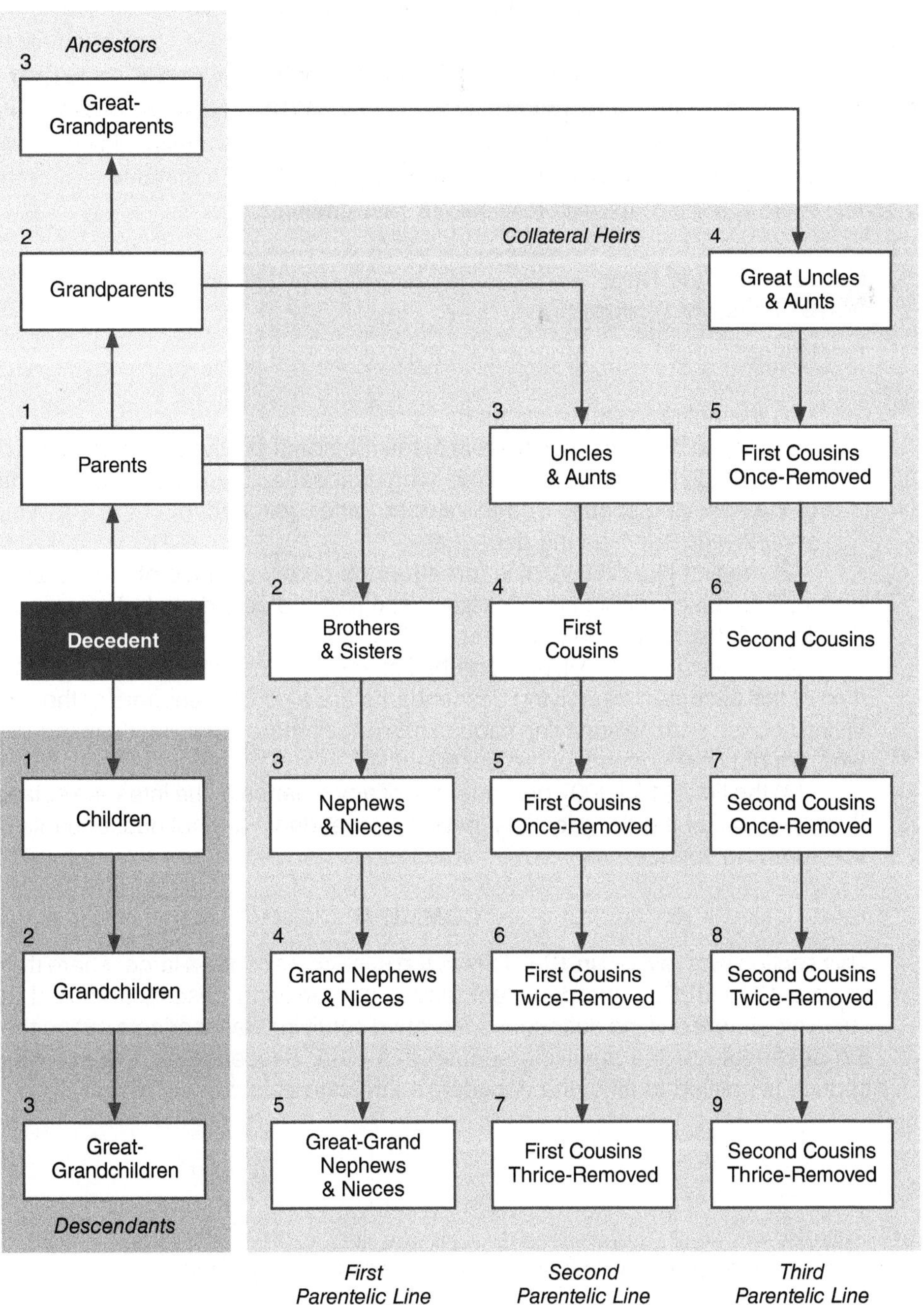

In all situations, collateral relatives are descendants of a decedent's ancestor. *First line collaterals* are descendants of the decedent's parents and are therefore said to be in the *first parentelic line. Second line collaterals* are descendants of the decedent's grandparents and are therefore said to be in the *second parentelic line*; and so on.[4]

Omitted from the Table of Consanguinity is the *surviving spouse* because there is no blood relationship between a decedent and surviving spouse.[5] In all jurisdictions, a surviving spouse takes priority, in both order and amount, as an intestate heir. A former spouse, however, inherits no part of the decedent's intestate estate. A legal marriage can terminate, thus ending an individual's status as "spouse," in only one of three ways: annulment, divorce, or death. With narrow exceptions, for purposes of intestate succession, a spouse remains a spouse during a divorce proceeding until the court enters a final decree of divorce. Thus, absent unusual circumstances (described in UPC §2-213), if a married person dies intestate during a divorce proceeding, the surviving spouse will inherit the same share of the intestate estate as if the couple had remained married and together.

Uniform Probate Code
§2-102 Share of Spouse

The intestate share of a decedent's surviving spouse is:

(1) the entire intestate estate if:

(A) no descendant or parent of the decedent survives the decedent; or

(B) all of the decedent's surviving descendants are also descendants of the surviving spouse and there is no other descendant of the surviving spouse who survives the decedent;

(2) the first [$300,000], plus three-fourths of any balance of the intestate estate, if no descendant of the decedent survives the decedent, but a parent of the decedent survives the decedent;

(3) the first [$225,000], plus one-half of any balance of the intestate estate, if all of the decedent's surviving descendants are also descendants of the surviving spouse and the surviving spouse has one or more surviving descendants who are not descendants of the decedent;

(4) the first [$150,000], plus one-half of any balance of the intestate estate, if one or more of the decedent's surviving descendants are not descendants of the surviving spouse.

COMMENT

This section was revised in 1990 to give the surviving spouse a larger share than the pre-1990 UPC. If the decedent leaves no surviving descendants and no surviving parent or if the decedent does leave surviving descendants but neither the decedent nor the surviving spouse has other descendants, the surviving spouse is entitled to all of the decedent's intestate estate.

---

4. The small numbers in the chart indicate the *degree of relationship* a relative has to the decedent. Some jurisdictions refer to degrees of relationship in determining intestate succession. The UPC does not.

5. The term "consanguinity" derives from the Latin word meaning "of common blood."

> If the decedent leaves no surviving descendants but does leave a surviving parent, the decedent's surviving spouse receives the first $300,000 plus three-fourths of the balance of the intestate estate.
>
> If the decedent leaves surviving descendants and if the surviving spouse (but not the decedent) has other descendants, and thus the decedent's descendants are unlikely to be the exclusive beneficiaries of the surviving spouse's estate, the surviving spouse receives the first $225,000 plus one-half of the balance of the intestate estate. The purpose is to assure the decedent's own descendants of a share in the decedent's intestate estate when the estate exceeds $225,000.
>
> If the decedent has other descendants, the surviving spouse receives $150,000 plus one-half of the balance. In this type of case, the decedent's descendants who are not descendants of the surviving spouse are not natural objects of the bounty of the surviving spouse.
>
> . . .
>
> Empirical studies support the increase in the surviving spouse's intestate share, reflected in the revisions of this section. The studies have shown that testators in smaller estates (which intestate estates overwhelmingly tend to be) tend to devise their entire estates to their surviving spouses, even when the couple has children.

Under the UPC, a surviving spouse is the most favored heir. If the decedent is survived by only a surviving spouse and no parents, the surviving spouse inherits the entire intestate estate. The same result occurs (even if the decedent is survived by a parent) if there is a surviving spouse and all of the decedent's surviving descendants are also descendants of the surviving spouse; here, the surviving spouse takes the entire intestate estate because the law presumes the surviving spouse will use the inheritance to care for the decedent's descendants or pass along the inherited assets to the joint descendants upon the surviving spouse's death. The surviving spouse, however, receives considerably less in blended families where the decedent is survived by descendants and either spouse has descendants from outside the marriage; here, the surviving spouse may have conflicting loyalties, so the intestate share is reduced to preserve adequate inheritance for the decedent's own descendants.

PROBLEM I

Petr and Wendell, both lifelong New Yorkers now in their 70s, were married ten years ago in Canada because same-sex marriage was not then legal in the United States. Although Petr and Wendell have been together for many decades, their relationship has recently been strained and they are now living separately. Petr's net worth is significantly higher than Wendell's, so Petr has been supporting Wendell financially even though they have separated. Petr and Wendell have no children, but they regard their long-haired calico as their "child" over whom they continue to share custody. Petr, who does not have a will, would not mind if Wendell shared in his estate, but Petr's primary concern is making sure that his cat be taken care of for the rest of its life. Petr's only blood relative is a sister, from whom he is estranged.

A. What would happen to Petr's estate if he died without a will, survived by Wendell, his cat, and his sister?

B. What, if any, relevance is the fact of Petr's separation from Wendell?

C. What would happen if Petr created a trust leaving his entire estate in trust for the benefit of his cat?

D. What would happen to Petr's estate if he divorced Wendell and then died, survived by Wendell, his cat, and his sister?

PROBLEM II

Arturo recently died intestate in a jurisdiction that has enacted the UPC. Under which of the following circumstances does his surviving spouse, Elvira, inherit Arturo's entire probate estate? If she does not inherit the entire probate estate, what is her share?

a. Arturo is survived by his wife; their son, Giorgio; and his mother, Henrietta.
b. Arturo is survived by his wife and by no parent or descendant.
c. Arturo is survived by his wife and his two children from a prior marriage.
d. Arturo is survived by his wife and her three children from a prior marriage.
e. Arturo is survived by his wife, her three children from a prior marriage, and his mother.
f. Arturo is survived by his wife, her three children from a prior marriage, and Giorgio, the son of Arturo and his wife.
g. Arturo is survived by his wife and his wife's child conceived during her extra-marital relationship with another man.

What is the rationale for the differing formulations in each of these examples?

UPC §2-103 addresses the situations in which an intestate decedent's surviving spouse does *not* inherit the entire estate.

Uniform Probate Code
§2-103 Share of Heirs Other than Surviving Spouse

(a) Any part of the intestate estate not passing to a decedent's surviving spouse under Section 2-102, or the entire intestate estate if there is no surviving spouse, passes in the following order to the individuals who survive the decedent:

(1) to the decedent's descendants by representation;

(2) if there is no surviving descendant, to the decedent's parents equally if both survive, or to the surviving parent if only one survives;

(3) if there is no surviving descendant or parent, to the descendants of the decedent's parents or either of them by representation;

(4) if there is no surviving descendant, parent, or descendant of a parent, but the decedent is survived on both the paternal and maternal sides by one or more grandparents or descendants of grandparents:

(A) half to the decedent's paternal grandparents equally if both survive, to the surviving paternal grandparent if only one survives, or to the descendants of the decedent's paternal grandparents or either of them if both are deceased, the descendants taking by representation; and

(B) half to the decedent's maternal grandparents equally if both survive, to the surviving maternal grandparent if only one survives, or to the descendants of the decedent's maternal grandparents or either of them if both are deceased, the descendants taking by representation;

(5) if there is no surviving descendant, parent, or descendant of a parent, but the decedent is survived by one or more grandparents or descendants of grandparents on the paternal but not the maternal side, or on the maternal but not the paternal side, to the decedent's relatives on the side with one or more surviving members in the manner described in paragraph (4).

(b) If there is no taker under subsection (a), but the decedent has:

(1) one deceased spouse who has one or more descendants who survive the decedent, the estate or part thereof passes to that spouse's descendants by representation; or

(2) more than one deceased spouse who has one or more descendants who survive the decedent, an equal share of the estate or part thereof passes to each set of descendants by representation.

COMMENT

This section provides for inheritance by descendants of the decedent, parents and their descendants, and grandparents and collateral relatives descended from grandparents; in line with modern policy, it eliminates more remote relatives tracing through great-grandparents. [Italics added.]

Under UPC §2-103, the intestate estate passes according to the following priority:

1. Descendants §(a)(1)
2. Parents §(a)(2)
3. First line collaterals (the first parentelic line) §(a)(3)
4. Grandparents §(a)(4)-(5)
5. Second line collaterals (the second parentelic line) §(a)(4)-(5)
6. Certain stepchildren §(b)

Note that UPC §2-103 does not provide for intestate succession beyond the second parentelic line. If there is no grandparent or descendant of a grandparent, the UPC does not extend inheritance rights to great-grandparents or their descendants (great uncles and aunts, second cousins, etc.). The UPC terminates heirship by blood relatives at second line collaterals to avoid the difficulties associated with what are called *laughing heirs*. This term refers to individuals related to a decedent so remotely that they may never have even known of or met the decedent and therefore are likely to laugh at the prospect of a windfall inheritance. The UPC's approach prevents laughing heirs from receiving a windfall, a sensible compromise in the absence of an expressed preference by the decedent. The policy justification for this limitation is premised on the evidentiary problems associated with determining the relationship between the intestate decedent and remote heirs, who may number in the thousands. The UPC takes the position that intestate inheritance by laughing heirs is presumptively inconsistent with the decedent's probable intent.[6]

If there are no takers within the first two parentelic lines, UPC §2-103(b) names the descendants of any deceased spouse of the decedent (that is, the decedent's step-children). Note that under UPC §2-103(b) only the descendants of a *deceased* spouse inherit; if a divorced spouse survives, neither the divorced spouse nor the divorced spouse's descendants inherit.

John Goodman in *King Ralph*

The UPC's treatment of laughing heirs avoids the situation depicted in the 1991 film *King Ralph*, in which an unrefined Las Vegas casino lounge singer (played by actor John Goodman, pictured above) was unexpectedly identified as the next successor in line to the British crown. An entire branch of the royal family had been accidentally electrocuted while sitting for a royal portrait, so the British government had to search far and wide for the next successor. Ralph was as shocked by the revelation of his royal heirship as the British aristocracy, which did not take well to Ralph's coronation. There are no "King Ralphs" under the UPC.

---

6. For discussion of the history and practice of "heir hunting," see David Horton & Andrea Cann Chandrasekher, Probate Lending, 126 Yale L.J. 102, 121-22 (2016) ("Heir hunters sift through probate records, which, like all court files, are available to the public, looking for wealthy intestate decedents who have no close family members. They then trace the decedent's family tree, identify her next of kin, and sell them information about the probate matter in return for a generous cut of their inheritance.").

If there is no taker under UPC §2-102 or 2-103, UPC §2-105 provides that the intestate estate passes to the state:

> **Uniform Probate Code**
> **§2-105 No Taker**
>
> If there is no taker under the provisions of this Article, the intestate estate passes to the [state].

PROBLEM III

Using the UPC statutory provisions as your guide, determine who takes what under each of the following examples in which the intestate decedent died leaving:

a. a surviving spouse, but no descendant or parent;
b. a surviving spouse and descendants;
c. a surviving spouse and a parent, but no descendant;
d. descendants but no surviving spouse;
e. a parent, but no surviving spouse or descendant;
f. two siblings, but no surviving spouse, descendant, or parent;
g. a grandparent, but no surviving spouse, descendant, parent, or sibling;
h. no surviving spouse, descendant, parent, sibling, grandparent, or descendant of grandparent;
i. two first cousins, descendants of the decedent's maternal grandparents; one first cousin, a descendant of the decedent's paternal grandparents.

What is the rationale for the differing formulations in each of these examples?

2.3 MODES OF DISTRIBUTION: REPRESENTATION

To inherit by intestacy, an heir must survive the decedent.[7] For this reason, intestacy statutes must account for the possibility that a predeceased relative may, herself, be survived by descendants (who are also relatives of the decedent). Suppose, for example, that the decedent, A, is a widow who had a daughter, B, and two grandchildren, C and D. Suppose further that B predeceased A. B's failure to survive A prevents B (or, more precisely, B's estate) from taking an intestate share of A's estate. The share of A's estate that B would have inherited had she survived passes, instead, to the next generation of descendants, C and D, who "represent" their parent in the distribution of the intestate estate. In this example, your intuition probably leads you to the correct distribution: C and D each take one half of A's intestate estate. This simple hypothetical illustrates the basic concept of "representation."

---

7. Under UPC §2-104, an heir must survive by at least 120 hours to inherit. See Chapter 6 for further discussion of the survival requirement and the problem of "simultaneous death."

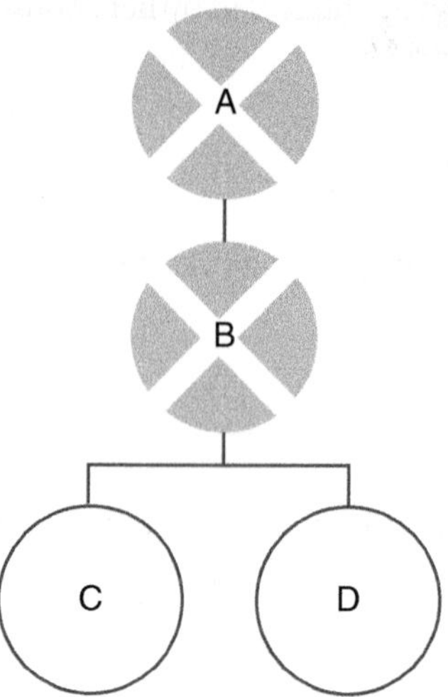

Representation refers to the rule-based methods for dividing property into shares among descendants and collaterals when a more closely related family member predeceases the decedent. There are three widely used systems of "representation": (1) *English* (or *"strict"*) *per stirpes*; (2) *modern per stirpes* (also referred to as *per capita with representation*); and (3) the UPC's method, known as *per capita at each generation*. Each of these approaches reflects a distinct preference of distribution from one generation to the next. These three systems may produce dramatically different results, depending on the composition of the decedent's surviving family.

Take the following example:

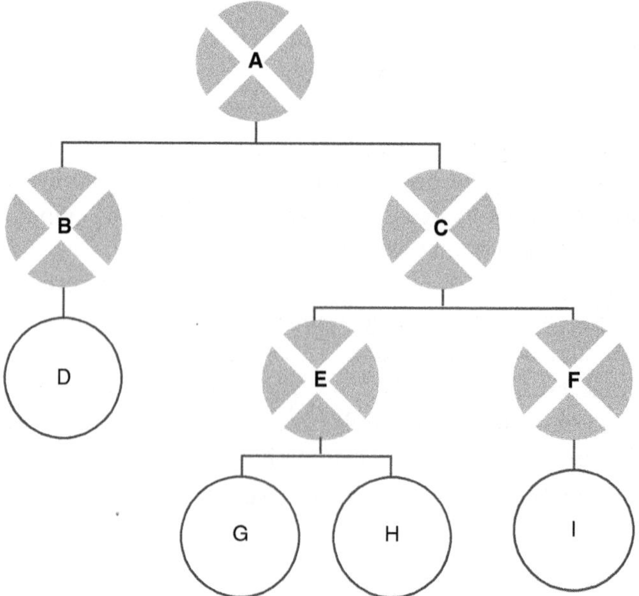

A has died intestate; she was predeceased by her spouse (who is not indicated in the diagram), two children (B and C), and two of her three grandchildren (E and F); she is survived by one grandchild (D) and three great-grandchildren (G, H, and I). Under these circumstances, what are the possibilities for distributing A's estate to her surviving descendants?

2.3.1 English Per Stirpes

An English/strict per stirpes approach emphasizes equality of distribution among the decedent's children, dead or alive. Thus, the estate is divided into as many shares as there are living children and predeceased children survived by living issue. The share of each predeceased child passes to that child's own line of descent. Under English per stirpes, it does not matter that some predeceased children produced more descendants than others. The stock of each child of the decedent receives the same allocation.

An English per stirpes distribution can be described as follows: Divide the decedent's estate into an equal number of shares such that one share is set aside for each *child* of the decedent who is then living and one share for each child who is not then living but has descendants who are living. Distribute the shares by representation.

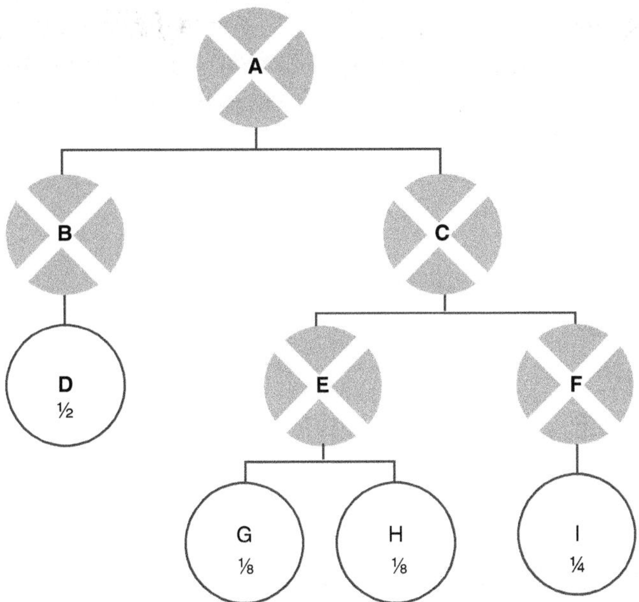

In this example, the initial division of A's intestate estate occurs at the first generation below the decedent, the generation of A's children, because, even though B and C predeceased A, both were survived by living issue. A's property is divided into two portions: one-half for the descendants of child B and one-half for the descendants of child C.

Child B's one-half share passes by *representation* to grandchild D: The grandchild is deemed to step up to the parental generation to represent and, therefore, to take B's share.

The same process is used in distributing C's share: In the generation immediately below C are two descendants, E and F. We therefore reserve a quarter share (after dividing C's half-share into two portions) for both E and F. Because E predeceased A, his quarter share passes by representation to his descendants, G and H, who each receive one-eighth. Similarly, because F predeceased A, his quarter share passes by representation to his descendant, I.

2.3.2 Modern Per Stirpes (UPC 1969)

Modern per stirpes is similar to English per stirpes with one key difference: Under modern per stirpes, the division into shares occurs in the first generation below the decedent in which there is at least one living individual. In cases where all of the decedent's children predecease but are survived by living issue, modern per stirpes treats the nearest generation with a living relative as the baseline for dividing the estate among the stocks.

A modern per stirpes distribution can be described as follows: Divide the decedent's estate into an equal number of shares in the first generation below the decedent in which there is at least one living relative. Set aside one such share for each member of that generation who is then living and one share for each member of that generation who is not then living but has descendants who are living. Distribute the shares by representation.

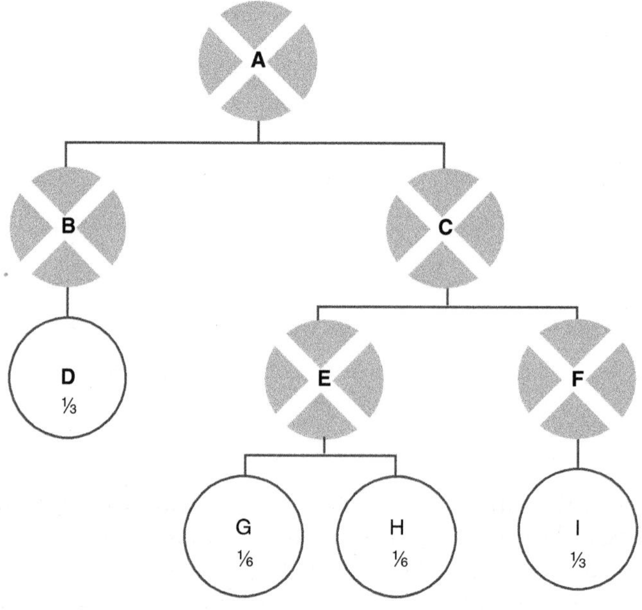

In this example, the initial division occurs at the generation of A's grandchild — D, E, and F — because both of A's children predeceased. Accordingly, a modern per stirpes distribution ignores A's children because there is no member of that generation who survived A. The division into shares occurs at the grandchild level, where there is one surviving grandchild and two deceased grandchildren who have left descendants who are alive. Thus, the estate is divided into three shares. Grandchild D receives one-third of A's intestate estate; E's one-third is divided into equal shares for E's descendants G and H, who receive a one-sixth share; F's one-third passes by representation to his descendant, I.

2.3.3 Per Capita at Each Generation (UPC 1990)

Per capita at each generation, which means "by head at each generation," emphasizes horizontal equality by giving the same share to each member of the same generation. That purpose is often described by the aphorism "equally near, equally dear."

A distribution pursuant to the UPC per capita at each generation can be described as follows: As with modern per stirpes (aka "per capita with representation"), divide the decedent's estate into an equal number of shares in the first generation below the decedent in which there is at least one living relative. Distribute one share to each member of that generation who is alive. Then, combine the remaining shares of predeceased members into a bucket. Pass the bucket down to the next generation with a living relative and repeat in the same manner until the entire estate is exhausted.

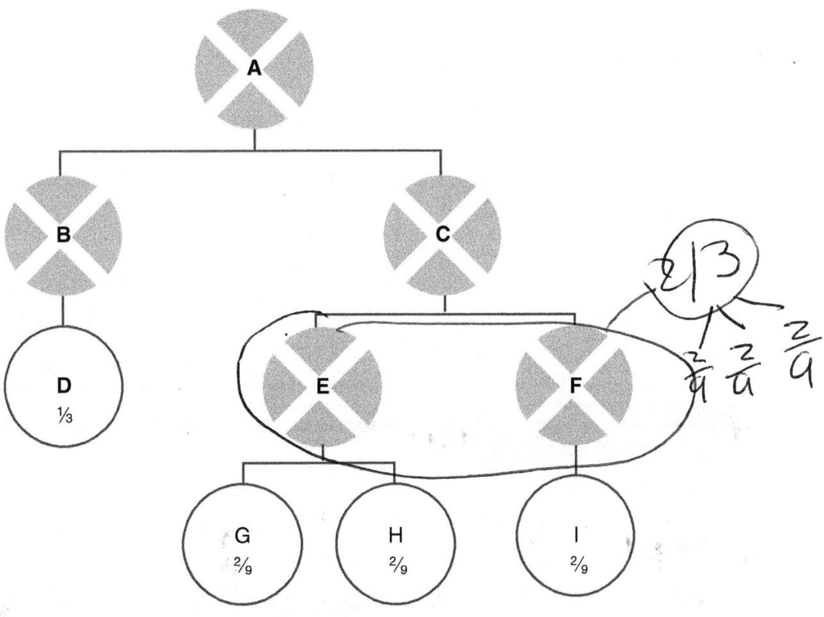

In this example, the initial division occurs at the generation of A's grandchild — D, E, and F — because both of A's children predeceased. Divide the estate into three shares and distribute one-third to D. Because E and F predeceased, the remaining two-thirds go into the bucket and passes to the next generation, G, H, and I, who each take two-ninths. Notice that heirs at each generation are treated identically. A's great-grandchildren each take two-ninths. Hence, equally near, equally dear.

The next case, *Estate of Mebust*, highlights the significance of differences among the various systems of representation. The trial court concluded that Montana law required distribution under the modern per stirpes system of representation. One of the decedent's nieces, however, argued that English per stirpes should apply. Note that because the decedent in *Estate of Mebust* was not survived by descendants of his own, this case illustrates the application of systems of representation to collateral relatives rather than descendants, as portrayed in the hypothetical above. As you read the case, you may find it helpful to refer to the diagram below of Berger O. Mebust's large family.

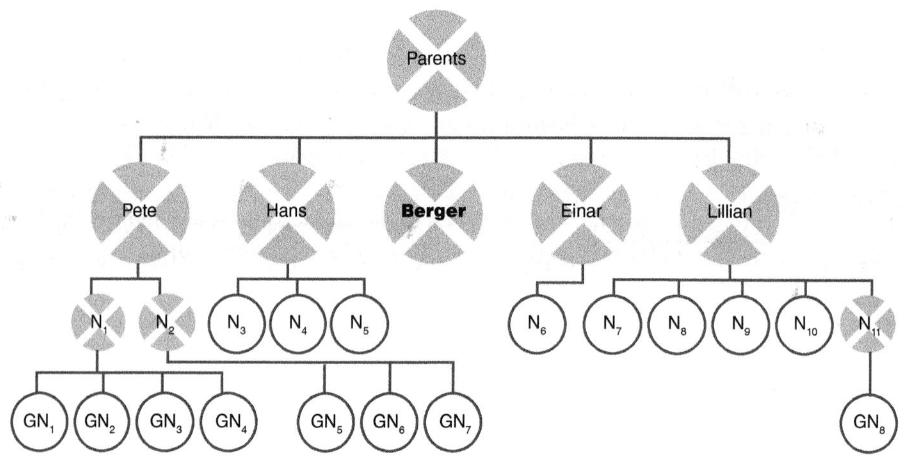

Estate of Mebust
843 P.2d 310 (Mont. 1992)

TURNAGE, Chief Justice.

Kristina Hanson, a niece of decedent Berger O. Mebust, appeals from an order of the District Court for the Twelfth Judicial District, Hill County, concerning distribution of Mebust's estate. We affirm.

The issue is: How does representation occur under Montana law when the only surviving heirs of an intestate decedent are the children and grandchildren of predeceased brothers and sisters?

Berger O. Mebust died intestate in February 1991. He left no surviving spouse or parents and had no children. He had three brothers, Pete, Hans, and Einar, and one sister, Lillian, all of whom predeceased him.

Pete had two children, both of whom are deceased, one leaving three children who survive and another leaving four children who survive. Hans had three children, all of whom survive. Einar had one child who survives. Lillian had five children, four of whom survive and one who is survived by a child.

In October 1991, the District Court entered an order indicating its intent to divide the estate into eleven equal shares, one for each of Mebust's nieces and nephews. It further indicated its intent to distribute a one-eleventh share to each of the eight surviving nieces and nephews and to divide the one-eleventh share of each of the three deceased nieces and nephews among his or her surviving children. The court allowed any interested person to argue why a different distribution should be made.

Four of the heirs, including appellant Kristina Hanson, petitioned the court to divide the estate into four equal shares, one for each of Mebust's brothers and sister, and to distribute the estate to the issue of such deceased sibling based on such sibling's one-fourth share. Under that scheme of distribution, Hanson, as the only child of Einar [N6, in the family tree above], would receive a one-fourth, rather than a one-eleventh, share of the estate.

After considering the arguments, the District Court reaffirmed its decision that under Montana's statutes, the distributable estate should be divided into eleven shares. The court certified its decision . . . to allow for immediate appeal to this Court.

Section 72-2-203, MCA, the applicable intestate succession statute, provides:

> The part of the intestate estate not passing to the surviving spouse under 72-2-202, or the entire intestate estate if there is no surviving spouse, passes as follows:
>
> . . .
>
> (3) if there is no surviving issue or parent, to the brothers and sisters and the children or grandchildren of any deceased brother or sister, by representation;
>
> (4) if there is no surviving issue, parent, brother, sister, or children or grandchildren of a deceased brother or sister, to the next of kin in equal degree, except that where there are two or more collateral kindred in equal degree but claiming through different ancestors, those who claim through the nearer ancestors must be preferred to those claiming through an ancestor more remote.

The District Court ruled that subsection (3) applies in this case. Hanson argues that both subsection (3) and subsection (4) apply.

Hanson supports her interpretation with an argument concerning the legislative intent and history of §72-2-203, MCA. However, Montana has long recognized that where the language of a statute is clear and unambiguous, other rules of statutory construction do not apply.

By its clear and unambiguous terms, subsection (4) of §72-2-203, MCA, applies only if there are no surviving "issue, parent, brother, sister, *or children or grandchildren of a deceased brother or sister.*" In this case, as the District Court pointed out, there are surviving children and grandchildren of Mebust's deceased brothers and sister. Therefore, we conclude the District Court was correct in applying only subsection (3).

The District Court applied the definition of "representation" provided at §72-2-204, MCA:

> If representation is called for by this code, the estate is divided into as many shares as there are surviving heirs in the nearest degree of kinship and deceased persons in the

> same degree who left issue who survive the decedent, each surviving heir in the nearest degree receiving one share and the share of each deceased person in the same degree being divided among his issue in the same manner.

Hanson claims the specific provisions of subsections (3) and (4) of §72-2-203, MCA, override the above definition of "representation." Relying on her argument concerning legislative intent, she asserts those provisions declare that the children or grandchildren of any deceased brother or sister will take the share their parent would have taken had the parent survived the decedent.

We have stated that clear statutory language controls over other rules of statutory construction and that subsection (4) does not apply in this case. Subsection (3) does not define "by representation," but the clear language of §72-2-204, MCA, does, and applies wherever "representation is called for by this code." Hanson's argument therefore fails.

Applying §72-2-204, MCA, to this case, the nearest degree of kinship in which there are surviving heirs is that including Mebust's nieces and nephews. Therefore, we hold that the District Court was correct in dividing the estate into equal shares for the nieces and nephews and, where the niece or nephew predeceased Mebust, dividing that person's share among his or her issue.

Affirmed.

QUESTIONS

1. Which of the three approaches to distribution did Kristina Hanson want the court to apply? Which of the three approaches to distribution did the court apply?

   ANSWER. Kristina, as the sole living heir to Berger's brother, Einar, wanted the court to apply a strict per stirpes approach. Under this approach, Berger's estate would be divided into four equal shares — one share for each of his siblings. The deceased siblings' heirs would then take by representation. The court instead followed the modern per stirpes approach, which divides the decedent's estate into equal shares in the first generation in which there is at least one descendant who is still living. Because none of Berger's siblings was still alive, his estate was divided into eleven equal shares, one for each of his nieces and nephews who survived Berger and one for each who did not survive Berger but had descendants who did survive him. Each share set aside for a niece or nephew who survived Berger received a 1/11 share. The 1/11 share set aside for a predeceased niece or nephew was then divided among his or her surviving children.

2. Is one of these approaches more "natural" to you than the other? What policies do each of these approaches promote?

   ANSWER. The strict or "English" per stirpes approach treats each line of descent as a distinct familial stock and is the oldest system of representation. The fundamental division takes place at the first generation, regardless of whether there is any person in that generation who survives the decedent. This approach promotes the closeness of the decedent and the decedent's children (or nearest kin if the decedent has no children) by dividing an estate equally among any surviving children and any predeceased children with surviving descendants. Under this approach, it does not matter whether one branch of the family contains more relatives than other branches. Each branch is treated the same for purposes of dividing the estate. English per stirpes mimics the distribution that the decedent probably would have chosen if his or her children had survived.

ANSWER. The other two approaches are more recent innovations to improve upon some of the perceived inequities resulting from the English per stirpes approach. The modern per stirpes approach gives more consideration to the nearest generation of the decedent still alive at the decedent's death. This approach recognizes that if a decedent is survived by multiple grandchildren, but no children, the grandchildren's interests should not be affected merely because of which deceased parent they inherit through. The UPC's per capita at each generation approach takes this approach one step further, ensuring that more removed generations are not prejudiced if they come from larger families. Per capita at each generation, however, also has the effect of rewarding more fertile branches of the family.

3. If the court applied the "English per stirpes" approach, what fractional share of Mebust's intestate estate would each heir receive?

   ANSWER. Under this scheme, the shares would be divided as follows: Kristina: 1/4 (Einar's share); Hans' three children: 1/12 each (Hans' 1/4 share divided equally); Lillian's four surviving children and one surviving grandchild: 1/20 each (Lillian's 1/4 share divided equally among her four surviving children and the one surviving grandchild of her predeceased child). Because neither of Pete's children survived Berger, but each left issue, Pete's share would be divided in the same manner. Because one of Pete's children left four children and the other left three, Pete's share would not be divided equally. Pete's grandchildren would either receive a 1/32 share (if one of four) or 1/24 share (if one of three), depending on their parentage.

4. If the court applied the "modern per stirpes" approach, what fractional share of Mebust's intestate estate would each heir receive?

   ANSWER. The court did apply the modern per stirpes approach. Under this scheme, each of the eight surviving nieces and nephews received a 1/11 share and the 1/11 share of each of the three deceased nieces and nephews was divided among his or her surviving children. The shares would be divided as follows: Kristina: 1/11; Hans' three children: 1/11 each; Lillian's four surviving children and one surviving grandchild: 1/11 each. Because neither of Pete's children survived Berger, but each left issue, the two remaining shares would be divided between Pete's grandchildren. Because one of Pete's children left four children and the other left three, their shares would not be divided equally. Pete's grandchildren would either receive a 1/44 share (if one of four) or 1/33 share (if one of three), depending on their parentage.

5. If the court applied a "per capita at each generation" approach, what fractional share of Mebust's intestate estate would each heir receive?

ANSWER. Had the court followed the UPC per capita at each generation approach, each of the eight surviving nieces and nephews would have received a 1/11 share. The three remaining shares would be divided into eight equal shares for each of the eight surviving grandnieces and grandnephews (3/88 of the entire estate each).

6. Were you persuaded by Hanson's arguments? Why do you think her lawyer brought this case all the way to the Montana Supreme Court?

ANSWER. Kristina's arguments were not particularly convincing to the court. Kristina's argument relied on her interpretation of legislative intent, but the court found the language of the statute to be unambiguous. Kristina's argument would require the court to ignore the language "or children or grandchildren of a deceased brother or sister" in subsection (4). Both the district court and the Montana Supreme Court were reluctant to do so. The case may have gone to the Supreme Court because of the size of the estate. If decided in Kristina's favor, she would have received 1/4 of the estate instead of 1/11 as determined by the district court. This would equate to a difference of approximately $15,910 for every $100,000 of estate value.

PROBLEM IV

Calculate how A's intestate estate will be distributed under each of the three systems of representation described above. Which method is preferable and why?

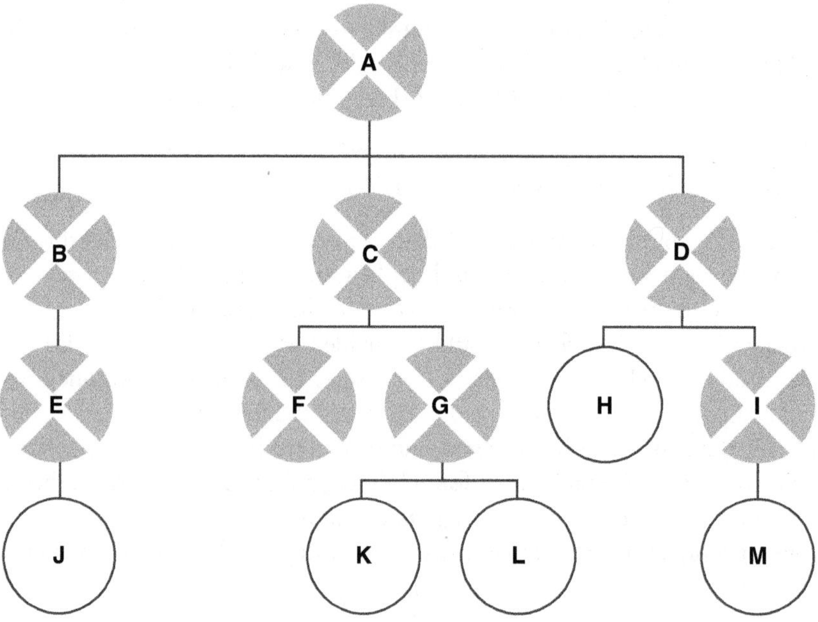

PROBLEM V

Under the UPC's per capita at each generation method of intestate distribution, who receives what portion of A's estate in the following two examples?

Per Capita at Each Generation (UPC 1990)
Two Examples

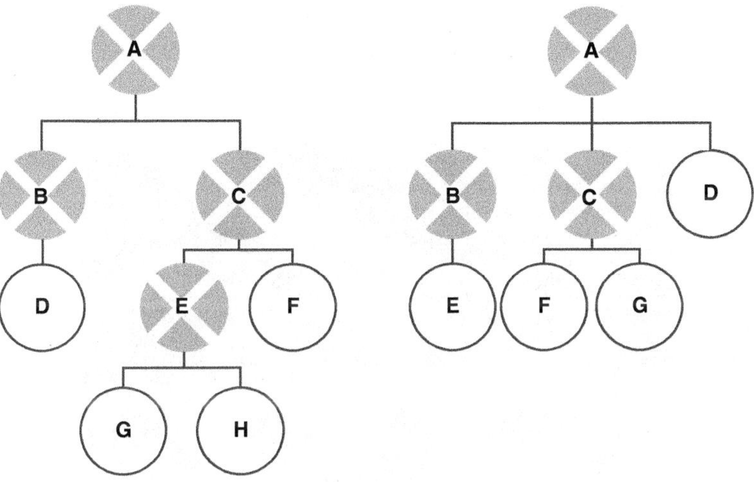

2.4 HALF-BLOOD

A relation by the half-blood exists between individuals who share one, but not both parents. For example, suppose Antonio had three children: Alvaro, Dino, and Carlos. Antonio had Alvaro and Dino with his first wife; after his divorce and remarriage, he then had Carlos with his second wife. Alvaro and Dino would be related by the whole blood, but Carlos would be related to Alvaro and Dino by the half-blood. If Alvaro subsequently died intestate, survived by Dino and Carlos, would each take an equal share of the estate?

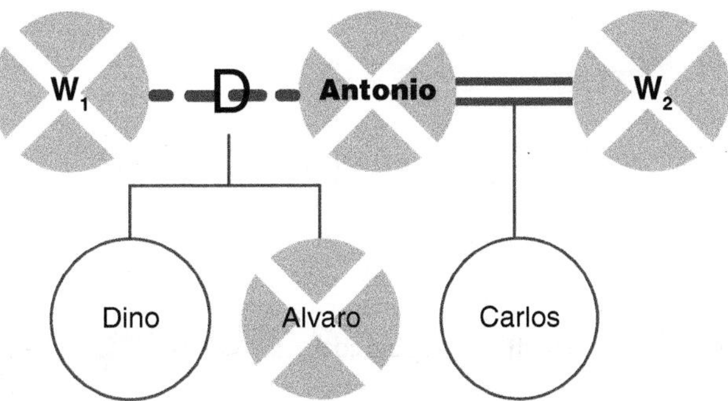

In some jurisdictions, such as Florida and Missouri, a relative of the half-blood inherits only half the amount of a full blood relative. Dino would take two-thirds; Carlos would inherit one-third. In UPC jurisdictions, however, Dino and Carlos would inherit equal shares of one-half.

Uniform Probate Code
§2-107 Kindred of Half Blood

Relatives of the half blood inherit the same share they would inherit if they were of the whole blood.

Applying the *minority* rule on kindred of the half-blood (in effect in a minority of U.S. jurisdictions), the next case illustrates the role of statutory interpretation in applying the intestacy statutes as well as the complexity and nuance sometimes required in computing intestate shares.

Music recording artist Prince died intestate on April 21, 2016 in his home state of Minnesota. Prince was survived by his sister and five half-siblings.

In re Estate of Thiemann
992 S.W.2d 255 (Mo. Ct. App. 1999)

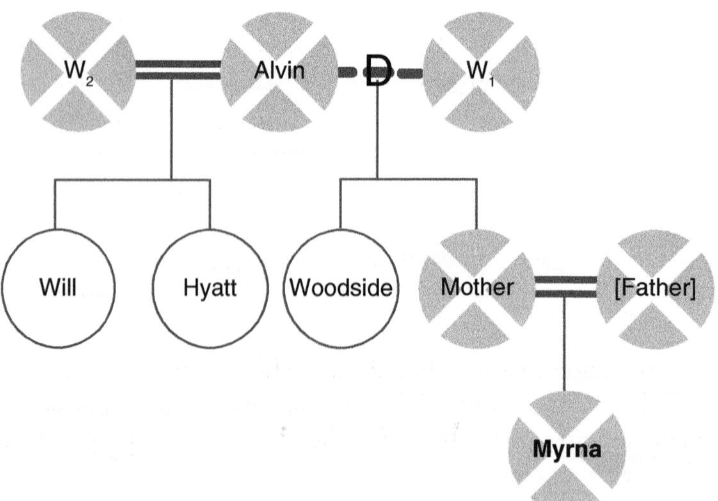

CLIFFORD H. AHRENS, Judge.

Eleanor M. Woodside ("Woodside") appeals from a judgment of the Circuit Court of St. Louis County, Probate Division, holding that she was to receive a one-third share of the estate of Myrna L. Thiemann ("Intestate"), and respondents Marcella M. Will ("Will") and Martha M. Hyatt ("Hyatt") would also each receive one-third. Woodside argues that since respondents are collateral kin of the half blood she should receive double the amount of the respondents' shares. We reverse and remand.

The facts are brief and not in dispute. Myrna L. Thiemann died intestate on May 9, 1997. Her closest surviving kindred were three aunts: Woodside, Will and Hyatt. Woodside and Intestate's mother were both born of the same parents, Alvin L. Meyer and his first wife. Will and Hyatt were born of the same father, Alvin L. Meyer, but their mother was Meyer's second wife.

Section 474.010 RSMo (Supp. 1998)[8] states, in part:

> All property as to which any decedent dies intestate shall descend and be distributed . . . as follows: . . . the entire intestate property, if there is no surviving spouse, shall descend and be distributed as follows: . . . (c) If there are no children, or their descendants, father, mother, brother or sister, or their descendants, then to the grandfathers, grandmothers, uncles and aunts or their descendants in equal parts. . . .

Section 474.040[9] reads as follows:

> When the inheritance is directed to pass to the ascending and collateral kindred of the intestate, if part of the collaterals is of the whole blood of the intestate, and the other part of the half blood only, those of the half blood shall inherit only half as much as those of the whole blood; but if all collaterals are of the half blood, they shall have whole portions, only giving to the ascendants double portions.

On July 16, 1998, the probate division entered an order-judgment determining heirs. The court found that Section 474.040 did not apply because (1) "the assets of the deceased do not pass to her ascending and collateral kindred, the condition of the statute, but only pass to collateral kindred," and (2) "only siblings can be half bloods or whole bloods." Therefore, the court held that the default intestacy scheme governed and section 474.040 was inapplicable. As a result, the court determined that Woodside, Will and Hyatt would all share equally in the disposition of Intestate's assets, each taking a one-third share.

Woodside argues on appeal that the trial court erred in holding that section 474.040 (1) only applies to estates in which there are heirs of both ascendant and collateral kindred, and (2) only applies to distributions between siblings of the intestate. We agree.

The trial court found that section 474.040 only applies in situations in which there are both existing ascending and existing collateral kindred. In this case, Woodside, Will and Hyatt are all collateral kindred, but there are no ascending kindred.[10] The trial court held that since section 474.040 applies "[w]hen the inheritance is

---

8. All subsequent references to "section 474.010" are to RSMo (Supp. 1998).

9. All subsequent references to "section 474.040" are to RSMo 1994.

10. A "collateral heir" is "[o]ne who is not of the direct line of deceased, but comes from a collateral line, as a brother, sister, an uncle, an aunt, a nephew, a niece, or a cousin of deceased." Black's Law Dictionary 262 (6th ed., 1990). An "ascendant" is a person "with whom one is related in the ascending line; one's parents, grandparents, great-grandparents, etc." *Id.* at 113.

directed to pass to the ascending and collateral kindred of the intestate," the statute was not applicable in a case where there were no existing ascending kindred.

We do not believe there must be existing ascending kindred to trigger the application of the half blood statute. Section 474.040 applies when the inheritance is "directed" to pass to ascending and collateral kindred, whether there are any existing ascending kindred or not. Missouri's basic rule of intestate distribution and descent, contained in section 474.010, states that under the facts of this case the intestate's property shall go "to the grandfathers, grandmothers, uncles and aunts or their descendants in equal parts." Thus the property is directed to go to ascendants (grandfathers and grandmothers) and collaterals (uncles and aunts) even though there are no living grandfathers or grandmothers. Therefore, since section 474.010 directs the property to go to ascending and collateral kindred of the estate, section 474.040 governs distribution among the heirs.

Previous Missouri cases have held that section 474.040 may be applicable in cases where there are no ascending heirs. Our holding is also in accord with the authoritative Missouri Practice manual, which states:

> A convenient method of determining the share of collaterals of the half blood *when no ascendants are involved* is to double the number of collaterals of the whole blood and add the result to the number of collaterals of the half blood. The resulting figure will be the denominator of the fractional share to which each half blood is entitled. Heirs of the whole blood will be entitled to twice that amount. . . . *If* an ascendant is involved the proper denominator may be determined by doubling the number of ascendants and adding that number to the number of collaterals.

5A John A. Borron, Jr. & Francis M. Hanna, Missouri Practice section 1232 (1990) (emphasis added). The manual clearly explicates how the statute would operate "when no ascendants are involved," thus suggesting that it is not necessary for there to be an ascending heir for the statute to be applicable. *Id.*

In Woodside's second point on appeal she argues that the trial court erred in holding that section 474.040 does not apply unless there is a distribution between siblings of the intestate. Will and Hyatt respond by arguing that in Missouri a "half blooded aunt" cannot exist by definition, and that only siblings can be half blooded.

In addressing respondents' argument we review the basic operation of Missouri's statutory intestacy scheme. When determining the manner in which an intestate's property will descend and be distributed, the court first applies Missouri's general intestacy statute, section 474.010. This statute determines a person or class of persons; in the case at bar this class consists of Intestate's "grandfathers, grandmothers, uncles and aunts or their descendants in equal parts." Section 474.010(2)(c). It is among the members of this class that section 474.040, if applicable, determines distribution. "As used in the law of inheritance, half-blood refers to the degree of relationship between two individuals who have the same mother or the same father but not both parents in common." Thomas E. Atkinson, Law of Wills 50 (2d ed. 1953). As previously noted, in this case Will and Hyatt have the same father as Woodside and Intestate's mother, but they do not all have both parents in common. As a result, they are only related by the half blood, and section 474.040 operates to determine distribution.

We reverse and remand for further proceedings consistent with this opinion.

QUESTIONS

7. As a matter of statutory interpretation, the appellate court held that the half-blood statute (§474.040) applied to cases involving only collateral kindred even though the statute is facially limited to cases "[w]hen the inheritance is directed to pass to the ascending and collateral kindred of the intestate." Why?

   ANSWER. The statute creates ambiguity because, on its face, it fails to provide a comprehensive rule governing intestate inheritance by half-bloods. Does the half-blood rule only apply if the decedent is survived by both collateral and ascendant relatives? Or does the half-blood rule apply if all surviving kindred are collaterals? The court examined prior case law interpreting the statute and found that Missouri courts apply the half-blood statute even when all surviving kindred are collaterals, that is, there are no surviving ascendants (ancestors). A broad construction of the half-blood statute may be necessary to implement the legislature's intent to provide different treatment for relatives of the whole and half-blood.

8. Did the appellate court agree with the trial court's holding that "only siblings can be half bloods or whole bloods"?

   ANSWER. No. The appellate court found that collateral relatives more remote than siblings can be half-blood. Here, two of the decedent's three aunts were relatives of the half-blood.

9. Compute the intestate shares of Woodside, Hyatt, and Will on remand.

   ANSWER. Woodside receives half the intestate estate; Will and Hyatt each receive a quarter.

10. What result under the UPC?

    ANSWER. Under the UPC, relatives of the half-blood receive the same share as relatives of the whole blood. Thus, Woodside, Will and Hyatt would each receive a third of the intestate estate.

11. Assume that Myrna's intestate heirs included her maternal aunts, Hyatt, and Will but not Woodside, as well as a paternal ancestor, a grandfather. How would you apply the last clause of §474.040, "but if all collaterals are of the half blood, they shall have whole portions, only giving to the ascendants double portions"?

    ANSWER. The statute appears to be poorly drafted. How can the material collateral half-bloods, Will and Hyatt, receive whole portions if the paternal ancestor, the decedent's grandfather, receives a "double portion"? Mathematically, it seems impossible.

PROBLEM VI

Refer to the facts in *In re Estate of Thiemann* and answer the following questions:

A. Suppose that after Myrna's death, Hyatt then died intestate. Who would receive what from Hyatt's estate?

B. What are the reasons for and against the UPC's rule treating relatives of the half-blood the same as relatives of the whole blood? Do you prefer the UPC's rule or the Florida rule? Why?

2.5 ADOPTION

Adoption, which allows individuals to alter and establish family relationships by legal decree rather than by birth or marriage, affects inheritance rights for purposes of intestate succession. Adoption creates an ancestor-descendant relationship between the adoptive parent and adopted individual. Upon adoption, the adoptee becomes an intestate heir apparent of the adoptive parent and vice versa. In many cases, adoption also severs intestate inheritance rights between the adopted individual and his or her genetic parents.

The intersection of adoption and inheritance law is quite complex and subject to great variation among the states. For example, in many but not all jurisdictions, adoption of a minor child is treated differently from the adoption of an adult under inheritance law. Family law generally permits the adoption of minor children to provide parental custody, support, and family life for children who would otherwise be parentless. For this reason, family law imposes upon adoptive parents legal obligations of support and care for the minor child, who becomes part of the adoptive parent's immediate family unit. This policy goal is reflected in the inheritance laws governing the adoption of minor children: An adopted minor child is typically treated as if naturally born to the adoptive parents and, therefore, eligible to inherit both *from* the adoptive parents and *through* the adoptive parents from ancestors, descendants, and collaterals of the adoptive family.

QUESTIONS

12. Suppose Alana adopts Patrick as a minor child and later dies intestate, survived by only Patrick and her sister, Sally. How would Alana's estate be distributed?

    ANSWER. Patrick would inherit Alana's entire estate because, under UPC §2-103, descendants take to the exclusion of collaterals (who are more distantly related). Patrick would be treated as Alana's descendant because she adopted him as a minor child.

13. Suppose further that, after Alana's death, her sister Sally also died intestate, survived by only Patrick and her cousin, Cary. How would Sally's estate be distributed?

    ANSWER. Patrick would inherit Sally's entire estate because, under UPC §2-103, nephews take to the exclusion of cousins (who are more distantly related). Because Alana adopted Patrick as a minor child, Patrick may inherit both from and through Alana, just as a natural child would.

In contrast to the adoption of minor children, adult adoption is treated differently under family law as a consensual relationship between two legally autonomous parties. Adult adoption does not impose any obligation of care or support upon the adoptive parent because adults are treated as legally autonomous upon reaching the age of majority. Indeed, often the sole purpose of adult adoption is to create inheritance rights between the adopted individual and adoptive parent.[11] Thus, in states that distinguish between child and adult adoption, the adoption of an adult creates inheritance rights only between the adoptee and adoptive parent. This principle, often described as the "stranger to the adoption" rule, holds that an adopted adult may inherit *from, but not through*, the adoptive parent. Other members of the adoptive parent's family are not consenting parties to the adult adoption (they are strangers to the adoption), so they are not bound by the adoption in the disposition of their estates.

Under the UPC, the intestacy rules governing adoption are the same whether the adopted individual is a child or an adult. For wills and trusts, however, UPC §2-705(f) applies the stranger to the adoption rule: Subject to a few narrow exceptions, the rule presumptively excludes an individual adopted as an adult from sharing in a class gift made by a transferor who is not the adoptive parent.

Uniform Probate Code
§2-116 Effect of Parent-Child Relationship

Except as otherwise provided in Section 2-119(b) through (e), if a parent-child relationship exists or is established under this [subpart], the parent is a parent of the child and the child is a child of the parent for the purpose of intestate succession.

§2-118 Adoptee and Adoptee's Adoptive Parent or Parents

(a) [Parent-Child Relationship Between Adoptee and Adoptive Parent or Parents.] A parent-child relationship exists between an adoptee and the adoptee's adoptive parent or parents.

. . .

§2-119 Adoptee and Adoptee's Genetic Parents

(a) [Parent-Child Relationship Between Adoptee and Genetic Parents.] Except as otherwise provided in subsections (b) through (e), a parent-child

---

11. Because adult adoption renders the adoptee a legal child of the adoptive parent, adult adoption can be useful in preventing a will contest by more remote heirs apparent who, because of their remoteness, would lack standing to contest the will. See Chapter 3 on will contests.

relationship does not exist between an adoptee and the adoptee's genetic parents.

(b) [Stepchild Adopted by Stepparent.] A parent-child relationship exists between an individual who is adopted by the spouse of either genetic parent and:

(1) the genetic parent whose spouse adopted the individual; and

(2) the other genetic parent, but only for the purpose of the right of the adoptee or a descendant of the adoptee to inherit from or through the other genetic parent.

(c) [Individual Adopted by Relative of Genetic Parent.] A parent-child relationship exists between both genetic parents and an individual who is adopted by a relative of a genetic parent, or by the spouse or surviving spouse of a relative of a genetic parent, but only for the purpose of the right of the adoptee or a descendant of the adoptee to inherit from or through either genetic parent.

(d) [Individual Adopted after Death of Both Genetic Parents.] A parent-child relationship exists between both genetic parents and an individual who is adopted after the death of both genetic parents, but only for the purpose of the right of the adoptee or a descendant of the adoptee to inherit through either genetic parent.

(e) [Child of Assisted Reproduction or Gestational Child Who Is Subsequently Adopted.] If, after a parent-child relationship is established between a child of assisted reproduction and a parent or parents under Section 2-120 or between a gestational child and a parent or parents under Section 2-121, the child is adopted by another or others, the child's parent or parents under Section 2-120 or 2-121 are treated as the child's genetic parent or parents for the purpose of this section.

Under UPC §2-118, an adoption decree creates a parent-child relationship between the adopted individual and the adoptive parents. Thus, the adopted individual may inherit both from and through the adoptive parents and vice versa. Under §2-119, an adoption decree generally severs the parent-child relationship between the adopted individual and his or her genetic parents, but the severance rule is subject to numerous exceptions, three of which are described below.

First, under §2-119(b), adoption by a stepparent does not affect inheritance rights between the adoptee and the genetic parent who is the adoptive parent's spouse. The adoptee also retains inheritance rights from and through the other genetic parent, but the other genetic parent may not inherit from or through the adoptee. Thus, in the diagram below, Mother and Father are divorced and Stepfather, Mother's new spouse, adopts Child. In this case, Child retains all inheritance rights from and through Mother and gains new inheritance rights from and through Stepfather. Child and Child's descendants also retain inheritance rights from and through Father, but Father loses inheritance rights from and through Child.[12]

12. Father loses inheritance rights from and through Child because he is no longer part of Child's immediate family unit.

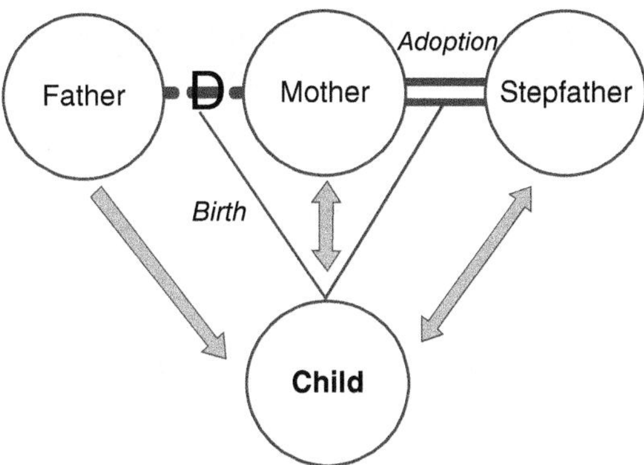

UPC §2-119(b)

Second, under §2-119(c), adoption by a relative of either genetic parent (or by the spouse or surviving spouse of a relative of a genetic parent) preserves the adopted individual's right to inherit from and through both genetic parents, but the genetic parents lose inheritance rights from and through the adopted individual. Thus, in the diagram below, upon Child's adoption by Aunt, Child may inherit from and through Aunt, Father, and Mother; however, Father and Mother may not inherit from or through Child. In this case, Child forms a new family unit with Aunt and partially severs relations with Father and Mother.

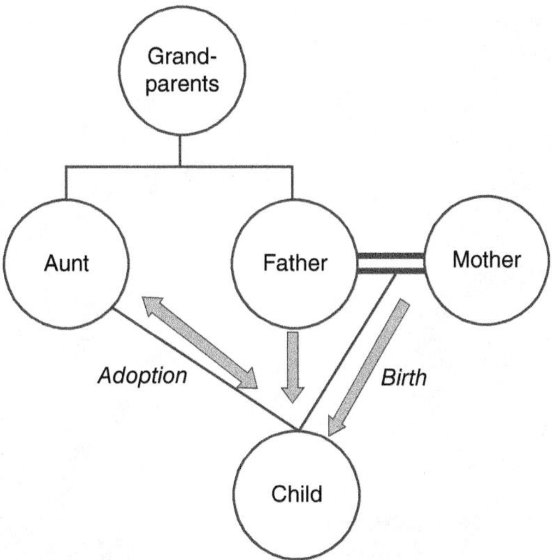

UPC §2-119(c)

Third, under §2-119(d), adoption following the death of both genetic parents preserves the adopted individual's right to inherit through both genetic parents, but the genetic parents' extended family lose inheritance rights from and through the adopted individual. Thus, in the diagram below, upon Child's adoption by Friend, Child may inherit from and through Friend, and through Father and Mother, but extended members of Child's genetic family may not inherit from or through Child.

In this case, Child forms a new family unit with Friend and partially severs relations with the extended members of the genetic family.

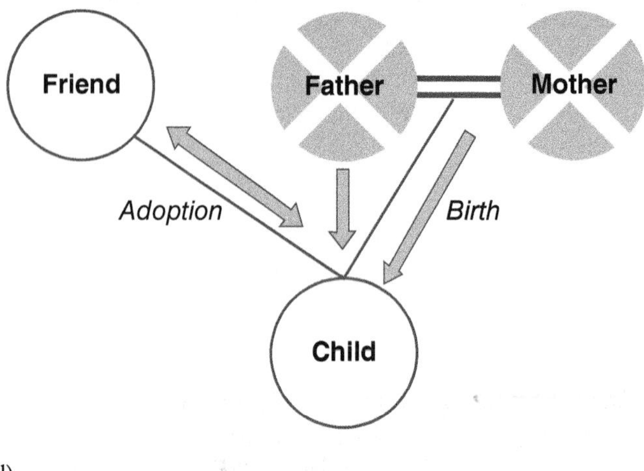

UPC §2-119(d)

President Bill Clinton was born in 1946 as William Jefferson Blythe III, three months after his father died in an accident. President Clinton's mother married Roger Clinton, Sr., who adopted Clinton as his son.

PROBLEM VII

A. Suppose Alana adopts her adult boyfriend Stuart and later dies intestate, survived by only Stuart and her sister, Sally. How would Alana's estate be distributed?

B. Suppose further that, after Alana's death, her sister Sally died *testate*, survived by only Stuart (Sally's nephew by adoption) and Sally's first cousin Cary. Sally's will devises everything to her nieces and nephews. How would Sally's estate be distributed?

C. Suppose instead that, after Alana's death, her sister Sally died *intestate*, survived by only Stuart (Sally's nephew by adoption) and Sally's first cousin Cary. How would Sally's estate be distributed?

2.6 ADVANCEMENTS

In distributing an intestate decedent's estate a question arises whether the decedent's inter vivos gifts to heirs were meant to be treated as advancements against the heirs' shares of the estate. An advancement refers to a lifetime gift from a donor to an intestate heir where the donor intends the lifetime gift to be in place of an inheritance by intestacy. At common law, lifetime gifts from a donor to an heir were presumed to be advancements that reduced an heir's portion of the intestate estate on the theory that an heir's inheritance should take into account the decedent's lifetime giving. The presumption could be rebutted only by evidence to the contrary. The underlying theory that an heir's inheritance should take into account lifetime giving, however, seems misplaced because most donors do not make lifetime gifts to members of their family as an inheritance advancement. Thus, the UPC reverses the common law presumption and, as a result, treatment of an inter vivos gift as an advancement is exceptionally rare.

Uniform Probate Code
§2-109 Advancements

(a) If an individual dies intestate as to all or a portion of his [or her] estate, property the decedent gave during the decedent's lifetime to an individual who, at the decedent's death, is an heir is treated as an advancement against the heir's intestate share only if (i) the decedent declared in a contemporaneous writing or the heir acknowledged in writing that the gift is an advancement, or (ii) the decedent's contemporaneous writing or the heir's written acknowledgment otherwise indicates that the gift is to be taken into account in computing the division and distribution of the decedent's intestate estate.

Example

Mackleberry has four children, Marlene, Meghan, Mia, and Michelle. Three of Mackleberry's children, Marlene, Meghan, and Mia, are identical triplets and have successful careers as singing circus entertainers. Michelle is also a talented singer, but she was never given the opportunity to perform with her singing triplets and, as a result, has struggled financially and lives alone in a boarding house down by the river. Mackleberry pities Michelle and sends her a check for $200,000 accompanied by the following note: "Please enjoy this gift. It is an advancement on your inheritance." A week later, Mackleberry dies intestate leaving an estate worth $1,000,000. Her only intestate heirs are Marlene, Meghan, Mia, and Michelle. What does each heir inherit?

Answer: Mackleberry made an advancement to her daughter Michelle by accompanying her $200,000 check with a "contemporaneous writing . . . indicat[ing] that the gift is to be taken into account in computing the division and distribution of the decedent's intestate estate." But for Mackleberry's advancement, the probate estate would be split equally into quarters, with each daughter taking $250,000. The advancement, however, is taken into account as follows:

Step 1: Add the advancement amount to the probate estate to form the "hotchpot."
$200,000 + $1,000,000 = $1,200,000

Step 2: Divide the hotchpot in equal shares, one for each intestate heir.
$1,200,000 ÷ 4 = $300,000

Step 3: Distribute one share to each intestate heir, but deduct the advancement from the inter vivos donee's share.

Marlene:	$300,000
Meghan:	$300,000
Mia:	$300,000
Michelle:	$300,000 – $200,000 = $100,000

Step 4: Proof
(3 × $300,000) + $100,000 = $1,000,000

3 | Wills: Protecting Testamentary Intent

3.1 INTRODUCTION

Previously, we discussed the freedom of testamentary disposition. It is exceptionally broad and limits testators only in special circumstances (e.g., to protect a surviving spouse or after-adopted/born children) or in situations where a testamentary provision is contrary to law or public policy. The question then arises, who can exercise this nearly unfettered right to convey property at death by will? The short answer is, any emancipated individual[1] who manifests testamentary intent and has the mental capacity to do so. The more complete answer also requires determining whether the will was the product of the testator's true volition in cases where a third party may have wrongfully exerted influence over the testator's estate plan. This chapter examines protective doctrines that set aside wills executed by a testator who lacked the cognitive capacity to formulate testamentary intent and wills procured by a third party who wrongfully interfered with the testator's estate plan.

We begin this discussion, however, with a note of caution: Litigation involving testamentary intent, capacity, and free will is notorious for undermining unconventional but valid estate planning choices deemed to be out of step with current social norms and values. Under the guise of protecting the testator's intent, judges and juries have superimposed their own views about how to distribute testators' estates by applying doctrines that set aside wills that embody nonconforming values. See, e.g., Melanie B. Leslie, The Myth of Testamentary Freedom, 38 Ariz. L. Rev. 235 (1996). For example, in an (in)famous case from 1947, sixteen years before Betty Friedan's *The Feminine Mystique* launched the modern movement for women's rights, a New Jersey court set aside the will of a woman who left her estate to the National Woman's Party on the grounds that it resulted from the testator's "insane delusions about the male." See In re Strittmater, 53 A.2d 205 (Ct. Errors & App. N.J. 1947). And, in a case decided five years before the 1969 Stonewall riot triggered the gay rights movement, a New York court held that a testator's will leaving his estate to his longtime same-sex partner, rather

1. In some jurisdictions individuals under the age of 18 can apply to the court for emancipation from parental control. Nevertheless, under the UPC, the minimum age to make a valid will is 18.

than to his estranged family, could not have been the expression of the testator's true desires but, rather, an unnatural disposition resulting from undue influence. See In re Kaufman's Will, 247 N.Y.S.2d 664 (App. Div. 1964). In both cases, courts applied doctrines, discussed below, that, ostensibly, protect a testator's exercise of dispositional freedom: the insane delusion doctrine in *Strittmater*, and the doctrine of undue influence in *Kaufman*. It is unlikely that courts today would reach similar conclusions, a shift that emphasizes the significance of social mores in judicial decision making.

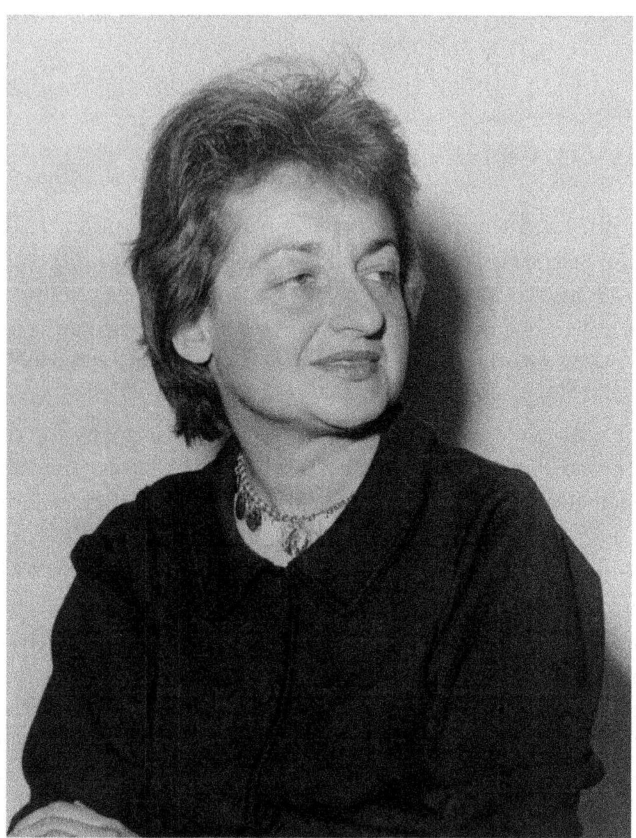

In *The Feminine Mystique*, Betty Friedan decried the inequality and unhappiness experienced by women in the 1950s and 1960s: "We can no longer ignore that voice within women that says: 'I want something more than my husband and my children and my home.'"

We should flag one other matter at the outset. A party can only challenge a will under the various protective doctrines discussed in this chapter if the party has legal standing. In general, parties have standing if they can establish a concrete stake in the outcome of the litigation. In a will contest, a party establishes standing by showing that the amount of their inheritance would change if a court invalidates all or part of a decedent's will. For example, suppose Teresa is unmarried, and has two children, Sally and Patrick. In 2016, Teresa makes a will leaving all of her property to Sally. Teresa's friend, Charles, lacks standing to challenge the 2016 will because Charles will not gain financially if a court strikes it down. That is because, in the absence of a will, Teresa's property would pass through intestacy to Sally and Patrick equally. Conversely, Patrick has the right to contest the 2016 will, because his status as an intestate heir means he would benefit from setting aside the will.

This chapter is organized in two parts. The first part involves a set of "internal" factors concerning the testator's mental capacity and manifestation of testamentary intent. We describe these factors as internal because they pertain to the testator's state of mind at the time the will is executed. The second part involves a set of "external" factors concerning the behavior of third parties in wrongfully influencing the testator's estate plan as memorialized in a will.

3.2 PROTECTIVE DOCTRINES: INTERNAL FACTORS

To create a valid will (and opt out of the default rules of intestacy), the law requires an individual to have both testamentary intent and capacity *at the moment the testator executes his or her will.* These requirements are internal because they concern the testator's state of mind and cognitive capacity to understand the legal significance of making a will.

3.2.1 Testamentary Intent

Testamentary intent, sometimes referred to by the Latin *animus testandi*, imposes the seemingly obvious requirement that a testator intend, at the time of execution, for the document signed as a will to be his or her will. The requirement of testamentary intent is necessary, in part, to distinguish between documents reflecting the decedent's preliminary considerations about a possible plan of disposition, such as unsigned drafts of a will, and the final testamentary instrument. By observing testamentary formalities, including the testator's signing of the will, the testator signifies that a particular document reflects testamentary intent.

Professor Mark Glover articulates a more nuanced taxonomy of testamentary intent and observes that the term implicates three related but distinct inquiries: (1) donative testamentary intent ("whether the purported will expresses an intent to make gifts that become effective upon the decedent's death"); (2) operative testamentary intent ("whether the decedent intended a document that expresses donative testamentary intent to be legally effective"); and (3) substantive testamentary intent (interpretation of the testamentary language expressed in the decedent's will). Mark Glover, A Taxonomy of Testamentary Intent, 23 Geo. Mason L. Rev. 569, 582-99 (2016).

Estate of Hand
73 N.E.3d 880 (Ohio Ct. App. 2016)

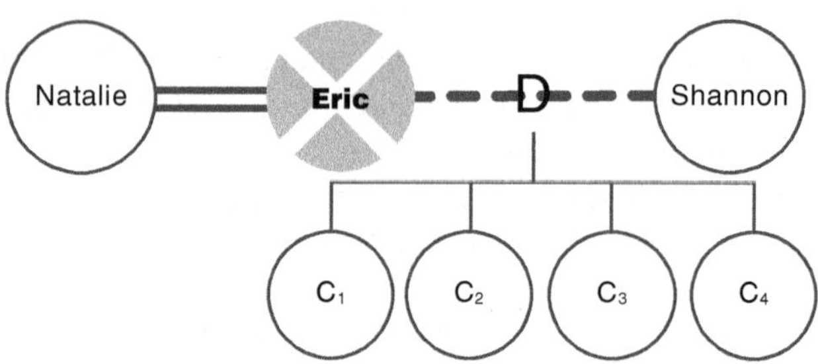

M. Powell, P.J.

Appellant, Natalie Hand, appeals a decision of the Butler County Court of Common Pleas, Probate Division, denying her application to admit to probate the purported will of her husband, Eric Anthony Hand (Decedent).

Appellant and Decedent were married in April 2014. Decedent died on September 7, 2014. He was survived by appellant and by his four minor children from a previous marriage. Shannon Hand ("Hand") is the children's mother and Decedent's former spouse.

In searching for a will, appellant discovered in a box of love letters she had received from Decedent over the years a three-page handwritten letter dated January 23, 2014 ("Love Letter Will"). Unlike Decedent's other love letters, this one was signed by Decedent with his full name. The letter included three paragraphs and a post-scriptum. The first two paragraphs professed Decedent's love for appellant; the last paragraph read as follows:

> As my last will and testament, I appoint you the primary beneficiary of all I have and all I have worked for. With the complete trust that you will look after the children, my business interests and all the other things that I have put together over the years and not let anyone try to deprive you of those things.
>
> I love you eternally,
>
> ERIC ANTHONY HAND
>
> s/ Eric Anthony Hand

. . .

It is well-established that one of the requirements of a valid will is that it be executed with testamentary intent, that is, disposition of property to take effect only at death. "Although a will cannot be established merely by showing an intent to make one, an instrument cannot be a will unless [testamentary intent] exists." In re Will of Mielke, 3d Dist. Paulding No. 11-76-5, 1977 WL 199309, *3 (June 30, 1977). The test is whether the instrument expresses the final testamentary purpose of the testator. In re Crowe's Will, 31 Ohio Law Abs. at 40.

. . .

Upon reviewing the record, we find that some credible, competent evidence supports the probate court's finding that appellant failed to prove . . . that Decedent intended the Love Letter Will to be his will.

The only language suggestive of a testamentary intent is found in the last paragraph of the Love Letter Will. The other two paragraphs profess Decedent's love for appellant as he had done many times before. Viewed as a whole, the Love Letter Will is consistent in style and content with the other love letters Decedent had written to appellant and reflects their emotional relationship and its highs and lows. In fact, appellant testified at the hearing that the Love Letter Will was Decedent's way of letting her know that he loved her and that their relationship was solid and forever. Appellant stored the Love Letter Will with the other love letters because "to [her] it was kind of like a love letter."

[A]ppellant [also] . . . testified that after Decedent wrote the Love Letter Will, he [said] . . . he was going to legally create a will at a later date. "To make a testamentary paper valid, the writer must have intended it as a will, as it stood, without further act, on his part, to complete it." In re Crowe's Will, 31 Ohio Law Abs. at 41. . . . The probate court, therefore, properly denied appellant's application to admit the Love Letter Will to probate.

QUESTION

1. The court notes that "[a]lthough a will cannot be established merely by showing an intent to make one, an instrument cannot be a will unless [testamentary intent] exists." This idea requires some explanation. As we discuss in Chapter 4, wills need to comply with certain formalities. In many states, these formalities include being written, signed by the testator, and signed by two people who witnessed the testator sign or acknowledge the instrument. Thus, it is entirely possible to have testamentary intent and yet fail to create a valid will by violating these directives. Do you think the outcome in *Hand* would have been different if the decedent had signed the Love Letter Will in front of two witnesses, who also signed the instrument?

ANSWER. Probably. The court concludes that the decedent did not intend the Love Letter Will to be his will because it was similar to other love letters that he had written in the past. But as the opinion observes, the Love Letter Will was different in one way: The decedent had signed it with his will name. If the Love Letter Will also boasted the signatures of two witnesses, it would seem much more like a formal legal document than a mere note.

PROBLEM I

Maria Gonzalez lives in a state that enforces holographic wills. (As we will see in Chapter 4, some states allow testators to make wills that are not signed by witnesses, provided that the "material provisions" (who gets what) are in the testator's handwriting, and that the testator signs the document.) While on vacation, Maria Gonzalez handwrote the following letter to her daughter, Rosa:

> I've thought a lot about my estate on this trip. When I return home next month, I'll see my lawyer and ask him to prepare a new will for me. Right now, under my current will, you get half of everything and your brother gets the other half. But I've changed my mind about that and want to write a new will. When I have a chance to formalize everything with my lawyer, I'll make sure you get it all.

Mrs. Gonzalez died in a train wreck while returning from her vacation. The letter was dated and signed by Mrs. Gonzalez, satisfying the formalities for a holographic will. Her daughter offered the letter for probate as Mrs. Gonzalez's will and claimed the entire estate for herself. Rosa's brother objects and claims that Mrs. Gonzalez called him shortly before her death to say that he would get at least half of her estate. What must Rosa prove to prevail?

3.2.2 Testamentary Capacity

What is testamentary capacity? The Uniform Probate Code is unusually laconic in its answer, which sets forth only the minimal age of capacity and the requirement that the testator execute a will with a "sound mind":

Uniform Probate Code
§2-501 Who May Make Will

An individual 18 or more years of age who is of sound mind may make a will.

The Restatement elaborates on the concept of "sound mind" by explaining the requirement of mental capacity:

Restatement (Third) of Property: Wills & Other Donative Transfers
§8.1 Requirement of Mental Capacity

(a) A person must have mental capacity in order to make or revoke a donative transfer.

(b) If the donative transfer is in the form of a will, a revocable will substitute, or a revocable gift, the testator or donor must be capable of knowing and understanding in a general way the nature and extent of his or her property, the natural objects of his or her bounty, and the disposition that he or she is making of that property, and must also be capable of relating these elements to one another and forming an orderly desire regarding the disposition of the property.

Note that the standard for testamentary capacity is not actual knowledge; instead, the testator merely must be "capable" of knowing and understanding "in a general way" the required elements. If the test required actual knowledge, failure to remember a particular asset or a member of the testator's family at the time of will execution could invalidate the will for lack of capacity. Moreover, the standard is not tied to intelligence or educational level: Testamentary capacity is determined without regard to an individual's intellectual gifts (or lack of them). Nor is capacity shown by the testator's dispositive plan alone: A will that might appear eccentric or even foolish may well have been executed with full mental capacity. As the West Virginia Supreme Court aptly summarized:

> It is not necessary, that a person should possess the highest qualities of mind, in order to make a will, nor that he should have the same strength of mind, which he may formerly have had; the mind may be in some degree debilitated, the memory may be enfeebled, the understanding may be weak, the character may be eccentric, and he may even want capacity to transact many of the ordinary business affairs of life; but it is sufficient, if he understand the nature of the business, in which he is engaged, has a recollection of the property, which he means to dispose of, the objects of his bounty, and the manner, in which he wishes to distribute it among them.

Nicholas v. Kershner, 20 W. Va. 251, 251-52 (1882).

Most prongs of the testamentary capacity test are relatively straightforward. However, the requirement that a testator be capable of knowing the "natural objects of one's bounty" is somewhat obscure.[2] Who are the natural objects of one's bounty? According to what criteria must the objects of the testator's bounty be "natural"? They are, primarily, those with whom the testator shared the closest relationships during life. Natural objects might include family members, whether related by blood or affinity, close friends, or, potentially, longtime business associates and colleagues. They might include charitable organizations to which the testator was devoted during lifetime such as the testator's school, religious institution, or favored museum. Importantly, the natural objects of one's bounty are not limited to heirs apparent. The Restatement emphasizes: "The natural objects of a testator's bounty include the testator's closest family members, who are not limited to blood or adoptive relatives or to those who would take by intestacy. . . ." Restatement (Third) of Property: Wills and Other Donative Transfers §8.1, comment c. At a time when less than 50 percent of U.S. households consist of married, opposite-sex couples,[3] the natural objects of one's bounty are now more likely than ever to include individuals who are not related by blood or marriage to the testator.

The capability requirement of understanding the natural objects of one's bounty does not impose a legal obligation on the testator to provide for those objects in his or her will:

> The requirement that the testator must, when executing a will, be capable of knowing and understanding in a general way the natural objects of his or her bounty does not suggest that a testator must devise his or her property to those persons or devise it to them in the shares embodied in the intestacy statutes. Indeed, one of the common reasons for making a will is

2. Indeed, the phrase "natural objects of one's bounty" invites difficult questions about *what* is "natural" and *who* decides what is natural in the context of the testator's relationships to other persons and organizations.

3. U.S. Census Bureau, Households and Families 2010 (2010 Census Brief issued April 2012), Figure 2.

> to create a dispositive plan that does not track the pattern of distribution in intestacy. A will that favors persons who are not close family members or a will that favors family members disproportionately to their relationship to the testator is not evidence that the testator did not know and understand in a general way the natural objects of his or her bounty.

Restatement (Third) of Property: Wills and Other Donative Transfers §8.1, comment c.

President Ronald Reagan and his longtime friend Charlton Heston (pictured with U.K. Prime Minister Margaret Thatcher) both suffered from Alzheimer's disease.

Practitioners generally encounter issues of testamentary capacity in two contexts: will execution and will contest litigation. In both contexts, the preliminary question is, who has an obligation to ascertain or prove the testator's cognitive status?

In the first context, supervising the preparation and execution of a will, attorneys have an ethical obligation to take precautions to prevent the execution of a will by a client who the attorney "reasonably believes" lacks testamentary capacity. Model Rule of Professional Conduct (MRPC) 1.14(b) provides:

> When the lawyer reasonably believes that the client has diminished capacity, is at risk of substantial physical, financial or other harm unless action is taken and cannot adequately act in the client's own interest, the lawyer may take reasonably necessary protective action, including consulting with individuals or entities that have the ability to take action to protect the client and, in appropriate cases, seeking the appointment of a guardian ad litem, conservator or guardian.

The American College of Trusts and Estates Counsel (ACTEC) provides further guidance on how to ascertain the client's cognitive status under the "reasonably believes" standard:[4]

> *Determining Extent of Diminished Capacity.* In determining whether a client's capacity is diminished, a lawyer may consider the client's overall circumstances and abilities, including the client's ability to express the reasons leading to a decision, the ability to understand the consequences of a decision, the substantive appropriateness of a decision, and the extent to which a decision is consistent with the client's values, long-term goals, and commitments. In appropriate circumstances, the lawyer may seek the assistance of a qualified professional.
>
> . . .
>
> *Testamentary Capacity.* If the testamentary capacity of a client is uncertain, the lawyer should exercise particular caution in assisting the client to modify his or her estate plan. The lawyer generally should not prepare a will, trust agreement, or other dispositive instrument for a client who the lawyer reasonably believes lacks the requisite capacity. On the other hand, because of the importance of testamentary freedom, the lawyer may properly assist clients whose testamentary capacity appears to be borderline. In any such case the lawyer should take steps to preserve evidence regarding the client's testamentary capacity.

In the second context, will contest litigation, the prevailing rule places the evidentiary burden on the party alleging lack of testamentary capacity. As the Restatement puts it:

> *Burden of proof.* The party contesting the validity of a donative transfer has the burden of persuasion in establishing that the donor lacked mental capacity to make the transfer. Section 3-407 of the Uniform Probate Code captures the prevailing view on the burden of proof and the view adopted in this Restatement. . . .

Restatement (Third) of Property: Wills and Other Donative Transfers §8.1, comment f.

This "prevailing rule," however, does not currently apply in several large jurisdictions such as New York or Texas. The minority rule, by contrast, places the burden on the will proponent to demonstrate testamentary capacity as part of the probate application process.

---

4. ACTEC Commentaries on the Model Rules of Professional Conduct 1.14, at http://www.actec.org/public/commentaries1.14.asp.

Estate of Nalaschi
90 A.3d 8 (Pa. Super. Ct. 2014)

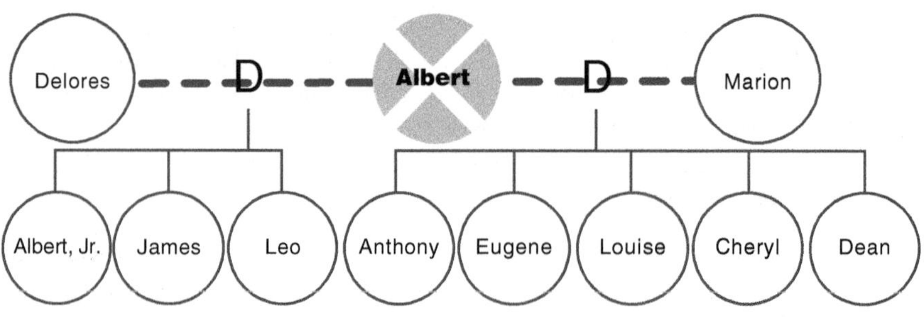

Opinion by DONOHUE, J.:

Eugene Nalaschi ("Eugene") appeals from the decree entered on June 19, 2013 by the Court of Common Pleas of Lackawanna County, Orphans' Court Division, granting the petition of Charles Witaconis, Esq. ("Witaconis") allowing the probate of the April 25, 2011 will of Albert Nalaschi, Sr. ("Decedent") and revoking the letters testamentary issued with respect to Decedent's January 28, 2010 will. We affirm.

Decedent died on July 6, 2012. Decedent was [unmarried and] survived by eight children, three of whom were from his first marriage to Delores Nalaschi — Albert Nalaschi, Jr., James Nalaschi ("James"), and Leo Nalaschi, and five of whom were from his second marriage to Marion Nalaschi — Anthony Nalaschi, Eugene, Louise Lokuta ("Louise"), Cheryl Wilson ("Cheryl"), and Dean Nalaschi. The controversy in this matter arises out of two wills executed by Decedent. The first will, dated January 28, 2010 ("the 2010 Will"), named Eugene the executor and Decedent's daughter Louise the sole beneficiary. The second will, dated April 25, 2011 ("the 2011 Will"), named Witaconis the executor and Decedent's son James the sole beneficiary.

. . .

Eugene first alleges that the trial court erred when it found that Decedent had testamentary capacity and was competent to execute the 2011 Will. Eugene relies on several examples in 2010 and early 2011 to demonstrate Decedent's lack of testamentary capacity. For example, from early 2010 to January 2011, Decedent lost nearly 40 pounds of weight, which was a possible indicator of dementia. In March 2010, Decedent reported his daughter Cheryl to the police, accusing her of stealing money from him. In July 2010, while Decedent was speaking with Detective Renee Castellani ("Detective Castellani") about Cheryl stealing from him, Decedent told Detective Castellani that he had stopped taking his medications. After speaking with Decedent, Detective Castellani referred Decedent's case to the Area Agency on Aging. As a result, Mary McAndrew ("McAndrew"), an Aging Care Manager at the Area Agency on Aging, began monitoring Decedent in July 2010. McAndrew testified that when she began monitoring Decedent, she would sometimes find him disheveled, hung-over, and agitated. In September 2010, Decedent accused Louise, another one of his daughters, of stealing food and money from him. Also in September 2010, Decedent missed an appointment with his primary care physician, Doctor Michael Jalowiec ("Dr. Jalowiec") because he got lost on the way to his office. In March of 2011, Decedent attempted to take a $2,300 cash advance from his credit card and instead wrote the check for $23,000. Additionally, when providing the names of his children for the 2011 Will, he spelled Cheryl's name incorrectly as "Sheryl," and despite the fact that both Cheryl and Louise were married, he used their maiden names.

Finally, in support of his assertions, Eugene relies heavily on the testimony of Doctor Eugene Turchetti ("Dr. Turchetti"). Dr. Turchetti reviewed all of Decedent's records and opined that Decedent suffered from alcohol-related dementia. Based on his review of Decedent's records, he contended that Decedent was not competent to execute the 2011 Will. Dr. Turchetti based his opinion on his belief that it is not possible to determine competence at one single point in time because dementia is a disease that progresses over time. Rather, Dr. Turchetti asserted that after examining Decedent's records, he believed that Decedent's behavior over the course of 2010 and early 2011 indicated that Decedent had a mental illness that had progressed to the point that by April 25, 2011, there was enough information to conclude Decedent was not competent to execute a will.

Testamentary capacity exists when a testator is aware of the natural objects of his bounty, the composition of his estate and what he wants done with it, even if his memory is impaired by disease. In re Bosley, 26 A.3d 1104, 1111-12 (Pa. Super. 2011). The testator "need not have the ability to conduct business affairs." *Id.* at 1112 (citation omitted). Courts evaluate testamentary capacity on the date of the execution of the contested will. *Id.* at 1112. "Evidence of such state of mind may be received for a reasonable time before and after execution as reflective of decedent's testamentary capacity. This information can be supplied by lay witnesses as well as experts." In re Agostini's Estate, 311 Pa. Super. 233, 457 A.2d 861, 867 (1983).

The record, when viewed in the light most favorable to Witaconis, supports the trial court's conclusion that Decedent had testamentary capacity. Although Eugene cites several questionable actions by Decedent in 2010, he provides little evidence of Decedent's incompetence from the time reasonably close to the execution of the 2011 Will. Moreover, Eugene fails to explain how his evidence of Decedent's mental deficiencies demonstrates that Decedent was not "aware of the natural objects of his bounty, the composition of his estate and what he wants done with it." See In re Bosley, 26 A.3d at 1111-12.

Furthermore, as this Court has previously stated,

> impressions of the Decedent on the very date he executed his will are more probative of the Decedent's testamentary capacity than those of someone . . . who never met the decedent and formulated an opinion of Decedent's mental state based solely on medical records.

Id. at 1112. In this case, most of the evidence that Eugene cites in support of his argument that Decedent lacked testamentary capacity to execute the 2011 Will is from 2010. This evidence is not from a reasonable time before or after the execution of the 2011 Will, but in some instances over a year before Decedent executed the 2011 Will on April 25, 2011. Additionally, Eugene relies heavily on the testimony of Dr. Turchetti, even though Dr. Turchetti never actually met with Decedent, but rather only reviewed his records.

Conversely, Witaconis provides ample testimony that Decedent was competent when he executed the 2011 Will. For example, Attorney James Zipay ("Zipay"), an Assistant Lackawanna County Solicitor with the Elder Law Project, met with Decedent in March 2011, approximately one month before he executed the 2011 Will. Decedent met Zipay regarding drafting a power of attorney. Zipay testified that whenever he meets with clients, he first determines that they have the capacity to execute a legal document. Zipay determined in March 2011 that Decedent was competent to execute a legal document.

Likewise, Witaconis testified that when Decedent came to his office in late March 2011 seeking his services to draft a will, Witaconis also determined that Decedent had testamentary capacity. Witaconis stated that on the date Decedent executed the 2011 Will, Decedent understood the makeup of his estate and to whom he was bequeathing his property. Therefore, Witaconis believed that Decedent was competent when he executed the 2011 Will.

. . .

Therefore, we find no abuse of discretion in the trial court's determination that Decedent had testamentary capacity when he executed the 2011 Will.

QUESTIONS

2. Who would have inherited Albert Nalaschi, Sr.'s property if the court had invalidated the 2011 will? What if the court had nullified both the 2011 will and the 2010 will?

   ANSWER. If the court had struck down the 2011 will, we would revert back to the 2010 will, which leaves everything to Albert's daughter Louise. If the court had annulled both wills, Albert's property would pass through intestacy to his children equally.

3. Although Albert had sufficient capacity to execute the will in April 2011, what is the most compelling evidence to the contrary?

   ANSWER. The test for capacity requires the testator to know roughly what he owns and who his friends and family are. In addition, evidence close in time to the execution of the will is more persuasive than evidence from other periods. Given this backdrop, the two most damning facts are probably the mistake with the check (writing $23,000 rather than $2,300) and the mix-up with his daughters' names. Both cast a sliver of doubt on his ability to comprehend the nature of his property and the natural objects of his bounty. In addition, both are from relatively close in time to when he executed the 2011 will.

PROBLEM II

Part A. In 1970, Harold Livingston III, then 42 years old, executed a will leaving his extensive art collection to the museum at his alma mater, Waterchester University. Since graduating from Waterchester, Mr. Livingston had made annual gifts of artwork, which had been in his family for generations, to the Waterchester Museum. In 1971, Mr. Livingston became a trustee of the City Art Museum (CAM), founded by one of his ancestors. In 1972, he began to make annual gifts of works from his art collection to CAM and suspended his pattern of making such gifts to the Waterchester Museum. In 1980, a court ruled that Mr. Livingston was mentally incapacitated and unable to manage his own affairs; the court appointed Mr. Livingston's son as his father's conservator. Mr. Livingston entered a private mental hospital, where he received in-patient care until his death in 2010. When Mr. Livingston's son probated the will, CAM asserted that it, not the Waterchester Museum, should receive the artwork remaining in Mr. Livingston's collections. CAM presented to the court a 1979 letter from Mr. Livingston that read in part: "I intend that my art collections find a permanent home at CAM after I'm gone."

Should the probate court give effect to the 1970 will? Of what relevance is the 1979 letter? Of what relevance is the 1980 court order declaring Mr. Livingston mentally incompetent?

Summary of Timeline

1970: Harold executes a will devising his art collection to Waterchester University.

1971: Harold joins the board of trustees of the City Art Museum.

1972: Harold ceases lifetime giving to Waterchester and begins making annual gifts to City Art Museum.

1979: Harold sends a letter to City Art Museum stating his intent "that my art collections find a permanent home at CAM after I'm gone."

1980: Court adjudicates Harold as mentally incapacitated and imposes a conservatorship; Harold enters in-patient care.

2010: Harold dies.

3.2.3 Lucid Intervals

The mental acuity of an incapacitated person often fluctuates from day to day or even hour to hour. Thus, even someone who suffers from a general condition of cognitive impairment may execute a valid will during a "lucid interval." That is, despite the mental incapacity, there may be a period in which the individual can form testamentary intent and demonstrate testamentary capacity. As a result, the lucid interval doctrine is often asserted as a defense to an incapacity claim.

In some states such as New Jersey, however, the lucid interval doctrine does not apply to an individual who has been adjudicated incompetent by court order. Following an adjudication of incapacity, an individual cannot execute a will "before a judgment has been entered adjudicating a return to competency." See N.J. STAT. ANN. §3B:12-27. Conversely, the Restatement provides that, in the absence of a rule like New Jersey's, a person suffering from mental incapacitation may execute a valid will during a lucid interval:

Restatement (Third) of Property: Wills & Other Donative Transfers §8.1, comment m

Lucid interval. A person who is mentally incapacitated part of the time but who has lucid intervals during which he or she meets the standard for mental capacity . . . can, in the absence of an adjudication or statute that has contrary effect, make a valid will or a valid inter vivos donative transfer, provided such will or transfer is made during a lucid interval.

In a recent New York case, the court stated its common law lucid interval doctrine as follows:

> The question of testamentary capacity concerns a person's mental condition only at the time of the execution of the will; evidence relating to the condition of the testator before or after the execution is only significant insofar as it bears upon the strength or weakness of the testator's mind at the exact hour of the day of execution. A testator needs only a lucid interval of capacity to execute a valid will, and this interval can occur contemporaneously with an ongoing diagnosis of mental illness, including depression or progressive dementia. Also, it has long been recognized that old age and physical weakness are not necessarily inconsistent with testamentary capacity.

In re Probate Proceeding, Will of Leon Feinberg, Deceased, 37 Misc. 3d 1206(A) (N.Y. Surr. Ct. Queens Cty. 2012).

PROBLEM II

Part B. Assume the facts as stated in Part A but with this addition: At the same time that CAM asserted its claim based on the 1979 letter, a lawyer for the hospital filed with the probate court a document purporting to be Mr. Livingston's last will. The document, dated December 1, 2008, was signed with a scribbled version of Mr. Livingston's signature and two attesting witnesses (both of whom were nurses at the hospital); it also was notarized. The document left all of Mr. Livingston's estate to "this wonderful hospital that has taken such good care of me for so many years."

Should the probate court give effect to the 2008 document? What would the hospital have to prove in order to show that the 2008 document was a valid testamentary instrument? Of what relevance is the 1980 court order declaring Mr. Livingston mentally incompetent under these circumstances?

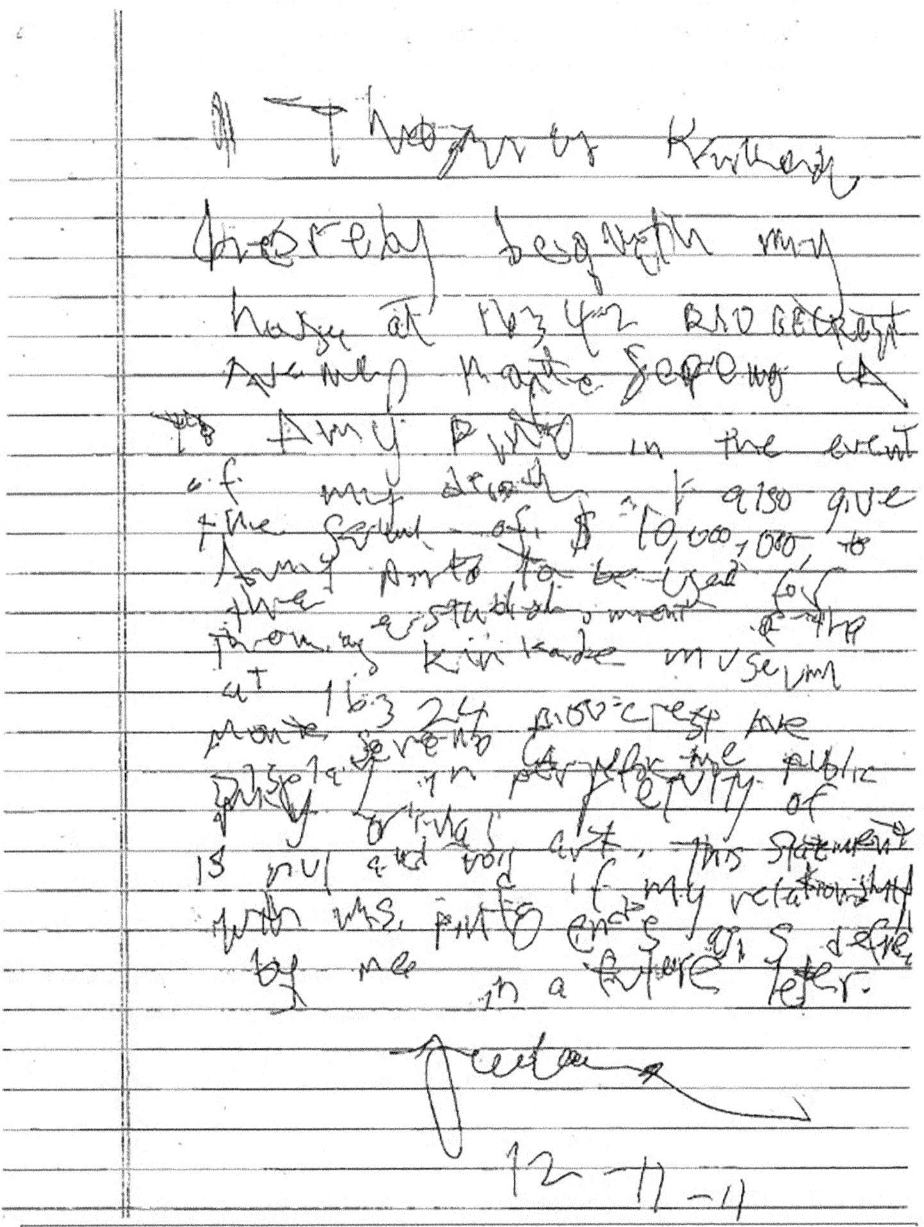

I Thomas Kinkade
hereby bequeath my
house at 16324 Ridgecrest
Avenue Monte Sereno CA
to Amy Pinto in the event
of my death. I also give
the sum of $10,000,000 to
Amy Pinto to be used for
the establishment of the
Thomas Kinkade museum
at
16324 Ridgecrest Ave
Monte Sereno for the public
display in perpetuity of
original art. This statement
is null and void if my relationship
with Ms. Pinto ends as determined
by me in a future letter.

12-11-11

A holographic will purportedly written by Thomas Kinkade

Artist Thomas Kinkade, who died in 2012 of acute intoxication at the age of 54, was survived by his estranged wife of thirty years, his girlfriend of eighteen months, and four daughters. Kinkade's surviving spouse offered for probate a will executed in 2000 in which Kinkade left $12.48 million in assets to his living trust settled in 1997. Kinkade's girlfriend, however, offered two handwritten purported wills, executed in

2011, in which Kinkade left substantial assets to her. Kinkade's artwork demonstrates a competent hand, but his alleged holographic wills are almost illegible. Kinkade suffered from alcoholism, and a handwriting expert opined that Kinkade was either suffering from Parkinson's disease "or was three sheets to the wind" when writing the documents.[5] If Kinkade was, in fact, intoxicated when he wrote the 2011 wills, could he have written them during a lucid interval?[6]

PROBLEM III

Marilyn lived alone with her cats. In her 80s, she was eccentric but fiercely independent. She had little contact with her remaining family. Her closest friends were her neighbors, Rick and Clara. Rick would often help Marilyn out by mowing her lawn, doing chores, arranging for contractor's work, and food shopping.

One day, Marilyn had a stroke. Rick found Marilyn and called for help. Marilyn survived, but began suffering from dementia and confusion. She now is often disoriented, has difficulty recognizing people, and suffers from mild hallucinations. Doctors have said that Marilyn is incapacitated due to irreversible dementia.

Two months after her stroke, Marilyn was moved to a rehabilitation hospital. Her cousin, Killeen, hired an attorney, Munnerlyn, to prepare a power of attorney naming Killeen as Marilyn's agent—her "attorney-in-fact." Over the next few weeks, Munnerlyn met with Marilyn several times to discuss her estate plans. He then prepared an irrevocable trust and a will to carry out Marilyn's wishes. Marilyn executed these documents while in the rehabilitation hospital; two of her nurses served as attesting witnesses.

After Marilyn died, Killeen discovered that Marilyn's will gave the majority of her estate to Rick and his wife, both of whom are just as surprised as Killeen when they learn the news. Upset, Killeen brought a claim before the probate court seeking to set aside the will for lack of testamentary capacity. At trial, she produced four of Marilyn's doctors, all of whom testified that during the period Marilyn executed the will she was incompetent and lacked the capacity to execute legal documents. The estate, on the other hand, produces testimony from Munnerlyn, who stated that he met with Marilyn numerous times, discussed her concerns, and believed her to be fully capable of meeting the standard for testamentary capacity. The two nurses who witnessed the will signing likewise testified that Marilyn was fully aware of what she was doing when she executed her will.

At the end of the bench trial, the estate's lawyer gave the following closing argument:

> Your Honor, this is a case about doctors and lawyers. Just as lawyers should not be dispensing medical advice, doctors should not be dispensing legal advice. Four doctors testified that the decedent was incompetent at the time she signed her will, but none was present when she actually *did* sign her will. None of the doctors talked with her about her property, her cats, her burial plans, her desire for an *in terrorem* clause to prevent probate

5. http://www.mercurynews.com/2012/06/18/painter-thomas-kinkades-estate-battle-centers-on-validity-of-hand written-wills/.

6. In Breeden v. Stone, 992 P.2d 1167 (Colo. 2000), the decedent, who committed suicide during a police standoff at his home, executed a holographic will while intoxicated with alcohol and cocaine. The will was upheld on grounds that he had testamentary capacity and was not suffering from an insane delusion (see below).

battles. Her orthopedic surgeon never asked her to identify the nature and extent of her bounty. None of the doctors can even testify if the will was executed during a lucid interval because none of them was present for the execution. The legal standard is whether the testator had the capacity to execute a will at the time the will was executed, not whether the testator was confused during the period in question. Her lawyer, familiar with the legal standard, was best equipped to determine whether she met the requirements for capacity at the time the will was executed. It was her doctors' job to look after her medical needs; it was her lawyer's job to look after her legal needs. Thus, it was her lawyer who was most capable of determine her capacity to execute legal documents, not her doctors.

A. Is the estate's lawyer correct? Who is in a better position to determine testamentary capacity: a doctor untrained in law or a lawyer untrained in medicine?

B. Would the result be different if Marilyn had been adjudged incompetent in a court of law prior to executing her will?

C. The two witnesses both said they talked with Marilyn for ten to fifteen minutes before she signed her will and she seemed fully aware the entire time. Is this a long enough period of time to determine if she was having a lucid interval? What if she was lucid during the execution, but had not been lucid when originally discussing her estate plans?

D. Could the court consider Marilyn's condition immediately before and immediately after the execution of the will to determine if she had proper testamentary capacity, or would the witness statements be sufficient to prove she was having a lucid interval?

E. Killeen argued that the disposition of the estate was further evidence of Marilyn's lack of capacity, because Marilyn left most of her estate to her "yardman." Another one of Marilyn's heirs questioned the validity of the will, claiming that Marilyn "was all about family." Should the fact that Marilyn gave a disproportionate amount of her estate to a friend rather than her family be a factor in determining her testamentary capacity?

3.2.4 Insane Delusion

Will contests are occasionally based on an assertion that the testator suffered from an "insane delusion." An insane delusion is a false belief from which an individual cannot be dissuaded despite all reason and evidence to the contrary. One commentator has added to the definition a component of action by the testator based on the false belief.[7] Examples of insane delusions include the erroneous belief that one's spouse is unfaithful, that one's son is the devil incarnate, or that one's daughter is a witch.

To invalidate a will on this basis, a contestant must show not only that the testator suffered from an insane delusion, but that the delusion *caused* the objectionable disposition.

7. See Julian R. Kossow, Probate Law and the Uniform Code: "One for the Money . . ." 61 Geo. L.J. 1357, 1362 (1973) ("[A]n insane delusion consists of a belief in the existence of certain facts which in reality do not exist, and which is held against all evidence, reason, or probability. *Additionally, there must be conduct by the believer on the assumption of the verity of the delusion.*").

This requires proof that the insane delusion "materially affected" the will, meaning that "the testator, if not laboring under the insane delusion, would have devised the property differently." In re Estate of Gassmann, 867 N.W.2d 325, 329 (N.D. 2015).

Finally, if a court finds that a testator suffered under an insane delusion that materially affected the will, the court has two options. First, the court may invalidate the provision that resulted from the insane delusion (e.g., disinheriting a purportedly unfaithful spouse). That is the Restatement's approach:

Restatement (Third) of Property: Wills & Other Donative Transfers §8.1, comment s

> Insane delusion. An insane delusion is a belief that is so against the evidence and reason that it must be the product of derangement. A belief resulting from a process of reasoning from existing facts is not an insane delusion, even though the reasoning is imperfect or the conclusion illogical. Mere eccentricity does not constitute an insane delusion.
>
> A person who suffers from an insane delusion is not necessarily deprived of capacity to make a donative transfer. A particular donative transfer is invalid, however, to the extent that it was the product of an insane delusion.

Alternatively, the court may invalidate the entire will. Courts generally choose that option only if they find that the insane delusion affected the entire dispositive plan or if invalidating the provision that resulted from the insane delusion would significantly disrupt the decedent's overall disposition.

Estate of Zielinski
208 A.D.2d 275 (N.Y. App. Div. 1995)

PETERS, Justice.

Appeals from . . . a decree of the Schenectady County Surrogate's Court (Mazzone, J.), entered April 15, 1994, which denied probate to an instrument purporting to be the last will and testament of decedent. . . .

Cecilia Zielinski (hereinafter decedent) was admitted to the hospital on May 30, 1992 and diagnosed with colon cancer shortly thereafter. While in the hospital, she was seen on a daily basis by her sister, Barbara Moczulski (hereinafter proponent) and her sister's husband. On or about June 23, 1992 while still in the hospital, decedent executed a will, in the presence of proponent, which provided for the distribution of her residuary estate in equal shares to proponent and proponent's husband. Neither decedent's only son, Eugene J. Zielinski ["Zielinski"], her two grandchildren, her five great-grandchildren nor any of decedent's other lineal decedents were named as beneficiaries. Her assets consisted of a house and approximately 200 savings bonds worth approximately $360,000.

. . . Decedent died on September 25, 1992. . . .

The expert testimony of Abdul Hameed, the consulting psychiatrist at the hospital where decedent had been admitted, indicated that decedent was diagnosed on the date of her admission as suffering from a delusional disorder regarding her son. Such psychiatrist testified that decedent told him that Zielinski had injected her in her buttocks and that her husband (since deceased) and her doctors had been involved in the plan. Hameed further testified that when he next examined decedent on June 9 and 10, 1992, she continued to verbalize these delusions. He opined that patients with this disorder could be competent in some respects and delusional with respect to others.

Testimony of a second psychiatrist, Zoser Mohammed, who examined decedent on June 15, 1992, confirmed Hameed's diagnosis. Decedent told Mohammed that her husband broke her legs and that Zielinski was getting instructions from a "device" that turned the world inside out. Mohammed confirmed that a person could exhibit appropriate behavior apart from the specific delusion. Testimony from decedent's attending nurses confirmed the delusional statements regarding decedent's son. Two additional psychiatrists, one proffered by proponent and the other by the challengers, confirmed such diagnosis after their review of the medical records. Both testified that such delusions may have directly affected decedent's decision to exclude Zielinski from the will.

Lay testimony included that of Patricia Russo, an employee of Zielinski, who knew decedent since 1979. She testified that decedent continuously made delusional statements from 1979 to 1992 regarding the placement of balloons in her stomach by Zielinski, that her husband ran over her legs and put someone else's legs on her, that Zielinski injected chemicals into her, and that there was a conspiracy by and between her husband, her son and her doctors. . . .

Zielinski's former spouse, Jean Smith, testified similarly and advised that such statements dated from 1973 when she first met decedent. She added that decedent advised her that her husband and doctors pushed her eyes back into her head and that decedent regularly spit into a jar to save as evidence of what Zielinski and her husband had done to her. Zielinski and one of his employees testified to finding approximately 25 to 30 one-gallon jars in decedent's closet, apparently filled with the saliva she had saved. Zielinski's current spouse, Lynn Zielinski, testified that when she met decedent in 1979, decedent told her about her legs being substituted and the balloons. She further confirmed prior testimony about the "devices" and the spitting into a jar. While she testified that decedent mostly blamed her husband, after decedent's husband became ill such witness testified that decedent's focus shifted to Zielinski. All such witnesses, including Zielinski, testified that there was no basis for such statements and that there existed a good relationship between Zielinski and decedent.

Recognizing that there was testimony indicating that decedent was capable of leading a normal life, we note that a person suffering from an insane delusion can still be competent to manage their own affairs and, if the person's behavior is not centered on the subject of the delusion, can appear to be normal. . . .

Even if it could be said that decedent had general testamentary capacity, she could, at the same time, have an insane delusion which controlled the testamentary act, thus rendering it invalid. "'In order to invalidate a will it is not necessary that the intellect . . . be in total eclipse. . . . There is a partial insanity and a total insanity. Such partial insanity may exist as respects particular persons . . . while as to others

> the person may not be destitute of the use of reason.'" We find that the testimony fully supports the conclusion that decedent was suffering from an insane delusion regarding her son and that this delusion directly affected her decision not to leave anything to him under her will. We further find that Surrogate's Court properly determined that proponent failed to show that the delusions had a rational basis. . . . Rather, there was sufficient credible evidence that Zielinski had a good relationship with decedent and that her delusions were chronic [even if] it could have been determined that decedent had the requisite testamentary capacity at the time of the execution of the will.

QUESTIONS

4. Why did Zielinski, the contestant, rely on the doctrine of insane delusion rather than pursue a contest based on the decedent's lack of testamentary capacity?

   ANSWER. New York law, which follows the minority rule of placing the burden of proving testamentary capacity on the proponent of the will, required the proponent to establish prima facie evidence of capacity, which apparently existed here. Although the appellate opinion above does not describe that prima facie evidence of capacity, it does state that there was evidence of the testator's ability to lead a normal life and deferred to the trial court's factual findings regarding testamentary capacity. Once the proponent satisfied this low evidentiary threshold, the burden then shifted to the contestant to prove lack of capacity, which would have required production of far more evidence of the decedent's mental state than would be necessary to prove an insane delusion, which involved a narrow inquiry into a particular strain of alleged derangement. Moreover, the facts here suggest that the decedent might have been capable of satisfying the test for testamentary capacity at the time she executed her will. There was no evidence that the decedent was disoriented as to her familial relations or the nature or extent of her property. Indeed, the testator's insane delusions about her late husband and son might have been the irrational basis for her decision to leave her entire estate to sister and brother-in-law. This further suggests that she understood the nature and extent of her property, the natural objects of her bounty, and, although tainted by the delusion, how she intended to dispose of her estate.

5. Why did Zielinski, the contestant, have standing to contest the decedent's will?

   ANSWER. A party has standing to contest a will if he would inherit from the estate upon a finding that the will (or a provision in the will) is invalid. A party contesting the will may therefore be a beneficiary under a previous will or an intestate heir. Although the opinion is not clear, the will in question appears to have been the decedent's only executed will. This means that invalidation of the will would result in intestate distribution of her estate. Given what we are told about the decedent's family, Zielinski, the decedent's son, would be appear to be her sole heir with standing to contest the will.

6. What is the significance of the court's finding at the end of the opinion that Zielinski and Cecilia "had a good relationship" when Cecilia was not in the grips of her delusion?

   ANSWER. As noted, the insane delusion must cause the testator to make a disposition different from one that he or she would otherwise make. Evidence that Zielinski and Cecilia were close suggests that Cecilia's delusions — and not some other factor — caused her to disinherit Zielinski.

PROBLEM IV

In New York, the proponent of a will has the initial burden of demonstrating that the decedent had testamentary capacity. Under the UPC, in an informal probate proceeding, "[a] will which appears to have the required signatures and which contains an attestation clause showing that the requirements of execution [under this Code] have been met shall be probated without further proof." UPC §3-303(c). In formal probate proceedings, "[c]ontestants of a will have the burden of establishing lack of testamentary intent or capacity, undue influence, fraud, duress, mistake or revocation." UPC §3-407. Which is the better presumption: New York's rule or the UPC's?

3.3 PROTECTIVE DOCTRINES: EXTERNAL FACTORS

Opportunists sometimes seek to override the freedom of disposition by manipulating the testator's estate plan for their own personal gain. This risk of exploitation is acute for the elderly, who often live in a state of isolation. Thus, one of the most commonly litigated issues in trusts and estates practice is whether a will expresses the testator's true intentions. Plaintiffs typically invoke a "protective doctrine" such as duress, fraud, or undue influence, which permit a court to strike down a purported will even if it was executed in compliance with the relevant formalities. Because these protective doctrines largely concern the interfering influence of third parties, we describe them as "external" factors.

Restatement (Third) of Property: Wills & Other Donative Transfers §8.3 Undue Influence, Duress, or Fraud

(a) A donative transfer is invalid to the extent that it was procured by undue influence, duress, or fraud.

(b) A donative transfer is procured by undue influence if the wrongdoer exerted such influence over the donor that it overcame the donor's free will and caused the donor to make a donative transfer that the donor would not otherwise have made.

(c) A donative transfer is procured by duress if the wrongdoer threatened to perform or did perform a wrongful act that coerced the donor into making a donative transfer that the donor would not otherwise have made.

(d) A donative transfer is procured by fraud if the wrongdoer knowingly or recklessly made a false representation to the donor about a material fact that was intended to and did lead the donor to make a donative transfer that the donor would not otherwise have made.

The Restatement's comments clarify that "donative transfer" means both the making and the revoking of a gift, so this section applies to both executing and revoking of a will or a codicil (a codicil is an amendment to a will).

Comment d summarizes the effect of undue influence, duress, or fraud, and reiterates the importance of carrying out a testator's intentions, as follows:

> Ordinarily, only the donative transfer that was procured by undue influence, duress, or fraud is invalid. Thus, if a devise in a will was procured by one of these wrongful acts, only that devise, not the entire will, is ordinarily invalid. The court may, however, hold the entire will invalid if it determines that complete invalidity would better carry out the testator's intent.

3.3.1 Undue Influence

The doctrine of undue influence protects testators — typically those suffering from diminished physical or mental ability — from wrongful pressure exerted by third parties. Although this section focuses on undue influence in the context of wills, the doctrine applies also to inter vivos gifts and trusts.

Of course, influence is inherent in all human relationships. Indeed, family members, close friends, and business associates significantly affect our behavior and decisions, often for the better. Those interactions might be called "due influence." Conversely, *undue* influence arises when the wrongdoer's volition overcomes the testator's, thereby causing the testator to do something he or she otherwise would not do (or fail to do something he or she otherwise would do). If asked, a testator acting under undue influence would say, as commentators have frequently noted, "this is not my free will, but I must do it."

Undue influence often presents difficult evidentiary issues for courts. The burden of establishing undue influence is on the contestant — the person or persons asserting that the will (or provisions of the will) are the product of undue influence. See Restatement Third of Property: Wills & Other Donative Transfers §8.3, comment b. Direct evidence of undue influence is often difficult to obtain because the best witness, the testator, is dead at the time of probate, and wrongdoers are often adept at covering their tracks. Occasionally, however, there is direct evidence of undue influence. Some wrongdoers document the process of drafting and executing a will, believing that this evidence will demonstrate the absence of undue influence. Such evidence, in fact, tends to backfire, especially on the numerous occasions when an attorney records the testator's signing of his or her will. In a recent Texas case, the harrowing recording shows a frail, disoriented woman in a hospital bed with her attorney and the two men who would have benefited from the will adjacent.[8]

---

8. In this case, the attorney was disbarred (see Olsen v. Comm'n for Lawyer Discipline, 347 S.W.3d 876 (Tex. App. 2011)) and one of the men who stood to benefit from the death-bed will was convicted of attempted theft. See McCay v. State, 476 S.W.3d 640, 643 (Tex. App. 2015). A copy of the video recording of the will execution is available at https://www.youtube.com/watch?v=C-maquqQT58.

Most cases are established by circumstantial evidence. The Restatement provides:

> In the absence of direct evidence of undue influence, circumstantial evidence is sufficient to raise an inference of undue influence if the contestant proves that (1) the donor was susceptible to undue influence, (2) the alleged wrongdoer had an opportunity to exert undue influence, (3) the alleged wrongdoer had a disposition to exert undue influence, and (4) there was a result appearing to be the effect of the undue influence.

Restatement (Third) of Property: Wills & Other Donative Transfers §8.3, comment e. Thus, some cases rely on circumstantial evidence to establish an inference of undue influence. The trier of fact may, but need not, accept the inference of undue influence as sufficient proof that it occurred.

Alternatively, a contestant alleging that a will or certain of its provisions were the product of undue influence may rely on the rebuttable presumption that arises "if the alleged wrongdoer was in a *confidential relationship* with the testator and there were *suspicious circumstances* surrounding the preparation, formulation, or execution of the [will]." Restatement Third of Property: Wills & Other Donative Transfers §8.3, comment f (italics added). The presumption is strengthened if the beneficiary of the alleged undue influence was not a natural object of the testator's bounty. When a contestant establishes the presumption, the burden shifts to the proponent to demonstrate that the will was procured in good faith and without undue influence. The two components of the presumption deserve explanation.

Confidential relationship: Comment g to Restatement §8.3 describes three kinds of confidential relationships: a *fiduciary relationship* (for example, a trustee and a trust beneficiary or an agent under a power of attorney and the principal); a *reliant relationship* (that is, a relationship based on special trust and confidence such as the relationship that might exist between a financial advisor and a client or between a physician and a patient); and a *dominant-subservient relationship* (for example, the relationship between a caregiver and a disabled, ill, or weakened individual). These relationships in any given case may overlap.

Suspicious circumstances: The Restatement provides a nonexclusive list of suspicious circumstances, as follows:

> (1) the extent to which the donor was in a weakened condition, physically, mentally, or both, and therefore susceptible to undue influence; (2) the extent to which the alleged wrongdoer participated in the preparation or procurement of the will or will substitute; (3) whether the donor received independent advice from an attorney or from other competent and disinterested advisors in preparing the will or will substitute; (4) whether the will or will substitute was prepared in secrecy or in haste; (5) whether the donor's attitude toward others had changed by reason of his or her relationship with the alleged wrongdoer; (6) whether there is a decided discrepancy between a new and previous wills or will substitutes of the donor; (7) whether there was a continuity of purpose running through former wills or will substitutes indicating a settled intent in the disposition of his or her property; and (8) whether the disposition of the property is such that a reasonable person would regard it as unnatural, unjust, or unfair, for example, whether the disposition abruptly and without apparent reason disinherited a faithful and deserving family member.

See *id.*, comment h. The Restatement emphasizes that this list is not comprehensive by noting that "all relevant factors may be considered." *Id.* For example, in holding there was insufficient evidence to establish that a testator's personal representative exercised undue influence, a recent Florida case described its criteria for determining whether there were suspicious circumstances (or, as the court described it, an "active procurement" of the will) as follows:

> These criteria include: (a) the beneficiary's presence at the execution of the will; (b) the beneficiary's presence when the testator expresses a desire to make a will; (c) the beneficiary's recommendation of an attorney to draw the will; (d) the beneficiary's knowledge of the contents of the will prior to execution; (e) the beneficiary's instructions to the attorney on the preparation of the will; (f) whether the beneficiary secured the witnesses to the will; and (g) whether the beneficiary has possession of the will subsequent to execution.

In re Estate of Flohl, 764 So. 2d 802, 804 (Fla. Dist. Ct. App. 2000).

If the presumption of undue influence is demonstrated and if the will proponent fails to rebut the presumption, the contestant is generally entitled to judgment. The court may then refuse to give effect to those provisions of the will resulting from undue influence or the court may refuse to admit the will to probate if doing so would better carry out the testator's true intentions. See Restatement (Third) of Property: Wills & Other Donative Transfers §8.3, comment d.

If undue influence rises to the level of a threat of physical (or other) harm, a court may find that the testator executed his or her will under duress.

Cases involving undue influence often turn on the jurisdiction's common (or statutory) law establishing burdens of proof. Perhaps nowhere else in the law of wills is the outcome of a case as subjective and as procedurally driven by shifting burdens of proof as under the doctrine of undue influence. The following case exemplifies these issues with particular clarity.

In re Estate of Kurrle

No. 295841, 2011 WL 1198198 (Mich. Ct. App. Mar. 31, 2011)

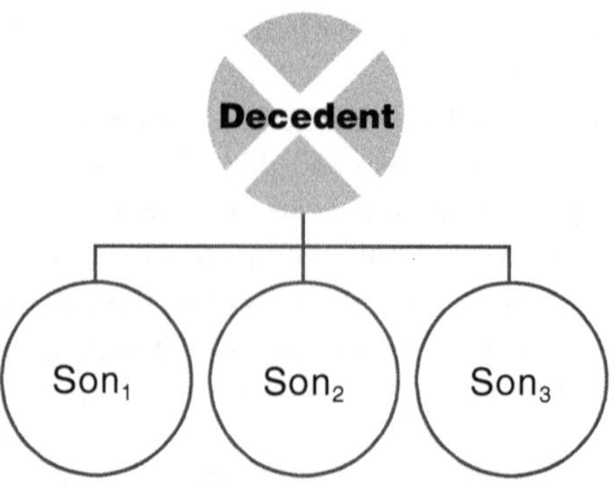

Per Curiam.

Respondent appeals by right the probate court's order setting aside a quitclaim deed and corresponding will executed by his mother, the decedent, on November 21, 2008. The executed documents purported to transfer the decedent's home and the entirety of her estate to respondent, effectively disinheriting the decedent's other two sons. Petitioner, one of the decedent's other sons, filed a petition to set aside the documents, in part, on the ground of undue influence. We affirm.

. . .

Respondent first challenges the probate court's finding that he, as the decedent's son, tenant, and joint account holder, had a fiduciary relationship with the decedent. Respondent correctly notes that a parent-child relationship, in and of itself, does not establish a fiduciary relationship or its corresponding presumption of undue influence. . . . In general, a fiduciary relationship . . . exists when there is a reposing of faith, confidence, and trust and the placing of reliance by one on the judgment and advice of another.

In support of his position that no fiduciary relationship existed, respondent relies heavily on Salvner v. Salvner, 349 Mich. 375 (1957), in which the plaintiff sought to have set aside certain conveyances to his children, the defendants, on the basis of undue influence. Our Supreme Court held in relevant part that no fiduciary relationship existed between the plaintiff and the defendants even though the defendants "unquestionably did many things to assist their father, a perfectly natural course of conduct in view of his physical condition." Instead, the critical issue in that case was whether the plaintiff was governed by the defendants' advice or dependent on them to make decisions. According to the *Salvner* Court, the plaintiff was not so governed; he capably made decisions on his own behalf and refused to act against his own inclinations. Accordingly, no fiduciary relationship existed because the defendants' assistance "amounted to no more than would be prompted normally by the existing relationship."

We note that the evidence tending to indicate the existence of a fiduciary relationship in the present case extends far beyond a child's friendly assistance to a parent. Unlike in *Salvner,* the evidence in this case strongly suggests that the decedent could not make sound decisions at the time that she executed the quitclaim deed and corresponding will, and that there existed a reposing of faith, confidence, and trust in respondent such that the decedent relied on his judgment and advice.

The decedent made respondent her joint bank account holder, trusting him to make financial decisions on her behalf should she become unable. Respondent also resided with the decedent, indicating a certain level of trust, and the decedent relied on respondent's presence so that she would not be alone. Moreover, although not apparently taken into consideration by the probate court, we note that the authority attendant a power of attorney creates a fiduciary relationship between the agent and the principal. As the holder of the decedent's financial power of attorney, respondent agreed to act only for the decedent's benefit, and a fiduciary relationship arose as a matter of law. The probate court did not err by determining that a fiduciary relationship existed between respondent and the decedent in this case.

As our Supreme Court explained in Kar v. Hogan, 399 Mich. 529 (1976), the existence of a fiduciary relationship is only the first element necessary to give rise to a presumption of undue influence:

> The presumption of undue influence is brought to life upon the introduction of evidence which would establish (1) the existence of a confidential or fiduciary relationship between the grantor and a fiduciary, (2) the fiduciary or an interest which he represents benefits from a transaction, and (3) the fiduciary had an opportunity to influence the grantor's decision in that transaction.

As indicated previously, the probate court properly determined that there existed a fiduciary relationship between the decedent and respondent in this matter. In addition, although not contested on appeal, we note that the other two elements are also established in this case. First, respondent clearly benefited from the transactions at issue, which transferred the decedent's home and the entirety of her estate to him, effectively disinheriting the decedent's other two sons. Respondent also had an opportunity to influence the decedent's decision to execute the disputed documents. Despite the decedent's compromised mental state, respondent admits that he obtained a notary and a witness and stood by as the decedent, suffering from confusion, transferred her home and the entirety of her estate to him. In addition, respondent had resided with the decedent for more than 13 years preceding her death. Based on the totality of the circumstances, we hold that sufficient facts existed to give rise to a rebuttable presumption of undue influence, and the probate court did not clearly err in this regard.

. . .

The establishment of a presumption of undue influence creates a mandatory inference of undue influence, shifting the burden of going forward with contrary evidence onto the person contesting the claim of undue influence. However, the burden of persuasion remains with the party asserting [undue influence]. If the defending party fails to present evidence to rebut the presumption, the proponent has satisfied the burden of persuasion.

. . .

As stated in Kouri v. Fassone, 121 N.W.2d 432 (Mich. 1963):

> [I]t is not possible to formulate a single definition embracing all forms of undue influence. The law is settled that we view each case largely upon its own circumstances. Particularly in search of undue influence, we look at the whole spectrum of circumstances, not at [one] facet. The ultimate question is whether the disposition was voluntary.

Another useful definition is provided in In re Estate of Willey, 9 Mich. App. 245, 255, (1967):

> Undue influence is the overpowering of the volition of the testator by another person whereby what purports to be the testator's will is in reality the will of the other person. While there need be no violence or threat of physical force, there must be unreasonable pressure upon the mind of the testator, amounting to psychological or moral coercion, compulsion, or constraint, so great that his free agency is destroyed and the volition of

the person applying the pressure is substituted. To be actionable, the unreasonable and improper pressure must result in a will which the testator would not otherwise have made. Such a testament does not represent the testator's true will at all, but, in reality, represents the will of the person who influenced him. [Citations omitted.]

To support his argument that the presumption of undue influence has been overcome in this case, respondent simply argues that there is no evidence that he exerted pressure upon the decedent through psychological or moral coercion, compulsion, or constraint such that she lacked free will. However, the mere absence of evidence supporting a presumed fact does not rebut that fact. Instead, rebuttal evidence requires some affirmative showing. Rather than merely assert a lack of evidence of undue influence, respondent was required to produce affirmative evidence proving the presumed fact to be false. Because defendant offered no proof in this regard, petitioner carried his ultimate burden of persuasion on the issue of undue influence as a matter of law, and the mandatory inference of undue influence remained intact.

Respondent's failure to rebut the presumption of undue influence aside, the evidence presented at trial fully supports the probate court's conclusion that the executed documents were the product of undue influence. The testimony suggested that respondent purposely concealed the execution of the documents from his family members and thereafter entered into an agreement to keep the executed documents a secret. Numerous witnesses testified regarding their belief that the executed documents were the result of respondent's manipulation of the decedent, and respondent's apparent remorse — hanging his head and stating, "it's too late now" — tended to support this testimony. The evidence plainly established that, rather than desiring to transfer all of her property to respondent, the decedent wished to divide her estate equally among her three sons. We must defer to the probate court's special opportunity to assess the credibility of the witnesses who appeared before it.

QUESTIONS

7. The first element necessary to raise a presumption of undue influence is that the wrongdoer stood in a confidential relationship with the testator. Would the respondent in *Kurrle* have met this test if the testator had lived alone and had not made respondent a joint bank account holder?

   ANSWER. Yes. The court holds that respondent and the testator were in a fiduciary relationship (one kind of confidential relationship) because Respondent lived with the testator and held a joint bank account with her. But even if those facts were not present, respondent held a power of attorney for the testator. This, by itself, would be sufficient to create a fiduciary (and thus confidential) relationship.

8. To trigger the presumption of undue influence, a contestant must not only show a confidential relationship; instead, he or she must prove that there were "suspicious circumstances." The court in *Kurrle* focuses on two such indicia of undue influence: that the wrongdoer benefited from a transaction and had the opportunity to influence the testator. However, most jurisdictions consider a wider range

of factors, such as the ones from the Restatement (on page 99 above). How many of the Restatement factors were present in *Kurrle*?

ANSWER. The first Restatement factor is whether the testator was susceptible to undue influence. In *Kurrle*, the testator was "could not make sound decisions" and apparently could not live alone. Factor two is that the wrongdoer actively participated in the execution of the will. Respondent "obtained a notary and a witness and stood by" when the decedent executed the will and the deed. Factor three is whether the donor received independent advice from an attorney or from other competent and disinterested advisors in preparing the will or will substitute. There is no such evidence in the opinion. Factor four is whether the will or will substitute was prepared in secrecy or in haste. Respondent "purposely concealed the execution of the documents from his family members and thereafter entered into an agreement to keep the executed documents a secret." Factor five is whether the donor's attitude toward others had changed by reason of his or her relationship with the alleged wrongdoer, and factor eight is whether the disposition of property seems unnatural. Evidence that pertains to both of these topics is that the decedent apparently intended to divide her property equally among her sons, rather than leaving everything to respondent.

9. Suppose respondent had called a witness at trial who testified that, in December 2008, the decedent had said to the witness: "I feel so much better now that I've got my estate plan and financial affairs exactly how I want." How might that have impacted the court's analysis?

   ANSWER. A presumption of undue influence can be rebutted by evidence that the testator was acting voluntarily. This after-the-fact confirmation that the will and deed reflect the testator's free will would be relevant for that issue.

10. As a lawyer, how can you guard against undue influence?

    ANSWER. A lawyer should always meet with the client in private to discuss whether the testator fully understands the disposition under the will and to provide the testator an opportunity to discuss with the attorney any pressure the testator may be under. If an attorney has any suspicion of undue influence, the attorney would also want to meet privately with the client to discuss those concerns and obtain reassurance that they are unfounded.

3.3.2 Duress

As the Restatement section above puts it, "[a] donative transfer is procured by duress if the wrongdoer threatened to perform or did perform a wrongful act that coerced the donor into making a donative transfer that the donor would not otherwise have made." A will resulting from a wrongdoer's infliction of duress does not express the free agency of the testator and is invalid. As our next case illustrates, duress both overlaps with and differs from undue influence in several important ways.

In re Estate of Rosasco
927 N.Y.S.2d 819 (Surr. Ct. 2011)

KRISTIN BOOTH GLEN, J.

This is a motion for summary judgment brought by John Cella, preliminary executor of the estate of his great-aunt, Mildred Rosasco, and proponent in a proceeding to probate her will. Objectants (four of decedent's nieces and nephews, including proponent's mother) oppose the motion. The facts of this case and the objections asserted present an opportunity to reexamine the tangled relationship in New York law between undue influence and duress as grounds for invalidating a will.

PROCEDURAL POSTURE

Decedent died on June 18, 2006, at age 93, survived by five nieces and nephews as her [intestate] distributees, leaving a $2.8 million estate. The propounded instrument, executed on September 16, 1997, nominated as co-executors Loretta, a predeceased sister, and proponent and left the entire probate estate to Loretta and Lillian, another predeceased sister, but, in the event neither survived decedent, to proponent. Accordingly, proponent is the only person with an interest under the propounded instrument.

Distributees Elissa Cella, Robert Rosasco, Arthur Rosasco and Ellin Learned objected to probate of the propounded instrument, alleging that the instrument . . . is the product of proponent's undue influence [and] . . . is the product of duress exercised by proponent on decedent. . . .

FACTS RELEVANT TO CLAIMS OF UNDUE INFLUENCE AND DURESS

Decedent, her sisters Lillian and Loretta, and proponent and his family all lived in various apartments in 45 Morton Street. . . . When proponent's parents threw him out of their home, proponent, according to his deposition testimony, simply moved from his parents' units, Apartments 7 and 8, into Apartment 2, which belonged to Lillian. Lillian resided with decedent in Apartment 5. Loretta lived in Apartment 4. In 1989, decedent gave proponent a key to Apartment 5.

In August 1997, proponent (along with Lillian and Loretta) attended a meeting between decedent and Joseph J. Cella, Esq., (no relation to proponent), the attorney who drafted the September 16, 1997 instrument, at which the terms of the proposed instrument were discussed. "In essence," proponent testified at his deposition, "she said she'd like to leave all her possessions to her sisters first and then to me."

In 1997, that same year, proponent's relationship with his sister Kate, according to his own deposition testimony, was "hostile." Proponent knew that decedent and her sisters provided Kate (who no longer was residing at 45 Morton Street) with financial support. It was "common knowledge"; besides, at the time, according to his deposition testimony, proponent had unfettered access to decedent's checkbook and monitored checks payable to Kate. Decedent's financial support of Kate infuriated proponent. [Proponent] berated decedent and her sisters loudly and often. [Proponent's] anger incited him to violence. He testified at his deposition that, in 1997, on one of Kate's weekly visits to Apartment 5 to ask decedent and her sisters for money, he struck Kate and "pushed" her to the floor.

45 Morton Street, New York, New York

Kate also testified at her deposition about the 1997 incident:

A. There was one time I believe in — I believe it was 97 when [proponent] hit me in the back while I was — while I was leaving the apartment and he was coming in. He just swung around and hit me. And it was in front of all three of my aunts. And that was one of the —

Q. As you were coming the [sic] apartment?

A. As I was going out.

Q. As you were going out the door?

A. Yes. And that was the one time that — well, not the one time; but it was, like, a major time when all three aunts got up and went after him. They were yelling at him to leave me alone. They were very agitated and they were very upset. They called the police.

The court notes that decedent was crippled from polio. In 1997, according to proponent's deposition testimony, decedent was 5′7″ and "skinny," weighing approximately 100 pounds, while proponent was 5′11″ tall, weighing 190 pounds.

According to Kate, the 1997 incident was not proponent's first act of violence against her in decedent's presence. As she testified at her deposition:

A. There were plenty of instances where he tried to intimidate me physically. But as for hitting me, it was confined to 97 and one in 94-95.

Q. Did you —

A. And that was in front of the aunts too.

Q. What happened then?

A. He started an argument with Mildred about giving me money and about me being around them, which is what he usually complains about. And when she told him to get out, he said, I'm not going anywhere. Then he promptly punched me in the stomach in front of them and I went down like a ton of bricks. He's a martial — he knew martial arts at this time. So he was pretty strong at that time. . . .

Proponent's violence and other intimidating behavior had a keen effect on decedent. Kate testified at her deposition:

> I remember the conversation happening at the end of August, beginning of September of 97 where she said one day — I came in one day to talk to her. She said — and I quote — I did a really stupid thing. I made your brother the executor of my estate and I should have made you that, meaning me. And I said, Well, easy thing to do. Call your lawyer and have it changed if that's what you want to do. [But decedent replied:] "Oh, no. If I do that, he'll hurt me." And I was, like, "Um, its your estate. You shouldn't have to be intimidated by him. If you're afraid of calling the lawyer, I'll call the lawyer." [But decedent said:] "No. If you do that, he's just going to end up making things a lot worse and he's going to hurt you and I don't want that on my conscience." . . . She kept saying that if she did that, John would hurt her. Which I could believe, because he intimidated her a lot over the years.

UNDUE INFLUENCE

Courts have long wrestled with the concept of undue influence. In the nineteenth century, the Court of Appeals noted:

> It is impossible to define or describe with precision and exactness what is undue influence; what the quality and the extent of the power of one mind over another must be to make it undue, in the sense of the law, when exerted in making a will. . . . [T]he influence exercised over a testator which the law regards as undue or illegal, must be such as to destroy his free agency; but no matter how little the influence, if the free agency is destroyed it vitiates the act which is the result of it. . . .

Rollwagen v. Rollwagen, 63 N.Y. 504, 519 (1876).

. . .

The New York State Pattern Jury Instructions provide:

> A will must be a true expression of the testator's wishes. If, instead, it reflects the desires of some person who controlled the testator's thoughts or actions, the will is invalid because of undue influence. To be undue, the influence exerted must amount to mental coercion that led the testator to carry out the wishes of another, instead of (his, her) own wishes, because the testator was unable to refuse or too weak to resist. The undue pressure brought to bear may consist of a play on the testator's emotions, passions, fears, weaknesses or hopes. It may consist of an appeal to (his, her) prejudices or a continual course of flattery. The exercise of undue influence may be slow and gradual, progressively gaining control over the testator.
>
> . . .

PJI2d 7:55 at 1429-1430 [2011].

This "classic" type of undue influence is difficult to prove. It tends to be practiced in secret (a "silent resistless power") on an individual who is enfeebled, isolated and moribund, someone susceptible to the effects of subtle importuning who, after executing her will, either loses capacity or dies while subject to the undue influence. On its face, it would not appear applicable to the instant case. Decedent here, at the time she executed her will, suffered no mental infirmity, lived communally with her sisters and survived an additional eight-and-three-quarter years. During that period, she was connected to, and received assistance from, many people other than proponent.

The burden of proving . . . undue influence is eased if objectants can establish that the testator was in a relationship of trust and dependence with a person who exploited that relationship. Such facts permit an inference of undue influence that obligates the person charged with undue influence to explain the bequest.

Unsurprisingly, objectants claim that decedent was in a relationship of trust and dependence with proponent; however, their non-specific and conclusory allegations fail to establish the existence of such relationship. Objectants claim that proponent was "a regular presence at [decedent's] apartment, a participant in her daily life," that he "assist[ed] her and [made] arrangements for her daily life" and that he "supervised her care." These allegations, inadequate in themselves to describe a confidential relationship, . . . undercut any claim of isolation or exclusive dependence. At most, proponent was part of decedent's support system.

In the absence of evidence of actual exercise of undue influence on a weakened mind or abuse of a confidential relationship, proponent . . . would be entitled to summary judgment. Yet . . . undue influence is not the only ground on which to determine whether a propounded instrument expresses testator's unconstrained choice. . . .

[DURESS]

The Restatement (Third) of Property distinguishes a bequest procured by undue influence from one procured by duress. As to the former:

> A donative transfer is procured by undue influence if the wrongdoer exerted such influence over the donor that it overcame the donor's free will and caused the donor to make a donative transfer that the donor would not otherwise have made.

Id. §8.3(b).

The latter is explained as follows:

> A donative transfer is procured by duress if the wrongdoer threatened to perform or did perform a wrongful act that coerced the donor into making a donative transfer that the donor would not otherwise have made.

Id. §8.3(c).

The Comment on Subsection (c) explains:

> An act is wrongful if it is criminal or one that the wrongdoer had no right to do. See Restatement Second, Contracts §§174-176. Although an act or a threat to do an

act that the wrongdoer had a right to do does not constitute duress, such a threat or act can constitute undue influence, for example, a threat to abandon an ill testator.

The Restatement of Contracts fleshes out the elements of duress. First, "the doing of an act often involves, without more, a threat that the act will be repeated" Restatement (First) of Contracts §492 Comment d. As stated in the Restatement (Second) of Contracts: "Past events often import a threat." *Id.* §175 Comment b.

Second, the standard for evaluating whether an "act or threat produces the required degree of fear is not objective," but subjective, that is, the issue is whether the threat of a wrongful act induced such fear in the testator "as to preclude the exercise by [her] of free will and judgment." Restatement (First) of Contracts §492 Comment a. As explained in the Restatement (Second) of Contracts: "The test is subjective and the question is, did the threat actually induce assent on the part of the person claiming to be the victim of duress." *Id.* §175 Comment c.

Finally, the motivation or intent of the person charged with duress is irrelevant: "duress does not depend on the intent of the person exercising it." Restatement (First) of Contracts §492 Comment a.

Objectants here have established a prima facie case for duress. The evidence adduced by objectants, if believed by the trier of fact, could establish that: (1) To decedent, proponent's wrongful act — his violence toward Kate — posed a threat of repeated violence. (2) That threat induced fear in decedent. (3) Decedent feared that, if she were to make a new will that favored Kate, not only would proponent harm decedent, if he were to learn of the new will during decedent's lifetime, but also, more significantly, upon decedent's death, proponent would physically harm Kate (and convert for himself any assets intended for Kate). And (4) Such fear precluded decedent from exercising her free will and judgment and naming Kate, a natural object of her bounty, a legatee.

CONCLUSION

The motion for summary judgment with respect to duress is denied. In all other respects, the motion is granted.

QUESTION

11. Why did the court grant summary judgment for John, the will proponent, on the issue of undue influence, but deny summary judgment on the issue of duress?

    ANSWER. The court holds that the proponent's past violence was a kind of implied threat that he would harm decedent or Kate if decedent's estate plan displeased him. That is sufficient to constitute duress. Conversely, undue influence usually requires proof of a confidential relationship and suspicious circumstances (such as the fact that the decedent had a weakened intellect or that the proponent was actively involved in the creation of the will). Neither of those facts seems to be present here.

3.3.3 Fraud

Fraud occurs when someone makes a false statement of a material fact, either intentionally or recklessly, that causes the victim to do something that he or she otherwise would not have done. In the context of wills, the Restatement defines fraud as follows:

> **Restatement (Third) of Property: Wills & Other Donative Transfers §8.3, comment j**
>
> Fraud. A donative transfer is procured by fraud if the wrongdoer knowingly or recklessly made a false representation to the donor about a material fact that was intended to and did lead the donor to make a donative transfer that the donor would not otherwise have made.
>
> Failure to disclose a material fact does not constitute fraud unless the alleged wrongdoer was in a confidential relationship with the donor.

Fraud can take two forms: "fraud in the inducement" or "fraud in the execution." Fraud in the inducement involves misrepresenting important factors, like falsely telling the testator that her daughter said that she can't wait until the testator dies because she is going to spend her inheritance on a lavish vacation. Fraud in the execution typically involves intentionally misleading a person about the contents of a document, such as asking them to sign a will but telling them it is really a birthday card. If a court determines that a provision in a will was procured by fraud, the court can invalidate the provision. The court may invalidate the entire will if it finds that doing so would better reflect the testator's intentions.

PROBLEM V

At the age of 85, Charlie, a widower, was befriended by Sally, a local antiques dealer fifty years his junior. Sally openly admired Charlie's collection of antique furniture and his Arts and Crafts period house built in 1895. Charlie, smitten by Sally's good looks and charm, said he would gladly leave Sally the house and antiques if not for his son, who was living hand to mouth as a struggling salesman. Charlie did not have a close relationship with his son, but he hoped to one day reestablish a rapport.

A. A few months after meeting Charlie, during one of her weekly visits, Sally presented Charlie with a fabricated obituary purporting to report the accidental death of Charlie's son during a sales call in Asia. Grief stricken, Charlie executed a duly attested will leaving his entire estate to Sally. He died a month later. Assuming Charlie's son can prove these facts, what is his strongest legal argument?

B. A few months after meeting Charlie, during one of her weekly visits, Sally presented Charlie with a document that purported to be his last will and testament. The instrument devised Charlie's entire estate to Sally. Seeking to trick Charlie into signing the document, Sally turned to the signature page and told Charlie he needed to sign a purchase order for a new collection of antiques he had planned to buy. Charlie signed the document and died a month later. Sally then forged the signatures of attesting witnesses and presented the instrument for probate. Assuming Charlie's son can prove these facts, what is his strongest legal argument?

Lear and Cordelia in Prison—William Blake circa 1779

In William Shakespeare's tragedy *King Lear* (1605), Lear declares his intent to devise his kingdom to those of his three daughters who love him the most. Goneril and Regan disingenuously declare their love for Lear while Cordelia refuses to participate in the spectacle. Lear then disinherits Cordelia and leaves everything to Goneril and Regan. For reasons that Lear later discovers (see painting above), Goneril and Regan were untruthful when they proclaimed their love. Had Cordelia survived her father, could she have asserted a claim for fraud against Goneril and Regan? If so, would the claim be fraud in the execution or fraud in the inducement?

4 | Wills: Formalities

4.1 FORMALITIES — INTRODUCTION

This chapter addresses formal requirements for the creation, revocation, and revival of a will.[1] Simply put, a will is a written expression of the decedent's intent to transfer property at death. Formal requirements help ensure that a document appearing to be a will is, in fact, an authentic and voluntary expression of the testator's intent. These requirements are, in part, designed to address the unique evidentiary problems inherent in the probating of wills: Questions about the document's authenticity and voluntariness must be resolved without live input from the decedent, who is no longer available to speak or testify. Likewise, questions about a testator's intent to revoke a will or revive a revoked will must be resolved without the decedent's testimony. Rather than resorting to dark arts or séance to answer such questions, the law of wills requires the observance of procedural formalities at the time of execution, revocation, and revival.

Testamentary formalities, known as "Wills Act" formalities, trace their origin to the English Statute of Frauds enacted in 1677, which required, among other things, that conveyances of land be in writing and that wills be written and witnessed. At that time, the English system of title conveyance was in a state of crisis, rife with forged deeds and fraud perpetrated against feeble testators executing deathbed wills.[2] By one account, "two-thirds of all real estate litigation in Westminster Hall involved concealed prior encumbrances. Land was often sold by people who did not own it. And those who did own it often sold it more than once. There was little way for a buyer to know whether he

1. For purposes here, "formal" refers to the requirements having to do with the forms to which various parts of a valid will must conform. It is not used as the antonym of "informal."

2. Professor John H. Langbein explains the Wills Act's origin as follows: "The Statute of Wills of 1540, 32 Hen. VIII, c. I (1540), made most real property devisable at common law for the first time. Although the statute required a writing, it was not primarily concerned with the formal requirements for such transfers. There were no formal requirements for wills of personalty, including leaseholds, until 1677. The Wills Act of 1837, 7 Will. 4 & 1 Vict., c. 26, (1837), sometimes called the Statute of Victoria, separated the law of wills from the Statute of Frauds and unified the formal requirements for wills of realty and of personalty." John H. Langbein, Substantial Compliance with the Wills Act, 88 Harv. L. Rev. 489, 490 n.1 (1975).

was purchasing enforceable title." James Lindgren, Abolishing the Attestation Requirement for Wills, 68 N.C. L. Rev. 541, 550 (1990) (quoting Philip Hamburger, The Conveyancing Purposes of the Statute of Frauds, 27 Am. J. Legal Hist. 354, 366 (1983)). Worse yet, the 1666 Fire of London, which destroyed St. Paul's Cathedral, incinerated countless land records. Meanwhile, the Great Plague of London (1665-1666) claimed so many lives that the city had to develop an orderly system for administering decedents' estates. The Statute of Frauds, including its provisions governing wills, was enacted in response to those crises.

The Great Fire of London (painter unknown)

Wills Act formalities are said to serve four functions. First, they impress upon the testator the legal significance of expressing testamentary intent ("the ritual function"). That is, requiring the testator to participate in a ceremonial act makes her more likely to treat the instrument with gravitas and seriously consider whether it reflects her intent with regard to the disposition of property at death. Second, formalities tend to enhance the reliability of wills as evidence of the decedent's intent by providing assurances of authenticity ("the evidentiary function"). Third, in some cases, formalities may protect the testator from fraud or undue influence committed by individuals seeking to override the decedent's free will for their own benefit ("the protective function"). And fourth, formalities tend to encourage standardization of wills, which, in turn, simplifies the task of identifying a will and deciphering its contents ("the channeling function").

Under the prevailing doctrine of "strict compliance," a court will refuse to admit a will to probate unless it was executed in exact conformity with Wills Act requirements. As we shall see, however, the Uniform Probate Code and a minority of jurisdictions no longer rigidly adhere to the doctrine of strict compliance.

4.1.1 Attested Wills

The UPC imposes three procedural requirements for the creation of an attested will: The instrument must be (1) in writing, (2) signed by the testator, and (3) either signed by two attesting witnesses or notarized.[3] Unlike the law of contracts, which enforces verbal agreements in all situations (other than those described in the Statute of Frauds), a will must be in writing.[4]

Uniform Probate Code
§2-502 Execution; Witnessed or Notarized Wills; Holographic Wills

(a) [Witnessed or Notarized Wills.] Except as otherwise provided in subsection (b) and in Sections 2-503 [Harmless Error], 2-506 [Choice of Law], and 2-513 [Tangible Personal Property], a will must be:

(1) in writing;

(2) signed by the testator or in the testator's name by some other individual in the testator's conscious presence and by the testator's direction; and

(3) either:

(A) signed by at least two individuals, each of whom signed within a reasonable time after the individual witnessed either the signing of the will as described in paragraph (2) or the testator's acknowledg[e]ment of that signature or acknowledgement of the will; or

(B) acknowledged by the testator before a notary public or other individual authorized by law to take acknowledgements.

(b) [Holographic Wills.] A will that does not comply with subsection (a) is valid as a holographic will, whether or not witnessed, if the signature and material portions of the document are in the testator's handwriting.

(c) [Extrinsic Evidence.] Intent that a document constitute the testator's will can be established by extrinsic evidence, including, for holographic wills, portions of the document that are not in the testator's handwriting.

The vocabulary of Wills Act formalities includes the following terms of art: *Attest* means "to authenticate by signing as a witness,"[5] so the term *attested will* is often used to describe a testamentary instrument signed by at least two witnesses who observed the testator's execution or acknowledgment of the will. *Acknowledgment* occurs when a testator declares before attesting witnesses that he or she has already executed the will; in some states, testators must acknowledge their signature on the will, not merely

---

3. The Uniform Probate Code introduced notarization as an alternative to witness attestation in 2008 although many states have yet to adopt this alternative. See generally Lawrence W. Waggoner, The UPC Authorizes Notarized Wills, 34 ACTEC J. 83 (2008).

4. Some jurisdictions provide a limited exception to the prohibition on oral wills. A "nuncupative" will is an oral declaration made close to the time of death. Nuncupative wills are exceedingly rare and are not recognized under the Uniform Probate Code. In jurisdictions that authorize nuncupative wills, they are given effect on the theory that the decedent lacked sufficient time to reduce her estate plan to writing. Statutes typically require that (1) the oral declaration be made by a person in imminent peril of death before disinterested witnesses; (2) the testator died from the impending peril; and (3) the oral declaration is reduced to writing by one of the witnesses and probated shortly after the testator's death. Many jurisdictions also restrict nuncupative wills to the transfer of personal property and severely limit the aggregate value of property subject to transfer.

5. http://www.merriam-webster.com/dictionary/attest.

the will itself. Once the testator has acknowledged the will and its signature, the witnesses may properly attest by adding their signatures to the instrument. Some jurisdictions impose a *simultaneous presence* requirement in which the testator and attesting witnesses must be simultaneously present at the time of execution (or acknowledgment) and attestation. The UPC, however, does not require simultaneous presence; attesting witnesses need sign the will only "within a reasonable time after the individual witnessed either the signing of the will . . . or the testator's acknowledg[e]ment of that signature or acknowledgement of the will." UPC §2-502(a)(3)(A). Some jurisdictions also require "subscription," which means that signatures must appear at the end of the will. See, e.g., N.Y. Est. Powers & Trusts Law §3-2.1(a)(1) ("[E]very will . . . shall be signed at the end thereof by the testator . . ."). Conversely, the UPC does not require subscription.

Although compliance with these requirements may seem like a simple task, there are many cases in which a noncompliant instrument is offered for, *and denied*, probate. Compliance problems most frequently concern the witness attestation requirement (hence our focus on attested wills). In a surprisingly large number of cases, defects of execution have resulted from the attorney's error. Courts, however, often reject claims of attorney error as grounds for probating a noncompliant will. In the majority of jurisdictions that apply the doctrine of strict compliance, even the slightest failure to satisfy Wills Act formalities can result in the instrument's denial to probate.

In re Estate of Henneghan
45 A.3d 684 (D.C. Ct. App. 2012)

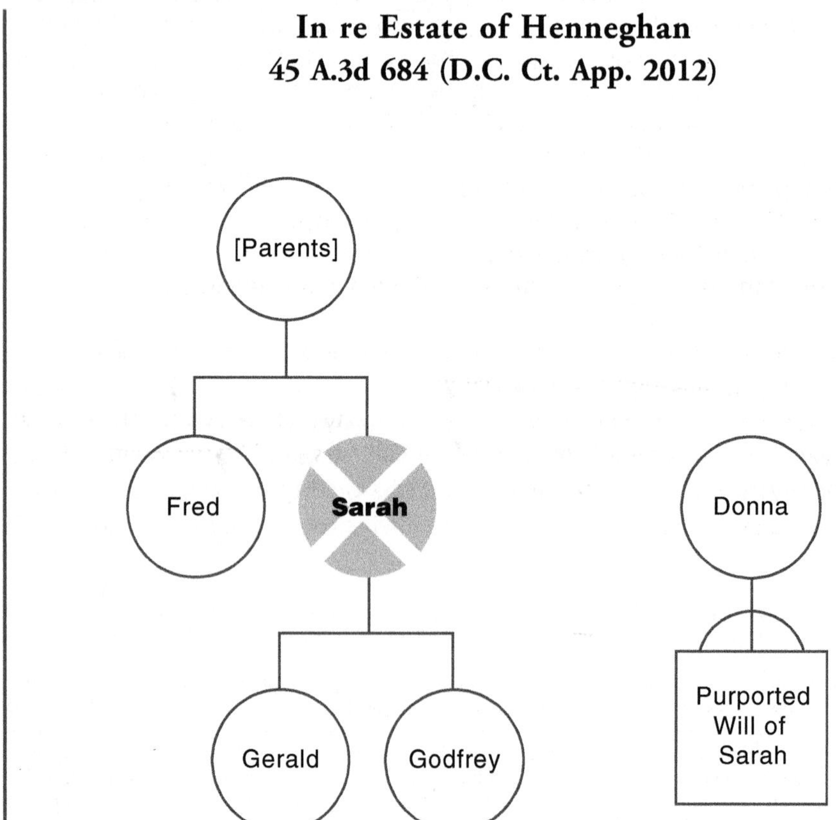

[The decedent, Sarah Ellen Henneghan, died June 17, 2010, with an estate valued at $273,134.[6] Sarah was survived by two sons, Gerald and Godfrey, who filed a joint petition five days after her death to probate the estate intestate. Donna Washington, whose relation to Sarah was not disclosed in the court's opinion, offered a notarized instrument signed only by Sarah for probate as Sarah's will.[7] In a local proceeding known as "Abbreviated Probate,"[8] Donna conceded that the instrument lacked two witness signatures as required by §18-103, but she offered affidavits of four individuals with knowledge of Sarah's will: (1) Ralph O. Turner, who was in the same building as the notary public at the time the decedent had her will notarized; (2) Fred N. Moses, Sarah's brother, who stated that he spoke with her many times regarding her will; (3) . . . Donna Washington, who stated that Sarah said she had finalized her will; and (4) Eugenia Robinson, who was present in the open reception area of the notary's office and saw Sarah execute her will. The probate court admitted the instrument to probate and Gerald appealed.]

. . .

. . . Under general probate principles, a testator must comply with statutes regulating due execution of the will, or the testator's intent, expressed by will, has no legal effect and is ignored by the courts. Almost all states require, by statute, that a duly executed will be signed by the testator, and attested to and subscribed by a certain number of witnesses in the testator's presence. See D.C. Code §18-103 (stating that a will in the District of Columbia is void unless: (1) in writing and signed by the testator, or by another person in his presence and by his express direction; and (2) attested and subscribed in the presence of the testator, by at least two credible witnesses). And so, unless both requirements are fully satisfied, the will is invalid.

The purpose of requiring strict statutory compliance is for the court to be certain that the testator had a definite and complete intention to pass along his or her property, and to prevent fraud, perjury, mistake, and the chance of one instrument being substituted for another. The question of whether the due execution requirement set forth in D.C. Code §18-103(2) can be substituted or be replaced by the abbreviated probate due execution presumption language of D.C. Code §20-312(b)(2) is a question of law which we review *de novo*.

We begin by examining the language of D.C. Code §18-103, which states that a will is properly executed only if it: (1) is in writing and signed by the testator (or by another person in the testator's presence and by his or her express direction); and (2) is

6. The decedent's estate consisted of $31,354.00 in cash, two automobiles worth $25,000.00 and $500.00, real property at 5814 Clay St., Northeast, Washington, D.C. worth approximately $214,780.00, and home furnishings estimated at $1,500.00.

7. At one point in the opinion, the court states that "appellant argues the submitted will contained only one witness' signature," 45 A.3d at 685, but all other references to the will in the opinion state that the testator was the only person to sign the will.

8. D.C. Code §20-312(b)(2) states that, in the case of a petition to admit a will in an abbreviated probate proceeding, due execution of the will is presumed and may be admitted into probate "upon the verified statement of any person with personal knowledge of the circumstances of execution, whether or not the person was in fact an attesting witness, reciting facts showing due execution of the will."

attested to and subscribed by at least two credible witnesses in the presence of the testator. Here, [Donna] concedes the will was not attested to and subscribed by two witnesses in the presence of the decedent; rather, the purported will only bore the decedent's signature and the raised seal of a notary public. However, [Donna] argues that the will is nonetheless valid, because, in the context of an abbreviated probate proceeding pursuant to D.C. Code §20-312(b)(2), the requirements for due execution, under D.C. Code §18-103, can be satisfied by affidavits from individuals with personal knowledge of the circumstances surrounding the will's execution, even if they were not attesting witnesses to the will. In the probate court's February 22, 2011 Order, the court apparently relied on this reasoning in admitting the will into probate.

We are not persuaded by this reading of D.C. Code §18-103 and D.C. Code §20-312, and conclude that affidavits from non-attesting witnesses, who cannot verify that they witnessed two attesting witnesses sign the will in the presence of the testator, fail to satisfy the statutory requirements for due execution of a will, pursuant to D.C. Code §18-103(2). Section 18-103 is unequivocal in its language that a will is void unless both due execution requirements are met. [Citation omitted.] The will must be in writing and signed by the testator (or by another person in his presence and by his express direction), and must be attested and subscribed in the presence of the testator, by at least two credible witnesses. Nothing in the plain language of D.C. Code §20-312 leads us to the conclusion that its provisions were intended to serve as a substitute for these requirements.

Moreover, D.C. Code §20-312's purpose was to streamline the abbreviated probate process by permitting, in certain circumstances, the verified statements of individuals with personal knowledge of the circumstances surrounding the due execution of a will, to substitute for the testimony of witnesses who actually attested and subscribed to the will in the presence of the testator. Here, the affidavits supporting the probate petition fail to satisfy the provisions of D.C. Code §20-312, because none of the affidavits were statements evidencing due execution of the will, as required under the statute. As such, the decedent's will was void because it lacked the signatures of two attesting witnesses subscribed in the presence of the testator, and the probate court's reliance on D.C. Code §20-312, in admitting the will into probate, was erroneous. Accordingly, we reverse the February 22, 2011 Order and remand to the probate court for proceedings consistent with this opinion.

QUESTIONS

1. In *Henneghan*, the relevant Wills Act provision required that the will be "attested and subscribed in the presence of the testator, by at least two credible witnesses." D.C. Code §18-103. Given that the instrument was notarized, why did the court refuse to treat the notary public's raised seal as a form of witness attestation?

   ANSWER. The District of Columbia has not adopted the Uniform Probate Code's provision allowing notarization as a substitute for witness attestation.[9] In the District of Columbia, an attesting witness must sign the will and, according to the opinion, the notary public applied a raised seal without signing the instrument. Perhaps if the notary public had signed the document in addition to applying the raised seal, a common notarization custom in other jurisdictions, the court would have treated the notary public's signature as a form of attestation, but the instrument would still need a second attesting witness's signature. Simply put, strict compliance is strict.

2. In *Henneghan*, Donna (the contestant) argued that, under the District of Columbia's abbreviated probate procedure, due execution is presumed if the will's proponent produces verified statements from individuals with personal knowledge of the circumstances surrounding the will's execution. The abbreviated probate procedure statute provides:

   > In the case of a petition to admit a will to abbreviated probate, due execution of the will shall be presumed and the Court may admit a will to probate either: (1) if the will appears to have been duly executed and contains a recital by attesting witnesses of facts constituting due execution; or *(2) upon the verified statement of any person with personal knowledge of the circumstances of execution, whether or not the person was in fact an attesting witness, reciting facts showing due execution of the will.*

   D.C. Code §20-312(b) (emphasis added). Why didn't the court apply the presumption of due execution based on the four affidavits offered by Donna to prove the will's validity?

   ANSWER. None of the affidavits contained a statement that Sarah's will had, in fact, been *signed* by two attesting witnesses. Ralph Turner, who was in the same building as the notary at the time, did not state that he witnessed the notarization, let alone execution by two attesting witnesses. Fred Moses and Donna, herself, offered statements about Sarah's intent to finalize her will, not about the execution of the instrument. Eugenia Robinson stated that she saw Sarah execute the will, but she did not report observing the attesting witnesses sign the will. Notably, because Eugenia observed Sarah execute the will, she could have potentially served as an attesting witness had she signed the will, but she did not sign it, and, thus, could not be treated as an attesting witness.

3. Did the court frustrate Sarah's testamentary intent to devise her estate to Donna by denying probate? If so, what did the court achieve in reversing the probate judge's decision and remanding with instructions to administer the estate intestate?

   ANSWER. The court likely frustrated Sarah's intent, but we will never know for sure. The court explained that the requirement of strict compliance is "to be certain that the testator had a definite and complete intention to pass along his or her property, and to prevent fraud, perjury, mistake, and the chance of one

9. UPC §2-502(a)(3)(B) (a will must be either signed by at least two individuals or "acknowledged by the testator before a notary public or other individual authorized by law to take acknowledgements").

instrument being substituted for another." While these goals are laudable, the assurance of certainty with regard to the will's authenticity and voluntariness often comes at the cost of denying probate of instruments whose defects of execution are not, in fact, indications of forgery or fraud. Scholars have criticized the doctrine of strict compliance and, as explained below, the UPC (and a minority of jurisdictions) rejects it by providing a "harmless error" rule as a curative doctrine.

PROBLEM I

Max was an elderly man who suffered from numerous physical disabilities and needed a wheelchair to get around. Max typed out a will at home and asked his niece, Sherry, to drive him to the local bank so he could sign it and have it witnessed. Before his retirement last year, Max had been the bank's longtime branch manager.

About one month ago, Sherry drove Max to the bank to execute his will. Inside the bank, they visited the office of Trisha, who served as the bank's assistant manager and notary public. Max asked Trisha to witness the execution of his will and she agreed. Seated at her desk across from Max and Sherry, Trisha (and Sherry) observed Max sign the will. Because of his disability, however, Max had trouble using a pen, so he signed with an "X" instead of his full signature. Trisha then took the will to the other side of the bank to the tellers' counter, while Max and Sherry remained seated in her office. At Max's request, Trisha asked two longtime tellers, David and Beth, to witness the will. They agreed and both signed the document below Max's signature while in presence of Trisha in the teller's lounge. After David and Beth had signed the will, Trisha returned to her office and delivered the executed instrument to Max, who put it inside his briefcase. Sherry and Max then left the bank.

Max died last week. Max's will left the bulk of his estate to Sherry and disinherited his own three children, who had neglected Max in his old age. Sherry offered the will for probate. Max's children objected on grounds that the will was not validly attested and, therefore, Max had died intestate. The applicable Wills Act provides as follows:

> No will shall be valid unless it be in writing and signed by the testator, or by some other person in his presence and by his direction, in such manner as to make it manifest that the name is intended as a signature; and moreover, unless it be wholly in the handwriting of the testator, the signature shall be made or the will acknowledged by him in the presence of at least two competent witnesses, present at the same time; and such witnesses shall subscribe the will in the presence of the testator, and of each other, but no form of attestation shall be necessary.

This jurisdiction applies the doctrine of strict compliance.

A. What result under this jurisdiction's Wills Act?
B. Assume, instead, that the jurisdiction strictly applies the Wills Act formalities contained in UPC §2-502(a). What result? What advice would you offer Sherry to improve her chances of probating the will under §2-502(a)?

PROBLEM II

Martina hired a lawyer to prepare her will. A few days after meeting with Martina, the lawyer composed a typewritten draft and mailed a copy to Martina's home address. The lawyer's secretary stamped the word "DRAFT" in red ink on the top of the first page. All of the will's distributive provisions appear on the first three pages. The fourth page contains an attestation clause followed by lines for two witness signatures. Martina reviewed the draft and liked it. A few days later, Martina's two adult children visited to celebrate her 76th birthday. After dinner, Martina retrieved the draft from her study, crossed out the word "DRAFT" in black ink, and, upon returning to the dinner table, asked her children to serve as attesting witnesses. They agreed and asked to review the will. Martina showed them the title of the document ("Last Will and Testament"); however, she refused to allow them to read the dispositive provisions, immediately turning to the signature page. Martina asked her children to sign the will, which they did. Martina then signed the will while her children watched. Martina then folded the document and, while holding it in the air, said, "This is my will and it's important that you respect my final wishes."

Martina died a few weeks ago, survived by her two adult children. A local homeless shelter, the sole beneficiary of Martina's will, offers the instrument for probate. Martina's children contest and file a petition seeking intestate administration.

You represent the homeless shelter, the proponent of the will. How would you respond to the following arguments asserted by Martina's children contesting the will's validity? Assume UPC §2-502(a) applies and that the court adheres to the doctrine of strict compliance.

a. Argument 1: "The document signed by Martina was marked as a draft and, therefore, cannot be treated as a final testamentary instrument."
b. Argument 2: "The attorney's cover letter accompanying the will instructed Martina to review but not sign the draft will. The cover letter stated, further, that the will execution ceremony had to take place in the attorney's office to ensure compliance with 'proper procedures.' Martina had an obligation to follow her attorney's instructions if she wished to use the document and, because she violated the attorney's instructions, the instrument cannot be probated as a valid will."
c. Argument 3: "Martina refused to allow her children to review the contents of the will, so they were unable to authenticate the document, as is required for proper witness attestation."
d. Argument 4: "The statute requires that attesting witnesses sign 'within a reasonable time *after* the individual witnessed either the [testator's] signing of the will . . . or the testator's acknowledgment of that signature or acknowledgment of the will.' The adult children signed the document before Martina signed it, not after, so the instrument was not properly attested."

PROBLEM III

Consider whether the following instruments strictly comply with the requirements of UPC §2-502(a)(1) and (2):

a. The words "I leave everything to my friend, Fred," written on the testator's bedroom wall in pencil, with the testator's signature written below in blue marker.
b. A video recording of the testator reciting the substantive provisions of her will preserved on a digital video disc, with the testator's signature on the paper insert of the plastic DVD case.
c. A typewritten will prepared by the testator on a word processing program and saved on the testator's hard drive; the text of instrument is written in Times New Roman font while the testator's name appears at the end of the document in cursive font; the document was not printed before the testator's death.
d. An email from the testator describing the disposition of his estate sent to all intended beneficiaries with the testator's name printed electronically at the end.
e. A typewritten will printed on thick stationery; the testator signed "Big Daddy" at the end instead of using his name, Harvey Pollitt; the will was also signed by two witnesses.
f. A photograph signed by the testator entitled, "My Will," depicting the testator standing in front of his house and gesturing toward his wife, who is also in the picture.

4.1.1.1 Witness Competency and "Purging" Statutes

The requirement of witness attestation implicates the related question of witness competency: Who, at law, can serve as a valid attesting witness? The UPC does not answer this question directly, but rather, incorporates principles from outside the law of wills: "An individual generally competent to be a witness may act as a witness to a will." UPC §2-505(a).

Uniform Probate Code
§2-502, comment o

The English Statute of Frauds of 1677 required the witnesses to be "credible." In this country, most non-UPC statutes require the witnesses to be either "credible" or "competent." Today in almost all states the conviction of a crime no longer renders a person an incompetent witness to a will. Mental incompetency, whether from mental deficiency, extreme intoxication, or the influence of drugs, remains a ground of disqualification as a witness. A few states specifically provide by statute a minimum age, such as 18, for attesting witnesses. More commonly, however, no age is specified in the statute. If no age is specified in the statute, a minor is a valid witness, unless the minor was not old enough to observe, remember, and relate the facts occurring at the execution ceremony.

An individual may meet the low threshold of witness competency, but if that individual is also a beneficiary under the will (an "interested witness"), he or she is arguably tainted by a conflict of interest. An interested witness has a stake in whether the will is admitted to probate and, therefore, an incentive to say whatever necessary to probate the will. One way to address such conflicts is to categorically disqualify all interested witnesses. In many cases, however, disqualification would leave an insufficient number of attesting witnesses to satisfy the requirements of the Wills Act and result in the will's denial from probate.

Most jurisdictions, instead, neutralize the conflict by validating the signature of an interested witness (thereby preserving the will's validity), but also purging some or all of the interested witness's right to take under the will absent an otherwise sufficient number of disinterested witness signatures. Most "purging" statutes, as they are known, limit their purging effect by precluding an interested witness from taking more than an intestate share under the will. If, however, there are at least two other disinterested witnesses, most jurisdictions treat the extra interested witness(es) as "supernumerary," or superfluous, and allow the beneficiary to inherit fully under the will.

Notably, the UPC does not have a purging statute. The UPC takes the position that an interested witness's participation in the execution of a will is typically a harmless mistake, not a concerted effort to defraud the probate court. UPC §2-505(b), adopted in a minority of jurisdictions, provides, "The signing of a will by an interested witness does not invalidate the will or any provision of it." Accordingly, under the UPC, a beneficiary may serve as a valid attesting witness and inherit under the will.

4.1.1.2 Attestation Clauses and Self-Proving Affidavits

It is customary, although not required by statute, for an attested will to include an *attestation clause* at the end of the instrument near the witness signatures. An attestation clause typically recites the circumstances surrounding the will's execution from the witnesses' perspective. Its purpose, in theory, is to memorialize the witnesses' observation of an authentic and voluntary will execution. Consider the following example:

> We, Jose Lopez and Maria Rodriguez, the witnesses, sign our names to this instrument, the Last Will and Testament of Juan de la Cruz, the testator, and hereby declare that the testator executed the instrument as his will, that he signed it willingly, that he executed it as his free and voluntary act for the purposes therein expressed, that each of the witnesses, in the presence and hearing of the testator and of each other, signed the will as witness, and that, to the best of the witnesses' knowledge, the testator was at that time 18 years of age or older, of sound mind, and under no constraint or undue influence.

An attestation clause is almost always drafted into the text of the will before the execution ceremony, so, as a practical matter, it is typically not an extemporaneous expression of the witnesses' observation. Rather, the witnesses are asked to read the attestation clause at the time of execution and, only if they agree with it, sign the will. Attesting witnesses are not entitled to examine the substantive provisions of the testator's will, but they must read the attestation clause. A witness's failure to understand the obligations recited in an attestation clause can create needless grounds for denial of probate.

Courts often treat an attestation clause as "*prima facie* evidence of the facts certified by it,"[10] thus creating a rebuttable presumption of a will's validity. If that presumption is rebutted, however, the proponent must prove due execution with other evidence of compliance with Wills Act formalities, such as the live testimony of the attesting witnesses.

Wills are often presented for probate many years after they were signed and witnessed. The passage of time increases the difficulty of locating witnesses or producing

10. Estate of Ruso, 212 A.D.2d 846 (N.Y. Sup. Ct. App. Div. 1995).

other evidence of proper execution and attestation. For this reason, it is now customary to prepare admissible proof of due execution at the time of execution in the form of a "self-proving affidavit." A self-proving affidavit looks similar to and serves all the purposes of an attestation clause, but, because it is also a sworn and notarized statement, it provides admissible evidence of due execution without further testimony of attesting witnesses. See, e.g., Bruce H. Mann, Self-Proving Affidavits and Formalism in Wills Adjudication, 63 Wash. U. L.Q. 39, 41 (1985).

The UPC supplies two statutory form self-proving affidavits. The first form, §2-504(a), is designed for use *at the time of* execution and attestation. This form should be drafted into the will itself; when the testator and witnesses sign the will, which includes the self-proving affidavit, they do so under oath to validate the sworn statement. Thus, the testator and witnesses sign only once, and the will itself is notarized.

The second form, §2-504(b), is designed for use *after* a will has been properly signed by the testator and the attesting witnesses. The form is designed to be a stand-alone affidavit; however, most attorneys attach it to the will. If this form is used, the testator and the witnesses must sign their names twice: once on the will and again on the affidavit.

Uniform Probate Code
§2-504 Self-proved Will

(a) A will that is executed with attesting witnesses may be simultaneously executed, attested, and made self-proved, by acknowledgment thereof by the testator and affidavits of the witnesses, each made before an officer authorized to administer oaths under the laws of the state in which execution occurs and evidenced by the officer's certificate, under official seal, in substantially the following form:

I, _______________ (name), the testator, sign my name to this instrument this _______________ day of _______________, and being first duly sworn, do hereby declare to the undersigned authority that I sign and execute this instrument as my will and that I sign it willingly (or willingly direct another to sign for me), that I execute it as my free and voluntary act for the purposes therein expressed, and that I am [18] years of age or older, of sound mind, and under no constraint or undue influence.

____

Testator

We, _______________ (name), _______________ (name), the witnesses, sign our names to this instrument, being first duly sworn, and do hereby declare to the undersigned authority that the testator signs and executes this instrument as (his)(her) will and that (he)(she) signs it willingly (or willingly directs another to sign for (him)(her)), and that each of us, in the presence and hearing of the testator, hereby signs this will as witness to the testator's signing, and that to the best of our knowledge the testator is [18] years of age or older, of sound mind, and under no constraint or undue influence.

____

Witness

____

Witness

State of ________________

County of ________________

Subscribed, sworn to and acknowledged before me by ___________, the testator, and subscribed and sworn to before me by ___________, and ___________, witness, this ___________ day of ___________.

(Seal)

____

(Signed)

____

(Official capacity of officer)

(b) A will that is executed with attesting witnesses may be made self-proved at any time after its execution by the acknowledgment thereof by the testator and the affidavits of the witnesses, each made before an officer authorized to administer oaths under the laws of the state in which the acknowledgment occurs and evidenced by the officer's certificate, under official seal, attached or annexed to the will in substantially the following form:

The State of _______________________

County of _________________________

We, ______________________ (name), ______________________ (name), and ________________ (name), the testator and the witnesses, respectively, whose names are signed to the attached or foregoing instrument, being first duly sworn, do hereby declare to the undersigned authority that the testator signed and executed the instrument as the testator's will and that (he)(she) had signed willingly (or willingly directed another to sign for (him)(her)), that (he)(she) executed it as (his)(her) free and voluntary act for the purposes therein expressed, and that each of the witnesses, in the presence and hearing of the testator, signed the will as witness and that to the best of (his)(her) knowledge the testator was at that time [18] years of age or older, of sound mind, and under no constraint or undue influence.

________________ Testator

________________ Witness

________________ Witness

Subscribed, sworn to and acknowledged before me by ___________, the testator, and subscribed and sworn to before me by ___________, and ___________, witnesses, this ___________ day of ___________.

(Seal)

____

(Signed)

____

(Official capacity of officer)

(c) A signature affixed to a self-proving affidavit attached to a will is considered a signature affixed to the will, if necessary to prove the will's due execution.

Estate of Griffith
30 So. 3d 1190 (Miss. 2010)

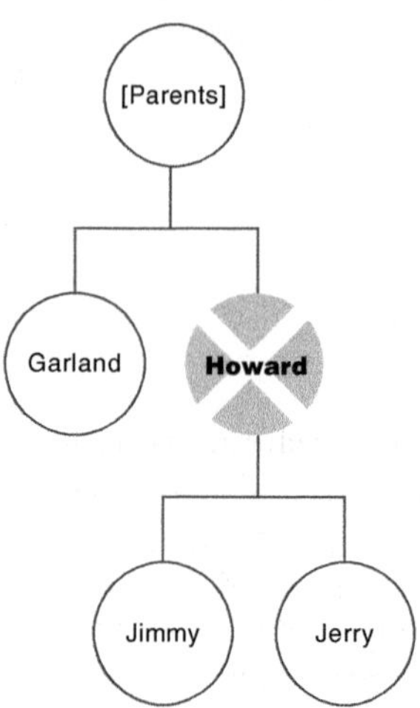

EN BANC.

LAMAR, Justice, for the Court:

¶1. In this will contest, . . . petitioner [Garland Griffith] appeals from the chancellor's order rejecting the probate of . . . decedent [Howard Griffith]'s alleged last will and testament. At issue is whether the last will and testament was properly executed under Mississippi Code Section 91-5-1 (Rev. 2004), when the two attesting witnesses claim they were unaware that the document they signed was a will. We affirm the trial court and find that attesting witnesses to a will must have knowledge of the purpose of their attestation.

FACTS

¶2. On February 27, 2006, Garland L. Griffith filed a petition to probate the purported last will of his brother, Howard Griffith. A copy of the purported, non-holographic will was attached to the petition. Under the will, Howard devised and bequeathed unto Garland his "home and its furnishings and furniture, together with the five acres, more or less, upon which it is situated . . . cash, bank accounts and certificates of deposit, and . . . [a] Maxima automobile, [a] truck, [a] Jeep automobile, [a] Ford 2000 tractor and [a] lawn mower . . . [and] two mobile homes and all furnishings and contents situated therein[.]" Relevant to these proceedings, Howard also devised and bequeathed to his sons, Jimmy L. Griffith and Jerry H. Griffith ("Contestants"), "that portion of [his] property upon which Griffith's Barber Shop is located . . . and all of [the] contents, fixtures and furniture in said business . . . [and the] rest remainder and residue of [his] estate[.]"

¶3. The purported will bears the signature of Howard Griffith and the signatures of Eric M. Scott and Patrick O. Bell as witnesses. Following the signatures of the witnesses, the will contains a "certificate" providing that:

> We, each of the subscribing witnesses to the Last Will and Testament of Howard Griffith, do hereby certify that said instrument was signed by the said Howard Griffith in our presence and in the presence of each of us, and that the said Howard Griffith declared the same to be his Last Will and Testament in the presence of each of us and that each of us signed as subscribing witnesses to said Last Will and Testament at the special request of Howard Griffith in his presence and in the presence of each other.

This "certificate" also bears the signatures of Eric M. Scott and Patrick O. Bell.

¶4. Additionally, the will contains an "affidavit of subscribing witnesses" which provides:

> that the said Howard Griffith, signed, published, and declared the aforesaid instrument to be his Last Will and Testament on July 6, 2005 in the presence of said Affiants . . . that the undersigned Affiants subscribed and attested said instrument as witnesses to the signature and publication thereof, at the special request of Howard Griffith, in his presence and in the presence of each other.

The affidavit concludes with the signatures and addresses of Eric M. Scott and Patrick O. Bell. The affidavit also contains the signature of the notary public, Judy C. Warren Lofton.

¶5. The Contestants filed a caveat against probate, alleging that their father "died without leaving a valid will, in that the purported will is . . . not supported by sworn witnesses."

¶6. Witnesses Scott and Bell filed affidavits ("2006 affidavits"), in which each asserted that he had not witnessed a will, but a power of attorney. Scott and Bell also claimed in their respective affidavits that they had never signed an "affidavit of subscribing witnesses."

¶7. Thereafter, the chancellor conducted a hearing to determine whether the will was duly executed. The chancellor heard testimony from Lofton, Scott, and Bell.

¶8. Lofton testified as to her normal procedure in notarizing a document, because she did not remember notarizing this particular document. Lofton testified that she normally requests identification from the parties; the parties sign the particular document; and she then notarizes the signatures. Lofton identified her signature on the will.

¶9. Scott testified that Elaine Coleman, Howard's niece, asked him to witness Howard's signature on "some documents." Scott agreed and met Howard, Garland, and Bell at a local bank. Scott testified that he never spoke with Howard at the bank other than a greeting. Scott testified that no one informed him what he was signing, and that the notary directed him where to sign. Scott further testified that his 2006 affidavit was incorrect, since he was unaware of what he was signing when at the bank. He stated that he did not read any of the documents prior to signing them, and that he would not have signed the documents had he known they constituted a will.

¶10. Bell testified that in July 2005 he worked at the Griffith Barber Shop. Bell further testified that Howard asked him to "witness something," and he agreed. Bell stated that he rode with Howard and Garland to the bank, and the notary directed him where to sign. Bell testified that he did not read the documents at the time he signed them, and that no one informed him that he was signing a will. He also testified that he would not have signed the documents had he known they constituted a will.

¶11. At the close of the hearing, the . . . chancellor entered an order rejecting the probate of the will based on the testimony of Scott and Bell. From this order, Garland appeals.

DISCUSSION

I. Whether the Chancellor Committed Manifest Error in His Findings of Fact

¶12. [T]he chancellor found that Scott and Bell were unaware that they had witnessed Howard's purported last will and testament. This Court has ruled that "the testimony of attesting witnesses denying or impeaching the execution of the will is to be considered and may be sufficient in some cases to prevent probate, [but it is] to be viewed with caution and suspicion and it is usually entitled to little credence." . . . Further, if either or both attesting witnesses deny the execution, then the proponents may introduce secondary evidence of the execution.

¶13. Bell's and Scott's testimony was the only evidence, other than the testimony of the notary public, submitted by the parties at the hearing. The proponent of the will, Garland, presented only the testimony of Lofton and failed to introduce any witness or other evidence showing that Bell and Scott had knowledge of the purpose of the attestation. The chancellor had before him conflicting evidence concerning whether the witnesses had knowledge that they were witnessing Howard's will, namely: (1) the will, which included the "certificate" and "affidavit of subscribing witnesses"; (2) Scott's and Bell's 2006 affidavits; and (3) Scott's and Bell's testimony at the hearing. This presented a question of fact for the court, and the chancellor resolved the conflict by ruling that the hearing testimony was the most credible. We have ruled that "when the trial judge sits as the finder of fact, he has the sole authority for determining the credibility of witnesses." . . . Further, we reiterate that our trial courts are entitled to deferential review in matters involving questions of fact. Because this Court reviews a chancellor's findings of fact under a standard of manifest error, we cannot say that the chancellor erred. . . . We additionally note that this case does not involve witnesses who cannot "recall the manner" of signing the purported will (see dissent at ¶36); this case involves two witnesses who testified that they had no knowledge of what they were signing, which we find to be a requirement, as explained infra.

II. Whether Attesting Witnesses to a Will Must Have Knowledge of the Purpose of Their Attestation

¶14. This Court also must determine whether the chancellor was correct in ruling that attesting witnesses to a will must have knowledge of the purpose of their attestation. In other words, this Court must decide whether the execution of the will complied with Mississippi Code Section 91-5-1, when the two attesting witnesses were unaware that the document they signed was a will. . . .

¶15. [Mississippi Code] §91-5-1 governs the execution of a last will and testament. It provides, in relevant part, that:

> [A] last will and testament, or codicil, [must] be signed by the testator or testatrix, or by some other person in his or her presence and by his or her express direction. *Moreover, if*

> *not wholly written and subscribed by himself or herself, it shall be attested by two (2) or more credible witnesses in the presence of the testator or testatrix:*

(emphasis added). Section 91-5-1 does not explicitly address any knowledge requirement on behalf of the attesting witnesses. However, we find that our caselaw addressing attestation and publication does address it and is determinative. . . .

¶16. This Court examined the meaning of ["attestation"] in [a previous case and] held that "[the term] includes not only the mental act of observation, but also . . . the manual one of subscription." In other words, not only must the witness observe the testator, he must also affix his signature to the document. In 1921, this Court discussed the requirement and purpose of attestation:

> The word "attested" is broader in meaning than the word "subscribed," and it was the purpose of the statute in requiring two witnesses to attest the will *to have more than the mere signatures of two persons to the will.* It was the duty of the attesting witnesses, under the statute, *to observe and see that the will was executed by the testator, and that he had capacity to make a will.* . . . Witnesses are not only to identify the paper which has been signed by the testator, but they are to prove the execution of the will. . . . [emphasis added]

The Court further explained:

> [T]he purpose of signing by the attesting witnesses in the presence of the testator is *that the testator will know that the witnesses are attesting the testator's will and not another document; that the witnesses will know the same*; these reasons to avoid imposition of fraud on either the testator or the witnesses by substitution of another will in place of that signed by the testator; *and that the witnesses will be reasonably satisfied that the testator is of sound and disposing mind and capable of making a will.*

. . .

[I]t is our hope that subscribing witnesses be advised by counsel of their corresponding duty to that testator. A witness to a will should be some person acquainted with the testator, and having no interest, direct or indirect, as a beneficiary. He should be impressed with the necessity of specifically observing the testator and other person sign the will. He should be impressed with the necessity of being satisfied that the testator understands it is a will, and that it expresses the wishes of the testator. Finally, the will should be signed in privacy, with no other persons present than the testator, his attorney and the witnesses, unless required by unusual and compelling circumstances. The presence of some persons who could cast a cloud or suspicion on this solemn occasion should be scrupulously avoided. In most of the will contest cases which come before this Court, we find one or more of these simple precautions have been ignored. [Citation omitted.]

¶17. In accord with . . . previous cases . . . we find that an attesting witness must have some knowledge that the document being signed is, in fact, the testator's last will and testament. Therefore, Scott and Bell were not "attesting" witnesses under Section 91-5-1 but merely subscribing witnesses. Curiously, the dissent finds that mere subscription is sufficient to satisfy the requirement of attestation without any citation in support thereof. Because Scott and Bell had no knowledge of the nature of the document, we agree with the trial court that the will was not properly executed.

. . .

¶21. We hold that the purported will was not duly executed, as the witnesses had no knowledge that the document they signed was the decedent's last will and testament. We affirm the lower court's order rejecting the probate of Howard Griffith's purported will.

¶22. Affirmed.

PIERCE, Justice, dissenting:

¶23. This Court was emphatically clear when it said:

> It is not the policy of the law to permit the defeat of the probate of a will because of the failure of the memory of an attesting witness. The right of a testator to make a will and devise his property as he pleases should not, in the execution of that right and the vesting of the property according to the desire of the testator, be conditioned upon any such fact that might so easily thwart and evade all of the intentions and purposes of the testator in regard to his property. . . . In other words, *if the policy of the law were otherwise, it would be quite possible for an heir who had been disinherited to fraudulently procure one of the subscribing witnesses to a will to testify that he had not subscribed the will as an attesting witness and thereby thwart the attempt of the testator to devise his property.* On account of this danger, it is established law that while the testimony of attesting witnesses denying or impeaching the execution of the will is to be considered and may be sufficient in some cases to prevent probate, it is, nevertheless, *to be viewed with caution and suspicion and it is usually entitled to little credence*, and a proponent, obliged to call an attesting witness as a witness, is not bound by his testimony.

Warren v. Sidney's Estate, 184 So. 806, 809 (Miss. 1938) (emphasis added).

. . .

¶31. Based on the less-than-consistent testimony of Bell and Scott at trial, and this Court's strong warning . . . that "testimony of attesting witnesses denying or impeaching the execution of the will . . . [should] be viewed with caution and suspicion and it is usually entitled to little credence," I am of the opinion that the trial court was manifestly in error for holding that the witnesses did not understand that the document they signed was Howard Griffith's Last Will and Testament and the will was not duly executed.

. . .

¶34. What is clear from the record, then, is that Scott and Bell signed Howard Griffith's will as witnesses, and signed both a CERTIFICATE and sworn statements in an AFFIDAVIT OF SUBSCRIBING WITNESSES that clearly indicated the document at issue was the Last Will and Testament of Howard Griffith. . . .

¶35. . . . Neither witness testified he was prohibited from reading the words on the document. From the record before this Court, it is clear "that enough [was] said and done in the presence and with the knowledge of the testator to make the witnesses understand that he desires them to know that the paper is his will, and that they are to be the witnesses thereto," as set forth in *Green*. The CERTIFICATE and the AFFIDAVIT OF SUBSCRIBING WITNESSES call attention to the fact that the document being witnessed was the Last Will and Testament of Howard Griffith as required for constructive publication by Maxwell.

¶36. Finally, the majority, perhaps unintentionally, has placed every will in this state on the crest of a very slippery slope, one which may fill the chancery courts of this state with witnesses who cannot recall the manner by which countless wills were subscribed and attested. For these reasons, I respectfully dissent. Because I would find that the will was validly executed under these particular facts, I would remand the matter to the trial court for a hearing on undue influence.

QUESTIONS

4. Howard's will divided his estate between his brother, Garland, and his two sons, Jimmy and Jerry. Because the court denied Howard's will to probate, Howard's estate was distributed by intestacy. Accordingly, Garland took nothing because Howard was survived by descendants, who inherit to the exclusion of more distantly related collateral relatives such as Garland. Assuming that Howard intended the estate plan in the signed instrument to be his will, what was he attempting to accomplish in his estate plan? Without knowing anything about Howard or his family, is there a rational explanation for the choices recited in the instrument?

   ANSWER. Howard left his personal residence, including all furnishings, and a number of vehicles, including two mobile homes, to his brother, Garland. Howard left his business, Griffith's Barber Shop, and the residue of his estate to his sons, Jimmy and Jerry. The will perhaps reflects Howard's intent to provide his brother with a comfortable place to live and his two sons with the family business. Howard may have taken into account the relative needs of his brother, on the one hand, and his two sons, on the other hand. If Jimmy and Jerry were self-sufficient adults but Garland had trouble paying his bills, it would have been rational for Howard to leave his business to his sons while providing his brother with an inheritance that would place a roof over his head and generate modest income through rental of the two mobile homes.

5. On July 6, 2005, Eric Scott and Patrick Bell, the subscribing witnesses, executed an affidavit in which they swore under oath that Howard had "signed, published, and declared the aforesaid instrument to be his Last Will and Testament." In 2006, Scott and Bell executed sworn affidavits stating that they had *not* signed an "affidavit of subscribing witnesses" on July 6, 2005, and they had *not* witnessed Howard's will, but rather, a power of attorney. At trial, sometime after February 27, 2006, Scott and Bell testified that they had not read the instrument they signed on July 6, 2005, that no one informed them they were signing a will, and, had they known the instrument was a will, they would not have signed it. The trial court found the trial testimony credible. Do you?

   ANSWER. While the dissent did not agree with the trial court's credibility finding, that finding is certainly plausible and the standard of review on appeal is deferential to findings of fact made by the trial court. Defects of execution are sometimes the result of the parties' failure to read or understand procedural requirements, which are typically recited in boilerplate attestation clauses and self-proving affidavit forms. If Scott and Bell failed to read both the attestation clause and the self-proving affidavit, then it is entirely possible that they did not know the document was Howard's will. In fact, Scott and Bell may not have known they were signing a sworn affidavit. Judy Lofton, the notary public, testified that she followed her normal notarization procedure in which she requests identification, instructs the parties to sign the document, and then notarizes the document. If she did not mention that one of the documents was a sworn affidavit, then Scott and Bell may not have realized they were under oath.

6. In Mississippi, long-standing precedent held that "the testimony of attesting witnesses denying or impeaching the execution of the will is to be considered and may be sufficient in some cases to prevent probate, [but it is] to be viewed with caution and suspicion and it is usually entitled to little credence." In *Griffith*, however, the state supreme court accepted the trial court's finding that Scott's and Bell's testimony denying the execution of Howard's will was credible. Do you agree with the dissent that *Griffith* "has placed every will in this state on the crest of a very slippery slope, one which may fill the chancery courts . . . with witnesses who cannot recall the manner by which countless wills were subscribed and attested"? Why is it difficult for the proponent to produce other evidence of due execution? Given the holding in *Griffith*, what purpose does the self-proving affidavit serve?

   ANSWER. The dissent is arguably correct in noting that an evidentiary standard that fails to discount the veracity of such renunciations increases the likelihood that reliable wills will be denied probate because it will be difficult for the proponent to produce other evidence of due execution. The Wills Act requires witness attestation in part because the observation and signature of witnesses creates and preserves evidence of due execution. If, at the time of probate, the witnesses deny due execution, then who else is likely to have personal knowledge of the circumstances surrounding the testator's execution of the document? Most attesting witnesses, however, do not renounce the will and, in the majority of cases, the self-proving affidavit serves the important function of relieving the proponent of the need to produce testimony from the attesting witnesses at the time of probate.

7. The court held that either actual or constructive publication is a necessary element of witness attestation. What is the difference between formal and constructive publication?

   ANSWER. A testator "publishes" her will by declaring to the attesting witnesses that she intends the instrument in question to be her will. Formal publication is an affirmative declaration by the testator that resolves all ambiguity regarding the document's identification without relying on attesting witnesses to read the document or its attestation clause. Constructive publication occurs when something other than the testator's affirmative declaration notifies the attesting witnesses that the testator intends the instrument in question to be her will. For example, if the attesting witnesses read the attestation clause, then they would have constructive notice that the testator intends the instrument to be her will even if the testator remains silent for the duration of the execution ceremony. Constructive publication would arguably also be satisfied by the testator's attorney supervising the execution ceremony and declaring, on the testator's behalf, that the instrument in question is the testator's will. In *Griffith*, the dissent argued that Scott's and Bell's execution of the affidavit should have served as constructive publication because the affidavit "call[ed] attention to the fact that the document being witnessed was the Last Will and Testament of Howard Griffith. . . ." The majority, however, did not agree.

8. The dissent argued that the majority's holding would permit "an heir who had been disinherited to fraudulently procure one of the subscribing witnesses . . . to testify that he had not subscribed the will as an attesting witness and thereby thwart the attempt of the testator to devise his property." If courts permit attesting witnesses to renounce due execution, then does the witness attestation requirement create the potential to generate as much fraud as it deters?

   ANSWER. Arguably, yes. Witness attestation is thought by some to improve the reliability of wills by deterring fraud, duress, and undue influence at the time of execution. Fraud, however, can occur at the time of probate as well. An attesting witness seeking to commit fraud at the time of probate gives the contestant an upper hand because his sworn renunciation discredits evidence relied upon by the now-deceased testator to preserve and establish due execution. The potential for fraud at the time of probate underscores the need for careful selection of attesting witnesses who are not related to testator or any beneficiary, as well as proper documentation and supervision of the execution ceremony.

PROBLEM IV

Thomas Grady Chastain, a citizen of Tennessee, died last year. Chastain is survived by his daughter, June Chastain Patterson, and six grandchildren from his two predeceased sons. Two weeks ago, Patterson offered a two-page document dated September 4, 2004, titled "Last Will and Testament," for probate as Chastain's will. The first paragraph of the instrument provides:

> I, *Thomas Grady Chastain* a resident of *Polk* County, *Tennessee* do hereby make, publish, and declare this to be my Last Will and Testament, hereby revoking any and all Wills and Codicils heretofore made by me.

Subsequent paragraphs on the first page recite the following devises: (1) Chastain's knife collection and the balance of certain insurance proceeds to be given to his grandchildren; and (2) the residue of his estate to be given to Patterson, who is also appointed as executor. The initials of Chastain and three witnesses appear at the bottom of the first page:

Initials:	*TGC*	*SJW*	*MT*	*NC*	*9.4.04*
	Testator	Witness	Witness	Witness	Date

The second page provides, in its entirety, as follows:

> IN WITNESS WHEREOF I declare this to be my Last Will and Testament and execute it willingly as my free and voluntary act for the purposes expressed herein and I am of legal age and sound mind and make this under no constraint or undue influence, this *4th* day of *September*, 2004 at *Ducktown* State of *TN.*
>
> The foregoing instrument was on said date subscribed at the end thereof by________________, the above name Testator who signed, published, and declared this instrument to be his/her Last Will and Testament in the presence of us and each of us, who thereupon at his/her request, in his/her presence, and in the presence of each other, have hereunto subscribed our names as witnesses thereto. We are of sound mind and proper age to witness a will and understand this to be his/her will, and to the best of our knowledge testator is of legal age to make a will, of sound mind, and under no constraint or undue influence.
>
> *Sammy J. Ware* residing at *Ducktown, TN 37326*
>
> *Missy Taylor* residing at *Coperhill, TN 37317*
>
> *NoreenCurtis* residing at *Ducktown, TN 37326*

The following affidavit is attached by paperclip to the first two pages:

> Self-Proved Will Affidavit
> (attach to Will)
>
> State of *TN*
> County of *Polk*
>
> I, the undersigned, an officer authorized to administer oaths, certify that *Thomas Grady Chastain*, the testator, and *Sammy Ware, Missy Taylor* and *Noreen Curtis*, the witnesses, whose names are signed to the attached or foregoing instrument and whose signatures appear below, having appeared before me and having been first duly sworn, each then declared to me that: 1) the attached or foregoing instrument is the last will of the testator; 2) the testator willingly and voluntarily declared, signed, and executed the will in the presence of the witnesses; 3) the witnesses signed the will upon the request of the testator, in the presence and hearing of the testator and in the presence of each other; 4) to the best knowledge of each witness, the testator was, at the time of signing, of the age of majority (or otherwise legally competent to make a will), of sound mind and memory, and under no constraint or undue influence; and 5) each witness was and is competent and of proper age to witness a will.

Thomas G. Chastain (testator)

Sammy J. Ware (witness)

Missy Taylor (witness)

Subscribed and sworn to before me by *Thomas Grady Chastain*, the testator, who is personally known to me or who has produced ________________ as identification, and by *Sammy Ware, Missy Taylor, and Noreen Curtis*, the witnesses, who are personally known to me, this *4th* day of *September*, 2004.

Candace Steen

Notary or other officer

Chastain's grandchildren have retained you to represent them in a proceeding to contest the will's validity. The Tennessee Wills Act provides as follows:

Tennessee Code
§32-1-104 Manner of execution

The execution of a will, other than a holographic or nuncupative will, must be by the signature of the testator and of at least two (2) witnesses as follows:

(1) The testator shall signify to the attesting witnesses that the instrument is the testator's will and either:

(A) The testator sign;

(B) Acknowledge the testator's signature already made; or

(C) At the testator's direction and in the testator's presence have someone else sign the testator's name; and

(D) In any of the above cases the act must be done in the presence of two (2) or more attesting witnesses.

(2) The attesting witnesses must sign:

(A) In the presence of the testator; and

(B) In the presence of each other.

The Tennessee Code also provides:

Tennessee Code
§32-2-110 Witnesses; affidavits

Any or all of the attesting witnesses to any will may, at the request of the testator or, after the testator's death, at the request of the executor or any person interested under the will, make and sign an affidavit before any officer authorized to administer oaths in or out of this state, stating the facts to which they would be required to testify in court to prove the will, which affidavit shall be written on the will or, if that is impracticable, on some paper attached to the will, and the sworn statement of any such witness so taken shall be accepted by the court of probate when the will is not contested as if it had been taken before the court.

§1-3-105(31) Definitions

"Signature" or "signed" includes a mark, the name being written near the mark and witnessed, or any other symbol or methodology executed or adopted by a party with intention to authenticate a writing or record, regardless of being witnessed.

Tennessee courts require strict compliance with these statutes.

A. What arguments will you assert to contest the will's validity?
B. How do you think Patterson, the will's proponent, will respond to your arguments?
C. How is the court likely to rule?

4.1.1.3 Safeguarding the Will

Original estate planning documents, such as wills and trusts that contain original signatures, should be marked clearly as "original" and filed in a safe location ascertainable by individuals who will eventually seek to administer the client's estate. Probate courts generally admit only original documents, so attorneys should exercise care in marking and preserving instruments that bear original signatures.

Some states treat original attorney-drafted documents as client property, and, if retained by the attorney, a professional responsibility of safekeeping is triggered. See, e.g., Model Rule of Professional Conduct 1.15(a) ("Other property [aside from client funds] shall be identified as such and appropriately safeguarded."). The American College of Trusts and Estates Counsel maintains that it is ethical for "[a] lawyer who has drawn a will or other estate planning documents for a client [to] offer to retain the executed originals of the documents subject to the client's instructions." ACTEC Commentaries on the Model Rules of Professional Conduct 170 (5th ed. 2016). However, the attorney should take precautions to avoid the appearance of retaining documents for the self-serving purpose of soliciting business from the client's estate, whose personal representatives will have to contact the attorney to retrieve the documents after the client's death. Thus, the attorney should advise the client in writing that the firm has retained original documents at the client's direction and disclose the attorney's possible conflict of interest in soliciting business from the client's estate. The attorney should also provide copies of all instruments, prominently marked as copies, to the client for his or her own records. Upon retirement or closure of the attorney's law practice, the attorney should notify and consult with the client regarding the transfer of documents to another custodian or to the client's own possession.

4.1.1.4 Acts of Independent Significance

Testators often anticipate changes that may occur after the will's execution by identifying a beneficiary or the subject of a devise by reference to future acts, events, or occurrences rather than by reference to a particular person or item of property. Consider, for example, the following devise: "I leave my car to the caregiver employed by me at the time of my death." This devise does not identify a particular car, such as "my 2013 Honda Accord," or a particular beneficiary, such as "my faithful caregiver, Martha Smith." Rather, the devise accounts for the possibility that both its subject and object (i.e., the car and beneficiary, respectively) may change between the will's execution and the testator's death. In this example, the will anticipates the possibility that the testator might trade her Honda for a Cadillac, or that Martha Smith's retirement might require the testator to hire a new caregiver. If, in subsequent years, the testator does trade her Honda for a Cadillac and hire a new caregiver after Martha Smith's retirement, the testator will have taken these actions to suit her lifetime preferences and needs. Although such acts during life would, in effect, alter the dispositive provisions of the will without witness attestation, this devise is valid without observing additional formalities because it refers to acts, events, or occurrences that have a significant lifetime motive independent of the testator's estate plan.

Under the doctrine of independent significance, a will may refer to acts, events, or occurrences that have independent significance apart from their effect on the testator's estate and the impact of such acts, events, or occurrences is not treated as an unattested change to the testator's will. If, however, the will refers to an act, event, or occurrence for the purpose of allowing the testator to make unattested changes to her estate, then the attempted gift is invalid. Consider, for example, the following devise: "I leave my house to the individual whose name will be written on a card inside a sealed envelope marked 'house beneficiary' to be found in the top drawer of my home office desk."[11] This devise refers to an act — the testator's written identification of the "house beneficiary" — that has no significance apart from its effect on the will. Unlike the first example, the sole purpose of this devise is to allow the testator to change the beneficiary without executing a new attested will. Under the doctrine of independent significance, this devise would not be given effect unless the card, itself, met all the requirements of an attested will.

Uniform Probate Code
§2-512 Events of Independent Significance

A will may dispose of property by reference to acts and events that have significance apart from their effect upon the dispositions made by the will, whether they occur before or after the execution of the will or before or after the testator's death. The execution or revocation of another individual's will is such an event.

PROBLEM V

Determine whether the following devises are valid under the doctrine of independent significance. Assume the relevant jurisdiction has adopted UPC §2-512.

a. "I leave all monies in my Atlantic Bank savings account to the woman I shall marry." On the date of the will's execution, the testator was married to Florence; on the date of the testator's death, the testator was married to Joan.
b. "I leave all monies in my Atlantic Bank savings account to the woman I shall marry." On the date of the will's execution, the testator was unmarried; on the date of the testator's death, the testator was married to Vicky.
c. "I leave the sum of $25,000 to each of my children who graduate from college." On the date of the will's execution, the testator's four young children were enrolled in elementary school; on the date of the testator's death, three of her children had graduated from college.

11. This devise implicates another doctrine, incorporation by reference, examined in Chapter 5.

d. "I leave the contents of my safe deposit box at Lakeside National Bank to the person or persons with whom I share my last Thanksgiving dinner." The testator ate his last Thanksgiving dinner at the counter of a roadside diner and sat next to a stranger. The safe deposit box contains a deed to real property.
e. "I leave $100,000 to the residuary beneficiary of my sister's estate." The testator's sister executed her will three years later and left the residue of her estate to charity.
f. "I leave the residue of my estate to the person whose photograph is stapled to this will at my death."

4.1.2 Holographic Wills

Roughly half the states have statutes authorizing "holographic" wills, testamentary documents that are handwritten and signed by the testator but not by witnesses. Holographic wills are exempt from the witness attestation requirement because the testator's handwriting sample is thought to provide sufficient evidence of authenticity. Early holographic will statutes required that the instrument be written *entirely* by the testator's own hand.[12] However, courts strictly applying this requirement sometimes reached absurd conclusions where a single typewritten word appeared on an otherwise handwritten instrument. For example, a document handwritten by the testator on personal stationery would be denied probate because the stationery contained the testator's printed name and address. Such results are absurd because they misconstrue the justification for holographic wills. Authentication is achieved through preservation of the testator's handwriting sample, an objective not necessarily thwarted by the existence of additional typewritten words on the document's face. Thus, over time, states began to relax the requirement.

Restatement (Third) of Property: Wills & Other Donative Transfers §3.2, comment a

Holographic will formality has evolved through three phases:

Typical first-generation holographic-will statute. "A holographic will is one that is entirely written, dated, and signed by the hand of the testator. It is subject to no other form, and need not be witnessed."

Second-generation holographic-will statute — Original Uniform Probate Code. "A will which does not comply with [the requirements for an attested will] is valid as a holographic will, whether or not witnessed, if the signature and the material provisions are in the handwriting of the testator."

Third-generation holographic-will statute — Revised Uniform Probate Code [Section 2-502(b)]. "A will that does not comply with [the requirements for an attested will] is valid as a holographic will, whether or not witnessed, if the signature and material portions of the document are in the testator's handwriting."

12. The word "holographic" derives from a Greek term meaning "wholly written."

Holographic will statutes are often invoked when a testator completes a preprinted form will by hand but fails to have the document signed by attesting witnesses. Preprinted form wills are generic templates that eliminate the need for legal draftsmanship. Typically, they direct the user to "fill in the blanks," such as the testator's name, the names of beneficiaries, and items of property to be devised. Commercial form wills can be purchased at stationery or office supply stores or downloaded from the internet. Recognizing the popular appeal of homemade wills, a handful of states have also enacted statutory form wills, which, in addition to providing an estate plan template, instruct the user on how to satisfy the requirements of the Wills Act. The use of statutory form wills is optional and commercial form wills may still be used in jurisdictions that have enacted a statutory form will. The first page of the California Statutory Will appears below:[13]

California Statutory Will
California Probate Code, Section 6240

INSTRUCTIONS

1. READ THE WILL. Read the whole Will first. If you do not understand something, ask a lawyer to explain it to you.

2. FILL IN THE BLANKS. Fill in the blanks. Follow the instructions in the form carefully. Do not add any words to the Will (except for filling in blanks) or cross out any words.

3. DATE AND SIGN THE WILL AND HAVE TWO WITNESSES SIGN IT. Date and sign the Will and have two witnesses sign it. You and the witnesses should read and follow the Notice to Witnesses found at the end of this Will.

CALIFORNIA STATUTORY WILL OF

Print Your Full Name

1. Will. This is my Will. I revoke all prior Wills and codicils.

2. Specific Gift of Personal Residence. (Optional-use only if you want to give your personal residence to a different person or persons than you give the balance of your assets to under paragraph 5 below.) I give my interest in my principal personal residence at the time of my death (subject to mortgages and liens) as follows:

(Select one choice only and sign in the box after your choice.)

a. Choice One: All to my spouse or domestic partner, registered with the California Secretary of State, if my spouse or domestic partner, registered with the California Secretary of State, survives me; otherwise to my descendants (my children and the descendants of my children) who survive me.

b. Choice Two: Nothing to my spouse or domestic partner, registered with the California Secretary of State; all to my descendants (my children and the descendants of my children) who survive me.

c. Choice Three: All to the following person if he or she survives me (Insert the name of the person.):

____

13. The complete document is available at http://www.calbar.ca.gov/Portals/0/documents/publications/Will-Form.pdf.

If a testator were to complete this form by hand but fail to follow the form's instruction regarding witness attestation, would the instrument comply with a holographic will statute requiring that its "material portions" be handwritten by the testator? Would such a document contain a valid manifestation of testamentary intent? If a court were to disregard all of the typewritten language and consider only the testator's handwritten words, could you identify this instrument as a will? All of the language expressing testamentary and donative intent (e.g., "This is my Will"; "Specific Gift of Personal Residence") is typewritten. Read in isolation, the handwritten words would amount to a list of names and items of property, not a will. Because it is obvious that the testator intended the handwritten words to be read alongside the typewritten words, modern holographic will statutes allow evidence of testamentary intent to be satisfied by extrinsic evidence.

Uniform Probate Code
§2-502(c) Extrinsic Evidence

Intent that a document constitute the testator's will can be established by extrinsic evidence, including, for holographic wills, portions of the document that are not in the testator's handwriting.

Under UPC §2-502(b), the testator's handwritten identification of beneficiaries and items of property constitutes "material portions." The Reporter's comment for §2-502(b) explains:

> By requiring only the "material portions of the document" to be in the testator's handwriting (rather than requiring, as some existing statutes do, that the will be "entirely" in the decedent's handwriting), a holograph may be valid even though immaterial parts such as date or introductory wording are printed, typed, or stamped.
>
> A valid holograph can also be executed on a printed will form if the material portions of the document are handwritten. The fact, for example, that the will form contains printed language such as "I give, devise, and bequeath to __________________" does not disqualify the document as a holographic will, as long as the testator fills out the remaining portion of the dispositive provision in his or her own hand.

In re Will of Morris
67 Va. Cir. Ct. 29 (2005)

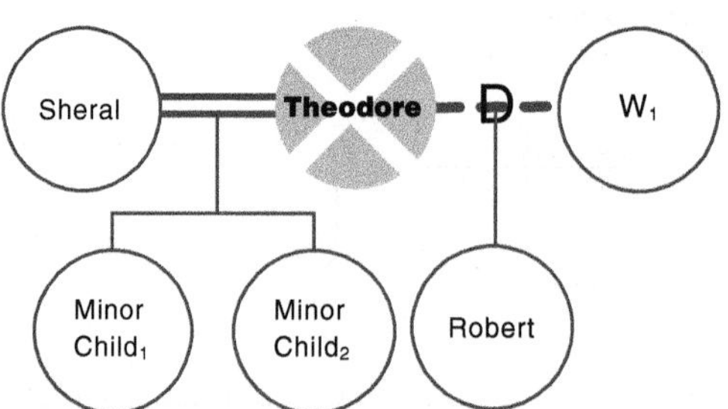

Ledbetter, J.

This case is before the court on appeal from the clerk's rejection of a document presented for probate. The issue is whether the pen-and-ink portion of the document is a valid holographic will.

Theodore John Morris died at age 48 on September 22, 2004, survived by his wife, Sheral Ann Morris, two minor children, and an adult child of a previous marriage.

On November 5, 2004 Sheral Ann Morris presented to the clerk a paper purporting to be the last will of her deceased husband. The paper is a preprinted form. Certain blank spaces are filled in. Below the preprinted section of the document there is a large space. Two numbered paragraphs, handwritten, appear in that space. In the first numbered paragraph, the author essentially disinherits his adult son.[14] In the second numbered paragraph, the author leaves his estate to his wife, Sheral Ann Morris "to do with as she sees fit" because "she knows my wishes." The paper is subscribed by the decedent and dated "1-28-97."

[There] is no controversy about the procedural status of the case. From the clerk's refusal to admit the paper to probate, Sheral Ann Morris noted a timely appeal pursuant to Virginia Code §64.1-78. Here, a guardian ad litem was appointed for the minor children[15] and all interested persons received proper notice.[16] The parties waived trial by jury and the case was tried de novo, as prescribed by Virginia Code §64.1-78, on January 24, 2005.

[I]t is undisputed that the handwriting and the signature on the paper were authored by the decedent. Sheral Ann Morris testified that she was present when her husband wrote and signed the paper, and she testified about the time, place and circumstances of the signing. The decedent's handwriting was established by the testimony of two disinterested witnesses, as required by Virginia Code §64.1-49.

The dispute centers on whether the handwritten portion of the document can be probated as the valid holographic will of the decedent. Sheral Ann Morris argues that the preprinted material can be disregarded and the handwritten portion should be accepted and admitted to probate as a holographic will. The decedent's two minor children, by their guardian ad litem, contend that the clerk correctly rejected the document because the handwriting is too connected to and dependent upon the preprinted material contained in the document.

In Virginia, with certain narrow exceptions, a will must be in writing and signed by the testator, the signature must be acknowledged by the testator in the presence of at least two witnesses who are present at the same time, and the witnesses must subscribe in the presence of the testator. Virginia Code §64.1-49. This is sometimes referred to as a "formal" will.

If the will is wholly in the handwriting of the testator and signed, attesting witnesses are unnecessary. Virginia Code §64.1-49. A will wholly in the handwriting of the testator is a "holographic" will.

---

14. The adult son, Robert P. Morris, received proper notice of this proceeding but did not appear.

15. If the decedent died intestate, the minor children would inherit. See Virginia Code §64.1-1, §64.1-11, etc.

16. As noted above, the decedent's other child, an adult, chose not to participate and told counsel for Sheral Ann Morris that he wanted no part of the estate.

The word "wholly" is not used in its absolute, utter, and rigidly uncompromising sense. Printed or typed material on the document can be disregarded so that if the handwriting contains a complete and entire testamentary disposition, the handwritten portion of the document can be admitted to probate as a valid holographic will.

Courts of other states that recognize holographic wills similarly hold that where a paper contains words not in the handwriting of the testator, those words can be ignored if the remaining handwritten portion of the paper would otherwise constitute a valid holographic will.

The [Virginia] Supreme Court seemed to take a narrow view of this principle [and] held [in a prior case] that the handwriting could be treated as a holographic instrument in itself because [it] was not interwoven with the typewriting nor did it immediately follow it; the handwriting was all on the other side of the paper; the testator did not intend any part of the typewriting as an integral part of the will in its final form; and there was no suggestion that the handwriting was a continuance of the typed material.

[In that case, t]he decedent wrote an entirely new will, in pencil, on the back of an old typewritten will. The [Virginia] Supreme Court affirmed the trial court's order admitting to probate the penciled portion of the document[:]

> The holograph instrument [i.e., the handwriting in pencil on the back of an older typed will] disposes of the entire estate . . . , names the parties and the amounts of property [the testator] desired each to receive. There is no uncertainty as to her dispositive intentions. It is quite true that the pencil writing does not contain an introductory paragraph and does not provide for the payment of debts. . . . While such paragraphs are usually found in wills prepared by those who have had more or less experience in writing such legal instruments, neither is necessary. If the testamentary intention may be determined from other parts of the will, the formal expression of such intention is not essential. . . . [Citation omitted.]

If that is the criteria [sic], the handwritten portion of Theodore John Morris' document complies.

Further, in the earlier *Gooch*[17] case, the facts were more akin to those in this case. In *Gooch*, the decedent had hand written a codicil on a preprinted form provided to him upon his initiation as a Mason. The court [held] that the printed portions of the form could be disregarded, leaving that portion of the writing that is wholly in the handwriting of the testator and signed by him. The Court said that the handwriting was "complete and entire in itself," and was made with testamentary intent, so it could be admitted to probate as a holographic instrument.

The handwritten portion of the document in this case is likewise "complete and entire in itself." It clearly is the testamentary act of the decedent. It disposes of all the decedent's property at his death, and it names the party to receive the property. There is no formal expression of testamentary intent, but that is not necessary. There is no provision for payment of debts, but such provision is not necessary. There is no appointment of a personal representative, but such appointment is not necessary.

17. Gooch v. Gooch, 134 Va. 21 (1922).

For these reasons, the court is of the opinion that the two numbered handwritten paragraphs at the bottom of the paper constitute the last will and testament of the decedent, and will be admitted to probate, disregarding the printed material on the paper. . . .

LAST WILL AND TESTAMENT

- of -

Theodore John Morris

I, Theodore John Morris, of 13560 Black Meadow Rd in the County of Spotsylvania and State of VA, do hereby revoke any and all wills and testamentary dispositions heretofore made by me and hereby make, publish and declare this as and for my Last Will and Testament.

FIRST: I nominate and appoint Sheral Ann Morris, of Spotsylvania VA as the executor of this my Last Will and Testament. I direct that no bond or other security shall be required of my said executor for the faithful performance of his or her duties in any jurisdiction in which he or she may be called upon to act.

I nominate and appoint Same, of Same, as the guardian of the person of my minor children if I should die as the role parent of such minor children. If Same shall predecease me, fail to qualify or cease to act as such guardian for any reason, I nominate and appoint William (Chip) Hart, of Spotsylvania, VA, as successor guardian. Any guardian so appointed shall be exempt from giving bond or other security.

SECOND: I direct that all of my just debts and funeral expenses be paid as soon after my death as shall be practicable.

I direct my executor to pay from my residuary estate all administration expenses and death taxes imposed on my estate.

THIRD: I give, devise, and bequeath my property as follows:

1) To my adopted Son Robert Morris, I leave the sum of $1.00 (one dollar). I leave this begrudgingly and with regret. I also leave him with my hope that he can be a better father than he was a son.
2) The balance of my estate I leave to my wife, Sheral Ann Morris, as she knows my wishes, to do with as she sees fit.

By: Theodore J. Morris
1-28-97

Witness: Sheral Morris

REDIFORM. 10235
© Copyright Rediform 1993-2

QUESTIONS

9. The relevant statute in Virginia provides, "A will wholly in the testator's handwriting is valid without further requirements, provided that the fact that a will is wholly in the testator's handwriting and signed by the testator is proved by at least two disinterested witnesses." Va. Code §64.2-403 (formerly codified at §64.1-49). How does this provision contrast with UPC §2-502(b), which provides, "A will that does not comply with subsection (a) is valid as a holographic will, whether or not witnessed, if the signature and material portions of the document are in the testator's handwriting"?

   ANSWER. There are two important distinctions. First, in Virginia, a holographic will is valid without attesting witnesses but the fact that a will was handwritten and signed by the testator must be proved by two disinterested witnesses. Under the UPC, a holographic will is valid without attesting witnesses, but the default evidentiary rules apply with regard to proof of the testator's handwriting and signature. A minimum of two disinterested witnesses is not required by statute under the UPC, but may be required by courts in particular cases. Second, in Virginia, the statute purports to require that a holographic will be "wholly in the testator's handwriting" whereas the UPC requires only that "material portions of the document are in the testator's handwriting."

10. In *Morris*, the document in question contained two parts: (1) a preprinted form with "certain blank spaces . . . filled in," and (2) two handwritten paragraphs in the large space between the preprinted form and the decedent's signature. Did the court give effect to any of the provisions in first part of the document, that is, the preprinted form? How did the court determine the document was testamentary in character?

    ANSWER. The court gave effect to only the handwritten paragraphs as a will "complete and entire in itself." The preprinted provisions were disregarded entirely; in fact, the opinion does not even recite the contents of those provisions. Although the preprinted portion did, in fact, contain a formal statement of testamentary intent ("I . . . hereby make, publish and declare this as and for my Last Will and Testament"), the court found that formal expression of testamentary intent was not necessary for a valid holographic will. The fact that the second part of the document, the handwritten paragraphs, functionally disposed of the decedent's estate and identified a beneficiary was enough to demonstrate testamentary intent.

11. Would the outcome in *Morris* have differed if the case were decided in a jurisdiction that had adopted UPC §2-502(b)?

    ANSWER. Perhaps. The UPC would have given effect to the first part of the document, provided the completed blanks were material and in the decedent's handwriting. Suppose, for example, that the preprinted portion contained the following provision completed in the decedent's handwriting (marked in italics below):

    I hereby appoint *Sheral Ann Morris* as executor of my estate.

    In a UPC jurisdiction, the court would give effect to this appointment because a material portion of the document, identification of the executor, was handwritten by the decedent; the fact that the handwritten portion is surrounded by preprinted words would not invalidate the document as a holographic will.

12. Why did the guardian ad litem appointed by the court to represent the decedent's minor children contest the will? If you were appointed guardian ad litem, would you have filed this contest on behalf of the minor children? Note that no party disputed that the handwriting on the document belonged to the decedent.

    ANSWER. Under the will, the decedent left his entire estate to his surviving spouse and nothing to his minor children, who were presumably in the care of his surviving spouse (their other parent). By contrast, if the will had been set aside and the estate administered by intestacy, the minor children would have received a share of the estate. Did the minor children truly benefit from litigating against their own mother for an intestate share of their father's estate while still in their mother's case? The guardian ad litem, who owed an uncompromising duty of care and loyalty to the minor wards, may have felt compelled to pursue an intestate share for the minor children out of concern for the guardian's own potential liability. Had the guardian waived this contest on the minor children's behalf, upon reaching the age of majority, the children could sue the guardian for failing to represent their interest properly in the probate proceeding. On the other hand, by asserting this claim, the guardian generated litigation expenses borne by the estate that depleted the amount ultimately inherited by the decedent's surviving spouse, thereby diminishing the amount of resources available to care for the minor children.

13. In a footnote, the court states, "[T]he decedent's other child, an adult, chose not to participate and told counsel for Sheral Ann Morris that he wanted no part of the estate." Why didn't the decedent's other adult child pursue a share of the estate?

    ANSWER. The first handwritten paragraph of the will states, "To my adopted son Robert Morris, I leave the sum of $1.00 (one dollar). I leave this begrudgingly and with regret. I also leave him with my hope that he can be a better father than he was a son." It is clear from this paragraph that relations between the decedent and his adult son were estranged. Perhaps the decedent's son chose not to participate in the will contest because he preferred to let the family conflicts pass with his father's death.

PROBLEM VI

Last year, Evan visited his elderly mother, Samantha, at her nursing home. Although Samantha suffered from numerous physical ailments, she was of sound mind and known to all as a sharp, independent thinker. Samantha had recently heard from another resident at the nursing home that holographic wills were valid in her state without the need for witnesses or notarization. During Evan's visit, Samantha asked him for help preparing a holographic will because her arthritis made it difficult for her to write. Evan closed the door so they could discuss the matter privately. Samantha then dictated her will while Evan recorded her words, verbatim, in his handwriting. After Evan left, Samantha, in shaky penmanship, handwrote and signed the following at the top of the page:

This is my will. Evan wrote it for me. Love to all, Samantha

Samantha died one month ago and the handwritten instrument was found in the top drawer of her dresser with other important papers. Evan, the primary beneficiary, has offered the instrument for probate as Samantha's will. Assume the relevant jurisdiction has adopted the UPC.

a. Does this instrument satisfy UPC §2-502(b)'s requirement that "material portions of the document" be in the testator's handwriting?
b. Given that Evan is the primary beneficiary, is it relevant or significant that he was also the scrivener of the instrument? (Evan is not a lawyer.)

4.1.3 Curative Doctrines

Centuries of experience applying Wills Act formalities eventually led to a realization that the underlying functions — cautionary, evidentiary, protective, and channeling — could be served without imposing the high costs associated with strict compliance. Namely, Wills Act formalities could remain in place and serve their functions without requiring courts to reject defectively executed but otherwise reliable expressions of testamentary intent. Strict compliance also imposes explicit costs on testators, particularly testators who are trying to execute wills without the assistance of counsel. See Alexander Boni-Saenz, Distributive Justice and Donative Intent, 65 UCLA L. Rev. ___ (forthcoming 2018). From this realization emerged a common sense legal reform movement to relax the formalities, but the adoption of curative doctrines has progressed in fits and starts and has yet to reach all U.S. jurisdictions.

4.1.3.1 Substantial Compliance

A judicial doctrine of substantial compliance developed in sporadic waves of early American court decisions in which wills were occasionally admitted to probate without literal compliance with the applicable Wills Act. In Sturdivant v. Birchett, 51 Va. 67 (1853), for example, the Virginia Wills Act applicable at the time required the simultaneous presence of the testator and attesting witnesses. The testator signed his will in the presence of two individuals, but those two individuals took the will into another room and signed the document outside the presence of the testator.[18] Thus, because the witnesses did not sign in the testator's presence, their attestation did not literally comply

18. Sturdivant v. Birchett, 51 Va. 67 (1853) ("For convenience, [the two witnesses] take it [i.e., the paper on which the testator has signed his name] into another room, out of the vision of the testator, and there subscribe their names to the paper as witnesses; and they immediately, within one or two minutes, return to the testator with the paper; and one of them, in the presence of the other, with the paper open in his hand, addresses the testator, and says, 'here is your will witnessed'; at the same time pointing to the names of the witnesses, which are on the same page and close to the name of the testator.").

with Virginia's simultaneous presence requirement. Notwithstanding this defect, however, the court admitted the will to probate:

> It is said . . . that a literal compliance with the terms of the statute of wills is not necessary; that a substantial compliance is all that is required. And it is said in another case, with great force and correctness, that the only sure guide for the court is to look at the substance, sense and object of the law, and with the aid of these lights to endeavor to ascertain if there has been a substantial compliance with its provisions.
>
> . . .
>
> Upon the whole, I think there has been a reasonable and substantial, if not a literal, compliance with the requirements of the statute shown in this case, sufficient for all practical purposes, and which in favor of the testamentary right ought to be sustained. To reject the will in such a case would be, as I think, to sacrifice substance to form, and the ends of justice to the means by which they are to be accomplished.

Id. at 74, 89. The *Sturdivant* court's refreshingly logical and pragmatic approach looked to the substance and totality of the acts performed rather than the observance of formalities in isolation. Over time, however, the substantial compliance doctrine began to stray from its pragmatic origins. Substantial compliance lost coherence as courts applied the doctrine inconsistently in an ad hoc manner without an underlying principle to distinguish harmless errors from execution defects calling into question the will's authenticity or voluntariness.

In 1975, Professor John Langbein proposed a broader test for substantial compliance that would treat a defectively executed document as compliant under the Wills Act:

> The finding of a formal defect should lead not to automatic invalidity, but to a further inquiry: does the noncomplying document express the decedent's testamentary intent, and does its form sufficiently approximate Wills Act formality to enable the court to conclude that it serves the *purposes* of the Wills Act?

John H. Langbein, Substantial Compliance with the Wills Act, 88 Harv. L. Rev. 489, 489 (1975) (italics added). Under Langbein's articulation, substantial compliance would apply to all defectively executed wills so long as the document expresses testamentary intent and the formalities observed are sufficient to serve the underlying purposes of testamentary formalities (i.e., cautionary, evidentiary, protective, and channeling). Substantial compliance could be applied without statutory amendment to the Wills Act because it allowed courts to deem instruments as compliant under existing statutory formalities; thus, the doctrine was said to construe the Wills Act without altering it.

To illustrate Langbein's version of substantial compliance, revisit the fact pattern in *Sturdivant*: The testator executed the will in the presence of two witnesses, the witnesses subscribed in a separate room, and then immediately returned the signed will to the testator. Under Langbein's approach, the court would ask the following questions: Did the document express the testator's intent to dispose of property at death? Was the execution ceremony sufficient to impress upon the testator the legal significance of his act? Was the written document sufficient to preserve evidence of the testator's estate plan? Did the presence of witnesses serve as deterrence against fraud and undue influence? If these questions could be answered Yes, then the instrument would be deemed to comply with the Wills Act and would be admitted to probate.

The New Jersey Supreme Court was the first high court to adopt Langbein's formulation of substantial compliance,[19] but other jurisdictions failed to follow New Jersey's lead. Langbein's own subsequent research revealed that courts tend to narrow their application of the doctrine over time and eventually construe "'substantial' to mean 'near perfect,'" thereby returning to a regime of strict compliance.[20] At present, several pre-Langbein articulations of substantial compliance persist in jurisdictions throughout the United States, but the doctrine's curative effect is severely limited in jurisdictions that, in effect, require nearly strict compliance. Even in New Jersey, courts have come to require a form of strict compliance notwithstanding the state supreme court's explicit adoption of Langbein's broad conception of substantial compliance. See In re Will of Ferree, 848 A.2d 81 (N.J. Ch. 2003), *aff'd*, 848 A.2d 1 (N.J. Super. Ct. App. Div. 2004).

Essex County Courthouse in Newark, New Jersey

19. In re Will of Ranney, 589 A.2d 1339 (N.J. 1991).

20. In 1987, Langbein published a study of probate files in Queensland, Australia, which had adopted the doctrine of substantial compliance in 1981. He concluded:

> It is now hard to imagine in what circumstances the Queensland courts might find an execution defect insubstantial, since they have (1) declared the most innocuous of the recurrent execution blunders, presence defects, as "most important"; and (2) refused to rescue the will of a testator whose failure to procure a second attesting witness was induced through official misrepresentation.

John H. Langbein, Excusing Harmless Errors in the Execution of Wills: A Report on Australia's Tranquil Revolution in Probate Law, 87 Colum. L. Rev. 1, 45 (1987).

4.1.3.2 Harmless Error

In contrast to substantial compliance, an alternative curative doctrine, the *"harmless error" rule*, excuses noncompliance with the Wills Act where there is adequate proof that the decedent intended the defectively executed instrument to be his or her will. Unlike substantial compliance, which considers whether the underlying purposes of testamentary formalities were served, the harmless error rule asks whether there is clear and convincing evidence that the decedent intended the writing as a will. Because the harmless error rule expressly authorizes courts to dispense with statutory formalities,[21] this type of curative doctrine must be adopted through legislation rather than judicial common law.

Uniform Probate Code
§2-503 Harmless Error

Although a document or writing added upon a document was not executed in compliance with Section 2-502, the document or writing is treated as if it had been executed in compliance with that section if the proponent of the document or writing establishes by clear and convincing evidence that the decedent intended the document or writing to constitute:

(1) the decedent's will,
(2) a partial or complete revocation of the will,
(3) an addition to or an alteration of the will, or
(4) a partial or complete revival of his [or her] formerly revoked will or of a formerly revoked portion of the will.

Only a handful of jurisdictions have enacted the harmless error rule (or some more restrictive form of it). A recent case from New York, which remains a strict compliance jurisdiction, provides a stark reminder of why testators must devote careful attention to observing Wills Act formalities in jurisdictions that have not adopted the harmless error rule:

> In October 23, 2016, the *New York Times* reported that Bill Cornwell, who died at the age of 88 in New York City, was survived by his same-sex partner of 55 years, Tom Doyle. Although same-sex marriage became legal shortly before Cornwell's death, the couple never married. For more than five decades, Cornwell and Doyle lived together in a West Village brownstone apartment building titled solely in Cornwell's name. Cornwell executed a will devising the house, worth more than $7 million, to Doyle. But Cornwell's will was signed by only one attesting witness, not two, as required by the New York Will's Act. And, because the couple never legally wed, Doyle was not entitled to an intestate share of Cornwell's estate as the surviving spouse. Instead, Cornwell's entire estate, therefore, passed by intestacy to his nieces and nephews, the sole heirs-at-law. One of the nieces, who suggested Cornwell and Doyle were not a couple but merely friends, argued that Cornwell "had 50 years to put [Doyle's] name on [the] papers. . . . The will was never a valid will."

Sarah Maslin Nir, A Brownstone and the Bitter Fight to Inherit It, N.Y. Times, Oct. 23, 2016, at A16. The Cornwell estate appears perfectly suited for relief under the harmless error rule because there is clear and convincing evidence that Cornwell intended the document to be his will. But as of 2017, New York has yet to adopt the rule.

21. For this reason, the harmless error rule is sometimes called the "dispensing power."

Estate of Ehrlich
47 A.3d 12 (N.J. Super. Ct. App. Div. 2012)

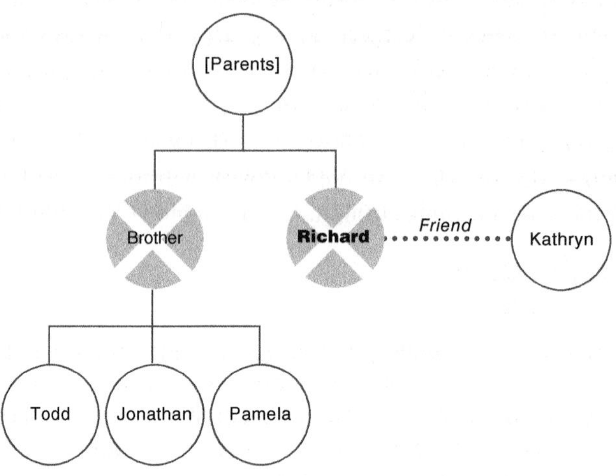

Before Judges PARRILLO, ALVAREZ and SKILLMAN.

PARRILLO, P.J.A.D.

Appellants Todd Ehrlich and Pamela Venuto appeal from an April 20, 2011 order of the General Equity Part admitting into probate the proffered Will of Richard D. Ehrlich and from the June 20, 2011 order denying their motion for reconsideration. . . . We affirm.

The material facts are not genuinely in dispute. Richard Ehrlich, a trust and estates attorney who practiced in Burlington County for over fifty years, died on September 21, 2009. His only next of kin were his deceased brother's children— Todd and Jonathan Ehrlich and Pamela Venuto. The decedent had not seen or had any contact with Todd or Pamela in over twenty years. He did, however, maintain a relationship with Jonathan, who, he had told his closest friends as late as 2008, was the person to contact if he became ill or died, and to whom he would leave his estate.

Jonathan learned of his uncle's death nearly two months after the passing. An extensive search for a Will followed. As a result, Jonathan located a copy of a purported Will in a drawer near the rear entrance of decedent's home, which, like his office, was full of clutter and a mess. Thereafter, on December 17, 2009, Jonathan filed a verified complaint seeking to have the document admitted to probate. His siblings, Todd and Pamela, filed an answer, objecting. . . . No other document purporting to be decedent's Will was ever located.

The document proffered by Jonathan is a copy of a detailed fourteen-page document entitled "Last Will and Testament." It was typed on traditional legal paper with Richard Ehrlich's name and law office address printed in the margin of each page. The document does not contain the signature of decedent or any witnesses. It does, however, include, in decedent's own handwriting, a notation at the right-hand corner of the cover page: "Original mailed to H. W. Van Sciver, 5/20/2000[.]" The document names Harry W. Van Sciver as Executor of the purported Will and Jonathan as contingent Executor. Van Sciver was also named Trustee, along with Jonathan and

Michelle Tarter as contingent Trustees. Van Sciver predeceased the decedent and the original of the document was never returned.

In relevant part, the purported Will provides a . . . bequest of $50,000 to Pamela and $75,000 to Todd. Twenty-five percent of the residuary estate is to pass to a trust for the benefit of a friend, Kathryn Harris, who is to receive periodic payments therefrom. Seventy-five percent of the residuary estate is to pass to Jonathan.

It is undisputed that the document was prepared by decedent and just before he was to undergo life-threatening surgery. On the same day this purported Will was drafted — May 20, 2000 — decedent also executed a Power of Attorney and Living Will,[22] both witnessed by the same individual, who was the Burlington County Surrogate. As with the purported Will, these other documents were typed on traditional legal paper with Richard Ehrlich's name and law office address printed in the margin of each page.

Years after drafting these documents, decedent acknowledged to others that he had a Will and wished to delete the bequest to his former friend, Kathryn Harris, with whom he apparently had a falling out. Despite his stated intention, decedent never effectuated any change or modification to his Will as no such document ever surfaced, even after the extensive search conducted of his home and law office after his death.

[T]he General Equity Judge granted Jonathan's motion [for summary judgment] and admitted the copy entitled "Last Will and Testament" of Richard Ehrlich to probate. The court reasoned:

> First, since Mr. [Richard] Ehrlich prepared the document, there can be no doubt that he viewed it. Secondly, while he did not formally execute the copy, his hand written notations at the top of the first page, effectively demonstrating that the original was mailed to his executor on the same day that he executed his power of attorney and his health directive is clear and convincing evidence of his "final assent" that he intended the original document to constitute his last will and testament as required both by N.J.S.A. 3B:3-3 and [In re Probate of Will and Codicil of Macool, 416 N.J. Super. 298, 310 (App. Div. 2010)]. . . .

I

At issue is whether the unexecuted copy of a purportedly executed original document sufficiently represents decedent's final testamentary intent to be admitted into probate under N.J.S.A. 3B:3-3 [New Jersey's harmless error rule] . . . .

N.J.S.A. 3B:3-2 contains the technical requirements for writings intended as wills[.][23]

A document that does not comply with the requirements of N.J.S.A. 3B:3-2 is nevertheless valid as a document intended as a Will and may be admitted into probate upon satisfaction of N.J.S.A. 3B:3-3, which provides:

> Although a document or writing added upon a document was not executed in compliance with N.J.S.[A.] 3B:3-2, the document or writing is treated as if it had been executed in compliance with N.J.S.[A.] 3B:3-2 if the proponent of the document or writing establishes by clear and convincing evidence that the decedent intended the document or writing to constitute: (1) the decedent's will. . . .

---

22. Jonathan is named the alternate agent to make health care decisions in the event his uncle became incapacitated and the primary agent was unavailable.

23. [The New Jersey Wills Act is similar to the formalities required by the UPC, except New Jersey does specifically authorize notarized wills. The statute is omitted for brevity. — Eds.]

The Legislature enacted N.J.S.A. 3B:3-3 in 2004, as an amendment to the New Jersey Probate Code. It is virtually identical to Section 2-503 of the Uniform Probate Code (UPC), upon which it was modeled. [Citation omitted.] The comments to that Section by the National Conference of Commissioners on Uniform State Laws express its clear purpose: "[s]ection 2-503 means to retain the intent-serving benefits of Section 2-502 formality without inflicting intent-defeating outcomes in cases of harmless error." Unif. Probate Code, cmt. on §2-503. Of particular note, the Commissioners' comments state that Section 2-503 "is supported by the Restatement (Third) of Property: Wills and Other Donative Transfers §3.3 (1999)." Recognizing that strict compliance with the statutory formalities has led to harsh results in many cases, the comments to the Restatement explain,

> . . . the purpose of the statutory formalities is to determine whether the decedent adopted the document as his or her will. Modern authority is moving away from insistence on strict compliance with statutory formalities, recognizing that the statutory formalities are not ends in themselves but rather the means of determining whether their underlying purpose has been met. A will that fails to comply with one or another of the statutory formalities, and hence would be invalid if held to a standard of strict compliance with the formalities, may constitute just as reliable an expression of intention as a will executed in strict compliance.
>
> . . .
>
> The trend toward excusing harmless errors is based on a growing acceptance of the broader principle that mistake, whether in execution or in expression, should not be allowed to defeat intention nor to work unjust enrichment.

Restatement (Third) of Property, §3.3 cmt. b (1999).

We recently had occasion to interpret N.J.S.A. 3B-3.3 in a case wherein we held that under New Jersey's codification of the "harmless error" doctrine, a writing need not be signed by the testator in order to be admitted to probate. In re Probate of Will and Codicil of Macool, 416 N.J. Super. 298, 311 (App. Div. 2010).

> [T]hat for a writing to be admitted into probate as a will under N.J.S.A. 3B:3-3, the proponent of the writing intended to constitute such a will must prove, by clear and convincing evidence, that: (1) the decedent actually reviewed the document in question; and (2) thereafter gave his or her final assent to it. Absent either one of these two elements, a trier of fact can only speculate as to whether the proposed writing accurately reflects the decedent's final testamentary wishes.

Id. at 310.

Thus, N.J.S.A. 3B:3-3, in addressing a form of testamentary document not executed in compliance with N.J.S.A. 3B:3-2, represents a relaxation of the rules regarding formal execution of Wills so as to effectuate the intent of the testator. This legislative leeway happens to be consonant with "a court's duty in probate matters . . . 'to ascertain and give effect to the probable intention of the testator.'" *Macool*, supra, 416 N.J. Super. at 307. As such, Section 3 dispenses with the requirement that the proposed document be executed or otherwise signed in some fashion by the testator.

Our dissenting colleague . . . discerns a specific requirement in Section 3 that the document be signed and acknowledged before a court may even move to the next step and decide whether there is clear and convincing evidence that the decedent intended the document to be his Will, and therefore excuse any deficiencies therein.

We find no basis for such a constrictive construction in the plain language of the provision, which in clear contrast to Section 2, expressly contemplates an unexecuted Will within its scope. Otherwise what is the point of the exception?

Because N.J.S.A. 3B:3-3 is remedial in nature, it should be liberally construed. [Citation omitted.] Indeed, if the Legislature intended a signed and acknowledged document as a condition precedent to its validation under Section 3, it would have, we submit, declared so expressly as did, for instance, the Colorado Legislature in enacting its version of UPC §2-503 and N.J.S.A. 3B:3-3.3 The fact that the Legislature chose not to qualify its remedial measure as the dissent suggests is also consistent with the Commissioners' commentary expressly citing those foreign jurisdictions that excuse non-compliance with the signature requirement, although "reluctant[ly]" so. And like the Commissioners' discussion, the comments to the Restatement also acknowledge that the absence of a signature is excusable, albeit the "hardest" deficiency to justify as it "raises serious, *but not insuperable doubt.*" Restatement (Third) of Property, §3.3 cmt. b (1999) (emphasis added).

To be sure, as a general proposition, the greater the departure from Section 2's formal requirement, the more difficult it will be to satisfy Section 3's mandate that the instrument reflect the testator's final testamentary intent. And while the dissent's concern over the lack of a signature and attestation is obviously understandable, their absence in this instance, as recognized by both sets of commentators and the express wording of Section 3, does not present an insurmountable obstacle.

Instead, to overcome the deficiencies in formality, Section 3 places on the proponent of the defective instrument the burden of proving by clear and convincing evidence that the document was in fact reviewed by the testator, expresses his or her testamentary intent, and was thereafter assented to by the testator. In other words, in dispensing with technical conformity, Section 3 imposes evidential standards and safeguards appropriate to satisfy the fundamental mandate that the disputed instrument correctly expresses the testator's intent.

Here, as noted, decedent undeniably prepared and reviewed the challenged document. In disposing of his entire estate and making specific bequests, the purported Will both contains a level of formality and expresses sufficient testamentary intent. As the motion judge noted, in its form, the document "is clearly a professionally prepared Will and complete in every respect except for a date and its execution." Moreover, as the only living relative with whom decedent had any meaningful relationship, Jonathan, who is to receive the bulk of his uncle's estate under the purported Will, was the natural object of decedent's bounty.

The remaining question then is whether, under the undisputed facts of record, decedent gave his final assent to the document. Clearly, decedent's handwritten notation on its cover page evidencing that the original was sent to the executor and trustee named in that very document demonstrates an intent that the document serve as its title indicates—the "Last Will and Testament" of Richard Ehrlich. In fact, the very same day he sent the original of his Will to his executor, decedent executed a power of attorney and health care directive, both witnessed by the same individual. As the General Equity judge noted, "[e]ven if the original for some reason was not signed by him, through some oversight or negligence his dated notation that he mailed the original to his executor is clearly his written assent of his intention that the document was his Last Will and Testament."

Lest there be any doubt, in the years following the drafting of this document, and as late as 2008, decedent repeatedly orally acknowledged and confirmed the dispositionary contents therein to those closest to him in life. The unrefuted proof is that decedent intended Jonathan to be the primary, if not exclusive, beneficiary of his estate, an objective the purported Will effectively accomplishes. Indeed, the evidence strongly suggests that this remained decedent's testamentary intent throughout the remainder of his life.

Moreover, decedent acknowledged the existence of the Will to others to whom he expressed an intention to change one or more of the testamentary dispositions therein. . . . Although there is no evidence whatsoever that decedent ever pursued this intention, the very fact that he admitted to such a document is compelling proof not only of its existence but of decedent's belief that it was valid and of his intention that it serve as his final testamentary disposition.

Given these circumstances, we are satisfied there is clear and convincing evidence that the unexecuted document challenged by appellants was reviewed and assented to by decedent and accurately reflects his final testamentary wishes. As such, it was properly admitted to probate as his Last Will and Testament.

. . .

Affirmed.

SKILLMAN, J.A.D. (retired and temporarily assigned on recall), dissenting.

I do not believe that N.J.S.A. 3B:3-3 can be reasonably construed to authorize the admission to probate of an unexecuted will. Therefore, I dissent.

By its plain terms, N.J.S.A. 3B:3-3 only allows the admission to probate of a defectively executed will, not an unexecuted will. N.J.S.A. 3B:3-3 provides that if "a document . . . was not executed in compliance with N.J.S.A. 3B:3-2," it may nonetheless be "treated as if it had been executed in compliance with N.J.S.A. 3B:3-2 if the proponent . . . establishes by clear and convincing evidence that the decedent intended the document or writing to constitute [his or her] will." Thus, N.J.S.A. 3B:3-3 may be invoked only in a circumstance where the document "was not executed in compliance with N.J.S.A. 3B:3-2"; it does not apply if the document was not executed at all.

. . .

In my view, Jonathan is entitled to prevail only if he can show, in conformity with the common law authority dealing with lost wills, that the unexecuted will found in the decedent's home is a copy of an original executed will sent to Van Sciver, which was lost and not revoked by the decedent. However, because this case was presented solely under N.J.S.A. 3B:3-3, the trial court did not make any findings of fact regarding these issues. Indeed, the trial court concluded that the copy of the will found in the decedent's home could be admitted to probate under N.J.S.A. 3B:3-3 "[e]ven if the original . . . was not signed by [the decedent]." Therefore, I would remand to the trial court to make such findings. I would not preclude the parties from moving to supplement the record to present additional evidence on the question whether the unexecuted copy of the will found in the decedent's home may be admitted to probate as a copy of the alleged executed original sent to Van Sciver.

. . .

QUESTIONS

14. How, if at all, did the decedent's will fail to comply with the requirements of the Wills Act?

    ANSWER. We do not know for sure what formalities were observed because the decedent's original will could not be located. The original will may have been properly signed and attested, but, because the person to whom it was sent predeceased, the document was presumed lost and not produced in this litigation. The copy of the original instrument offered for probate did not comply with Wills Act formalities because it was not signed by the testator or attesting witnesses.

15. Did the decedent intend the unsigned document to constitute his will?

    ANSWER. The decedent most likely did not intend for the unsigned copy to be probated as his will. He presumably signed the original instrument and sent it to his executor because he intended that original instrument, not the copy, to be probated. The majority, however, found that a copy could be probated in place of the original under these circumstances: "The fact that the document is only a copy of the original sent to decedent's executor is not fatal to its admissibility to probate. Although not lightly excused, there is no requirement in [the harmless error rule] that the document sought to be admitted to probate be an original. Moreover, there is no evidence or challenge presented that the copy of the Will has in any way been altered or forged." Does the majority's reasoning undermine testamentary intent if we presume that the decedent most likely did not intend for the unsigned copy to be probated as his will? The test for testamentary intent generally focuses on whether a specific document was intended by the decedent to be a will, so how, if at all, should this test apply to copies?

16. As explained in the dissent (and later this chapter), a lost will may be probated if its contents can be adequately proved. Why didn't the proponent argue for probate of the original lost will and use the unsigned copy to prove the contents of lost document?

    ANSWER. To probate the unsigned copy under the lost will doctrine, the proponent would have to prove not only the contents of the original but the fact that the original will was itself validly executed. No party to this litigation knew for certain whether the decedent had executed the original will, so the fact of execution was impossible for the proponent to prove. The proponent could have argued that the harmless error rule should apply to the original will, but again, it would be difficult to produce clear and convincing evidence with regard to a document that none of the parties could locate or had ever seen.

17. The majority found clear and convincing evidence that the decedent intended the unsigned copy to be his will. Some of the evidence on which the majority relied included oral statements by the decedent in which he "acknowledged and confirmed the dispositionary contents therein." In one of those oral acknowledgments, the decedent stated that he "wished to delete the bequest to his former friend, Kathryn Harris, with whom he apparently had a falling out." Why didn't the court give effect to the decedent's intent to delete the bequest to his former friend, Ms. Harris?

ANSWER. The harmless error rule, by its terms, applies only to documents; it does not apply to oral statements. Implicit in this rule is a notion that the testator's failure to reduce expressions of testamentary intent to writing is not a harmless error. Thus, inquiry into the decedent's intent is confined to the question of whether the decedent intended the noncompliant document to serve as her will. The harmless error rule does not authorize a court to give effect to unwritten expressions of testamentary intent, even if those expressions can be proved by clear and convincing evidence.

PROBLEM VII

In 1995, Louise executed a will leaving her entire estate to her husband, Elmer, if he survived her, and, if he predeceased, to Elmer's six children from a prior marriage in equal shares. Louise had no children of her own, but maintained a close relationship with her niece, Mary, who was not named in the 1995 will. Last year, Elmer died and Louise decided to revise her will to include Mary as a beneficiary. Louise scheduled an appointment with her lawyer and, before meeting, handwrote the following notes:

1. *Niece*
   Mary Smith
   123 Cherry Lane
   Newport, West Dakota
   If anything happens to Mary, her share goes to her daughter Angela Smith. If anything happens to Angela, it goes to her 2 children. 1. Nikos 2. Jade

House to stay in Elmer's family.
My stepchildren:

1. *Mike*
2. *Merle*
3. *Bill*
   Take

Louise brought the note with her to the appointment and told the lawyer that she wanted to divide her estate in seven equal shares: one for Mary and one for each of Louise's six stepchildren. While Louise remained in the office, the lawyer dictated a draft of the will. After Louise left for lunch, the lawyer's secretary prepared a typewritten draft will from the lawyer's dictation. However, Louise died at the restaurant before returning to review or sign the typewritten draft.

One of Louise's stepchildren offers the 1995 will for probate and Mary asks you to represent her in seeking a share of Louise's estate under the unsigned document prepared by the lawyer. How will you proceed?

4.2 WILL AMENDMENT AND REVOCATION

A will may be freely amended or revoked until the testator dies or loses the mental capacity to make a will. This section examines the amendment of a prior will by codicil and the revocation of a prior will by subsequent writing, physical act, and operation of law. In each of the following subsections, refer to the UPC provisions below:

Uniform Probate Code
§2-507 Revocation by Writing or by Act

(a) A will or any part thereof is revoked:

(1) by executing a subsequent will that revokes the previous will or part expressly or by inconsistency;

(2) by performing a revocatory act on the will, if the testator performed the act with the intent and for the purpose of revoking the will or part or if another individual performed the act in the testator's conscious presence and by the testator's direction. For purposes of this paragraph, "revocatory act on the will" includes burning, tearing, canceling, obliterating, or destroying the will or any part of it. A burning, tearing, or canceling is a "revocatory act on the will," whether or not the burn, tear, or cancellation touched any of the words on the will.

(b) If a subsequent will does not expressly revoke a previous will, the execution of the subsequent will wholly revokes the previous will by inconsistency if the testator intended the subsequent will to replace rather than supplement the previous will.

(c) The testator is presumed to have intended a subsequent will to replace rather than supplement a previous will if the subsequent will makes a complete disposition of the testator's estate. If this presumption arises and is not rebutted by clear and convincing evidence, the previous will is revoked; only the subsequent will is operative on the testator's death.

(d) The testator is presumed to have intended a subsequent will to supplement rather than replace a previous will if the subsequent will does not make a complete disposition of the testator's estate. If this presumption arises and is not rebutted by clear and convincing evidence, the subsequent will revokes the previous will only to the extent the subsequent will is inconsistent with the previous will; each will is fully operative on the testator's death to the extent they are not inconsistent.

Restatement (Third) of Property: Wills & Other Donative Transfers
§8.1, comment c

Although many statutes of wills do not expressly say that a testator must be "of sound mind" to revoke a will, the same requirement of mental capacity applies. To revoke a will by revocatory act, the testator must have intent to revoke. An intent to revoke is only recognized if the testator has mental capacity when performing the revocatory act. To revoke a will by subsequent will, the testator must have capacity to make a will when executing the will that revokes the prior will.

A purported will or revocation of a will by a person who lacks the mental capacity to make a will is void.

4.2.1 Codicils

A codicil is a testamentary instrument that (a) amends or supplements a previously executed will, and (b) satisfies Wills Act formalities or meets statutory requirements for a holographic will. The requirement of testamentary capacity applicable to wills governs the creation of a codicil. It is recommended, but not necessary, for a codicil to refer explicitly to the will it amends because the will and codicil will be interpreted together. Practitioners, however, discourage the use of codicils: It is preferable to create a new will than revise an old one. The late Professor Thomas Atkinson explains:

> As a whole, codicils should be avoided since they may lead to difficulties in construing the various instruments together, as well as an additional burden of probate. It is better to prepare an entirely new instrument when a change of testamentary scheme is desired. At any rate, a codicil should never be prepared until the original will has been carefully studied and the effect of the codicil accurately forecast. The principal occasion for a codicil is when time does not permit the drafting of a complete new will. It has also been suggested that the codicil should be employed if there has been a change for the worse in testator's mental condition since execution of his prior will.

Thomas E. Atkinson, Law of Wills 835 (West 2d ed. 1953). Our discussion of codicils will summarize the law governing holographic codicils, partial revocation of a prior will by inconsistency with a later codicil, and the doctrine of republication by codicil.

Holographic codicils: In most jurisdictions that recognize holographic wills, a testator may create a holographic codicil by making handwritten, signed alterations to a typewritten will. But see Estate of Foxley, 575 N.W.2d 150 (Neb. 1998) ("handwritten changes on the photocopy of [decedent's] will do not constitute a valid holographic codicil and may not be incorporated into her will by reference"). "If necessary, the handwritten codicil can derive meaning, and hence validity as a holographic codicil, from nonhandwritten portions of the document." UPC §2-502, comment c. Handwritten alterations need not form a complete sentence, but they must supply a sufficient handwriting sample to assess the genuineness of the codicil. In the example below, the testator's handwritten alteration would constitute a holographic codicil because it amends the prior typewritten will, it was handwritten and signed by the testator, and there is enough handwriting to establish the genuineness of the sample. Thus, the testator's cousin, Cory, would receive a legacy of $25,000.

> Article III: Bequests
> I hereby give, devise, and bequeath:
>
> (a) My gold Rolex watch to my son, Samuel;
> (b) My collection of 18th Century portrait paintings to the Parkside Museum;
> (c) My personal residence to my wife, Wanda;
> (d) All the rest, residue, and remainder to my daughter, Dolly.
> (e) *I give the sum of twenty-five thousand dollars ($25,000) to my cousin, Cory. Signed, David Prescott 12/16/2013*
>
> Article IV: Executor Appointment

Partial revocation by inconsistency: Because a codicil supplements or amends a prior will, a codicil supersedes all inconsistent provisions in the prior will. Inconsistencies with the prior will are resolved in favor of the codicil, leaving all other provisions of the prior will intact. Under UPC §2-507(c), however, an instrument that makes a *complete disposition* of the testator's estate is treated as a revocation and replacement of the prior will rather than as a codicil.

Republication by codicil: Under the doctrine of *republication by codicil*, a prior will is treated as re-executed as of the date of its most recent codicil if (and only if) such treatment would be consistent with the testator's intent. As the Restatement cautions, "[t]he doctrine of republication by codicil is to be applied unless the effect would be inconsistent with the testator's intent. That a codicil contains a provision expressly republishing the prior will does not require the doctrine to be applied. The doctrine is still inapplicable if the effect of applying it would be inconsistent with the testator's intent." Restatement (Third) of Property: Wills & Other Donative Transfers §3.4, comment b. Consider the following example:

> 2000: Alan executes a typewritten will with the following provision: "I leave the sum of $25,000 to my dear friend Suzy." The will appoints his brother, Barry, as executor of his estate. Although Alan signed his will, he did so without obtaining signatures of two attesting witnesses.
>
> 2012: Alan executes a valid holographic codicil appointing Suzy as the new executor but making no other dispositions from his estate.
>
> 2013: Alan dies.

Alan's 2000 will lacks the signatures of two attesting witnesses and therefore does not comply with Wills Act formalities. We are told, however, that Alan's 2012 holographic codicil was validly executed. Under the doctrine of republication by codicil, the 2000 will is republished and treated as re-executed in 2012 codicil, the date of the codicil, because republication is consistent with Alan's testamentary intent.[24] The 2012 codicil, therefore, ratifies the 2000 will and amends it to the extent of any inconsistency: Suzy replaces Barry as executor of Alan's estate and receives the $25,000 bequest.

---

24. This result is true is some but not all states. For example, under Florida law, "an improperly executed will can be saved by a properly executed codicil that ratifies the improperly executed will." In re Guardianship of Mull, 56 N.E.3d 270, 279 (Ohio Ct. App. 2015) (applying Florida law). In New York, by contrast, a "codicil does not republish an unattested will, nor an instrument which has been mutilated and effectively revoked." In re Rosenberg's Will, 205 Misc. 528, 530 (N.Y. Surr. Ct. 1953).

PROBLEM VIII

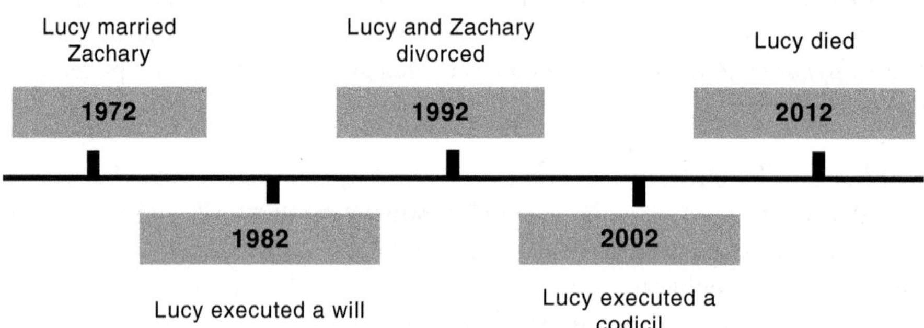

In answering the questions below, refer to the following timeline of events:

1972: Lucy marries Zachary.

1982: Lucy executes a will leaving her entire estate to Zachary if he survives her, and if not, to her adult children from a prior marriage, Mitch and Connor.

1992: Lucy and Zachary divorce.

2002: Lucy executes a valid codicil in which she devises her real estate holdings to her sister, Sarah. The codicil states further, "Except as expressly modified by this codicil, all remaining terms and provisions of my LAST WILL and TESTAMENT identified above shall remain in full force and effect."

2012: Lucy dies.

For purposes of this problem, assume that the law in Lucy's jurisdiction provides that a testator's divorce revokes all dispositions in favor of the divorced spouse by operation of law.[25]

A. Who inherits Lucy's real estate holdings?
B. Who inherits Lucy's bank account?

4.2.2 Revocation by Subsequent Writing

A will may be partially or wholly revoked by the execution of a subsequent will satisfying Wills Act formalities. Revocation may be express or implied. Express revocation is an affirmative statement such as, "I hereby revoke all prior wills and codicils." Well-drafted wills include an express revocation clause to set a clean slate for any revisions to the testator's estate plan. Absent an express revocation clause, revocation is implied when a subsequent

25. Revocation by operation of law is discussed below in Section 4.2.4.

will contains inconsistent distributive or administrative provisions when compared with the prior will. Consider the following will and codicil in Example 1, below:

Revocation Example 1

Will of December 19, 2013	Codicil of January 19, 2014
Article III: Bequests I hereby give, devise, and bequeath: (a) My gold Rolex watch to my son, Samuel; (b) My collection of eighteenth-century portrait paintings to the Parkside Museum; (c) My personal residence to my wife, Wanda; (d) All the rest, residue and remainder to my daughter, Dolly.	This codicil hereby amends my Will dated December 19, 2013 as follows: I hereby give, devise, and bequeath my personal residence to my daughter, Dolly. All other provisions of the Will remain in full force and effect.

Article III(c) of the 2013 will, which devises the testator's personal residence to his wife, is implicitly revoked by the 2014 codicil, which devises the testator's personal residence to his daughter Dolly. Revocation is implied because, although there is no express revocation clause, the 2014 codicil is inconsistent with the 2013 will regarding the devise of the personal residence. Dolly inherits the testator's personal residence.

Now, consider the following two wills in Example 2, below:

Revocation Example 2

Will of May 11, 2013	Will of June 11, 2014
Article III: Bequests I hereby give, devise, and bequeath: (a) My gold Rolex watch to my son, Samuel; (b) My collection of eighteenth-century portrait paintings to the Parkside Museum; (c) My personal residence to my wife, Wanda; (d) All the rest, residue and remainder to my daughter, Dolly.	This Will hereby amends my prior Will dated May 11, 2013 as follows: I hereby give, devise, and bequeath my entire estate to my daughter, Dolly.

Under UPC §2-507(c), a subsequent will that makes a complete disposition of the estate is treated as a replacement for, rather than an amendment to, the prior will. Thus, the June 2014 will amends the 2013 will, but the 2014 will is not a codicil because it makes a complete disposition of the testator's estate. The 2014 will devises the testator's entire estate to Dolly, so the following inconsistent devises in the 2013 will are implicitly revoked: (a) the gold Rolex watch to Samuel; (b) the eighteenth-century art collection to the Parkside Museum; and (c) the personal residence to Wanda. Dolly inherits the entire testate estate.

4.2.3 Revocation by Physical Act

A will may be revoked by the testator's performance of a revocatory act upon the will with revocatory intent. UPC §2-507(a)(2) defines the term "revocatory act" as "burning, tearing, canceling, obliterating, or destroying the will or any part of it"; the statute explains further that a "burning, tearing, or canceling is a 'revocatory act on the will,' whether or not the burn, tear, or cancellation touched any of the words on the will." Revocatory intent (animus revocandi) is the testator's intent to revoke a will. "Determining whether a revocatory act was accompanied by revocatory intent may involve exploration of extrinsic evidence, including the testator's statements as to intent." UPC §2-507, comment.

The following case, *Estate of Gushwa*, involves both revocation by physical act and revocation by subsequent will. The decedent, George Gushwa, attempted to revoke his will, which was in the possession of Ted, his son-in-law, who refused to relinquish it. Without access to the original document, George tried to revoke his will another way: by executing a document titled "Revocation of Missing Will(s)." The question in this case is whether the latter document revoked Gushwa's will under these unique circumstances. As noted in the opinion, the holding is based on New Mexico's distinctive and restrictive statute governing the revocation of wills by subsequent writing. As such, the law of this case may not represent the majority rule. We include this case, as well as some of the underlying documents in the litigation, to deepen your understanding of revocation and analysis of revocatory intent. As you read the case, think about what else Gushwa could have done to revoke his will.

Estate of Gushwa
197 P.3d 1 (N.M. 2008)

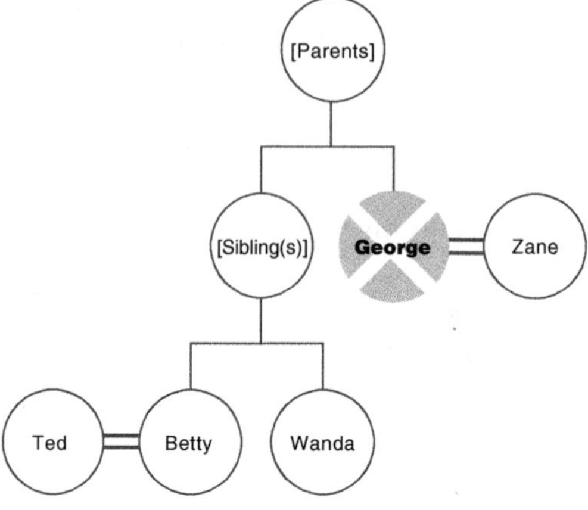

BOSSON, Justice.

{1} The New Mexico Probate Code specifies the means by which a testator may revoke a prior will. See NMSA 1978, §45-2-507(A) (1993) (stating that a will may be revoked by either executing a subsequent will or by performing a revocatory act on the will). The district court, concluding that the purported revocation in this case was legally ineffective, granted summary judgment, and the Court of Appeals affirmed in a well-reasoned opinion. On certiorari, we affirm most of that opinion. . . .

BACKGROUND

{2} In June 2000, Decedent George Gushwa executed his Last Will and Testament (the Will) while his wife, Zane Gushwa, the Petitioner in this appeal, was in the hospital. Decedent was assisted in preparing the Will by his niece, Betty Dale, and her husband, Ted Dale (Ted). The Will provided that Decedent's separate property be held in trust for the support of Wife,[26] during her life, and upon her death it was to be distributed to Decedent's nieces and nephews. Wife received no permanent distribution under the Will. Decedent named Ted as the trustee, and gave the original Will to him for safekeeping. The Dales were not beneficiaries under the Will.

{3} Shortly thereafter, it appears that Decedent decided he wanted to revoke the Will. According to Wife, Decedent called Ted to regain possession of the original Will, but Ted refused to send it. Ted denies receiving such a request from Decedent. Instead, Ted submitted an affidavit stating that Wife called him and requested that he send *her* the original Will. Ted then notified Decedent's attorney and asked whether he should send Wife the original Will, because Ted knew that Decedent did not want her to see it. Decedent's attorney told Ted to contact Decedent, which Ted did. According to Ted, Decedent asked him to discuss the Will only in general terms with Wife, and told Ted which pages of the Will to send to Decedent. Ted then sent photocopies of those pages to Decedent.

{4} In January 2001, Decedent contacted another lawyer to help him revoke the Will. In February 2001, his new lawyer assisted him in drafting a document entitled "Revocation of Missing Will(s)," in which Decedent repeatedly stated that he wanted to revoke his previous Will. At the same time, on the advice of counsel Decedent wrote "Revoked" on the copy of three pages of the Will, presumably the same three pages that he received from Ted, and attached those pages to the Revocation of Missing Will(s) document. That document was signed by Decedent and two witnesses and was notarized. In April 2001, Decedent received a photocopy of the entire Will from his previous attorney and wrote "Revoked" on each page of that copy of the Will.

{5} Decedent died in 2005. After his death, Wife filed an application for informal appointment of a personal representative. Wife asserted that her husband died intestate and that she was not aware of any unrevoked testamentary instruments. In her application, Wife listed the names of several interested parties, including Wanda Hunt (Wanda), Decedent's niece, the Respondent in this appeal. Wanda objected to Wife's application, arguing that the June 2000 Will had not been

26. [The court's opinion capitalizes "Wife" but does not define the term. — EDS.]

revoked and was still in force, because Decedent had failed to follow the statutory formalities for revocation set forth in the Probate Code.

{6} In response to Wanda's objections, Wife argued that the June 2000 Will had been revoked by the Revocation of Missing Will(s) document, and also by Decedent's act of writing "Revoked" on the photocopied pages of the Will. She further contended that Ted's behavior prevented Decedent from obtaining possession of the original Will so that he could write "Revoked" on the original instead of just a copy. Wife asked the district court to impose a constructive trust upon Decedent's estate if the court found that the Will had not been successfully revoked under the statute. In July 2006, the district court agreed with Wanda that Decedent's will had not been revoked in a manner consistent with the requirements of the Probate Code and granted summary judgment in her favor and against Wife.

{7} The Court of Appeals affirmed the district court, concluding that the Revocation of Missing Will(s) document was not testamentary in nature; it was not a subsequent will as required by statute, and therefore it did not revoke Decedent's prior Will. In re Estate of Gushwa, 168 P.3d 147. The Court of Appeals also agreed that the act of writing "Revoked" on the photocopied will was not a legally effective revocatory act because such an act must be done on an original or a duplicate original and not a photocopy. Id. ¶29. Finally, the Court of Appeals concluded that Ted's refusal to surrender the original will did not preclude summary judgment. Id. With the exception of the last point, we agree with much of the Court of Appeals' analysis.

DISCUSSION

{8} This appeal raises two questions under the Probate Code and one question of equity. First, we consider whether Decedent's execution of the Revocation of Missing Will(s) document satisfies the requirements of Section 45-2-507(A)(1), dealing with revocation by writing. Second, we determine whether Decedent's act of writing "Revoked" on a photocopy is a revocatory act within the meaning of Section 45-2-507(A)(2). Finally, we examine whether the allegations of fraud against Ted create a genuine issue of material fact that, if proven, might justify relief and preclude summary judgment.

{9} We review a district court's grant of summary judgment de novo. . . .

{10} Our Probate Code provides that a will or any part thereof may be revoked in one of two ways. See §45-2-507. A testator may revoke a previous will "by executing a subsequent will that revokes the previous will or part expressly or by inconsistency." Section 45-2-507(A)(1). A testator may also revoke a previous will "by performing a revocatory act on the will if the testator performed the act with the intent and for the purpose of revoking the will or part." Section 45-2-507(A)(2). A "revocatory act on the will" includes "burning, tearing, canceling, obliterating or destroying the will or any part of it." Id. For purposes of this appeal, we concentrate on the word "canceling," but we turn first to the requirement in Section 45-2-507(A)(1) for revocation by a "subsequent will."

Revocation by Writing

{11} In this case, the district court specifically found that "[n]either party proposes the revocation document satisfies the requirements of §45-2-507A(1)." Nevertheless, the court conducted its own analysis of the Revocation of Missing Will(s) document and concluded that the document was not a "subsequent will" as set forth in Subsection 507(A)(1). The court specifically noted that the document "act[ed] instanter and not upon [Decedent's] death[,]" and therefore could not be a testamentary disposition.

{12} [T]he Court of Appeals agreed that the Revocation of Missing Will(s) document was not a subsequent will within the meaning of the Code. The Court noted that "although some portions of the document may arguably contain testamentary language, the document itself was not intended to be a subsequent will."

{13} At the outset, we note that our Probate Code, unlike that of other states, does not allow for revocation of a will by any "other writing." Compare §45-2-507(A)(1) ("A will or any part thereof is revoked . . . by executing a subsequent will that revokes the previous will or part expressly or by inconsistency. . . .") with Fla. Stat. §732.505(2) (2002) ("A will or codicil, or any part of either, is revoked . . . [b]y a subsequent will, codicil, or other writing executed with the same formalities required for the execution of wills declaring the revocation." (Emphasis added.)). As our Court of Appeals has previously explained:

> Generally, the question whether a will can be revoked by a writing not testamentary in character depends upon the provisions of the governing statute. . . . [W]here the statute omits the clause "some other writing" or its equivalent, and simply states that no will shall be revoked except by some other "will, testament or codicil in writing, declaring the same," it has been held that a will may not be revoked by a writing not testamentary in character.

{14} Wife argues that the Revocation of Missing Will(s) document should be given the effect of a subsequent will because of its language expressly revoking Decedent's prior will. Wife relies on the definition of "will" contained in the definitions section of the Probate Code. See NMSA 1978, §45-1-201(A)(53) (1995) (defining a will as "any testamentary instrument that . . . revokes or revises another will").

{15} Wife's position, however, is at odds with the Code's specific language describing the only legally effective methods of revocation. If a will could be revoked by any writing that simply revoked another will, without the necessary testamentary language — or that it be in fact a "subsequent will" — then a will could be revoked by "any other writing," contrary to the Code's specific language and the legislative intent to limit the available means of revocation. Because our Probate Code requires revocation by a subsequent will, we are guided by this more specific statement rather than a generic definition. Accordingly, we reject Wife's argument that the Revocation of Missing Will(s) document satisfies the requirements of Section 45-2-507(A)(1). It clearly does not, regardless of Decedent's intent. Our Probate Code requires an exacting attention to form as well as intent to validate a revocation. See *Martinez*, 1999-NMCA-093, ¶11.

{16} Similarly, Wife's argument that other language in the Revocation of Missing Will(s) document gives it the effect of a subsequent will does not persuade us. Instead, the language chosen by Decedent clearly shows that he knew he was not drafting a subsequent will.

{17} First, in the Revocation of Missing Will(s) document, Decedent explained in writing his correct understanding of the two methods by which a testator can revoke a will — drafting a subsequent will or performing a revocatory act on the will. Decedent then listed acceptable revocatory acts, including burning or canceling. After establishing that he knew how to revoke a will, and what acts constitute a revocatory act on a will, Decedent then "attest[ed] that [he] canceled the first three (3) pages of the will executed . . . on or about June 6, 2000, with the express intent to revoke the same." Thus, it is clear from the Revocation of Missing Will(s) document that if Decedent intended to revoke the Will, it was not by drafting a subsequent will, but by performing a revocatory act on the photocopy of the Will.

{18} Additionally, Decedent used conditional language in the Revocation of Missing Will(s) document which strongly suggests that he did not intend the Revocation document to act as a subsequent will. Decedent wrote that he retained the option of drafting a subsequent will. Decedent stated that he knew that his property would pass through intestate succession "*if* [he did] not make a subsequent will." (Emphasis added.) In other words, the Revocation of Missing Will(s) document, though an expression of intent, was not a subsequent will in Decedent's mind. In addition, while Decedent excluded Ted and Betty from inheriting any of his property, he explained that they were not to inherit "whether by will or by intestate succession," leaving open the possibility of a subsequent will.

{19} Our review of the statutory requirements for revocation by a subsequent will, along with our analysis of the language Decedent selected for use in the Revocation of Missing Will(s) document, persuades us that the Revocation of Missing Will(s) document was never intended to be a subsequent will and should not be given the effect of a subsequent will by this Court. Therefore, as a matter of law consistent with the clear language of the Probate Code, this document did not revoke Decedent's prior will.[27]

The Effect of a Revocatory Act on a Photocopy of the Will

{20} In addition to revoking a will by executing a subsequent will, the Probate Code provides that a will may be revoked by performing a revocatory act on the will. Section 45-2-507(A)(2). ("A will . . . is revoked . . . by performing a revocatory act on the will if the testator performed the act with the intent and for the purpose of revoking the will. . . ."). The district court concluded that Decedent's act of writing "Revoked" on

27. In considering the thoughtful dissent authored by Chief Justice Chávez, we emphasize that under Section 45-2-507(A) of our Probate Code only a subsequent will may serve to revoke an existing will. As noted earlier, the district court found, without objection on appeal, that neither party put forth the Revocation of Missing Will(s) document as a subsequent will. Wife did not submit the document to probate, instead claiming that Decedent died without a will, intestate. Given these and other circumstances, the district court correctly concluded as a matter of law that Decedent did not comply with Section 45-2-507(A)(1) despite Decedent's indications that he may have wanted to revoke by this or some other means.

a photocopy was insufficient to revoke the Will because a photocopy of a will does not have the same legal status as an executed copy of a will. The Court of Appeals agreed.

{21} The Court of Appeals first noted that an executed copy differs from a photocopy because an executed copy, or duplicate original, is executed with the same formalities as the original; the executed copy is signed, witnessed, and notarized at the same time as the original. Because each copy is signed and witnessed, the executed or duplicate copy has the legal effect of the original. . . .

{22} Wife argues that a majority of modern courts hold that a testator's revocation of a copy of a will is a legally effective revocation of the original will. In support of her argument, Wife relies on an annotation that contains only six cases, all decided prior to 1952. See 79 Am. Jur. 2d Wills §516 (2002). These cases do not support Wife's position because the courts were considering the legal efficacy of fully executed duplicate copies, not photocopies of an original will. . . .

{23} Wife acknowledges that these cases address duplicate originals, but she contends that under our rules of evidence the distinction between a duplicate original and a photocopy "is a distinction without a difference." Relying on Rule 11-1003 NMRA, "Admissibility of Duplicates," Wife argues that a photocopy of a will should have the same evidentiary value as a duplicate original will.

{24} We disagree. Our rules of evidence require admission of an original "[t]o prove the content of a writing, recording or photograph." Rule 11-1002 NMRA. Our rules also provide that a duplicate, which includes a photocopy, may be admitted in lieu of an original to prove the contents of a document unless there is a genuine question about the authenticity of the original or unless it would be unfair to admit the duplicate. Rule 11-1003. Based on this evidentiary principle, courts have admitted a photocopy of a will in lieu of an original as evidence to prove the contents of a lost will.

. . .

{27} [O]ur Probate Code mandates that a revocatory act be performed "on the will." Section 45-2-507(A)(2). While the Code does not explicitly require that the act be performed on the original or on an executed original, such a requirement is implicit in the statutory term "will."

. . .

{29} [W]e agree with our Court of Appeals that treating photocopies differently from originals is important as a matter of policy. As that Court explained, the requirement of an original can protect against fraudulent reproduction of unauthorized wills. Photocopies can be readily produced and the existence of multiple copies of a will can engender confusion, especially when the issue is whether the will has been validly revoked.

{30} We are also informed by case law from other jurisdictions where courts have held that a revocatory act performed on a mere photocopy is legally ineffective. . . . Accordingly, we hold that Decedent's revocatory acts performed on a mere photocopy of his original Will do not comport with the statutory requirements of Section 45-2-507(A)(2).

. . .

{38} It is so ordered.

CHÁVEZ, Chief Justice (dissenting).

{39} Decedent George Gushwa executed a document (the Revocation of Missing Will(s) document) explaining that he wanted his prior will to be revoked and describing how he wished his property to be distributed upon his death. He was careful to follow all of the formalities required of a testator under the New Mexico Probate Code. After his death, the district court, without any specific fact-finding, refused to give effect to Decedent's clearly expressed desires. The majority gives this decision its seal of approval, relying on the formalities of the Probate Code, which were designed to *capture* the intent of testators, not to frustrate it.

{40} I recognize that the Revocation of Missing Will(s) document is not an ideal will, and indeed that Decedent apparently believed that it did not constitute a will under New Mexico law. Decedent used language suggesting that he did not consider the document a will and that he intended to revoke his prior will by the ineffective means of performing a revocatory act on a partial photocopy of his prior will. Because of this confusion, the majority concludes as a matter of law that Decedent's document was not a will, and as such failed to satisfy New Mexico's statutory requirements for the revocation of a prior will. I respectfully disagree. The document met all of the formalities necessary to create a will, and the district court's responsibility was simply to determine the testator's intent. . . . Given the document's ambiguity, we should remand to the district court to determine, on the basis of extrinsic evidence of the testator's intent, whether the Revocation of Missing Will(s) document should be considered a will for the purposes of NMSA 1978, Section 45-2-507(A)(1) (1993) (providing that a prior will can be revoked "by executing a subsequent will that revokes the previous will or part expressly or by inconsistency"). . . . Accordingly, I respectfully dissent.

. . .

{42} Had Decedent executed, in accordance with the statutory formalities, a document purporting to be a will requesting that his property be disposed of through the intestacy laws, but specifying that nothing from his estate would be given to certain relatives, I see no reason why our courts should refuse to give effect to his desires. . . . In other words, such a document would be a valid will. Furthermore, if Decedent executed such a subsequent will, it seems clear that the New Mexico Probate Code would obligate us to conclude that the previous will had been revoked, even if the new will did not explicitly recite language revoking the previous will. . . . Unfortunately, our decision is not so simple, since the disputed Revocation of Missing Will(s) document contains additional language suggesting that Decedent did not perceive it to be a will.

{43} Because of this additional language, the majority has concluded that the Revocation of Missing Will(s) document "was not a subsequent will *in Decedent's mind.*" (Emphasis added.) I agree with the majority that this language supports such an inference. However, since Decedent is unavailable to explain his understanding of what constitutes a "will," I find it impossible to conclude as a matter of law that his understanding coincides with the definition of "will" under the New Mexico Probate Code. . . . Can we be so confident, then, that Decedent did not intend to create what our law recognizes as a will? I prefer to simply acknowledge that the Revocation of Missing Will(s) document is ambiguous in this respect.

. . .

REVOCATION OF MISSING WILL(S)

I, George Gushwa, a resident of Elda, Roosevelt County, New Mexico, being of legal age and of sound mind and memory, and acting of my own will, free from any duress or undue influence, do hereby revoke any and all former wills and codicils made by me at anytime heretofore, and specifically the Last Will and Testament executed by me on or about June 6, 2000.

I understand that pursuant to the New Mexico Probate Code, a will is revoked by executing a subsequent will that revokes a previous will or by performing a revocatory act, which includes burning, tearing, cancelling, obliterating or destroying the will. I further understand that a burning, teaching or cancelling is a "revocatory act of the will" whether or not the burn, tear, or cancellation touches any of the words on the will. I attest that I have canceled the first (3) pages of the will executed by me on or about June 6, 2000, with the express intent to revoke the same, a copy which is attached hereto as Exhibit A and incorporated by reference. I do not have possession of the remaining pages of this will and by this instrument expressly revoke the will in its entirety.

It is my express intent in revoking this and any and all other wills and codicils executed by me that my nephew, Ted Dale, and my niece, Betty Dale, inherit nothing from me or my estate, whether by will or by intestate succession.

I understand that by not revoking any and all other wills executed by me through a subsequent will that my estate will pass as provided by the New Mexico laws of intestate succession if I do not make a subsequent will. I declare that it is my intent, as expressed in this instrument, to revoke any and all wills and codicils made by me at any time heretofore without making a subsequent will.

IN WITNESS WHEREOF, I have hereunto subscribed my name this 28th day of February, 2001, in the presence of witnesses.

George Gushwa
George Gushwa

[Notarized "Verification," signed by attesting witnesses, omitted.]

QUESTIONS

18. In New Mexico, revocation by subsequent writing must be in the form of a "will that revokes the previous will or part expressly or by inconsistency." Unlike other jurisdictions, revocation by "other writing" is not sufficient. What is the significance of the distinction between revocation by subsequent will and revocation by subsequent "other writing"?

ANSWER. New Mexico appears to draw a distinction between a will that contains affirmative dispositions of property and an "other writing" whose sole function is to revoke a prior will or codicil. As a general rule, a will provision revoking all prior wills and codicils is operative at the time of execution while a provision making dispositions of property is operative at death. Under *Gushwa*'s holding, an instrument that only revokes a prior will without making affirmative dispositions of property is not testamentary in character.

19. Why did the court find the "Revocation of Missing Will(s)" document did not satisfy the statutory requirement of revocation by will?

    ANSWER. A revocation must be executed according to Wills Act formalities and must be testamentary in character, meaning that it reflects the testator's intent to govern the disposition of property at the time of death. Here, although the revocatory document complied with Wills Act formalities because it was in writing, signed by the testator, and two witnesses, the court found that the language of the Revocation of Missing Will(s) document was ambiguous as to whether Gushwa regarded the document as a will. Thus, according to the court, these ambiguities precluded a finding that the instrument was testamentary in character. Although the majority correctly identifies ambiguous language in the document, it does not acknowledge the unambiguous statement of revocatory intent at the beginning of the instrument: "I George Gushwa, . . . being of legal age and of sound mind and memory, and acting of my own will, free from any duress of undue influence, do hereby revoke any and all former wills and codicils made by me at anytime heretofore, and specifically the Last Will and Testament executed by me on or about June 6, 2000."

20. The "Revocation of Missing Will(s)" document stated that the testator retained the option of drafting a subsequent will. Does this fact help determine whether the document constitutes a valid revocation?

    ANSWER. No. Wills are freely revocable, provided that the testator revokes in a manner that complies with the statute. Thus, all testators implicitly retain the option to draft and execute a subsequent will so long as they retain testamentary capacity. For this reason, it is not necessary for a will to expressly retain the right to execute a subsequent will. Reservation of such a right would seem merely to restate the law, not negate testamentary intent.

21. Suppose a testator executes the following instrument observing all statutory formalities: "I hereby revoke all prior wills and codicils." The instrument otherwise contains no affirmative devises or bequests. Would this document validly revoke all prior wills and codicils?

    ANSWER. In most jurisdictions, the answer would be Yes; a testamentary instrument may revoke a prior will or codicil without making dispositions of property, such as devises and bequests. In New Mexico, however, the answer would appear to be No absent evidence that the decedent regarded the document as a will.

22. How would this case have been decided under the harmless error rule, UPC §2-503?

    ANSWER. In New Mexico, the doctrine of strict compliance applies to both the execution and revocation of wills. *Gushwa*, ¶15 ("Our Probate Code requires an exacting attention to form as well as intent to validate a revocation."). Under UPC §2-503, by contrast, a defectively executed revocatory writing is treated as executed in compliance with the Wills Act if the proponent establishes by clear and convincing evidence "that the decedent intended the document or writing to constitute . . . a partial or complete revocation of the will." Here, not only was the Revocation of Missing Will(s) document executed in compliance with UPC Wills Act formalities, but there is ample clear and convincing evidence that Gushwa intended the document effect a revocation of his June 2000 will. Although muddied by some ambiguous language, the document itself clearly articulates Gushwa's revocatory intent and the surrounding circumstances show that he tried to do everything within his power to revoke the 2000 will notwithstanding Ted's refusal to return the original document.

23. Assuming the testator could not obtain the original copy of his will, what else could he have done to revoke it?

    ANSWER. The testator, perhaps with the genius of hindsight, could have (1) executed a new will devising property to his intended beneficiaries; or (2) executed a new will stating only his intent to revoke all prior wills and codicils, thereby omitting the lengthy discussion of revocation law that the court found ambiguous. Had Gushwa confined his Revocation of Missing Will(s) document, which ran for three pages, to only the first sentence articulating his revocatory intent, perhaps the court would have construed the document as a valid revocation. In this case, it appears, less is more.

24. Why must a revocatory act be performed on the original will rather than a duplicate?

    ANSWER. A requirement that the revocatory act be performed on the original will rather than an unexecuted duplicate copy lessens the opportunity for fraudulent revocation. Revocation by physical act does not need to be witnessed and, because the revocation is an act rather than a writing, it is not signed by the testator. Questions may therefore arise as to who performed the revocatory act. By limiting the doctrine's application to acts performed on the original will, the requirement ensures that individuals holding copies of the will cannot fraudulently revoke the instrument. On this point, the court's majority and dissent expressed agreement.

PROBLEM IX

Marcia executes a valid will in 1994 and a valid codicil in 2008. Marcia dies in 2017. What is the effect on Marcia's will and codicil of the following, assuming they occurred in 2016:

a. Marcia tears the codicil in half with intent to revoke it.
b. Marcia tears the will in half with intent to revoke it.
c. Marcia directs her attorney to revoke the will.

d. Marcia draws a diagonal line across the first page of the will with intent to revoke it.
e. Marcia's house was destroyed by fire. The fire marshal determines that Marcia caused the fire intentionally for the purpose of committing insurance fraud. Marcia survives the fire but does not collect insurance proceeds. The original will and codicil were inside her house and there are no copies.

4.2.3.1 Lost Wills

When a will cannot be found, there are three possible reasons: (1) the will was lost or unintentionally destroyed; (2) someone other than the testator destroyed the will intentionally for the fraudulent purpose of preventing its admission to probate; or (3) the testator revoked the will by physical act and disposed of it.[28] When a will is lost or unintentionally destroyed, it may be probated upon proof of its contents, such as production of a reliable duplicate copy. Likewise, a will that is fraudulently destroyed may be probated upon proof of the fraud and contents of the will. The next case illustrates the common law presumption that arises when a will cannot be found among the testator's personal effects and was last known to be in the testator's possession.

In re Estate of Conley
753 N.W.2d 384 (N.D. 2008)

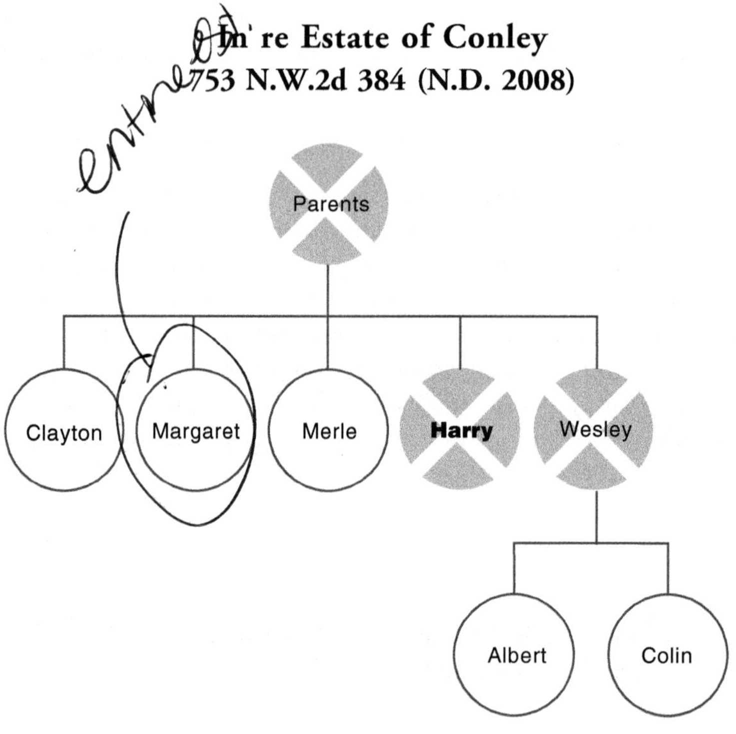

28. If the testator had revoked the will by subsequent writing, then the subsequent writing would have been produced at the time of probate.

KAPSNER, Justice.

[¶1] Albert and Colin Conley, as personal representatives of the estate of Harry Wayne Conley ["Harry"], appeal a district court order [admitting to probate Harry's will]. Because the district court erroneously failed to apply the common law presumption that a missing will is revoked, we reverse. . . .

I

[¶2] Harry died on April 21, 2001, in Jamestown, North Dakota. [He] never married and had no children. He was survived by his brother, Clayton Conley ["Clayton"], and his sisters, Margaret York ["Margaret"] and Merle McKinney ["Merle"]. His parents and one brother, Wesley Conley, predeceased him. Wesley Conley was survived by two sons, Albert Conley ["Albert"] and Colin Conley ["Colin"].

[¶3] Harry executed a will on January 19, 1982[, which] could not be found at the time of and after his death, but a conformed copy was obtained from the files of the lawyer who prepared it. Under the provisions of this missing will, Harry's sister, Margaret, would receive his entire estate. If Harry's estate passed [by] intestacy, [his] estate would . . . be shared among his [siblings, Clayton, Margaret, and Merle, and his two nephews, Albert and Colin].

[¶4] Four years after Harry's death in 2001, [his] nephews, Albert and Colin, [petitioned for letters of administration to probate the estate by intestacy]. The district court granted their appointments [as personal representatives] in September 2005. . . .

[¶5] In May 2006, Margaret filed a Petition to Establish Testacy and Right of Succession to the Estate Assets, and she requested that a conformed copy of Harry's 1982 will be admitted into probate. The co-personal representatives [objected, arguing] that no original will had been found and that it is presumed that Harry had revoked all prior wills and died intestate.

. . .

[¶7] Clayton's affidavit provided that he knew of the existence of the will and had seen it as late as Christmas 2000. His affidavit provided that he helped Harry take care of his paperwork, that the original will had been placed inside a particular folder in a filing box, and that until Christmas 2000, Clayton saw the will there a few times each year. [I]n early 2001, Harry requested Clayton take him to a lawyer so he could make a new will [but died before contacting the lawyer]. Clayton . . . thinks perhaps Harry may have destroyed the will, because when Clayton asked Harry about [it], Harry said he had "taken care of it."

. . .

[¶9] Alma Lulay provided that she had been in custody of documents that belonged to Harry's mother, Winnifred Conley, from May 1981 to September 1982, she thoroughly reviewed the documents in her possession, and she did not find an original or copy of the 1982 will.

[¶10] Margaret's affidavit provided she was aware Harry had created a will in 1982, and Winnifred Conley had given her a signed copy of Harry's original will shortly after it was created. [S]he had kept the copy of Harry's signed will in her closet, along with some of her personal documents, but the will and several other documents were removed from her closet, without her permission or knowledge, sometime after Harry's death. . . . Clayton had a key to her apartment, and Clayton was the only person who would have had an interest in taking the documents. . . . Harry never told her about any intention to revoke his will, but rather that he intended the property in the will go to her.

[¶11] The deposition testimony of Carol Nelson related to the storage and retention of documents by the attorney who drafted the will, a conformed copy of which was admitted in this proceeding. The attorney who drafted the 1982 will provided deposition testimony related to the creation of the 1982 will.

. . .

[¶14] [The district court held that] Harry's 1982 will was not presumed to be revoked. . . . The district court awarded Margaret the entirety of Harry's estate as provided by his will. Following the order, the co-personal representatives filed a notice of appeal. . . .

II

. . .

[¶17] North Dakota has adopted section 2-507 of the [Uniform Probate] Code as N.D.C.C. §30.1-08-07[.][29]

This statute does not specifically speak to the effect of losing or misplacing a will. . . . This provision is merely silent as to the loss of a will. . . .

. . .

[¶19] [The North Dakota Code does not] provide specific presumptions for admitting a missing will, but these statutes clearly indicate the drafter's intent to allow, under certain circumstances, the probate of lost or missing wills.

[¶20] To date, this Court has not had an opportunity to interpret any of the statutes related to the probate of missing wills. . . . [U]nlike a majority of jurisdictions, [North Dakota] has not formally adopted or discussed the presumption of animo revocandi, which presumes a missing will has been intentionally destroyed and thus revoked by the testator, since the adoption of the Code. . . .

[¶21] The amino revocandi presumption is founded upon the observation that

> [p]ersons in general keep their wills in places of safety, or . . . among their papers of moment and concern. They are instruments in their nature revocable: testamentary intention is ambulatory till death; and if the instrument be not found in the repositories of the test[at]or, where he had placed it, the common sense of the matter, prima facie, is that he himself destroyed it, meaning to revoke it. . . .

. . . The presumption . . . protect[s] the testator's right to "change [his will] at pleasure" and recognizes "that wills are almost always destroyed secretly." Consequently, when a will cannot be found upon the death of the testator [among the testator's personal effects], the presumption arises that the testator secretly chose to revoke the missing will. The fact that a conformed copy of the missing will is in the office of the attorney who drafted it does not alter the rationale for the presumption.

. . .

---

29. [Statutory text omitted. See page 157 for UPC §2-507 on Revocation by Writing or by Act. — Eds.]

We adopt the presumption and must turn to the question of what standard of evidence is required to rebut the presumption.

[¶28] In a majority of jurisdictions, the courts employ something akin to a clear-and-convincing evidence standard . . . . We note a clear-and-convincing standard is consistent with several evidentiary standards required in the North Dakota Uniform Probate Code for rebutting other presumptions . . . . However, N.D. R. Evid. 301(a) provides that in presumptions arising in civil proceedings not otherwise provided for by statute, [the burden of proof is by preponderance of the evidence]. N.D. R. Evid. 301(a) requires the party seeking to probate the missing will to demonstrate, by a preponderance of the evidence, that the testator did not destroy or revoke the missing will animo revocandi.

[¶29] . . . After meeting the [applicable procedural] requirements . . . , the party petitioning for the probate of a missing will must demonstrate, by a preponderance of the evidence, that the will existed at the time of the testator's death, that the will was fraudulently destroyed in the lifetime of the testator, or by other evidence demonstrating the testator did not intend to revoke the missing will. . . .

III

[¶30] We . . . conclud[e] the district court erroneously failed to apply the common law presumption that a missing will is revoked, and we remand for further proceedings consistent with this opinion.

QUESTIONS

25. What presumption arises when the decedent's will is believed to have been lost?

    ANSWER. A lost will, standing alone, does not trigger a presumption of revocation because there are many plausible reasons for the will's disappearance. When a will is last known to be in the testator's possession and it cannot be found among the testator's personal effects at death, however, the will is presumed revoked on the theory that the reason it cannot be found is that the testator revoked it by physical act. Importantly, the presumption does not apply to all lost wills, but rather, to a will last known to be in the testator's possession that cannot be found among the testator's personal effects at death. Although the *Conley* court did not emphasize this important aspect of the common law doctrine applied in other jurisdictions, the 1982 will was last known to be in the decedent's possession, so the revocation presumption was properly applied. If, however, someone other than the testator, such as the attorney, had been last in possession of the will, then the revocation presumption does not apply.

26. Why is the presumption of revocation rebuttable by preponderance of the evidence rather than the higher standard of clear and convincing evidence?

    ANSWER. Jurisdictions are split on whether to apply a preponderance or clear and convincing evidence standard to rebut the revocation presumption. The lower preponderance standard may be justified on grounds that there are many reasons other than the testator's revocation for why the will disappeared and it may be difficult to ascertain proof of why the will cannot be found among the testator's personal effects. In *Conley*, once the trial court applies the presumption, how could Margaret prove Harry had not revoked the missing will? Absent proof that one of Harry's intestate heirs had access to and destroyed the will, Margaret will have trouble rebutting the presumption. The higher clear and convincing evidence standard may be justified on grounds that this is the standard typically applied to establish facts in the context of wills. The Restatement (Third) of Property: Wills & Other Donative Transfers §4.1, comment j applies the preponderance standard. In *Conley*, the clear and convincing evidence standard would make it even more difficult for Margaret to rebut the presumption of revocation.

PROBLEM X

You have been retained by Margaret York, the proponent of the will in *In re Estate of Conley*, to represent her in the remand proceedings.

A. What arguments will you assert to rebut the presumption that Harry revoked his will?
B. Draft a petition on Margaret's behalf to establish the testacy of her deceased brother Harry.

4.2.3.2 Partial Revocation by Physical Act

Partial revocation by physical act is the cancellation of one or more provisions within a will without effecting a revocation of the entire instrument. Consider, for example, the revocatory act of cancellation.[30] A testator who crosses out a specific devise with intent to revoke it has performed the revocatory act of cancellation upon the stricken devise, but intends for the rest of the instrument to remain in effect. The UPC §2-507 and a majority of jurisdictions recognize this as a partial revocation by physical act. A minority of jurisdictions do not permit partial revocation by physical act on the theory that, by revoking a particular devise or bequest, the testator has, in effect, made an unattested testamentary gift to someone else, such as a residuary beneficiary or intestate heir.

30. According to Professor Atkinson, "[c]ancellation is derived from a Latin word meaning lattice. Hence our ordinary concept of the verb cancel is to draw criss-cross lines across an instrument." Thomas E. Atkinson, Law of Wills 438 (West 2d ed. 1953).

In re Estate of Schumacher
253 P.3d 1280 (Colo. Ct. App. 2011)

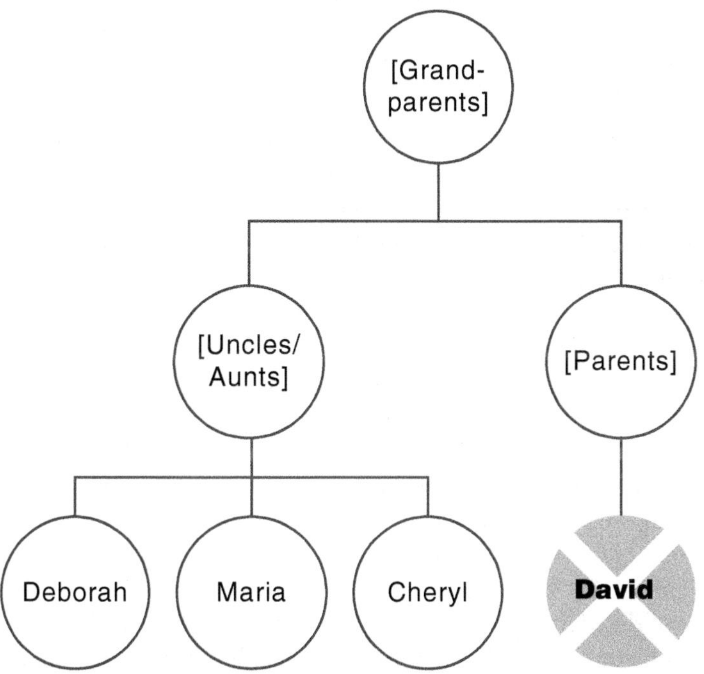

J. Marquez:

Petitioner, Maria Caldwell, appeals the probate court's order giving testamentary effect to words crossed out on decedent's holographic will. We affirm.

I. BACKGROUND

On December 1, 2004, David Schumacher (decedent) executed a holographic will, which contained a clause devising shares of Meyers Land & Cattle stock to decedent's cousins, petitioner, Maria Caldwell, Cheryl Smart, and respondent, Deborah Caldwell.

On January 12, 2006, decedent met with his attorney, Michael Gilbert, to create a typed will. In a later hearing, attorney Gilbert testified he had no specific recollection whether he saw the original will or only the photocopy. Attorney Gilbert's copy of the will included lines crossing out the names of petitioner and Cheryl as remainder devisees of all the shares of the stock. Attorney Gilbert testified:

> What [decedent] told me was that . . . he had prepared a holographic will and subsequent to preparing it he had decided that he did not want his . . . stock to be

> given to two of his three cousins . . . and those names had been crossed out on the copy of the will which I had. . . .

Attorney Gilbert also testified:

> I asked [decedent] about the change, why Maria and Cheryl's names had been deleted and essentially what he told me was that he felt closest to his cousin, Deborah, and he had changed his mind and he wanted the stock . . . after the death of his mother to go to Deborah alone.

However, attorney Gilbert did not ask decedent who made the cross-outs.

Attorney Gilbert then drafted a typed will pursuant to decedent's instructions and transmitted it to decedent. Decedent died on July 3, 2007 without ever executing the typed will. After decedent's death, attorney Gilbert tendered the copy of the holographic will to the probate court.

Approximately six months prior to his death, decedent had sent several boxes of his personal records to his secretary with instructions that she store them in her garage and sort them out. When decedent died, decedent's secretary, her sister, and decedent's personal representative found, in an unopened box, the original holographic will signed by decedent and containing the lines crossing out the names of Maria and Cheryl as devisees of the stock. The personal representative took the original holographic will to attorney Gilbert, who tendered it to the probate court.

On April 14, 2008, the personal representative filed a petition for determination of validity of decedent's holographic will dated December 1, 2004. Petitioner and Cheryl later filed a petition for construction of the holographic will to determine the validity of the markings on the will.

The probate court held a hearing in June 2009 in which attorney Gilbert and a handwriting expert testified. The probate court later issued a written order, finding that decedent performed a "revocatory act" on the will by crossing out petitioner's and Cheryl's names, with the intent and for the purpose of revoking part of his holographic will. The court ordered that "the strikethroughs in the Holographic Will . . . can and must be given effect in probate."

Both Cheryl and Maria appealed the probate court's order. However, Cheryl's appeal was dismissed, and Maria remains as the sole petitioner[, who] contends that the probate court erred in giving testamentary effect to the cross-outs. . . .

II. STANDARD OF REVIEW

"Decisions of a trial court regarding factual disputes are accorded great deference, and, therefore, a reviewing court applies the clear error standard." Therefore, "we will not disturb the trial court's determinations of factual questions that are necessary to carrying out the testator's expressed intent unless they are clearly erroneous." Clearly erroneous means the findings of fact are unsupported by substantial evidence in the record considered as a whole. . . .

III. DISCUSSION

A. Sufficiency of the Evidence

On appeal, petitioner contends that (1) the evidence contradicts and does not support a finding that decedent made the cross-outs and (2) there is no evidence to support the finding that decedent made the cross-outs with the intent and purpose to revoke the devise as required under section 15-11-507, C.R.S. 2010. We disagree.

A will can be revoked only in the manner provided by statute, and the statutory provisions for revocation of wills must be strictly construed.

Prior to 1995, section 15-11-507 only allowed for total revocation of a will. However, the General Assembly revised the statute to allow part of a will to be revoked if certain formalities have been satisfied. Accordingly, now, under C.R.S. 15-11-507(1), C.R.S. 2010[, Colorado has adopted the language of UPC §2-507].

Here, the probate court found that decedent made the cross-outs with the intent and purpose to effectuate a partial revocation of the devise of the stock to petitioner and Cheryl. It based its decision primarily upon the testimony and affidavit of attorney Gilbert, who was "certain in [his] mind that the cross-outs that appear on the machine copy were cross-outs that [decedent] wanted changed in his will." Additionally, attorney Gilbert "was aware that [the will] was the most recent expression of [decedent's] testamentary intent" and the attorney "was very clear in [his] understanding that that's what decedent wanted. That change was from what he had originally stated in his holographic will." The court concluded that the intent was clearly and convincingly proved through the affidavit and testimony of attorney Gilbert, and found that decedent "was still in possession and/or control of the will because he employed the secretary."

Petitioner's expert handwriting analyst, whose testimony was based on a comparison of the photocopy of the will and the original, opined that "it was not possible to determine who wrote the cross-outs" on the will. To this, the court stated:

> This would be significant if the issue[s] confronting the Court included who had made the strikethroughs. Attorney Gilbert's testimony was unequivocal that the Decedent told him that he (the Decedent) had crossed out the . . . names with the intent and purpose of removing them from the provision of the . . . Will.

1. Performance of Act

. . .

As noted, section 15-11-507(1)(b) provides that a revocatory act on a will includes burning, tearing, canceling, obliterating, or destroying the will or any part of it. Canceling a part of a will can be accomplished "by drawing lines through one or more words of the will."

Attorney Gilbert testified that when decedent visited him, decedent showed him the cross-outs on a copy of the holographic will and told attorney Gilbert he did not want his "stock to be given to two of his three cousins" and "those names had been crossed out on the copy of the will which [attorney Gilbert] had." Attorney Gilbert also testified that he "was certainly aware that [decedent] had changed his mind and he decided he wanted the stock to just go to his cousin, Deborah." Decedent told him that "except for those deletions," decedent wanted him to prepare a will that contained the same dispositive provisions as his original will. Decedent also responded to attorney Gilbert's question "about the change, why Maria and Cheryl's names had been deleted." That testimony, together with the evidence, as discussed below, that the original will with the crossed-out portions was found in decedent's possession, is sufficient evidence to demonstrate that decedent made the cross-outs.

2. Possession

[Petitioner asserts that the probate court erroneously found that decedent was in possession of the will upon his death, and therefore, a presumption that decedent made the cross-outs should not apply.]

Neither petitioner nor respondent disputes that if a properly executed will containing tears or cancellations is known to be in the possession of the testator at the time of death, the testator is presumed to have revoked all or some of it. . . . Rather, what is contested is whether the original holographic will was in fact in decedent's possession upon his death.

Here, the probate court found that the will was in decedent's possession when it was at his secretary's house "because he employed the secretary." Petitioner, however, contends that the decedent must have been in exclusive possession of the will for the presumption to apply, and because the will was found at decedent's secretary's house, it was not in his exclusive possession. We conclude petitioner views possession too narrowly.

. . .

In this case, we conclude that the probate court's finding that decedent had been in possession of his will upon death is supported by the record and is not clearly erroneous. The record contains evidence that decedent had given the boxes of his own effects to his secretary to organize and keep on his behalf, and the will was found among many of his other personal items. Unbeknownst to the secretary, the boxed items included the will. There is no evidence that anyone but the secretary, her sister, and the personal representative had access to the will. Additionally, none of them benefited under the will, and all three signed affidavits averring that at no point did they alter the will. Thus, the record supports the court's finding that it was in decedent's possession upon death.

The probate court also properly concluded that "decedent hired the secretary and as such, the [d]ecedent was still in possession and/or control of the will because he employed the secretary." An employee acts on behalf of his or her employer when the employee is acting within the scope of his or her employment. Here, the probate court determined the secretary stored decedent's effects based on his instructions and her position as his employee, and because the question whether an employee is acting within the scope of the employment is a question of fact for the trial court, we must accept its determination. Id.

Based on the facts of this case, we are satisfied that the probate court did not err in finding the will was still in decedent's possession upon his death. Accordingly, any error in the court's finding that decedent told attorney Gilbert he made the cross-outs is harmless in light of other evidence and the court's finding concerning possession.

3. Intent and Purpose

Petitioner also contends that there is no evidence to prove that decedent made the cross-outs with the intent and purpose to revoke the devise of stocks to her. We disagree.

Extrinsic evidence is admissible to establish the testator's intent. . . .

Here, the court determined that clear and convincing evidence established decedent's intent and purpose to revoke the devise of stock through the cross-outs. The court's determination was based on attorney Gilbert's testimony. . . .

We conclude that the court's finding is adequately supported by sufficient evidence in the record. The court's finding that decedent was in possession of the will at the time of his death also establishes a presumption the he made the cross-outs with the intent and purpose of partial revocation.

. . .

Because both elements of partial revocation as required by section 15-11-507 have been met and are adequately supported by the record, the probate court's decision to give the cross-outs testamentary effect was not erroneous.

. . .

The order is affirmed.

QUESTION

27. Why is the testator's possession of the will necessary to trigger the presumption that the revocatory act was performed by the testator? If the presumption does not require uninterrupted, exclusive possession by the testator, as held by the court, does the presumption accomplish its purpose?

    ANSWER. Revocatory acts are presumed to have been performed by the testator if the testator was in possession of the will. The testator's possession and control over the document limits the possibility that anyone other than the testator could have performed the revocatory act. In *Schumacher*, the court recognized a narrow exception to this general rule because, although the testator's will was not in his exclusive, uninterrupted possession, it remained securely in the files of his secretary who safeguarded his files within the scope of her duties of employment. Under these circumstances, it is unlikely that anyone other than the testator could have performed the revocatory acts described in the case.

4.2.4 Revocation by Operation of Law

As a general rule, a change in circumstances relevant to the testator's estate does not revoke the testator's will or codicil. UPC §2-508. However, there are a few exceptions to this general rule for life changes affecting the composition of the testator's family. Divorce, marriage, and the birth of children may revoke (or partially revoke) by operation of law because it is presumed that the testator would want to account for changes in family status, even if the testator neglected to update the will. Suppose, for example, Testator executes a will leaving his entire estate to Spouse A. Two years later, Testator and Spouse A divorce. A few years after that, Testator and Spouse B marry and have two children. If the testator dies without updating his will, Spouse A (his former spouse) could potentially inherit his entire estate to the exclusion of Spouse B (his surviving spouse) and children. Revocation by operation of law prevents this result because to do otherwise would be contrary to the testator's presumed intent.

UPC §2-804 provides that divorce or annulment of a marriage revokes, by operation of law, all probate and nonprobate transfers to a former spouse (and to relatives of a former spouse) unless otherwise provided by the governing instrument (e.g., will or trust), court order, or a contract relating to the division of the marital estate. The former spouse is treated as having disclaimed his or her share.

Uniform Probate Code
§2-804 Revocation of Probate and Nonprobate Transfers by Divorce; No Revocation by Other Changes of Circumstances

(a) [Definitions.] In this section:

(1) "Disposition or appointment of property" includes a transfer of an item of property or any other benefit to a beneficiary designated in a governing instrument.

(2) "Divorce or annulment" means any divorce or annulment, or any dissolution or declaration of invalidity of a marriage, that would exclude the spouse as a surviving spouse within the meaning of Section 2-802. A decree of separation that does not terminate the status of husband and wife is not a divorce for purposes of this section.

(3) "Divorced individual" includes an individual whose marriage has been annulled.

(4) "Governing instrument" means a governing instrument executed by the divorced individual before the divorce or annulment of his [or her] marriage to his [or her] former spouse.

(5) "Relative of the divorced individual's former spouse" means an individual who is related to the divorced individual's former spouse by blood, adoption, or affinity and who, after the divorce or annulment, is not related to the divorced individual by blood, adoption, or affinity.

(6) "Revocable," with respect to a disposition, appointment, provision, or nomination, means one under which the divorced individual, at the time of the divorce or annulment, was alone empowered, by law or under the governing instrument, to cancel the designation in favor of his [or her] former spouse or former spouse's relative, whether or not the divorced individual was then empowered to designate himself [or herself] in place of his [or her] former spouse or in place of his [or her] former spouse's relative and whether or not the divorced individual then had the capacity to exercise the power.

(b) [Revocation Upon Divorce.] Except as provided by the express terms of a governing instrument, a court order, or a contract relating to the division of the marital estate made between the divorced individuals before or after the marriage, divorce, or annulment, the divorce or annulment of a marriage:

(1) revokes any revocable

(A) disposition or appointment of property made by a divorced individual to his [or her] former spouse in a governing instrument and any disposition or appointment created by law or in a governing instrument to a relative of the divorced individual's former spouse,

(B) provision in a governing instrument conferring a general or nongeneral power of appointment on the divorced individual's former spouse or on a relative of the divorced individual's former spouse, and

(C) nomination in a governing instrument, nominating a divorced individual's former spouse or a relative of the divorced individual's former spouse to serve in any fiduciary or representative capacity, including a personal representative, executor, trustee, conservator, agent, or guardian; and

(2) severs the interests of the former spouses in property held by them at the time of the divorce or annulment as joint tenants with the right of survivorship [or as community property with the right of survivorship], transforming the interests of the former spouses into equal tenancies in common.

. . .

(d) [Effect of Revocation.] Provisions of a governing instrument are given effect as if the former spouse and relatives of the former spouse disclaimed all provisions revoked by this section or, in the case of a revoked nomination in a fiduciary or representative capacity, as if the former spouse and relatives of the former spouse died immediately before the divorce or annulment.

(e) [Revival if Divorce Nullified.] Provisions revoked solely by this section are revived by the divorced individual's remarriage to the former spouse or by a nullification of the divorce or annulment.

(f) [No Revocation for Other Change of Circumstances.] No change of circumstances other than as described in this section and in Section 2-803 ["Slayer Statute"] effects a revocation.

New additions to the testator's family are treated differently. Although some jurisdictions retain the old rule that marriage revokes all premarital wills, most jurisdictions now provide the testator's spouse with a "pretermitted" share, discussed in Chapter 7. Briefly, when the testator's spouse is omitted from a premarital will, the omitted spouse receives an intestate share of the estate (subject to several conditions and qualifications). The testator's premarital will is therefore revoked, by operation of law, to the extent necessary to furnish the omitted spouse's pretermitted share, but the rest of the will remains in effect. A similar rule applies to pretermitted children, that is, omitted children born after the will's execution. The testator's will is revoked, by operation of law, to the extent necessary to furnish the omitted child's pretermitted share.

4.2.5 Dependent Relative Revocation (Doctrine of Ineffective Revocation)

Dependent relative revocation — often referred to by its initials "DRR" and rechristened by the Restatement (Third) of Property: Wills & Other Donative Transfers as *ineffective revocation*—"unrevokes" a revoked will under certain circumstances. The trigger for DRR is that the testator revoked a will in whole or in part because of *some mistaken belief.* DRR typically applies in two situations. The first is where the testator's revocation was predicated on an incorrect factual or legal assumption (such as revoking a will that leaves everything to Mary based on the false impression that Mary has died). The false assumption must be established by clear and convincing evidence or stated explicitly in the revoking instrument. Second, DRR governs if the testator tries to implement a different testamentary plan that fails as a matter of law (such as revoking will 1 in order to execute will 2, but failing to execute will 2 validly).

Once a court has concluded that the testator revoked a will due to a mistake, it must ask whether upholding the revocation or reversing the revocation would be more consistent with the testator's probable intention. If the court concludes that, in hindsight, the testator would not have revoked her will if she had known all relevant facts, DRR disregards the revocation and admits the instrument into probate.

Restatement (Third) of Property: Wills & Other Donative Transfers §4.3 Ineffective Revocation (Dependent Relative Revocation)

(a) A partial or complete revocation of a will is presumptively ineffective if the testator made the revocation:

(1) in connection with an attempt to achieve a dispositive objective that fails under applicable law, or

(2) because of a false assumption of law, or because of a false belief about an objective fact, that is either recited in the revoking instrument or established by clear and convincing evidence.

(b) The presumption established in subsection (a) is rebutted if allowing the revocation to remain in effect would be more consistent with the testator's probable intention.

Here are three more examples of the contexts in which DRR typically applies.

Example 1

Ayana and her husband had three children, but they separated when Ayana discovered her husband's extramarital affair. After the separation, neither filed for divorce and Ayana moved in with her elder son in Chicago. While there, she validly executed attested will #1. A year later, Ayana moved to live with her younger son in Texas where she validly executed will #2 that expressly revoked will #1. Following a fight with her younger son's wife, Ayana moved to live with her daughter in Missouri. Ayana happily became a part of her daughter's family and vowed never to move again. Ayana then validly executed a new attested will #3 that expressly revoked all prior wills. The beneficiaries of all three wills were Ayana's children, however the wills differed in the amounts each child would receive. Ayana made no provision for her husband in any of the wills.

A few years later, after a falling out with her daughter in Missouri, Ayana decided she was dissatisfied with will #3 and tore it into pieces with the intent of revoking it. She placed the torn will and a note to her children in a sealed envelope and wrote on the back, "OPEN WHEN I'M GONE." After Ayana died, the children found the envelope with the torn will and note. The note said, "I revoked will #3 because it gave too much to my daughter. Will #2 now stands. AND DO NOT GIVE YOUR FATHER A PENNY OF MY PROPERTY!"

The law in effect where Ayana died provides that a previously revoked will is not revived unless re-executed or republished by codicil.[31] Ayana did neither.

Without DRR, Ayana would die intestate because she revoked all three of her wills. And, because Ayana never actually divorced her husband and all of their children belong to each other, her husband is her sole intestate heir. DRR, however, better effectuates Ayana's intent by setting aside her revocation of will #3 because she did so under the mistaken belief that will #2 would be revived. DRR's relief is limited to setting aside the mistaken revocation, which, in this case, Ayana performed on will #3. Thus, even though Ayana preferred the estate plan contained in will #2, probating will #3 is more consistent with Ayana's intent than allowing her estate to be distributed by intestacy to her surviving spouse. DRR would permit the court to admit will #3 to probate, subject to her husband's right to an elective share.

Example 2

Amir executed a valid attested will #1, but a year later, he tore the will in half with the intent of revoking it. He then wrote and signed a valid holographic will #2 in New Jersey, which permits holographic wills. Subsequently, Amir retired to Florida, where he died without having executed any other wills or codicils. Florida does not recognize holographic wills even when executed in a jurisdiction where such wills are valid. Accordingly, will #2 fails because it does not comply with Wills Act formalities and Amir's estate passes by intestacy to his heirs under Florida law. If, however, the Florida probate court were to apply DRR, Amir's revocation of will #1 would be considered ineffective because it was based on his belief that will #2 would be given effect. Thus, a court would apply DRR unless an intestate distribution would more closely carry out Amir's probable intent.

Example 3

Makeda Skibba validly executed an attested will with the following provision:

> ARTICLE II.
>
> A. I give my only brother Alexander $500.
>
> B. I give my first cousin Semer $400.
>
> C. I give my first cousin Retta $400.

---

31. We discuss the revival of revoked wills in the next section of this chapter.

Makeda kept the will in her desk drawer and told her brother Alexander to find it there if anything happened to her. Following Makeda's death, Alexander found the will, however, Article II contained the following handwritten modifications:

ARTICLE II.

A. I give my only brother Alexander ~~$500~~. *$650 because I love him so much. Signed: Makeda*

B. I give my first cousin Semer ~~$400~~. *$500 because of her sister's death. Signed: Makeda*

C. I give my first cousin Retta ~~$400~~. *NOTHING because she died too young! Signed: Makeda*

Some months earlier, Makeda's aunt told her that Retta had died. The aunt, however, was mistaken. Retta had secretly eloped with a boyfriend without telling anyone and was still alive.

The jurisdiction where Makeda was domiciled at her death permits partial revocation by physical act and holographic wills. The original legacies to Alexander, Semer, and Retta are all revoked because they were cancelled by hand and, because the will was in Makeda's possession, she is presumed to have made the cancellations. Alexander and Semer will likely receive the handwritten amounts because Makeda signed those changes and the jurisdiction permits holographic codicils. But what happens to the revoked gift of $400 to Retta?

Without the doctrine of DRR, Retta would receive nothing because the jurisdiction permits partial revocation by physical act. Application of DRR, however, would allow the cancellation to be set aside because it was expressly predicated on Makeda's false belief that Retta had died. DRR applies only if setting aside the revocation would more closely approximate the testator's intent. Thus, if evidence were presented that Makeda would never have forgiven Retta for running away, that evidence might rebut the DRR presumption, meaning that Retta would receive nothing.

4.3 REVIVAL OF REVOKED WILLS

Testators who make and revoke multiple wills must clearly and expressly identify the document intended to govern at death. This identification is often accomplished on the face of the will itself by titling the instrument "Last Will and Testament," and by reciting the standard opening declaration: "I [Name] do hereby make, publish, and declare this document to be my last will and testament and I hereby revoke all prior wills and codicils heretofore made by me." Given the ubiquity of "Last Will and Testament," identifying what is truly the "last" one (on occasion, a task that differs from determining which among a series of wills should be offered for probate) is not always simple. Why lawyers continue to use "Last Will and Testament" most likely results from habit, tradition, and client expectation. Those reasons, however, are insufficient to continue to identify a testator's multiple wills with the phrase, as the excerpt below explains.

Using the Language of the Law

David Mellinkoff
331-33 (2004 reprint)

LAST WILL AND TESTAMENT

[W]hich *last will* is the *last will*? Calling it the *last will* does not make it so. These words do not of themselves revoke an earlier will, but — like it or not — they do give room for an argument that that was the intention. When a testator has been made will-conscious, and likes the habit, *last will* adds spice to a will contest. For example: will No. 1 revoked by will No. 2; a later ". . . codicil to my last will" held to refer to No. 1, reviving it and revoking No. 2. The testator was talking about his first, not his second, when he said his *last will.*

Trying to remember just what it was you called a *last will* is no easier for lawyers than for laymen. Thus subdivision No. 1 of a statute speaks of a *last will in writing* to "dispose of his estate" and a later added subdivision No. 2 speaks of only a *will* to dispose of the testator's body. Does the *last* make a difference?

Last will and testament is redundant, confusing, and usually inaccurate. The first American professor of law came closer to ordinary experience when he wrote of ". . . my testament, probably the last."

But what happens when a will that revokes a prior will is itself revoked? Consider the following example:

1970: Clara executes a will devising her entire estate to her sister.

1975: Clara has a child and executes a new will devising her entire estate to her child.

1980: Clara's child dies. Clara revokes her 1975 will by physical act.

Does Clara's revocation of the 1975 will *revive* her 1970 will?

Under the UPC, the answer depends on (1) whether the 1975 will revoked the 1970 will in whole or in part, and (2) whether it is evident from the circumstances of revocation that the testator intended revival.

UPC §2-509 provides for the revival of a previous will revoked by physical act (subsections (a) and (b)) and revival of a previous will revoked by subsequent will (subsection (c)):

Uniform Probate Code
§2-509 Revival of Revoked Will

(a) If a subsequent will that wholly revoked a previous will is thereafter revoked by a revocatory act under Section 2-507(a)(2), the previous will remains revoked unless it is revived. The previous will is revived if it is evident from the circumstances of the revocation of the subsequent will or from the testator's contemporary or subsequent declarations that the testator intended the previous will to take effect as executed.

(b) If a subsequent will that partly revoked a previous will is thereafter revoked by a revocatory act under Section 2-507(a)(2), a revoked part of the previous will is revived unless it is evident from the circumstances of the revocation of the subsequent will or from the testator's contemporary or subsequent declarations that the testator did not intend the revoked part to take effect as executed.

(c) If a subsequent will that revoked a previous will in whole or in part is thereafter revoked by another, later will, the previous will remains revoked in whole or in part, unless it or its revoked part is revived. The previous will or its revoked part is revived to the extent it appears from the terms of the later will that the testator intended the previous will to take effect.

PROBLEM XI

In 1990, Dara executed a will devising her entire estate to Charity ABC. In 2003, Dara married Chet and executed a new will devising her entire estate to Chet. In 2013, Dara and Chet divorced. After the divorce, Dara emailed her attorney and explained that she wanted to execute a new will leaving her entire estate to Charity ABC, the sole beneficiary of her 1990 will. Dara died shortly after sending the email to her attorney.

A. Was Dara's 2003 will revoked in whole or in part upon her 2013 divorce from Chet?
B. In a jurisdiction that has adopted UPC §2-509, is Dara's 1990 will revived?

4.4 CONTRACTS CONCERNING TESTAMENTARY SUCCESSION

Contracts concerning testamentary succession involve a decedent's promise to make a will, not revoke a will, or die intestate. The enforceability and interpretation of contracts concerning succession are generally governed by the law of contracts, but the formation of such agreements is subject to formality requirements under the law of wills. The UPC, for example, requires that contracts concerning succession be in writing and signed by the decedent. When a person makes an enforceable promise concerning her estate and dies without having implemented the promised estate plan, the injured promisee may be entitled to damages from the promisor's estate or, in the absence of a written contract, equitable relief in the form of a constructive trust[32] or quantum meruit.

Uniform Probate Code
§2-514 Contracts Concerning Succession

A contract to make a will or devise, or not to revoke a will or devise, or to die intestate, if executed after the effective date of this [article], may be established

32. For discussion of constructive trusts, see Chapter 9.

only by (i) provisions of a will stating material provisions of the contract, (ii) an express reference in a will to a contract and extrinsic evidence proving the terms of the contract, or (iii) a writing signed by the decedent evidencing the contract. The execution of a joint will or mutual wills does not create a presumption of a contract not to revoke the will or wills.

Contracts concerning succession often arise in the context of personal services performed for the decedent in exchange for the decedent's promise to make a devise at death rather than payment at the time of performance. The common case of this involves a caregiver's promise to provide lifetime care for the testator in exchange for a testamentary gift. If the caregiver performs, but the testator fails to include the promised bequest, the caregiver will sue the testator's estate for breach of contract. When the caregiver is a member of the testator's family, some courts refuse to enforce the contract on grounds that the agreement lacked consideration; however, scholars have criticized this exception because it tends to discourage the provision of end of life care. See Thomas Gallanis & Josephine Gittler, Family Caregiving and the Law of Succession: A Proposal, 45 U. Mich. J.L. Reform 761 (2012); Joshua C. Tate, Caregiving and the Case for Testamentary Freedom, 42 U.C. Davis L. Rev. 129 (2008).

In other contexts, contracts concerning succession may be motivated by tax objectives. Consider the following illustration: An elderly testator desires to purchase real property from his friend but lacks sufficient cash on hand to pay the purchase price. The bulk of the testator's wealth consists of a large portfolio of securities acquired decades ago and the testator would prefer not to liquidate the securities now because a sale would realize significant taxable capital gains on the portfolio's appreciation in value. If, however, the testator were to retain the portfolio until death, his estate would be entitled to a stepped-up tax basis equal to the portfolio's date-of-death value, thereby allowing the unrealized capital gains to escape income taxation. 26 U.S.C. §1014. Suppose the testator asks his friend if he would accept consideration for the property in the form of a promise to execute a will devising the securities portfolio to his friend. The favorable tax treatment from the stepped-up basis would place the inherited portfolio's value roughly at par with the friend's asking price for the property. If the friend accepts the offer and conveys title to the testator, but the testator dies without having executed the promised devise, the friend would be entitled to damages or equitable relief arising from the testator's breach of promise.

Implied contracts concerning succession have generated a fair amount of litigation in the context of reciprocal wills. Married couples often execute reciprocal wills naming each as the other's primary beneficiary and their children as contingent beneficiaries. This estate plan structure, however, fails to anticipate the possibility of remarriage by the surviving spouse following the death of the first spouse. Upon remarriage, may the surviving spouse execute a new will in favor of the new spouse? The new will, in effect, may channel the deceased spouse's estate to the surviving spouse's new partner rather than the deceased's spouse's children. Do reciprocal arrangements between the initial spouses imply the existence of an agreement not to revoke? Under UPC §2-514 and in most jurisdictions, the execution of reciprocal wills does not imply a contract not to revoke. Instead, there must be a provision manifesting agreement not to revoke in the will itself or in an external writing signed by the decedent.

5 | Wills: Components and Provisions

5.1 INTRODUCTION

This chapter looks at the contents of wills. It begins by examining three closely related topics: integration (which defines the physical contours of the will); incorporation by reference (which lets testators weave existing, extrinsic documents into their instruments); and the personal property memorandum (a flexible device allowing testators to dispose of tangible personal property). It then explains how testators use particular provisions to distribute their property, delegate this task to someone else through a power of appointment, nominate an executor, deter litigation, dispose of their corporeal remains, name guardians for their minor children, and specify who should bear responsibility for their debts.

5.2 COMPONENTS OF WILLS

5.2.1 Integration: Staple Rule

Usually, it is not difficult to determine the physical "four corners" of a testator's will. The pages of an attested will are customarily held together with a staple; some attorneys still tie the pages of a will together with ribbon and sealing wax. However, in unusual cases involving an attested will — and, increasingly more often, holographic wills — a question develops as to which pages constitute the testator's will. The answer in those situations is provided by a fairly straightforward two-prong test: the pages that the *testator intended to be part* of his or her will *and* that were *physically present when the testator executed the will* constitute the testator's will.

Restatement (Third) of Property: Wills & Other Donative Transfers
§3.5 Integration of Multiple Pages or Writings into a Single Will

To be treated as part of a will, a page or other writing must be present when the will is executed and must be intended to be part of the will.

Under the doctrine of integration, the physical connection of the pages of the will (say, by staple) or the internal coherence of the language of the will (for example, sentences running over from one page to the next in a continuum) raises an inference that the connected or internally coherent pages were all present at the time of execution. Extrinsic evidence is admissible to determine whether pages offered for probate as a will were (a) all present at the time of execution and (b) intended to be part of the will.

PROBLEM I

In 2010, Tommy prepared an unsigned six-page document titled "Last Will and Testament." The document recites dispositive provisions on the first five pages. The top of page six reads, "Dated this _____ day of _____, 201_____. I hereby sign my name and declare this document to be my last will and testament," followed by signature lines for the testator and attesting witnesses. Tommy, however, did not date or sign page 6. In 2015, Tommy prepared a new signature page identical to page 6 of the draft will and stapled it to the back of the six-page document with a notation of "p. 7" in the top right corner. On July 19, 2015, Tommy entered the date on page 7 and then executed the new signature page before attesting witnesses who also entered their signatures. Tommy died earlier this year and the executor submits the entire seven-page document for probate. Is this document a valid will? Would the result differ if Tommy and two witnesses signed page 7 in his office at work, but pages 1-6 were on Tommy's desk at home?

5.2.2 Incorporation by Reference

The doctrine of *incorporation by reference* permits a court to give testamentary effect to an extrinsic writing (i.e., an unintegrated writing that is not a physical part of the will) even if the writing was not executed in accordance with applicable Wills Act formalities.

Uniform Probate Code
§2-510 Incorporation by Reference

A writing in existence when a will is executed may be incorporated by reference if the language of the will manifests this intent and describes the writing sufficiently to permit its identification.

Three issues arise in incorporation by reference cases. First, the writing must be "in existence" at the time the testator makes her will. If testators execute a will that refers to a memorandum that they intend to create in the *future*, the memorandum cannot be incorporated. Second, the language of the will must signal that the testator wants to incorporate the writing. And third, the will must identify the writing relatively clearly. Courts are not always finicky about the last two prongs (intent to incorporate and describing the writing). They sometimes ignore uncertainty about whether the testator wanted to incorporate a particular document and overlook minor discrepancies between the will's incorporation language and the incorporated document itself.[1]

One potential source of confusion is the fact that incorporation by reference partially overlaps with the doctrine of integration (the "staple rule"), discussed in Section 5.2.1. Integration requires a writing to be physically present when the testator executes the will. When the doctrine applies, the integrated document becomes *part of the will* if the testator so intended. Conversely, incorporation by reference applies even if the referenced document is *not* physically present when the testator executes the will. Moreover, the incorporated document is not actually considered part of the will itself, although its language is effective to, among other matters, distribute the testator's property. Thus, unless the administration is contested or the external document concerns the transfer of real property, the external writing generally need not be offered for probate and does not become a matter of public record.

Gifford v. Gifford
805 S.W.2d 71 (Ark. 1991)

HAYS, Justice.

The question for decision is whether a memorandum in the handwriting of the testatrix was incorporated into her will by reference. The probate judge found that it was. We sustain that finding.

Mary Ella Gifford died on February 26, 1989. Mrs. Gifford's daughter, Julia Gifford Haines, proffered four instruments as the decedent's last will and testament: a two page handwritten note dated January 1980, another handwritten note, also in two pages, dated June 1986; a typewritten will dated July 2, 1986; and a typewritten codicil dated November 21, 1986. The probate judge accepted all four as constituting the last will of Mrs. Gifford. By this appeal, Mrs. Gifford's son, Joel S. Gifford, Jr., challenges only the admission of the January 1980 memorandum.

Appellant [Gifford, Jr., the contestant,] maintains the January 1980 note was not incorporated by reference into his mother's will. . . . [He] argues it was her intent for her estate to be distributed in accordance with the June 1986 note, the will and the codicil.

The incorporating language of the [July 2, 1986 typewritten] will reads as follows:

> Having survived my husband, Joel S. Gifford, Sr., and being mindful of his desires, it is my intention herein to equally divide our properties which passed to me at his death in equal shares to our beloved children.
>
> I first direct my Executrix hereinafter appointed to carry out the provisions of the handwritten bequest, which I have attached hereto and which was prepared by me in June of 1986, relative to items of personal property, which I want each of the children to receive.

1. For instance, in Clark v. Greenhalge, 582 N.E.2d 949, 950 (Mass. 1991), the testator's will tasked her executor with distributing some items as she "designate[d] in a memorandum left by [her] and known [by] the [the executor,] or in accordance with [her] known wishes." The testator then prepared a writing labelled "memorandum" and a separate notebook that disposed of some of her personal property. See *id.* The court held that *both* the "memorandum" and the notebook were incorporated by reference. See *id.* at 953-54.

> Secondly, I give, devise and bequeath all the rest, residue and remainder of my estate, whether real, personal or mixed, to my said children, Julia M. Gifford Haines and Joel S. Gifford, Jr., share and share alike. If either of them, however, shall predecease me, then the share herein devised to them shall go to their children and likewise in equal shares.

The codicil, executed some five months later, has the identical provision except that it contains four specific bequests: $5,000 to Mrs. Gifford's former daughter-in-law, $2,000 to the First United Methodist Church of Rose Bud, $500 to the Baptist Church of Rose Bud and $500 to Ouachita Baptist University.

Ark. Code Ann. §28-25-107 (1987) provides that any writing in existence when a will is executed may be incorporated by reference if the will's language manifests such interest and describes the writing sufficiently to identify it. The writing must either be in the handwriting of the testator or be signed by her and must describe the items and devisees with reasonable certainty.

It is undisputed that the June 1986 writing was incorporated by reference and while the January 1980 note is not specifically identified in the will, it was in existence when the will was executed, and is unmistakeably connected to the 1986 writing. The two writings are physically attached to the will itself and their combined four pages are numbered by page, 1, 2, 3 and 4. Pages 1 and 2 are the 1980 memorandum and pages 3 and 4, the 1986 memorandum. Both deal with various items of personalty, primarily household and personal effects, and are clear and specific as to item and devisee. Moreover, the 1986 writing specifically refers to "earlier lists of 1973, 1976 and 1980," noting that some items might be duplicated on the several lists. The June 1980 note bears the caption, "1st section of bequests 1973, 1976 & 1980," removing any doubt that the 1986 note refers to the January 1980 note. Both notes are entirely in Mrs. Gifford's handwriting and conclude with her signature. That, plus their physical attachment to the will, their pagination and the express allusion of one to the other satisfies us entirely that the probate judge ruled correctly.

. . .

Finding no merit in the points argued for reversal, we affirm the order appealed from.

QUESTIONS

1. Suppose that Mary Ella had not signed the 1980 note. Could it be incorporated by reference under Arkansas law? Under the UPC? Would either result change if she had not signed it *and* it was typewritten, not handwritten?

    ANSWER. Arkansas law is unusual because it requires the incorporated document either to be signed by the testator or in her handwriting. The UPC does not impose either requirement. Thus, if Mary Ella had not signed the 1980 note, it could still be incorporated under Arkansas law because it was handwritten. If she had neither signed it nor written it by hand, it could not be incorporated under Arkansas law, although it could be incorporated under the UPC because "the language of the will manifests this intent and describes the writing sufficiently to permit its identification."

2. Assume that Mary Ella had written and signed the note not in 1980, but on November 22, 1986. Could it be incorporated under either Arkansas law or the UPC? How would the result change if she had written and signed the note on November 20, 1986?

   ANSWER. Under both Arkansas law and the UPC, a document must be in existence to be incorporated by reference. If Mary Ella had written and signed the note on November 22, 1986, it would post-date all of her wills and codicils, and thus not be in existence on November 21, 1986, when she executed her last testamentary instrument (the codicil). She could not incorporate it. However, if she had written and signed the note on November 20, 1986, it would have been created after her July 2, 1986 will but before her November 21, 1986 codicil. Recall from Chapter 4, under the doctrine of republication by codicil, a prior will is treated as re-executed on the date of its most recent codicil if (and only if) such treatment would be consistent with the testator's intent. Because the November 21st codicil would have republished the July 2nd will referencing the November 20th note, the note, although created after the will, would then be deemed in existence when the will was executed and validly incorporated.

3. Could the court have ruled that the 1980 note was integrated with the 1986 will?

   ANSWER. Maybe. Although the opinion is not crystal clear, it appears that the note was physically attached to the will, present at the time of execution, and intended to be part of the will. Thus, it seems to meet the requirements of the integration doctrine as well as incorporation by reference.

PROBLEM II

Owen Smith had been married for three decades to his high school sweetheart, Kristin. They had one child together named Robin. One of Owen's most prized possessions was a rare stamp that bears an inverted picture of former President Richard Nixon.

Owen died in 2012. In his desk drawer are two sheets of paper. The first one, which is entirely typewritten, but not signed by Owen or any witnesses, reads: "I LEAVE MY INVERTED RICHARD NIXON STAMP TO MY DAUGHTER, ROBIN. DATED: MAY 1, 2009." The second is entirely handwritten (and also not signed by witnesses), and reads: "I want my wife, Kristin, to have everything (other than my

Richard Nixon stamp, for which I have other plans) after I die. Signed: Owen Smith. Dated: Oct. 1, 2010."

What result in a jurisdiction that recognizes holographic wills but does not recognize the curative doctrine of harmless error (UPC §2-503)?

5.2.3 Lists of Tangible Personal Property

Among the many challenges testators confront when preparing a will, one of the more difficult is deciding what to do with their *things*. Whether an individual possesses famous artwork or lavish jewels or items that merely have enormous sentimental value, it is often difficult to make decisions about who should get what. Moreover, people fear that once a decision is memorialized in a will, changes may be time-consuming and expensive, requiring visits to the attorney and the execution of new wills or codicils.

To simplify this process, UPC §2-513 gives testators the flexibility to dispose of tangible personal property through an unattested "separate writing." Critically, unlike the doctrine of incorporation by reference, the separate writing rule does *not* require a document to be in existence at the time the testators execute their wills. This innovation allows testators to execute a will referencing an external writing, which then may be created or revised later without amending the will. UPC §2-513 limits this opportunity to the disposition of tangible personal property *other than money*.

Uniform Probate Code
§2-513 Separate Writing Identifying Devise of Certain Types of Tangible Personal Property

Whether or not the provisions relating to holographic wills apply, a will may refer to a written statement or list to dispose of items of tangible personal property not otherwise specifically disposed of by the will, other than money. To be admissible under this section as evidence of the intended disposition, the writing must be signed by the testator and must describe the items and the devisees with reasonable certainty. The writing may be referred to as one to be in existence at the time of the testator's death; it may be prepared before or after the execution of the will; it may be altered by the testator after its preparation; and it may be a writing that has no significance apart from its effect on the dispositions made by the will.

One way to think of the separate writing rule is to view it as an exception to the acts of independent significance doctrine, which we discussed in Chapter 4. Writing a list of who gets your things when you die is a classic example of an act *without* independent significance apart from the list's effect on the testator's estate. Yet the separate writing rule carves out an exception for testators to make testamentary dispositions without complying with Wills Act formalities.

How do testators express their intent to invoke this mechanism? The comment to UPC §2-513 provides this sample language for insertion into a will:

> I might leave a written statement or list disposing of items of tangible personal property. If I do and if my written statement or list is found and is identified as such by my Personal Representative no later than 30 days after the probate of this will, then my written statement or list is to be given effect to the extent authorized by law. . . .

In re Last Will and Testament and Trust Agreement of Moor 879 A.2d 648 (Del. Ch. 2005)

STRINE, Vice Chancellor.

In this opinion, I conclude that a testator is not forbidden by Delaware or Florida law from directing, in a personal property memorandum referenced in a valid will, that certain personal property be sold by her executors and that the sale proceeds be given to specific persons.

. . .

I. FACTUAL BACKGROUND

Betty R. Moor ("Mrs. Moor") died on April 5, 2002, when she was a resident of Rehoboth Beach, Delaware. Mrs. Moor had executed a will (the "Will") on February 4, 1998 in Fort Lauderdale, Florida, where she resided at that time. The Will named Jerome A. Bauman and April Hudson as Mrs. Moor's executors. The second article of the Will provides for the attachment of a written statement disposing of tangible personal property. . . .

In 2000, Mrs. Moor moved from Fort Lauderdale to Rehoboth Beach, Delaware. . . . On March 9, 2001, Mrs. Moor executed a personal property memorandum (the "Property Memo") that, as described in the second article of her Will, made several specific bequests of personal property to specific persons. . . .

II. THIS DISPUTE: IS THE "CAPITAL GAIN CLAUSE" OF MRS. MOOR'S PROPERTY MEMO EFFECTIVE?

The penultimate clause of Mrs. Moor's Property Memo is the source of the current dispute. That clause provides the following instruction: "Any items not listed in this WILL are to be auctioned, the capitol gain [sic] from the auction is to be dispersed to those stated in the aforesaid document." I will refer to that provision of the Property Memo as the "Capital Gain Clause" for ease of reference. The Property Memo was signed by Mrs. Moor and notarized by a single witness. In accordance with the Property Memo, eighteen items are to be distributed to five persons.

. . .

III. UNDER EITHER DELAWARE OR FLORIDA LAW, THE CAPITAL GAIN CLAUSE IS EFFECTIVE

. . .

I agree with the parties that there appears to be no material difference between the Delaware and Florida statutes bearing on this issue, and therefore, no definitive choice of law needs to be made. Both states require that, in order to be valid, a will must be signed by two witnesses. Both states also permit bequests of tangible personal property in a separate writing 1) if the separate writing is referred to in the will, and 2) if, as here, the separate writing is signed by the testator.

The types of disposition that may permissibly be made by separate writing are limited under 12 Del. C. §212, which states in part that: "A will may refer to a written statement or list to dispose of items of tangible personal property not otherwise specifically disposed of by the will, other than money, evidences of indebtedness, documents of title, and securities, and property used in trade or business." The analogous Florida statute, Fla. Stat. §732.515, is substantially similar, stating in part that: "A written statement or list referred to in the decedent's will shall dispose of items of tangible personal property, other than property used in trade or business, not otherwise specifically disposed of by the will."

The executors argue that the Capital Gain Clause of Mrs. Moor's Property Memo exceeds the scope of these statutes by attempting to devise money gained from the sale of personal property, rather than the personal property itself. Both Delaware and Florida law, they say, forbid the use of a separate writing to dispose of intangible property, like cash[2] and securities. Therefore, because the Property Memo was not executed in compliance with the requisite formalities applicable to the execution of wills — that is, because the Property Memo was signed by one witness instead of two — the Capital Gain Clause is void. I am not persuaded by this argument, for the following reasons.

Initially and most importantly, the executors' argument would read into the statutory text words of restriction that were not included by the relevant legislatures, contrary to the law of statutory construction in both Delaware and Florida. Both the Delaware and Florida statutes use the broad term "dispose of" in reference to the power that a testator might exercise in a personal property memorandum. The executors contend that this capacious phrase can only be read as meaning "to devise directly to" rather than "to sell and distribute the sale proceeds to." But the term "dispose of" has been employed by the legislatures of both Delaware and Florida in other contexts to refer to an elastic range of activities. Accordingly, I find no basis for interpreting the words of the pertinent statutes here in the cramped manner that the executors advocate. Under a literal reading of those statutes, Mrs. Moor "disposed of" her personal property by directing her executors to sell that property and distribute the proceeds to specific persons. Importantly, there is no contention that Mrs. Moor attempted, through the Capital Gain Clause, to devise by her Property Memo a species of property — intangible property — that Delaware or Florida law explicitly preclude from being devised through a separate writing. All of the property covered by the Capital Gain Clause was tangible, identified by the executors, and has, in fact, already been sold by them, generating a substantial amount of cash.

The executors seek to convince me that a more restricted definition of the term "dispose of" should be read into §212 because the relevant Delaware [and Florida] statute[s] explicitly [prohibit] a testator from disposing of money via a separate writing. Under both Delaware and Florida law, the executors say, testators must use the body of their wills to distribute intangible property, particularly pure financial assets like cash, negotiable instruments, and securities. . . .

---

2. [UPC §2-513 also precludes the use of an unattested writing to dispose of property "other than money." — Eds.]

The point of both the Delaware and Florida statutes is to provide testators with a more flexible means by which to devise their [tangible] personal property. That legislative intention was accomplished, as are most public policy judgments, by a compromise between competing values. The more rigorous formalities required of the body of a will itself were relaxed, permitting a testator to dispose of personal property by a simple, unwitnessed writing that becomes an annex to the will. By that tradeoff, both legislatures made the judgment that the flexibility and convenience of this method were, on balance, worth the enhanced possibility that such a writing might not reflect the uncoerced, free will of the testator.

There is, of course, risk in this sort of tradeoff. One can easily imagine persons who possess items of personal property — works of art, period piece furniture, sports memorabilia — that are more valuable than their cash and securities. Because a personal property memorandum may be executed without the procedural protections of a will, there is an increased chance that such a memorandum might be induced by designing persons. Under both the Delaware and Florida statutes at issue, the public policy judgment is that this increased chance is worth taking. . . .

With this public policy judgment having been made, I fail to see what purpose is served by acceding to the executors' demand to engraft a restriction on the term "dispose of" that does not arise naturally from the statutory text. To do so would do nothing to better protect testators from undue influence.

The executors concede that a testator may convey an expensive painting directly in a separate writing, thereby giving the recipient ownership and the right to sell the painting for cash profit. As a result, it is difficult to conceive of what public policy offense occurs if the testator instead directs her executors to sell the painting and to convey the sale proceeds to certain persons. In either case, the economic incentives for designing persons, and the corresponding economic risk to the testator and other possible objects of her testamentary good wishes, remain the same.

. . .

IV. CONCLUSION

For the foregoing reasons, the executors shall convey the net proceeds of the sale of the personal property covered by the Capital Gain Clause to the five individuals referred to in Mrs. Moor's Property Memo, with each beneficiary receiving 20 percent of the total. . . .

QUESTIONS

4. Under the UPC, does it matter that Betty's "Property Memo" does not actually contain a list of any specific property?

   ANSWER. No. The UPC does not require a list of items — it permits a "written statement . . . to dispose of items of tangible personal property not otherwise specifically disposed of by the will."

5. Suppose on March 10, 2001, Betty added a clause to her Property Memo giving her baby grand piano to her nephew Ralph. Would that clause be valid?

    ANSWER. Yes. Testators can change their separate writings after they make them. As UPC §2-513 states, the writing can be "altered by the testator after its preparation" and "may be prepared before or after the execution of the will."

6. What if Betty had tried to transmit stock certificates through a separate writing? Would the result depend on whether the UPC, Delaware, or Florida law applied?

    ANSWER. Delaware expressly excludes securities, so Betty could not have used a separate writing to transfer her stock certificates. Under the UPC and Florida law, the issue is whether stock certificates are tangible personal property. The answer is probably No. Tangible personal property is "personal property that can be seen, weighed, measured, felt, or touched, or is in any other way perceptible to the senses, such as furniture, cooking utensils, and books." Black's Law Dictionary 1254 (8th ed. 2004). Nevertheless, "[a]lthough stock certificates might fall within the literal definition of tangible personal property, they are generally regarded as intangible property because their value is derived from the intangible rights they represent." Steen & Berg Co. v. Berg, 713 N.W.2d 87, 91 (N.D. 2006).

7. Is cash tangible or intangible personal property? What distinction, if any, is there between cash and a stock certificate?

    ANSWER. Cash is typically classified as intangible personal property. See, e.g., CAL. COM. CODE §9102(42) (West) ("'General intangible' means any personal property, including things in action, other than accounts, chattel paper, commercial tort claims, deposit accounts, documents, goods, instruments, investment property, letter-of-credit rights, letters of credit, money, and oil, gas, or other minerals before extraction."). For purposes of validating an unattested separate writing under the Wills Act, cash is therefore functionally indistinguishable from a stock certificate.

PROBLEM III

Shelly owns an antique silver ring. Shelly's valid will, dated February 24, 2016, leaves the ring "in accordance with a writing that will be found in the small pocket of my backpack, which is in a closet in my attic." After Shelly dies, a handwritten note is found exactly where Shelly described. It states: "After I die, I leave my silver ring to Adam," and is signed and dated February 26, 2016. Which of the following arguments would allow Adam to take the ring and why? (i) That the will incorporated the note by reference; (ii) That the note is a codicil (assuming that Shelly lives in a state that recognizes holographic wills); (iii) That the note is an act of independent significance; (iv) That the note is a separate writing passing tangible personal property.

5.3 DISPOSITIVE PROVISIONS

This section examines *dispositive* provisions, which contain a devise that disposes of property from the testator's probate estate. Our discussion of dispositive provisions begins with the *classification of devises*, followed by *powers of appointment*, in which donors delegate ultimate selection of beneficiaries and timing of a gift to a third party.

5.3.1 Classification of Devises

Wills may use four kinds of devises. First, they may make *specific devises*: dispositions of particular pieces of property. Examples include "I leave my house to my wife," "I leave my used television to my friend Bob," and "I leave my bank account to my son, Ernesto." Second, they may use *general devises* to make gifts of cash, such as "$10,000 to my former Trusts and Estates professor." Third, they may create *demonstrative devises*. These are payments of specified amounts of money to be paid from a specified source (e.g., "I leave $10,000 to my former Trusts and Estates professor to be paid from the sale of my diamond collection"). Finally, they should always include a *residuary devise*: safety nets that sweep up all property that the testator has not effectively disposed of elsewhere in her will. Residuary devises take one of two forms. Some come at the end of a list of specific, general, or demonstrative devises, and say: "All the rest, residue, and remainder of my estate, I leave to. . . ." Alternatively, residuary devises can take the form of simple wills that divide the testator's entire estate among designated beneficiaries, such as "I leave everything I own to Ismael and Irene," or "I leave my entire estate to my spouse."

We mention these concepts here merely to introduce them. We will revisit them in Chapter 6. As we will see then, the classification of bequests matters for a broad range of doctrines, such as ademption by extinction, abatement, and the "no residue of a residue rule."

Aldrich v. Basile
136 So. 3d 530 (Fla. 2014)

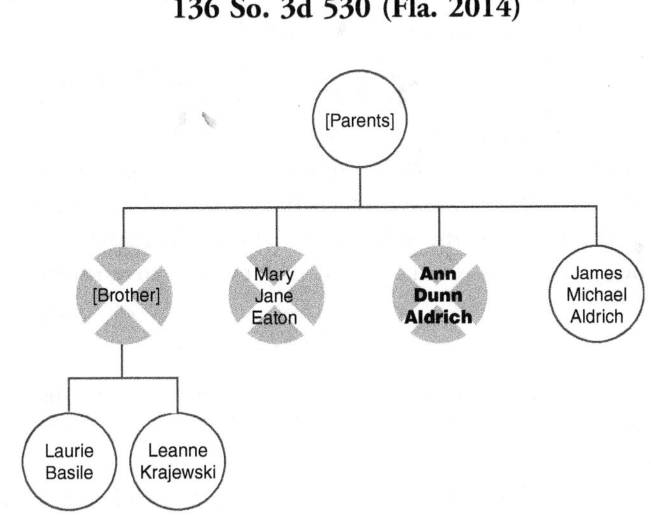

QUINCE, J.

. . .

FACTS AND PROCEDURAL HISTORY

On April 5, 2004, Ms. [Ann Dunn] Aldrich wrote her will on an "E-Z Legal Form." In Article III, entitled "Bequests," just after the form's pre-printed language "direct[ing] that after payment of all my just debts, my property be bequeathed in the manner following," she hand wrote instructions directing that all of the following "possessions listed" go to her sister, Mary Jane Eaton:

—House, contents, lot at 150 SW Garden Street, Keystone Heights FL 32656
—Fidelity Rollover IRA 162-583405 (800-544-6565)
—United Defense Life Insurance (800-247-2196)
—Automobile Chevy Tracker, 2CNBE 13c916952909
—All bank accounts at M & S Bank 2226448, 264679, 0900020314 (352-473-7275).

Ann also wrote: "If Mary Jane Eaton dies before I do, I leave all listed to James Michael Aldrich, 2250 S. Palmetto 114 S Daytona FL 32119." Containing no other distributive provisions, the will was duly signed and witnessed.

Three years later, Ms. Eaton did die before Ann, becoming her benefactor instead of her beneficiary. Ms. Eaton left cash and land in Putnam County to Ms. Aldrich, who deposited the cash she inherited from Ms. Eaton in an account she opened for the purpose with Fidelity Investments. On October 9, 2009, Ann Dunn Aldrich herself passed away, never having revised her will to dispose of the inheritance she had received from her sister.

After being appointed as personal representative of Ms. Aldrich's estate, Mr. Aldrich [Ms. Aldrich's brother] sought to have a court determine who would inherit the property that Ms. Aldrich acquired after the execution of her will. Laurie Basile and Leanne Krajewski, Ms. Aldrich's nieces from a predeceased brother, asserted an interest in the probate action. Mr. Aldrich initiated an adversary proceeding in the probate case and argued that the most reasonable and appropriate construction of the will was that Ms. Aldrich intended for her entire estate, including what she had acquired from her sister, to pass to him. . . .

The nieces argued that . . . in the absence of a residuary clause, Ms. Aldrich's will contained no mechanism to dispose of the after-acquired property or any other property not mentioned in the will, so that she died intestate as to the Putnam County property and the cash in the non-IRA Fidelity Investments account. . . .

ANALYSIS

The events that led to this case were based on the following timeline: Ann Aldrich executed her will on April 12, 2004. Ms. Aldrich's sister, Ms. Eaton, died on November 10, 2007. Administration of Ms. Eaton's estate was concluded and an Order of Discharge was entered on July 23, 2008, leaving Ann Aldrich personal and real property. Two days later, Ann Aldrich opened an investment account to deposit the inherited money. Evidence in the record suggests that, later that year, Ms. Aldrich attempted to draft a codicil to her original will. Along with the original will was a piece of paper bearing the printed title "Just a Note" and dated November 18, 2008, below Ms. Aldrich's handwriting and signature. The handwritten note read as follows:

> This is an addendum to my will dated April 5, 2004. Since my sister Mary jean [sic] Eaton has passed away, I reiterate that all my worldly possessions pass to my brother James Michael Aldrich, 2250 S. Palmetto, S. Daytona FL 32119.
>
> With her agreement I name Sheila Aldrich Schuh, my niece, as my personal representative, and have assigned certain bank accounts to her to be transferred on my death for her use as she seems [sic] fit.

Although Ms. Aldrich signed the "addendum," the signature of Sheila Schuh, Mr. Aldrich's daughter, was the only other signature that appeared on the face of the document; therefore, the document was not an enforceable testamentary instrument under the Florida Probate Code.[3] In October 2009, Ann Aldrich passed away.

Mr. Aldrich essentially argues that the testator's intent to dispose of her entire estate should lead this Court to construe her will as devising all of her property to the sole heir [sic] in the will, including the property not mentioned in the will. The testator's nieces argue that the property that the testator acquired after the execution of the will should pass through intestacy, since the testator did not mention the property in the will and, therefore, had no clear intention as to the property. A similar view is expressed in an amicus brief filed by the Real Property Probate and Trust Law Section of The Florida Bar, which found no general bequest in the will that would indicate the testator's intent for the after-acquired property to pass under the will.

The legislative history of Florida law regarding wills and after-acquired property supports th[is] conclusion. . . . Prior to June 13, 1892, a will was ineffective to devise real property in Florida that the testator had no interest in at the time the will was executed. Upon the effectuation of the Revised Statutes of 1892, any will containing a residuary clause has been effective to transfer property acquired after the execution of the will, if the testator has an interest in the property at the time of death, unless the testator expressly states in the will that such is not his or her intention.

It has been well established that "in construing a will the intention of the testator is the controlling factor and it should be gleaned from the four corners of the will unless the language employed by the testator is ambiguous, in which case the testimony of competent witnesses may be received and considered as an aid to the court in its quest for the testator's intent." Adams v. Vidal, 60 So. 2d 545, 547 (Fla. 1952). The testator's intention as expressed in the will controls, not that which she may have had in her mind.

---

3. [Florida law does not recognize any form of holographic wills. See, e.g., Malleiro v. Mori, 182 So. 3d 5, 8 (Fla. Dist. Ct. App. 2015). — Eds.]

It is clear from the language of Ms. Aldrich's will that she intended to leave all of the property listed to her brother, Mr. Aldrich, in the event her sister, Ms. Eaton, predeceased her. Ms. Aldrich expressed no intent as to any property that she may have acquired after the execution of her will, as the document did not include a residuary clause, nor did it include any general bequests that could encompass the inherited property. Mr. Aldrich is asking this Court to infer from the four corners of the will that the testator intended to devise all of her property to the sole person mentioned in the will, including the inherited property which was not mentioned in the will, based on the assertion that the testator did not intend to die intestate as to any of her property. This conclusion is simply not supported by the four corners of the document.

Ms. Aldrich's will states that she intended for all of the property that she listed to pass to her brother. Although it was not disputed that the property listed in the will was substantially all, if not completely all, of the property owned by the decedent at the time she executed the will, Ms. Aldrich did not explicitly state that her identified beneficiaries were to receive all of the property that she owned at her death, only the property that she listed in her will. If Ms. Aldrich did in fact intend to devise all of the property she owned at death to her named devisee, her intent would have been better served through the use of a residuary clause or general devises of personal and real property in the will.

The testator had nearly two years to decide how the after-acquired property would be distributed. She inherited approximately $122,000 in cash, which she deposited into an account she opened with Fidelity Investments days after she received it. At the time of her death, the investment account containing the after-acquired money had an approximate balance of $87,000. The decedent did not "effectively dispose of" the Fidelity Investments account as she had done with the accounts listed in the will. It is possible that in the years that passed between executing the first will and receiving the inheritance from Ms. Eaton, that Ms. Aldrich's testamentary intent may have changed and that she became less eager to disinherit any additional heirs. Or, perhaps, Ms. Aldrich intended to sell the land and spend or gift all the inherited money during her lifetime, leaving none of this money to be disposed of by will. If Ms. Aldrich intended for the inherited money to pass to her named beneficiaries through the will, she could have simply deposited said money into one of the already-existing accounts that were expressly disposed of in her will. Instead, she chose to deposit the after-acquired money into a new investment account, which would seem to indicate that she intended for that property to be separate from the money that she had already mentioned in her will.

. . .

QUESTIONS

8. How would you classify each of the devises in Ann's will?

ANSWER. These are all specific devises: gifts of particular items of property.

9. Would the result have been different if Ann had used a residuary devise? Why do you think she did not include one?

ANSWER. The result would have been different because a residuary devise transmits all property not mentioned in the will to a particular beneficiary. As the opinion notes, a residuary devise would have transmitted Ann's after-acquired property and any property she owned when she executed her will but did not specifically devise in the will. Ann probably did not include one because she filled out a form will without the advice of an attorney.

10. In reaching its decision, the court fails to consider the November 18, 2008, document other than to observe that it fails as a valid testamentary instrument under Florida law. What do you think Ann intended to happen to her estate?

ANSWER. Ann probably intended to transmit the inherited property to her brother rather than to her intestate heirs. The addendum note, signed and notarized less than a year before Ann's death, states, "Since my sister Mary jean [sic] Eaton has passed away, I reiterate that all my worldly possessions pass to my brother James Michael Aldrich."

11. What would the result have been in a state that follows the UPC's harmless error rule?

ANSWER. Under the harmless error rule, Ann's handwritten and signed "addendum" would likely have been treated as a valid holographic codicil. James would inherit all of Ann's estate.

5.3.2 Powers of Appointment: General and Special

Powers of appointment are a valuable estate planning tool often used in wills and other types of donative transfers (particularly trusts). When individuals create a power of appointment, they give a third party the right to decide how to distribute property governed by the power. The third party can usually exercise this right either in his own will, or by executing a deed during his lifetime.

By delegating to a trusted person with good judgment the selection of beneficiaries and the decision of when to make a distribution, donors can use powers of appointment to build flexibility into their dispositions. The person who holds the power can make an informed choice about how to transmit the testator's (or settlor's) wealth after the testator or settlor dies. Powers of appointment can also provide useful techniques for tax planning and asset protection purposes.

Restatement (Third) of Property: Wills & Other Donative Transfers
§17.1 Power of Appointment Defined

A power of appointment is a power that enables the donee of the power to designate recipients of beneficial ownership interests in or powers of appointment over the appointive property.

5.3.2.1 Definitions

Powers of appointment have their own idiosyncratic vocabulary. The individual who creates the power, whether by will, trust, deed, or other conveyance, is the "donor." The "donee" is the individual who holds the power and has the ability to appoint the property subject to the power (the "appointive property"). The "appointee" is the person who receives the appointed property. The "permissible appointees" or "objects" are the people to whom the donor has authorized the donee to appoint the appointive property. And the "takers in default" receive the appointive property if the donee does not exercise the power or fails to exercise it correctly. Sometimes the donor will expressly name takers in default. ("I leave my house to my husband for life, then to such of my sisters as he shall appoint by will, and in default of appointment, to my nephew, Hank.") If the donor does not name takers in default, the appointive property reverts to the donor's estate, often passing through intestacy.[4]

Powers of appointment can be either general or special. This distinction allows the donor to restrict the identity of the permissible appointees. A *general power* is "exercisable in favor of the donee, the donee's estate, or the creditors of either, regardless of whether the power is also exercisable in favor of others." Restatement (Third) of Property: Wills & Other Donative Transfers §17.3. That is, the hallmark of a general power is that the appointive property *basically belongs to the donee*. If the donee wants to keep the appointive property, the donee can appoint it to him- or herself. In addition, the donee can appoint it to other people or entities that are the functional equivalent of the donee: the donee's creditors (who otherwise would have a valid claim on the donee); the donee's estate (where it will be distributed as if it always belonged to the donee); or the creditors of the donee's estate (which will increase the value of the donee's net estate). If the permissible appointees include *either* the donee *or any one* of those donee-substitutes, then the power is general *even if there are other permissible appointees*. Because the donee of a general power of appointment is, in effect, the owner of the appointive property, the donee is generally treated as the owner for purposes of tax and creditor claim liability.

For example, suppose Carol's will states: "I give my house to my brother, Greg, for life, and then to such individuals as Greg shall appoint by will." The clause following Greg's life estate creates a testamentary general power of appointment: The power is testamentary because Greg can exercise it only by an express provision of his will. The power is general because Greg can appoint the house (the appointive property) to his own estate. Greg will be taxed on income generated by the house during life and, at his death, the value of the house will be included in his gross estate for purposes of the estate tax.

Conversely, in a *special power* (sometimes called a *nongeneral power*), the donee is a custodian who has the mere ability to determine who gets the appointive property and in what proportions. The donor may identify, restrict, or define a class of permissible appointees. The donee of a special power cannot appoint the assets to him- or herself

4. There is one exception: If the power is general, and the donee makes an ineffective appointment, a court still may find that the donee intended the appointive property to pass through the *donee's* estate (rather than revert to the donor or the donor's estate). The donee's ineffective exercise of the power reflects the donee's intent to assume control over the appointed property, so the "capture doctrine" treats the donee as having made an implied appointment to her own estate. See Restatement (Third) of Property: Wills & Other Donative Transfers §19.21 (2011).

(or his or her creditors, or his or her estate, or the creditors of his or her estate). Thus, broadly defined, a special power is any power that is not a general power. The donee of a special power of appointment is not the effective owner of the appointive property and is usually not treated as its owner for purposes of tax and creditor claim liability.

For example, suppose Carol's will states: "I give my house to Forest Bank & Trust Company in trust to pay the income, if any, and to distribute as principal to descendants of my brother, Greg, whom Greg shall appoint during his life." This provision creates a lifetime special power of appointment in Greg: The power must be exercised by Greg during his life and he cannot exercise the power in favor of himself, his estate, his creditors, or creditors of his estate. The fact that Greg may exercise the power in favor of his own descendants, who might be included as beneficiaries of his estate, does not change the character of the power from special to general. The permissible appointees were selected by the donor, not the donee, of the power, so the donee's power is not equivalent to the rights and liabilities associated with outright ownership. While held in trust, income generated by the house will be imposed on the trust (not Greg) and Greg will not incur gift tax liability upon exercising the power during life.

In re Estate of Muchemore
560 N.W.2d 477 (Neb. 1997)

GERRARD, Justice.

The decedent, G. Robert Muchemore, died testate in 1992 leaving a will and a revocable trust agreement. The trust agreement, as amended, created a pecuniary credit shelter trust and a marital deduction trust.[5] The county court entered an order declaring that the property passing to the decedent's surviving spouse, Agnes B. Muchemore, the appellee, pursuant to the will and the trust agreement was not subject to Nebraska inheritance tax. The district court affirmed the order of the county court. Douglas County appealed the judgment of the district court to the Nebraska Court of Appeals. Pursuant to our authority to regulate the caseloads of the Court of Appeals and this court, we removed the case to our docket. For the following reasons, we affirm.

FACTUAL BACKGROUND

The decedent died testate on August 4, 1992. The decedent's will devised all personal effects to the appellee and the remainder of his estate to the First National Bank of Omaha as trustee of the G. Robert Muchemore revocable trust. This revocable trust was created pursuant to a February 12, 1980, revocable trust agreement, as amended on July 23, 1982. Article VII, sections B and C, of the revocable trust agreement, as amended, created both a "Pecuniary Credit Shelter Trust" and a

5. [Credit shelter trusts and marital deduction trusts are techniques used to minimize estate tax liability. See Chapter 12 on wealth transfer taxation. — EDS.]

"Marital Deduction Trust." The appellee is the decedent's surviving spouse and the personal representative of his estate.

. . .

Article VII, section C, subsections 2 and 3, of the trust agreement provides as follows:

> 2. On the death of the [appellee], the Trustee shall pay the then remaining principal and the income [of the MARITAL DEDUCTION TRUST] to, or hold the same for the benefit of, such person or persons or the estate of the [appellee] . . . as the [appellee] shall appoint by a Will, executed after the [decedent's] death, referring specifically to the power given to the [appellee].[6]
>
> 3. On the death of the [appellee], if, or to the extent that, the [appellee] doesnot [sic] exercise her power to appoint by Will, the Trustee shall dispose of the then remaining principal and income [of the MARITAL DEDUCTION TRUST] according to the terms and conditions, and as a part of the CREDIT SHELTER TRUST set forth in B of this ARTICLE.

Thus, under the terms of the trust, the appellee has the power to appoint by will the property remaining in the marital deduction trust at the time of her death, but if she does not exercise this power, the property will be placed in the credit shelter trust and distributed according to its terms. Under section B of article VII, if the appellee has not exercised the power of appointment at the time of her death, the credit shelter trust is to be paid in equal proportions to the decedent's nephew and nieces.

The appellee filed a petition for the determination of inheritance tax in the county court. The appellee contended that Neb. Rev. Stat. §77-2008.03 (Reissue 1996) requires that the assets in the marital deduction trust that are subject to the power of appointment in the appellee be deemed transferred to the appellee as of the time of the decedent's death and are, accordingly, not subject to inheritance taxation.

. . .

ANALYSIS

The decedent had obviously planned his estate to minimize federal estate and state inheritance taxation. The decedent's assets were divided in two portions through a trust agreement with First National Bank of Omaha. The first portion (a pecuniary credit shelter trust) received the $600,000 amount which was exempt from federal estate taxation by virtue of the federal unified credit. See 26 U.S.C. §2010 (1994). The balance passed to a marital deduction trust in order to qualify for the federal unlimited marital deduction. See 26 U.S.C. §2056 (1994). Such planning, when done correctly, results in the elimination of federal estate taxation on the first spouse's death and, presumably, the elimination of Nebraska inheritance taxation with respect to the marital trust deduction on the first death.

---

6. [Specific reference requirements, in which the donor requires the donee to expressly refer to the power of appointment to exercise it, are discussed in the next subsection, 5.3.2.2 (Exercise of a Power of Appointment). — Eds.]

In the instant case, the marital deduction trust required that all income be paid annually to the appellee and required the corporate trustee to pay to the appellee such amounts of principal as were necessary and in the best interests of the appellee. The marital deduction trust also provided a testamentary power of appointment to the appellee. . . .

Douglas County contends that these provisions in the marital deduction trust devised only a life interest to the appellee, with the power to dispose of by will [sic] the residual property at death or to allow the residual property to descend to the decedent's nephew and nieces. Thus, the remainder interest of the beneficiaries of the credit shelter trust would be subject to inheritance tax under §77-2008.01. Conversely, the appellee asserts that the marital deduction trust provided a general testamentary power of appointment resulting in a transfer of the property and the marital deduction trust to the appellee pursuant to §77-2008.03. Therefore, the appellee contends that the property is not subject to inheritance tax.

Section 77-2008.01 provides, in pertinent part, as follows:

> When property is devised, bequeathed, or otherwise transferred or limited in trust or otherwise in such a manner as to be subject to the tax prescribed in sections 77-2001 to 77-2008, and the rights, interests, or estates of the transferees, legatees, devisees, or beneficiaries are dependent upon contingencies or conditions whereby they may be wholly or in part created, defeated, extended, or abridged, an inheritance tax shall be imposed upon such transfer at the highest rate which, on the happening of any of the contingencies or conditions, would be possible. . . .

Douglas County argues that the property at issue must be taxed at the highest rate possible given the contingencies. Douglas County contends that the highest taxed contingency would occur if the appellee failed to exercise her power of appointment and the property passed to the beneficiaries of the credit shelter trust. Thus, Douglas County argues that this remainder interest ought to be subject to inheritance taxation. In such a case, the tax would be charged against the trust corpus, and if a refund becomes necessary at the time of the appellee's death, it would be paid back into the trust corpus. See Neb. Rev. Stat. §77-2008.02 (Reissue 1996).

The appellee relies . . . on §77-2008.03, which provides, in pertinent part, as follows:

> Whenever any person . . . shall be given a power of appointment [over property subject to these sections], such power of appointment shall be deemed a transfer of the interest in the property which is subject to such power from the donor to the donee of such power at the date of the donor's death; Provided, if at the date of the donor's death, the power of appointment is limited, in whole or in part, to be exercised in favor of one or more specific beneficiaries or classes of beneficiaries, then, to the extent it is so limited, such power of appointment shall not be deemed a transfer from the donor to the donee of the power. . . .

The appellee contends that because the trust instrument created a general testamentary power of appointment in the appellee that was not limited in favor of any specific beneficiaries, the application of this section results in a transfer of interest in the property to the appellee.

This case requires us to decide whether the power of appointment at issue is a general testamentary power of appointment, such that an interest in the property subject to the power passes to the appellee, or whether it is a special (or limited) power of appointment, such that an interest in the property is not treated as passing to the appellee, but to the beneficiaries of the credit shelter trust. Neb. Rev. Stat. §77-2004 (Reissue 1996) provides, in relevant part, that "[i]nterests passing to the surviving spouse by will . . . shall not be subject to [inheritance] tax." Thus, if all property contained in the marital deduction trust is treated as passing to the appellee, then no inheritance tax is currently due on the transfer. However, if the property subject to the power of appointment is not treated as passing to the appellee, inheritance tax would now be due on the remainder interest of the nephew and nieces.

Douglas County claims that the power of appointment devised to the appellee in the instant case is not the general power of appointment that is contemplated by §77-2008.03, because the power of appointment is a testamentary power only and may not be exercised inter vivos. However, Douglas County's argument fails to recognize the fundamental distinction between general powers of appointment and special (or limited) powers of appointment. The basic distinction between powers of these two types consists in the difference in the extent of dispositive power over the appointive property.

It is well recognized that even though a power of appointment may be exercisable by will only, so that the donee cannot appoint to himself or herself, the power is nonetheless regarded as general if the donee can appoint the property in such a way that it will be distributed as a part of his or her own estate. Where no restriction on the possible appointees is indicated in the instrument creating the power, it is presumed that a general power is intended. On the other hand, a power is special (or limited) when the donee's appointment is limited to a group . . . which does not include himself or herself.

The donee of a general testamentary power of appointment must be able to appoint the property to anyone, including his or her own estate. In the instant case, the appellee was given complete control over the ultimate disposition of the property in the marital trust. The power of appointment gave the appellee the right to determine the person or persons who would ultimately receive the marital trust property. . . . Thus, we conclude that the power of appointment in the marital trust was a general testamentary power of appointment because of its virtually unlimited power of disposition.

Section 77-2008.03 clearly provides that property passing to a surviving spouse subject to a general power of appointment shall be deemed a transfer from the decedent to the surviving spouse at the date of the decedent's death. . . . We hold that the district court was correct in affirming the county court's determination that such an interest in property passing to a surviving spouse is exempt from Nebraska inheritance tax.

. . .

QUESTIONS

12. Suppose the power that Robert gave Agnes allowed her to appoint the property only to "any of her siblings." Is that a general or a special power?

    ANSWER. This is a special power. Agnes's siblings are a class that does not include Agnes, her estate, her creditors, or the creditors of her estate.

13. Now suppose the power allowed Agnes to appoint the property to "any of her siblings," but one of Agnes's siblings alleges that Agnes owes her $10,000. Does the fact that Agnes's sister is one of Agnes's creditors change the nature of the power to special?

    ANSWER. No. Courts define powers formally, not functionally. To be a general power, the permissible appointees must expressly include the donee or the other individuals or entities that are closely associated with the donee.

5.3.2.2 Exercise of a Power of Appointment

There are three requirements for exercising a power. First, the donee's exercise must be in a legally effective document. For example, donors sometimes give donees the ability to exercise a power in the donee's will (a testamentary power of appointment). But if the donee does not make a will or if the donee's will is invalid, the power has been effectively exercised.

Second, the donee's exercise of the power must fulfill any requirements imposed by the donor. Donors sometimes use a "specific reference requirement," which insists that the donee include language in the document that exercises the power referring back to the instrument that created the power (i.e., the donor's will or trust). The purpose of requiring the donee to recite these magic words is to prevent the donee from inadvertently exercising the power.[7] For example, if Izzie makes a trust in 2016 that gives Brenda a power to appoint property by will, Izzie can impose a specific reference requirement that Brenda refer back to the 2016 trust in order to exercise the power. If Brenda then makes a will in 2017 that says, "I exercise any power of appointment that I hold," she has *not* complied with the specific reference requirement (there's no references to the 2016 trust) and thus she has *not* exercised the power.

A specific reference requirement can prevent a particular type of ambiguity created by the following combination of facts: (1) the donor does not impose any procedural requirement other than that the power is exercisable only by will, and (2) the donee's will says nothing about exercising the power, but contains a residuary clause. To be sure, the donee's will is completely silent on whether the donee intends to exercise the power. At the same time, though, the purpose of a residuary clause is to pass on everything that the donee could plausibly think that he or she owns—which, arguably, includes the appointive property. Nevertheless, the majority rule is that residuary clauses, standing alone, are insufficient to exercise a testamentary power of appointment. Yet there is also a

7. The trust agreement in *In re Estate of Muchemore*, above, contains such a requirement ("[T]he trustee shall pay the then remaining principal and the income . . . to . . . such person or persons . . . as the [appellee] shall appoint by a Will . . . *referring specifically to the power given to the [appellee].*").

minority approach that allows residuary clauses to exercise a general power provided that the residuary beneficiaries are also permissible appointees.

Third, at the risk of saying the obvious, the donee's attempt to exercise the power must be in favor of permissible appointees. For example, if a power can be exercised in favor of the donor's cousins, but the donee tries to appoint the appointive property to the donor's grandchildren, the exercise fails.

Finally, remember that in any case where the donee's attempt to exercise the power is ineffective, the takers in default receive the appointive property.

Restatement (Third) of Property: Wills & Other Donative Transfers
§19.1 Requisites for Exercise of a Power of Appointment

A power of appointment is exercised to the extent that:

(1) the donee manifests an intent to exercise the power in an otherwise effective document;

(2) the donee's expression of an intent to appoint satisfies the formal requirements of exercise imposed by the donor and by applicable law; and

(3) the donee's appointment constitutes a permissible exercise of the power.

Hargrove v. Rich
604 S.E.2d 475 (Ga. 2004)

HUNSTEIN, Justice.

In her last will and testament, Cecil H. Rich, the mother of Frances Rich and appellee Jack Rich, granted a power of appointment over one-fourth of her estate to Frances by providing in Item III(B):

> [Frances] shall have the power at any time and from time to time, by instrument in writing signed by her and delivered to the Trustees, or at death by her Last Will and Testament, making express reference to this power, to direct the Trustees to turn over any part or all of the property in this Trust to her brothers or sisters or her nieces and nephews, or descendants of deceased nieces and nephews, and in such manner, in Trust or otherwise, as [Frances Rich] may in such instrument direct or appoint, provided that she shall have no power to appoint such property to herself, to her estate, to her creditors or the creditors of her estate.

In her will Frances exercised the power of appointment in favor of her niece, appellant Hargrove, to the exclusion of other nieces and nephews. Frances's will specifically referred to the power of appointment in Item III(B) of her mother's will as follows:

> It is specifically my intent to exercise that certain power of appointment granted to me pursuant to Item III(B)(4) of the Last Will and Testament of Cecil H. Rich in favor of Frances Ann Hargrove.

Jack Rich filed a declaratory judgment action claiming an interest in the trust property his sister attempted to transfer to Hargrove on the ground that the power of appointment granted by his mother's will did not permit the exclusive transfer of the entire gift corpus to Hargrove. He also contended that the method by which Frances attempted to exercise the power of appointment was ineffective because she failed to direct the transfer in the manner specified in the power. The trial court entered declaratory judgment in favor of Jack Rich finding that the language in Frances's will was ineffective to exercise the power of appointment to Hargrove because (1) it did not follow the specific requirements of Cecil H. Rich's will requiring Frances to direct the trustees to turn over any part or all of the property in this trust, and (2) it improperly excluded all other nieces and nephews contrary to the express intention of Cecil H. Rich. For the reasons that follow, we affirm.

1. The sole question on appeal is whether the quoted language in Frances's will was a valid and effective exercise of the power of appointment reposed in her by Item III(B) of Cecil H. Rich's will. Under Georgia law, a power of appointment can be exercised only in the manner specified by the donor. At the same time,

> the donee of a power may execute it without expressly referring to it, or taking any notice of it, provided that it is apparent from the whole instrument that it was intended as an execution of the power. The execution of the power, however, must show that it was intended to be such execution; for if it is uncertain whether the act was intended to be an execution of the power, it will not be construed as an execution. The intention to execute a power will sufficiently appear (1) when there is some reference to the power in the instrument of execution; (2) where there is a reference to the property which is the subject matter on which execution of the power is to operate; and (3) where the instrument of execution would have no operation, but would be utterly insensible and absurd, if it was not the execution of a power.

May v. Citizens & Southern Bank of LaGrange, 223 Ga. 614, 615, 157 S.E.2d 279 (1967). Applying the above principles, we find that pursuant to the unambiguous language of Cecil H. Rich's will, Frances was authorized to exercise the power of appointment granted to her either during her life by instrument signed by her and delivered to the trustees or upon her death, by including in her will language making express reference to the power. Accordingly, the language in Frances Rich's will stating her specific intent to exercise the power of appointment granted to her under Item III(B) of the will of Cecil H. Rich was sufficient to exercise the power of appointment.

We cannot agree with the trial court that the language of Item III(B) imposed upon Frances a more formal requirement that she "direct" the trustees to turn over the property. A review of the language of Item III(B) demonstrates that the donor created a power of appointment authorizing Frances to direct the trustees to turn over any part or all of the trust property and prescribed specific formalities for the exercise of such power. The power granted by the donor was the power to direct the trustees and the method of direction was specifically restricted by the donor to the creation of an instrument in writing signed by Frances and delivered to the trustees or via language in her last will and testament making express reference to the power. To require a different or more formal method of communication would impermissibly expand or alter the formalities imposed by the donor.

2. Although we hold that the language of Frances's will was sufficient to exercise the power of appointment, we nevertheless agree with the trial court that Frances did

not have the authority to exercise the power of appointment in favor of only one niece. Where a power of appointment is limited to the nomination of certain persons from a class or from persons named or indicated by the donor, the selection of outsiders cannot be sustained as a valid exercise of the power. Under the plain language of Item III(B) Frances had only limited authority to exercise the power in favor of "her brothers or sisters or her nieces and nephews, or descendants of deceased nieces *and* nephews." The donor's use of the conjunctive "and" in the phrase "nieces and nephews" indicates her intent to limit the power of appointment to preclude Frances from exercising the power in favor of one niece to the exclusion of other nieces and nephews. . . . Inasmuch as the donee of a power can do only what she is empowered to do, Frances was without authority to exercise the power of appointment solely in favor of Hargrove.

Judgment affirmed.

QUESTIONS

14. Is the power that Frances Rich held a general or a special power?

    ANSWER. It is a special power, because it specifically excludes Frances, her estate, her creditors, and the creditors of her estate as permissible appointees.

15. Would Frances Rich have effectively exercised the power if she tried to appoint the property in favor of "her nieces and nephews," rather than Frances Ann Hargrove?

    ANSWER. Yes — because nieces and nephews, collectively and as a class, constitute permissible appointees under the special power.

16. Frances Rich's will stated: "It is specifically my intent to exercise that certain power of appointment granted to me pursuant to Item III(B)(4) of the Last Will and Testament of Cecil H. Rich in favor of Frances Ann Hargrove." Instead, suppose that Frances Rich's will had not contained this language, but left all of her property to her nieces and nephews. Would that have exercised the power?

    ANSWER. No. The donor — Frances's mom, Cecil — imposed a specific reference requirement by specifying that Frances could exercise the power in an instrument "making express reference to this power." If Frances's will did not contain a reference to the power, it probably would not have satisfied this requirement.

PROBLEM IV

Roger and Sally are married with two children, Wendy and Paul. Roger executes a valid will that leaves a vacation home he inherited from his aunt to Sally, and then to such of their children as Sally shall appoint by will. Roger then dies. Later, Sally signs a valid will that makes no mention of the power, but leaves "the rest, residue, and remainder" of her estate to Wendy. Sally then dies. What type of power is created by Roger's will? Is the residuary clause of Sally's will sufficient to exercise the power? Who takes Roger's vacation home?

5.4 ADMINISTRATIVE PROVISIONS

In this section, we examine *administrative* provisions, which regulate the procedural aspects of estate administration. We will focus on the appointment of fiduciaries to administer the estate, powers and duties of the personal representative, and the testator's preferences regarding the bonding requirement.

5.4.1 Appointment of Fiduciaries

One advantage to making a will, as opposed to dying intestate; is the privilege of naming an executor and successor executors. Executors step into decedents' shoes, manage their assets, deal with the beneficiaries, and interact with the probate court for the duration of the estate's administration. Given the importance of these tasks, courts generally defer to the testator's wishes regarding the selection of an executor.[8]

However, there are grounds for finding a proposed executor to be unqualified. In most states, statutes bar people handpicked by the testator from serving if they are underage or incapacitated, have been convicted of a felony, or have demonstrated a propensity for dishonesty.

In addition, once a probate matter has begun, beneficiaries can petition to remove an executor. The standards for removal are similar to the rules for a preliminary objection to the appointment of an executor. Yet there is one difference: Petitions for removal tend to focus on the executor's actual track record during the course of the case. They are often coupled with allegations that the executor has breached her fiduciary duties. Although we will discuss fiduciary duties in more depth later in Chapter 11,[9] for now it is enough to understand that executors must prudently manage the decedent's property, refrain from self-dealing and conflicts of interest, avoid commingling funds, keep the beneficiaries informed, and otherwise act in the best interests of the estate.

Disputes concerning the appointment, performance, or removal of personal representatives are among the most commonly litigated probate matters, although a recent empirical study found that such disputes are more common in intestate estates as compared to testate estates. David Horton, Wills Law on the Ground, 62 UCLA L. Rev. 1094, 1128 (2015). The testator's careful selection of an executor can and, in many cases does, prevent beneficiaries from fighting in court over the right to administer the estate.[10]

---

8. Occasionally, no one who is named in the will can serve as executor. Courts fill this gap by applying the principles for naming administrators in intestate proceedings. Most jurisdictions have a set hierarchy of people who can serve, usually starting with the decedent's surviving spouse, and then cycling through the decedent's issue, parents, siblings, nieces and nephews, and so on. See, e.g., CAL. PROB. CODE §8461 (West 2015); cf. TEX. TRUSTS & ESTATES CODE §304.001 (West 2015) (giving the beneficiaries of the will priority after the decedent's surviving spouse).

9. The fiduciary duties imposed on the personal representative of a decedent's estate are generally the same as the fiduciary duties imposed upon trustees. See, e.g., UPC §3-703(a) ("A personal representative is a fiduciary who shall observe the standards of care applicable to trustees as described by Section 7-302.").

10. Ice cream king Tom Carvel, who died in 1990, appointed seven executors to administer his estate initially valued at $67 million. The numerous executors have been at odds with each other for decades and approximately $28 million has been spent on legal fees. See http://abcnews.go.com/Business/story?id=8129259&page=1.

Uniform Probate Code
§3-611 Termination of Appointment by Removal; Cause; Procedure

(a) A person interested in the estate may petition for removal of a personal representative for cause at any time. . . .

(b) Cause for removal exists when removal would be in the best interests of the estate, or if it is shown that a personal representative or the person seeking his appointment, intentionally misrepresented material facts in the proceedings leading to his appointment, or that the personal representative has disregarded an order of the court, has become incapable of discharging the duties of his office, or has mismanaged the estate or failed to perform any duty pertaining to the office. . . .

In re Estate of Jones
93 P.3d 147 (Wash. 2004)

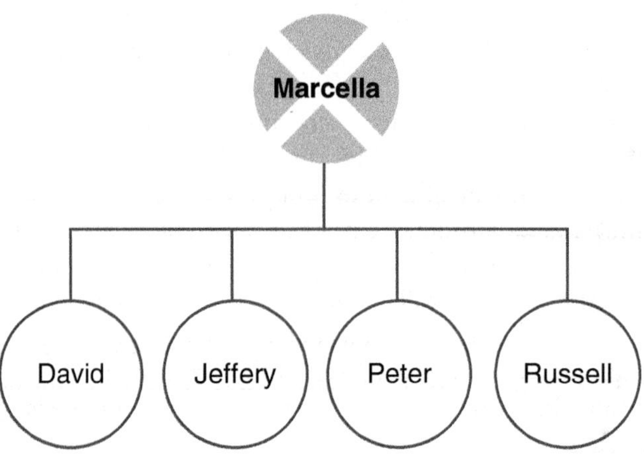

OWENS, J.

. . .

FACTS

Marcella Louise Jones died testate September 2, 1995, with property in Spokane, Washington. Marcella's will transferred her estate in equal shares to her four sons, David, Russell, Jeffery, and Peter, and named Russell the personal representative. . . . The will was admitted to probate on September 25, 1995, Russell was appointed the personal representative, and an order of probate . . . was entered. The estate included real estate in Spokane, securities and investments, an interest in a mortgage/real estate contract, personal property, and a 1987 Buick automobile. Although the brothers met on May 4, 1996, to distribute property, the meeting was unsuccessful due to continuing unresolved conflicts between the brothers that have endured over the last 40-50 years.

. . .

ANALYSIS

. . . RCW 11.28.250 provides:

> Whenever the court has reason to believe that any personal representative has wasted, embezzled, or mismanaged, or is about to waste, or embezzle the property of the estate committed to his charge, or has committed, or is about to commit a fraud upon the estate, or is incompetent to act, or is permanently removed from the state, or has wrongfully neglected the estate, or has neglected to perform any acts as such personal representative, or for any other cause or reason which to the court appears necessary, it shall have power and authority, after notice and hearing to revoke such letters.[11]

The superior court must have valid grounds for removal and these grounds must be supported in the record. Further, if even one ground for removal is valid, the decision should be upheld on appeal.

. . . The trial court's removal of Russell Jones as a personal representative was based on several breaches of fiduciary duty. These breaches included using estate property for personal use, [and] commingling estate funds. . . .

a. The Estate House

It is undisputed that Russell lived in the estate property and practiced law from the house from the mid-1980's until the time of trial, rent free. On September 20, 1996, about one year after his mother's death, Russell deeded himself the property but did not record the deed. At that time, there was no agreement between the four brothers that Russell would take the property as his distributive share or live in the house rent free during probate. Peter Jones even offered to buy the house in May and September of 1996. . . .

Russell breached his fiduciary duty by . . . using the property as his own before the estate closed and failing to pay rent. Until an estate is closed, the heirs may not treat estate real property as their own. Therefore, until the estate was closed Russell had the rights of only an executor in the property. An executor is entitled to possess and control estate property during the administration of the estate and has a right to it even against other heirs. However, as a general rule, an executor is accountable for his use of the deceased's real property. Where a person's only right to possession of the property arises from his status as executor, he does not have a right to remain on and use the property when there are other reasonable alternatives open (e.g., renting the property). If he chooses to use the house for his own benefit he must pay rent. . . . This is true even where an executor claims to remain on the property to protect it from vandalism and decay. Because Russell chose to live on the property and used the property for his own personal benefit while only entitled to an executorship interest, Russell breached his fiduciary duty and owes the estate rent.

---

11. ["Letters" refers to "letters testamentary," the term used to describe a probate court's order identifying and appointing the personal representative of a decedent's estate. — EDS.]

b. Piano and Car

In addition to Russell's misuse of the estate house, the trial court noted that Russell put 17,000 miles on the estate car and found that Russell breached his fiduciary duty by revaluing an estate piano. The record supports Russell's excessive use of the car. However, although Russell's use of the car may constitute personal use of estate property, it appears the car was sold for approximately its fair market value, so waste to the estate did not occur. . . .

[T]he way Russell went about revaluing the piano indicates unfaithfulness to the estate. Russell seeks to revalue the piano at approximately $15,000 based on expert advice he received from an antique piano restorer and appraiser. It is unclear from the record if this appraiser has even examined the piano. . . .

Standing alone, Russell's actions involving the piano and car are insufficient to remove Russell. However these actions are indicative of his unfaithfulness to the estate. Further, in light of our previous findings regarding Russell's use of the estate house, removal of Russell is still proper.

c. Commingling, Sale of Securities, and Bank Records

The trial court found that Russell Jones breached his fiduciary duty by commingling his personal funds and estate funds. An executor should keep [estate] funds in a bank account and not commingle them with his own money. However, ultimately, if all funds are accounted for, the executor is not guilty of misconduct and the beneficiaries are not injured. Here, there is evidence that several bank accounts were used and that Russell made distributions from his personal account and repaid himself with estate funds. However, a final accounting has not been completed, and if all funds are accounted for at that time, then no breach occurred.

Additionally, the court found discrepancies in the selling of investments and securities, the estate's tax records, and Marcella Jones's personal checking account. Although there is evidence in the record of the discrepancies, there is also evidence that there is a reasonable explanation for the discrepancies. We remand to the trial court for a final accounting to determine whether these discrepancies exist and if all estate funds have been accounted for.

. . .

With the removal of Russell Jones, we affirm the trial court's appointment of James Woodard as the new personal representative of the estate. Under RCW 11.68.070, if a personal representative is removed, the court has the power to appoint his successor. . . . [I]f the letters of administration are revoked before the settlement of an estate, the letters shall be granted "to those to whom administration would have been granted if the original letters had not been obtained, or the person obtaining them had renounced administration." [*Id.*]

Here, if Russell had not been appointed as the personal representative, David would have been appointed, as he was the alternative personal representative named in the will.

However, any person interested in a will may object to the granting of testamentary letters to the persons named as executors. Moreover, the right of beneficiaries to have an estate distributed by law is a primary right, and if a particular person serving as a personal representative may interfere with this right, that person should not be appointed. It is the court's job to guard against waste or loss to the estate. Therefore, where a conflict of interest exists which would contravene the rights of the beneficiaries and result in waste of the estate, a potential representative should be disqualified.

Here, the record shows that David was in league with Russell during the administration of the estate. David believed that Russell was "doing an honest, competent, and thorough job in the closing of the estate." David testified that Russell had been "fair and equitable in the distribution of the estate" and that an accounting was unnecessary. David's statements exhibit his trust and comfort in Russell's methods of distributing the estate. This evidence, combined with Russell's multiple breaches of his fiduciary duty, supports the trial court's denial of David's appointment based on David's conflict of interest with the estate. Further, in light of the conflicting relationship between the brothers that David himself testified to, appointing any family member would result in further litigation and a delay in closing the estate. Therefore, we affirm James Woodard's appointment.

. . .

QUESTIONS

17. Is there anything in the record that suggests that Marcella (Russell's mom) might have expected that Russell would continue to live and practice law in the house after she died?

    ANSWER. Marcella had allowed Russell to occupy the house rent-free from "the mid-1980s" until her death in 1995. Arguably, then, she did not mind him treating the home as his own.

18. What language in either the UPC or the Washington statute supports the court's refusal to appoint David successor executor?

    ANSWER. Both the Washington statute and the UPC give the court a great deal of leeway in deciding to remove (or to refuse to appoint) an executor. The Washington legislation authorizes judges to remove an executor "for any other cause or reason which to the court appears necessary." WASH. REV. CODE §11.28.250. Likewise, the UPC allows removal if it "would be in the best interests of the estate." UPC §3-611. Arguably, this justifies the Washington Supreme Court's refusal to appoint David given the contentious relationship between the brothers and the likelihood of further litigation.

5.4.2 Personal Representative Powers

In many states, the personal representative's default powers are enumerated by statute. For example, the Pennsylvania Consolidated Statutes contain more than twenty subsections conferring various default statutory powers including investment of estate funds, procurement of liability insurance, settlement of estate claims, proxy voting of stock contained in the estate, and so on. PA. CONS. STAT., title 20, chapter 33, subchapter B. The statutory default powers are generally broad so as to permit the personal representative to perform most aspects of estate administration without returning to court for authorization to act. In an attempt to confer the broadest scope of authorized powers upon the personal representative, most wills contain provisions reciting specific powers of the personal representative. These provisions sometimes contain elaborate detail and are nearly always in the form of boilerplate stock language reused from one will to the next. When including personal representative powers in a will, unless otherwise directed by the testator, practitioners should clearly state that such powers enumerated in the will are in addition to and do not restrict the default powers conferred by statute.

Rather than enumerating specific default powers of the personal representative, the UPC takes the position that a personal representative enjoys the same power over estate property as an absolute owner.

Uniform Probate Code
§3-711 Powers of Personal Representatives; In General

(a) Until termination of his appointment a personal representative has the same power over the title to property of the estate that an absolute owner would have, in trust however, for the benefit of the creditors and others interested in the estate. This power may be exercised without notice, hearing, or order of court.

(b) A personal representative has access to and authority over a digital asset of the decedent to the extent provided by [the Revised Uniform Fiduciary Access to Digital Assets Act] or by order of court.

5.4.3 Bond

Traditionally, probate courts have required a decedent's personal representative to take out a bond from a bonding company. The purpose of the bond is to protect the decedent's heirs, beneficiaries, and creditors from fraud and embezzlement. If the personal representative loots the estate, the bonding company is on the hook for the loss.

Testators can waive the bonding requirement in their wills. Bonds can be expensive, and testators usually choose executors whom they love and trust — not those who might steal their assets. Thus, it is not surprising that testators almost always waive bond.

The UPC requires bonds in informal proceedings only under unique circumstances, such as when the will expressly requires it or an interested party demands it. See UPC §§3-603, 3-605. In formal proceedings, bonds are not necessary unless an interested party requests it "and the court is satisfied that it is desirable." *Id.* §3-603.

5.5 OTHER PROVISIONS

5.5.1 In Terrorem or No Contest Clauses

Individuals sometimes try to insulate their estates from litigation through the use of "no contest" or "in terrorem" clauses. These provisions state that any beneficiary who files any claim (or a particular claim) forfeits his or her bequest. Thus, no contest clauses give prospective plaintiffs a choice: either back down, or sue and risk losing their inheritance unless they prevail in the contest.

No contest clauses raise delicate policy considerations. On the one hand, they can be useful in discouraging beneficiaries from litigating will disputes in court. Probate and trust litigation is notorious for draining estates and exposing family skeletons. Thus, no contest provisions can help testators and settlors achieve the vital goal of buying peace. But on the other hand, no contest clauses have the potential to deter well-founded complaints. To be sure, a litigant who overturns a will or trust on grounds such as fraud, duress, or undue influence also nullifies the no contest clause within the instrument, and thus cannot be penalized. Yet the specter of being disinherited may be enough to keep parties with solid cases from coming forward.

A few jurisdictions have decided that the costs of no contest clauses trump the benefits, and thus hold that they violate public policy. See FLA. STAT. ANN. §732.517 (West 2016) ("A provision in a will purporting to penalize any interested person for contesting the will or instituting other proceedings relating to the estate is unenforceable."); IND. CODE ANN. §29-1-6-2 (West 2016) ("[S]uch provision or provisions shall be void and of no force or effect."). Conversely, the UPC tries to balance these concerns by imposing a probable cause standard for the enforcement of such clauses.

Uniform Probate Code
§2-517 Penalty Clause for Contest

A provision in a will purporting to penalize an interested person for contesting the will or instituting other proceedings relating to the estate is unenforceable if probable cause exists for instituting proceedings.

Dustin Hoffman and Tom Cruise in a scene from *Rain Man*

In the 1988 Oscar Award–winning film *Rain Man*, Charlie Babbitt (played by actor Tom Cruise) was estranged from his father, who died when Charlie was young. The father's will left Charlie a car and "outright title to my prizewinning hybrid rose bushes" to remind Charlie of "the possibility of perfection." The father left the balance of his $3 million estate to a trust that did not include Charlie as a beneficiary. Should Charlie's father have included a no contest penalty clause in his will?

In re Estate of Shumway
9 P.3d 1062 (Ariz. 2000)

FELDMAN, Justice.

We granted review to determine whether the penalty, or so-called in terrorem clause in a will should be enforced against those who contest the will. [The clause stated:

> If any beneficiary under this Will in any manner, directly or indirectly, contests or attacks this Will or any of its provisions, any gift or other provision I have made to or for that person under this Will is revoked and shall be disposed of in the same manner provided herein as if that contesting beneficiary had predeceased me without issue.]

Per A.R.S. §14-2517, the penalty clause is unenforceable if probable cause existed to contest the will. Under the facts of this case of first impression and according to what we conclude to be the proper definition of probable cause, we find that the penalty clause should not be enforced. . . .

FACTS AND PROCEDURAL HISTORY

Ralph V. Shumway (Decedent) executed a will [dated June 26, 1997,] six days before his death. The will had been prepared at his request by his helper and bookkeeper, Adelida Rodriguez. The will nominated Rodriguez, who was neither related to Decedent nor a beneficiary under his prior will, as personal representative and left her twenty-five percent of Decedent's estate. Decedent was survived by a brother and four children. Virginia Gavette, one of his daughters, filed a petition for appointment as personal representative; the other survivors agreed to that appointment. After Gavette's appointment, Rodriguez filed an objection, offering the [June 26,] 1997 will for probate. Gavette contested that will. . . . The trial judge found that the will was valid; that Rodriguez proved by clear and convincing evidence that she had not exerted undue influence. . . . The judge also enforced a penalty clause contained in the will.

. . .

DISCUSSION

A. The Statute

There is a significant divergence of views as to whether an in terrorem clause is enforceable when a contest is brought in good faith. We need not concern ourselves with this because our statute provides:

> A provision in a will purporting to penalize an interested person for contesting the will or instituting other proceedings relating to the estate is unenforceable if probable cause exists for that action.

A.R.S. §14-2517 (1995). The court of appeals' opinion is the first published decision to construe this statute. The statute is based on Uniform Probate Code §2-517. . . .

The rationale behind the rule on enforceability of penalty clauses in wills balances several policy factors. Public policy reasons to support penalty clauses include preserving the transferor's donative intent, avoiding waste of the estate in litigation, and avoiding use of a will contest to coerce a more favorable settlement to a dissatisfied beneficiary. These must be balanced with the public policy interests of allowing access to the courts to prevent probate of wills procured by or resulting from fraud, undue influence, lack of capacity, improper execution, forgery, or subsequent revocation by a later document. Thus, the Uniform [Probate] Code, the Restatement [(Third) of Property], and the Arizona statute all refer to probable cause as the key issue in deciding whether to enforce a penalty clause.

. . .

B. Probable Cause — The Standard

. . .

"[P]robable cause" is defined as

> the existence, *at the time of the initiation of the proceeding*, of evidence *which would lead a reasonable person, properly informed and advised*, to conclude that there is a substantial likelihood that the contest or attack will be successful. The evidence needed . . . should be less where there is strong public policy supporting the legal ground of the contest or attack. . . . A factor which bears on the existence of probable cause *is that the beneficiary relied upon the advice of disinterested counsel sought in good faith after a full disclosure of the facts.*

Restatement §9.1 cmt. j (emphasis added). . . .

We believe the Restatement standard for probable cause properly balances the conflicting policy interests and therefore adopt it over the other potential standards. . . . We will apply the Restatement test flexibly, especially when strong policy supports grounds for challenge — as in the case of suspected undue influence, the principal ground for contest in the present case. The Restatement's standard of a "reasonable person, properly informed and advised" who concludes there is a substantial likelihood of success in the contest is, of course, a question initially for the trial court. In addressing that question, the trial judge should, as the Restatement requires, refer to the evidence known at the time the contest was initiated.

C. Whether Probable Cause Existed in the Present Case

Penalty clauses work a forfeiture, which is disfavored in the law. Because of this, the statute should be liberally construed, especially when the grounds include such matters as undue influence. . . . [T]he absence of findings and lack of any comment or explanation in the trial judge's orders leaves us not only to speculate as to the standard she applied in a case of first impression, but also to our own devices in attempting to find support for her unexpressed but implicit conclusion that there was no probable cause.

Prior to filing the present action, Gavette obtained a written opinion by Decedent's doctor that he was "borderline competent" during the last week of his life, that he showed "marked deterioration," was "waxing and waning," and that by June 30 (four days after the will was signed), he "clearly was incompetent." One important factor used to determine whether the will contest was filed with probable cause is that the beneficiaries relied on the advice of disinterested counsel, sought in good faith after a full disclosure of the facts. The attorney advised Gavette of the legal presumption of undue influence when one who occupies a confidential relationship to a decedent is active in procuring the execution of the will and is one of the principal beneficiaries.

The facts also showed that Rodriguez, as she concedes, had a confidential relationship with Decedent. "[W]here a confidential relationship is shown the presumption of invalidity can be overcome only by clear and convincing evidence that the transaction was fair and voluntary." Stewart v. Woodruff, 19 Ariz. App. 190, 194, 505 P.2d 1081, 1085 (1973). This is a difficult standard of proof. Though Rodriguez met it to the trial judge's satisfaction after presentation of all evidence, when Gavette filed the contest she could reasonably have questioned Rodriguez' ability to do so, given the other circumstances surrounding execution of the will.

These circumstances include the following: Rodriguez helped Decedent prepare his will with computer software she had previously purchased; she was named the personal representative; and she arranged for Decedent to sign the will in the hospital six days before his death, with two of her relatives as the only witnesses. Rodriguez was not a beneficiary under Decedent's prior will and was not related to him, but she would inherit twenty-five percent of his estate under the will she prepared. . . .

Decedent was legally blind, and Gavette may reasonably have believed that he did not truly know what the will said. A previous draft had been prepared and read in her presence on June 25, the day before the contested will was executed. Decedent seemed to be asleep during this reading and did not agree that the will expressed his testamentary desires. The will was revised overnight and then read only in the presence of Rodriguez' relatives. The person who notarized the will's signatures did not witness its reading. Cole said Decedent could not remember things when she was talking with him prior to Rodriguez' arrival on the day the will was executed. It is also unclear whether Decedent intended to include the penalty clause. The software program used by Rodriguez did not allow the user to pick and choose which clauses were desired, so the penalty clause very well may have been included automatically. In fact, Decedent may not have known it was there. Thus, whether the will expressed Decedent's testamentary intent was in question. It is therefore impossible to conclude as a matter of law that a reasonable person would not have believed there was a substantial likelihood of success in contesting this will.

Rodriguez argues that Decedent was not close to Gavette, that he was a very strong-willed person, and that she provided clear and convincing evidence that he was competent to execute this will. However, the definition of probable cause does not require certainty of success. The question is whether Gavette had enough facts to establish probable cause at the time the contest was filed. Simply because the trial judge concluded there was no undue influence does not mean no probable cause existed to contest the will. If that were the case, the only contestants to a will would be either those who were absolutely certain of the will's invalidity or those who had little or nothing to lose should the contest fail. Any person who had a substantial interest under a will would face the choice of letting a questionable will stand or forfeiting his or her share of the estate should the challenge fail.

In light of the undue influence challenge, including the presumption applicable in this case and the public policy militating against forfeiture and favoring access to the courts, the factors that weighed against a probable cause finding do not overcome the information known to Gavette at the time the contest was filed. Based on the circumstances surrounding the drafting and execution of this will, the doctor's concern regarding Decedent's competence, the lack of clarity of Decedent's intent, the presumption of undue influence, and the policy of Arizona law on this subject, we conclude there was probable cause to contest the will.

. . .

CONCLUSION

The implicit finding by the trial judge of no probable cause for this will contest is unsupported and must be set aside. . . .

QUESTIONS

19. Can a no contest clause deter a person who is completely disinherited from suing?

    ANSWER. No. No contest clauses are not an effective stick unless they also have a carrot: some gift that the litigious beneficiary risks losing if she sues and violates the clause.

20. Suppose that on the same day Shumway had signed his will, he had also taken out a life insurance policy and made Rodriguez the sole beneficiary. Gavette unsuccessfully challenged the validity of the life insurance contract on the grounds of undue influence and incapacity. Does it matter whether she had probable cause to file this claim?

    ANSWER. Probably not. The no contest clause only governs challenges to the "[w]ill or any of its provisions." The attempt to overturn the life insurance contract does not seem to fall within its scope.

PROBLEM V

Floyd, who is an estate planning lawyer, lives in a jurisdiction that recognizes holographic wills. Floyd's kids have always teased him about his sloppy, barely legible handwriting. After Floyd dies, his children find in his fireproof safe at work a document written in Floyd's distinctive handwriting that purports to be his will. It gives his daughter Murriel $10,000, and his six other children $50,000 each. It also contains a no contest clause:

> If any one person or persons named or referred to in this instrument contest my will, that person or persons will automatically be dropped from my will and their part will be equally divided among the other parties named and/or referred to herein.

The will ends with Floyd's signature and is dated June 11, 2015.

Shortly after the probate of Floyd's estate begins, Murriel files a petition to validate a handwritten document she found in the glove compartment of Floyd's car as Floyd's holographic will. In neat block letters, this document gives all of Floyd's property to Murriel. Rather than culminating with Floyd's signature, it ends with an X. It is dated August 1, 2015.

The trial court enforces the June 11 will and rejects the August 1 handwritten document. Can Murriel take $10,000, or does the no contest clause bar her from inheriting from Floyd?

5.5.2 Minor Children

Parents often choose specific people to act as guardians for their minor children. The UPC allows them to do so in wills and also in unattested but signed written instruments. These appointments can become effective upon not only the parents' death but also their disability. The fact that a parent names an individual creates a rebuttable presumption that the individual should be confirmed by the court. However, interested parties can object to such an appointment, forcing the court to decide what is in the best interests of the child.

Uniform Probate Code
§5-202 Parental Appointment of Guardian

(a) A guardian may be appointed by will or other signed writing by a parent for any minor child the parent has or may have in the future. The appointment may specify the desired limitations on the powers to be given to the guardian. The appointing parent may revoke or amend the appointment before confirmation by the court.

. . .

(c) Subject to Section 5-203, the appointment of a guardian becomes effective upon the appointing parent's death, an adjudication that the parent is an incapacitated person, or a written determination by a physician who has examined the parent that the parent is no longer able to care for the child, whichever first occurs.

. . .

(g) The appointment of a guardian by a parent does not supersede the parental rights of either parent. If both parents are dead or have been adjudged incapacitated persons, an appointment by the last parent who died or was adjudged incapacitated has priority.

. . .

(i) The authority of a guardian appointed under this section terminates upon the first to occur of the appointment of a guardian by the court or the giving of written notice to the guardian of the filing of an objection pursuant to Section 5-203.

§5-203 Objection by Minor or Others to Parental Appointment

Until the court has confirmed an appointee under Section 5-202, a minor who is the subject of an appointment by a parent and who has attained 14 years of age, the other parent, or a person other than a parent or guardian having care or custody of the minor may prevent or terminate the appointment at any time by filing a written objection in the court in which the appointing instrument is filed. . . . The objection does not preclude judicial appointment of the person selected by the parent.

§5-204 Judicial Appointment of Guardian: Conditions for Appointment

(a) A minor or a person interested in the welfare of a minor may petition for appointment of a guardian.

(b) The court may appoint a guardian for a minor if the court finds the appointment is in the minor's best interest, and:

(1) the parents consent;

(2) all parental rights have been terminated; or

(3) the parents are unwilling or unable to exercise their parental rights.

. . .

In re R.M.S.
128 P.3d 783 (Colo. 2006)

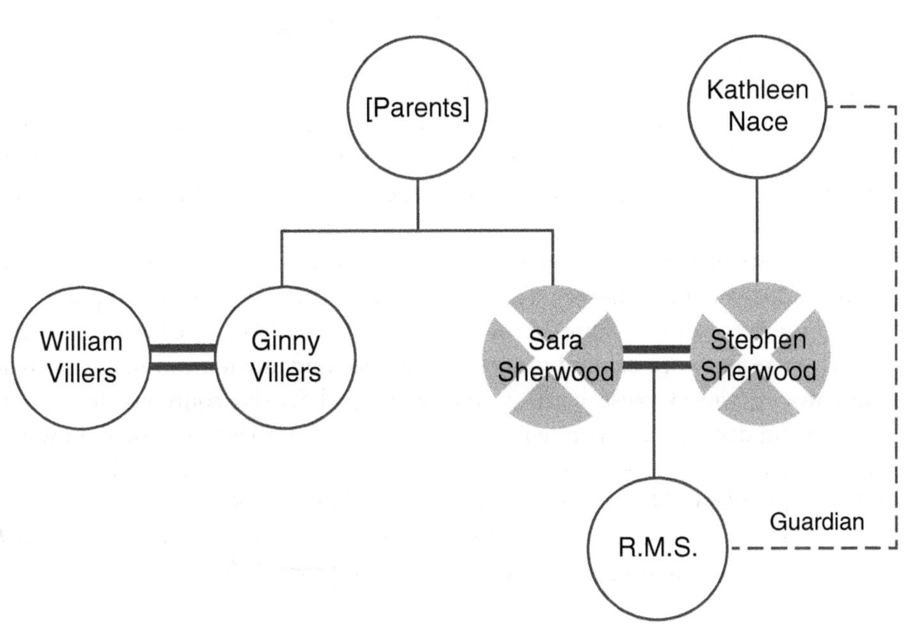

MARTINEZ, Justice.

Petitioners, Ginny Villers and William Brian Villers (collectively, "the Villers"), filed this original proceeding under C.A.R. 21 seeking to vacate the trial court's order awarding guardianship of R.M.S., a minor, to Respondent, Kathleen Nace, after the deaths of R.M.S.'s parents, Sara Sherwood and Stephen Sherwood. The trial court enforced the terms of Stephen Sherwood's will, which appointed Nace guardian for R.M.S., based on its legal conclusion that a court can set aside a valid testamentary appointment only to avoid potential harm or injury to the minor. The Villers, as persons with the care and custody of R.M.S., objected to the testamentary appointment and seek a new order appointing a guardian for R.M.S. pursuant to the best interest of the child standard. . . .

I. FACTS AND PROCEEDINGS

On the afternoon of August 3, 2005, Larimer County law enforcement officials responded to a 911 call reporting sounds of gunfire in the home of Sara and Stephen Sherwood. Upon entry, officials discovered the Sherwoods' bodies. Nine days after returning from active combat duty in Iraq, Stephen Sherwood shot and killed his wife, Sara Sherwood, and then killed himself.

The Sherwoods' daughter, R.M.S., was at a neighbor's home during the shootings. Authorities subsequently placed R.M.S. in the care of Ginny Villers, Sara Sherwood's sister, and Ginny Villers' husband, William Brian Villers. R.M.S. has remained in the Villers' care and custody since the deaths of her parents. . . .

Kathleen Taylor Nace, Stephen Sherwood's mother, petitioned for appointment of guardianship on the basis that she was appointed by the will of the last parent to die, Stephen Sherwood, and the appointment had not been prevented or terminated. . . .

The Villers objected to Nace's petition for the appointment of guardian and advanced a best interest of the child standard to the guardianship determination. Under this standard, the Villers argued it would be in R.M.S.'s best interest to remain in their care and custody.

After a hearing on both guardianship petitions, the trial court entered an oral ruling appointing Nace guardian of R.M.S. The trial court concluded the relevant statute, while providing a court some degree of discretion in determining the appointment of a guardian, did not provide it with the discretion to employ a "best interests of the child standard." The court instead applied a harm standard: it concluded Stephen Sherwood's will controlled the guardianship appointment unless "the appointment causes harm or injury" to R.M.S. Because Nace was willing to accept the appointment and the court could not find any indication that such an appointment would cause harm or injury to R.M.S., the court granted Nace's petition and denied the Villers' emergency petition. The trial court noted, however, that if it had applied a best interest standard, it might have appointed the Villers as R.M.S.'s guardian. The trial court stayed removal of R.M.S.

The Villers seek a rule to show cause requiring the trial court to vacate its ruling and enter a new ruling based upon the best interests of R.M.S.

II. ANALYSIS

Sections 15-14-201 to -210, C.R.S. (2005), of the Colorado Probate Code govern the appointment of guardians.[12] A guardian may be appointed by a parent under section 15-14-202 (a "testamentary appointment") or by a court under section 15-14-204, C.R.S. (2005) (a "judicial appointment"). Although a parent may make a testamentary appointment, a person with the care or custody of the minor may object to the appointment under section 15-14-203(1), C.R.S. (2005).

To determine the issue before us — whether an objection under section 15-14-203(1) to a parental appointment requires judicial appointment of a guardian determined on the best interest of the child standard — we review de novo the statutory provisions governing parental appointments, objections and judicial appointments. . . .

We first discuss uncontested testamentary appointments made under section 15-14-202 and note that a court's role is limited to confirming the appointment. Next, we consider objections to parental appointmensts [sic] under section 15-14-203(1) and conclude an objection triggers the judicial appointment statute. We then discuss judicial appointments made under section 15-14-204, C.R.S. (2005), and observe that the legislature has clearly conditioned all judicial appointments on the minor's best interests. Finally, we conclude that a judicial appointment, made subsequent to an objection to a testamentary appointment, is to be made pursuant to the best interest of the child standard.

A. Testamentary Appointment of a Guardian

Section 15-14-202 confers authority on a parent to appoint a guardian by will or other signed writing. . . . A testamentary appointment is generally effective upon the death of the appointing parent. Although a parent may appoint a guardian, whose appointment will be effective upon his or her death, the court must be petitioned to confirm the appointment.

. . .

B. Objection to a Testamentary Appointment

Section 15-14-203(1) addresses objections by others to a parental appointment. By statute, an objection may be filed only by the other parent or, as relevant here, "a person other than a parent or guardian having care or custody of the minor," §15-14-203(1). Significantly, an objection under section 15-14-203(1) to a testamentary appointee terminates, and may prevent, the appointment. . . . Once a person with the care or custody of the minor terminates the testamentary appointment by objection, the parental appointment is ineffective and the appointee has no authority. Since the testamentary appointee has no authority, no guardian exists for the minor and a guardian must be appointed by a mechanism other than the testamentary appointment.

We conclude it is plain in subsection 15-14-203(1) that an objection triggers a judicial appointment under section 15-14-204. . . . Thus, an objection under

12. [The Colorado statutory scheme is the same as the UPC's. — Eds.]

section 15-14-203(1) has two interrelated effects on a parental appointment: (1) it terminates and may prevent the appointment; and (2) requires judicial appointment of a guardian. The parties agree that an objection to a parental appointment triggers a court's involvement in the guardianship process beyond confirmation, but disagree as to the scope of the involvement. The Villers argue a guardian must be judicially appointed pursuant to a best interest of the child standard. Nace asserts a valid testamentary nomination pursuant to section 15-14-202 removes all discretion from the trial court and requires the trial court to enforce the terms of the will unless such an appointment would cause harm or injury to the child. We agree with the Villers and conclude that an objection triggers the judicial appointment statute's best interest standard, to which we now turn.

C. Conditions for the Judicial Appointment of a Guardian

Section 15-14-204 conditions the judicial appointment of a guardian on a finding that the appointment will be in the minor's best interest. . . . In fact, no mention of a standard other than the best interest of the child is made in section 15-14-204. We see no reason to deviate from the best interest standard when the judicial appointment is made subsequent to an objection to a testamentary appointment.

We therefore decline to employ the harm standard advanced by Nace and adopted by the trial court. Indeed, applying a harm standard would require us to read language into the statute. The judicial appointment statute makes no mention of a harm standard and does not direct that a trial court, in making its appointment, should apply any standard other than the best interests of the child, the standard that applies to all judicial appointments. Nor does the judicial appointment statute identify any exceptions for a judicial appointment made subsequent to an objection by a person with the care or custody of the minor. Had the legislature intended a court to appoint a guardian pursuant to a harm standard, it could have so stated. Instead, the statute repeatedly provides a consistent standard by which to make a judicial appointment: the best interest of the child. Hence, when the trial court has jurisdiction over appointment of a guardian, its responsibility is to provide for the best interest and welfare of the minor.

Although we recognize the strong public policy in favor of encouraging parents to make testamentary selections in the first instance, we conclude the legislature did not intend to preclude the court from considering the best interests of the child who has been in the care or custody of persons other than the testamentary guardian. Hence, the testamentary nomination is not binding where the trial court determines in its sound discretion that a party with the care or custody of the minor is better suited to act as guardian.

Parental intent as to who should care for their minor children may nonetheless be a relevant factor to be considered in appointing a guardian under the best interest standard. A court may consider all relevant facts and circumstances to determine the best interest of the child. Hence, the best interest of the child standard does not preclude a court from considering the desires of the pertinent parties, including the wishes of the minor's parent as expressed through a testamentary appointment. Thus, a court may weigh such wishes, keeping in mind the fluid and changing nature of interpersonal relationships and the frequency with which the will was reviewed after its election.

However, the paramount consideration is the best interest of the child and a testamentary appointment must yield to this overriding concern when the court resolves a guardianship dispute subsequent to an objection by a person with the care or custody of the minor under section 15-14-203(1). Accordingly, to appoint a guardian for a minor when a person with the care or custody of the child objects to the testamentary appointment, the court shall appoint a guardian under section 15-14-204 pursuant to the best interest of the child standard.

III. APPLICATION

Here, Stephen Sherwood effected a valid will appointing Nace as R.M.S.'s testamentary guardian. Although Nace accepted the testamentary appointment, the timely objection of the Villers, as persons with the care and custody of R.M.S. terminated Nace's appointment. Consequently, the court must make a judicial appointment of a guardian for R.M.S. pursuant to the best interest of the child standard.

IV. CONCLUSION

The rule to show cause is made absolute. The case is remanded with the directions to the district court to appoint a guardian under section 15-14-204 pursuant to the best interest of the child standard.

QUESTIONS

21. Who would have been appointed R.M.S.'s guardian if the Villers had not objected to Nace's petition? Would that result change if the court believed, as the trial court found, that it would be better for R.M.S. to remain with the Villers than to live with Kathleen Nace?

ANSWER. In an uncontested appointment of a guardian for a minor under a parent's will, the parent testator's choice governs. Nace would have been appointed guardian. Even if it was in R.M.S.'s best interests to remain with the Villers, UPC §5-202 and COLO. STAT. ANN. §15-14-202, the court has no power to rule that an appointment is not in the minor's best interests.

22. Could R.M.S. have objected to Kathleen Nace's petition if R.M.S. was 15 years old? What if R.M.S. was 13 years old?

ANSWER. Under UPC §5-203 and COLO. STAT. ANN. §15-14-203, minors need to be at least 14 years old to object to a parent's testamentary appointment under UPC §5-202 and COLO. STAT. ANN. §15-14-202. Thus, R.M.S. could have objected if she were 15, but not 13.

PROBLEM VI

Scott and Laraya, who live in a UPC jurisdiction, have a 3-year-old daughter, Ginny. Tragically, Scott and Laraya are involved in a serious car crash. Ginny goes to stay with Scott's mom, Sara. In fact, Scott's will nominates Sara as Ginny's guardian. However, Laraya has signed a one page, typed, and unwitnessed piece of paper that names her dad, Reggie, as Ginny's guardian.

A. If Scott is killed instantly, and Laraya dies later in the hospital, who presumptively becomes Ginny's guardian?

B. Would the outcome change if Laraya had written the piece of paper nominating Reggie as guardian before she was pregnant with Ginny?

C. Suppose Laraya never executes the piece of paper nominating Reggie. The court appoints Scott's mother, Sara, as Ginny's guardian under Scott's will. Laraya's sister, Kim, has never gotten along with Sara. Kim firmly believes that it is in Ginny's best interest to live with her, Kim, not Sara. Can Kim object to Sara's appointment?

5.5.3 "Just Debts"

Wills almost always contain a clause that empowers the executor to pay the testator's "just debts." These directives are unnecessary, because executors are required to honor legitimate claims by creditors even if a will does not impose this duty. See, e.g., N.Y. Surr. Ct. Proc. Act Law §1811 (McKinney 2014) ("Every fiduciary must proceed with diligence to pay the debts of the decedent."). In fact, "just debts" clauses are worse than superfluous. Sometimes they create confusion about a decedent's wishes with respect to mortgages on real property.

In the eighteenth century, the common law exoneration doctrine allowed beneficiaries to take a decedent's real property free of any amount owed to a bank or lender. That meant that the other beneficiaries — for example, those that received the residue of the estate — had the unpaid mortgage balance deducted from their shares. Gradually, state legislatures began to rethink this rule. They adopted statutes that called for exoneration only when the testator specifically requested it. Here, however, the prevalence of boilerplate "just debts" clauses reared its head. Courts often construed these provisions as evidence that the testator wanted to discharge any outstanding mortgage. Thus, in a widely adopted reform, the UPC took the additional steps of (1) making nonexoneration the norm and (2) trying to prevent rote "just debts" clauses from overriding this default.

Uniform Probate Code
§2-607 Nonexoneration

A specific devise passes subject to any mortgage interest existing at the date of death, without right of exoneration, regardless of a general directive in the will to pay debts.

In re Estate of Vincent
98 S.W.3d 146 (Tenn. 2003)

FRANK F. DROWOTA, III, C.J.

In this will construction case, we address the question of whether or not the doctrine of exoneration applies to a mortgage on real property passing by right of survivorship where the decedent's will directed that his personal representative pay all his "just debts." We find that the general direction to pay "just debts" is not sufficient to require that the estate pay the remaining balance on the mortgage of non-probate property. . . .

FACTUAL BACKGROUND

The facts in this case are uncontested. On January 22, 1993, George Vincent (the "decedent") purchased a house and lot for $255,000.00 in Deerfield Resort, Campbell County, Tennessee (the "Deerfield property"). On the day of purchase, the decedent signed an adjustable rate note (the "note") with Home Federal Bank ("Home Federal") for $150,000. The note was secured by a Deed of Trust on the property (the "mortgage"), which was recorded on January 26, 1993.

On June 17, 1993, the decedent executed a deed conveying full title and interest in the Deerfield property to himself and the plaintiff, William J. Vincent ("Vincent"), his nephew, as joint tenants with right of survivorship. The deed was recorded on July 7, 1993. The decedent alone made all monthly installment payments up until his death.

George Vincent died testate on February 22, 2001. The Last Will and Testament of George Vincent (the "will"), dated February 1, 2001, contains the following general instructions with regard to the payment of his debts:

> Second: I direct my Executor to pay all my just debts and funeral expenses; provided, however, any installment debts secured by real estate may, in the discretion of my executor, continue to be paid on an installment basis for so long as my Executor deems such method of payment to be beneficial to my estate.

In the will, the decedent directed that all of his real and personal property go to John Oliver ("Oliver"). There was no mention of Vincent, the Deerfield property, or the mortgage.

After the decedent's death, no further installment payments were made, and the mortgage on the Deerfield property went into default. Following the will's admission to probate, Home Federal filed a claim against the estate for the balance of the mortgage, $128,341.62. On June 25, 2001, Vincent instituted this action for declaratory judgment, seeking a declaration from the chancery court that he was entitled to exoneration of the mortgage debt on the property he had acquired by right of survivorship. On August 3, 2001, Reid Troutman, Personal Representative of the decedent's estate, filed an exception to Home Federal's claim. The trial court held that the property was not a part of the estate and that Vincent was not entitled to exoneration of the mortgage debt.

The Court of Appeals reversed the trial court, finding that the decedent "was solely responsible for the indebtedness to Home Federal" and that "the indebtedness to Home Federal is a 'just debt' of the estate." The Court of Appeals concluded that its decision "results in the exact situation which would have occurred had the decedent not passed away and continued to make monthly payments, as he did until his death, until the mortgage was paid."

We granted the defendants' application for permission to appeal and now reverse the judgment of the Court of Appeals and reinstate the judgment of the trial court. . . .

ANALYSIS

Under the common law doctrine of exoneration, an heir or devisee is generally entitled to have encumbrances upon real estate paid by the estate's personalty unless, in the devisee's case, the will directs otherwise. Vincent, despite taking title by deed and not through devise or descent, argues that the doctrine of exoneration should be applied to his situation as well, and that this Court should extend the doctrine to apply to mortgages on property passing outside probate.

. . .

[However], a number of jurisdictions have abrogated the common law doctrine of exoneration, requiring that wills specifically direct that exoneration is intended for encumbered property. Some statutes, like those of Nebraska, New York, and the Uniform Probate Code, stipulate that a general direction to pay debts is not enough to exonerate specifically devised property. See Neb. Rev. Stat. §30-2347 (2002); N.Y. Est. Powers & Trusts Law §3-3.6(a) (McKinney 1981); Uniform Probate Code, §2-609.

We find that the general language in the decedent's will, directing his personal representative to pay all of his "just debts," is not sufficiently clear to justify the exoneration of a mortgage on property passing by right of survivorship. . . . [G]iven the trend in other states to limit the common law doctrine by requiring specific language indicating an intent to exonerate devised property, it would be inappropriate to interpret general language such as "just debts" as evincing an intent to exonerate property passing outside probate. In the absence of guidance from the General Assembly, we decline to extend the common law doctrine of exoneration in this manner.

The plaintiff argues further that the additional language regarding installment debts following the directive to pay "just debts" supports his contention that the decedent meant for all of his outstanding mortgages — on both probate and non-probate property — to be paid by his estate.

However, the cardinal rule for interpreting and construing a will is to ascertain the intent of the testator and to give effect to that intent unless prohibited by law or public policy. . . . In this case, the clearly stated intent of the decedent is to benefit the sole beneficiary of the will. Furthermore, the decedent had two opportunities to direct that Vincent was to receive the Deerfield property free and clear: he could have purchased the property outright, avoiding a mortgage altogether, or else expressly directed in his will that the Deerfield property mortgage be paid from his estate. The brevity of the will, the direction to give all his property, both real and personal, to

John Oliver, and the absence of language mentioning either the plaintiff or the Deerfield property in the will require this Court to infer that the decedent intended that his entire estate pass to the stated sole beneficiary. This Court believes that it would be overreaching to find that the language regarding installment payments applies to unnamed, non-probate property.

. . .

Were this Court to order the estate to pay the balance on the Deerfield property mortgage, the sole beneficiary of the will would suffer. On the other hand, the plaintiff is not harmed by taking the property subject to the mortgage. The plaintiff has several options. He can continue ownership of the property by paying the mortgage, or he can sell the property and redeem any existing equity, or he can allow the bank to foreclose.

Therefore we find that the mortgage on the Deerfield property is not an obligation of the estate. This is the correct result as a matter of public policy because it gives effect to the stated intent of the testator. Under these facts, having taken the property subject to the mortgage, Vincent must continue to pay the mortgage in order to continue to enjoy ownership.

CONCLUSION

For the reasons stated herein, the judgment of the trial court is reinstated, and the judgment of the Court of Appeals is reversed.

The Deerfield Property was located on Norris Lake, a man-made body of water created in 1933 when the Tennessee Valley Authority built the Norris Dam (pictured above).

QUESTIONS

23. In most disputes over "just debts" clauses and exoneration, the issue is whether the recipient of land under the will is entitled to have the will's other beneficiaries pay off the mortgage. But in *Vincent*, William, the party seeking exoneration, received the real estate through a deed. Do you think the court's analysis would have been different if William took the real property under the will?

ANSWER. The court might have been slightly more willing to find exoneration. For example, it emphasizes its unwillingness to "extend" the common law exoneration doctrine to nonprobate transfers. Arguably, this implies that the court might have invoked the common law exoneration rule (bucking the UPC's trend) if the facts of the case did not call for such an extension.

24. Why does the clause giving the executor discretion to pay "installment debts" not apply?

ANSWER. Most likely because the executor can only invoke this provision if he or she determines that paying installment debts is "beneficial to the estate." Here, William is not a beneficiary of the estate—only John is. It is hard to see how John would benefit from paying the mortgage on William's property.

PROBLEM VII

Carmel died, leaving a valid will that gives her house to her daughter, Kristi, and the residue of her estate to her son, Brandon. The house is subject to a $100,000 mortgage. Carmel also owned $200,000 in cash. Under the UPC, who gets what in the following scenarios?

a. Carmel's will requires her executor to "pay her just debts."
b. Carmel's will requires her executor to "pay her just debts, other than those relating to real property."
c. Carmel's will requires her executor to "pay her just debts, including those relating to real property."
d. Carmel's will says nothing about paying her debts.

5.6 NEGATIVE WILLS: THE RIGHT TO EXCLUDE INTESTATE HEIRS

UPC §2-101(b) permits what are known as *negative wills*. A negative will is a will (or a provision in a will, sometimes referred to as an *exclusionary clause*) that expressly disinherits potential heirs in the event of an intestacy. Under the common law, such negative wills were given no effect, despite a decedent's explicit statement of intent.

Uniform Probate Code
§2-101 Intestate Estate

. . .

(b) A decedent by will may expressly exclude or limit the right of an individual or class to succeed to property of the decedent passing by intestate succession. If that individual or a member of that class survives the decedent, the share of the decedent's intestate estate to which that individual or class would have succeeded passes as if that individual or each member of that class had disclaimed his [or her] intestate share.

COMMENT

. . .

New subsection (b) authorizes the decedent, by will, to exclude or limit the right of an individual or class to share in the decedent's intestate estate, in effect disinheriting that individual or class. By specifically authorizing so-called negative wills, subsection (b) reverses the usually accepted common-law rule, which defeats a testator's intent for no sufficient reason.

The Restatement concurs with the UPC:

Restatement (Third) of Property: Wills & Other Donative Transfers §2.7 Negative Wills

A decedent's will may expressly exclude or limit the right of an individual or class to succeed to property of the decedent passing by intestate succession.

The following case indicates the common law's—and still today many jurisdictions'—contrary approach to the position taken in both the UPC and the Restatement.

Cook v. Estate of Seeman
858 S.W.2d 114 (Ark. 1993)

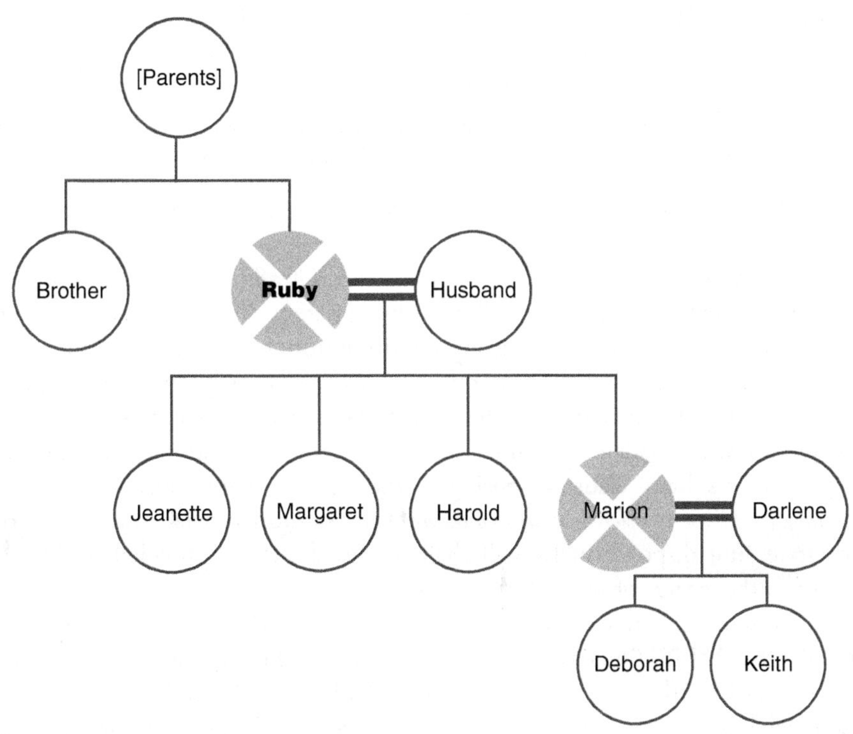

Holt, Chief Justice.

This case presents the novel issue of whether an exclusionary clause in a will lacking a residuary clause controls intestate property held by the testatrix. We hold that it does not and reverse the findings of the Probate Court.

On May 7, 1987, the decedent, Ruby Seeman, executed a will distributing her assets to her husband, brother and three surviving children. The will, which does not have a residuary clause, fails to dispose of her residence, but it does explicitly exclude the widow and children of her late son, Marion Seeman, from inheriting any part of her estate: "Whereas, my son, Marion Seeman, has preceded me in death, I direct that no part of my estate shall go to his Widow, Darlene Seeman, or to their children Deborah Seeman Jones and Keith Seeman."

Mrs. Ruby Seeman died on March 10, 1992, and proof of will documents were filed by the two witnesses. The Executrix for the Estate petitioned the court for authority to sell the decedent's residence and asked the court to determine to whom the proceeds of the sale should be distributed. After a hearing the Arkansas County Probate Court determined:

> That the decedent's residence was not disposed of by her will, and the decedent's will did not contain a residuary clause.
>
> . . .
>
> As it was the Testatrix's specific intent to exclude Deborah Seeman Jones and Keith Seeman from sharing in her estate, the will should be construed so that the proceeds from the sale of the house are distributed to the decedent's three surviving children, Jeanette Seeman Tuthill, Margaret Seeman Schafer and Harold Seeman, Jr.
>
> IT IS, THEREFORE, BY THE COURT, CONSIDERED, ORDERED ADJUDGED AND DECREED that the proceeds from the sale of the decedent's residence are to be distributed to the decedent's three surviving children, Jeanette Seeman Tuthill, Margaret Seeman Schafer and Harold Seeman, Jr.

It is from this order that Debra (Seeman Jones) Cook and Keith Seeman bring this appeal.

This is a case of first impression for this court. Clearly, the decedent's residence was not disposed of through her will; it is also apparent that Mrs. Seeman intended to prevent her two grandchildren from inheriting from her estate. Traditionally, the cardinal principle of will interpretation is that the testator's intent governs and that intention is to be gathered from the four corners of the instrument, and if at all possible, we will broaden or enlarge a residuary clause to avoid intestacy. Yet, here, there is no residuary clause disposing of the balance of the decedent's estate *so intestacy as to the residence is unavoidable*. Our statutes provide that any part of the estate "not disposed of by will shall be distributed as provided by law with respect to the estates of intestates."

Although there are no Arkansas cases deciding whether the intent to disinherit should affect distribution of intestate property, we have mentioned this issue on one occasion. In Quattlebaum v. Simmons Nat'l Bank, 184 S.W.2d 911 (Ark. 1945), a case involving questions of whether certain bequests had lapsed and, if so, whether certain legatees could also share in the residual intestate property, we stated in obiter dictum, "The fact that a person is disinherited by the will does not prevent his sharing, as heir at law or distributee, in property, a legacy or devise of which has failed by lapse."

In other jurisdictions it is well settled that although the testator's intent to disinherit is clearly and unambiguously expressed in the will, such exclusionary language will not be given effect as against the distribution of intestate property. A good reason given for this rule, expressed by the court of appeals of a sister state, is that because the intestate property passes by law rather than by will, the statute and not the testator controls the distribution of this property. . . .

We hold that although the will excluded the appellants from the estate, it did not alter their entitlement under the laws of intestate succession, provided in Ark. Code Ann. §28-26-103 (1987). Accordingly, we reverse the decision of the Probate Court.

Reversed and remanded.

QUESTIONS

25. Mrs. Seeman did not want her grandchildren, Deborah and Keith, to share in her estate, but because Arkansas does not recognize negative wills, they did inherit from Mrs. Seeman as intestate heirs. What, if anything, could Mrs. Seeman have done to effectuate her intent notwithstanding Arkansas's position on negative wills?

    ANSWER. Mrs. Seeman should have made a complete disposition of her estate by including a residuary clause in favor of beneficiaries other than Deborah and Keith. Had she done so, none of her property would pass by intestacy, thereby avoiding the need to exclude affirmatively Deborah and Keith from her estate. All well-drafted wills include a residuary clause, as discussed in Chapters 5 and 7. She should also have included an exclusionary clause because she might have died domiciled in a jurisdiction that recognized negative wills or Arkansas law could have been amended to permit negative wills.

26. The court cited *Quattlebaum v. Simmons National Bank*, in which both residuary beneficiaries of a will predeceased the testator, thus causing the residuary devise to "lapse" (see Chapter 6) and pass by intestacy. The *Quattlebaum* court held that beneficiaries who received specific gifts of money under the will were not precluded from also taking part of the lapsed residue as intestate heirs. There was a partial intestacy, but no express disinheritance clause. Given this context, do you find the *Quattlebaum* dictum quoted by the court helpful in resolving the question of whether to enforce a negative will?

    ANSWER. The *Quattlebaum* dictum, which is itself a quotation from a general legal encyclopedia, does not seem particularly helpful because the underlying case did not implicate disinheritance.

27. Do you agree with the court that "because the intestate property passes by law rather than by will, the statute and not the testator controls the distribution of this property"?

    ANSWER. This passage reflects an important distinction between the right to transmit and the right to receive. Testamentary freedom confers individuals with the power to direct the disposition of property at death, including the power to transmit property to beneficiaries who are not intestate heirs. Upon an individual's failure to exercise testamentary freedom by executing a will, heirs at law succeed to the decedent's property interests by intestacy and therefore have a right to inherit.

28. Does recognition of negative wills facilitate or inhibit the donor's freedom of disposition?

    ANSWER. Recognition of negative wills facilitates the freedom of disposition by providing donors with another way of opting out of the default rules of intestacy. A negative will allows the donor to exclude certain intestate heirs without making affirmative dispositions in a will. Negative wills contain direct evidence of the decedent's intent, so if the goal of intestacy is to carry out the decedent's probable intent, then recognition would facilitate the freedom of disposition rather than inhibit it.

PROBLEM VIII

Rachael Lieberman, a 70-year-old widow, has been estranged from her only son, Jacob, for the last twenty-five years. She has, however, developed a close relationship with two first cousins who, aside from Jacob, are her closest blood relations. She has also been a longtime supporter of her local synagogue, Kesher Israel, to which she has considered donating her property at death. Ms. Lieberman is sure that her son, Jacob, should not receive any property upon her death, but she is not prepared to decide whether to devise her estate entirely to her synagogue or partially to her synagogue and her cousins. What advice would you offer Ms. Lieberman?

negative will ~~to~~ Jacob and may appoint personal rep for resid & if PP - could be a list of tangible PP

6 | Will Drafting Principles and Default Rules

6.1 INTRODUCTION

This chapter explores principles of will drafting and, more broadly, how to structure and interpret the testator's estate plan. As in other areas of the law, these drafting principles operate against a backdrop of default rules of construction that apply when a will *fails* to address the most common interpretive problems, conflicts, and questions. Good estate planning, at a minimum, requires a solid understanding of default rules so that the attorney can provide advice on whether to incorporate a default or draft customized language in the will to suit the testator's contrary preference.

Our discussion will focus on two unifying themes. First, wills are inherently forward-looking instruments, so they must be drafted with a keen understanding of the facts, contingencies, and conditions that are likely, if not inevitably, to change with the passage of time. Second, when testamentary language falls short of absolute precision and accuracy (as it too often does), the interpretive problems are compounded by the testators' unavailability, at the time of probate, to clarify their intention.

In Sections 6.1-6.4, we discuss default rules applicable when factual circumstances change between the will's execution and administration. This passage of time is often accompanied by changes in both the subject (i.e., property) and object (i.e., beneficiaries) of the will's various devises. Property in testators' probate estates may change: New property will come in, and other property will be lost, stolen, destroyed, sold, or otherwise disposed of. So too with named beneficiaries: Some will survive the testator and some will not; new members of testators' families will be born or adopted. For testators' wills to remain effective in carrying out testators' intentions, these situations should be clearly addressed in testators' wills. More often than not, however, precautions are not taken, resulting in the development of the doctrines discussed below, often described as doctrines that address the problem of a "stale will": default rules governing the death of a beneficiary before the testator (lapse in Section 6.2; antilapse in Section 6.3; and class gifts in Section 6.4) and changes in the composition of the testator's estate (ademption, abatement, and accession in Section 6.5).

In Section 6.6, we discuss the limitations of language and problems that arise when lawyers fail to ask the right questions, confirm the answers, and proofread wills with meticulous care: issues of ambiguous and mistaken language.

6.2 FAILURE TO SURVIVE—LAPSE

A testamentary instrument must anticipate the possibility that one or more beneficiaries may not outlive the testator. A beneficiary who fails to survive the testator cannot enjoy the intended testamentary gift, so it is essential that the testator contemplate alternative beneficiaries to take in the predeceased beneficiary's absence. This consideration is so central to the art of will drafting that the phrase "if she survives me" has become one of the most familiar idioms in estate planning. Indeed, as the Restatement explains, the requirement that a beneficiary survive the testator is so fundamental to the law of donative transfers that the principle applies even without use of the famed idiom:

> A donative transfer cannot be made to a person who is deceased, because a decedent lacks juridical personality. This is a mandatory rule, not a rule of construction. Consequently, language in a donative document expressly requiring survival until the time when the donative document takes effect is surplusage. The requirement of survival derives from the law, not from the document. An attempt to confer a property interest on a beneficiary who dies before the donative document takes effect as a dispositive instrument is ineffective. Although the transferor cannot override the rule of this section, he or she can create an express gift over to a substitute taker, even to the "estate" or "executor" of a predeceased beneficiary. . . .

Restatement (Third) of Property: Wills & Other Donative Transfers §26.1, comment b. Under the survivorship requirement, a testamentary gift is said to *lapse*[1] when a beneficiary predeceases the testator.

The effect of lapse on a testamentary gift is that the gift "fails." It cannot be distributed to the predeceased beneficiary's estate unless the testator explicitly provides gift-over in the bequest. For example, "I give $1,000 to my sister Susan if she survives me by thirty days but if she does not survive me by thirty days, the gift to my sister Susan shall be paid instead to her estate."

Although little can be done to prevent a gift from lapsing because the intended beneficiary predeceases the testator, a great deal can be done to avoid a lapsed gift. Good principles of estate planning and will drafting require consideration of what *should* happen to a gift in the event of lapse. In some cases, the testator will designate an alternative beneficiary to take in place of the predeceased beneficiary. In other cases, the anti-lapse provisions of UPC §2-603 (below) may create a substitute gift in alternative

1. We will repeatedly run into the word "lapse." The word derives from the Latin word *lapsus*, meaning "slip."

beneficiary or the gift may lapse, in which case disposition of the gift will be governed by default rules (UPC §2-604, below) that redistribute the gift to other beneficiaries depending on the type of devise: Upon lapse of a specific, general, or demonstrative devise, the lapsed gift falls into the residuary estate. Upon lapse of a residuary devise, if there is more than one residuary beneficiary, in most states and under the UPC, the lapsed residuary devise is reallocated among the surviving residuary beneficiaries. However, in a minority of states that continue to apply the common law "no-residue-of-a-residue" rule, a lapsed residuary devise passes by intestacy even if there are other surviving residuary beneficiaries. If there is only one residuary beneficiary, a lapsed residuary devise passes by intestacy.

Uniform Probate Code
§2-604 Failure of Testamentary Provision

(a) Except as provided in Section 2-603 [Antilapse], a devise, other than a residuary devise, that fails for any reason becomes a part of the residue.

(b) Except as provided in Section 2-603, if the residue is devised to two or more persons, the share of a residuary devisee that fails for any reason passes to the other residuary devisee, or to other residuary devisees in proportion to the interest of each in the remaining part of the residue.

The default survivorship rules for determining whether a testamentary provision has lapsed is codified under UPC §2-702: When a donative instrument conditions the beneficiary's disposition on surviving a particular event, such as the testator's death, the beneficiary is deemed to have predeceased the event absent clear and convincing evidence of survival by 120 hours (five days), the same survivorship period required under the corresponding intestacy rule, UPC §2-104. However, UPC §2-702(d) contains four exceptions, the most important of which declares the 120-hour survivorship rule to be a default. Thus, the testator may specify a longer survivorship period or explicitly provide that a bequest to a predeceased beneficiary be paid to the beneficiary's estate. Indeed, it is common for well-drafted wills to opt out of the 120-hour rule in favor of a longer survivorship period of thirty days or more. Do you see the benefits of opting for a longer survivorship period?

PROBLEM I

Arthur and Betsy were married but had no children. Arthur's will devised his estate to Betsy if she survived him by ten days, and if not, to his parents. Betsy's will devised her estate to Arthur if he survived her by ten days, and if not, to her parents. A year ago, Arthur and Betsy were involved in a catastrophic automobile accident. Betsy died at the scene of the accident. Arthur sustained a severe brain injury and fell into a coma. He was taken to the hospital and placed on life support. At the behest of Arthur's parents, he remained on life support for eleven days, at which point they concluded that the prospects for recovery were unlikely. Who inherits Betsy's estate?

Carpenter v. Miller
26 S.W.3d 135 (Ark. Ct. App. 2000)

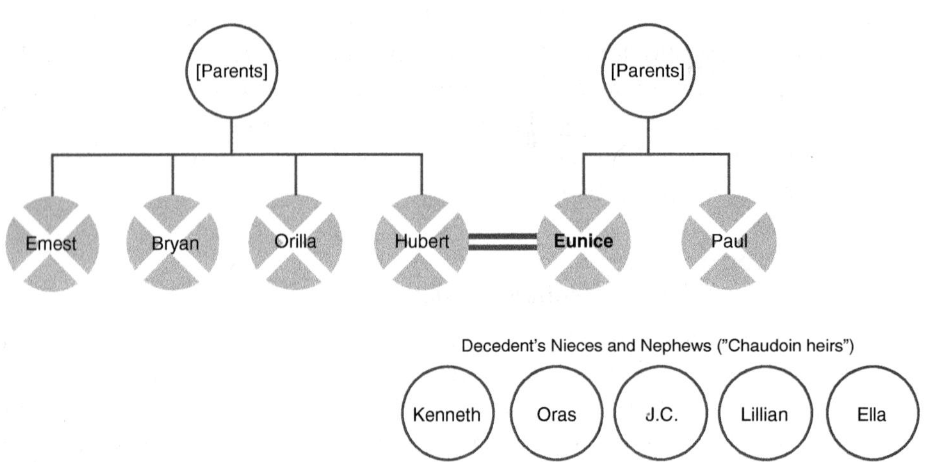

K. Max Koonce, II, Judge.

In this case, we are asked to review the probate judge's interpretation of the will of Eunice Carpenter, deceased. The judge found that the will unambiguously devised the residue of the decedent's estate to five particular individuals. Appellant C.J. Carpenter, a co-executor of the decedent's estate, argues that the judge erred in determining that no ambiguity existed. We affirm.

Eunice Carpenter died in 1999, leaving an estate valued at approximately $361,000. Her husband, Hubert Carpenter, predeceased her. In her will, decedent devised virtually all of her property to her husband but declared that, should he predecease her, her estate would pass as provided in articles four and five of her will. Article four bequeathed $1,000 to each of twenty-three nieces and nephews. Article five then devised the residue of the estate as follows:

> In the event that my husband, HUBERT C. CARPENTER, should predecease me, after the payment of the TWENTY-THREE THOUSAND DOLLARS ($23,000.00) above-mentioned in paragraph "IV", I hereby give, devise and bequeath my entire estate to ERNEST L. CARPENTER; BRYAN A. CARPENTER; ORILLA CARPENTER PINKSTON and PAUL L. CHAUDOIN.
>
> In the event that either of the above-named brothers of HUBERT C. CARPENTER, or the above-named sister of HUBERT C. CARPENTER should predecease me, then in that event his or her interest shall lapse and the surviving beneficiaries of the FOUR (4) beneficiaries above-named shall take the interest that the deceased beneficiary would have received had he or she survived me; except that in the event of the death of PAUL L. CHAUDOIN, his interest shall not lapse, but the interest that he would have taken had he survived my death shall be given to the following parties, share and share alike.

1. KENNETH CHAUDOIN, my nephew;

2. ORAS MILLER, my nephew;

3. J. C. MILLER, my nephew;

4. LILLIAN MILLER PROVINCE, my niece; and

5. ELLA JEAN MILLER VEST, my niece.

Of the four primary beneficiaries listed above, three of them — Ernest Carpenter, Bryan Carpenter, and Orilla Carpenter Pinkston — were siblings of the decedent's late husband. The fourth primary beneficiary — Paul Chaudoin — was the decedent's brother. The five individuals listed as taking Paul Chaudoin's interest in the event of his death were the decedent's only heirs-at-law at the time of her death. They will be referred to hereafter as the "Chaudoin heirs."

The language at issue in this case is the phrase which reads, "in that event [that Ernest, Orilla, or Bryan should predecease the testatrix] his or her interest shall lapse and the surviving beneficiaries of the FOUR (4) beneficiaries above-named shall take the interest that the deceased beneficiary would have received had he or she survived me." The language is important because all four of the primary beneficiaries predeceased Eunice Carpenter — Ernest in 1991, Orillia in 1996, Paul in 1997, and Bryan in 1998.

Appellant, who is co-executor of the estate and whose interest is aligned with the children of Ernest Carpenter, Bryan Carpenter, and Orilla Pinkston (hereafter "Carpenter heirs"), argues that article five is ambiguous and may be interpreted to mean that, upon the deaths of Ernest, Bryan, and Orilla, each of their one-fourth interests passed to their own heirs or legatees. Under this interpretation, the Carpenter heirs would receive three-fourths of the residue of the estate and the five individuals listed as taking Paul's interest would receive one-fourth. Appellee, who is the other co-executor of the estate and whose interest is aligned with the Chaudoin heirs, argues that the will is susceptible to only two interpretations, either of which would result in the Chaudoin heirs receiving the entire residuary estate. His first interpretation is that the shares bequeathed to Ernest, Orilla, and Bryan lapsed upon their deaths, in which case their shares passed to the Chaudoin heirs by intestate succession. His alternative interpretation is that, upon the death of each primary beneficiary other than Paul, that beneficiary's bequest lapsed and served to increase the shares of the surviving primary beneficiaries. The practical result of this interpretation is that, upon the death of Ernest in 1991, his bequest lapsed and served to increase the shares of Orilla, Paul, and Bryan so that each of them was then beneficiary of a one-third interest; upon the death of Orilla in 1996, her bequest lapsed and served to increase the shares of Paul and Bryan so that each of them was then a beneficiary of a one-half interest; upon Paul's death in 1997, his bequest did not lapse because the Chaudoin heirs became entitled to take Paul's share; and then upon Bryan's death in 1997, his share lapsed and the Chaudoin heirs, who stand in Paul's stead, became the sole beneficiaries inasmuch as Paul's share is determined as if Paul had survived the testatrix, and had he survived her, he would have been the sole surviving primary beneficiary.

After a hearing on the issue, the probate judge determined that there was no ambiguity in the will and that the Chaudoin heirs were the beneficiaries of the entire residue of the estate. Appellant appeals from that ruling.

Probate cases are reviewed de novo on appeal. However, we do not reverse a probate court's findings unless they are clearly erroneous. A finding is clearly erroneous when, although there is evidence to support it, the reviewing court on the entire evidence is left with the definite and firm conviction that a mistake has been committed. In the interpretation of wills, the paramount principle is that the intent of the testator governs. The testator's intent is to be gathered from the four corners of the instrument itself. However, extrinsic evidence may be received on the issue of the testator's intent if the terms of the will are ambiguous. An ambiguity has been defined as an indistinctness or uncertainty of meaning of an expression in a written instrument.

We hold that the language in article five is not ambiguous. It provides that, upon the deaths of Ernest, Orilla, and Bryan, their interests shall "lapse" if they predecease the testatrix. The term "lapse" is a technical one, with a specific meaning in probate law. It means that a devise fails or takes no effect. Thus, a lapsed devise will not pass to a devisee's heirs. Consistent with this, Arkansas law provides that, when a bequest to a residuary legatee lapses, his interest passes to the other residuary legatees in proportion to their interests. The technical meaning of the term "lapse" as used in this case means that any bequest to Ernest, Bryan, or Orilla would cease to exist if they predeceased the testatrix and would not be passed on to their respective heirs but would increase the shares of the remaining residuary legatees.

We also hold that the decedent's express declaration that, upon the deaths of Ernest, Bryan, or Orilla, his or her interest would pass to "the surviving beneficiaries of the FOUR (4) beneficiaries above-named" is not ambiguous. The phrase refers to the survivors from among the four primary beneficiaries, i.e., upon Ernest's death in 1991, the interest he was bequeathed lapsed and served to increase the shares of Bryan, and Orilla, and Paul, who were the "surviving beneficiaries of the four." The language used by the decedent is similar to that used in Chlanda v. Estate of Fuller, 326 Ark. 551, 932 S.W.2d 760 (1996). There, the testator declared that his estate would be shared equally among certain beneficiaries "or the survivor thereof." The supreme court held that the words "the survivor thereof" did not mean the heirs of any beneficiary but unambiguously referred to the person among the designated class who outlived the other.

Affirmed.

ROBBINS, C.J., and JENNINGS, MEADS, and ROAF, JJ., agree.

JOHN F. STROUD, JR., Judge, dissenting.

I disagree with the majority's conclusion that article five of the will is unambiguous. It is susceptible to at least two and possibly three interpretations. Even appellee, in his brief, suggests two possible interpretations of the will. Both of his interpretations and the interpretation suggested by appellant are reasonable and merit further exploration with the aid of extrinsic evidence, especially in light of the complex and somewhat confusing language used by the testatrix.

The majority relies in part on the decedent's use of the term "lapse" to describe what would happen to the interests of those who predeceased her. Although it is possible that she meant to employ this term in its technical sense, it is equally possible that she was using it in a more generic sense. This is evidenced by the fact that, soon after declaring that her bequests to Ernest, Bryan, and Orilla would lapse, she felt the need to designate those to whom their lapsed interests would pass. If she was using "lapse" in its technical sense, her instruction that the lapsed interest would pass to the "surviving beneficiaries of the four" was superfluous. The confusion in the use of the word "lapse" is further amplified by the next paragraph of the will. The testatrix again uses the word "lapse," but this time says "in the event of the death of Paul L. Chaudoin, his interest shall not lapse. . . ." Although providing that the bequest shall not lapse, she also proceeds to name who shall receive the bequest.

In light of the foregoing, it is worth considering that the testatrix was not speaking technically when using that term. Technical terms need not be construed in their technical sense when the testator uses explanatory words to give them a different meaning.

I also disagree that the *Chlanda* case is dispositive here. The testator in that case used different language than the testatrix used in this case. Our testatrix did not refer to "the survivors of the four" or "the survivors among the four" but "the *surviving beneficiaries* of the four." (Emphasis added.) That language creates an ambiguity not present in *Chlanda*.

QUESTIONS

1. Based on your reading of *Carpenter*, can you determine whether Arkansas has repealed or retained the common law no-residue-of-a-residue rule as the default governing a lapsed residuary devise?

   ANSWER. The opinion recites a rule that rejects the common law no-residue-of-a-residue rule: "[A] lapsed devise will not pass to a devisee's heirs. Consistent with this, Arkansas law provides that, when a bequest to a residuary legatee lapses, his interest passes to the other residuary legatees in proportion to their interests." Under this system, a lapsed residuary devise does not pass by intestacy as at common law but, rather, is reallocated among the surviving residuary beneficiaries, which today is the majority rule.

2. How, if at all, did the residuary clause in *Carpenter* differ from the default rule in Arkansas?

   ANSWER. Under the Arkansas default rule, when a residuary beneficiary predeceases the testator, the share of the predeceased beneficiary is reallocated among the surviving residuary beneficiaries. Mrs. Carpenter's residuary clause is consistent with and incorporates aspects of the default, but differs in at least one important respect. The clause reallocates shares of her late husband's predeceased siblings among the four primary residuary beneficiaries (i.e., her three siblings-in-law and her brother, Paul), but in the event that Paul were to predecease Mrs. Carpenter, his share passes to an alternative slate of residuary beneficiaries and is not reallocated among the testator's husband's predeceased siblings.

3. Based on the language present in the will, what do you think Mrs. Carpenter was trying to accomplish by structuring the residuary clause as it appeared in her will? Did the court's interpretation give effect to Mrs. Carpenter's intent?

   ANSWER. It appears that Mrs. Carpenter wanted her residuary estate to pass to the surviving siblings of her husband and herself. If her husband's siblings failed to survive, however, she did not want her residuary estate to pass to more remote relatives of her husband's family. Instead, she preferred to leave her estate to a select group of her own blood relatives. Here, all of the primary residuary beneficiaries predeceased, so the testator's most likely intent was to pass her entire residuary estate to that select group of blood relatives identified in the will as alternate residuary beneficiaries. The inclusion of a residuary clause with an alternate slate of residuary beneficiaries shows (an arguably) clear intent *not* to pass any part of the estate by intestacy. The court's interpretation, which treated the lapsed interests of the testator's siblings as passing first to Paul, and then, because Paul predeceased, to the alternative slate of residuary beneficiaries, appears consistent with Mrs. Carpenter's intent.

4. Do you agree with the dissent that the residuary clause of Mrs. Carpenter's will is ambiguous?

   ANSWER. The residuary clause is ambiguous to the extent it does not expressly address what would happen if all the residuary beneficiaries predeceased the testator. The majority's analysis, however, offers a plausible interpretation to address that contingency.

PROBLEM II

After reading *Carpenter v. Miller*, above, review the residuary clause of the testator's will, reproduced below:

> In the event that my husband, HUBERT C. CARPENTER, should predecease me, after the payment of the TWENTY THREE THOUSAND DOLLARS ($23,000.00) above-mentioned in paragraph "IV," I hereby give, devise and bequeath my entire estate to ERNEST L. CARPENTER; BRYAN A. CARPENTER; ORILLA CARPENTER PINKSTON and PAUL L. CHAUDOIN.
>
> In the event that either of the above-named brothers of HUBERT C. CARPENTER, or the above-named sister of HUBERT C. CARPENTER should predecease me, then in that event his or her interest shall lapse and the surviving beneficiaries of the FOUR (4) beneficiaries above-named shall take the interest that the deceased beneficiary would have received had he or she survived me; except that in the event of the death of PAUL L. CHAUDOIN, his interest shall not lapse, but the interest that he would have taken had he survived my death shall be given to the following parties, share and share alike.

1. KENNETH CHAUDOIN, my nephew;
2. ORAS MILLER, my nephew;
3. J. C. MILLER, my nephew;
4. LILLIAN MILLER PROVINCE, my niece; and
5. ELLA JEAN MILLER VEST, my niece.

How, if at all, could the residuary clause have been drafted more clearly to avoid what was arguably ambiguous language?

PROBLEM III

In 2004, Edith executes a will with a residuary clause naming five residuary beneficiaries. In 2005, Luella, one of the residuary beneficiaries (a friend of Edith), dies. In 2008, Edith executes a codicil in which she reduces the number of residuary beneficiaries from five to four. Luella, although by this point deceased, is one of the four residuary beneficiaries named in Edith's 2008 codicil even though Edith had been aware of Luella's death (indeed, Edith attended Luella's funeral). Edith dies in 2017. Luella's children claim that, because Edith knew that Luella was dead when she executed the 2008 codicil, Edith intended for Luella's share to pass to them through Luella's estate. Edith's children, the other three residuary beneficiaries under Edith's will, object. What result? Should the gift to Luella be treated as having lapsed under these circumstances or should the court interpret this devise as "to Luella, but if she predeceases me, to Luella's estate"?

6.3 SIMULTANEOUS DEATH

Sometimes two people who stand to inherit from each other — for example, spouses — die at roughly the same time. As we have just discussed, under the lapse doctrine, a beneficiary of a will or an intestate heir needs to survive the decedent to share in the decedent's estate. In fact, under the common law, one must outlive a decedent *for only a fraction of a second* to satisfy this condition. Traditionally, this rule meant that when an accident claimed the lives of closely related people, the distribution of their property depended on who survived the other — even if that survival was for an exceedingly short period.

There are three problems with the traditional approach. First, when the cause of death was a car accident or airplane crash, it was often impossible to determine the order of death. Second, the survivorship rule created an incentive to litigate the order of death, and such litigation would inevitably dredge up gory and unpleasant details concerning a family tragedy. And third, the survive-for-an-instant rule led to seemingly arbitrary results contrary to the decedent's probable intent. For example, suppose that Thomas is married to Juan-Pierre. Thomas's will leaves everything to Juan-Pierre, but if Juan-Pierre dies first, to Thomas's son from another relationship, Bob. Juan-Pierre's will leaves everything to Thomas, but if Thomas dies first, to Juan-Pierre's mother, Allison. Thomas and Juan-Pierre die when their boat capsizes. If Allison is able to prove that Juan-Pierre survived Thomas — even if for only a heartbeat — then, in that split second, Juan-Pierre would inherit all of Thomas's property. As a result, when

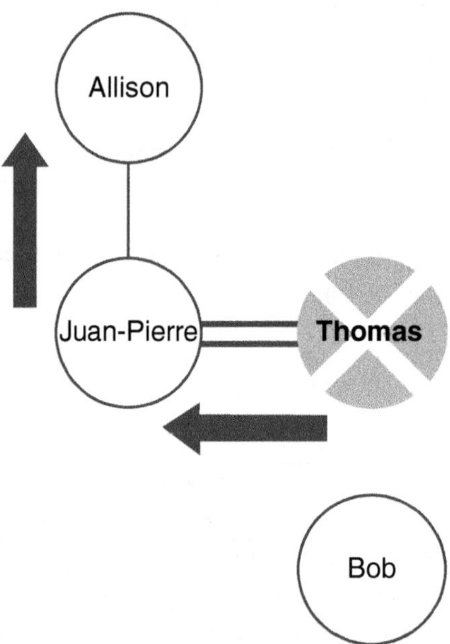

Juan-Pierre died a moment later, both his *and Thomas's* property would pass to Allison. From Thomas's perspective, this outcome is less than ideal: As he stated in his will, he would prefer Bob to inherit from him if Juan-Pierre cannot.

Today, lawmakers have solved this dilemma by enacting Simultaneous Death Acts. These statutes impose a default rule that beneficiaries under wills and intestate heirs must survive the decedent by 120 hours (five days) to inherit from them. If there is clear and convincing evidence that one person survived the other by 120 hours (or more), the survivor takes from the decedent. But if there is no evidence of survival by 120 hours, courts apply a legal fiction that each decedent outlived the other; therefore, each decedent transmits property through his or her own estate to other heirs and beneficiaries. Put another way, because each decedent is deemed to have predeceased the other, neither estate inherits property from the other decedent's estate.

To see why this is an elegant solution to the simultaneous death conundrum, return to the example of Thomas and Juan-Pierre. Assume that it is undisputed that Thomas survived Juan-Pierre by only two days. Because this period is less than 120 hours, it triggers the simultaneous death fiction. For the purposes of Thomas's estate, the probate court will hold that Thomas survived Juan-Pierre. Bob, Thomas's son, will inherit Thomas's property. For the purposes of Juan-Pierre's estate, the judge will find that Juan-Pierre survived Thomas, and give Juan-Pierre's assets to Allison. That is probably what both Thomas and Juan-Pierre would have wanted.

The simultaneous death fiction — failure to survive by 120 hours — is a default rule. Testators frequently state in their wills that any beneficiary must survive them for a longer period of time to inherit. (Thirty to ninety days seems to be the norm.) In addition, testators sometimes include "common disaster" provisions that expressly distribute property in a particular fashion when it is impossible to determine whether the testator or a beneficiary died first. The materials that follow flesh out these nuances.

Uniform Probate Code
§2-104 Requirement of Survival by 120 Hours; Individual in Gestation

(a) For purposes of intestate succession . . . the following rules apply:

(1) An individual born before a decedent's death who fails to survive the decedent by 120 hours is deemed to have predeceased the decedent. If it is not established by clear and convincing evidence that an individual born before a decedent's death survived the decedent by 120 hours, it is deemed that the individual failed to survive for the required period.

(2) An individual in gestation at a decedent's death is deemed to be living at the decedent's death if the individual lives 120 hours after birth. If it is not established by clear and convincing evidence that an individual in gestation at the decedent's death lived 120 hours after birth, it is deemed that the individual failed to survive for the required period.

§2-702 Requirement of Survival by 120 Hours

(a) [Requirement of Survival by 120 Hours Under Probate Code.] For the purposes of this [code], except as provided in subsection (d), an individual who is not established by clear and convincing evidence to have survived an event, including the death of another individual, by 120 hours is deemed to have predeceased the event.

(b) [Requirement of Survival by 120 Hours under Governing Instrument.] Except as provided in subsection (d), for purposes of a provision of a governing instrument that relates to an individual surviving an event, including the death of another individual, an individual who is not established by clear and convincing evidence to have survived the event, by 120 hours is deemed to have predeceased the event.

(c) [Co-owners with Right of Survivorship; Requirement of Survival by 120 Hours.] Except as provided in subsection (d), if (i) it is not established by clear and convincing evidence that one of two co-owners with right of survivorship survived the other co-owner by 120 hours, one-half of the property passes as if one had survived by 120 hours and one-half as if the other had survived by 120 hours. . . . For the purposes of this subsection, "co-owners with right of survivorship" includes joint tenants, tenants by the entireties, and other co-owners of property or accounts held under circumstances that entitles one or more to the whole of the property or account on the death of the other or others.

(d) [Exceptions.] Survival by 120 hours is not required if:

(1) the governing instrument contains language dealing explicitly with simultaneous deaths or deaths in a common disaster and that language is operable under the facts of the case;

(2) the governing instrument expressly . . . requires the individual to survive the event by a specified period; but survival of the event or the specified period must be established by clear and convincing evidence;

. . .

(4) the application of a 120-hour requirement of survival to multiple governing instruments would result in an unintended failure or duplication of a disposition; but survival must be established by clear and convincing evidence.

. . .

In re Leete Estate
803 N.W.2d 889 (Mich. Ct. App. 2010)

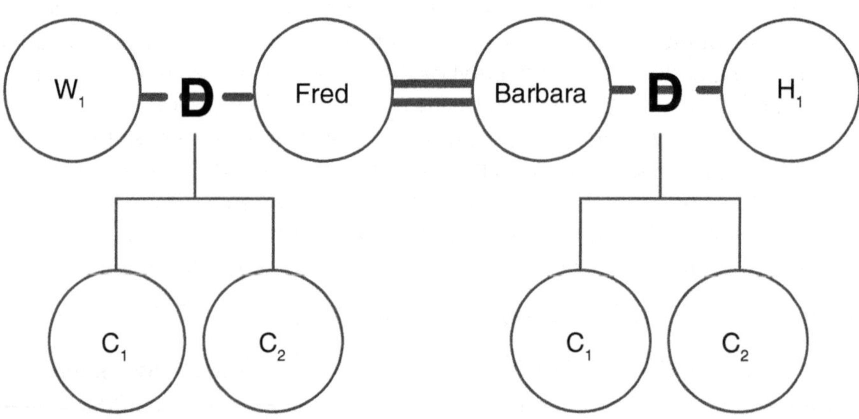

Per Curiam.

In this probate case, we must decide whether the probate court correctly interpreted and applied the Estates and Protected Individuals Code (EPIC), MCL 700.1101 et seq., and its simultaneous-death provision, MCL 700.2702.

In 2008, Frederick DeLand Leete III and Barbara R. Leete, 80 and 75 years old respectively, had been married for 34 years and lived in Brownsburg, Indiana. They had no children from their marriage, but each had children from previous marriages. The Leetes owned, as tenants by the entirety, a cottage located in Mackinaw City in Emmet County, Michigan, which is the property that is the subject of this dispute. Apparently, Frederick had inherited this property, which had been in the Leete family for about 100 years. Nonetheless, Frederick and Barbara executed a quitclaim deed, dated October 29, 1996, which indicated that Frederick and Barbara would own [it] as tenants by the entirety.

On February 28, 2008, at an unknown time, Frederick allegedly left his vehicle running in the garage after returning from the store. That same day, Barbara's daughter went to Barbara and Frederick's home and discovered Barbara dead and Frederick unconscious. At the time, the car's engine was still warm, but it was no longer running because it had run out of gas. Frederick was taken to the hospital, but he expired on March 3, 2008, at 9:10 p.m. Barbara's death certificate lists her date of death as February 28, 2008, time "unknown." The cause of their deaths was carbon monoxide poisoning. Barbara died intestate, but Frederick had a will, dated September 20, 1974.

With regard to the disputed property, Frederick's will provided:

> I give and bequeath to my wife, Barbara R. Leete, if she shall survive me for a period of more than thirty (30) days, all real estate and improvements thereon of which I may die

> the owner or par[t] owner, specifically including the real estate and improvements located on Lot 62, Block "A," Mackinaw City, Emmett County, Michigan. In the event my said wife shall not survive me for a period of more than thirty (30) days, then I give and bequeath such real estate to my aforenamed children who survive me for a period of more than thirty (30) days. . . .
>
> . . .

On November 24, 2008, appellee, who was Barbara's daughter and the personal representative of Barbara's estate, filed an appearance in the case, giving notice to Frederick's estate that Barbara's estate sought a one-half interest in all jointly owned property because Frederick had not survived Barbara by more than 120 hours.

. . .

At the outset, we note that the 120-hour rule, or simultaneous-death provision, is not new to Michigan probate law. Its origin is related to the problematic administration of the common-law rule that an heir or devisee had to survive the testator by only an instant in order to receive a donative transfer under the testator's will. Administration of this common-law concept became problematic in the early twentieth century when vehicular accidents resulting in simultaneous deaths became more common. Thus, in the context of simultaneous deaths, some new rule was necessary to ensure that each decedent's property passed to his or her heirs and avoid the expense of double probate administration. Michigan first adopted a survival requirement in 1941 and a survival-period requirement of 120 hours in 1978. The latter requirement is meant to ensure that a decedent's property passes to a beneficiary who can personally benefit, as opposed to a beneficiary who became deceased a short time later, meaning that the property would ultimately pass to that beneficiary's heirs.

In Michigan, the 120-hour survival requirement did not always apply to nonprobate transfers, such as joint estates with rights of survivorship. While the 120-hour rule was only applicable to wills under the Revised Probate Code, see former MCL 700.132, EPIC expanded the 120-hour rule to cover all events, governing instruments, and co-ownerships. . . .

. . .

MCL 700.2702(3) [EPIC's simultaneous death provision], provides, in relevant part:

> Except as provided in subsection (4), *if it is not established by clear and convincing evidence that 1 of 2 co-owners with right of survivorship survived the other co-owner by 120 hours, 1/2 of the co-owned property passes as if 1 had survived by 120 hours and 1/2 as if the other had survived by 120 hours.* . . . For the purposes of this subsection, "co-owners with right of survivorship" includes joint tenants, tenants by the entireties, and other co-owners of property or accounts held under circumstances that entitles 1 or more to the whole of the property or account on the death of the other or others. [Emphasis added.]

There is no dispute between the parties regarding the meaning of this language and, indeed, we are of the view that this language is clear. If two coowners with rights of survivorship die within 120 hours of one another, then the property does not pass in whole to the last surviving coowner but is divided in equal shares between each coowner's estate. Conversely, if clear and convincing evidence shows that one coowner survived the other by 120 hours or more, then the estate of the longer surviving coowner receives the whole property consistently with his or her right of survivorship.

MCL 700.2702(4) provides a list of exceptions to the general rule established in MCL 700.2702(3). It states:

> Survival by 120 hours is not required under any of the following circumstances:
>
> (a) The governing instrument contains language dealing explicitly with simultaneous deaths or deaths in a common disaster and that language is operable under the facts of the case. . . .
>
> (b) The governing instrument expressly . . . requires the individual to survive the event by a specified period. Survival of the event or the specified period, however, must be established by clear and convincing evidence.
>
> . . .
>
> (d) The application of a 120-hour requirement of survival to multiple governing instruments would result in an unintended failure or duplication of a disposition. Survival, however, must be established by clear and convincing evidence.

Thus, under these limited, articulated circumstances, the 120-hour rule is inapplicable.

Because there is no evidence in the present case demonstrating that Frederick survived Barbara by more than 120 hours—and appellant identifies no such evidence on appeal, in the record or otherwise, and makes no argument relating to the substance of this issue—the 120-hour rule applies and one-half of the Mackinaw City property vested in Barbara's estate, unless appellant can substantiate that one of the exceptions in MCL 700.2702(4) is applicable. The only exception that appellant argues is applicable is MCL 700.2702(4)(d). However, we disagree. While this case does involve multiple governing instruments—Frederick's 1974 will and the 1996 deed—we are not of the view that application of the 120-hour rule would result in an "unintended failure . . . of a disposition." Certainly, Frederick indicated in his 1974 will that Barbara must survive him by more than 30 days in order to receive a full ownership interest in the Mackinaw City property. At the time, Frederick was presumably the sole owner of the property. However, Frederick and Barbara executed a quitclaim deed in 1996 that conveyed the Mackinaw City property to Barbara and Frederick as tenants by the entirety. Clearly, as is evident from the execution of the deed, Frederick's intent with respect to the disposition of the Mackinaw City property changed in 1996. "A conveyance by a testator of . . . his property after making his will revokes the will." Thus, a portion of Frederick's will was effectively revoked with respect to this particular property because the conveyance was inconsistent with the will's provision regarding the disposition of the Mackinaw City property at Frederick's death. And, accordingly, it cannot be said that the application of the 120-hour rule under the present circumstances would result in an unintended failure of disposition. Rather, adherence to the 1974 will would have that effect.

Accordingly, appellant has failed to show that any of the exceptions to the 120-hour rule are applicable. The trial court did not err by applying the 120-hour rule to the present circumstances. And because clear and convincing evidence does not show that Frederick survived Barbara by 120 hours or more, the Mackinaw City property is properly divided between their respective estates.

Affirmed.

QUESTIONS

5. Frederick's 1974 will required Barbara to survive him by thirty days in order to inherit from him. Yet the court holds that Frederick implicitly revoked the portion of his will dealing with the Mackinaw City cottage in 1996, when he deeded it to himself and Barbara as tenants in the entirety. We covered implied revocation in Chapter 4.2.2. For now, though, the critical point is this: The court decides the case as though Frederick and Barbara both died intestate with respect to the cottage. Would Barbara's estate have owned any part of the cottage if Frederick had not executed the 1996 deed?

   ANSWER. If Frederick had not executed the 1996 deed, he would have owned 100 percent of the cottage, and the 1974 will would have controlled. The will gave the cottage to Barbara if she survived Frederick by thirty days. Because she did not, her estate would have had no entitlement to the cottage.

6. Because the 120-hour rule applies, Frederick's estate and Barbara's estate split the cottage. However, Frederick's children argued that the 120-hour rule did not govern because the case fell within the exception for causing "an unintended failure or duplication of a disposition." The court disagrees, essentially reasoning that two co-owners would probably want to divide an asset 50/50 if they died at the same time. Suppose, however, that Frederick and Barbara executed mutual wills, leaving all of their property to each other. In addition, because they wanted to make a $10,000 gift to their church, Frederick's will gave $10,000 to the church if he survived Barbara, while Barbara's will gave $10,000 to the church if she survived Frederick. If both spouses die, and there is not clear and convincing evidence that one survived the other by 120 hours, should the church receive $20,000? Or would that be "an unintended . . . duplication of a disposition"?

   ANSWER. This is a textbook example of "an unintended . . . duplication of a disposition." Frederick and Barbara intended to make one $10,000 gift to the church. But because they died at the same time, the simultaneous death fiction applies, and we treat each one as surviving the other for the purposes of their own estate plan. That means that the church would get two $10,000 gifts instead of one.

7. The Simultaneous Death Act also addresses situations when "the governing instrument contains language dealing explicitly with simultaneous deaths or deaths in a

common disaster and that language is operable under the facts of the case." "Common disaster" is a term of art that means "[a] event that causes two or more persons . . . to die at very nearly the same time, with no way of determining the order of their deaths." Black's Law Dictionary 333 (10th ed. 2014). In Stephens v. Beard, ___ So. 3d ___, No. 14-0406, 2016 WL 1069089, at *1 (Tex. Mar. 18, 2016), a married couple, Venice and Melba Beard, signed nearly identical wills that each made specific cash devises to certain people only "[i]f both [of us] die in a common disaster. . . . " In a tragic turn of events, Venice shot Melba and then himself. However, Venice survived Melba by two hours. Should the "common disaster" clause in their wills apply?

ANSWER. The court held that the common disaster clause did not apply. Because Venice outlived Melba, the case did not involve a scenario in which there was "no way of determining the order of their deaths."

PROBLEM IV

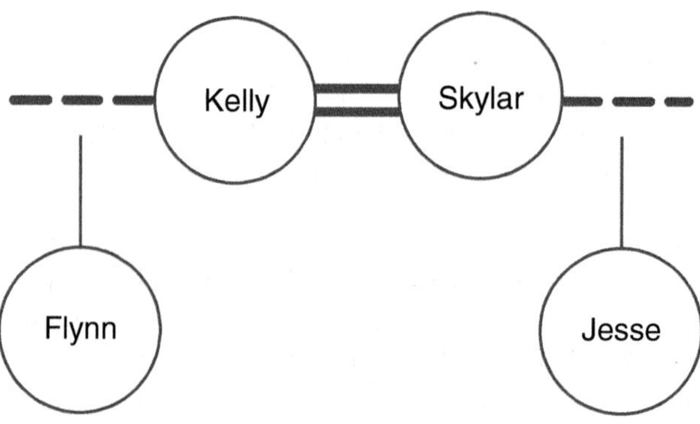

Kelly and Skylar are married. Kelly has a child from a previous relationship, Flynn. Skylar has a child from a previous relationship, Jesse. Each has an estate worth $200,000, and neither of them has a will. They live in a state that has enacted the following statute:

> If a decedent dies intestate, then: (1) The decedent's surviving spouse shall be entitled to all of the decedent's property if the decedent has no surviving children; (2) The decedent's surviving spouse shall be entitled to half of the decedent's property if the decedent has at least one surviving child who is not also a descendant of the surviving spouse. The remaining property shall pass to the decedent's surviving child or children. (3) If the decedent has no surviving spouse, the decedent's surviving child or children inherit all of the decedent's property.

A. On July 1, Kelly dies. On July 10, Skylar dies. What result?

B. On July 1, Kelly dies. On July 4, Skylar dies. What result?

6.4 ANTILAPSE

The law of wills has long presumed that when a beneficiary closely related to the testator predeceases, the testator's preference is to pass the gift to the predeceased beneficiary's descendants rather than to other beneficiaries or intestate heirs. This presumption reflects a preference for preserving lines of descent within the testator's own family. As Professors Halbach and Waggoner explain:

> [C]ommon dispositive preferences instinctively favor representation among different lines of descent. When a deceased child leaves children or more remote descendants, most parents would not want to disinherit that child's line of descent. From the earliest of times, this human instinct has been embedded in the patterns of distribution in intestacy, under which descendants take by representation.

Edward C. Halbach, Jr. & Lawrence W. Waggoner, The UPC's New Survivorship and Antilapse Provisions, 55 Alb. L. Rev. 1091, 1101 (1992). Antilapse statutes effectuate that preference by providing a substitute testamentary gift to the predeceased beneficiary's descendants where the original beneficiary is closely related to the testator. Antilapse rules vary considerably across jurisdictions, but typically share three distinct features.

First, antilapse rules apply only when the predeceased beneficiary fits within a statutorily defined relationship to the testator. Under UPC §2-603(b), for example, the rule applies only to predeceased beneficiaries who are "a grandparent, a descendant of a grandparent, or a stepchild of . . . the testator." Notably, under the UPC, neither the testator's surviving spouse nor the surviving spouse's family (other than the testator's own stepchildren) falls within the scope of the antilapse rules, but other jurisdictions apply the rule more broadly. For example, the California antilapse rule applies to "a person who is kindred of the [testator] or kindred of a surviving, deceased, or former spouse of the [testator]." Cal. Prob. Code §21110(c) (West).

Second, antilapse rules pass the lapsed devise to the predeceased beneficiary's *descendants*, not the predeceased beneficiary's heirs or beneficiaries under a will. Under UPC §2-603(b)(1), for example, "a substitute gift is created in the devisee's surviving descendants. They take by representation the property to which the devisee would have been entitled had the devisee survived the testator." This principle is consistent with the presumption that the typical testator would want to preserve lines of descent rather than allow a lapsed devise to pass to a predeceased beneficiary's surviving spouse, more remote kin, or individuals unrelated to the testator. Query, however, whether this presumption is well placed.

Third, antilapse statutes operate by default, not by command. Thus, the testator may opt out of the antilapse rule through express language in the will indicating a contrary intention. A reliable technique for expressing contrary intent is to provide an alternative devise. Inclusion of an alternative devise clarifies the testator's intent that the predeceased beneficiary's share should not pass to that beneficiary's descendants, but rather, to the alternative devisee named in the will. Another reliable technique is to state expressly that a devise shall not pass to the devisee's descendants or shall lapse and be distributed as part of the testator's residuary estate.

Actress Carrie Fisher (above left) died December 27, 2016 after suffering an in-flight heart attack while flying from London to Los Angeles. Fisher was survived by her daughter, Billie Lourd, and mother, Debbie Reynolds (above right). Tragically, however, Reynolds died one day after Fisher's death. Under the common law rule of lapse, a devise in Reynolds's will to Fisher would fail because Fisher failed to survive Reynolds. Under the antilapse rule, however, a devise in Reynolds's will to Fisher would not fail, but rather, pass to Fisher's descendants (here, Lourd, Fisher's daughter and Reynolds's granddaughter). The rationale for applying the antilapse rule here is that Reynolds would have wanted Lourd to take in the event that Fisher predeceased, thereby preserving a line of descent for Fisher and her stock. Would the antilapse rule apply to a devise in Fisher's will to Reynolds?[2]

---

2. Yes, antilapse would apply. Even though Reynolds survived Fisher and would otherwise have been eligible to inherit a testamentary gift under Fisher's will, Reynolds failed to survive Fisher by 120 hours. Thus, under UPC §2-702 (see above), Reynolds would be deemed to have predeceased Fisher unless Fisher's will provided a shorter survival requirement (an unlikely case). UPC §2-603(a)(8) defines "surviving devisee" as "devisees . . . who neither predeceased the testator nor are deemed to have predeceased the testator under Section 2-702."

A less reliable technique for expressing contrary intent is so-called *words of survivorship*, such as "if he survives me." There is a split of authority whether words of survivorship, standing alone, manifest the testator's intent to opt out of the antilapse rule. In most jurisdictions, words of survivorship are interpreted to mean that the beneficiary must survive in order to take, so a failure to survive the testator means that neither the beneficiary nor her descendants inherits under the devise. In California, for example, the antilapse statute provides that words of survivorship manifest the testator's intent to opt out of the antilapse rule:

> The issue of a deceased [beneficiary] do not take in the [beneficiary]'s place if the instrument expresses a contrary intention or a substitute disposition. A requirement that the initial [beneficiary] survive the [testator] or survive for a specified period of time after the death of the [testator] constitutes a contrary intention. A requirement that the initial [beneficiary] survive until a future time that is related to the probate of the [testator]'s will or administration of the estate of the [testator] constitutes a contrary intention.

CAL. PROB. CODE §21110(b) (West). Most jurisdictions follow some form of this approach, either by statute or common law.

A minority of states, however, follows UPC §2-603(b)(3), which disregards standalone words of survivorship as meaningless boilerplate: "words of survivorship, such as in a devise to an individual 'if he survives me,' or in a devise to 'my surviving children,' are not, in the absence of additional evidence, a sufficient indication of an intent contrary to the application of this section." UPC §2-603(b)(3). The Reporter's comment explains the UPC's rationale:

> A much-litigated question is whether mere words of survivorship — such as in a devise "to my daughter, A, if A survives me" or "to my surviving children" — automatically defeat the antilapse statute. Lawyers who believe that the attachment of words of survivorship to a devise is a foolproof method of defeating an antilapse statute are mistaken. The very fact that the question is litigated so frequently is itself proof that the use of mere words of survivorship is far from foolproof.
>
> . . .
>
> [A common] objection to applying the antilapse statute [to a devise containing words of survivorship] is that mere words of survivorship somehow establish a contrary intention. The argument is that attaching words of survivorship indicates that the testator thought about the matter and intentionally did not provide a substitute gift to the devisee's descendants. At best, this is an inference only, which may or may not accurately reflect the testator's actual intention. An equally plausible inference is that the words of survivorship are in the testator's will merely because the testator's lawyer used a will form with words of survivorship. The testator who went to lawyer X and ended up with a will containing devises with a survivorship requirement could by chance have gone to lawyer Y and ended up with a will containing devises with no survivorship requirement — with no different intent on the testator's part from one case to the other.

Sharply criticized by scholars,[3] the UPC's approach remains a minority rule.

Under the UPC, antilapse applies both to wills and certain nonprobate transfers. UPC §2-706, for example, extends antilapse treatment to nonprobate beneficiary designations in a "governing instrument," defined (in UPC §1-201) as "an insurance or annuity policy, . . . an account with POD designation, . . . a security registered in beneficiary form (TOD), or . . . a pension, profit-sharing, retirement, or similar benefit plan, or other nonprobate transfer at death." UPC §2-707 extends antilapse treatment to certain future interests in trust.[4]

Lorenzo v. Medina
47 So. 3d 927 (Fla. Dist. Ct. App. 2010)

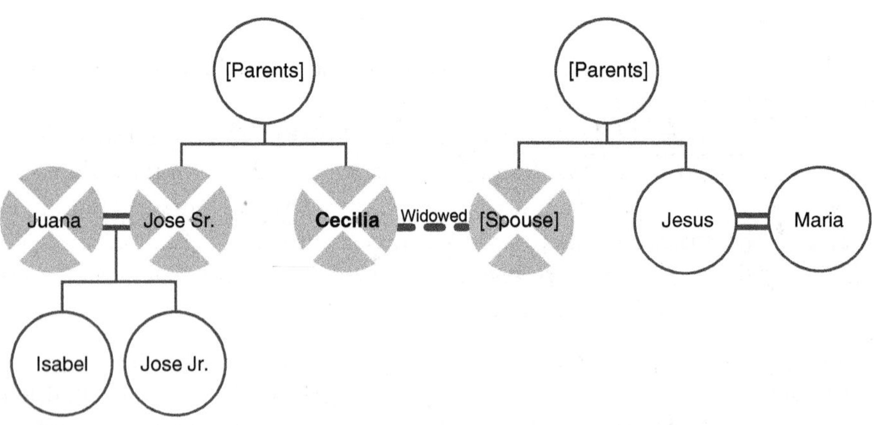

Before SUAREZ, ROTHENBERG, and SALTER, JJ.

ROTHENBERG, J.

We reverse an order construing the will of Cecilia Lorenzo ("the Testator").

---

3. See, e.g., Mark L. Ascher, The 1990 Uniform Probate Code: Older and Better, or More Like the Internal Revenue Code?, 77 Minn. L. Rev. 639, 654-55 (1993) ("Instead of allowing 'if he survives me' to mean what almost everyone would expect it to mean, the revisers have translated it into, 'if he survives me, and, if he does not survive me, to his issue who survive me.' For those unfamiliar with estate planning esoterica, therefore, it has become yet more difficult to figure out what the words in a will actually mean. The uninitiated apparently have three options: hire a competent estate planner, go to law school, or curl up with *Alice in Wonderland.*").

4. By contrast, the Uniform Trust Code does not address the issue of antilapse. In a bracketed provision signifying non-uniformity among the states, UTC §112 provides that "[t]he rules of construction that apply in this State to the interpretation of and disposition of property by will also apply as appropriate to the interpretation of the terms of a trust and the disposition of the trust property." The comment explains: "Because of the wide variation among the States on the rules of construction applicable to wills, this Code does not attempt to prescribe the exact rules to be applied to trusts but instead adopts the philosophy of the Restatement that the rules applicable to trusts ought to be the same, whatever those rules might be."

The Testator passed away on October 20, 2008, with an estate consisting of a parcel of residential property in Hialeah. In 2009, the Testator's will was admitted to probate. The Testator's will provided for a bequest of the entire estate as follows:

> [T]o my brother, JOSE R. MEDINA and to my brother in law, JESUS LORENZO, in equal shares. If either of them do not survive me, the share of the deceased shall be given to their surviving spouse, JUANA R. MEDINA or MARIA LORENZO respectively.

Without question, the operation of the will provides for a minimum fifty percent share of the Testator's estate to . . . Jesus Lorenzo ("the brother-in-law"), who survived the Testator. The issue in this appeal is who is entitled to the remaining fifty percent of the Testator's estate since the intended recipients, the Testator's brother, Jose R. Medina, and his wife, Juana R. Medina, both predeceased the Testator. The trial court's order awarded this disputed portion of the Testator's bequest to the appellees, Isabel Medina and Jose Antonio Medina ("the niece and nephew"), who are the surviving children of Jose R. Medina and Juana R. Medina.

In December 2009, the brother-in-law filed a petition for construction of the Testator's will, arguing that the bequest to the two deceased relatives, Jose and Juana R. Medina, lapsed, and therefore, he was entitled to an undivided interest in the property. The niece and nephew argued that pursuant to section 732.603(1), Florida Statutes (2008), the anti-lapse statute, they were entitled to a fifty percent share of the property. The trial court issued the instant order finding that the niece and nephew were entitled to a fifty percent share, and the brother-in-law was entitled to a fifty percent share. The brother-in-law's appeal followed.

As a matter of common law, when a will provides for a bequest to a person who predeceases the testator, the gift lapses. The potentially harsh effects of this common law rule are ameliorated to an extent by the operation of statute. When the predeceased devisee is a descendant of the testator's grandparents, section 732.603 will "save" the lapsed gift by creating a substitute gift in the devisee's descendants. §732.603(1). Because section 732.603 is in derogation of the common law, we must strictly construe its provisions.

In this case, the operation of the Testator's will prevents any recovery by the niece and nephew. At the moment of the Testator's death, her will provided for a bequest of fifty percent of the Testator's estate to Jose R. Medina. Jose R. Medina, however, predeceased the Testator. The will also provided that in the event that Jose R. Medina predeceased the Testator, Jose R. Medina's share would pass to his wife, Juana R. Medina. Thus, upon the death of the Testator, the named devisee was Juana R. Medina. Juana R. Medina, however, also predeceased the Testator.

Pursuant to the common law rule outlined above, the bequest lapsed. And because Juana R. Medina is not a descendant of the Testator's grandparents, the niece and nephew cannot invoke the operation of section 732.603(1) to "save" the bequest and provide them with a substitute gift. Thus, we conclude that the niece and nephew are not entitled to the Testator's lapsed bequest. Accordingly, we reverse the order under review.

Reversed.

In re Edwards
13 Misc. 3d 210 (N.Y. Surr. Ct. 2006)

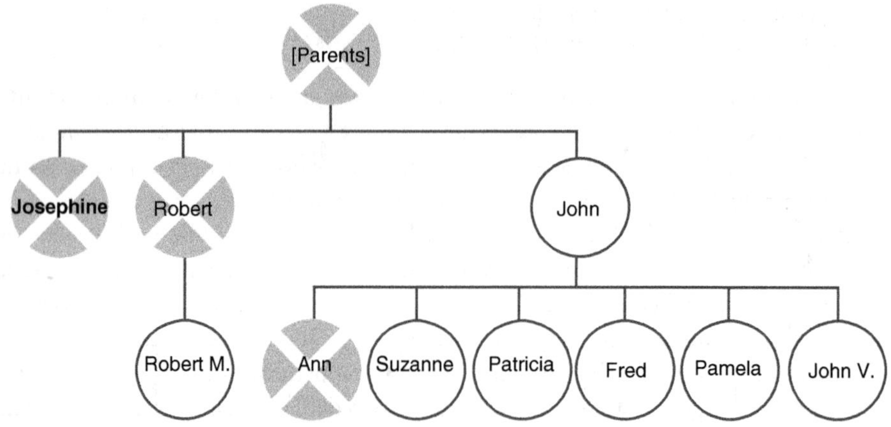

JOHN B. RIORDAN, J.

This petition for construction of a will . . . requires the construction of . . . EPTL 3-3.3. . . .[5]

The decedent, Josephine Edwards, died on June 26, 2005 leaving a last will and testament which was duly admitted to probate by a decree of this court.

The will provides in part:

> "article second: I hereby give, devise and bequeath all the rest, residue and remainder of my estate, real, personal or mixed, wheresoever situated, whereof I may be seized or possessed or to which I may be in any manner entitled or in which I may be interested at the time of my death as follows:
>
> "A. a twenty-five (25%) percent share to my brother, robert edwards, per capita, absolutely and forever;
>
> "B. a twenty-five (25%) percent share to my brother, john edwards, per capita, absolutely and forever;
>
> "C. a twenty-five (25%) percent share to my niece, ann kaufman, per capita, absolutely and forever;
>
> "D. a twenty-five (25%) percent share to my nieces and nephews, robert m. edwards, suzanne ingrasia, patricia purrman, fred koestlich, pamela heidtmann and john v. edwards, share and share alike, per capita, absolutely and forever."

Robert Edwards and Ann Kaufman predeceased the testator. There are several issues of construction raised in this petition.[6]

---

5. ["EPTL" is the abbreviation for New York's Estates, Powers, and Trusts Law. — EDS.]
6. [We have edited out all but one issue from this opinion. — EDS.]

The first issue of construction concerns the operation of the antilapse statute (EPTL 3-3.3) in connection with the words "per capita" in the bequest to Robert Edwards.[7] If the words "per capita" are considered to be an "otherwise provision" (EPTL 3-3.3[a][2]), the antilapse statute does not apply and Robert M. Edwards does not succeed to his father's share of the residuary estate under the statute. If the words "per capita" have no effect, Robert M. Edwards succeeds to his father's share of the residuary estate.

A distribution "per capita" is an equal division among beneficiaries (EPTL 1-2.11). When used in connection with the words "issue" or "descend[a]nts," the term per capita may describe a substitutional gift. Standing alone, "per capita" does not indicate a substitutional gift.

In the context of a gift to one person, without substitution, the words "per capita" are not descriptive. Words employed by a testator should not be rejected as meaningless if by any reasonable construction they may be made consistent and significant. In this case, however, it appears that the words "per capita" were added inadvert[e]ntly and should be disregarded.

The words "absolutely and forever" are not words of substitution and do not prevent application of the antilapse statute. . . .

Therefore, the bequest to Robert Edwards vests in Robert M. Edwards.

. . .

QUESTIONS

8. In *Edwards*, the court found that the words "per capita" did not manifest the testator's intent to provide a substitute testamentary gift, so the share of Robert Edwards, the predeceased beneficiary, passed under the antilapse statute to his son, Robert M. Edwards. The court explained further that, "[i]n the context of a gift to one person, without substitution, the words 'per capita' are not descriptive. Words employed by a testator should not be rejected as meaningless if by any reasonable construction they may be made consistent and significant. In this case, however, it appears that the words 'per capita' were added inadvert[e]ntly and should be disregarded." How did the court know that the testator used the words "per capita" inadvertently?

ANSWER. As the court correctly notes, "[w]hen used in connection with the words 'issue' or 'descend[a]nts,' the term per capita may describe a substitutional gift." Perhaps the testator used the term "per capita" to denote that, if Robert predeceased, his share would pass to his descendants by representation and the system of representation chosen by the testator was per capita (query: per capita with representation or per capita at each generation?). While it is impossible to

7. [The New York antilapse statute provides, "*Unless the will . . . provides otherwise*: . . . Whenever a testamentary disposition . . . is made to a beneficiary who is one of the testator's issue or a brother or sister, and such beneficiary dies during the lifetime of the testator leaving issue surviving such testator, such disposition does not lapse but vests in such surviving issue, by representation." N.Y. Est. Powers & Trusts Law §3-3.3(a)(2) (McKinney) (emphasis added). — Eds.]

know for sure whether the testator included "per capita" inadvertently, it is a common drafting error that should be avoided. See Reid K. Weisbord & David Horton, Boilerplate and Default Rules in Wills Law: An Empirical Analysis, ___ Iowa L. Rev. ___ (forthcoming 2017). ("Bizarrely, . . . many of the Sussex County wills invoke language of representation in gifts to individual beneficiaries, not multi-generational classes. For instance, four testators left property to single recipients "per capita." Because "per capita" means "[d]ivided equally among all individuals . . . in the same class," it is a non-sequitur in a devise to one person. An additional forty-four wills — nearly one out of every five in our sample — contained a similarly illogical devise to an individual "per stirpes."").

9. In *Edwards*, how would the share of Ann Kaufman, who predeceased the testator, be distributed?

ANSWER. New York, like the UPC, has abrogated the common law "no residue of a residue rule," so upon the lapse of a residuary devise, unless saved by the antilapse statute, the share is reallocated proportionately among the surviving residuary devisees. Ann's share lapses because she predeceased the testator and was not survived by issue. Thus, Ann's residuary devise is reallocated proportionately among the surviving residuary beneficiaries as follows: The testator split the balance of the residue equally among Robert Edwards (para. A), John Edwards (para. B), and her nieces and nephews (para. D), so Ann's share will be split into three shares. A one-third share is reallocated to Robert Edwards, but since he predeceased, that share passes to his son, Robert M. Edwards, under the antilapse statute. A one-third share is reallocated to John Edwards, who survived the testator and therefore takes under both paragraph B and paragraph D. A one-third share is reallocated and divided equally among the nieces and nephews named in paragraph D, including Robert M. Edwards. Thus, Robert M. Edwards takes under paragraphs A, C, and D.

PROBLEM V

After reading *In re Edwards*, above, review the residuary clause of the testator's will, reproduced below:

> "article second: I hereby give, devise and bequeath all the rest, residue and remainder of my estate, real, personal or mixed, wheresoever situated, whereof I may be seized or possessed or to which I may be in any manner entitled or in which I may be interested at the time of my death as follows:
>
> "A. a twenty-five (25%) percent share to my brother, robert edwards, per capita, absolutely and forever;
>
> "B. a twenty-five (25%) percent share to my brother, john edwards, per capita, absolutely and forever;

"C. a twenty-five (25%) percent share to my niece, ann kaufman, per capita, absolutely and forever;

"D. a twenty-five (25%) percent share to my nieces and nephews, robert m. edwards, suzanne ingrasia, patricia purrman, fred koestlich, pamela heidtmann and john v. edwards, share and share alike, per capita, absolutely and forever."

Assuming that the testator would have agreed with the outcome in the case, how would you redraft the residuary clause to clarify the language that led to litigation in this case?

PROBLEM VI

Review the following testamentary provisions. Assume that all beneficiaries (except for spouses) have the requisite statutory relationship to the testator for antilapse purposes and that at least one beneficiary in each will has predeceased. Would the antilapse rule apply under the majority rule? Under UPC §2-603(b)(3)? Why or why not?

Words of Contrary Intent?	Majority Rule	UPC §2-603(b)(3)
"All the rest, residue and remainder of my estate, of all kind and description and wheresoever situate, I give, devise, and bequeath to be divided equally among my three (3) sisters, Anna Harmath Kovacs, Mary Harmath Kish, and Helen Harmath Laitos, share and share alike, to the express exclusion of any other person or persons."		
". . . one-half of the residue of my property to my step-daughter, Hazel Brennan of Guilford, Connecticut, if she survives me."		
"All the rest, residue, and remainder of my property, . . . I give, devise, and bequeath to my wife, ESTHER Z. BULGER, and in the event my wife, ESTHER Z. BULGER, shall predecease me, all of my said property shall go and the same is hereby given, devised, and bequeathed to my children, EDWARD G. BULGER, VERONICA STEDMAN, EMMETT BULGER and CHARLES BULGER, to share and share alike, or to the survivor or survivors of them, in equal shares." [Assume that the testator's wife, Esther, and son Emmett predeceased. Emmett was survived by descendants.]		

6.5 CLASS GIFTS

A class gift allows a testator to identify a group of beneficiaries in relation to their status or membership in a defined class. On the date that the class closes, only those members who remain in the class share in the gift. Class gifts are a dynamic estate planning technique that accounts for the possibility that the size and membership of a class may fluctuate. Thus, a class gift is preferable to a gift to several individual beneficiaries because the testator need not revise his or her will every time the class membership changes.

Consider the following example: Thalia, the testator, executes a will leaving the residue of her estate to "my maternal nieces and nephews who survive me." On the date of the will's execution, Thalia had four maternal nieces and nephews: A, B, C, and D. Three new maternal nieces, E, F, and G, were born after Thalia executed her will. On the date of Thalia's death, two maternal nephews, A and B, were no longer living. Had Thalia instead drafted her residuary clause with individual devises to each maternal niece and nephew, she would have had to revise her will upon the death of A and B, and upon the birth of E, F, and G. By treating her maternal nieces and nephews as a class closing on the date of her death, Thalia effectuates her intent to include all maternal nieces and nephews without having to amend the will in response to each birth and death.

Observe, however, the interplay between class gifts and antilapse, as the doctrines tug in opposite directions. Class gifts *extinguish* devises to predeceased class members while antilapse rules *create* a substitute devise for certain predeceased beneficiaries' descendants. The law generally harmonizes the two doctrines by applying antilapse first and class gift treatment second.

When should class gift treatment apply to a devise to multiple beneficiaries? The Restatement, reproduced below the following excerpt, explains that a "disposition is *presumed* to create a class gift if the terms of the disposition identify the beneficiaries only by a term of relationship or other group label. The presumption is rebutted if the language or circumstances establish that the transferor intended the identities and shares of the beneficiaries to be fixed." The article below elaborates.

What's in the Third and Final Volume of the New Restatement of Property That Estate Planners Should Know About

Lawrence W. Waggoner
38 ACTEC L.J. 23, 25 (2012)

IS IT A CLASS GIFT OR NOT?

Does a disposition "to my children" in a will or trust create a class gift? What about a disposition "to my three children, A, B, and C"? And, what difference does it make? The short answers are that the disposition "to my children" presumptively creates a class gift, the disposition "to my three children, A, B, and C" presumptively does not create a class gift, and it makes a lot of difference whether it is a class gift or not.

The presumption that a disposition "to my children" creates a class is rarely rebutted. Assuming that the presumption is not rebutted, and that the disposition is classified as a class gift, the identities and shares of the beneficiaries are not static, but are subject to fluctuation until the time when a class member is entitled to distribution; and upon distribution, the property is divided among the then-entitled class members on a fractional basis. Thus, if the transferor has another child, D, that child becomes a beneficiary (a class member): A, B, C, and D take a one-fourth share.

Assuming that the presumption that a disposition "to my three children, A, B, and C" does not create a class prevails, the identities and shares of the beneficiaries are fixed. Thus, if the transferor has another child, D, that child does not become a beneficiary: A, B, and C take a one-third share. How strong is the presumption? Because of the inflexibility of a gift to individuals whose shares and identities are fixed, as compared with the flexibility of a class gift, the Property Restatement makes it clear that presumption against class-gift classification is not strong. For estate planners, the drafting lesson is clear: If a transferor really does want the shares and identities of the beneficiaries to be fixed, the disposition should be drafted so that it states that intent clearly and directly: "one-third to my daughter A, one-third to my son B, and one-third to my daughter C." Drafting "to my three children, A, B, and C" is never a good idea.

Restatement (Third) of Property: Wills & Other Donative Transfers
§13.1 Class Gift Defined; How Created

(a) A class gift is a disposition to beneficiaries who take as members of a group. Taking as members of a group means that the identities and shares of the beneficiaries are subject to fluctuation.

(b) A disposition is presumed to create a class gift if the terms of the disposition identify the beneficiaries only by a term of relationship or other group label. The presumption is rebutted if the language or circumstances establish that the transferor intended the identities and shares of the beneficiaries to be fixed.

6.6 DISCREPANCIES BETWEEN DISPOSITIVE PROVISIONS AND THE PROBATE ESTATE

This section addresses discrepancies between property identified in the will and property found in the testator's estate at death. Wills generally refer to property owned by the testator on the date of the will's creation, but significant time typically passes between that date and the testator's death. In the interim, the testator may have acquired or disposed of property without updating the will. A will should anticipate such changes through careful drafting; indeed, some wills avoid the issue altogether by devising the estate in shares rather than by specific items of property. Many wills, however, overlook the issue entirely. Commentators describe this oversight as another aspect of the "stale will" problem.

There are four default rules of construction applicable when property identified in the will differs from property found in the testator's estate at death: ademption by extinction; ademption by satisfaction; abatement; and accession. Each of these doctrines, in turn, relies on the following classification of devises:

Restatement (Third) of Property: Wills & Other Donative Transfers §5.1 Classification of Devises

(1) A specific devise is a testamentary disposition of a specifically identified asset.

(2) A general devise is a testamentary disposition, usually of a specified amount of money or quantity of property, that is payable from the general assets of the estate.

(3) A demonstrative devise is a testamentary disposition, usually of a specified amount of money or quantity of property, that is primarily payable from a designated source, but is secondarily payable from the general assets of the estate to the extent that the primary source is insufficient.

(4) A residuary devise is a testamentary disposition of property of the testator's net probate estate not disposed by a specific, general, or demonstrative devise.

PROBLEM VII

Sonia Felipe's holographic will provides as follows:

I, Sonia Felipe, am of sound mind and body and, now that my husband has died, I am writing this to be my final WILL.

My life insurance policy will go to the people I put on the form from the insurance company. Otherwise, here is what I want.

1. *I give my car to my son, Ricardo.*
2. *I give my gold wedding ring inscribed OF and SH 12/2/90 to my daughter, Maria.*
3. *I give $2,000 to my mother.*
4. *I give $1,000 from my teachers' credit union account to my father.*
5. *I give 200 shares of the Westinghouse Corporation to my good friend, Salvador.*
6. *I give $1,000 to be divided up equally for my nieces and nephews.*
7. *I give $500 to my poodle, Happy (Maria is to take this money and use it for Happy).*
8. *I give EVERYTHING else I have to Ricardo and Maria to split up evenly between them.*

Please bury me next to my parents (I have already paid for my funeral with Hernandez Funeral home).

I love you all,

[Signed] *Sonia Felipe*

September 30, 2011

How would you classify the devises in the numbered paragraphs 1 through 8?

6.6.1 Ademption by Extinction

Ademption refers to the nullification of a dispositive testamentary provision. The term "adeem" means to nullify a testamentary gift.

Ademption by extinction applies when property described in a specific devise is not found in the testator's estate at death. Under the common law "identity" theory of ademption by extinction, a specific devise adeems (or fails) if property specifically named in the devise cannot be identified in the estate. When a specific devise is extinguished under this doctrine, the beneficiary takes nothing under the adeemed gift. Notably, the common law identity theory does not invite inquiry into *why* specifically devised property cannot be found in the testator's estate.[8] Thus, it does not matter whether the testator sold the property with the intent of extinguishing the gift or whether the property was destroyed for reasons beyond the testator's control. In both cases, the specific devise fails, and the beneficiary receives no replacement property as a substitute for the original gift because the testator manifested no such intent in the will. Had the testator intended to provide a substitute gift, the testator would have manifested that intent in the will.

By precluding factual inquiry into the matter, the identity theory is easy to apply but sometimes conflicts with the testator's probable intent. Suppose, for example, a testator devises "my beach house at the Jersey Shore to my friend, Fanny." Suppose further that, on the date of the will's execution, the testator owned a beach house in Avalon, but shortly before her unexpected death, the testator sold the Avalon property because she was in the process of buying a new beach house in nearby Stone Harbor. If the testator received the proceeds from sale of the Avalon property but died before closing on the purchase of the Stone Harbor property, the specific devise of the Avalon property adeems under the identity theory.[9] The estate contains no "beach house at the Jersey Shore" at the time of the testator's death, so there is nothing for the beneficiary to take. But does that result implement the testator's probable intent under these circumstances? If the testator had a chance to update her will before her unexpected death, wouldn't she have given Fanny a substitute devise in place of the Avalon property?

To align this doctrine more closely with probable testamentary intent, courts developed an alternative "intent" theory of ademption by extinction: The beneficiary receives the specifically devised property (if any) plus a substitute pecuniary devise (typically, a monetary gift drawn from the residuary estate) equal to the value of property disposed of by the testator during life, so long as there is evidence the testator did not intend to extinguish the gift. The UPC and Restatement follow the intent theory:

---

8. Thomas E. Atkinson, Law of Wills 742 (2d ed. 1953) ("[E]ver since the leading case of Ashburner v. Macguire, [Bro. C.C. 108, 29 Eng. Rep. 62, 1786,] the orthodox position has been that intent has nothing to do with the matter, and that the sole question is whether the subject matter of the specific [devise] is in the testator's estate at his death, and if it is not the [devise] is adeemed, and the [devisee] gets nothing.").

9. In this case, however, the doctrine of equitable conversion, which treats the buyer's interest as an inheritable real property interest after execution of the contract but before closing, might apply.

Uniform Probate Code
§2-606(a)(6) Nonademption of Specific Devises

A specific devisee has a right to specifically devised property in the testator's estate at the testator's death and to . . . a pecuniary devise equal to the value as of its date of disposition of other specifically devised property disposed of during the testator's lifetime but only to the extent it is established that ademption would be inconsistent with the testator's manifested plan of distribution or that at the time the will was made, the date of disposition or otherwise, the testator did not intend ademption of the devise.

Restatement (Third) of Property: Wills & Other Donative Transfers
§5.2(c) Failure ("Ademption") of Specific Devises by Extinction

[I]f specifically devised property is not in the testator's estate at death, the specific devise fails unless failure of the devise would be inconsistent with the testator's intent.

Although the intent theory may be more likely to effectuate probable testamentary intent, the identity theory remains the prevailing majority rule. The Restatement, however, observes that courts have found ways to bend the rule: "Although the testator's intent is nominally irrelevant under the identity theory, it is well documented in the case law that courts purportedly following the identity theory frequently manipulate doctrine to effectuate intent anyway. By adopting the intent theory, this Restatement prefers the more candid analysis of the problem." Restatement (Third) of Property: Wills & Other Donative Transfers §5.2, comment b. Legislatures have also softened the identity theory through statutory exceptions for insured casualty losses, condemnation awards, sale by a legal guardian on behalf of an incapacitated person (and a few others).

In re Estate of Sagel
901 A.2d 538 (Pa. Super. Ct. 2006)

[In 1998, Henry Sagel died in an air crash disaster while piloting his Piper Aerostar 600 aircraft. At the time of the crash, Henry was wearing his Rolex watch. Both the aircraft and watch were insured and the estate recovered insurance proceeds for the loss of both items. Henry's will contained the following specific devise:

> Article 1.3: I give all tangible personal property that I own at my death, including but not limited to, all household furniture and furnishings, automobiles, books, pictures, jewelry, art objects, hobby equipment and collections, wearing apparel and other articles of household or personal use or ornament, to my son, Gregory Sagel.

Henry devised the residue to beneficiaries other than his son, Gregory.

At the time of his death, Henry was domiciled in Pennsylvania, which enacted the following statute:

> Rules of Interpretation, 20 Pa. C. S. §2514 (2012):
> In the absence of a contrary intent appearing therein, wills shall be construed as to real and personal estate in accordance with the following rules:
>
> . . .

(18) Nonademption; balance. — A devisee or legatee of property specifically devised or bequeathed has the right to any of that property which the testator still owned at his death and:

> (i) any balance of the purchase price or balance of property to be received in exchange, together with any security interest, owing from a purchaser to the testator at his death by reason of a sale or exchange of the property by the testator;
> (ii) any amount due for the condemnation of the property and unpaid at the testator's death;
> (iii) any proceeds unpaid at the testator's death on fire or casualty insurance on the property; and
> (iv) property owned by the testator at his death as a result of foreclosure, or obtained in lieu of foreclosure, of the security for a specifically bequeathed obligation.

Henry's son Gregory claimed that, since the aircraft and watch were "tangible personal property" devised under Article 1.3, he was entitled to the insurance proceeds obtained by the estate for those items under 20 Pa. Cons. Stat. Ann. §2514(18)(iii). Opposing Gregory's claim, the estate argued that the specific devises of Henry's watch and plane adeemed because they were destroyed in the crash and therefore were not owned by Henry at the time of his death. The estate interpretation claimed, therefore, that the insurance proceeds passed under the residuary clause to other beneficiaries. The trial court held that the specific devises did not adeem and that Gregory was entitled to the insurance proceeds. The estate appealed. — Eds.]

Lally-Green, J.:

. . .

Appellant first argues that the doctrine of ademption extinguished decedent's bequest to his son of his airplane and watch, as those items did not exist at the time of decedent's death. The trial court found that the watch and airplane existed at the time of decedent's death. Therefore, the trial court found that ademption did not apply.

Our courts have described the doctrine of ademption as follows:

> It has long since been decided in this jurisdiction that a specific legacy or devise is extinguished if the property is not in existence or does not belong to the testator at the time of his death. Testator's intent is not relevant where the property devised or bequeathed in his will is not part of his estate at death. Where the legacy has been determined to be specific the legatee is entitled to the very thing bequeathed if it be possible for the executor to give it to him; but if not, he cannot have money in place of it. This results from an inflexible rule of law applied to the mere fact that the thing bequeathed does not exist, and it is not founded on any presumed intention of the testator. This rule is equally applicable where the specifically devised or bequeathed property is removed from testator during his lifetime by an involuntary act or by operation of law. Thus, where it is established that the bequest or devise was specific and the [item was nonexistent] in the testator's estate at the time of death, an ademption results.

In re Estate of Balter, 703 A.2d 1038, 1041 (Pa. Super. 1997) [brackets in original]. This language espouses the "identity" theory of ademption. That theory is that, if the testator does not have the item at the time of his death, or if the item no longer exists, it is adeemed. There is no inquiry into the testator's intent.

In addition to *Balter*, we must consider 20 Pa. C. S. A. §2514, which governs interpretation of wills:

> (18) Nonademption; balance.—A devisee or legatee of property specifically devised or bequeathed has the right to any of that property which the testator still owned at his death and: . . . (iii) any proceeds unpaid at the testator's death on fire or casualty insurance on the property. . . . 20 Pa. C. S. A. §2514(18)(iii).

The parties do not dispute that the decedent made a specific bequest of his personal property, including the airplane and watch, to his son. The decedent's will did not contain an anti-ademption clause. The sole issue before us is whether, for purposes of §2514(18) and the ademption doctrine, the decedent owned the airplane and watch at the time of his death. Our research uncovered no binding precedent governing the instant facts.

Appellant argues that the decedent owned the airplane and watch immediately before his death, but at the time of his death those two items no longer existed.[10] The record does not support Appellant's contention. It is clear that the airplane and watch still existed, albeit in a severely damaged state. Moreover, the plain language of §2514(18) makes such a determination unnecessary, inasmuch as the relevant inquiry is whether the decedent owned the property at the time of his death. We find no authority for the proposition that accidental damage or destruction of property contemporaneous with decedent's death divests the decedent of ownership in that property, nor does Appellant attempt to argue that such is the case. We therefore conclude, pursuant to §2514(18), that the decedent's son is entitled to the insurance proceeds from the decedent's airplane and watch.

. . .

Order affirmed.

QUESTIONS

10. Applying the identity theory of ademption, the *Sagel* court concludes that the plane and watch existed at the time of Henry's death, so the specific devises did not adeem. Was Gregory entitled to the casualty insurance proceeds because the devises did not adeem?

    ANSWER. No, Gregory received the insurance proceeds because of the statutory provision permitting a specific devisee to recover insurance proceeds from property destroyed before the testator's death but covered by casualty insurance. Many jurisdictions, including the UPC, follow this rule and provide that if the subject of a specific devise is destroyed and insured, the beneficiary is entitled to insurance proceeds unpaid at the time of the testator's death. UPC §2-606(a)(3).

---

10. Appellant's argument regarding the "existence" of the property is based on *Balter*. Appellant essentially argues that, since the property in question was damaged or destroyed simultaneously with the decedent's catastrophic death, the property no longer existed for purposes of ademption. Appellant does not address §2514(18) in its brief.

11. What would Gregory have received if Pennsylvania had not enacted 20 Pa. Cons. Stat. Ann. §2514(18)?

ANSWER. The Pennsylvania statute, 20 Pa. Cons. Stat. Ann. §2514(18), is the only basis for Gregory's claim to the insurance proceeds because Pennsylvania follows the identity theory of ademption by extinction and there is otherwise no basis for Gregory to take a substitute pecuniary devise. Thus, Gregory would inherit the damaged property but the insurance proceeds would pass under the residuary clause.

12. Suppose Pennsylvania followed the *intent* theory and that Henry's plane or watch were not covered by insurance. What would Gregory receive?

ANSWER. Under the intent theory, Gregory would take the destroyed plane and watch, as well as a substitute pecuniary devise equal to the value of the plane and watch on the date of their destruction. Under these circumstances, we presume that Henry did not intend to extinguish the devise of his plane and watch to Gregory upon their destruction in the air crash disaster.

13. What result if Henry's will contained the following provision: "The doctrine of ademption by extinction shall not apply to Article 1.3"?

ANSWER. If Henry had wanted to avoid application of the ademption rule and provide for replacement property, he could have done so by stating his intent in the will. See Raley L. Wiggins, Adeemed If You Do, Adeemed If You Don't: The Testator's Intent to Passively Revoke a Specific Devise, 61 Ala. L. Rev. 1163, 1181 (2010) ("Even without legislative action, however, it may be possible for a drafting attorney to include a non-ademption provision as part of standard will language. While there does not appear to be any authority addressing the validity of such a provision, a provision providing for non-ademption under specific circumstances would certainly serve to clarify the testator's intent.").

14. What result if Henry had landed safely in Myrtle Beach, and, upon landing, sold the aircraft and watch, and then died?

ANSWER. Under the identity theory, both gifts would adeem because they were not owned at the time of death. Gregory would not be entitled to any of the sales proceeds. Under the intent theory, Gregory would have to prove that Henry did not intend for the gifts to adeem when he sold the watch and plane.

15. What result if Henry died just after landing safely in Myrtle Beach, and his will contained the following devise: "$300,000 to my son, Gregory, to be paid from proceeds from the sale of my Piper Aerostar 600 and Rolex watch"?

ANSWER. This is a demonstrative devise. Ademption does not apply to demonstrative devises. See, e.g., In re Estate of Lung, 692 A.2d 1349, 1350 (D.C. 1997). If the proceeds from the sale of the plane and watch were not sufficient to satisfy the $300,000 gift, the balance would be payable from the residuary estate.

16. What result if Henry had landed safely in Myrtle Beach and, upon landing, exchanged his Piper Aerostar 600 for a Piper Aerostar 700, and then died?

 ANSWER. Even under the strict identity theory, Gregory would probably take the Piper 700. "Even though a specifically devised asset is not in the testator's estate in its original form, the specific devise does not fail if the asset is in the testator's estate in a changed form. By well-established authority, the change-in-form principle applies if the change in form is insubstantial. It is not possible to give a comprehensive list of what types of post-execution transactions amount to a mere change in form and what types do not. It is clear, however, that if the testator gives the property to the devisee or to another, the change-in-form principle cannot operate because the testator has received nothing in return for the gift. The testator's estate owns no product into which the subject of the original devise was changed." Restatement (Third) of Property: Wills & Other Donative Transfers §5.2, comment d.

PROBLEM VIII

In 1992, Beatrice executes a will with the following devise: "I give the sum of 15,000 shares of OPM Corporation to my dear friend Betty if she survives me." In 1995, Beatrice gives Betty a pin made of precious stones but shortly thereafter Beatrice realizes that she had previously promised the same pin to her granddaughter. Beatrice asks Betty to return the pin and promises to leave jewelry of equal value to Betty in her will. Betty returns the pin. In 1996, Beatrice executes a codicil with the following devise: "I give my large, multi-diamond dinner ring to my dear friend Betty." Beatrice dies in 2017. Beatrice's estate contains neither a multi-diamond ring nor any shares of OPM Corporation.

A. To what, if anything, is Betty entitled? Would the result depend on whether the jurisdiction applied the identity or intent theory of ademption?

B. What outcome under the identity or intent theory if there were found in Beatrice's estate a large, multi-*sapphire* dinner ring?

PROBLEM IX

In 2006, Jennifer executes the following will: "Blackacre to my son, Sam; the rest, residue, and remainder of my estate to my daughter, Debby." In 2008, Jennifer is declared incompetent and placed in a nursing home. A court appoints Debby as Jennifer's legal guardian. In 2009, to pay for Jennifer's nursing home expenses, Debby, in her capacity as Jennifer's guardian, sells Blackacre with court approval and receives $500,000 in net proceeds from the sale. Debby deposits the $500,000 into Jennifer's bank account (for which Debby has authority as guardian to make deposits and withdrawals on Jennifer's behalf). In 2012, Debby withdraws $100,000 from Jennifer's bank account to pay for Jennifer's care. In 2017, Jennifer dies leaving a net estate worth $700,000.

What, if anything, does Sam take under:

a. the identity theory;
b. the intent theory; and
c. UPC §2-606(b), which states:

If specifically devised property is sold or mortgaged by a conservator or by an agent acting within the authority of a durable power of attorney for an incapacitated principal, or a condemnation award, insurance proceeds, or recovery for injury to the property is paid to a conservator or to an agent acting within the authority of a durable power of attorney for an incapacitated principal, the specific devisee has the right to a general pecuniary devise equal to the net sale price, the amount of the unpaid loan, the condemnation award, the insurance proceeds or the recovery.

PROBLEM X

Adam owns valuable collections of art and rare books. Tanya, Adam's daughter, has long served as an informal, amateur curator of the collections and has grown deeply attached to many of the items. Adam has always promised Tanya she would inherit the collections. Last year, Adam's house caught fire. Adam died of smoke inhalation, and the collections were entirely destroyed. Adam's estate obtained insurance proceeds of $10 million for the loss of the art and rare books. For the following questions, assume that the jurisdiction recognizes the *intent* theory of ademption by extinction.

A. Suppose Adam died intestate, survived only by his five children. To what would Tanya be entitled?

B. Suppose Adam's will provided, "I devise my collections of art and rare books to Tanya." To what would Tanya be entitled?

C. Suppose Adam's will provided, "I devise my collections of art and rare books to my art dealer, Sarah." To what would Tanya be entitled? To what would Sarah be entitled?

D. Suppose Adam's will provided, "I devise my collections of art and rare books to Tanya for her lifetime, so long as she maintains the collections in her home. Should the collections not remain in her home, then I direct my executor to sell the collections and distribute the proceeds to my other four children." To what would Tanya be entitled?

6.6.2 Ademption by Satisfaction

Ademption by satisfaction, or simply *satisfaction*, applies when the testator changes the timing of a gift from testamentary to inter vivos, but fails to amend the will accordingly.[11] Suppose, for example, a testator executes a will with a general devise of $100,000 to her favorite charity. A year later, the testator decides it would be better to give her the

11. The doctrine of satisfaction can apply to specific and general devises, although some courts limit the doctrine to general devises.

$100,000 to charity during life rather than at death, so she makes an inter vivos gift of $100,000. If the testator forgets to revoke the original devise of $100,000 in her will, should the inter vivos gift of $100,000 be treated as satisfying the devise? Under ademption by satisfaction, the answer is generally No, unless the testator manifested her intent to satisfy (and therefore extinguish) the devise by making the inter vivos gift.

Most jurisdictions presume that inter vivos gifts are *not* made in satisfaction of a testamentary devise. Like UPC §2-109, the analogous rule governing advancements in intestate estates, under UPC §2-609(a), ademption by satisfaction applies only if the testator manifests intent to satisfy affirmatively in writing or if the devisee has made a written acknowledgment of the satisfied devise:

Uniform Probate Code
§2-609(a) Ademption by Satisfaction

Property a testator gave in his [or her] lifetime to a person is treated as a satisfaction of a devise in whole or in part, only if (i) the will provides for deduction of the gift, (ii) the testator declared in a contemporaneous writing that the gift is in satisfaction of the devise or that its value is to be deducted from the value of the devise, or (iii) the devisee acknowledged in writing that the gift is in satisfaction of the devise or that its value is to be deducted from the value of the devise.

Restatement (Third) of Property: Wills & Other Donative Transfers
§5.4 Post-Execution Events Affecting Wills

An inter vivos gift made by a testator to a devisee or to a member of the devisee's family adeems the devise by satisfaction, in whole or in part, if the testator indicated in a contemporaneous writing, or if the devisee acknowledged in writing, that the gift was so to operate.

When satisfaction does apply, an inter vivos gift may satisfy a devise partially or completely. An inter vivos gift may satisfy a testamentary devise even if it is not the same property mentioned in the will. Some jurisdictions presume satisfaction when a testator makes an inter vivos gift to her own child even in the absence of a written manifestation of such intent. Thus, litigation involving the doctrine of ademption by satisfaction often involves factual inquiry into the testator's intent.

Estate of Condon
715 N.W.2d 770 (Iowa Ct. App. 2006)

[In 1989, Marguerite Condon executed a will with several pecuniary bequests to members of her family and charity. In one such bequest, Marguerite gave $10,000 to her niece and nephew, Mary and Charles, with a direction that, "in the event either of my niece or nephew predecease me, then the share of the one so dying shall go to the survivor." The will left the residue to Robert, Marguerite's son, and appointed him executor. Charles, the nephew, predeceased Marguerite in 1992. In 1996, Marguerite wrote a $5,000 check to Mary, the niece, with the words "will payment" in the memo. Marguerite died in 2003.

As executor of Marguerite's estate, Robert argued that Mary was not entitled to her $5,000 share of the bequest because the gift had been satisfied during life. Robert testified that Marguerite "wanted to have the satisfaction of knowing that she gave the money to the people she wanted to receive it." Robert offered Mary $5,000 for Charles's share of the original bequest and kept the other $5,000 for himself as the residuary beneficiary. Mary objected. The district court held that Mary was entitled to the entire $10,000 bequest. Robert appealed. — EDS.]

BEEGHLY, S.J.:

. . .

The executor raises the alternative theory of ademption by satisfaction. [T]he law regarding advancements generally only applies in cases of intestacy, "but the doctrine of ademption [by satisfaction], though strictly speaking applying only to personal property or to legacies, is resorted to carry out the apparent or presumed intention of a testator. . . ." The term "ademption" generally applies to a specific legacy, while "satisfaction" is applied when the legacy is general. A legacy is the testamentary disposition of personal property. Iowa Code §633.3(25).

The doctrine of ademption by satisfaction is explained as follows:

> When a general legacy is given of a sum of money without regard to any particular fund, and thereafter testator pays this legacy to the legatee or advances him even a small sum with intent to discharge the legacy or to substitute the advancement for the bequest, the legacy is satisfied, or, as it is sometimes said, adeemed. When the amount of the advancement or gift is smaller than the legacy, the satisfaction is held complete, not for the reason that the smaller sum is regarded as payment of the larger, but by reason of the intent of the testator to substitute the smaller for the larger, and to reduce the amount of the general legacy. The doctrine of satisfaction depends very largely, if not altogether, upon the intent of the testator.

"[A]pplication of the doctrine of satisfaction of legacies ultimately depends upon evidence of the decedent's intent at the time the lifetime gift is made." 1 Sheldon F. Kurtz, Kurtz on Iowa Estates §15.26, at 615 (3d ed. 1995). The doctrine of satisfaction depends upon the intention of the testator, as inferred from his or her acts.

It is not essential that the decedent's will specifically provides for satisfaction based on inter vivos gifts. The court should consider all the facts and surrounding circumstances to determine the intent of the testator. A party may show through extrinsic evidence that the testator intended a payment to be considered as satisfaction for a bequest.

"Since proof of a decedent's intent is frequently difficult, the Iowa courts have adhered to two presumptions in applying the doctrine." Kurtz on Iowa Estates §15.26, at 615. In the first instance, when the testator is a parent or stands in loco parentis to the legatee, a subsequent gift to the legatee is presumed to be in satisfaction of the legacy.

On the other hand, where the testator is a stranger to the legatee, such a presumption does not arise. A party may still show that satisfaction was intended, however, by clear proof that satisfaction was intended. The intention to satisfy a legacy may be shown if the benefit subsequently conveyed is the same or so far identical in character as to be ejusdem generis.[12] The intention has also been shown where there was a receipt attached to the will showing satisfaction of the legacy.

Since Marguerite and Mary did not have a parent-child relationship, there is no presumption that Marguerite intended the 1996 payment to be a satisfaction of the legacy in her will. We consider all the facts and surrounding circumstances to determine Marguerite's intent. The executor may show, through extrinsic evidence, that Marguerite intended to satisfy the legacy. On this issue we consider the notation of "will payment" on the [check] and Robert's testimony as to Marguerite's intent. We also note that the [payment] made by Marguerite [was] for the precise amount of the specific [bequest] in her will. On our de novo review, we find clear evidence that Marguerite intended the 1996 [payment] to be in satisfaction of the [bequest] she made in her will. We find the factual differences ascribed to the cases concerning the doctrine of satisfaction by the district court do not overcome the application of that doctrine to the facts in this case.

Based on the doctrine of satisfaction, we reverse that portion of the district court opinion which determined Mary was entitled to $10,000 from the estate. The bequest of $5,000 to Mary has been satisfied. Mary is still entitled to receive the $5,000 which represented the share of her brother, Charles, because this bequest has not been satisfied.

Reversed and remanded.

QUESTIONS

17. What result if Marguerite had given Mary a valuable piece of jewelry instead of the $5,000 check?

    ANSWER. In jurisdictions with a contemporaneous writing requirement, ademption by satisfaction would not apply. In this case, the only written documentation of Marguerite's intent to satisfy the bequest was on the check (i.e., "will payment"), so without that notation, there would be no contemporaneous writing to meet the requirement. In Iowa, however, there is no statutory writing requirement. Satisfaction must be proven by clear and convincing evidence of the testator's intent. Here, without the check memo, the evidence of Marguerite's intent to satisfy the $5,000 bequest by giving Mary jewelry is not clear and convincing, in part, because Robert's testimony is self-serving (he stands to inherit the unpaid $5,000 through the residuary clause).

18. What result if Marguerite had given Mary a check for $2,500 with "will payment" written in the memo?

    ANSWER. In most jurisdictions and under UPC §2-609(a), this would be considered a partial satisfaction and Mary would be entitled to the remaining $2,500 of her share of the bequest. In Iowa, according to the law quoted by the

12. [The Latin phrase "ejusdem generis" means "of the same kind." — EDS.]

court, the smaller inter vivos gift would be construed as the testator's intent to substitute a smaller gift for the larger bequest; Mary would not be entitled to the remaining balance of her share of the bequest. Which is the better rule and why?

PROBLEM XI

Ursula executes a will devising $50,000 to her best friend, Harold. Two years after executing the will, Ursula gives Harold's daughter a check for $50,000 with "inheritance satisfaction" written on the check. When Ursula dies, to what, if anything, is Harold entitled?

PROBLEM XII

In 2004, John gives his cousin Mary a gift of $10,000 accompanied by a note stating the following: "This is an advancement on your inheritance." As of 2004, John has not yet made a will. In 2009, John executes a will containing a devise of $5,000 to Mary. John dies in 2017. To what, if anything, is Mary entitled? Would the result differ if John had made the same gift and devise to his own son?

6.6.3 Abatement

The term "abate" means to reduce in amount. In the context of wills, the doctrine of abatement provides an orderly system for reducing testamentary gifts when the probate estate does not contain sufficient assets to cover estate expenses, creditor claims, and devises to beneficiaries as recited in the instrument. Recall that creditors of the estate are entitled to payment before the distribution of assets to beneficiaries, so a common reason for the application of abatement is the existence of claims against the estate. Abatement also applies when the will makes general bequests that exceed the value of property contained in the estate.

Abatement establishes the order in which testamentary gifts are reduced (abated) in these circumstances. A testator can modify the statutory default order by will; however, careful drafting is necessary to avoid unintentional consequences, such as charging certain beneficiaries for expenses the testator did not realize would be deducted before distribution.

Uniform Probate Code
§3-902 Distribution; Order in Which Assets Appropriated; Abatement

(a) Except as provided in subsection (b) . . . shares of distributees abate, without any preference or priority as between real and personal property, in the following order:

(1) property not disposed of by the will;[13]

(2) residuary devises;

13. The term "property not disposed of by the will" refers to probate property that transfers by intestacy. For example, if the will does not include a residuary clause, the residue of the estate would pass to the testator's heirs by intestacy.

(3) general devises;
(4) specific devises.

For purposes of abatement, a general devise charged on any specific property or fund is a specific devise to the extent of the value of the property on which it is charged, and upon the failure or insufficiency of the property on which it is charged, a general devise to the extent of the failure or insufficiency. Abatement within each classification is in proportion to the amounts of property each of the beneficiaries would have received if full distribution of the property had been made in accordance with the terms of the will.

(b) If the will expresses an order of abatement, or if the testamentary plan or the express or implied purpose of the devise would be defeated by the order of abatement stated in subsection (a), the shares of the distributees abate as may be found necessary to give effect to the intention of the testator.

PROBLEM XIII

In 2000, Melvin executes a will with the following material provisions:

> FIRST: I do hereby direct that all of my just debts and all expenses of my last illness, funeral, and the administration of my estate shall be paid out of my estate by my executrix hereinafter appointed as soon after my death as may be practicable.
>
> SECOND: Subject to the provisions of the foregoing paragraph, I give: (a) all money, stocks and bonds to my beloved sister Hazel if she survives me; if she should predecease me, then to her issue by representation; and (b) all the rest, residue, and remainder of my estate, including my 115-acre ranch, to my friends Bryan and Marie.

Melvin dies in 2017 and his estate contains a substantial amount of debt.

Bryan and Marie offered the will for probate and argued that claims against the estate should be paid using the estate's liquid assets. Hazel objected to this interpretation because all of Melvin's debts would be paid out of her share of the estate since money and stock are liquid assets. The probate court held that Article First of the will, which directed that debts "be paid out of my estate," expressed Melvin's intent that his debts be apportioned *pro rata* from each category of bequest. All parties appeal and you are one of the appellate judges assigned to the case. Under UPC §3-902, how would you rule? Should you affirm, allowing bequests to abate ratably? Or should some other principle of abatement apply? Consider the following questions to guide your analysis.

A. Did the probate court correctly interpret Article First of the will by holding that Melvin intended to vary the default order of abatement?

B. If you conclude the default order of abatement should apply, whose devise would abate first?

C. Is the 115-acre ranch the subject of a specific or residuary devise? Why would this matter?

PROBLEM XIV

In 2010, Susan, a widow, executes a will with the following bequests: "(1) $50,000 to my faithful nurse, Nancy; (2) $50,000 to my son, Stanley; (3) my summer home in East Hampton to my daughter, Dorothy; and (4) all the rest, residue, and remainder to my companion, Charlie." In 2017, Susan dies leaving the following estate: (1) $100,000 in cash and marketable securities; and (2) a summer home in East Hampton (worth $1.2 million on the date of death). Susan's funeral and burial cost $50,000, and creditors asserted valid claims against the estate for $1.2 million arising from Susan's tortious conduct. Applying UPC §3-902, determine what, if anything, Nancy, Stanley, Dorothy, and Charlie take from Susan's estate.

6.6.4 Accession

Accession refers to an increase or addition to property. In the context of wills, the doctrine of accession applies when a testator devises shares of stock or securities and, after the will's execution, those securities produce additional shares because of a stock split, stock dividend, corporate merger, or subsidiary spinoff. A stock split occurs when the issuing corporation increases the total number of outstanding shares by declaring that each existing share will be divided into multiple shares. In a 3-for-1 stock split, for example, each shareholder will receive two additional shares for each existing share; after the split, each shareholder will hold three shares for each pre-split share. Since a stock split is merely a change in form, the value of three post-split shares is equal to the value of one pre-split share.

As a general rule, under the doctrine of accession, the beneficiary receives additional shares produced by the devised securities after the will's execution. The doctrine, however, does not entitle the devisee to take cash dividends distributed during the testator's lifetime. In some jurisdictions, the devisee does not take additional shares produced by stock dividends distributed during the testator's lifetime. See In re Estate of Sheldon, 42 Misc. 2d 1091 (N.Y. 1964).

Uniform Probate Code
§2-605 Increase in Securities; Accessions

(a) If a testator executes a will that devises securities and the testator then owned securities that meet the description in the will, the devise includes additional securities owned by the testator at death to the extent the additional securities were acquired by the testator after the will was executed as a result of the testator's ownership of the described securities and are securities of any of the following types:

(1) securities of the same organization acquired by reason of action initiated by the organization or any successor, related, or acquiring organization, excluding any acquired by exercise of purchase options;

(2) securities of another organization acquired as a result of a merger, consolidation, reorganization, or other distribution by the organization or any successor, related, or acquiring organization; or

(3) securities of the same organization acquired as a result of a plan of reinvestment.

(b) Distributions in cash before death with respect to a described security are not part of the devise.

COMMENT

The rule of subsection (a), as revised, relates to a devise of securities (such as a devise of 100 shares of XYZ Company), regardless of whether that devise is characterized as a general or specific devise.

Restatement (Third) of Property: Wills & Other Donative Transfers §5.3 Effect of Stock Splits, Stock Dividends, and Other Distributions on Devises of a Specific Number of Securities

A devise of a specified number of securities carries with it any additional securities acquired by the testator after executing the will to the extent that the post-execution acquisitions resulted from the testator's ownership of the described securities.

Some jurisdictions, unlike the UPC, limit a beneficiary's entitlement to additional shares to specific devises of securities. As noted in the UPC comment, however, the modern approach applies accession to any increase in shares attributable to stock splits, whether the underlying devise is specific or general. The following case illustrates accession in a jurisdiction that limits the doctrine to the specific devise of securities.

Polson v. Craig
570 S.E.2d 190 (S.C. Ct. App. 2002)

[The decedent, Martha Broadbent, inherited 400 shares of Standard Oil Company from her husband, William, who died in 1965. William stated in his will, "it is my request that [Martha] give said shares to my daughter, Norma B. Polson, at my wife's demise." Martha's 1967 will devised "400 shares of capital stock of Standard Oil Company" to Norma. In 1984, Martha signed a new will, which included the same gift to Norma, although in 1972, Standard Oil Company had become Exxon. Martha kept the shares she had inherited from her husband in an account separate from her other stock holdings. At the time of Martha's death in 1997, as the court noted, "the original four hundred shares [had] greatly increased in number."

The executors of Martha's estate argued that Norma was entitled to only 400 shares of Exxon. Norma claimed she was entitled to the 400 shares and all additional shares resulting from stock splits. The probate court characterized Martha's gift to Norma as a general devise and, as a result, that Norma would receive 400 shares of Exxon stock. The circuit court reversed after determining that the gift was a specific devise and, accordingly, that Norma was entitled to the additional shares produced by the stock splits. The executors brought this appeal. — Eds.]

Goosby, J.:

[The executors] argue the probate court's finding that Martha intended a general devise of only four hundred shares is supported by the evidence. They further contend Polson failed to present any evidence of Martha's intent to devise Polson more than four hundred shares of Exxon stock.

. . .

[The South Carolina accession statute] accords with the general rule that the legatee of a specific bequest of shares of corporate stock, as distinguished from the legatee of a general bequest, is entitled to any accretions to the bequeathed shares which are received by the testatrix, as a result of a stock split, subsequent to the making of such bequest. The rationale behind this rule is that a stock split in no way alters the substance of the [testatrix's] total interest or rights in the corporation. It is merely a dividing up of the outstanding shares of a corporation into a greater number of units without disturbing the stockholder's original proportional participating interest in the corporation. If the legatee is not awarded the additional shares, the value of the specific bequest would be substantially reduced, contrary to the testatrix's intent.

. . .

We therefore look to the evidence to determine whether there is an indication, however "slight," of Martha's intent to make the legacy specific. Martha's last will states in pertinent part:

> ITEM II. I hereby will and bequeath unto Norma B. Polson, daughter of my late husband, four hundred (400) shares of capital stock of Standard Oil Company.

The probate court held the lack of a possessive term such as "my stock" or "the stock which I own" demonstrates the bequest is general. Appellants argue Martha's use of the term "four hundred" evidences an intent to limit the devise to four hundred shares.

In examining the record to see if the probate court's finding that Martha intended only a general devise of stock or its monetary equivalent is supported by the evidence, we can find no evidence Martha intended anything other than to give Polson the stock she received from [her husband] William Broadbent's will. All of the evidence indicates Martha's reference to "four hundred" shares is a specific reference to the four hundred shares of Standard Oil stock she received from William Broadbent. Martha's early will, written shortly after William's death, and Martha's reference to "four hundred" shares in her later will indicate Martha intended to comply with the request in William's will that she return the shares to Polson in the event she had no need of them.

Jean DuBose testified Martha "wanted to return the 400 shares that Bill gave to her — back to Norma." There is evidence that Martha kept this Exxon stock separate from her stock portfolio. Even Pam Yarborough's deposition and testimony stating that Martha intended to give Polson four hundred shares of stock does not support the finding that the devise of "four hundred" shares is not a specific reference to the four hundred shares Martha received from William Broadbent. Standard Oil of New Jersey did not exist at the time Martha executed the will. The only possible reason for the description of the stock as Standard Oil stock was that the stock Martha intended to give Polson is the same Standard Oil stock William devised to her in his will. Martha's two wills and all the evidence support the conclusion that Martha intended to return to Norma the same stock she received from William, not merely its monetary equivalent, if it remained in her estate at the time of her death. This stock is clearly separable and distinct from the rest of the property in Martha's estate.

. . .

[The accession statute] entitles Polson to "any additional or other securities of the same entity owned by the testator by reason of action initiated by the entity excluding any acquired by exercise of purchase options." This subsection permits Polson to claim the additional stock resulting from stock splits. Had Martha not intended this result, she could have included a statement to the contrary in her will. We therefore conclude the probate court's finding that the devise is a general one, not subject to section 62-2-605, is not supported by reasonable evidence and is governed by an error of law regarding the application of the presumption in favor of a general devise. We accordingly affirm the circuit court's order holding that Polson is entitled to the original four hundred shares and all additional stock resulting from subsequent stock splits.

Affirmed.

Standard Oil Company stock certificate

Standard Oil Company, founded by John D. Rockefeller in 1870, was the parent company of the famed petroleum giant before numerous corporate spin-offs, including the Standard Oil Company of New Jersey. In 1911, the U.S. Supreme Court held that Standard Oil Company of New Jersey had violated the Sherman Antitrust Act by asserting its vast market size and power anticompetitively. See Standard Oil Co. of New Jersey v. United States, 221 U.S. 1 (1911). Standard Oil Company of New Jersey was divested into thirty-four separate companies, but over the years, many of those corporate entities recombined through mergers and acquisitions into the modern-day ExxonMobil.

QUESTIONS

19. Do you agree with the following assessment by the court: "The only possible reason for the description of the stock as Standard Oil stock was that the stock Martha intended to give Polson is the same Standard Oil stock William devised to her in his will"?

    ANSWER. Not necessarily. The description most likely matched the stock certificates Martha kept in her portfolio. Before the advent of electronic markets and stock trading over the internet, stock certificates were issued in paper form. Martha's will most likely provided a proper description of the devised securities.

20. What drafting techniques would help avoid the dispute litigated in this case?

    ANSWER. Stock portfolios should be devised in shares. Here, the decedent and her late husband appeared to attach special significance to this devise, but why would Norma (the beneficiary) care whether she received 400 shares of Standard Oil, 4,000 shares of Exxon, or 25 shares of Berkshire Hathaway, assuming they were of similar value? The beneficiary is likely to care only if the devise of securities constitutes a controlling stake in the company or the securities were issued by a close or family-owned business where corporate control is important.

PROBLEM XV

For the following items, refer to Problem VII above.

A. Sonia Felipe was killed during a botched car-jacking. Despite numerous witnesses, the police never found Sonia's murderer or her car. The car was not insured. Under devise #1 of Sonia's will, what does her son, Ricardo, receive?

B. A few weeks before Sonia died, she gave her mother $500 in cash. Under devise #3 of Sonia's will, what would her mother receive?

C. Some months before Sonia died, she closed out her account at the teachers' credit union. Under devise #4, what would Sonia's father receive?

D. One month after executing her will, Westinghouse Corporation announced a 2-for-1 stock split. Under devise #5 of Sonia's will, what would Salvador receive?

E. Sonia's life insurance policy paid out $5,000 in equal shares of $2,500 to each of Ricardo and Maria who were the only beneficiaries Sonia had named on the beneficiary designation form. After Ricardo and Maria paid off Sonia's debts, Sonia's total estate consisted only of household furnishings and clothing with no commercial value; Sonia's wedding ring; and $1,500 in cash. Under these circumstances, which of Sonia's beneficiaries receive what under Sonia's will?

6.7 LIMITATIONS OF LANGUAGE: RULES OF CONSTRUCTION AND EXTRINSIC EVIDENCE

> **Words strain, Crack and sometimes break, under the burden, Under the tension, slip, slide, perish, Decay with imprecision, will not stay in place, Will not stay still.**
>
> **T.S. Eliot, Four Quartets (Burnt Norton)**

Words have multiple connotative and denotative meanings. Those meanings derive from the context in which the words are used, the person using them, and the document in which they appear. Although courts talk of the "testator's" language, except for holographic wills, words in a will are almost always those of the attorney who wrote it. It is common practice today for an estate planning attorney to meet with a client, take notes regarding the client's family, property, and wishes, and then — often with the help of standard forms and word-processing programs — to assemble a will that the attorney believes accurately reflects the testator's directions and intentions. The attorney then usually sends a draft of the will accompanied by a letter explaining its terms to the client for review. Clients (usually) review the draft and either request changes or indicate that the draft is fine. The lawyer subsequently prepares the will in final form for execution. Given this process — it is hard to say that it is *really* the "testator's" words that appear on the will. Nevertheless, courts treat the words of a will — and any problems that develop from the choice of those words — as if they had been written by the testator.

Disputes over the meaning of a word, expression, name, address, or phrase almost always occur after the will is offered for probate. By then, of course, the testator (who could offer the best clarification of meaning and intent) is unavailable to testify. Thus, the question becomes whether a court will limit the evidence it considers in resolving the dispute to the "four corners" of the will, that is, only the words in the will, or whether a court will consider evidence *extrinsic* to the will — such as testimony from the scrivener, prior drafts of the will, previously executed but subsequently revoked wills, friends' and family members' recollections of the testator's references to the will, and so on.

At common law, courts were reluctant to admit extrinsic evidence to clarify a testator's intent even in situations involving clear error. That reluctance led to results that were often contrary to testators' intentions but provided relatively simple rules for judges: a textual Procrustean bed.[14] The modern trend of inheritance law reform has liberalized the rules of construction and both the Restatement and the UPC now permit courts to admit extrinsic evidence in a broad range of circumstances. Although not yet fully adopted in a majority of jurisdictions, this shift reflects the reality that when a living person's intentions are reduced to fragile words, those words do not always convey the testator's true intentions.

---

14. In Greek mythology, Procrustes, the son of Poseidon, would invite weary travelers to stay the night, but he would then torture his guests either by stretching them to fit an iron bed or cutting them down to size to fit. In the modern vernacular, a Procrustean standard has come to mean an arbitrary one, without regard to circumstances that would otherwise require a more particularized inquiry.

6.7.1 Common Law Rules of Construction

The common law generally prohibited most rules of interpretation that modified the words of a validly executed will. This prohibition, consistent with the "strict compliance" approach to Wills Act formalities, was rooted in the belief that no form of unattested action or writing should be admissible as part of a decedent's will because unattested material was deemed inherently unreliable and rendered the estate vulnerable to fraud and false claims. The common law approach disfavoring modification of testamentary language was embodied in three traditional rules of construction: (1) the "plain meaning" rule; (2) the "no reformation" rule; and (3) doctrines distinguishing patent and latent ambiguities. The first two of these are described in this section; ambiguities are treated in the next section.

First, under the so-called *plain meaning rule* (sometimes referred to as the "*no extrinsic evidence*" rule), courts barred the admission of extrinsic evidence to alter the plain meaning of the words unless the words of the will were susceptible to more than one meaning, in which case there was an ambiguity, or the words altogether lacked a plain meaning. The plain meaning rule often produced harsh results. In one case, a testator told her attorney that she wanted her residuary estate to pass in equal shares to her twenty-five first cousins. See Mahoney v. Grainger, 186 N.E. 86 (Mass. 1933). The attorney, after asking the testator to clarify that the twenty-five first cousins were indeed her closest relations, drafted the following residuary clause: "[I give my residuary estate to] . . . my heirs at law living at the time of my decease, absolutely; to be divided among them equally, share and share alike. . . ." The testator died shortly after executing this will. Only then was it discovered that the testator's cousins were *not*, in fact, her closest relations: She was survived by a maternal aunt, who was, at the testator's death, her sole heir at law. Only if the aunt had predeceased the testator would the first cousins have met the description "heirs at law living at the time of my decease."[15] Despite strong evidence of the testator's actual intent, the Massachusetts Supreme Judicial Court refused to consider evidence proffered by the drafting attorney that would have altered the clear meaning of the words in the will. Thus, the maternal aunt inherited to the exclusion of the testator's intended beneficiaries, her twenty-five first cousins.

Second, under the *no reformation rule*, courts were prohibited from modifying the words of a will to correct a mistake. It made no difference whether the mistake occurred because of the testator's error (if, for example, the testator told the attorney that she had five nephews when, in fact, she had six) or because of an error by the person writing the will — commonly referred to as a "scrivener's error" (for example, the testator said she wanted her property at 123 Main Street to be given to her sister, but the will read "*132* Main Street" instead of 123). Today, however, under the modern trend in a growing number of jurisdictions, the "plain meaning" and "no reformation" rules have given way to doctrines that are more amenable to extrinsic evidence and, therefore, better suited to carrying out the testator's intent.

15. Recall the discussion in Chapter 2 explaining that no living person has heirs but, rather, only heirs apparent. Not until the moment of death does an heir apparent become an heir at law for purposes of testamentary distributions.

The consideration of extrinsic evidence to determine the meaning of a will is governed by the substantive law of wills rather than the generally applicable evidentiary rules governing admissibility. To emphasize the applicability of substantive inheritance law, the Restatement does not describe allowable evidence as "admissible," but rather uses the phrase, "may be considered." Restatement (Third) of Property: Wills & Other Donative Transfers §10.2, comment c. Thus, although under the modern approach, extrinsic evidence may be considered to resolve an ambiguity or to correct a mistake, the evidentiary rules that generally apply in civil litigation—for example, the attorney-client privilege, hearsay, and Dead Man's statutes—also apply to a dispute over the meaning of words in a will.

6.7.2 Ambiguities

Language is ambiguous when words are susceptible to more than one meaning. At common law, courts distinguished between two types of ambiguity: patent and latent. The characterization of an ambiguity as patent or latent determined the admissibility of extrinsic evidence. In general, patent ambiguities in dispositive provisions did not provide grounds for admitting extrinsic evidence and therefore often led to a failure of the bequest; by contrast, courts generally resolved latent ambiguities by considering extrinsic evidence and upholding the bequest. As we will see, the modern trend (albeit still a minority rule) collapses the distinction between patent and latent ambiguities and allows courts to consider extrinsic evidence to resolve all ambiguous testamentary language.

A *patent* ambiguity is an uncertainty of meaning discernable directly from the language of the will. At common law, courts excluded extrinsic evidence to resolve a patent ambiguity primarily because the extrinsic evidence necessary to resolve the ambiguity would directly contradict the attested language of the will. Consider, for example, a general devise containing the following language: "I give One Thousand Dollars ($10,000) to my cousin Steve." The ambiguity is apparent: No extrinsic evidence is needed to establish the existence of the ambiguity since it is evident on the face of the will. At common law, courts would exclude extrinsic evidence showing that the testator intended to devise "One Thousand Dollars" because it would literally contradict language in the will purporting to bequeath $10,000; similarly, extrinsic evidence showing that the testator intended to bequeath $10,000 would, likewise, directly contradict the testator's gift of "One Thousand Dollars." Without extrinsic evidence to resolve the patent ambiguity, the bequest would fail, meaning that whatever amount the testator had intended to give her cousin Steve, that amount would pass instead to the testator's residuary beneficiaries.

A *latent* ambiguity, by contrast, is not apparent from the face of the will. Latent ambiguities are hidden, so they can be revealed only by extrinsic evidence. For example, suppose a testator bequeaths the residuary estate to her "cousin John." After the testator's death, the executor of the estate discovers, through inquiries about the testator's relatives (i.e., facts derived from outside the four corners of the will), that the testator had two cousins named John. The bequest is treated as a latent ambiguity because it presents two possible interpretations that derive from extrinsic evidence — a family tree. Each of those interpretations favors a different cousin named John. Thus, because the ambiguity reveals itself from extrinsic evidence and, more importantly, because neither possible interpretation directly contradicts the will's language (regardless of outcome, the gift will pass to one of the testator's cousins named John) courts traditionally would consider extrinsic evidence to resolve the ambiguity thereby preventing failure of the gift.

We will look more carefully at the distinction between patent and latent ambiguities below.

6.7.2.1 Patent Ambiguities

Patent ambiguities appear in various forms. For example, a will may contain a patent ambiguity when language in one section conflicts with language in another section.

> **Example A**
> Article II, paragraph (a) of decedent's will devises "the residuary of my estate to Abigail." Article VIII devises the "rest, residue, and remainder of my estate to Beatrice."

In Example A, who is the residuary beneficiary, Abigail or Beatrice? The inconsistency is apparent from the face of the instrument and therefore constitutes a patent ambiguity.

> **Example B**
> Article II, paragraph (a) of decedent's will devises "$12,500 (Two Thousand Five Hundred Dollars) to my friend Abigail."
>
> Article II, paragraph (e) devises "$2,500 (Twelve Thousand Five Hundred Dollars) to my friend Abigail."

In Example B, the language is patently ambiguous in at least two respects: first, on account of the discrepancy between the dollar amounts expressed in words and the dollar amounts expressed in numerical form; second, because the will contains nearly — but not exactly — identical, repetitive language within the same Article. Did the testator intend to give Abigail one or two gifts? Were the gifts intended to be $2,500 or $12,500? Was one gift intended to be $2,500 and the other $12,500? What was the total amount the testator intended Abigail to receive? Was the gift in the later paragraph (e) meant for someone else with Abigail's name appearing by mistake? Or, were there two Abigails whom the testator wanted to benefit and, if so, how would the court determine which gift went to whom and in what amount? For examples of the many kinds of patent ambiguities, see Restatement (Third) of Property: Wills & Other Donative Transfers §11.2, comments n-q.

Of course, whether an ambiguity is patent or latent is often a matter of interpretation.

6.7.2.2 Latent Ambiguities

Latent ambiguities arise when the language of the will appears to be unambiguous, but extrinsic evidence renders terms of the will to be uncertain. At common law, extrinsic evidence was allowed to clarify latent ambiguities under the theory that, since "a latent ambiguity is only disclosed by extrinsic evidence, it may be removed by extrinsic evidence." Patch v. White, 117 U.S. 210, 217 (1886).

There are two basic kinds of latent ambiguities. The first occurs when a will clearly refers to a person or thing, but two or more persons or things fit that description. This kind of ambiguity is referred to as an *equivocation.*

Example C
George F. leaves $50,000 "to my son, George." George F. has five sons named George.

Example D
Talal leaves his collection of antique coins "to my dear Jimmy." Talal has a brother, close friend, and grandson all named James.

Sometimes, latent ambiguities can be resolved through the "personal usage" exception. Restatement (Third) of Property: Wills & Other Donative Transfers §11.2, comment on Subsection (b)(3). The personal usage exception applies when the testator habitually used a name or word in an idiosyncratic way or referred to a person by an idiosyncratic term. For example, in Example C, if the testator always referred to his first-born son named George as "George," but to the other Georges always by nicknames (e.g., "Big George," "Skinny George," "Georgie," "Hothead," etc.), a court might determine that the gift was intended for the eldest son George and not for any of his brothers named George. In Example D, evidence of the testator's consistent use of the various nicknames might also, under the personal usage exception, resolve the ambiguity, even if the testator were the only person who referred to the particular James as "Jimmy."

The second type of latent ambiguity exists when no person or thing exactly fits the description, but two or more persons or things could fit the description in whole or part.

Example E
Dora leaves $5,000 in stock certificates to "my nephew, Evan Franklin Grimaldi." Dora has a nephew named Evan Fitzpatrick Grimaldi and a nephew named Ethan Franklin Grimaldi.

Example F
Lanying gives "my car to my cousin Shaozu." Lanying's executor discovers that Lanying owned three cars, a Volkswagen, a Tesla, and a Bentley.

In Example E, a court would consider extrinsic evidence to determine which nephew the testator intended to benefit from the bequest. Likewise, in Example F, a court would consider extrinsic evidence to determine which of Lanying's three cars she intended Shaozu to receive. Notice that in both of these cases — as in all latent ambiguities — the extrinsic evidence clarifies the testamentary language but never directly contradicts it.

PROBLEM XVI

Article I of the decedent's will provides a general description of assets in the estate and describes the testator's collection of rare books and manuscripts as, "by far, the most valuable and important asset in my estate." Article III, paragraph (a) of the decedent's will gives "my personal property to my daughter, Sonya." The residuary clause of the decedent's will gives "all the rest, residue, and remainder of my estate to my beloved husband, Desi, for it is he who should benefit most from my estate." If the decedent's most valuable asset was a collection of rare books and manuscripts, then would that collection pass as the decedent's "personal property" to her daughter, Sonya, or as part of the residuary estate to her husband, Desi, "who should benefit most from [the testator's] estate"? What kind of ambiguity is created by this kind of sloppy drafting? Patent? Latent? Something else?

6.7.2.3 Resolving Ambiguities: The Introduction of Extrinsic Evidence

Because the ultimate aim of testamentary interpretation today is to determine testamentary intent, the modern trend eliminates the patent/latent distinction and permits consideration of extrinsic evidence to clarify all ambiguities. The Restatement and the following case take this approach.

Restatement (Third) of Property: Wills & Other Donative Transfers
§11.1 Ambiguity Defined

An ambiguity in a donative document is an uncertainty in meaning that is revealed by the text or by extrinsic evidence other than direct evidence of intention contradicting the plain meaning of the text.

Notice that the Restatement abolishes, as a definitional matter, the distinction between patent ambiguities (those that are "revealed by the text") and latent ambiguities (those that are revealed "by extrinsic evidence"). Although it remains the minority rule, the Restatement's position has been adopted by many courts, as we will see below. Notice, too, however, that the Restatement's definition does not abrogate, but instead continues, the common law rule barring consideration of extrinsic evidence that directly contradicts the attested language of the will, to the extent the language has a plain meaning.

For example, a bequest to the testator's "sisters" would contain a latent ambiguity if, in fact, the testator never had more than one biological or adopted sister and had maintained a close relationship with her graduating class of college sorority sisters, whom she always referred to as her "sisters." Courts would admit extrinsic evidence to resolve the question of whether the bequest should pass to the testator's sole biological sister or to her sorority sisters as a group. If, by preponderance of the evidence, the testator's intent could be proved one way or the other, then the ambiguity could be resolved. Courts, however, would not admit extrinsic evidence purporting to show that the testator, in fact, intended the bequest to benefit her three *brothers* because that interpretation would, in effect, rewrite the will with language directly contradicting the testamentary language referring to "sisters." If the testator mistakenly included a bequest to her "sisters" when, in fact, she intended to provide for her brothers, then the language is mistaken, not ambiguous. As we will see, the modern approach to correcting mistakes permits the admission of extrinsic evidence to reform a will, but only under the higher evidentiary standard of clear and convincing evidence.

Restatement (Third) of Property: Wills & Other Donative Transfers
§11.2 Resolving Ambiguities in Accordance with the Donor's Intention

> (a) An ambiguity to which no rule of construction or constructional preference applies is resolved by construing the text of the donative document in accordance with the donor's intention, to the extent that the donor's intention is established by a preponderance of the evidence.
>
> (b) Ambiguities to which no rule of construction or constructional preference applies include those arising when:
>
> > (1) the text or extrinsic evidence (other than direct evidence contradicting the plain meaning of the text) reveals a mistaken description of persons or property.
> >
> > (2) the text reveals an apparent mistaken inclusion or omission.
> >
> > (3) extrinsic evidence (other than direct evidence contradicting the plain meaning of the text) reveals that the donor's personal usage differs from the ordinary meaning of a term used in the text.

The following case addresses the problem of ambiguity in the context of an inter vivos trust, but it discusses and applies the substantive law of wills governing patent and latent ambiguity to the trust. This is consistent with the Restatement's approach governing donative transfers, which includes both wills and trusts.

University of Southern Indiana Foundation v. Baker
843 N.E.2d 528 (Ind. 2006)

Opinion

BOEHM, Justice.

SHEPARD, C.J., and DICKSON, SULLIVAN, and RUCKER, JJ., concur.

We hold that the trust created by Marian Boelson left her tangible personal property and any interest she retained in her individual retirement accounts to her brother and gave the remaining assets to the University of Southern Indiana Foundation.

FACTUAL AND PROCEDURAL HISTORY

In 1996 Marian Boelson created an inter vivos trust.[16] Section 7 expressly declined to make any provision for Boelson's brother, Richard Baker, or any other potential intestate heirs. Section 8 provided a bequest of $50,000 to Faye Rucks, a friend of Boelson's, and Section 9 left the residue to the University of Southern Indiana Foundation ("USIF"). In August 2001, Boelson amended the trust, revoking Sections 7 and 8 and replacing them with new Sections 7 and 8:

> 7. Upon the death of Trustor, the Trustor's brother, Richard A. Baker, if living, shall receive any and all proceeds and assets that were held in Trustor's individual retirement accounts, if any, as well as, all of Trustor's automobiles, furnishings and other personal property.
>
> 8. After payment of [expenses of trust administration], the Trustee shall distribute to Trustor's friend, Faye Rucks, presently residing at 850 Cherokee Road, Henderson, Kentucky, the sum of Ten Thousand Dollars ($10,000.00), if living, and if not living, then said funds shall become part of the residue of the Trust and be distributed according to the terms and conditions set forth in Section 9 of this Trust Agreement.

No other substantial changes were made and the provision in Section 9 leaving the residue to USIF remained unchanged. Boelson died on August 29, 2003, leaving a will that poured her assets over into the trust.[17] At death Boelson owned a condominium in Indiana, a one-acre lot in Florida, bank accounts, certificates of deposit, treasury notes, bonds, and two individual retirement accounts in which her brother was the designated beneficiary. There was also an automobile and tangible personal property (furniture, etc.) in the condominium.

Following Boelson's death, the trustee petitioned for an interpretation of the amended trust. No one challenged the $10,000 provision for Rucks, but Baker and USIF disagreed as to the disposition of the remaining assets. Baker alleged he was the beneficiary of all of the remaining personal property, and that USIF was the beneficiary of Boelson's real property only. USIF responded that the trust left Boelson's "personal effects" to Baker but gave all of Boelson's real property and all intangible personal property to USIF. USIF moved for summary judgment, designating the following affidavits and exhibits: (1) the affidavit of Boelson's attorney stating that "my understanding [was] that Mrs. Boelson intended for her brother to receive the personal property located in her residence"; (2) the affidavit of Boelson's trustee stating that Boelson told the trustee that Boelson hoped she would live

16. [As we will discuss in Chapter 8, an individual (the "donor") may transfer his or her property during lifetime to trustees to manage the property during the donor's lifetime; at the donor's death, the trust instrument acts as a will substitute, distributing the trust property in accordance with the donor's instructions. Such inter vivos trusts are almost always revocable or amendable by the donor during his or her lifetime. A person who creates this kind of inter vivos revocable trust may be referred to as the "donor," "settlor," or — as in this case — the "trustor." — Eds.]

17. [This kind of "pour-over" will assures that any of the trustor's property that had not been transferred to the trustees during the trustor's lifetime will be transferred to the trustees when the trustor dies. — Eds.]

long enough to see the gift to USIF grow to be worth one million dollars; (3) the affidavit of Boelson's companion stating that Boelson had told him shortly before her death that after her death, USIF would receive almost all of Boelson's property, including her stocks; (4) typed instructions given by Boelson to her attorney which state, "Brother is beneficiary of and to receive two IRA accounts, automobile and any furnishings and personal property in the condo that he would like"; and (5) Boelson's attorney's handwritten notes stating "3. Item 7—Brother now gets: 1. Both IRAS / 2. Auto / 3. furniture from residence / 4. other personal property in residence."

Based on USIF's affidavits and exhibits, the probate court concluded that Boelson's intention was to give the bulk of her personal property to USIF and to limit Baker to the IRAs, the automobile, and the household furnishings and personal effects in Boelson's condominium. However, the probate court concluded that because the language of the trust unambiguously devised "personal property" to Baker without limitation, it could not give effect to that intention. Specifically, the probate court held that the term "personal property" unambiguously encompassed all of Boelson's tangible and intangible personal property. The probate court therefore granted Baker's motion to strike USIF's designated evidence on the ground that the proffered evidence and exhibits were inadmissible parol evidence. The trustee was instructed to pay trust administration costs and to distribute $10,000 to Rucks, all remaining tangible and intangible personal property to Baker, and the real property to USIF. USIF appealed and the Court of Appeals affirmed. . . .

I. Standard of Review

The interpretation of a will or trust is a question of law for the court. . . .

II. Interpretation of Boelson's Amended Trust

The primary purpose of the court in construing a trust instrument is to ascertain and give effect to the settlor's intention. Indiana follows "the four corners rule" that "extrinsic evidence is not admissible to add to, vary or explain the terms of a written instrument if the terms of the instrument are susceptible of a clear and unambiguous construction." Accordingly, where a trust is capable of clear and unambiguous construction, under this doctrine, the court must give effect to the trust's clear meaning without resort to extrinsic evidence. Baker argues that the trial court and the Court of Appeals correctly ruled that the trust unambiguously devises all personal property to him and therefore all property except the realty was properly distributed to him. USIF argues that the trust unambiguously devises only "personal effects" to Baker. We disagree with both Baker and USIF and conclude that the term "personal property" is ambiguous in the context of this trust instrument.

A document is not ambiguous merely because parties disagree about a term's meaning. Rather, language is ambiguous only if reasonable people could come to different conclusions as to its meaning. Baker argues that the trust contains no ambiguity. He is correct that the term "personal property" means "Any movable or intangible thing that is subject to ownership and not classified as real property."

Baker cites the rule of construction that, particularly where an attorney familiar with technical terms has drafted an instrument, courts will give terms their technical meaning.

USIF also claims that the trust is unambiguous, but that "personal property" means "personal effects" and does not include cash, certificates of deposit or bonds. USIF cites authority for the view that courts should interpret terms in the context of the entire instrument and should not give terms their technical meaning where it clearly appears that the testator did not intend to employ the terms in their technical sense. USIF notes that the provision for Baker lists individual retirement accounts as well as Boelson's "automobiles, furnishings and other personal property" and argues that specific mention of the IRAs would be superfluous if Boelson intended "personal property" to include intangible property. We do not find that last point conclusive. . . .

USIF makes a final argument that we find more persuasive. USIF points to the internal structure of the trust. USIF contends that the syntax of the provision for Baker limits the scope of property conveyed. Specifically, USIF argues that because "other personal property" appears as a more general item at the end of a list of specific tangible items (automobiles and furnishings), it should be interpreted to include only personal effects of like kind to the automobiles and furnishings. USIF points out that if "automobiles, furnishings and other personal property" means, as Baker contends, "all personal property," there is no need to name any single item. Moreover, the trust as amended called for the "personal property" to go to Baker under Section 7. Section 8 follows, calling for a gift of $10,000 to Rucks to be paid after the payment of the expenses of the trust, but not mentioning any antecedent provision for Baker. This fairly plainly contemplates that the earlier provision for Baker was not thought to have a higher call on available cash than the gift to Rucks, which was subordinate only to payment of administrative expenses. Though it is conceivable that a trust could be set up to give all intangible property to one beneficiary, and then provide for a specific cash devise to another to be funded by sale or borrowing against real property, if that were Boelson's intent, we think it highly probable it would have been spelled out in a far less oblique manner than the language of this trust. It seems at least as likely that "other personal property" meant other tangible property, and the cash bequest to Rucks, establishes an assumption that intangible property would be available to fund the payment for Rucks of $10,000.

We conclude that the meaning of "personal property" in the trust is ambiguous and reasonable persons could come to different conclusions as to its meaning in this instrument. We agree that the term has the technical legal meaning Baker urges but find that the document as a whole creates substantial doubt that Boelson intended this technical meaning. Accordingly, we find the trust ambiguous and must address whether USIF's proffered exhibits and affidavits may be admitted to resolve the ambiguity. USIF argues that its exhibits and affidavits that bear directly on Boelson's intentions are admissible and resolve any ambiguity in its favor. Baker responds that we may not consider USIF's proffered extrinsic evidence because any ambiguity in the Boelson trust is "patent," not "latent," and under existing Indiana law, extrinsic evidence of the settlor's intent is not admissible to resolve a patent ambiguity. Earlier decisions of this Court drew the distinction Baker urges between patent and latent ambiguities. A patent ambiguity is an uncertainty created by the text of the donative instrument. A patent ambiguity can arise in a variety of settings, for example, where two portions of a document conflict with one another; or where it is unclear to which portion of a document a provision applies; or where a word has more than one dictionary meaning. A latent ambiguity is not apparent from reading the text of the donative document but is established by extrinsic evidence other than direct evidence of the settlor's intention. As an example, a will devising property "to my cousin John" has a latent ambiguity if extrinsic evidence reveals that the testator had no cousin named John but did have a nephew named John and a cousin named James. In Indiana, extrinsic evidence — both circumstantial and direct evidence of intention — has been held admissible to establish the existence of a latent ambiguity and also to resolve it. Indiana courts have traditionally refused to admit extrinsic evidence to aid in the resolution of a patent ambiguity on the ground that the language used conveys either no definite meaning or a confused meaning and the courts should not engage in conjecture and rewrite a donative instrument where the settlor has failed to adequately express his or her intent.

We agree with Baker that the ambiguity in the Boelson trust arises from the text of the document and therefore is patent under these authorities. We agree with USIF, however, that the distinction between patent and latent ambiguities is not useful, and it is proper to admit extrinsic evidence to resolve any ambiguity. USIF notes that the current version of the Restatement of Property allows for admission of all extrinsic evidence — both direct and circumstantial — relevant to determining a settlor's intent. Consistent with this view, several jurisdictions have abandoned the latent/patent distinction. Under this approach, whether an ambiguity is deemed patent or latent has no significance. We agree with USIF and these authorities that the latent/patent distinction has not been consistently applied and no longer serves any useful purpose. Accordingly, we conclude that where an instrument is ambiguous, all relevant extrinsic evidence may properly be considered in resolving the ambiguity.

The extrinsic evidence offered by USIF establishes unequivocally that Boelson's intention was to give the majority of her property to USIF. Indeed, the trial court so found, but regarded itself bound by earlier precedent to disregard the evidence. Boelson's own notes indicate "Brother is beneficiary of and to receive two IRA accounts, automobile and any furnishings and personal property in the condo that he would like." Boelson's attorney's affidavit and her notes of her meeting with Boelson reflect the attorney's understanding that Boelson wanted the gift to Baker to be the IRAs and the tangible personal property in Boelson's condominium and nothing more. Further proof of Boelson's intent is found in the affidavits of the trust officer and Boelson's companion. Both state that Boelson expressed to them her intention to give the bulk of her estate to USIF. There is no conflicting extrinsic evidence of Boelson's intent. There is therefore no genuine issue of material fact. We conclude that Boelson intended to limit her brother's share of her estate to IRAs, automobiles, and furnishings and other personal effects contained in her condominium. Baker offers nothing to contradict any of these affidavits, so the issue is resolvable on summary judgment.

CONCLUSION

The probate court's order directing the trustee to distribute all of Boelson's personal property to Baker and the real property to USIF is reversed. This case is remanded with instructions to order the trustee to pay the trust's administrative expenses, to distribute $10,000 to Rucks, to distribute Boelson's IRAs and any asset that passes under Boelson's will and all automobiles, furnishings and the other personal property contained in Boelson's condominium to Baker, and to distribute the trust's remaining real and personal property to USIF.

QUESTIONS

21. If the settlor intended to give her brother all intangible personal property including all liquid assets of the trust, from what source would the trustee pay Ms. Rucks her $10,000 gift?

    ANSWER. If the settlor had intended to give all liquid assets of the trust to her brother, the $10,000 gift to Ms. Rucks would have to come from the remaining assets of the trust. Because Article 7 gave to the settlor's brother all of her "automobiles, furnishings, and other personal property," if "other personal property" is interpreted to include all intangible personal property such as bank accounts and other liquid assets, then the $10,000 gift would have to come from the sale of the settlor's real property, which would otherwise pass to USIF. Do you think the testator would have intended the trustee to liquidate real property when there were so many liquid assets in the trust? Might this suggest that the testator did not intend to give all liquid assets to her brother?

22. Is the trust's mention of "personal property" in Article 7 patently ambiguous, as the court found? Can you determine the uncertainty of meaning without the extrinsic evidence proffered by USIF?

    ANSWER. Courts routinely struggle with interpreting the phrase "personal property" (see Problem XVI) because the term has both a technical meaning (all non-real property) and a colloquial meaning (personal effects and household furnishings). Testators who use the term personal property may fail to understand the implications of using the term. Here, the only indication from the trust itself that the settlor did not intend to give her brother all personal property was the otherwise inconsistent gift of $10,000 to Mrs. Rucks. This suggests that the ambiguity may have been patent, but extrinsic evidence revealed far more about the uncertainty of meaning in this instrument. The admission of extrinsic evidence to determine the decedent's intent where there are conflicting interpretations appears to be sound policy.

23. Given what the settlor's attorney swore under oath (in the affidavit submitted by USIF) that she knew about the settlor's assets and intentions regarding those assets, how should the attorney have drafted Article 7?

 ANSWER. The settlor's attorney stated that her understanding was that "Mrs. Boelson intended for her brother to receive the personal property located in her residence." The attorney's notes further states, "Brother is beneficiary of and to receive . . . any furnishings and personal property in the condo that he would like." From this extrinsic evidence, we understand the settlor's intent was to give her brother household furnishings and personal effects, not all personal property according to the technical definition of the term. As a first principle, an attorney generally should not use a technical term unless the term is defined within the instrument itself, plainly sets forth the settlor's intent, or conforms to an accepted usage under statutory or common law. The attorney could have also employed more specific language to articulate the settlor's intention, such as a provision giving her brother "all of Trustor's automobiles, furnishings, and other personal property located in her residence." Even clearer would be using the term tangible personal property.

6.7.3 Mistake

The inevitability of human error generates a constant stream of mistaken language in wills that, as a result of the textual error, requires court attention to determine a testator's intent. Of course, not all mistakes are attributable to the attorney: Often a client will give incomplete or incorrect information or fail to review a draft will carefully. Regardless, mistakes of fact and of law are not uncommon as the following examples demonstrate. Before studying the law on modification to correct mistaken language, consider what principles you would apply in determining whether extrinsic evidence should be admitted to clarify the language in the following examples.

Example G
Elise leaves her daughter "my house at 415 Robinson Avenue." Elise does not own any property at that address, but has a home at 145 Robinson Ave.

Example H
Florence leaves her car "to Ricardo Garcia of 1101 110th St." There is a Ricardo Garcia who lives at that address, but he did not know Florence, and Florence had never heard of him, much less ever met him. Florence had a very close friend named Ricardo Garcia who lived at 1001 110th Ave.

Example I
Gertrude, who is quite sick with cancer, is told that her only nephew has died on a trip to collect dinosaur bones in a remote part of Mongolia. Gertrude's will had left a gift of $100,000 to her "beloved nephew." Gertrude signs a codicil that deletes the

gift to her nephew and inserts a bequest that states, "I give $100,000 to the City Natural History Museum to name a gallery in memory of my beloved nephew." One day after Gertrude dies, word arrives that her nephew is, in fact, still alive. He had merely gone missing from his university expedition to spend time "alone in the mountains meditating." The nephew flies home just in time to attend his aunt's funeral.

6.7.3.1 Reformation to Correct Mistakes

Although the majority of jurisdictions has retained the common law "no reformation" rule, the modern trend, reflected in both the Restatement and the UPC, permits a will to be reformed to correct a mistake.

Restatement (Third) of Property: Wills & Other Donative Transfers
§12.1 Reforming Donative Documents to Correct Mistakes

A donative document, though unambiguous, may be reformed to conform the text to the donor's intention if it is established by clear and convincing evidence (1) that a mistake of fact or law, whether in expression or inducement, affected specific terms of the document; and (2) what the donor's intention was. In determining whether these elements have been established by clear and convincing evidence, direct evidence of intention contradicting the plain meaning of the text as well as other evidence of intention may be considered.

Uniform Probate Code
§2-805 Reformation to Correct Mistakes[18]

The court may reform the terms of a governing instrument, even if unambiguous, to conform the terms to the transferor's intention if it is proved by clear and convincing evidence what the transferor's intention was and that the terms of the governing instrument were affected by a mistake of fact or law, whether in expression or inducement.

Just as the modern trend has the law moving away from strict compliance with statutory formalities, for example, UPC §2-503 (harmless error), so too has the law moved away from strict construction of a donative instrument if a mistake can be proven by clear and convincing evidence. Professor John Langbein gives four reasons for this trend:

1. the rise of the nonprobate system, which permits reformation in a number of contexts similar to wills;
2. experience in other jurisdictions that permit reformation to correct mistaken content;
3. growing embarrassment that failure to cure well-proved mistakes inflicts unjust enrichment; and

18. This section of the UPC was added only in 2008, bringing the UPC in line with Uniform Trust Code §415 and the Restatement section quoted above. Both the UTC and the Restatement had allowed for reformation of a donative instrument if there was clear and convincing evidence that a mistake thwarted the donor's intent.

4. acknowledgement that it is often more efficient to correct a scrivener's error during the probate process than to probate a will containing mistaken language and later subject the attorney to malpractice liability.

John H. Langbein, Curing Execution Errors and Mistaken Terms in Wills: The Restatement of Wills Delivers New Tools (and New Duties) to Probate Lawyers, 18 Prob. & Prop. 28, 30 (2004).

Similarly, there has been a trend toward allowing reformation to accomplish a donor's tax objectives. See UPC §2-806; UTC §416; Restatement (Third) of Property: Wills & Other Donative Transfers §12.2. The clear and convincing standard required by the Restatement and the UPC sharply limits the courts' authority to reform wills. The evidentiary standard reduces the likelihood of granting reformation in doubtful cases of purported mistake and also prevents courts from being flooded with frivolous petitions for reformation.

The next case provides an example of judicial adoption of the reformation doctrine in a jurisdiction that has not adopted the UPC.

Estate of Herceg
193 Misc. 2d 201 (N.Y. Surr. Ct. 2002)

EUGENE E. PECKHAM, S.[19]

The residuary clause of the will of Eugenia Herceg, dated December 2, 1999, which was admitted to probate on August 16, 2001, reads as follows:

> All the rest, residue and remainder of the property which I may own at the time of my death, real and personal, and wheresoever the same may be situate.

There is no more. The name of the intended beneficiary of the residuary is missing. As a practical matter, the residuary clause amounts to only 10% of the estate, since the will made pre-residuary bequests of 90% of the net estate.

Colomba Pastorino, as Executrix of the will, has petitioned for construction of the will by reading the residuary clause to be the same as decedent's prior will dated June 18, 1997. The residuary clause of the 1997 will provided:

> All the rest, residue and remainder of the property which I may own at the time of my death, real and personal, and wheresoever the same may be situate . . . I give, devise and bequeath to my nephew, Sergio Pastorino, per stirpes. In the event that my nephew, Sergio Pastorino, does not survive me, his share shall go to his wife, Colomba Pastorino.

In fact, Sergio Pastorino died on November 25, 2000, without issue and Eugenia Herceg died on November 30, 2000. The persons who would take the decedent's estate in intestacy are a niece, Josephine D'Angelo, and a great nephew, Sergio Rossello. Josephine D'Angelo has filed a consent to the relief requested in the

19. [The abbreviation "S." stands for "Surrogate," which is how New York refers to judges overseeing cases in the Surrogate's Court, New York's name for its probate courts. — EDS.]

petition for construction. Sergio Rossello defaulted in appearing on the return day of the proceeding.

Daniel Gorman, the attorney draftsman of the will, has filed an affidavit stating that when the 1997 will was redrafted in 1999, using computer software "some lines from the residuary clause were accidentally deleted."

Obviously a mistake has been made. The question presented is whether the mistake can be corrected. For the reasons set forth below, we hold that the testator intended the residuary beneficiary to be Colomba Pastorino, wife of decedent's nephew and that her name should be inserted into the will.

The difficulty in this case is that there is a line of cases holding that where the name of the beneficiary is missing it cannot be supplied by construction or reformation of the will. In other words, the Court cannot supply missing names to correct a mistake, whether of the draftsperson of the will or the testator.

There is also another line of cases that hold that extrinsic evidence cannot be admitted unless there is an ambiguity in the will. If extrinsic evidence is not admitted, the prior wills of testatrix cannot be considered, nor the affidavit of the attorney draftsman.

Of course, the paramount objective in interpreting a will is to determine the intention of the testator from a reading of the whole will. Furthermore, the testator is presumed to intend to avoid intestacy[—]otherwise he or she would not have bothered to make a will. Even more[:] "The presumption against intestacy is particularly weighty where the subject of the gift is the residuary estate." Matter of Bieley, supra at 525, 673 N.Y.S.2d 38, 695 N.E.2d 1119. The *Bieley* court then quotes Matter of Hayes, 263 N.Y. 219 at 225, 188 N.E. 716 rearg. denied 264 N.Y. 459, 191 N.E. 513 and says:

> The idea of anyone deliberately purposing to die testate as to a portion of his estate, and intestate as to another portion, is so unusual, in the history of testamentary dispositions, as to justify almost any construction to escape from it.

Thus we have a conflict between two long-standing policies of the Law of Wills. On the one hand the court is not supposed to supply what the testator has not, through extrinsic evidence or otherwise. On the other hand, the primary objective is to ascertain the intention of the testator in order to avoid intestacy. If we follow the first line of precedent, the fact that no one is named in the residuary clause of Eugenia Herceg's will would mean no residuary beneficiary exists and the residue passes by intestacy to her heirs at law. The second line of precedent would lead to the conclusion that any thing possible should be done to avoid intestacy and carry out the testator's intent which would mean considering the extrinsic evidence pointing to Colomba Pastorino as the intended residuary beneficiary after the death of her husband, Sergio Pastorino.

As is often the case, Chief Judge Cardozo indicated the path to follow when he said:

> One principle or precedent, pushed to the limit of its logic, may point to one conclusion; another principle or precedent, followed with like logic, may point with equal certainty to another. In this conflict, we must choose between the two paths, selecting one or

> other, or perhaps striking out upon a third, which will be the resultant of the two forces in combination, or will represent the mean between extremes.

Cardozo, The Nature of the Judicial Process, pp. 40-41.

Actually, the law has started to move away from the [former] rigid rule . . . and toward the principle of considering all available evidence, including any available extrinsic evidence, to effectuate the intent of the testator.

Tentative Draft No. 1 of the Restatement of the Law of Property (Donative Transfers) §12.1 provides:

> A donative document, thought unambiguous, may be reformed to conform the text to the donor's intention if the following are established by clear and convincing evidence: (1) that a mistake of fact or law, whether in expression or inducement, affected specific terms of the document; and (2) what the donor's intention was.

"There would be no restriction as to the kind of evidence that could be considered for this purpose; the oral statements of the testator and the attorney who drafted the instrument would be admissible. The theory of this approach is that the testator's intention is better served and unjust enrichment of unintended legatees prevented, while the fraud-preventing purpose of the Statute of Wills is accomplished by requiring clear and convincing proof of the necessary elements." [citation omitted.]

Thus the Restatement provides for considering any evidence of testator's intent, but raising the standard of proof from a preponderance of the evidence to clear and convincing evidence.

In actuality, the New York courts have already moved in this direction. In Matter of Snide, . . . 418 N.E.2d 656 (1981) the decedent and his wife each signed the other's will. The Court of Appeals held that the decedent's will should be admitted to probate with the mistake corrected by reading both wills together and substituting the wife's name into the decedent's will wherever necessary, as if the decedent had signed the correct will.

Other cases have held that language missing from a will due to typographical or other error can be supplied to carry out the testator's intent.

Similarly, a number of cases have held that where the name of the beneficiary is wrong and extrinsic evidence establishes who was really intended to be the beneficiary, the court will order the correction.

It is a significant step beyond the cases just cited to say that not only can omitted language be added and the name of a beneficiary be corrected, but also that the name left out of the will can be added to the provisions of the will. Nevertheless, it seems logical to this court to choose the path of considering all available evidence as recommended by the Restatement in order to achieve the dominant purpose of carrying out the intention of the testator.

In this case, the court is persuaded that the evidence is *clear and convincing* that Colomba Pastorino is the intended beneficiary of the residuary of the estate of Eugenia Herceg. As stated above, the previous 1997 will provides for the residuary to pass to decedent's nephew, Sergio Pastorino, if he survives me, and if not to his wife, Colomba Pastorino. Additionally, two other prior wills dated October 1, 1992 and August 6, 1990, contain an identical residuary clause. This supports the contention of the petition that the identical residuary clause was intended to be included in the 1999 will admitted to probate.

Equally convincing is the fact that Colomba Pastorino was named the alternate executrix in the will admitted to probate in the event of the death of her husband. The testatrix had sufficient confidence in Colomba to name her as executrix in the event, which actually happened, of her husband, Sergio, predeceasing the testatrix. This demonstrates that Colomba had not fallen out of favor with the testatrix and been deliberately removed from the residuary. The consent by Josephine D'Angelo, the niece of the testatrix, and one of the persons who would take in intestacy confirms this saying "I acknowledge that the omission of the name of the residuary was a typographical error, and my aunt continued to have Sergio Pastorino, or his wife, Colomba Pastorino, if he was deceased, as the residuary beneficiary." Further confirmation comes from the attorney-draftsperson's affidavit which states "Mrs. Herceg's express intention was to continue the remainder of her property distribution as it was in the previous will."

This conclusion is buttressed by the presumption against intestacy. Mrs. Herceg disposed of 90% of her estate in various percentage bequests. As the Court of Appeals [has] said . . . almost any construction is justified to avoid the unusual result of testatrix dying intestate as to the 10% of her estate remaining for the residuary. It is equally illogical to think the attorney-draftsman put into the will the standard language for a residuary disposition and then deliberately left out the name of the beneficiary. Rather what makes sense is to construe the will to add the missing provision by inserting the names of the residuary beneficiaries from the prior will.

Accordingly, the residuary clause, Paragraph Eighth, of the will of Eugenia Herceg is construed to insert the name of Colomba Pastorino as the beneficiary (her husband, Sergio Pastorino, having predeceased).

QUESTIONS

24. The court demonstrates reluctance to add the name of a beneficiary not explicitly listed in the will. Did the fact that the will was drafted by an attorney rather than the testator affect the outcome?

    ANSWER. A court may or may not take into consideration whether a will was professionally drafted. In *Herceg*, it helped that the will was drafted by an attorney because the attorney was alive and available to testify about the source of the error and to admit that the mistake was his fault, an admirable act.

25. Are courts more likely to reform wills if to do so will avoid a partial or complete intestacy?

    ANSWER. There is both strong public policy and judicial canon favoring the avoidance of intestate estates, particularly when the decedent attempted to make a will.

26. If a jurisdiction does not allow for reformation of a will, what argument might the attorney make in the alternative to correct a mistake in a will?

    ANSWER. The lawyer can argue that there is no mistake, but rather, a latent ambiguity that can be resolved by a court's considering extrinsic evidence. Because the two doctrines are closely related, courts may be willing to analyze the problem as a latent ambiguity rather than a mistake. See, e.g., Kaplan v. Fair (In re Estate of Herron), No. L-03-1300, 2004 WL 1468547 (Ohio Ct. App. June 30, 2004) (unpublished) (case resolved as latent ambiguity even though there was no equivocation nor could two or more persons fight the description of the incorrectly named beneficiary).

6.7.3.2 Probable Intent

As we saw in the first part of this section, under the common law, courts generally refused to reform the language in a will to correct a mistake and would permit bequests written with a patent ambiguity to fail (with the result that the property described in the bequest would pass under the will's residuary clause or, if the will did not contain a residuary clause, by intestacy). The common law permitted extrinsic evidence to be considered to resolve only a latent ambiguity under the theory that extrinsic evidence brought the ambiguity to light and therefore only with extrinsic evidence could the ambiguity be resolved. We have seen how the modern trend permits courts to consider extrinsic evidence to resolve any ambiguity and to reform a mistake.

New Jersey has taken matters a step further by statutorily enacting the Doctrine of Probable Intent, a doctrine that had been recognized by New Jersey courts for decades:

> The intention of a testator as expressed in his will controls the legal effect of his dispositions, and the rules of construction expressed . . . shall apply unless the probable intention of the testator, as indicated by the will and relevant circumstances, is contrary.

N.J. STAT. ANN. 3B:3-33.1(a) (2004). The doctrine, particularly useful in cases where there is an unexplained gap or missing provision in the testator's estate plan, is succinctly explained by the New Jersey Supreme Court in *In re Estate of Payne*:

> In interpreting a will, our aim is to ascertain the intent of the testator. "[W]hen we say we are determining the testator's intent, we mean his probable intent." Fidelity Union Trust Co. v. Robert, 36 N.J. 561, 564, 178 A.2d 185 (1962) (citation omitted). We continue to adhere to the view of the doctrine of probable intent expressed in *Fidelity Union*. In that case, the Court stated that in determining the testator's subjective intent, "courts will give primary emphasis to his dominant plan and purpose as they appear from the entirety of his will when read and considered in the light of the surrounding facts and circumstances." The trial court should "ascribe to the testator 'those impulses which are common to human nature and . . . construe the will so as to effectuate those impulses.'" More recently, this Court emphasized that "[c]ourts are enjoined to 'strain' toward effectuating the testator's probable intent 'to accomplish what he would have done had he envisioned the present inquiry.'"

> The trial court is not "limited simply to searching out the probable meaning intended by the words and phrases in the will." Extrinsic evidence may "furnish[] information regarding the circumstances surrounding the testator [and] should be admitted to aid in ascertaining [the testator's] probable intent under the will." To be sure, the testator's own expressions of his or her intent are highly relevant. Once the evidence establishes the probable intent of the testator, "the court may not refuse to effectuate that intent by indulging in a merely literal reading of the instrument."

895 A.2d 428, 434 (N.J. 2006).

QUESTIONS

27. How might the Doctrine of Probable Intent undermine the public policy promoting the efficient and speedy settlement of decedents' estates?

    ANSWER. The plain meaning rule is easily applied and therefore promotes the efficient and speedy settlement of estates, but its application can lead to intent-defeating results. The doctrine of probable intent may lead to more accurate interpretations of testamentary intent, but judicial inquiry into probable intent can delay and increase the cost of a probate proceeding. In order to determine the testator's probable intent, the court must examine extrinsic evidence, including hearing testimony from individuals who may able to shed light on the testator's intent. In some instances, these cases are not decided until many years after the testator's death. See, e.g., In re Estate of Payne, 895 A.2d 428 (N.J. 2006) (decided four years after testator's death); In re Estate of Branigan, 129 N.J. 324 (1992) (same). For beneficiaries, this delay can cause numerous problems. As the case drags on, administration costs for the estate may significantly reduce the size of the estate.

PROBLEM XVII

In a famous rhyme, Dr. Seuss has Horton the Elephant repeatedly say (as Horton fulfills his promise to sit on a bird's egg until it hatches), "I meant what I said, and I said what I meant. An elephant's faithful, one hundred percent." Dr. Seuss, Horton Hatches the Egg passim (1940). To what extent do you consider the modern shift from the common law approach to patent ambiguities and mistakes to be a step forward? A step back? Is there an argument to be made that the language of a testator's will should be interpreted strictly — should be interpreted under Horton's simple, direct approach? Would you apply the doctrines of reformation or probable intent to Horton's will?

7 | Family Status and Family Protection

7.1 INTRODUCTION

As we have already seen, family status looms large in trusts and estates law. For instance, as we discussed in Chapter 2, intestacy statutes presume that decedents want to leave their estates to their families. Likewise, when we examined antilapse in Chapter 6, we observed that the law applies special rules when a predeceasing beneficiary is closely related to the testator. In this chapter, we consider yet another cluster of issues that involve a decedent's family. First, we examine the impact of divorce upon a will. Second, we consider one of the few ways that American law denies property owners unfettered freedom of testation: statutes that give a surviving spouse a mandatory share of a decedent's estate. Third, we analyze rules that protect husbands, wives, and children from being accidentally disinherited.

7.2 CHANGES IN FAMILY STATUS

Married people often select their spouse as the primary beneficiary of their estate plan. But what happens if the couple divorces without updating their estate plan? This question has tremendous practical importance given the prevalence of divorce. See, e.g., Lawrence W. Waggoner, The Multiple-Marriage Society and Spousal Rights Under the Revised Uniform Probate Code, 76 Iowa L. Rev. 223 (1991). In general, there is a strong presumption that a divorce wipes out any benefit that the former spouse would have received from a decedent under both probate and nonprobate transfers. The assumption behind this rule is that most decedents no longer want their now-former husband or wife to inherit from them.[1]

1. Occasionally, couples divorce and then remarry. That revives any devise to the once-former, now-current spouse. See Uniform Probate Code §2-804(e) ("[Revival if Divorce Nullified.] Provisions revoked solely by this section are revived by the divorced individual's remarriage to the former spouse or by a nullification of the divorce or annulment.").

Uniform Probate Code
§2-802 Effect of Divorce, Annulment, and Decree of Separation

(a) An individual who is divorced from the decedent or whose marriage to the decedent has been annulled is not a surviving spouse unless, by virtue of a subsequent marriage, he [or she] is married to the decedent at the time of death. A decree of separation that does not terminate the status of husband and wife is not a divorce for purposes of this section. . . .

§2-804 Revocation of Probate and Nonprobate Transfers by Divorce . . .

. . .

(b) [Revocation Upon Divorce.] Except as provided by the express terms of a governing instrument,[2] a court order, or a contract relating to the division of the marital estate made between the divorced individuals before or after the marriage, divorce, or annulment, the divorce or annulment of a marriage:

(1) revokes any revocable

(A) disposition or appointment of property made by a divorced individual to his [or her] former spouse . . . [or] a relative of the divorced individual's former spouse.[3]

. . .

(C) nomination in a governing instrument, nominating a divorced individual's former spouse or a relative of the divorced individual's former spouse to serve in any fiduciary or representative capacity, including a personal representative, executor, trustee, conservator, agent, or guardian; and

(2) severs the interests of the former spouses in property held by them at the time of the divorce or annulment as joint tenants with the right of survivorship [or as community property with the right of survivorship], transforming the interests of the former spouses into equal tenancies in common.

Lincoln Benefit Life Co. v. Guerrero
No. 14-1077 JCH/WPL, 2016 WL 4547157 (D.N.M. June 27, 2016)

JUDITH C. HERRERA, United States District Judge.

This insurance dispute is before the Court on Defendant Imara Guerrero's Motion for Summary Judgment, in which she seeks a ruling that the Estate of the Decedent, Neftaly Guerrero, is entitled to the proceeds from the life insurance policy issued by Lincoln Benefit Life Company. Neftaly Guerrero's ex-wife, Bertha Guerrero, and Lincoln Benefit Life Company, have filed response briefs, to which Imara Guerrero has replied. After considering the briefs, the evidence, and the

2. A reminder: In the UPC, the term "governing instrument" includes wills, trusts, insurance or annuity policies, POD accounts, TOD deeds, etc. See UPC §1-201(18).

3. The UPC comment explains why the statute revokes dispositions in favor of a relative of the divorced individual's former spouse: "In several cases, . . . the result of treating the former spouse as if he or she predeceased the testator was that a gift in the governing instrument was triggered in favor of relatives of the former spouse who, after the divorce, were no longer relatives of the testator. . . . Given that, during divorce process or in the aftermath of the divorce, the former spouse's relatives are likely to side with the former spouse, breaking down or weakening any former ties that may previously have developed between the transferor and the former spouse's relatives, seldom would the transferor have favored such a result. This section, therefore, also revokes these gifts."

applicable law, the Court concludes that the motion should be granted, and judgment should be entered in favor of Imara Guerrero as Personal Representative of the Estate of Neftaly Guerrero.

MATERIAL FACTS

Most of the facts of this case are undisputed, unless otherwise noted.

Plaintiff, Lincoln Benefit Life Company ("Lincoln Benefit"), issued life insurance policy No. 01N1088144 ("the Policy") on the life of Neftaly Guerrero ("the Decedent"), for a death benefit in the amount of $125,000.00. The Decedent designated his then wife, Defendant Bertha Guerrero ("Bertha") as the primary beneficiary in the event of his death. He designated Bertha's mother, Defendant Ignacia Cisneros ("Cisneros"), as the contingent beneficiary.

In 2003, the Decedent and Bertha divorced. The order entered by the Second Judicial District Court, Bernalillo County, New Mexico, dissolved their marriage but did not provide that Bertha would remain the primary beneficiary; indeed, it made no mention of the policy whatsoever. In June of 2008, Decedent and Bertha met with Christopher Rael, an insurance agent contracted with Lincoln Mutual, regarding the Policy as well as the policy covering Bertha's life. The purpose of the meeting was to sever the policies so that they could each own separate, independent life insurance policies.

According to Rael, at that meeting Bertha completed an Application for Term Conversion. The Decedent was not required to, and did not, complete such an application himself, though he did sign Bertha's application, thereby authorizing the insurance split. The Application identifies Bertha as the "Person Proposed for Conversion." It sets forth "Policy Information," such as the new face amount and the current term policy face amount. It names Bertha as the primary insured, sets forth premium amounts for her new policy, and states that Bertha already owns insurance which will be changed as a result of the Application. The Decedent's signature appears at the bottom of each page. On the final page, Decedent signed on the line marked "Signature of Previous Owner." There is nothing in the Application stating that the owner of the original Policy is in any way reaffirming its terms.

The Decedent did not make any new beneficiary designation for his own life insurance policy in June of 2008, or at any time after the divorce. In fact, other than authorizing the split by signing the Application for Term Conversion, the Decedent made no alterations to his policy after the divorce. However, it was Rael's "understanding" or belief that by signing the Application for Term Conversion (as he was required to do to authorize the split in the policies), the Decedent "adopted" the information contained therein, including the beneficiary designations, and "no further action was required of him." After Decedent signed the Application for Term Conversion, Rael informed Decedent that he could change his beneficiary designation by filling out certain forms, but he declined. The Decedent said nothing to Rael about wanting to change the beneficiary designation on his policy and did not fill out a change of beneficiary form. On the other hand, at no time after the divorce did Decedent ever expressly tell Rael that he wanted to keep Bertha as his beneficiary.

In her own affidavit, Bertha avers that the Decedent's desire was that she "would continue on as the primary beneficiary and [Ignacia] would continue on as a contingent beneficiary, despite the split of the policy." She states that both she and Decedent "were led to believe that all he needed to do for [Bertha] to continue to be listed as his previously listed beneficiary designation, as listed in the Application for Insurance, was to sign the Application for Term Conversion on August 1, 2008." Bertha avers that she and Decedent signed the Application for Term Conversion only after Rael advised Decedent "that if he wished to change the designated beneficiary as part of the split that he needed to complete a Change of Beneficiary, which he declined to do." Finally, Bertha asserts that after the policy split and continuing until May 21, 2012, she paid the monthly premiums on the policy held by the Decedent, with the reasonable expectation and understanding that she was the designated beneficiary who would receive the policy proceed in the event of his death.

The Decedent died on March 2, 2014. In August of 2014, Lincoln Benefit received notice of the Decedent's death, as well as the fact of his previous divorce from Bertha. In August of 2014, Lincoln Benefit received a copy of the order dissolving the marriage, as well as a claim from Bertha for the proceeds under the Policy. Lincoln Benefit took the position that, based on a New Mexico statute, Bertha and Cisneros' beneficial interests may have been revoked upon the dissolution of the marriage between Bertha and Decedent. According to Lincoln Benefit, it cannot determine what right, if any, Bertha and Cisneros have to the Policy proceeds, and that if neither has a right to those Proceeds, then Decedent's estate has a potential right to the proceeds.

On June 18, 2015, Defendant Imara Guerrero ("Imara") filed her answer to the Amended Complaint. Imara is the Personal Representative of Decedents (sic) estate. In her answer, Imara asserted that neither Bertha nor Cisneros has a right to the Policy proceeds, and that in the absence of a named beneficiary those proceeds should accrue to the estate. She argues that under New Mexico law, the Decedent's designation of Bertha as the beneficiary of the Policy was automatically revoked at the time of their divorce, and he never took any affirmative action after the divorce to rename Bertha as the beneficiary. On January 19, 2016, Imara filed the motion for summary judgment currently at issue before the Court, asserting that the estate—not Bertha—is entitled to the Policy proceeds.

...

DISCUSSION

The question raised by the motion for summary judgment is whether or not Bertha is the beneficiary of the Policy under New Mexico law. As Personal Representative of the estate, Imara argues that under NMSA 1978, §45-2-804, the Decedent's designation of Bertha as the beneficiary was legally revoked at the time of the divorce, and that Decedent never took affirmative steps to redesignate her (or anyone else) as beneficiary. Thus, Imara argues that the Policy proceeds should inure to the Decedent's estate. In response, Bertha does not dispute the applicability of §45-2-804, or its effect in revoking her designation as beneficiary. Instead, Bertha argues that after the divorce, the Decedent evidenced his intent to have her remain as the beneficiary of the Policy, and the Court should give effect to that intent. Thus, the motion presents the following legal issues: (1) does §45-2-804 create a bright line rule requiring revocation of a beneficiary designation upon divorce, or does it merely create a rebuttable presumption that the donor intended revocation, and (2) if §45-2-804 creates a rebuttable presumption, what amount of proof is required to rebut it?

I. The New Mexico Revocation Statute

In 1993, the New Mexico Legislature enacted §45-2-804, which provides that a divorce automatically rescinds any existing revocable disposition or appointment of property made by a divorced person to his or her former spouse. Specifically, NMSA 1978, §45-2-804(B) states, in relevant part:

> B. Except as provided by the express terms of a governing instrument, a court order or a contract relating to the division of the marital estate made between the divorced individuals before or after the marriage, divorce or annulment, the divorce or annulment of a marriage: (1) revokes any revocable: (a) disposition or appointment of property made by a divorced individual to the former spouse in a governing instrument and any disposition or appointment created by law or in a governing instrument to a relative of the divorced individual's former spouse[.]

Thus, the only exceptions to the automatic revocation outlined above are for (1) the express terms of the governing instrument, (2) a court order (such as a divorce decree that expressly exempts the governing instrument from revocation), and (3) a contract relating to the division of the marital estate. There is no argument by any party that any of these three exceptions applies in this case.

The statute defines "governing instrument" as an instrument "executed by the divorced individual before the divorce or annulment of the divorced individual's marriage to the former spouse." §45-2-804(A)(4). None of the parties dispute that a life insurance policy such as the Policy at issue in this case is a "governing instrument" within the meaning of the statute. "Disposition or appointment of property" includes "a transfer of an item of property or any other benefit to a beneficiary designated in a revocable trust or other governing instrument." §45-2-804(A)(1). The statute also defines the term "revocable." . . .

None of the parties dispute that appointment of a spouse as a beneficiary to a life insurance policy is a revocable appointment.

II. Analysis

The New Mexico state courts have had no occasion to interpret §45-2-804(B). However, the New Mexico statute is based upon Section 2-804 of the Uniform

Probate Code ("UPC"). Many other states have adopted this UPC provision, or ones nearly identical thereto. As a result, this Court has the benefit of several decisions from state and federal courts in those jurisdictions interpreting the statute in situations similar to the facts in this case.

In Stillman v. Teachers Ins. and Annuity Ass'n College Retirement Equities Fund, 343 F.3d 1311 (10th Cir. 2003), the Tenth Circuit examined the impetus behind Utah Code Ann. §75-2-804(2) (which is virtually identical to its New Mexico counterpart) and the Uniform Probate Code provision upon which both state statutes are based. The Court noted that the discord that drives a couple to divorce usually also signifies a desire to remove the alienated spouse as a beneficiary on a will, insurance policy, retirement account, or other donative instrument, but often individuals fail to take affirmative action to change the beneficiary designation. . . .

The *Stillman* court observed that the approach under the UPC was to withdraw the prior emphasis on legal formalism in interpreting wills, trusts, and other transfers in favor of policies that fulfilled the intent of the donor. Recognition of that intent means that usually a donor must take some affirmative action after a divorce if he or she wishes a former spouse to remain a beneficiary. The question is what action can be considered sufficient.

For example, in State Farm Life Ins. Co. v. Davis, 2008 WL 2326323 (D. Alaska 2008) (unpublished), after their divorce the ex-husband verbally told his insurance agent that he wanted his former wife to remain as the beneficiary. Just as in this case, because the wife had already been designated as beneficiary, the agent did not believe that it was necessary for the husband to fill out a new beneficiary designation form, and so the husband did not do so. In ruling on a motion for summary judgment, the court stated that Alaska's revocation-upon-divorce statute created only a rebuttable presumption of revocation, "not a strict and inflexible rule." *Id.* at *4. The court further found that in order to rebut the presumption of revocation, the wife must present proof by a preponderance of the evidence of the decedent's intent for her to be the beneficiary after the divorce. *Id.* In *Davis*, the court found that the wife's proof—an oral statement by the decedent made to the insurance agent— . . . rebutted the statutory presumption of revocation. *Id.*

However, in In re Estate of Lamparella, 109 P.3d 959 (Arizona Ct. App. 2005), the Arizona Court of Appeals took a slightly different approach in interpreting that state's version of UPC §2-804. In that case, in 1996 the husband purchased a deferred annuity policy naming the wife as the beneficiary. *Id.* at 960. In 2000, the couple divorced, but the decree made no mention of the annuity policy. *Id.* at 961. The decedent never changed the beneficiary designation after the divorce, though he did withdraw part of the value of the annuity. *Id.* He died in 2002. *Id.* Both the ex-wife and the husband's estate made claims to the annuity proceeds. *Id.* In support of her claim, the ex-wife submitted an affidavit averring that decedent told her he intended that she remain as the beneficiary on the annuity policy, as he had hoped for a reconciliation and still loved her. *Id.* at 962. There was no other witness to this statement of the ex-husband's intent. The Arizona court concluded that if the donor wishes to rebut the presumption of revocation and retain a former spouse as the beneficiary post-divorce, the donor must evidence this intention in writing "and must otherwise comply with applicable policy terms." *Id.* at 967. The court reasoned:

> the purpose of A.R.S. §14-2804(A) would be eviscerated if a former spouse could circumvent the automatic revocation effected by the statute by submitting self-serving testimony that the decedent spouse's inaction reflected an intention to revive his or her designation of the ex-spouse as the beneficiary. Even if Angelo told Pamela he intended to retain her as his beneficiary, he was required, if the statute is to have any effect, to confirm that decision in writing with Jackson National Life.

Id. at 966.

. . .

In the case presently before this Court, under NMSA §45-2-804(B)(1)(a) the Decedent's designation of Bertha as his beneficiary was revoked by operation of law at the time of their divorce. The question is whether Decedent took the necessary affirmative action to re-designate Bertha as his beneficiary at some point after the divorce. As explained above, most courts require such a re-designation to occur in writing in a form that is in compliance with the terms of the life insurance policy. Bertha argues that the Decedent made a written re-designation here, when he signed the Application for Term Conversion to authorize the creation of two policies from the single policy the couple previously shared. However, the Court disagrees. A review of the Application reveals that the information in it is almost entirely about the new policy being created and separated from the original policy. There is absolutely nothing in the Application for Term Conversion form signed by Decedent that would indicate to the signatory that he was "adopting" the same named beneficiary set forth in the original Policy application, or somehow re-designating Bertha as his beneficiary. Thus, Decedent's signature authorizing the split is not sufficient to act as a written re-designation of beneficiary.

Similarly, the Decedent's inaction is not enough to overcome the presumption of revocation created by §45-2-804. Here, Bertha argues that Decedent's inaction — that is, his refusal to fill out a form designating a new beneficiary — demonstrates his intent to keep her as the beneficiary on his policy. As the Tenth Circuit observed in *Stillman*, "[r]evocation-upon-divorce statutes reflect the legislative judgment that when the transferor leaves unaltered a will or trust or insurance beneficiary designation in favor of an ex-spouse, this failure to designate substitute takers more likely than not represents inattention rather than intention." 343 F.3d at 1317-18. It is this same legislative judgment that has prompted courts to hold that a failure to act is insufficient evidence of intent, and a donor must take affirmative steps to re-designate a former spouse as his beneficiary. . . .

Bertha's final argument is that the presumption of revocation created by NMSA 1978, §45-2-804 is rebutted by Decedent's verbal expression of his desire to retain her as the beneficiary. It is true that some courts permit a would-be beneficiary to rebut the presumption of revocation through a preponderance of admissible evidence, including the donor's verbal statements, expressing his or her intent. This Court agrees that it makes sense to permit the presumption of revocation to be rebutted in this manner. In this way, the statute can best meet its purpose: to give force to the expressed intent of the divorced donor. However, courts must exercise caution in determining what evidence is acceptable. In this case,

Bertha avers that the Decedent verbally expressed to her his intent to keep her as beneficiary. However, there is no evidence that Decedent made that statement to a disinterested third party, such as Rael. In fact, Rael testified that Decedent never expressly told him that he wanted to keep Bertha as his beneficiary. Instead, Rael merely inferred that intent from the Decedent's inaction on the matter.

The Court holds that Bertha's evidence is insufficient to carry her burden to present proof, by a preponderance of the evidence, that Decedent actually intended her to be the beneficiary of the Policy despite their divorce. . . .

Because Bertha has failed to rebut the presumption that her divorce from Decedent revoked his designation of her as beneficiary on the Policy, the Court concludes that summary judgment should be granted in favor of Decedent's estate.

QUESTIONS

1. The opinion does not say when the decedent bought the life insurance policy listing his then-wife Bertha as the beneficiary, but let us imagine that it was in 2000. The decedent and Bertha then divorced in 2003, and the decedent did not remove Bertha as the beneficiary of the policy. Would the outcome have been the same if the decedent had purchased the policy listing Bertha as the beneficiary not in 2000, but rather in 2010?

   ANSWER. The outcome would be different. The revocation-on-divorce statute applies only to estate planning choices made by married individuals who then divorce. In this question, the decedent would have purchased the 2010 policy after he and Bertha divorced, which means that the statute does not govern.

2. Suppose the decedent had placed $100,000 in an irrevocable trust — one that he lacked the power to amend or terminate — in 2000. The trust provided that when the decedent died, Bertha, his then-wife, would receive the money. Then, three years later, the decedent and Bertha divorced. Who takes the $100,000: Bertha or the decedent's estate?

   ANSWER. The revocation-on-divorce statute applies only to "revocable" dispositions of property. Very roughly, those are ones that the decedent can cancel or change. An irrevocable trust does not fall within that definition, which means that the statute does not apply. Bertha takes the $100,000.

3. The toughest issues in the case are (1) whether the revocation-on-divorce statute is a bright-line rule or a mere presumption, and (2) assuming that the statute is a mere presumption, what evidence is sufficient to rebut it? How does the court answer these questions? What would the result in the case have been if the undisputed facts established that the decedent had written Bertha a letter in 2009 in which he stated that he wanted her to continue to be the beneficiary of his life insurance policy?

   ANSWER. The court holds that (1) the revocation-on-divorce statute is a mere presumption that (2) can be rebutted by any evidence, but usually will require more than self-serving testimony from the former spouse. Indeed, on the last point, the court strongly implies that Bertha would have rebutted the presumption if the life insurance agent, Rael, had corroborated Bertha's account of the decedent's statements. Under this standard, a letter from the decedent setting forth his intent to benefit Bertha would be sufficient.

PROBLEM I

In 2015, Elizabeth and Debra marry. They buy a house, which they hold as joint tenants with the right of survivorship. In 2016, Elizabeth makes a will that leaves \$100,000 to Debra, \$25,000 to Debra's mom, Nancy, and the residue to Elizabeth's dad, Brad. Elizabeth's will names Debra as the executor, Nancy as the alternate executor, and Brad as the second alternate executor.

A. In 2016, Elizabeth and Debra separate. In 2017, Elizabeth dies. Who inherits what from Elizabeth? Who serves as executor of her will?
B. Same facts as above, with the following change: In 2016, Elizabeth and Debra divorce. Who inherits what from Elizabeth? Who serves as executor of her will?

7.3 FAMILY PROTECTION

All American jurisdictions prohibit deceased spouses from completely disinheriting their surviving husband or wife. However, they disagree about how to accomplish this goal. The root of this problem is dueling conceptions of the nature of the institution of marriage itself.

Traditionally, marriage was seen as imposing an obligation upon the spouses to support each other. As a result, many states passed "elective share" statutes that gave a surviving husband or wife the right to receive a share of their deceased spouse's estate. These laws were animated by the idea that the deceased spouse owed a duty to continue to provide support for the surviving spouse after death. In many states, the elective share is one-third of the deceased spouse's estate, typically far less than the surviving spouse would receive by intestacy.

More recently, the "support theory" of marriage has been supplanted by the "partnership theory." Under this view, marriage creates an economic partnership, so surviving spouses are generally entitled to a fair share of the partnership rather than the bare minimum necessary for their support. Under the partnership theory of marriage, the surviving spouse is entitled to a share of the estate that is more closely linked to his or her contributions during the marriage. Most states have adopted one of two ways of calculating this sum. First, in *separate property states*,[4] a surviving spouse can choose to

4. In separate property states, except for jointly titled property, married persons own property separately. Divorcing spouses in separate property states, therefore, leave the marriage with only the separate property titled in their name, although this rule is softened by equitable distribution rules in which courts are empowered to order the redistribution of property in settlement of divorce. Married persons who remain married until one spouse dies enjoy testamentary power over all separate property titled in their own name, subject to the elective share described in this chapter.

receive a more generous elective share (up to one-half) than would be available under a support theory of marriage (typically, one-third). Second, in *community property states*,[5] each spouse owns one-half of all the earnings during marriage regardless of nominal title. For more discussion, see generally Laura A. Rosenbury, Two Ways to End a Marriage: Divorce or Death, 2005 Utah L. Rev. 1227.

The following passage from the UPC fleshes out the partnership theory and the policy rationales behind separate property and community property regimes. We then examine the elective share (for separate property states) and contrast it with the community property rubric.

Uniform Probate Code
Part 2 Elective Share of Surviving Spouse

THE PARTNERSHIP THEORY OF MARRIAGE

The partnership theory of marriage, sometimes also called the marital-sharing theory, is stated in various ways. Sometimes it is thought of "as an expression of the presumed intent of husbands and wives to pool their fortunes on an equal basis, share and share alike." M. Glendon, The Transformation of Family Law 131 (1989). Under this approach, the economic rights of each spouse are seen as deriving from an unspoken marital bargain under which the partners agree that each is to enjoy a half interest in the fruits of the marriage, i.e., in the property nominally acquired by and titled in the sole name of either partner during the marriage (other than in property acquired by gift or inheritance). A decedent who disinherits his or her surviving spouse is seen as having reneged on the bargain. Sometimes the theory is expressed in restitutionary terms, a return-of-contribution notion. Under this approach, the law grants each spouse an entitlement to compensation for non-monetary contributions to the marital enterprise, as "a recognition of the activity of one spouse in the home and to compensate not only for this activity but for opportunities lost." Id. See also American Law Institute, Principles of Family Dissolution §4.09 Comment c (2002).

No matter how the rationale is expressed, the community-property system . . . recognizes the partnership theory, but it is sometimes thought that the common-law system denies it. In the ongoing marriage, it is true that the basic principle in the common-law (title-based) states is that marital status does not affect the ownership of property. The regime is one of separate property. Each spouse owns all that he or she earns. By contrast, in the community-property states, each spouse acquires an ownership interest in half the property the other earns during the marriage. By granting each spouse upon acquisition an immediate half interest in the earnings of the other, the community-property regimes directly recognize that the couple's enterprise is in essence collaborative.

---

5. In community property states, all property acquired by married persons with earnings generated during the marriage becomes community property owned in equal shares by each spouse regardless of nominal title. Divorcing spouses in separate property states, therefore, leave the marriage with the separate property they owned before marriage and half the community property. Married persons who remain married until one spouse dies enjoy testamentary power over all separate property titled in their own name plus half of the community property. The surviving spouse owns the other half of the community property.

7.3.1 The Elective Share

In separate property states (except Georgia), spouses are protected through the elective share. Absent a valid marital agreement between the spouses that provides otherwise, the elective share effectively precludes decedents from completely disinheriting their spouses. In certain circumstances, it allows the survivor to "elect" to inherit a preset amount of his or her deceased spouse's assets.

There are two basic elective share regimes: the original UPC, which was promulgated in 1969, and the revised UPC, which was published in 1990. We will address each in turn.

7.3.2 The 1969 UPC

The UPC's original elective share statute, based on spousal protection statutes in New York and Pennsylvania, is still in effect in several jurisdictions. It grants the decedent's surviving spouse the right to take a one-third share of the deceased spouse's estate rather than the property devised by will. The 1969 UPC is notable because it establishes a bright-line rule for determining which transfers fall within the "estate" subject to the elective share.

Early elective share statutes applied only to the decedent's probate estate, so they left a gaping loophole for nonprobate transfers to parties other than the surviving spouse. When the bulk of a decedent's property passes to third parties by nonprobate transfers, an elective share limited to the probate estate provides little or no protection against spousal disinheritance. To prevent a decedent's use of nonprobate transfers to defeat the elective share, courts applied equitable doctrines to determine whether a decedent had defrauded the surviving spouse, but those doctrines yielded inconsistent results because they relied on evidence of the decedent's subjective intent. By contrast, the 1969 UPC adopted the concept of an "augmented estate," which uses an objective bright-line rule to capture both the decedent's probate estate as well as certain nonprobate transfers in calculating the elective share. The augmented estate also prevents a surviving spouse from electing a forced share when the decedent provided adequately for the surviving spouse outside the will.

Specifically, the 1969 UPC's augmented estate includes four kinds of property. The first is the decedent's net probate estate. The second is certain nonprobate transfers to third parties made during marriage that are essentially will substitutes, such as assets placed in inter vivos revocable trusts or held in joint tenancy with right of survivorship.[6] The third is significant outright gifts made by the decedent to third parties within two years of death. The fourth is the surviving spouse's own property (and property transferred by the surviving spouse during the marriage to third parties), but only to the extent that the property was derived by gift or nonprobate transfer (e.g., trust, joint

6. The 1969 UPC's augmented estate, however, does *not* include life insurance payable to a person other than the surviving spouse on the (questionable) theory that life insurance "is not ordinarily purchased as a way of depleting the probate estate and avoiding the elective share of the surviving spouse." UPC §2-202, comment (1969).

tenancy, life insurance) from the decedent.[7] Under the 1969 UPC, the augmented estate is the aggregate value of these categories of property. The elective share is one-third of the augmented estate.

Once we have calculated the value of one-third of the augmented estate, we need to figure out how to *satisfy* the surviving spouse's elective share. The first step in satisfying the elective share is to "charge" the surviving spouse for property received from the augmented estate. Charging the surviving spouse for this property is necessary to account for property conveyed by the decedent outside the will and, therefore, reduces the total elective share amount payable to the surviving spouse. Then, if there is still an outstanding elective share amount payable to the surviving spouse, we need to dip into property earmarked by the decedent for other beneficiaries. We satisfy the outstanding elective share amount by reducing shares of the augmented estate payable to other beneficiaries in proportion to the value of what those beneficiaries were supposed to receive.

Uniform Probate Code
§2-201 Right of Elective Share

(a) If a married person domiciled in this state dies, the surviving spouse has a right of election to take an elective share of one-third of the augmented estate under the limitations and conditions hereinafter stated. . . .

§2-202 Augmented Estate

The augmented estate means the [net probate] estate . . . , to which is added the sum of the following amounts:

(1) The value of property transferred to anyone other than a bona fide purchaser by the decedent at any time during marriage, to or for the benefit of any person other than the surviving spouse, to the extent that the decedent did not receive adequate and full consideration in money or money's worth for the transfer, if the transfer is of any of the following types:

(i) any transfer under which the decedent retained at the time of his death the possession or enjoyment of, or right to income from, the property;

(ii) any transfer to the extent that the decedent retained at the time of his death a power, either alone or in conjunction with any other person, to revoke or to consume, invade or dispose of the principal for his own benefit;

(iii) any transfer whereby property is held at the time of decedent's death by decedent and another with right of survivorship; . . .

(3) The value of property owned by the surviving spouse at the decedent's death, plus the value of property transferred by the spouse at any time during marriage to any person other than the decedent which would have been includible in the spouse's augmented estate if the

7. The augmented estate includes this fourth category of property to prevent the surviving spouse from taking an elective share despite having been provided for adequately by the decedent through transfers outside the will.

> surviving spouse had predeceased the decedent . . . to the extent the owned or transferred property is derived from the decedent by any means other than testate or intestate succession without a full consideration in money or money's worth. . . .

§2-207 Charging Spouse with Gifts Received; Liability of Others for Balance of Elective Share

> (a) In the proceeding for an elective share, values included in the augmented estate which pass or have passed to the surviving spouse . . . are applied first to satisfy the elective share and to reduce any contributions due from other recipients of transfers included in the augmented estate. . . .
>
> (b) Remaining property of the augmented estate is so applied that liability for the balance of the elective share of the surviving spouse is equitably apportioned among the recipients of the augmented estate in proportion to the value of their interests therein. . . .

Consider the following illustration: Suppose that Henry and Wanda were married in 2010 and live in a separate property state. In 2013, Henry makes a will leaving $325,000 to his friend Flavio. In 2014, Henry places his house, worth $50,000, into a revocable living trust that names himself as the primary beneficiary during life, and then passes outright to Wanda when he dies. In 2016, Henry dies, owning $325,000 cash and his house. Wanda has a separate bank account with $25,000 of her own money earned during the marriage.

First, we need to calculate the augmented estate. We add up the decedent's probate estate, the decedent's transfers to others (including the surviving spouse), the surviving spouse's transfers to others, and the surviving spouse's own property derived by gift or nonprobate transfer from Henry. Here, Henry's augmented estate is worth $375,000 because it consists of $325,000 cash and his $50,000 house. Wanda's separate bank account balance of $25,000 is not included in the augmented estate because, although she earned the money during the marriage, it was not derived by gift or nonprobate transfer from Henry.

Second, we compute Wanda's elective share amount, which is one-third of the augmented estate, or $125,000.

Third, to satisfy the elective share, we reduce this amount by the value of property Wanda received from the augmented estate. Here, Wanda is charged only for the $50,000 house that Henry conveyed to her in trust. Thus, Wanda is entitled to receive $75,000 ($125,000 – $50,000) under the 1969 UPC elective share statute. This money comes from the only other beneficiary of Henry's estate plan: Flavio. Ultimately, Flavio takes $250,000 (the original $325,000 devise to Flavio minus Wanda's elective share of $75,000) and Wanda takes $125,000 (the $50,000 house plus $75,000 under the elective share).

Alternatively, if Henry's will had left $260,000 to Flavio and $65,000 to his cousin, Carly, the executor would satisfy Wanda's elective share by reducing the devises to

Flavio and Carly proportionately. That involves taking the new amount to be disbursed under the will, $250,000 ($325,000 (devises to Flavio and Carly) minus Wanda's elective share of $75,000), and adjusting each beneficiary's share to preserve Henry's intent that Flavio inherit four times as much as Carly. Ultimately, Flavio would take $200,000 and Carly would receive $50,000.

Hooters restaurant, Morrisville, North Carolina

Robert Brooks, founder of the Hooters restaurant chain, died of a heart attack in 2006 at the age of 69. Brooks was survived by his second wife, Tami, and two children (one from each of his marriages). Brooks's will left Tami $20 million, but Brooks's stake in the Hooters business was estimated at more than $250 million. Tami sued under the South Carolina elective share statute, which provided the surviving spouse with a right to one-third of the decedent's augmented estate. Tami later settled with the estate, but the settlement led to the sale of the Hooters business.[8]

7.3.3 The 1990 UPC

In 1990, the UPC's drafters sought to bring the elective share system more in line with the partnership theory of marriage. Recall that, under the partnership theory of marriage, married spouses are treated as co-equal members of an economic marital

---

8. See Dan Primack, Has Hooters Found Its Wingman, Fortune (Nov. 23, 2010), at http://fortune.com/2010/11/23/has-hooters-found-its-wingman/.

partnership, so the 1990 UPC revisions increase the potential elective share from one-third to one-half. The 1990 revisions also take into account two variables not factored into the original 1969 elective share statute: (1) the length of the marriage, and (2) the separate property of the surviving spouse. In deference to the support theory of marriage, the 1990 revisions provide a safety net in the form of a "supplemental elective share" if the surviving spouse's post-estate assets fall below $75,000; the supplemental elective share is equal to the amount necessary to bring the surviving spouse's assets to the minimum of $75,000. See UPC §2-202(b) (1990).

Consider the following illustration: Suppose that Henry and Wanda, who live in a separate property jurisdiction, marry in early 2010. In 2012, Henry makes a will leaving his entire probate estate to his child from another marriage, Claire. In late 2015, Henry dies. His probate assets are worth $500,000, and his $500,000 life insurance policy lists his nephew Nate as the sole beneficiary. Wanda owns $200,000 of her own property.

First, as before, we begin by determining the value of the decedent's "augmented estate." We follow the same path as before, adding up the decedent's probate estate, the decedent's transfers to others (including the surviving spouse), the surviving spouse's transfers to others, and the surviving spouse's own property. Under the 1990 UPC revisions, however, there are two notable differences. First, life insurance proceeds payable to beneficiaries other than the surviving spouse are included in the augmented estate. This revision closes a loophole that previously allowed a spouse to use life insurance naming third-party beneficiaries to skirt the policy prohibiting spousal disinheritance. Second, the surviving spouse's separate property is included in the augmented estate even if that property was not derived by gift or nonprobate transfer from the decedent spouse. After increasing the elective share from one-third to one-half, inclusion of the surviving spouse's separate property in the augmented estate was necessary to ensure that each spouse receives an equal share of the economic partnership. Here, therefore, Henry's augmented estate consists of $500,000 in his probate estate, $500,000 in proceeds from his life insurance policy, and Wanda's separate property valued at $200,000. The augmented estate adds up to $1,200,000.

Second, the 1990 UPC then instructs us to calculate the "marital-property" component of the augmented estate. The purpose of this step is to ensure that the elective share is applied only to property acquired from earnings during the economic partnership of marriage. But rather than requiring the executor to conduct a potentially messy post-mortem inventory of property to determine which assets were acquired before or after the marriage, the 1990 UPC uses the length of marriage as a rough proxy of what portion of the augmented estate to treat as marital property. The marital property portion is a fixed percentage of the augmented estate that is keyed to the length of the marriage. It can be found in the UPC §2-203(b) table, reproduced below. The longer the marriage, the greater proportion of the augmented estate will be treated as marital property regardless of nominal title or time of acquisition. In a short marriage, a relatively small share of the couple's assets is likely to have been acquired from earnings during the marriage. In a long marriage, most if not all of the couple's assets is likely to have been acquired during the marriage. For example, for a couple that was married for a year and half, the marital-property portion is 6 percent of the augmented estate. If a couple had been married for ten years, the marital-property portion is 60 percent of the augmented estate. If the length of the marriage if fifteen years or more, the marital-property portion is 100 percent of the augmented estate. To return to the illustration involving Henry and Wanda, recall that the couple was married for more than five but fewer than six years. Thus, to compute the marital-property portion, we multiply the augmented estate ($1,200,000) by 30 percent (the percentage stated in UPC §2-203(b)). This gives us $360,000.

Third, to calculate the surviving spouse's elective share, we divide the marital-property portion of the augmented estate in half. See *id.* §2-209(a). That means that Wanda's elective share is $180,000 (50 percent of $360,000).

Fourth, we satisfy Wanda's elective share amount of $180,000 first from the marital-property portion of the augmented estate received by, payable to, or already owned by the surviving spouse. If there is a remaining balance of elective share payable to her, the elective share is satisfied from property passing to other beneficiaries from the deceased spouse. Here, Wanda's elective share amount is satisfied first from the marital-property portion of her separate property of $200,000. We therefore deduct $60,000 (30 percent of $200,000) against the elective share amount. This leaves Wanda with an outstanding elective share amount of $120,000 payable from other beneficiaries of Henry's estate.

Fifth, as before, we satisfy the remaining elective share amount by deducting contributions from other beneficiaries of the estate in proportion to what they would have received but for the elective share. This means that we adjust Henry's estate plan to accommodate Wanda's elective share while leaving intact the relative proportions of Claire's and Nate's devises. Because Claire and Nate were supposed to receive equal amounts of Henry's combined probate and nonprobate assets, they share equally in the burden of contributing to Wanda's elective share amount of $120,000. Accordingly, Wanda is entitled to $60,000 from Henry's probate estate and $60,000 from his life insurance policy. Claire takes $440,000 from the probate estate and Nate takes $440,000 in life insurance proceeds.

Uniform Probate Code
§2-202 Elective Share

(a) [Elective-Share Amount.] The surviving spouse of a decedent who dies domiciled in this state has a right of election, under the limitations and conditions stated in this [part], to take an elective-share amount equal to 50 percent of the value of the marital-property portion of the augmented estate.

§2-203 Composition of the Augmented Estate; Marital-Property Portion

(a) . . . [T]he value of the augmented estate . . . consists of the sum of the values of all property, whether real or personal; movable or immovable, tangible or intangible, wherever situated, that constitute:

(1) the decedent's net probate estate;

(2) the decedent's nonprobate transfers to others;

(3) the decedent's nonprobate transfers to the surviving spouse; and

(4) the surviving spouse's property and nonprobate transfers to others. . . .

(b) The value of the marital-property portion of the augmented estate consists of the sum of the values of the four components of the augmented estate as determined under subsection (a) multiplied by the following percentage:

If the decedent and the spouse were married to each other:	The percentage is:
Less than 1 year	3%
1 year but less than 2 years	6%
2 years but less than 3 years	12%
3 years but less than 4 years	18%
4 years but less than 5 years	24%
5 years but less than 6 years	30%
6 years but less than 7 years	36%
7 years but less than 8 years	42%
8 years but less than 9 years	48%
9 years but less than 10 years	54%
10 years but less than 11 years	60%
11 years but less than 12 years	68%
12 years but less than 13 years	76%
13 years but less than 14 years	84%
14 years but less than 15 years	92%
15 years or more	100%

§2-209 Sources from Which Elective Share Payable

(a) [Elective-Share Amount Only.] In a proceeding for an elective share, the following are applied first to satisfy the elective-share amount and to reduce or eliminate any contributions due from the decedent's probate estate and recipients of the decedent's nonprobate transfers to others:

(1) amounts included in the augmented estate . . . which pass or have passed to the surviving spouse by testate or intestate succession and amounts included in the augmented estate [stemming from nonprobate transfers]

(2) the marital-property portion of amounts included in the augmented estate . . .

(b) [Marital-Property Portion.] The marital-property portion under subsection (a)(2) is computed by multiplying the value of the amounts included in the augmented estate . . . by the percentage of the augmented estate set forth in the schedule in Section 2-203(b) appropriate to the length of time the spouse and the decedent were married to each other.

(c) [Unsatisfied Balance of Elective-Share Amount . . .] If, after the application of subsection (a), the elective-share amount is not fully satisfied . . . amounts included in the decedent's net probate estate, other than assets passing to the surviving spouse by testate or intestate succession, and in the decedent's nonprobate transfers to others . . . are applied first to satisfy the unsatisfied balance of the elective-share amount. . . . The decedent's net probate estate and that portion of the

> decedent's nonprobate transfers to others are so applied that liability for the unsatisfied balance of the elective-share amount . . . is apportioned among the recipients of the decedent's net probate estate and of that portion of the decedent's nonprobate transfers to others in proportion to the value of their interests therein.

PROBLEM II

A. Trent and Juanita have been married in a separate property jurisdiction for four years and three months when Trent dies. Trent's will leaves his entire probate estate — which is worth $200,000 — in equal shares to his best friend, Clarke, and his daughter from a previous marriage, Darlene. Juanita owns no assets. What is her elective share under both the 1969 UPC and the 1990 UPC? How much do Clarke and Darlene take under each rubric?

B. Same facts as Question A, with the following differences: (a) Trent and Juanita have been married for twenty years when Trent dies, (b) Trent's will leaves his probate estate (worth $150,000) entirely to Clarke, but Trent also has a $150,000 life insurance policy payable to Darlene, and (c) Juanita owns $100,000 in assets when Trent dies. What is Juanita's elective share under the 1969 UPC and the 1990 UPC? How much do Clarke and Darlene take?

C. Benny and Dora have been married for thirty years when Dora dies. Her will leaves half of her probate estate of $500,000 to Benny and half to her alma matter, UCLA. She also shared a joint bank account with her father that is worth $400,000. Benny owns $300,000 in property. Under the 1990 UPC, can Benny choose an elective share?

7.3.4 Community Property

Unlike separate property states, nine states (Arizona, California, Idaho, Louisiana, Nevada, New Mexico, Texas, Washington, and Wisconsin) are community property jurisdictions. The community property system takes the partnership theory of marriage quite seriously: Its basic premise is that each spouse acquires a one-half interest in the assets earned by the couple during the marriage. As a result, when first spouses die, they have the right to dispose of their one-half share of the community's assets; meanwhile, surviving spouses already own the other one-half share. There is no need for the elective share because surviving spouses are already protected by direct ownership of their portion of the community.

Not all wealth acquired during marriage is community property. Property acquired before the marriage or received by gift, inheritance, or some tort claims during the marriage are classified as separate property. However, earnings from separate property are usually classified as community property. In addition, spouses can contract to change the status of property. And if separate property is commingled with community property, separate property is then treated as community property.

Thorny questions can arise when couples move to another state. In general, the law of the jurisdiction where assets are obtained governs the character of those assets. This creates a serious problem when spouses move from a separate property jurisdiction to a community property jurisdiction.[9] Husbands or wives who have accumulated separate property are entitled to continue holding those assets as separate property in their new state. But their spouse, who was previously protected by the elective share, no longer has any independent claim to that wealth. To prevent this inequitable result, some community property states have created "quasi-community property," which is a label given to possessions that would have been community property but were acquired in a separate property state. Quasi-community property is often treated like community property when the first spouse dies. See, e.g., CAL. PROB. CODE §101 (West 2016).

Benavides v. Mathis
433 S.W.3d 59 (Tex. App. 2014)

Opinion by: SANDEE BRYAN MARION, Justice.

. . . The dispositive issue in this appeal is whether income distributions paid to Carlos [Y. Benavides, Jr.] from a family trust are his separate property or are community property. Because we hold the distributions are Carlos's separate property, we affirm.

BACKGROUND

Leticia [Benavides] is the wife of Carlos Y. Benavides, Jr. There are no children from their marriage; however, Carlos has three adult children from his first marriage. Years before Carlos and Leticia's marriage, the Benavides Family Mineral Trust was created, in 1990, to hold in trust, manage, and control approximately 126,000 acres of mineral estate for its beneficiaries. Carlos, who is one of several participating beneficiaries under the trust, receives monthly payments of the net balance (after payment of certain expenses) of revenues from the trust estate.

On October 14, 2011, a Webb County Court at Law appointed [Shirley Hale] Mathis as temporary guardian of Carlos's person and estate. Subsequently, Mathis notified the trust's co-trustees of her appointment and demanded that all funds distributable to Carlos be distributed to her. In February 2012, counsel for Leticia wrote to the co-trustees asking that they deliver to Leticia one-half of all distributions owed to Carlos on the grounds that all trust distributions during the marriage were community property; thus, one-half of the distributions were owed to her. The co-trustees refused. About a month later, counsel for Leticia then made the same demand of Mathis. Mathis refused, and Leticia filed the underlying lawsuit. . . .

---

9. Conversely, fewer complexitics arise when spouses migrate from community property states to separate property states. The Uniform Disposition of Community Property Rights at Death Act, 8A ULA 121 (1971), provides that community property retains its character even in a separate property regime.

DISCUSSION

. . .

We begin with the general rules regarding community property and separate property, which are well-established. Community property consists of the property, other than separate property, acquired by either spouse during marriage. Tex. Fam. Code Ann. §3.002 (West 2006). A spouse's separate property consists of the property owned or claimed by the spouse before marriage, acquired by the spouse during the marriage by gift, devise, or descent, and the recovery for personal injuries sustained by the spouse during marriage (except for recovery for loss of earning capacity). *Id.* §3.001. Earnings from the separate estate of one spouse are community property. A party claiming separate property has the burden of rebutting the community property presumption by clear and convincing evidence.

With these general rules in mind, we next turn to the issue of whether the trust income in this case is community or separate. Here, the distributions to Carlos are from a family trust created before Carlos and Leticia married. A trust is a method used to transfer property. "Courts have held that distributions from testamentary or inter vivos trusts to married recipients who have no right to the trust corpus are the separate property of the recipient because these distributions are received by gift or devise." Sharma v. Routh, 302 S.W.3d 355, 361 (Tex. App.-Houston [14th Dist.] 2009, no pet.). We agree with our sister court's conclusion in *Sharma* that, "in the context of a distribution of trust income under an irrevocable trust during marriage, income distributions are community property only if the recipient has a present possessory right to part of the corpus, even if the recipient has chosen not to exercise that right, because the recipient's possessory right to access the corpus means that the recipient is effectively an owner of the trust corpus." [*Id.*] at 364. Therefore, in this case, if the trust is irrevocable and if Carlos has no present, possessory right to any part of the corpus, then, as a matter of law, the income distributions are his separate property. The answer to this question lies in the unambiguous terms of the document that created the Benavides Family Trust.

A. Is the Trust Irrevocable?

The trust document provides as follows:

> This Trust is expressly irrevocable, but may be amended from time to time, except as to the duration hereof, with the written consent of three-fourths (3/4) in interest or more of all of the then participating beneficiaries. . . .

Despite the "expressly irrevocable" language, Leticia asserts the trust is revocable because it can be amended. "No specific words of art are needed to create an irrevocable trust." Vela v. GRC Land Holdings, Ltd., 383 S.W.3d 248, 250 (Tex. App.-San Antonio 2012, no pet.). However, the instrument must clearly reflect the settlor's intent to make the trust irrevocable. *Id.* Also, even with a revocable trust, an amendment does not result in the trust being revoked unless the words used in the amendment clearly show the settlor's intent to revoke the trust. An intent to revoke the trust can be evidenced if an inconsistent disposition of property between the trust and the amendment means both cannot stand. Revocation by implication is disfavored.

Here, the trust language is clear: the trust is "expressly irrevocable." *See McCauley*, 336 S.W.2d at 881 (holding "express use of the word 'irrevocably' in the granting clause meets the requirements of the statute and is legally sufficient to make the trust agreement irrevocable"). "We cannot conceive of any other purpose or explanation for the use of such word[s]." *Id.* Nor do we believe the ability to amend the trust transforms an "expressly irrevocable" trust into a revocable trust. Therefore, we conclude the trust is irrevocable. We next consider whether Carlos has a present, possessory interest in the trust corpus.

B. Present, Possessory Interest

Leticia argues Carlos has a present, possessory right because he has the right to transfer his interest, receive a portion of the corpus, and receive all of his share of the corpus on termination of the trust. Leticia's arguments that Carlos has a present, possessory interest lack merit primarily because her argument in part confuses a present, possessory interest in the income from the trust with a present, possessory interest in the corpus of the trust. Nevertheless, to the extent part of her contention is that Carlos has a present, possessory interest in the trust corpus, we disagree with her arguments.

First, Leticia points to the trust's definition of "revenue," which includes all bonuses and royalties. Leticia argues that because bonuses and royalties are corpus, any bonuses or royalties paid as income to Carlos constitute distributions of the trust corpus; therefore, he has a present, possessory interest in the trust corpus, making the income community property. We disagree with Leticia's argument.

Minerals are a part of the land; therefore, as a general rule, royalties are considered corpus. However, in any given case, the question of whether royalties constitute the corpus of the estate or constitute income can be decided only by reference to the trust document as a whole. If the trust document's language is not ambiguous and expresses the settlor's intent, we need not construe the trust. . . .

The corpus of the trust at issue here constitutes all right, title, and interest in and to all oil, gas, and other minerals in and under certain lands (defined in the trust as "family mineral rights"). "Trust estate" is defined as

> all rights, title and interests of the participating beneficiaries in and to all of the oil, gas, and all other minerals of every kind and character (whether similar or dissimilar, hard or soft) in, and under all of the lands described in attached Exhibit "A" as well as any other lands or estates which may hereafter be added to this trust estate.

The income to which the participating beneficiaries are entitled consists of net revenues. "Revenue" is defined as

> all monies received by the Trust produced directly or indirectly by the trust estate or other property hereafter forming a part of the trust estate, including but not limited to,

> all bonuses, rentals, royalties, production payments and any other monies or things paid to the trust or earned by the trust on any short term investments of trust income prior to distribution.

The trust document then expressly states what constitutes "income" and not "corpus":

> all natural resources from all such lands, including all oil and gas and other minerals, and all rentals, royalties, overriding royalties, limited royalties, working interests, bonuses, oil or gas payments, and all manner of mineral rights and interests, and all manner of revenue or receipts or proceeds therefrom, . . . shall constitute income of the Trust. . . .

We conclude the trust unambiguously "speaks for itself," and the clear intent of the settlors was that royalties and bonuses would not become a part of the trust "corpus." . . . Therefore, under the terms of this trust, the fact that Carlos receives royalties and bonuses as revenue does not mean he has a present, possessory interest in the trust corpus.

. . .

CONCLUSION

We conclude the trust is irrevocable, and Carlos does not have a present, possessory interest in the corpus of the irrevocable trust. Therefore, we conclude, as a matter of law, the distributions Carlos receives are not community property. Accordingly, the trial court did not err in rendering summary judgment in favor of Mathis.

QUESTIONS

4. Put aside complex issues of classifying the payments that Carlos received from the trust for a minute. Suppose instead that Carlos received a $100,000 gift from a rich aunt and a $50,000 bonus from his employer. Would these assets be classified as separate or community property? Now assume that Carlos invested the $100,000 gift in a particular company's stock and earned a $5,000 dividend. Would the dividend be separate or community property? What if Carlos transferred the $100,000 gift into a bank account that he owned jointly with his wife?

   ANSWER. Community property includes all income generated through work, while separate property includes anything that a spouse receives as a gift. In addition, earnings from separate property are themselves community property. So the $100,000 from the aunt would be separate property but the $50,000 bonus would be community property. However, when Carlos invests the $100,000 and earns income from it, that $5,000 dividend would be community property. Likewise, if Carlos had placed the $100,000 gift into a bank account he owned with his wife, his commingling of the funds would transform it into community property.

5. Although we study trusts in depth in Chapter 9, a few points about them might help clarify why the court asks the questions it does about the payments to Carlos. A "settlor" creates a trust by transferring property to a trustee, who holds the property (the "corpus") for the benefit of the beneficiaries. Trusts are often used as "will substitutes": The trustee can hold, manage, and distribute the corpus after the settlor dies. Often, trusts are revocable during the life of the settlor but irrevocable afterwards, when they implement the settlor's estate planning wishes. In addition, the beneficiaries typically do not enjoy all the rights of outright owners of the trust corpus. For instance, they generally cannot decide to end the trust or exercise control over the corpus. How do these additional facts inform the court's disposition of the case? Do they explain why it matters for the purposes of classifying Carlos's payments from the trust whether the trust is revocable and whether he has a present possessory interest in it?

   ANSWER. The critical question is whether Carlos's income from the trust is a kind of inheritance (in which case it would be separate property) or income from an asset that he owns. If the trust is irrevocable, it is more akin to a will: It is likely serving an estate planning function for a deceased settlor. That tips the scales toward the payments being an inheritance. In addition, if Carlos has the right to demand the corpus, he is basically an outright owner of the trust property. This would make income generated from the property into community property, like money earned from an investment. But because Carlos has no present possessory interest in the corpus, the income he receives is again more like an inheritance than income from an asset he owns.

PROBLEM III

A. John and Marcy have been married for five and a half years. John has $400,000 in property and Marcy owns $200,000. All of this money was earned by their respective jobs. John executes a valid will leaving his entire estate to his favorite charity. He then dies. Assuming that John and Marcy live in a separate property jurisdiction that follows the 1990 UPC, what does Marcy receive from John's estate? How would the answer change if John and Marcy live in a community property jurisdiction?

B. How would your answer to Question A change if $100,000 of John's $400,000 was money that he earned before he married Marcy?

7.3.5 Additional Protections

Most jurisdictions supplement the elective share or their community property system with three additional protections. These rights are generally immune from a decedent's creditors and other claimants.

First, there is the *homestead allowance*. Many states give the surviving spouse special rights relating to the couple's primary residence. These entitlements vary tremendously among jurisdictions. See, e.g., Gregory J. Duncan, Home Sweet Home? Litigation Aspects to Minnesota's Descent of Homestead Statute, 29 Wm. Mitchell L. Rev. 185, 194-200 (2002). Homestead rights are enshrined in constitutions in some states and are created by statute in others. They run the gamut from a fee simple or life estate in the couple's home to a lump sum payment meant to help keep the family living there. The UPC gives a surviving spouse a flat amount of $22,500. See UPC §2-402. This allowance from the deceased spouse's estate is "in addition to any share passing to the surviving spouse . . . by the will of the decedent, . . . by intestate succession, or by way of elective share." *Id.* As a result, a surviving spouse can receive the $22,500 homestead allowance even if he or she already owns or inherits the family home from the decedent. See In re Estate of Martelle, 32 P.3d 758 (Mont. 2001).

Second, a surviving spouse (or if there is none, the decedent's surviving children) can receive a *tangible property set-aside*: up to $15,000 "in household furniture, automobiles, furnishings, appliances, and personal effects." UPC §2-403.

Third, a decedent's surviving spouse and children can collect a *family allowance* of a maximum of $27,000. This allowance is designed to sustain the family during the administration or probate of the decedent's estate. *Id.* §§2-404 to 2-405.

7.4 PROTECTION AGAINST ACCIDENTAL OMISSION

What if a testator creates a will and *then* gets married or has children? Absent unusual foresight, it is unlikely the testator will mention a future spouse or children in a will. Of course, some testators do adjust their estate plan to reflect their new marital or parental status. But others do not, even if they fully intend to give the new spouse or child a share of their estate. In many cases, as we will see, the law presumes that a testator's failure to update a will after getting married or having a child to be unintentional.

As a result, the law sometimes protects omitted spouses and children—who are sometimes called "pretermitted" spouses or children—by giving them a share of the decedent's property. This rule applies when there is reason to believe that the testator *inadvertently* left his or her husband, wife, or child out of the will. Thus, including the pretermitted spouse or child in the estate is presumed to reflect what the testator would have wanted if he or she had been aware of the omission.

A few points can help clarify the pretermission rules at the outset. First, under the UPC, they do not apply if a testator marries or has a child and *then* subsequently makes a will that omits the spouse or child. In that context, policymakers assume that the testator *intentionally* did not provide for the omitted party because the testator knew about the spouse or child when making the will. Second, these statutes generally apply only to *wills*. See, e.g., Fox v. Lincoln Fin. Grp., 109 A.3d 221, 227 (N.J. Super. Ct. App. Div. 2015) (noting that "the omitted spouse statute . . . does not extend to nonprobate assets such as a life insurance policy"); see also Adam J. Hirsch, Text and Time: A Theory of Testamentary Obsolescence, 86 Wash. U. L. Rev. 609, 655 (2009).

7.4.1 Omitted Spouse

In most states, a pretermitted spouse is entitled to recover a portion of the testator's probate estate. However, there are three exceptions. The omitted spouse statute does not apply if (1) the testator made the will with full awareness of the impending marriage, (2) the will expressly declares that it is designed to stay the same even if the testator marries after the will is executed, or (3) the testator provides for the spouse through nontestamentary transfers in lieu of a devise under the will.

If none of these factors is present, then the surviving spouse is protected by the doctrine of pretermission, but how do we calculate the pretermitted spouse's share? We start by taking the decedent's probate estate and exempting any assets that the decedent devised to a child who (1) was born *before* the decedent married the surviving spouse and (2) is *not* also a child of the surviving spouse. We also carve out any property devised to a descendant of any such child. Then we give the omitted spouse an intestate share of what remains in the probate estate.

In separate property states, it is possible for a pretermitted spouse to recover *both* under the omitted spouse *and* elective share statutes. See UPC §2-301, comment. However, recall that when calculating the elective share, we deduct property that the surviving spouse has received from the deceased spouse. Thus, any amount that a surviving spouse takes as an omitted spouse reduces the amount he or she receives under the elective share. See *id.*

Uniform Probate Code
§2-301 Entitlement of Spouse; Premarital Will

(a) If a testator's surviving spouse married the testator after the testator executed his [or her] will, the surviving spouse is entitled to receive, as an intestate share, no less than the value of the share of the estate he [or she] would have received if the testator had died intestate as to that portion of the testator's estate, if any, that neither is devised to a child of the testator who was born before the testator married the surviving spouse and who is not a child of the surviving spouse nor is devised to a descendant of such a child . . . unless:

(1) it appears from the will or other evidence that the will was made in contemplation of the testator's marriage to the surviving spouse;

(2) the will expresses the intention that it is to be effective notwithstanding any subsequent marriage; or

(3) the testator provided for the spouse by transfer outside the will and the intent that the transfer be in lieu of a testamentary provision is shown by the testator's statements or is reasonably inferred from the amount of the transfer or other evidence.

(b) In satisfying the share provided by this section, devises made by the will to the testator's surviving spouse, if any, are applied first, and other devises, other than a devise to a child of the testator who was born before the testator married the surviving spouse and who is not a child of the surviving spouse . . . abate. . . .

Bell v. Estate of Bell
181 P.3d 708 (N.M. 2008)

CASTILLO, Judge.

Petitioner Appellant Vivan Bell (Mrs. Bell) is the surviving spouse of Ralph M. Bell (Decedent), who executed a will and created a revocable trust approximately five months prior to his marriage to Mrs. Bell. Neither the will nor the revocable trust mentions Mrs. Bell or Decedent's anticipated marriage to Mrs. Bell. Following Decedent's death, Mrs. Bell filed a petition for adjudication of intestacy in the district court and asserted, among other things, a claim under NMSA 1978, §45-2-301 (1995), as an omitted spouse. The district court determined that Decedent devised his estate to his adult children of a prior marriage via the will and revocable trust, and that Mrs. Bell's claim under Section 45-2-301 must therefore fail. The district court certified the issue for interlocutory appeal. For the reasons set forth below, we reverse and remand with instructions.

I. BACKGROUND

Decedent executed his will and created the Ralph Morris Bell Family Revocable Trust (Trust) on September 14, 2000. The will provides the following: "All of my estate of whatsoever kind . . . I devise to the Trustee of the [Trust] to be held by said Trustee . . . to be distributed as part of that Trust." In turn, the Trust provides that "[u]pon the death of [Decedent], the . . . Trustee shall distribute the entire [T]rust estate, principal and accumulated income[ ] to [Decedent's] children, RALPH MACK BELL and DIXIE ROBERTA HECKENDORN, in equal shares." . . . Neither the will nor the Trust refers to Mrs. Bell in any manner, nor do they indicate that Decedent was contemplating getting married.

In February 2001, approximately five months after executing the will and the Trust, Decedent married Mrs. Bell. Decedent died four years later on April 5, 2005. In addition to Mrs. Bell, Decedent was survived by two children from a prior marriage, Ralph Mack Bell (Son) and Dixie Roberta Heckendorn (collectively, Children).

On November 30, 2005, Mrs. Bell filed a petition for adjudication of intestacy, determination of heirship, and formal appointment as personal representative. Mrs. Bell asserted, among other things, that Decedent died intestate with respect to Mrs. Bell under Section 45-2-301. Son filed an objection to Mrs. Bell's petition, in which he claimed that Decedent devised all of his property to Children by will and thus died testate. Son asked the district court to appoint him as personal representative and to admit Decedent's will to probate. On April 25, 2006, the district court entered an order concluding that Decedent died testate and appointing Son as personal representative.

On October 19, 2006, Mrs. Bell filed a "Motion for Summary Judgment or for Finding of Law" regarding her theory that the Trust property should either be included in Decedent's estate for the purposes of calculating Mrs. Bell's intestate share under Section 45-2-301, or should be used for payment of her intestate share to the extent the probate estate proves to be inadequate. Mrs. Bell asserted that under

Section 45-2-301, if the surviving spouse of a decedent married the decedent after he executed his will, the surviving spouse is entitled to receive, as an intestate share, no less than the value of the share of the estate she would have received if the decedent had died intestate. Mrs. Bell further claimed that no material facts were in dispute and that none of the exceptions to Section 45-2-301 applied.

Respondent-Appellee the Estate of Ralph M. Bell (Estate) filed a response in opposition to Mrs. Bell's motion and claimed that Section 45-2-301 only applies to that portion of the testator's estate that is not devised to the testator's child born before the testator married the surviving spouse and who is not a child of the surviving spouse. The Estate asserted that Decedent devised all of his property to Children via the Trust and that Decedent provided for Mrs. Bell by transfer outside of the will, thus triggering one of the exceptions listed in Section 45-2-301. More specifically, the Estate claimed that Decedent provided Mrs. Bell with $7,000.00 in life insurance proceeds, approximately $2,900.00 per month in retirement income, medicare coverage through Decedent's social security account, and long-term health care. Mrs. Bell filed a reply in which she asserted that these benefits did not constitute a transfer outside of the will under Section 45-2-301 and that Children are not devisees of Decedent's property, but instead are beneficiaries under the Trust.

Following a hearing on Mrs. Bell's motion for summary judgment, the district court found that the will and Trust taken together indicated Decedent's intent to devise his property to Children. The district court further concluded that Mrs. Bell was not entitled to a share of Decedent's estate as an omitted spouse. . . .

The district court's order denying Mrs. Bell's motion for summary judgment recited, in relevant part, the following:

> [Mrs.] Bell is the surviving spouse of [Decedent] and married . . . Decedent after he executed his Will, which was admitted to probate in this matter. There was no provision made for [Mrs.] Bell in the Will or the Trust. However, the [c]ourt finds under [Section] 45-2-301 . . . the Will and the . . . Trust . . . reflect that the property of . . . Decedent was devised to children of [Decedent] who were born before [Decedent] married [Mrs.] Bell, and who are not children of [Mrs.] Bell; therefore, [Mrs.] Bell is not entitled to take any intestate share under [Section] 45-2-301 as an omitted spouse. As a result of the [c]ourt's ruling on the basis of the Will and the Trust . . . , the [c]ourt finds it does not need to hear any evidence regarding the intent of [Decedent] for purposes of [Section] 45-2-301.

. . .

II. DISCUSSION

A. Definition of "Devisee" Under Section 45-2-301

. . .

Section 45-2-301 provides, in relevant part, the following:

> A. If a testator's surviving spouse married the testator after the testator executed his will, the surviving spouse is entitled to receive, as an intestate share, no less than the value of the share of the estate he would have received if the testator had died intestate as to that portion of the testator's estate, if any, that neither is devised to a child of the testator who

> was born before the testator married the surviving spouse and who is not a child of the surviving spouse nor is devised to a descendant of such a child . . . unless: (1) it appears from the will or other evidence that the will was made in contemplation of the testator's marriage to the surviving spouse; (2) the will expresses the intention that it is to be effective notwithstanding any subsequent marriage; or (3) the testator provided for the spouse by transfer outside the will and the intent that the transfer be in lieu of a testamentary provision is shown by the testator's statements or is reasonably inferred from the amount of the transfer or other evidence.

In the present case, the following is undisputed: (1) Mrs. Bell married Decedent after he executed his will, (2) the will contained no provision for Mrs. Bell, (3) the will does not reflect that it was made in contemplation of Decedent's marriage to Mrs. Bell, and (4) the will does not express the intention that it is to be effective notwithstanding Decedent's marriage to Mrs. Bell. Therefore, the only question that remains regarding the application of Section 45-2-301 in the present appeal is whether Decedent's devise of his property to the Trust constituted a devise to Children.

Black's Law Dictionary defines "devise" as the following:

> n. 1. The act of giving property by will. . . . 2. The provision in a will containing such a gift. 3. Property disposed of in a will. 4. A will disposing of property.
>
> . . .
>
> vb. To give (property) by will.

Black's Law Dictionary 483-84 (8th ed. 2004). . . .

These definitions focus on the transfer of property through a will; nothing in the definitions suggests that the beneficiaries of a trust are also "devisees" of the trust assets. . . . In the present case, Decedent's will unambiguously devised his entire estate to the Trustee of the Trust, not to the Trust's beneficiaries. Therefore, under the plain language of Section 45-2-301, Decedent's estate was not "devised" to Children.

The Estate argues that this is an overly technical reading of the statute that cuts against Decedent's intent—as reflected in the will and the Trust—to leave his assets to Children. This argument fails. . . . [N]either the will nor the Trust reflects Decedent's intent with respect to Mrs. Bell, as required by Section 45-2-301. It is clear from the statute that an omitted spouse is entitled to receive an intestate share, unless the testator expresses an intent to the contrary, either in the will itself or through a transfer outside of the will in lieu of a testamentary provision. See §45-2-301(A). As mentioned previously, neither the will nor the Trust mentions Mrs. Bell, nor has the record been fully developed with respect to whether there has been a transfer outside of the will under Section 45-2-301(A)(3). By drafting Section 45-2-301 and the exceptions contained therein, the legislature obviously understood that a will executed prior to the testator's marriage might not reflect the testator's intent with regard to the omitted spouse. Therefore, the Estate's argument merely begs the question regarding Decedent's intent with respect to Mrs. Bell.

. . .

We have already stated that the record before us in this case does not reflect that any of the exceptions in Section 45-2-301 have been met. On remand, the district court should hold an evidentiary hearing to determine whether Decedent made a transfer outside of the will with the intent that the transfer be in lieu of a testamentary provision under Section 45-2-301(A)(3). If that exception is not met, the legislative intent of protecting the omitted spouse must control, and Mrs. Bell is entitled to receive an intestate share of Decedent's estate. We now turn to the questions regarding the application of the Trust assets to the satisfaction of the intestate share — questions we address to provide guidance on remand if necessary.

B. Trust Assets and Intestate Share

... Mrs. Bell ... contends that the Trust assets should be included in the probate estate for purposes of calculating and satisfying her intestate share. ...

Mrs. Bell points out that the New Mexico Uniform Probate Code defines the term "estate" to include generally "the property of the decedent, trust or other person whose affairs are subject to the Uniform Probate Code as originally constituted and as it exists from time to time during administration." Section 45-1-201(A)(12). Section 45-1-201(A) provides definitions for the entire Probate Code — to be applied, "unless the context otherwise requires." While Mrs. Bell is correct that the term "estate" can include the property of a trust, her argument disregards the distinction between a trust estate and a probate estate.

The Restatement (Third) of Property: Wills and Other Donative Transfers §1.1(a) (1999) defines "probate estate" as "the estate subject to administration under applicable laws relating to decedents' estates." This section continues as follows: "The probate estate consists of property owned by the decedent at death and property acquired by the decedent's estate at or after the decedent's death." *Id.* Decedent funded the Trust before he died. After funding the Trust, Decedent no longer owned those assets because they became the property of the Trust and because the title to the assets was thus in the Trustee. Decedent's continued control over the assets as Trustee did not make these assets a part of the probate estate. Upon Decedent's death, the Trust directed that the property in the Trust was to be transferred to the beneficiaries; the Trust property never became a part of the probate estate. We conclude that the Trust assets are not a part of the probate estate and therefore cannot be used to calculate or satisfy the intestate share.

...

Accordingly, we conclude that (1) a funded revocable trust is not a part of the probate estate and (2) an omitted spouse may not access the assets of a non-testamentary revocable trust in order to satisfy his or her intestate share. We therefore hold that Mrs. Bell may not invade the corpus of the Trust in order to calculate or satisfy her intestate share under Section 45-2-301.

...

III. CONCLUSION

We reverse the district court's order and remand for further proceedings consistent with this opinion.

QUESTIONS

6. Suppose Vivan and Ralph had married first and *then* Ralph had executed his will and trust. Would Vivan be entitled to protection under the pretermitted spouse statute? What is the logic behind this result?

   ANSWER. No. Omitted spouse statutes apply only when a decedent makes a will and only later marries. The logic here is that a decedent who marries first and then makes a will is unlikely to accidentally omit his or her spouse. That is, any omission is probably intentional. Conversely, a decedent who makes a will and then marries might forget to amend his or her estate plan to reflect the marriage.

7. Vivan argues that she is entitled to a share of Ralph's estate as a pretermitted spouse. Do we know enough about the factual background to conclusively determine whether her claim will succeed?

   ANSWER. No. Pretermitted spouse statutes do not apply if the decedent intended to provide for the spouse through transfers outside of the will. Here, Ralph's children allege that, instead of giving Vivan property under the will, Ralph provided Vivan with life insurance, retirement income, and health insurance. On remand, the court must determine whether Ralph wanted these benefits to act as a substitute for a gift under the will.

8. Why do Ralph's children argue that Ralph "devised" his property to them in the trust? What is the purpose of the rule that Ralph's children seek to invoke?

   ANSWER. The pretermitted spouse statute allows the accidentally omitted spouse to recover a portion of the decedent's probate estate. The portion is the amount of property that the spouse would have received in intestacy. However, it excludes an amount that the testator "devised" to a child of the testator who was born before the testator married the surviving spouse (and who is not a child of the surviving spouse). Thus, Ralph's children—who were born before Ralph married Vivan—are trying to argue that Ralph devised his entire probate estate to them by leaving it to the trust, leaving nothing for Vivan to take as a pretermitted spouse. The purpose of this rule is to protect the testator's children from a previous marriage from being effectively disinherited.

9. Once again, it can be helpful to review the basics of trusts to understand the consequences of the court's holding. Recall that settlors create a trust by transferring property to trustees, who must manage the trust property for the benefit of the trust beneficiaries. After this transfer, the settlor does not own the property—the trustees do. In addition, well-counseled settlors often execute a "pour over will," which leaves everything to the trustees of their trust. The purpose of a pour over will is to ensure that any asset that the settlor fails to transfer during life to the trustees nevertheless passes through probate at death to the trustees to be distributed under the terms of the trust. This is exactly what Ralph did with his will. Although the opinion does not say what assets Ralph actually placed in his trust before he died, and which assets

passed under Ralph's pour over will, can you see why that would be a critical distinction if the court finds that Vivan is a pretermitted spouse on remand?

ANSWER. The court holds that assets already in the trust are immune from Vivan's omitted spouse claim. Thus, if Ralph had placed an asset in the trust, Vivan could not reach it. But Vivan is entitled to a share of the assets that pass under Ralph's pour-over will, because they are part of his probate estate.

PROBLEM IV

A. In 1995, Frankie marries Jasper. In 1996, they have a child, Harry. In 1998, they divorce. In 1999, Frankie executes a valid will leaving her property half to Harry and half to her best friend, Rudolph. In 2000, Frankie marries Lance. In 2016, Frankie dies, leaving an estate worth $1,500,000. Can Lance take a share of Frankie's estate as an omitted spouse? If so, how much can Lance take under the statute? (You might want to review the UPC's intestacy statute, §2-102, which we discussed previously in Chapter 2.)

B. How would your answer to Question A change if Frankie's will declared that she wanted to provide for her children to the exclusion of anyone she would later marry?

C. How would your answer to Question A change if Frankie left all her property to Harry?

D. How would you calculate Lance's total inheritance, including the elective share, under the facts of Question A? Assume that (1) Frankie and Lance lived in a separate property state that adopted the 1990 UPC revisions, (2) Frankie had no nonprobate assets and made no lifetime transfers, and (3) Lance owned $100,000 at Frankie's death. (You might want to review the spousal elective share discussed earlier in this chapter.)

7.4.2 Omitted Children

Pretermitted children are also entitled to recover a share of the decedent's probate estate. The rationale behind pretermitted child statutes is the same as the one underlying pretermitted spouse laws: If the decedent made a will and then had a child, the will likely no longer reflects the decedent's intent if it does not mention the child.

Given this symmetry, it is not surprising that the pretermitted child statutes resemble their pretermitted spouse counterparts. For instance, the UPC's pretermitted child statute[10] does not apply if a testator omits an *existing* child born or adopted after the will is executed. Likewise, even if the will precedes the birth, the child takes nothing if either

10. Pretermitted child statutes vary widely between jurisdictions. For instance, some states protect omitted children who are born both *before* and after the execution of the will. See, e.g., ARK. CODE ANN. §28-39-407 (West 2016); NEV. REV. STAT. §133.170 (West 2016); N.H. REV. STAT. ANN. §551:10 (West 2016).

(1) the will explains that the omission is intentional or (2) the testator provides for the child through nontestamentary transfers in lieu of an inheritance from the will.

However, pretermitted child statutes feature unique rules for calculating the accidentally omitted child's share. One important variable is whether the testator had other living children when he or she executed the will. If the testator was childless, the pretermitted child takes the share that the child would have received in intestacy. However, the pretermitted child does not inherit if the testator gave most of his or her estate to the child's other parent.[11]

Conversely, if the testator had at least one other child when he or she executed the will, and the testator left some property to this child, the pretermitted child's share is different. In this scenario, the pretermitted child is entitled to a *pro rata* share of the amount that the testator left to his or her existing children.

For example, assume that T executed a will when she had two children, A and B, and left them \$75,000 each for a total devise of \$150,000. Then T had another child, C, and died without having updated her will. As one of three children, C is entitled to take one-third of the total amount that T left to T's children (\$150,000), or \$50,000. (A and B also take \$50,000 each, as they share the burden of paying for C's inheritance.) Alternatively, if T had given \$100,000 to A and \$50,000 to B, C would also take \$50,000, because that is a proportionate share (one-third) of all the property that T left to T's children (\$150,000). A (who received two-thirds of the original bequest) would contribute two-thirds of \$50,000, or \$33,333, to C's share (leaving A with \$66,666) and B (who received one-third of the original bequest) would kick in one-third of \$50,000, or \$16,666, to C's share (leaving B with \$33,333).

Uniform Probate Code
§2-302 Omitted Children

(a) Except as provided in subsection (b), if a testator fails to provide in his [or her] will for any of his [or her] children born or adopted after the execution of the will, the omitted after-born or after-adopted child receives a share in the estate as follows:

(1) If the testator had no child living when he [or she] executed the will, an omitted after-born or after-adopted child receives a share in the estate equal in value to that which the child would have received had the testator died intestate, unless the will devised all or substantially all of the estate to the other parent of the omitted child and that other parent survives the testator and is entitled to take under the will.

(2) If the testator had one or more children living when he [or she] executed the will, and the will devised property or an interest in property to one or more of the then-living children, an omitted after-born or after-adopted child is entitled to share in the testator's estate as follows:

11. Compare this rule with UPC §2-102(1)(b), which gives the surviving spouse the entire intestate estate if all of the decedent's descendants also belong to the surviving spouse. Are these rules based on similar presumptions about the decedent's probable intent? What are those presumptions?

(A) The portion of the testator's estate in which the omitted after-born or after-adopted child is entitled to share is limited to devises made to the testator's then-living children under the will.

(B) The omitted after-born or after-adopted child is entitled to receive the share of the testator's estate, as limited in subparagraph (A), that the child would have received had the testator included all omitted after-born and after-adopted children with the children to whom devises were made under the will and had given an equal share of the estate to each child. . . .

(D) In satisfying a share provided by this paragraph, devises to the testator's children who were living when the will was executed abate ratably. . . .

(b) Neither subsection (a)(1) nor subsection (a)(2) applies if:

(1) it appears from the will that the omission was intentional; or

(2) the testator provided for the omitted after-born or after-adopted child by transfer outside the will and the intent that the transfer be in lieu of a testamentary provision is shown by the testator's statements or is reasonably inferred from the amount of the transfer or other evidence. . . .

Estate of Maher v. Iglikova
138 So. 3d 484 (Fla. Dist. Ct. App. 2014)

FERNANDEZ, J.

Lyudmila Taran, guardian of her son, P.M., a minor and beneficiary of the Estate of James P. Maher, III, appeals the trial court's denial of her motion for summary judgment, wherein the trial court found that A.M.I., appellee Olga Valerievna Iglikova's daughter, is a pretermitted child. We reverse because A.M.I. does not qualify as a pretermitted child because she was born before the execution of the decedent's will.

This case arises out of the probate of the estate of James P. Maher, III, who disappeared in 2004. On August 3, 2009, the trial court entered an order on Petition for Order Declaring Death of Missing Person and a presumptive Death Certificate. Maher's last will and testament dated July 11, 2001 was admitted to probate on December 1, 2009. [James's will left his property, in part, to his "children."]

The decedent fathered two children during his lifetime: P.M., the decedent's son, of whom Taran is the legal guardian, born April 29, 1999; and A.M.I., Iglikova's daughter, born on December 15, 2000. The decedent did not become aware of A.M.I.'s existence until either June or July of 2002. A paternity test conducted in either late 2002 or early 2003 confirmed the decedent's paternity of A.M.I. The decedent thereafter made monthly child support payments to Iglikova for the benefit of A.M.I. These payments continued until the filing of the Petition for Administration on December 1, 2009. On August 10, 2005, a court order from the Commonwealth of Massachusetts directed that A.M.I.'s birth certificate be amended to reflect the decedent as the father.

. . .

1. There are three elements that must be satisfied for a child to be pretermitted. The child must be: (1) omitted from the will, (2) born or adopted after the making of the will, and (3) have not received a part of the testator's property equivalent to a child's part by way of advancement. §732.302, Fla. Stat. (2010). Section 732.302 specifically provides:

> When a testator omits to provide by will for any of his or her children born or adopted after making the will and the child has not received a part of the testator's property equivalent to a child's part by way of advancement, the child shall receive a share of the estate equal in value to that which the child would have received if the testator had died intestate, unless:
>
> (1) It appears from the will that the omission was intentional; or
>
> (2) The testator had one or more children when the will was executed and devised substantially all the estate to the other parent of the pretermitted child and that other parent survived the testator and is entitled to take under the will.

. . .

2. Taran argues that A.M.I. is not a pretermitted child because she benefits from the will in that she shares in a class gift for "children" surviving the decedent, and she was born [before] the execution of the will. We agree.

Although not specifically named, A.M.I. is not "omitted" from the will because she stands to inherit from the will in the form of a class gift as a child of the decedent. Section 732.302 does not speak to the sufficiency or to the amount of the child's beneficial interest. It only states that the child must be "omitted" to be pretermitted.

3. Furthermore, under the plain and obvious meaning of the statute, A.M.I. is not a pretermitted child because she was born before the execution of the decedent's will. Iglikova argues that an adjudication of paternity should be equated with an adoption that took place after the execution of the will. We decline to adopt such a rationale, as the two are distinct. "'Adoption' means the act of creating the legal relationship between parent and child where it did not exist." However, adjudication of paternity merely acknowledges an existing relationship. In addition, it is not within the purview of this Court to expand the meaning of the statute when its language is clear and unambiguous. Accordingly, we hold that the trial court erred when it denied Taran's motion for summary judgment and determined A.M.I. is a pretermitted child.

Reversed and remanded for further proceedings consistent with this opinion.

QUESTIONS

10. The court holds that A.M.I. is not entitled to inherit from James's estate as a pretermitted child for two reasons: (1) she stands to inherit from James's will under the clause leaving property to James's "children," and (2) she was born before James executed his will. But suppose that James had not included the devise to his "children." In that situation, can you think of a colorable argument that it is unfair to hold that James intentionally omitted A.M.I. from his will?

ANSWER. The policy basis of the pretermitted child statute is that a decedent's will becomes "stale" when it does not mention a child who is born after the decedent executes the instrument. By giving the pretermitted child a cut of the testator's estate, the law tries to carry out the testator's unstated intent. Here, James apparently did not know that A.M.I. existed—let alone was his child—when he executed his will in 2001. Thus, he had no reason to provide for A.M.I. in the document. This suggests that there is no meaningful distinction between A.M.I. and a child who is born after the testator signs the will. Moreover, when James learned the results of the paternity test in 2002 or 2003, he began to pay child support, suggesting that he wanted to provide for A.M.I.

11. Is James's son, P.M., entitled to a share of James's property as a pretermitted child?

ANSWER. P.M. cannot inherit from James's estate for the same reasons as A.M.I: (1) he stands to inherit from James's will under the clause leaving property to James's "children," and (2) he was born before James executed his will.

PROBLEM V

A. In 2009, Evelyn and Kevin marry. In 2010, Evelyn executes a valid will that leaves her entire estate, which is worth $1,000,000, to Kevin. In 2012, Evelyn and Kevin have a child, Bruce. In 2016, Evelyn dies, survived by Kevin and Bruce. Can Bruce take a pretermitted child's share under the UPC? What is the likely rationale for this outcome?

B. What if Evelyn had left $300,000 to Kevin and $700,000 to her best friend, Claire? (Again, you might want to review the UPC's intestacy statute, §2-102, which we discussed previously in Chapter 2.2.)

C. How would your answer to Question B change if Bruce's father was not Kevin?

D. Now suppose that Bruce's parents are Evelyn and Kevin, and that the couple also had another child, Sally, who was born in 2009. Is Sally entitled to a pretermitted child's share under the UPC? Is Bruce?

E. How would your answer to Question D change if Evelyn had left $20,000 to Sally and $80,000 to Kevin?

F. How would your answer to Question E change if Evelyn's will stated, "I hereby make no disposition for any child born after this will"? Alternatively, what if Evelyn's will did not contain this clause, but Evelyn had given Bruce a $50,000 gift with the intent that it serve as a substitute for a disposition under the will?

Actor Heath Ledger died of a drug overdose in 2008 at the age of 28. Ledger's will, executed in 2003, left everything to his parents and siblings. In 2005, however, Ledger had a daughter with actress Michelle Williams and never updated his will.

8 | Trust Formation and Elements

8.1 TRUSTS: INTRODUCTION

The trust, an infinitely adaptable relationship among people and property, is one of the common law's great achievements.[1] Trusts provide asset and estate planning opportunities limited only by the human imagination. Trusts may be inter vivos (created during lifetime) or testamentary (created at death by will). They may last for a few years or, following recent statutory changes in some jurisdictions, potentially in perpetuity.[2] Trusts can provide financial support and the legal infrastructure for property supervision on behalf of incapacitated or disabled persons without threatening the beneficiary's qualification for public assistance. They can assure a wife that, if she dies before her husband, he will be taken care of financially but lack the ability to divert her estate to a subsequent wife to the exclusion of her children. Trusts can shield wealth, for generations, from beneficiaries' creditors. They can shepherd property for minor children until they attain the age of majority. In short, trusts are stunningly flexible and, in the hands of a creative attorney, a remarkable means of managing property for even the most idiosyncratic goals. The only limits on trust purposes are that they be neither illegal nor contrary to public policy.[3]

A trust is a relationship as to property that vests *legal title* to the trust property in a trustee. The trustee, in turn, holds that property according to the trust's terms for the beneficial enjoyment of one or more beneficiaries, who have *equitable title*. In its simplest form, a trust is created (or "settled") when, with the present intent of creating a trust, a *settlor*[4] transfers property to one or more *trustees* to hold and manage for the

1. "If we were asked what is the greatest and most distinctive achievement performed by Englishmen in the field of jurisprudence I cannot think that we should have any better answer to give than this, namely, the development from century to century of the trust idea." F. Maitland, Selected Essays 129 (1936).

2. Indeed, a majority of U.S. states have now eliminated the Rule Against Perpetuities or substantially expanded the Rule's vesting period. See Howard M. Zaritsky, ACTEC, The Rule Against Perpetuities: A Survey of State (and D.C.) Law 7-8 (updated through March 2012). http://www.actec.org/assets/1/6/Zaritsky_RAP_Survey.pdf [http://perma.cc/KRD4-9QKU] (last updated March 2012).

3. "A trust may be created only to the extent its purposes are lawful, not contrary to public policy, and possible to achieve. A trust and its terms must be for the benefit of its beneficiaries." Uniform Trust Code (UTC) §404.

4. The terms *grantor, donor*, and *trustor* are interchangeable with the term *settlor*.

benefit of one or more *beneficiaries*.[5] The trust property is known as the trust *corpus* or *res*.[6] If the settlor transfers property to himself as trustee, and if the trust relationship is recorded in writing (as they almost always are), the trust document is known as a *declaration of trust*. If the settlor transfers property to one or more third parties as trustees, the trust document is known as a *deed of trust*.[7]

Trusts can be used instead of a will to dispose of property at death. However, unlike wills, which become effective only upon the testator's death,[8] inter vivos trusts are effective upon creation and allow trustees to manage the trust property during the settlor's lifetime. When the settlor of an inter vivos trust dies, the trust property is either distributed to the beneficiaries as nontestamentary (nonprobate) transfers or held by the trustees for future distribution. Today, the inter vivos revocable trust is a common means of providing for both lifetime management *and* nonprobate disposition of property at death.

Most of the trusts we discuss in this chapter are "express" trusts because they reflect the settlor's affirmative, voluntary, and intentional act of creating a trust.[9] Express trusts are governed by the settlor's chosen terms and impose fiduciary duties on the trustees. "Implied" trusts, by contrast, arise by operation of law or by court order. Thus, implied trusts are not actually trusts, but rather, equitable remedies that invoke the concept, but not the legal substance, of trust law. The primary function of implied trusts is to prevent unjust enrichment. As such, they do not generally impose the full range of fiduciary duties on the implied trustee. We will discuss implied trusts, including constructive trusts, resulting trusts, and honorary trusts, in Chapter 9.

For centuries, trust law was a matter of common law, originating in the common law chancery courts of equity. In 2000, however, the Uniform Law Commissioners promulgated the Uniform Trust Code (UTC), now adopted, at least in part, in thirty-one states. Accordingly, trust law in the United States has moved markedly toward statutory law, and the UTC provides the primary source of statutory law for this chapter. We will also draw upon the Restatement (Third) of Trusts and The Restatement (Third) of Property: Wills & Other Donative Transfers because there are numerous important common law principles of trust law not addressed by statute.

---

5. Today, the term "cestui que trust," meaning the beneficiary (who holds an equitable interest in the trust property), is rarely seen. Nevertheless, it is a term that occurs from time to time.

6. *Res* is Latin for "thing" or "matter." It is pronounced "race," although one occasionally hears the odd "rez." The term appears in many other legal contexts such as *res judicata*, *res nullius*, *res ipsa loquitor*, etc.

7. The doctrine of merger generally prohibits a sole trustee to be also the sole beneficiary of a trust. In those circumstances, the law treats the legal and equitable titles to the trust corpus as having "merged," thereby destroying the unique characteristic of trusts: the separation of legal and equitable titles.

8. Wills are effective as of the date of the testator's death with one exception: An explicit revocation clause in a will (e.g., "I hereby revoke all wills and codicils I have made prior to this will.") is effective in most jurisdictions to revoke prior wills.

9. South Dakota Codified Laws §55-1-3 (2016) provides a common understanding of this term: "An express trust is an obligation arising out of a personal confidence reposed in and voluntarily accepted by one for the benefit of another."

8.2 THE DISTINCTION BETWEEN GIFTS AND TRUSTS

To understand the law of trusts, one must also understand the related law of gifts. Gifts and trusts are both donative transfers — voluntary acts accompanied by donative intent that results in the transfer of title to property from a donor to a donee without consideration.[10] Gifts and trusts differ, however, in the manner through which possession and control of property transfers to the donee.

We begin our discussion here with the foundational concept of donative intent, a common element shared by both gifts and trusts. Donative intent refers to the donor's present intention to transfer ownership of property gratuitously to a donee.[11] The manifestation of donative intent, however, is not always clearly documented in a written instrument, nor immediately evident from the surrounding circumstances. Consider, for example, Person A, who delivers property to Person B, and receives nothing in return. From this fact, alone, can we presume that Person A intended this delivery to Person B as a gift? Such determination depends on Person A's subjective intent at the time of delivery, so, without additional facts, we cannot answer the question. Think about the wide range of possible explanations for such a transfer: When you check your overcoat at a restaurant, you deliver it to the coatroom attendant who takes it from you, but you have no intention of giving the attendant title to the coat.[12] When you lend an umbrella to a friend on a rainy day, you demonstrate thoughtfulness, not generosity, because you expect the friend to return your umbrella; you do not intend to make a gift of it. If you deliver a work of art to an art dealer to sell on your behalf, that action constitutes a consignment; you do not intend to give the dealer title to the work but, rather, only the authority to transfer your title to the eventual purchaser. If the work does not sell, however, you expect the dealer to return the artwork, not to keep it for herself.[13] Thus, a finding of a current intention to make a gratuitous transfer is essential for a delivery of property to constitute a gift or trust and, thus, to effect a valid transfer of title to the property from a donor to a donee. Ascertaining donative intent, if not evident from a written instrument documenting the transfer, requires an evaluation of the facts and circumstances surrounding the delivery of property.

---

10. There are, of course, exceptions. For example, parents might sell a work of art to a child for less than its fair market value. In that situation, the parents make a gift to the child to the extent that the work's fair market value exceeds the amount the child pays to the parents.

11. The Restatement (Third) of Property (Wills & Donative Transfers) distinguishes between donative intent and donative motive:

> To be a gift, a transfer must be made with donative intent. The requirement of donative intent is the essence of a gift.
>
> Donative intent is to be distinguished from donative motive. The motive for making a gift is a complex matter and does not determine whether or not a gift was intended.

§6.1, comment b.

12. "A *bailment* is an agreement, either express or implied, that one person will entrust personal property to another for a specific purpose and that when the purpose is accomplished the bailee will return the property to the bailor." Milbank Ins. Co. v. Indiana Ins. Co., 56 N.E.3d 1222, 1231 (Ind. Ct. App. 2016) (emphasis added).

13. Of course, there are exceptions to this example. See Uniform Commercial Code §2-403(2).

At common law, a valid gift generally requires (1) donative intent, (2) delivery, and (3) acceptance of the gifted property. Donative intent is generally ascertained from the legal instrument evidencing the transfer, if in writing, and, if not, from extrinsic evidence of the surrounding circumstances. Delivery, through which the donor surrenders dominion and control over gifted property, can be actual (a physical transfer of the property), or, when actual delivery is impracticable or impossible, delivery can be symbolic or constructive. Symbolic delivery is accomplished when the donor has performed a symbolic act in place of actual delivery, such as the donor's execution of a *deed of gift* identifying the gifted property and delivery of the deed to the donee. Constructive delivery is accomplished when the donor delivers to the donee a means of taking possession of the gifted property. For example, a donor might give the donee keys to a bicycle's lock as constructive delivery of the bicycle itself. Acceptance, the final element of a gift, is generally presumed and rarely contested, as most donees do not look a gift horse in the mouth. The Restatement tracks these common law requirements for an outright gift of property:

Restatement (Third) of Property: Wills & Other Donative Transfers
§6.1 Requirements Applicable to All Gifts of Property

(a) To make a gift of property, the donor must transfer an ownership interest to the donee without consideration and with donative intent.

(b) Acceptance by the donee is required for a gift to become complete. Acceptance is presumed, subject to the donee's right to refuse or disclaim.

Gifts of real property, governed by the Statute of Frauds, must be documented with deeds indicating transfer of title. Gifts of most forms of intangible personal property (such as bank accounts or shares of stock) are documented when the donor retitles the account or shares in the donee's name. Gifts of tangible personal property, however, and particularly gifts of valuable works of art, require particular attention to the formalities of delivery and acceptance, as *Peterson v. Peck*, excerpted below, illustrates.

To create an effective inter vivos trust, by contrast, the settlor must demonstrate a present intention to create a trust relationship and deliver the trust corpus to the trustees, who must accept the property and their appointments to serve as trustees. Delivery of trust property is typically achieved when the settlor signs and delivers to the trustees a trust document that describes the trust property; acceptance is typically accomplished when the trustees indicate their willingness to serve as trustees by signing the trust document.

Although in many ways similar, trusts differ from gifts in several important respects, three of which we survey below. As you consider these distinctions between outright gifts and transfers in trust, bear in mind that the settlor's primary reason for choosing the trust form rather than an outright gift is almost always to exert more control over the beneficiaries' use of gifted property:

First, in a gift, the donor transfers legal title directly to the donee, but in a trust, the settlor transfers legal title to trustees, who serve as intermediaries between the settlor and beneficiaries. Thus, the donee of an outright gift obtains both legal and equitable title to the gifted property whereas, in a trust, the trustees hold legal title subject to the equitable title held by the beneficiaries.

Second, trusts are often infinitely preferable to outright gifts for the gratuitous transfer of future interests and gifts that take place over extended periods of time. Although it is possible to transfer a future interest in property by gift,[14] future interest gifts are confined to the original form of property conveyed by the donor, they are typically impractical if the subject of the gift is not real property, and they lack the supervision of a third party responsible for managing the property and facilitating continuity of ownership. Trusts, by contrast, are not limited to the original form of the gifted property — the trustee, unless prohibited by the trust, may sell the original property in exchange for new property when it is prudent to do so. Trusts are, therefore, especially appropriate for gifts of certain assets such as marketable securities, which require supervision by a legally responsible person with authority to adjust investments when market conditions change. Trusts, unlike outright gifts of future interests, are also structurally well suited for facilitating continuity of ownership over time when there are multiple beneficiaries.

For example, consider a grandparent who has one adult child and four minor grandchildren. Suppose the grandparent settles an inter vivos trust for the benefit of her descendants. The trust instrument could require the trustees (a) to distribute income generated by the trust property to the settlor's adult child during his lifetime and, (b) upon the adult child's death, to distribute the remaining trust property to that child's children — the settlor's grandchildren (or, if a grandchild predeceases, to more remote descendants). In this example, the grandparent would retain no interest in the trust property. Instead, legal title would transfer to the trustees and equitable title would transfer to the settlor's descendants. Unlike an outright gift, however, the descendants do not immediately acquire full control over the trust property. Rather, a current possessory interest in the trust's *income* would vest immediately in the settlor's child, and a contingent future interest in the *remainder* of the trust assets would vest in the settlor's grandchildren. Following the adult child's death, the trust would terminate because the trust requires the trustees to distribute the remaining corpus to the settlor's grandchildren outright at that time. All of this would take place under the care and watchful eye of the trustees.

Third, gifts are legally unsuitable for transfers intended to take place at death whereas trusts are perfectly suited for this purpose. A gift intended by the donor to take place at death is generally not valid unless it otherwise complies with the statutory requirements for making a will. Postponement of a gift in this manner is usually treated as an ineffective testamentary transfer. By contrast, an inter vivos trust can provide for the disposition of property upon the settlor's death without complying with testamentary formalities because title passes to the trustees during the settlor's lifetime.

---

14. For example, the donor could convey Blackacre to A for life, then to B for life, and then to C in fee simple absolute.

Peterson v. Peck
430 S.W.3d 797 (Ark. App. 2013)

WALMSLEY, Judge.

This appeal involves a dispute over the ownership of a piece of artwork created by Alexander Calder. Robert Peck was the owner of the artwork before his death in 2006. Appellant Capi Peterson is Robert Peck's daughter. Appellee Hannah Peck is Robert Peck's widow. After a bench trial, the Pulaski County Circuit Court found that the artwork was not the subject of an inter vivos gift to Peterson from Robert Peck and that it was not given to Peterson through Peck's trust.[15] . . . We affirm.

Peterson's grandparents purchased a mobile by Alexander Calder known as "Autumn Leaves" ("the Calder") in the 1950s. Robert Peck had possession of the Calder after the deaths of his parents. Peck created the Peck Family Trust, a revocable trust, on May 8, 2001. The purpose of the trust was to provide for the support, education, maintenance, and preservation of the health of Hannah Peck during her lifetime. Robert Peck was to be the trustee during his lifetime, with Hannah Peck named as trustee upon his death.

On June 15, 2001, Robert Peck . . . executed a Declaration of Trust Ownership conveying "[a]ll tangible articles of a household or personal nature . . . including . . . works of art" to the trust. The declaration also stated that it was intended to revoke all prior declarations of ownership.

In January 2005, Robert Peck amended and restated the May 2001 trust. He also executed a will that left all artwork and most of his other personal property to Hannah Peck if she should survive him. The rest of Robert Peck's property was to pour over into the trust. The will specifically referenced the May 2001 trust and incorporated it by reference.

Robert Peck passed away in 2006 while living in Hawaii and married to Hannah Peck. Hannah Peck maintained that she received the Calder mobile under her husband's will and sold it for $3.7 million.[16]

---

15. [The court's discussion of Peterson's argument that she received the Calder mobile under the terms of the trust is omitted. — EDS.]

16. [The Calder mobile sold at public auction at Sotheby's, New York, on November 14, 2007 for $3,737,000 (the hammer price plus the buyer's premium). Its presale estimate was $1,500,000-2,500,000. The printed catalog states the mobile's provenance (that is, its history of ownership) as follows:

> **Provenance:** Edward Durrell Stone (acquired directly from the artist)
>
> Sam Peck (gift from the above)
>
> Robert Peck (acquired from the above by descent)
>
> Acquired by the present owner from the above by descent

On its website, Sotheby's states the work's provenance merely as "Edward Durrell Stone (acquired directly from the artist)" and no longer carries a photograph of the work. See http://www.sothebys.com/en/auctions/ecatalogue/2007/contemporary-art-evening-n08363/lot.51.html. However, an image of it appears at http://www.invaluable.com/auction-lot/alexander-calder-,-1898-1976-untitled-autumn-lea-51-c-qocs4jxt1h. — EDS.]

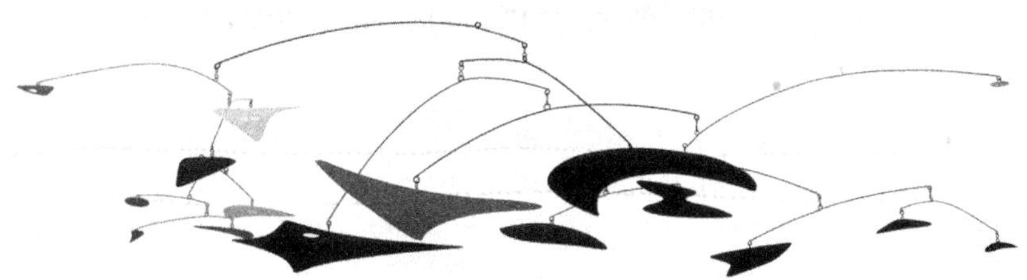

Alexander Calder, *Autumn Leaves*, c. 1955. © *2017 Calder Foundation, New York / Artists Rights Society (ARS), New York.*

On October 25, 2010, Peterson filed suit against Hannah Peck, as trustee, alleging that she was the owner of the Calder mobile and that Hannah Peck wrongfully sold it to a third party and was liable to Peterson for its value. Peterson sought . . . damages for the sale of the mobile.

Hannah Peck answered the complaint and counterclaimed for a declaratory judgment to determine . . . ownership of the Calder. . . . Hannah Peck acknowledged that she sold the mobile and invested the proceeds in what turned out to be Allen Stanford's offshore Ponzi scheme. . . .

At trial, Peterson asserted that she was the owner of the mobile by virtue of an inter vivos gift from her father. This assertion was based on an April 2001 letter Robert Peck wrote to Peterson, stating that he gave Peterson the Calder artwork, although he retained the right to display it during his lifetime. In the letter, Peck characterized it as "an attachment to, and pursuant to Section 3.3 of the Peck Family Trust created in April of 2001." In the alternative, Peterson asserted that she received the artwork under the [terms of the] trust. In doing so, she relied on another letter from her father, written in July 2004 to attorney Joe Polk in which he reaffirmed that he had given the Calder to Peterson. The letter also suggested changes to Peck's trust and will.

. . . On September 13, 2012, the circuit court entered its order dismissing Peterson's complaint. The court found that there was no valid inter vivos gift of the Calder mobile and that it was not given to Peterson through the trust. . . . This appeal followed.

. . .

Peterson's first two points are argued in the alternative. In those points, she contends that she is the owner of the artwork as a result of an inter vivos gift from her father or, that she received the artwork under the [terms of the] trust.[17]

Under Arkansas law, a valid inter vivos gift is effective when the following elements are proved by clear and convincing evidence: (1) the donor was of sound mind; (2) an actual delivery of the property took place; (3) the donor clearly

17. [See note 15, above: Peterson's contention that she received the Calder through the trust is not included in this edited version of the court's opinion. — Eds.]

intended to make an immediate, present, and final gift; (4) the donor unconditionally released all future dominion and control over the property; and (5) the donee accepted the gift. The rule with respect to delivery of gifts is less strictly applied to transactions between family members. Even so, delivery must occur for a gift to be effective. Our supreme court further explained . . . that the gravamen of delivery is a showing of an act or acts on the part of the putative donor displaying an intention or purpose to part with dominion over the object of the gift and to confer it on some other person. Express words or particular conduct are not required when reasonable minds would conclude from attending circumstances that the purpose was present. An inter vivos gift may be delivered in a constructive manner. The circuit court found that the facts fell short of satisfying two of the inter vivos gift elements, specifically, that Peck lacked the intent to make an immediate, present, and final gift, and that by retaining the right to display the Calder mobile, Peck did not unconditionally release all future dominion and control over the property.

Citing Bellis v. Bellis, 56 S.W.3d 396 (Ark. App. 2001), and Gruen v. Gruen, 496 N.E.2d 869 (N.Y. 1986), Peterson argues that one may make a present inter vivos gift of personal property while retaining a life estate in the property. Neither *Bellis* nor *Gruen* helps Peterson.

In *Bellis*, a father gave a music box to his son. The son decided that, for safekeeping purposes and his mother's enjoyment, the music box would be best left temporarily with his parents. The circuit court distinguished the present case from *Bellis* by noting that, in *Bellis*, it was the donee who decided to leave the music box with his parents, while here, the donor decided he would retain possession of the Calder for display purposes. *Gruen* is not persuasive because New York does not require proof of the same inter vivos gift elements as Arkansas law requires.

Peterson testified that she never had possession of the Calder itself, just the April 2001 letter purporting to give her the artwork. She acknowledged that her father had possession of the piece. Peterson also testified about a conversation with her father where her father told her that he wanted her to have the Calder after his death. Peterson's argument focuses on evidence of Robert Peck's intent to give her the Calder; however, that is only one of the elements necessary to establish an inter vivos gift. A gift inter vivos cannot be made to take effect in the future, as such a transaction would only be a promise or an agreement to make a gift. Peterson's own testimony showed that Robert Peck had not unconditionally released all future dominion and control over the Calder. She testified in her deposition that Peck could have transferred possession of the Calder to anyone. Based on our standard of review, we cannot say that the circuit court was clearly erroneous in determining that the elements of an inter vivos gift of the Calder had not been established.

. . .

Affirmed.

QUESTIONS

1. At the time of his death, to whom did Robert Peck think the Calder mobile belonged? What might Robert Peck's attorney have advised Peck and his daughter to do to assure that the Calder was treated as a completed gift to his daughter?

 ANSWER. From the court's opinion, it seems that Robert Peck thought he had made a valid, lifetime gift of the Calder to his daughter. The letter Peck wrote to his attorney in July 2004 confirmed that Peck had given the Calder to his daughter. Moreover, the letter "suggested changes to Peck's trust and will."

 The court, however, was not convinced that Peck had the intent of making a present, lifetime gift of the mobile, particularly in light of Peck's failure to part with his possession of it. To clarify Peck's intention of making the gift (if, indeed, that is what Peck intended), Peck's attorney could have prepared a deed of gift documenting Robert Peck's gift of the Calder to his daughter and had Peck sign the document as donor and his daughter, as donee. The deed would have satisfied evidentiary requirements to prove donative intent and served as constructive delivery of the mobile. Subsequently, the daughter should have been advised to document that she was lending the mobile to her father. She also should have been advised to take action demonstrating her dominion and control over the mobile while it was in her father's possession. For example, the daughter could have listed the mobile on her own fine arts insurance policy and paid the insurance premiums. Additionally, the daughter could have arranged to lend the mobile to a museum for a short period being certain that the loan documents indicated that she was the owner.

PROBLEM I

For her family's new house, Leah purchased a piano and an expensive sculpture to place on top of it. Leah's husband, Jose, a musician, was excited to have a piano in the house. Leah's daughter, Fatima, fell in love with the sculpture. Happy with their reactions, Leah told them the piano was a gift for Jose, and the sculpture, a gift for Fatima. Jose said it would be better if he had the piano in his studio, a separate structure in the back yard. Leah watched happily as Jose and some friends moved the piano to the studio. The sculpture got moved to a shelf in the living room. At dinner that night, Leah told friends she had given Jose a piano. After dinner, Leah sent Jose a text saying "So happy I gave you the piano!!! And isn't the sculpture great?!" A week later, Leah died unexpectedly. Who owns the piano? Who owns the sculpture?

PROBLEM II

To prove an inter vivos gift of property, the court in *Peterson v. Peck*, above, identifies five elements that must be supported by clear and convincing evidence.

Why must the evidence meet this higher standard rather than the usual civil standard of "preponderance of the evidence"?

Unlike works of art, for which there exists neither a comprehensive registry of ownership nor statutory requirements to register title, ownership of some forms of tangible personal property are documented with registration certificates. For example, federal law requires that aircraft be registered before being flown in the United States (49 U.S.C. §44101(a)), and the Federal Aviation Administration maintains a registry of such aircraft. State laws require registration of automobiles and boats, and states maintain registries for complying with those requirements. Thus, unlike most other forms of tangible personal property, delivery and acceptance of a gift of aircraft, automobiles, and boats are generally accomplished by recording a new registration certificate in the donee's name with the appropriate federal or state agency.

8.3 ELEMENTS OF PRIVATE TRUSTS

The UTC draws a distinction between two general categories of express trusts: non-charitable trusts (more commonly referred to as "private" trusts) and charitable trusts. Most aspects of trust law (and most provisions of the UTC) applicable to private trusts apply also to charitable trusts. Our discussion of trust law principles in this section, therefore, applies generally to both categories of express trusts.[18]

The law imposes relatively few formal requirements for creating a valid trust. The UTC enumerates three ways to do so:[19]

Uniform Trust Code
§401 Methods of Creating Trust

A trust may be created by:

(1) transfer of property to another person as trustee during the settlor's lifetime or by will or other disposition taking effect upon the settlor's death;

(2) declaration by the owner of property that the owner holds identifiable property as trustee; or

(3) exercise of a power of appointment in favor of a trustee.

---

18. We will discuss distinctions between private and charitable trusts in Section 8.5, "Charitable Trusts," below.

19. The Restatement is less succinct and includes a broader range of circumstances.

> . . . [A] trust may be created by:
>
> (a) a transfer by the will of a property owner to another person as trustee for one or more persons; or
>
> (b) a transfer inter vivos by a property owner to another person as trustee for one or more persons; or
>
> (c) a declaration by an owner of property that he or she holds that property as trustee for one or more persons; or
>
> (d) an exercise of a power of appointment by appointing property to a person as trustee for one or more persons who are objects of the power; or
>
> (e) a promise or beneficiary designation that creates enforceable rights in a person who immediately or later holds those rights as trustee, or who pursuant to those rights later receives property as trustee, for one or more persons.

Restatement (Third) of Trusts §10. Methods of Creating a Trust.

Thus, trusts may be created by performing one of three actions: transferring property to a trustee, making a declaration of trust, or exercising a power of appointment in favor of a trustee.[20] Although all three methods are, in practice, almost invariably recorded in a written instrument, nothing in UTC §401 requires a trust to be in writing.[21] Indeed, UTC §407 validates oral trusts but sets the bar for proving it at the highest civil standard of proof: clear and convincing evidence. Nevertheless, oral trusts are rare, and it is always preferable to record the terms of a trust in writing. A trust created under UTC §401(1), in which the settlor transfers property to at least one third-party trustee, is known as a "deed of trust." A trust created under UTC §401(2), in which the settlor declares him- or herself as the owner of certain property in trust, is known as a "declaration of trust."[22]

QUESTIONS

2. UTC §407 begins with the clause "[e]xcept as required by a statute other than this [Code]. . . ." What kind of statute might the UTC be referring to and why?

   ANSWER. All jurisdictions have enacted or recognize at common law some form of the English Statute of Frauds. Typically, those statutes require a writing for creating, granting, or transferring an interest in real property. Accordingly, although the UTC may not require that a trust be in writing, if a jurisdiction enacts §407 and has enacted a Statute of Frauds, a writing would be required if the trust holds (or is expected to hold) any interest in real property. Additionally, some jurisdictions require a writing to create a valid trust that holds only personal property.

3. Why does the UTC require that proof of an oral trust be established by clear and convincing — rather than by a preponderance of the — evidence?

   ANSWER. As with many other relaxations of formalities in the UPC and UTC, the clear and convincing standard guards against fraud. By relying on strict formalities in creating a valid will or trust relationship, prior law permitted a lower evidentiary standard. With a loosening of the formalities, the risk of potential fraudulent claims increases. Thus, the higher clear and convincing standard is required in proving an oral trust or an element of wills acts requirements under the "harmless error" rule set out in UPC §2-503.

UTC §402 imposes five required elements for the creation of a trust: (1) capacity, (2) intent, (3) one or more beneficiaries, (4) active duties imposed upon one or more

20. A "power of appointment," discussed in Chapter 5, is the authority to direct the ownership of property to a described group of donees ("limited power of appointment") or to anyone ("general power of appointment"). UTC §401(3) clarifies that it is permissible to appoint property to a trustee to be held for the benefit of the trust beneficiaries.

21. Some UTC jurisdictions, such as New Jersey and New York, nevertheless require a written instrument for the creation of a valid trust. See, e.g., N.J. Stat. §3B:31-18 (requiring a written trust instrument); N.Y. Est. Powers & Trusts Law §7-1.17 (requiring a revocable, inter vivos trust to be in writing; signed by a settlor of the trust (and by at least one trustee if the settlor is not the sole trustee); and acknowledged by a notary or signed in the presence of two witnesses).

22. Trusts created under UTC §401(3) will be in a form set out in the instrument that creates the power of appointment. For powers of appointment, see Chapter 5.

trustees, and (5) that the sole beneficiary is not the same person as the sole trustee. Each of these elements is examined in greater depth below.

Uniform Trust Code
§402 Requirements for Creation

(a) A trust is created only if:
(1) the settlor has capacity to create a trust;
(2) the settlor indicates an intention to create the trust;
(3) the trust has a definite beneficiary or is:
(A) a charitable trust;
(B) a trust for the care of an animal, as provided in Section 408; or
(C) a trust for a noncharitable purpose, as provided in Section 409;
(4) the trustee has duties to perform; and
(5) the same person is not the sole trustee and sole beneficiary.
. . .

8.3.1 Trust Settlor's Capacity and Intent

Legal capacity requirements protect individuals with diminished cognitive abilities who are incapable of safeguarding their own interests. Capacity requirements are generally higher in contexts where there is an increased risk of harm to persons requiring protection. Thus, contracts and outright gifts are subject to higher capacity requirements than wills because the risk of a cognitively impaired person impoverishing herself during life by improvidently transacting away her property is a greater concern than the risk of such a person executing a false will leaving property to unintended beneficiaries at death. Similarly, the capacity required to establish a trust depends on whether the trust is revocable or irrevocable: The law imposes a lower capacity standard for revocable trusts and a higher capacity standard for irrevocable inter vivos trusts.

Revocable trusts are commonly used as will substitutes, so they are governed by the same capacity requirement as wills. The settlor of a revocable trust retains the power to amend or to revoke the trust during his lifetime without the consent of any third party (such as the trustee). Thus, the risk of a cognitively impaired settlor inadvertently impoverishing himself is low and, in any event, not materially higher than that of a testator making a will.[23]

Uniform Trust Code
§601 Capacity of Settlor of Revocable Trust

The capacity required to create, amend, revoke, or add property to a revocable trust, or to direct the actions of the trustee of a revocable trust, is the same as that required to make a will.

By contrast, irrevocable inter vivos trusts are governed by a higher capacity standard because such trusts cannot be revoked by the settlor once they are created. In an

---

23. If the settlor of a revocable trust permanently releases the right to revoke, the trust becomes irrevocable. If the settlor of a revocable trust revokes the trust, the trust terminates, and the trustees convey the trust property to the settlor.

irrevocable inter vivos trust, the settlor's transfer of property takes effect during the settlor's own lifetime. Lifetime gifts, whether outright or in trust, can deplete the owner's stock of assets available for her own lifetime support or the support of her dependents. The comment to UTC §601, citing the Restatement provisions below, articulates the capacity standard for the creation of an irrevocable inter vivos trust by incorporating the capacity standard applicable to lifetime gifts: "To create an irrevocable trust, the settlor must have the capacity that would be needed to transfer the property free of trust."

Restatement (Third) of Trusts
§11 Capacity of a Settlor to Create a Trust

(3) A person has capacity to create an irrevocable inter vivos trust by transfer to another or by declaration to the same extent that the person has capacity to transfer the property inter vivos free of trust in similar circumstances.

Unlike the Restatement (Third) of Trusts, above, the Restatement (Third) of Property: Wills & Other Donative Transfers, below, makes clear that the settlor of an irrevocable trust must have both testamentary capacity and the capacity to understand the economic implications of making a lifetime gift:

Restatement (Third) of Property: Wills & Other Donative Transfers
§8.1 Requirement of Mental Capacity

(c) If [a] donative transfer is in the form of an irrevocable gift, the donor must have the mental capacity necessary to make or revoke a will and must also be capable of understanding the effect that the gift may have on the future financial security of the donor and of anyone who may be dependent on the donor.

Trusts cannot be formed by accident. For a trust to be valid, the settlor must have *intended* to create it.

Restatement (Third) of Trusts
§13 Intention to Create Trust

A trust is created only if the settlor properly manifests an intention to create a trust relationship.

The hallmark of the trust relationship is the imposition upon one or more trustees of *fiduciary duties* that are enforceable by the beneficiaries.[24] It is not always easy to determine whether a putative settlor's language manifests an intention to create a trust. Merely stating that a gift is "in trust" may not, as the case below illustrates, be sufficient. And limitations on a gift that express the donor's preference but fail to impose legally enforceable restrictions cannot change an outright gift into a gift in trust.

Precatory language—language suggesting a course of action but not legally binding—does not create a trust relationship. Take, for example, a decedent's will that says, "I give everything to my wife, hoping she will use this gift not just for her own

24. We examine fiduciary duties in Chapter 11.

benefit, but also to care for our children." The clause beginning with "hoping" is precatory because the children have no legally enforceable interest in the bequest to the decedent's wife. This will expresses the testator's wish, but does not *require* the wife to comply with the testator's preference that she use the property, at least in part, to care for their children. The absence of such a requirement is significant because it precludes the testator's children from bringing suit against the wife (as trustee) to enforce the testator's preference, expressed in the form of precatory language. If the testator's language imposes anything at all, it is merely a moral obligation on his surviving spouse to care for their children.

Benjamin Franklin's will provides another example of precatory language that neither manifests an intention to create a trust nor imposes any enforceable restriction on his daughter's enjoyment of her bequest.

> The king of France's picture, set with four hundred and eight diamonds,[25] I give to my daughter, Sarah Bache, requesting, however, that she would not form any of those diamonds into ornaments either for herself or [her] daughters, and thereby introduce or countenance the expensive, vain, and useless fashion of wearing jewels in this country; and those [diamonds] immediately connected with the picture may be preserved with the same.

Franklin's request clearly manifests his opinion about fashion, but not an intention to impose either a trust relationship or an enforceable restriction on his daughter's use or enjoyment of the picture. As owner of the portrait, free of trust, Franklin's daughter could have had the diamonds set in a necklace to wear on special occasions had she wished to do so. After Franklin's death, his daughter and more remote descendants did, in fact, remove and sell all but one of the many diamonds. In 1959, a descendant of Franklin gave the portrait with its one remaining diamond to the American Philosophical Society, where it remains today in Franklin's adopted hometown of Philadelphia.[26]

Louis Marie Sicardi. Miniature Portrait of Louis XVI, 1784. *American Philosophical Society. Gift of the Richard Bache Duane Family of New York, 2014.*

25. The miniature portrait was encased in a gold locket and was surrounded by two concentric circles of diamonds.
26. See http://www.benfranklin300.org/frankliniana/result.php?id=77&sec=2.

The Restatement (Third) of Trusts §13, comment d, lists the following considerations for ascertaining a settlor's intent to create a trust:

> (1) the specific terms and overall tenor of the words used; (2) the definiteness or indefiniteness of the property involved; (3) the ease or difficulty of ascertaining possible trust purposes and terms, and the specificity or vagueness of the possible beneficiaries and their interests; (4) the interests or motives and the nature and degree of concerns that may reasonably be supposed to have influenced the transferor; (5) the financial situation, dependencies, and expectations of the parties; (6) the transferor's prior conduct, statements, and relationships with respect to possible trust beneficiaries; (7) the personal and any fiduciary relationships between the transferor and the transferee; (8) other dispositions the transferor is making or has made of his or her wealth; and (9) whether the result of construing the disposition as involving a trust or not would be such as a person in the situation of the transferor would be likely to desire.

As the following case demonstrates, however, merely using the words "in trust" may not suffice to manifest intent to create a trust.

In re Estate of Mannara
5 Misc. 3d 556 (N.Y. Surr. Ct. N.Y. Cty. 2004)

EVE PREMINGER, J.

Petitioner, administrator c.t.a.[27] of the will of Lydia Mannara, has asked the Court to construe the sole dispositive provision of the will and find a valid trust.

The entire text of the will is:

> I, Lydia Mannara, hereby give my power of attorney to my friend, Christodoulas Pelaghias, [*sic*] I empower him to make decisions concerning my health, life support and any medical arrangements.
>
> I hereby appoint him Executor of my last will and testament.
>
> I hereby bequeath all of my assets to my two nephews in trust for their education.

The testator executed the will while *in extremis*. A friend who happened to be visiting the testator the day before her death handwrote the will; and although the friend is an attorney, it is clear from the affidavits of attesting witnesses filed in the probate proceeding that the friend served merely as an amanuensis for the testator who was a layperson.

Petitioner, who is testator's sole distributee and father of [testator's] infant nephews, contends the will creates two residuary trusts[,] one for the benefit of each nephew[,] and would have the Court imply certain detailed provisions: that the trustees are petitioner and one Hormoz Lashkari, each of whom may designate his own successor trustee, that the trustees may make discretionary payments for the

27. [An administrator cum testamento annexo (with the will annexed) is appointed as the personal representative of an estate when the will does not appoint an executor or the executor appointed in the will does not accept the appointment or otherwise cannot serve as the personal representative. — EDS.]

benefit of the beneficiary's education, and that each trust shall terminate when the beneficiary attains the age of twenty-two, with the remainder payable to the beneficiary. Petitioner has also provided for the disposition of property in the event a beneficiary dies before attaining the age of twenty-two.

The guardian *ad litem,* appointed to represent the interests of the two nephews, posits that the will creates a "passive" or invalid trust and that the residuary bequest therefore vests directly in her wards.

A trust is a "fiduciary relationship in which one person holds a property interest, subject to an equitable obligation to keep or use that interest for the benefit of another" [citation omitted]. There are four essential elements of a trust: (1) a designated beneficiary; (2) a designated trustee;[28] (3) a fund or other property sufficiently designated or identified to enable title thereto to pass to the trustee; and (4) actual delivery or legal assignment of the property to the trustee, with the intention of passing legal title to such property to the trustee. No formulaic expression is required to create a trust; not even the words "trust" and "trustee" are mandatory. Conversely, mere inclusion of the phrase "in trust for" does not effectuate a trust. What matters is the testator's intent to create a trust relationship. The test is objective rather than subjective, a question of manifestation of intent rather than actual intent.

The instant will lacks fundamental attributes of a trust. It neither designates a trustee, nor confers upon anyone who could be construed to be a trustee the duties of managing the fund. Other than the words "in trust for," there is no language that would sustain or give color to the construction of a trust. The testator does not distinguish income from principal, exhibit any conception of a trust remainder, or otherwise provide for the use and duration of the fund in terms which would limit qualitatively or quantitatively her nephews' interest in the property. Certainly, the testator has not manifested an intent to impose upon a transferee of property the equitable duties of holding such property for the benefit of another.

. . .

In the instant will, use of the term "in trust for" is . . . indiscriminate and inadvertent . . . [and] the reference to the education of testator's nephews [is] an expression of her motivation for the bequest. [The court states that the testator] . . . contemplated a guardianship rather than a trust.

Even if the Court were to find the testator had manifested an intent to create a trust and were to imply a trustee[29] but not fabricate additional terms now proposed by petitioner, it would be unavailing. A trust involving no active duties on the part of the trustee is only a passive trust. By operation of law, title to property bequeathed to the trustee of a passive trust vests in the beneficiary.

There being no valid testamentary trust, the net residuary estate vests in the testator's two nephews.

This decision constitutes the order of the Court.

---

28. [In the absence of a designated trustee, a court may appoint one. — EDS.]

29. [As will be discussed below, a trust will not fail simply because no trustee is appointed in the trust instrument or because the appointed trustee declines to serve. A court with jurisdiction over the trust has authority to appoint a willing trustee. — EDS.]

QUESTIONS

4. What interests were at stake in this case for opposing parties: the father of the testator's two nephews (who argued that the holographic will created valid trusts) and the guardian ad litem (who represented the minor children and argued that the will left the children property outright and free of trust)?

   ANSWER. It is difficult to know for certain but consider what would happen if the father had prevailed in court. The father extrapolated specific terms he believed were implied by the testator's will and asked the court to be appointed as a co-trustee of the trusts for his children. Assuming the father had the best interests of his children in mind, the father assumed that establishing the trusts would be the most efficient means of managing the bequeathed assets and applying them for the educational benefit of the children. Although trustees are entitled to compensation for their service as fiduciaries, often in close family circumstances trustees serve without compensation. Here, however, the guardian ad litem prevailed and the property passed to the infant beneficiaries outright under the will. The minor children do not have the capacity to own property, so the property must be administered for the children by a conservator or guardian. Depending on the laws of the jurisdiction, court approval may be necessary for the conservator's or guardian's decisions as to investments, expenditures, compensation, etc. Those court proceedings are expensive and sometimes generate greater benefits for the conservator or guardian (and his or her attorneys) than for the wards.

PROBLEM III

What do you think the testator in *Mannara* intended by her words, "to my two nephews in trust for their education"? Do you agree with the court's assessment that the language of the holographic will did not impose any active duties on a trustee?

PROBLEM IV

A testator's will contains the following language:

> I give all of my property and estate to my father, Hans Beducker, if he survives me, and if he does not survive me, I give all of my property and estate to my step-mother, Molly Beducker, if she shall survive me. If either my father or my step-mother survive me, I give nothing to my three children, namely: Hans Beducker III, Albertus Beducker, and Ashley Beducker, or to any descendant of any child who shall not survive me. I make this provision for the reason that I feel confident that any property which either my father or my step-mother receive from my estate will be used in the best interests of my children as my father or step-mother may determine in their exclusive discretion.

The testator died one month ago. The testator's father predeceased him, but the testator was survived by his stepmother. The testator's children consult with you and ask if their father's will creates a trust for their benefit. What do you tell them?

QUESTIONS

5. What is the legal effect of the following language in a donative instrument (assume that the property X has been delivered and accepted by person A):
   A. I give X to A.
   B. I give X to A with the hope that A will distribute X to my friends.
   C. I give X to my trustees to hold for the benefit of A upon the following terms and conditions . . .

ANSWER. a. This language recites an outright gift.

b. This language recites an outright gift with additional precatory language ("with the hope . . ."). A is under no legal obligation to distribute any of X to the donor's friends.

c. This language creates a trust of property X, which will be held by trustees for the benefit of A as provided by the trust instrument.

One final comment on precatory language: An absolute gift or devise accompanied by precatory language is, in some cases, legally enforceable and deemed to impose trust-like duties on the recipient. Consider, for example, the will of Marilyn Monroe, which contains the following bequest:

> I give and bequeath all of my personal effects and clothing to LEE STRASBERG, or if he should predecease me, then to my Executor hereinafter named, it being my desire that he distribute these, in his sole discretion, among my friends, colleagues and those to whom I am devoted.

Lee Strasberg, Monroe's acting coach, survived, but contrary to Monroe's wish, he kept all of her personal effects and clothing for himself and, at his death, that property passed to Strasberg's widow. Strasberg may have had a moral obligation in accepting the bequest to follow Monroe's "desire," but he was under no legal obligation to do so because the language was precatory rather than mandatory. However, what if Strasberg had predeceased Monroe? What would have happened to the bequest? The devise to Strasberg would have lapsed and, according to Monroe's will, the property would have passed to the executor. The executor's status as devisee is significant because a bequest accompanied by precatory language to a personal representative in his or her fiduciary capacity creates a "power coupled with a trust." Under these circumstances, a personal representative holds gifted property under rules applicable to trusts and the precatory language becomes legally binding to prevent the personal representative, whose role is that of fiduciary rather than beneficiary, from being unjustly enriched. In Monroe's case, however, a court could not enforce her preference to distribute personal property to her "devoted" "friends" because the sole criterion for membership in a class gift to Monroe's friends fails to identify an ascertainable class of beneficiaries.[30] That is, how could a court ascertain Monroe's friends without a more specific definition of the term?

---

30. We discuss the requirement of an ascertainable beneficiary for a valid private trust later in this chapter.

8.3.2 Trust Property

A trust must generally hold some property, known as the trust *corpus* or *res*, to form a valid trust. Trust property must be in existence and ascertainable when the trust is created. Restatement (Third) of Trusts §2, comment i. If there is no trust property (a problem known as a *dry trust*), there are no duties for the trustee to perform and the trust will fail. The trust corpus can consist of any interest in property, so long as the property is not merely the settlor's hope or expectancy that he or she will come to own the property in the future.

Uniform Trust Code
§103 Definitions

"Property" means anything that may be the subject of ownership, whether real or personal, legal or equitable, or any interest therein.

Restatement (Third) of Trusts
§40 Any Property May Be Trust Property

Subject to [the rule invalidating unlawful provisions], a trustee may hold in trust any interest in any type of property.

Restatement (Third) of Property: Wills & Other Donative Transfers
§41 Expectancies; Nonexistent Property Interests

An expectation or hope of receiving property in the future, or an interest that has not come into existence or has ceased to exist, cannot be held in trust.

Trust property must be sufficiently and specifically identified in the trust instrument. This requirement enables the trustees to definitively ascertain the property under their care and for which they will be held responsible upon breaching a fiduciary duty. For example, a settlor could create a trust consisting of "my entire art collection" or just a few specifically identified pieces, but the settlor could not create a valid trust consisting of "some of my art collection" because it would be unclear which pieces belong to the trustees.

Trust property, like any other gift, must generally be delivered to the trustee. Physical delivery is not always possible, but the transfer of the trust property from the settlor to the trustee must be evident. Typically, delivery is symbolic: It is recited in the trust instrument, which is given to the trustee. For any property subject to the Statute of Frauds, an effective transfer to the trustee requires a signed writing manifesting the settlor's intention and reasonably identifying the trust property, the beneficiaries, and the purposes of the trust. Restatement (Third) of Trusts §22(1). For real property, deeds recording the transfer of ownership from the settlor to the trustee satisfy the delivery requirement. Similarly, personal property can be transferred to the trustee by symbolic delivery, such as a description of particulars recited in the trust instrument delivered to the trustee. For intangible personal property, such as bank or securities accounts, delivery is accomplished by retitling the accounts from the settlor's name to the name of the trustee(s). A typical title to such an account would appear as, "Trustees of the [XYZ] Trust u/d/t[31] dated [DATE]" or "John Doe, Trustee, of the [XYZ] Trust u/d/t dated [DATE]."

An exception to the delivery requirement is a declaration of trust in which the settlor recites that she holds property currently in her possession in trust for the benefit of the beneficiaries. In that situation, delivery from the settlor to the settlor-trustee is unnecessary because the settlor already holds the property. However, to document the settlor's voluntary self-imposition of fiduciary duties and, therefore, the settlor's intent to create a trust, it is better practice to retitle the property from the name of the settlor to the name of the settlor *as trustee*. For example, Keiji has a $50,000 certificate of deposit (CD) titled in his name. He tells his daughter, Noriko, that he now holds the CD in trust solely for her benefit. Keiji instructs his bank to reissue the CD in the name of "Keiji, as Trustee for Noriko." The retitling of the CD provides clear and convincing evidence that Keiji has created a valid oral trust and now holds the CD for Noriko's benefit.[32]

The following case illustrates the significance of the trust property requirement.

Cate-Schweyen v. Cate
303 Mont. 232 (2000)

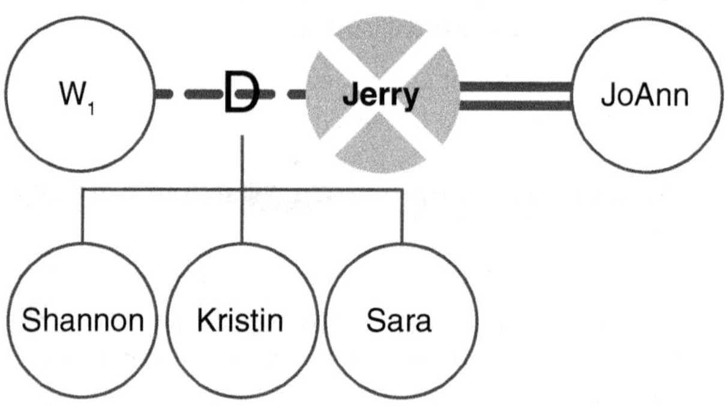

Justice James C. Nelson.

¶1 This is an appeal from an Order and Rationale . . . denying Personal Representative JoAnn Cate's (JoAnn) motion for summary judgment and granting a motion for summary judgment in favor of Shannon Cate-Schweyen, individually, and as Conservator of Sara Cate, a minor (collectively referred to herein as Shannon). The Order provided that JoAnn would convey various assets to Shannon and take other actions with respect thereto, and also awarded Shannon her costs.

¶2 We reverse and remand for further proceedings consistent with this opinion.

31. "u/d/t" is an abbreviation for "under deed of trust."

32. See In re Estate of Zukerman, 218 Ill. App. 3d 325 (1991). For examples of ineffective inter vivos transfers, see Restatement (Third) of Trusts §16.

¶3 On appeal, JoAnn raises the following [issue]:[33]

Whether the District Court erred in finding that the 1988 document represents a testamentary trust as opposed to an *inter vivos* trust which failed for lack of delivery of the document or the trust property to the trustee.

. . .

FACTUAL AND PROCEDURAL BACKGROUND

¶4 The focus of this controversy is a handwritten document drafted by Jerome J. Cate (Jerry), a practicing attorney in Montana for nearly 30 years and now deceased, entitled "Irrevocable Trust Reserving Income For Life." The document was signed by Jerry and dated January 2, 1988. Jerry died intestate on April 4, 1995.

¶5 The trust document purported to "sell, assign and convey" various mineral interests, which Jerry had inherited from his mother and her brother, to a trust for the benefit of his daughters from his first marriage, Shannon, Kristin, and Sara, with Shannon serving as trustee. Jerry reserved a life interest for himself, and then, upon his death, the three daughters would receive a term of years interest for 20 years, and then the corpus would be distributed outright to the daughters or their heirs pursuant to a "per stirpes" declaration. The trust document apparently was drafted by Jerry in anticipation of his remarriage to the Appellant, JoAnn, in February of 1988. The document reflects this, providing that "bearing in mind specifically that I intend to marry again on the 14th of February, 1988, [I] do hereby sell, assign and convey. . . ." The undisputed facts show that Jerry never transferred or conveyed the named mineral interests to the trust or otherwise delivered the trust property to Shannon, the named trustee.

¶6 At the time of his death, JoAnn, in her capacity as personal representative of Jerry's estate, refused to convey the alleged trust property upon the request of the daughters. Consequently, Shannon . . . request[ed] that the District Court declare that either an express or resulting trust in the mineral interests existed. (The eldest daughter, Kristin, is not a party to this action.) At that time, the handwritten document had not been located; rather, a 1993 bill of sale document executed by Jerry indicated the existence of the trust.

¶7 The 1993 bill of sale . . . provided: "This Bill of Sale and Assignment does not include any mineral interests owned by Jerome J. Cate, a/k/a Jerry Joseph Cate, which have heretofore been placed in trust for the benefit of Shannon and Sara Cate." Kristin's name was apparently omitted from this reference due to a rift between her and Jerry. Thus, Shannon pursued the legal theory that the referenced trust was testamentary in nature, and therefore JoAnn, as personal representative of Shannon's father's estate, must fund the testamentary trust with the mineral interests owned by Jerry at the time of his death.

---

33. [This case presents a succinct discussion of the distinctions between an inter vivos and a testamentary trust as a necessary component of the principal issue addressed in the edited form of this opinion. We have omitted the second issue the Montana Supreme Court addressed, whether either of two non-trust equitable doctrines, a resulting trust and a constructive trust, applies to the facts presented. We discuss those doctrines in different contexts in Chapter 9. — Eds.]

¶8 Once the 1988 trust document was found, Shannon did not alter her legal theory, maintaining that the handwritten trust document was testamentary as well.

¶9 In response to Shannon's petition, JoAnn contended that the handwritten document was not a valid testamentary trust. She argued that the document intended to create an *inter vivos* trust, which Jerry never executed by conveying or otherwise transferring the interests to the trust or Shannon [in her capacity as trustee]. Therefore, according to JoAnn, the handwritten trust document is unenforceable, and the identified mineral interests should be included within Jerry's estate.

¶10 Both parties moved for summary judgment. Following a July 29, 1998 hearing, the District Court denied JoAnn's motion for summary judgment and granted summary judgment in favor of Shannon.

¶11 The District Court concluded that to qualify as a testamentary disposition, the document need only comply with Montana's statutory requirements for a will. The court concluded that the handwritten trust document was testamentary. The court stated that "[t]he fact that Decedent chose to reserve income for life when he created the trust is not inconsistent with an intention to create a testamentary disposition." The court further concluded that the "evidence is clear, convincing and overwhelming that the intent of Decedent Jerome J. Cate was to establish a testamentary trust with his daughters to be the beneficiaries thereof." The court also ruled that "Respondent's contention that the instrument is a failed attempt to create an *inter vivos* transfer of the property is belied by the holographic nature of the instrument."

. . .

¶13 JoAnn appealed.

STANDARD OF REVIEW

¶14 This Court reviews an order granting summary judgment *de novo*. . . .

¶15 Here, no material facts remain in dispute. Rather, both parties contend that they are, respectively, entitled to judgment as a matter of law, in light of the District Court's conclusion that the trust document in question was testamentary, rather than *inter vivos.* As with the judicial interpretation and construction of any instrument, the question of whether any particular language creates an express trust, given the circumstances under which the trust was executed, is a question of law for the court to decide. Thus, accepting the facts found by the District Court, we will proceed to determine if either party was entitled to judgment as a matter of law.

DISCUSSION

Whether the District Court erred in finding that the 1988 document represents a testamentary trust as opposed to an inter vivos trust which failed for lack of delivery of the document [or] the trust property to the trustee.

¶16 JoAnn argues that the trust document in dispute is *inter vivos,* rather than testamentary, and is therefore unenforceable because no property was ever transferred or conveyed to it by her deceased husband, Jerry, as required by law. Thus, the named trust property should remain in Jerry's estate. . . .

¶17 Shannon contends that the District Court's conclusion that the trust document was testamentary is correct, and therefore the trust is valid because her father intended that the trust would remain "dry" until his death at which time his estate would transfer the mineral interests. . . .

¶18 The theories set forth by both parties comport with statutory law governing creation of trusts in Montana. Under §72-33-203, MCA, a trust is created "only if there is trust property." Under §72-33-201(2), MCA, a valid *inter vivos* trust requires that the owner transfer the subject property to a trustee during the owner's lifetime. In contrast, under subsection (3), a valid trust may be created when the property is identified as a "testamentary transfer" to a trustee. Under §72-33-216, MCA, a court may exercise its equitable powers and impose a "resulting trust" to fulfill the manifest intent of the trustor if the trust fails to fulfill this intent.

¶19 Further, Montana's statutory requirements generally comport with the Restatement (Second) of Trusts (1959), which often has been relied on by this Court, and has been presented as persuasive authority by the parties here.

¶20 As a preliminary matter, we shall first dispense with the fundamentally flawed argument that the trust document at issue was testamentary. We conclude that as a matter of law the trust document clearly and convincingly expresses an intent to create an *inter vivos* trust that would take effect during Jerry's lifetime, notwithstanding whatever alleged misunderstandings or intentions that he may have expressed or exercised at a later date.

¶21 Our examination of the construction of the trust in question here is guided by several steadfast rules. . . . First, we must seek out the trustor's "intent," so far as possible. Second, we must look to the language of the trust agreement itself to ascertain this intent. Third, the words used in the instrument are to be taken in their ordinary and grammatical sense unless a clear intention to use them in another sense can be ascertained. Finally, the burden of proof to establish the existence of a trust— or in this case a particular "kind" of trust— is upon the party who claims it, and must be founded on evidence which is unmistakable, clear, satisfactory, and convincing.

¶22 Removing superfluous verbiage, the handwritten document, identified as an "Irrevocable Trust Reserving Income For Life" provides:

> I Jerome J. Cate . . . do hereby sell, assign and convey all of my oil gas and mineral interests . . . to my daughter, Shannon Cate, to hold in trust for her benefit and the benefit of her sister Kristin Cate and her sister Sara Cate, as Shannon in her sole discretion shall see fit, for a period of time twenty years subsequent to the date of my death, at which time she shall distribute those mineral interests in equal shares . . . reserving, however, to myself the income from this trust for my lifetime.

¶23 Shannon argues at length that the foregoing writing technically satisfies statutory requirements for a holographic will, and is therefore "testamentary."

¶24 A testamentary trust, however, not only must comply with the statutory requirements for a will, but also must take effect "only upon the testator's death."

. . .

¶26 Suffice to say, to construe the foregoing document as "testamentary" would require an alchemist's crucible. While not nimbly drafted, the document nevertheless expresses a clear and convincing intent that it would take effect *inter vivos*, or during Jerry's lifetime. Rather than anticipating a future testamentary transfer by such common language as "give, devise, and bequeath," the transfer is that of an ordinary, present conveyance: "I . . . do hereby sell, assign and convey. . . . " Further, there is no preceding or subsequent qualification of this transfer language by other language such as "upon my death" or "when I die" or "in the event of my death." Rather, the "twenty years subsequent to the date of my death" language which appears later merely serves as a fixed termination date—rather than a commencement date—for the trust itself. Although Jerry did in fact retain legal title over the trust property, he did not name himself as trustee; rather, this duty is expressly accorded to his daughter, Shannon, meaning the document expresses a clear intent that Jerry planned to divest himself of legal title over the named trust property and thereby transfer a present interest. In turn, the "income from this trust for my lifetime" language indicates that the trust would come into existence during Jerry's lifetime, and he would become the trust's first beneficiary. Finally, the document itself is identified as "irrevocable," which in light of the accompanying language indicates an unmistakable intent to pass legal title to the trust during Jerry's lifetime, and thereby remove the property from his estate.

¶27 Taken as a whole, the evidence that the trust document is testamentary does not rise to the level of being unmistakable, clear, satisfactory, or convincing. Rather, the opposite is true: the trust document convincingly displays all the attributes of an *inter vivos* transaction that the trustor intended would take place at the time the document was drafted or soon thereafter. We therefore hold that the District Court erred in concluding that Jerry Cate's handwritten trust document was testamentary.

¶28 [W]e next turn to the issue of "delivery" to determine whether the trust in question was ever made legally effective, or instead remained a "phantom" or "dry" trust and therefore unenforceable.

¶29 This Court has concluded that, under the common law, in order to establish an *inter vivos* trust, there must be a transfer of property. We quoted from the Restatement of Trusts that "if the owner of property makes a conveyance *inter vivos* of the property to another person to be held by him in trust for a third person and the conveyance is not effective to transfer the property, no trust of the property is created." *See also* Am. Jur. 2d, *Trusts* §49 (1992) (stating general rule that a separation of legal title and equitable ownership of the trust property is necessary to the formation of an express trust); Am. Jur. 2d, *Trusts* §52 (1992) (stating general rule that in order to create a valid trust, there must be an actual conveyance or transfer of property).

¶30 The undisputed facts clearly reveal that Jerry never delivered, or conveyed, or otherwise attempted to transfer the identified trust property to the named trustee, his daughter Shannon, or to the trust itself with or without her knowledge.

¶31 Further, the trust document itself is insufficient to serve as an instrument of conveyance. Although the property is clearly identified in the handwritten document, we concluded under . . . similar circumstances [in an earlier case] that in order for a trust document to serve as an instrument of conveyance, the person executing the trust document must subsequently redeliver, confirm, ratify, or adopt the transfer.

¶32 The reasons for Jerry's omissions, as JoAnn indicates in her brief, are known only to Jerry. That the undisputed facts clearly show that Jerry intended to create some form of a trust that would benefit only his three daughters unfortunately does not alter the fact that he never took the affirmative legal steps necessary for the trust to become enforceable as either a testamentary or *inter vivos* trust.

. . .

¶37 Accordingly, we conclude that the *inter vivos* trust document at issue failed due to the lack of a transfer of property to the trust during Jerry Cate's lifetime, and therefore no enforceable trust existed. Based on this conclusion, we hold that the District Court erred when it determined that Shannon was entitled to judgment as a matter of law, and denied JoAnn's motion for summary judgment.

¶38 This matter is reversed and remanded for further proceedings consistent with this opinion.

KARLA M. GRAY, WILLIAM E. HUNT, and TERRY N. TRIEWEILER, JJ., concur.

Chief Justice J.A. TURNAGE, dissenting.

¶39 I respectfully dissent from the majority opinion.

¶40 The District Court concluded that the handwritten trust document executed by Jerome Cate met the requirements of the Montana Statute of Wills and would be valid as a holographic will. It further concluded that JoAnn Cate had produced no persuasive authority that an otherwise valid testamentary disposition which was never revoked is invalid simply because the testator chose to designate the disposition as "irrevocable."

¶41 Under long-settled rules of construction of testamentary instruments, including trusts, the testator's intent controls. On this record, Jerome Cate's intent is crystal clear — to create a testamentary trust for his daughters. The reason for that intent is also clear — to pass on to his blood descendants mineral interests which he himself had inherited from his mother and her brother as part of his family legacy. If the majority cannot discern that intent, then their vision is fogged.

¶42 I would affirm the decision of the District Court.

. . .

QUESTIONS

6. Why did Jerome Cate include in the putative trust document the statement, "bearing in mind specifically that I intend to marry again on the 14th of February, 1988 . . ."?

   ANSWER. Although only Mr. Cate knew for certain why he included that language, we assume he did so to prevent the doctrine of pretermission from applying to the instrument. Recall that, under pretermission, a spouse omitted from a will executed before the marriage is entitled to an intestate share of the decedent's probate estate (subject to exceptions and limitations described in Chapter 7). Since, in most jurisdictions, pretermission applies only to wills and not to inter vivos trusts, perhaps implicitly in Mr. Cate's inclusion of this language is his belief that he was making a will, although the court concluded otherwise.

7. Was the trial court judge incorrect in stating that the "evidence is clear, convincing and overwhelming that the intent of Decedent Jerome J. Cate was to establish a testamentary trust with his daughters to be the beneficiaries thereof"?

   ANSWER. No. The trial court's finding is correct under the facts presented but mere intent to establish a testamentary trust is not sufficient to create such a trust. Mr. Cate never took the actions required to transform his intent into a legally effective donative transfer. As the Montana Supreme Court states in its opinion, "[t]hat the undisputed facts clearly show that Jerry intended to create some form of a trust . . . unfortunately does not alter the fact that he never took the affirmative legal steps necessary for the trust to become enforceable as either a testamentary or inter vivos trust." Mr. Cate expressed intent to create a trust during life but never delivered the trust property or the trust instrument to the trustee, his daughter Shannon.

8. Is Justice Turnage's dissent convincing? If so, why? If not, why not?

   ANSWER. Justice Turnage's dissent offers a compelling case to apply the doctrine of reformation. If it was indeed "crystal clear" that Mr. Cate intended his handwritten document to constitute a will that created a testamentary trust and the words of Mr. Cate's document failed to articulate that intent properly, why not reform the words of the instrument to conform the language to Mr. Cate's actual intent? Had the court been willing to apply reformation to correct what Justice Turnage implies was mistaken language, how would the document in question be rewritten?

There is an important and well-recognized exception to the requirement of trust property as necessary for a valid trust: a dry inter vivos trust to be funded upon the settlor's death by a "pour-over will." In this estate planning technique, the testator uses the inter vivos trust as the primary donative instrument and the testator's will names the trustees as the beneficiaries of the testator's probate estate. Thus, the testator's probate property is said to "pour over" into the trust. In this context, a testator may create a valid inter vivos revocable trust without a trust res. The requirement of a trust corpus, for these purposes, is satisfied by the trustee's entitlement to inherit property under the testator's will. A post-mortem transfer of the testator's probate property under the pour-over will "funds" the trust, bringing it fully into existence. This practice is expressly authorized under the

Uniform Testamentary Additions to Trusts Act and the UTC.[34] The use of trusts in conjunction with pour-over wills is further discussed below in Chapter 10.

8.3.3 Deeds and Declarations of Trusts

The UTC does not require a written instrument (or, for that matter, a *signed or attested* writing) to create a valid trust, but in practice, oral trusts are rare (for good reason!).[35] Trusts almost always are documented in writing under a declaration or deed of trust. Because any trust relationship established without a writing is suspect, the existence of an oral trust must be proven by clear and convincing evidence.

Uniform Trust Code
§407 Evidence of Oral Trust

Except as required by a statute other than this [Code], a trust need not be evidenced by a trust instrument, but the creation of an oral trust and its terms may be established only by clear and convincing evidence.

Restatement (Third) of Trusts
§20 Validity of Oral Inter Vivos Trusts

Except as required by a statute of frauds, a writing is not necessary to create an enforceable inter vivos trust, whether by declaration, by transfer to another as trustee, or by contract.

Oral trusts can be formed in real property only if allowed by state law.[36] As with written trusts, no specific language is required to form an oral trust — another reason

---

34. See Restatement (Third) of Trusts §19. "Pour-Over" Dispositions by Will, comment a(3):

> In addition to the usual case of a pour-over to an existing inter vivos trust [i.e., an inter vivos trust holding trust property], this Section is also concerned with situations in which the testamentary "pour-over" disposition is to provide the initial funding for, *and thereby to create upon the testator's death*, a trust the terms of which are set out in an independent writing. . . . [Italics added.]

Compare Restatement (Third) of Property: Wills & Other Donative Transfers §3.8, Pour-Over Devises:

> (a) A "pour-over" devise is a provision in a will that (i) adds property to an inter vivos trust or *(ii) funds a trust that was not funded during the testator's lifetime but whose terms are in a trust instrument that was executed during the testator's lifetime.* [Italics added.]
>
> (b) A pour-over devise may be validated by statute, by incorporation by reference, or by independent significance.

See also UPC §2-511. Uniform Testamentary Additions to Trusts Act.

35. In In re Estate of Fournier, 902 A.2d 852 (Me. 2006), the Maine Supreme Court affirmed the trial court's enforcement of an oral trust based on clear and convincing evidence drawn primarily from witness testimony, but after the parties discovered a handwritten note evidencing the settlor's contrary intent, the parties returned to court for a new trial. In this second proceeding, the court found that the settlor did not intend the terms of the oral trust to be enforced (on the basis of clear and convincing evidence!) in the prior proceeding. In re Estate of Fournier, 966 A.2d 855 (Me. 2009).

36. See, e.g., Ellis v. Vespoint, 102 N.C. App. 739, 741 (1991) ("Because North Carolina has never adopted the Seventh Section of the English Statute of Frauds which requires all trusts in land to be manifested in writing, real property may be made the subject of parol trusts.") (internal quotation marks and citations omitted); but see In re Estate of Gates, 876 So. 2d 1059, 1063 (Miss. Ct. App. 2004) ("An express trust may be oral, but only if real property is not involved. If the corpus of the purported trust estate consists both of real and personal property, an express oral trust is ineffective to impose a trust on either.").

courts apply the clear and convincing standard. As one court stated, to find a valid oral trust:

> The acts or words relied upon must be so unequivocal as to lead to but one conclusion, and if the evidence is doubtful or capable of reasonable explanation upon any other theory, it is not sufficient to establish an oral express trust. . . . Yet, no particular form of words is necessary to create a trust, when the writing makes clear the existence of a trust. Wherever an intention to create a trust can be fairly collected from the language of the instrument and the terms employed, such intention will be supported by the courts.

In re Estate of Zukerman, 218 Ill. App. 3d 325, 330 (1991). Some jurisdictions, by contrast, do not recognize oral trusts.[37]

The preceding case, *Cate-Schweyen v. Cate,* demonstrates that a trust document may be handwritten: There, the putative trust failed for lack of a trust corpus; it did not fail as a trust because the instrument was handwritten. Unlike wills, which generally require witness attestation (unless handwritten), there is no equivalent attestation requirement for trusts.

8.3.4 Trust Beneficiaries

The beneficiary, sometimes referred to as the *cestui* or *cestui que trust,* is the person or entity for whose benefit the trustee holds, manages, and administers the trust property. A beneficiary is an absolute necessity for a valid trust. Without at least one beneficiary, there is no one for whom the trustee holds the trust property and no one to enforce the fiduciary duties of trusteeship. The requirement of a trust beneficiary is so central to the concept of the trust relationship that UTC §404 states expressly that "[a] trust and its terms must be for the benefit of its beneficiaries."

For ***private*** trusts, the beneficiary may be a person (e.g., "my sister Rachel"), an entity ("the XYZ association"), or an identifiable class (e.g., "my children"). There may be one or more beneficiaries and, in the case of multiple beneficiaries, the beneficial interests may be concurrent or successive. A settlor of a trust may also be a beneficiary, as is usually the case in revocable inter vivos trusts. So, too, a trustee of a trust can be a beneficiary, provided there is at least one additional co-trustee or at least one other beneficiary. Restatement (Third) of Trusts §43, comment a. However, a predeceased person cannot be a beneficiary at the time the trust is created. *Id.* §44, comment d.

The settlor does not need to articulate the individual identity of each beneficiary nor must each beneficiary be in existence when creating the trust. A trust created for the

37. See, e.g., N.Y. EST. POWERS & TRUSTS LAW §7-1.17 (requiring all inter vivos trusts to be in writing and executed with the formalities of a conveyance of real property or the formalities of will execution); GA. CODE ANN. §53-12-20(a) ("An express trust shall be created in writing and signed by the settlor or an agent for the settlor acting under a power of attorney containing express authorization."); N.J. STAT. §3B:31-18 (all three methods of creating a trust require a written instrument).

benefit of a class of beneficiaries, for example, does not typically identify the individual class members by name. This is permissible so long as the settlor has identified beneficiaries who are *ascertainable* or capable of becoming ascertainable. UTC §402(b) ("A beneficiary is definite if the beneficiary can be ascertained now or in the future, subject to any applicable rule against perpetuities.").

Restatement (Third) of Trusts
§44 Definite-Beneficiary Requirement

A trust is not created, or if created will not continue, unless the terms of the trust provide a beneficiary who is ascertainable at the time or who may later become ascertainable within the period and terms of the rule against perpetuities.

To understand the ascertainable definite beneficiary requirement, consider the provision of James Boyer's will reproduced below. Mr. Boyer, who died at the age of 91, made a will that purported to establish a trust consisting of his entire probate estate, with a named individual, George Morrison, to serve as trustee:

> SECOND: I give, devise and bequeath all of my estate and property, real, personal and mixed, wheresoever situated, of which I may be possessed, or to which I may be entitled at the time of my death, to my Trustee, George A. Morrison, in Trust.
>
> THIRD: I direct my Trustee to distribute all of my estate according to my instructions which I may give to him from time to time in my own handwriting or otherwise, but nonetheless signed or initialed by me. In the event, by whatever circumstance, I fail to leave such instructions to my Trustee, then I direct my Trustee to distribute my estate according to his discretion, bearing in mind the many conversations we have had together in which I have named those who are the objects of my generosity.

Matter of Estate of Boyer, 117 N.M. 74, 76 (1994). The New Mexico Supreme Court held that Article Third did not establish an ascertainable class of beneficiaries and, accordingly, Mr. Boyer did not create a valid trust:

> The elements of a valid trust include . . . a sufficiently ascertainable beneficiary or beneficiaries. . . . Because the identity of the persons intended to be "the objects of [the decedent's] generosity" are not capable of reasonably being ascertained, we agree with the trial court that the provisions of the decedent's will attempting to create a testamentary trust were not effective to establish an express trust.
>
> . . .
>
> The provisions of the Second and Third Articles of the decedent's will specified that the beneficiaries of his estate were to be selected by Morrison. However, the identity of the individuals eligible to be selected as beneficiaries were not capable of being drawn from any specifically identifiable class or category specified by the decedent. Under this posture the attempted trust was unenforceable.

Id. at 78-79. The differing rules for beneficiaries of *charitable* trusts are treated later in this chapter.

8.3.5 Trustees

A trustee is an individual or corporate person who holds legal title to the trust corpus. The trustee is responsible for carrying out the terms of the trust, managing trust assets, and distributing property to beneficiaries as directed by the settlor.[38] The trustee's obligations with respect to the trust commence upon acceptance of the trusteeship. UTC §801 ("Upon acceptance of a trusteeship, the trustee shall administer the trust in good faith, in accordance with its terms and purposes and the interests of the beneficiaries, and in accordance with this [Code].").

Although most trust instruments appoint a trustee—and usually one or more successor trustees—if no trustee is named (or if the designated trustee cannot or will not serve) *a trust will not fail for lack of a trustee.* Restatement (Third) of Trusts §31. If the trust instrument does not appoint a trustee or there is a vacancy in the office of trustee, a court having jurisdiction over the trust will appoint a willing trustee if one can be found.[39] Alternatively, a trust may provide instructions or procedures for the selection of a trustee or successor trustee. The court also has equitable powers to appoint a trustee "whenever the court considers the appointment necessary for the administration of the trust." UTC §704(c).

Any individual who has the capacity to take and hold property as a true owner has the capacity to serve as a trustee. Restatement (Third) of Trusts §32. A corporation can serve as trustee, but only if the property is transferred to the corporation in trust "for a purpose germane to the purposes for which the corporation is created." *Id.* §33, comment b. Indeed, banks and trust companies often serve as a corporate trustee either as sole trustee or as a co-trustee with one or more individual co-trustees.

Service as a trustee of an express trust is voluntary: It cannot be imposed. A person who is named in a trust may decline to accept a trusteeship. Restatement (Third) of Trusts §35. However, one who has agreed to serve as trustee but subsequently wants to resign must do so "properly" by (a) complying with the term provided in the trust document, (b) obtaining consent of all beneficiaries, or (c) obtaining court approval. *Id.* §36.

Trustees are entitled to compensation. The amount of compensation is either set forth in the trust instrument, in which case a trustee's compensation generally is limited to that amount, or is subject to a legal standard of reasonableness under the circumstances. Of course, what is reasonable can be a matter of dispute.

---

38. UTC Article 7 addresses issues relating to the "Office of Trustee." In the General Comment to Article 7, the editors note that all of its provisions are default rules with one exception: a court's authority to order a trustee to post a bond. Other than that exception, a settlor may modify the default positions taken in the UTC.

39. However, a court will not appoint a trustee upon the vacancy of one trustee position if the trust provides for co-trustees and there is at least one remaining trustee in office. UTC §704(b).

In re Estate of Rauschenberg
20th Judicial Cir. Ct., Lee Cty., Fla.
Case No.: 08-CP-2479 (Aug. 1, 2014)

ORDER GRANTING TRUSTEES' FEES

THIS CAUSE comes before the Court following a trial to determine the reasonable trustees' fees for the Trustees of the Robert Rauschenberg Revocable Trust (Trust). Having reviewed testimony and evidence presented at trial, the case file, and the applicable law, and having heard argument by the parties, the Court finds as follows:

Robert Rauschenberg

1. Robert Rauschenberg was born on October 22, 1925, in Port Arthur, Texas. He died on May 12, 2008, at the age of 82 at his home on Captiva Island, Florida. Rauschenberg was an iconic, highly respected, prolific artist, producing pieces in a variety of formats, including painting, photographs, silkscreening, collage, and what he called combines — combinations of painting and sculpture, using found materials. He also provided costumes and set designs for various performances. The prominence of Rauschenberg as an artist has been compared to that of artists such as Picasso. His artwork has been exhibited, and sought after by museums and galleries for exhibition, all over the world. Robert Rauschenberg is regarded as one of the most influential American artists and influential forces in Twentieth Century art.

2. Robert Rauschenberg was well known for his philanthropy. He donated artwork to organizations and causes he supported. He created Change, Inc., an organization that provided grants to artists. He founded the Rauschenberg Overseas Culture Interchange to foster art in countries around the world, initiating cross-border communication and promoting peace. One of Rauschenberg's long term goals was the creation of the Robert Rauschenberg Foundation (Foundation), to continue his philanthropic efforts after his death.

Procedural Background

3. Rauschenberg appointed . . . Darryl Pottorf, Bennet Grutman, and Bill Goldston, [as co-trustees of his revocable trust] in the 1990s, and withdrew himself as a trustee in 2005.

4. After his death on May 12, 2008, a Petition for Administration of his estate was filed on September 5, 2008. The will devised the residuary estate to the Trust.[40] The Trust assets at the time of Rauschenberg's death were valued at $605,645,595.00. Upon disbursement to the Foundation in 2012, the Trust assets were valued at approximately $2,179,000,000.00.

40. [The remainder of the trust's assets, after distribution of several relatively small gifts to individuals, was directed to be distributed to the Foundation. — EDS.]

5. The Foundation filed a "Petition to Determine Trustees' Fees" on June 21, 2011.

. . .

7. The parties attended voluntary mediation on January 26, 2012, but were unable to reach a resolution. The parties attended court-ordered mediation on October 1, 2013, and were unable to reach a settlement.

8. After a lengthy period of discovery, along with a number of pre-trial motions and hearings, trial was held on the issue of a reasonable trustees' fee. . . . The Court heard testimony, in person and through deposition, of 21 witnesses, and over 300 exhibits were admitted.

Trustees' Argument

9. The Trustees argued that the method to be used to determine their reasonable fee should be a consideration of the factors set forth in West Coast Hospital Association v. Fla. National Bank of Jacksonville, 100 So. 2d 807, 811 (Fla. 1958). Those factors are:

a. The amount of the capital and income received and disbursed by the trustee;
b. The wages or salary customarily granted to agents or servants for performing like work in the community;
c. The success or failure of the administration of the trustee;
d. Any unusual skill or experience which the trustee in question may have brought to his work;
e. The fidelity or disloyalty displayed by the trustee;
f. The amount of risk and responsibility assumed;
g. The time consumed in carrying out the trust;
h. The custom in the community as to allowances to trustees by settlors or courts and as to charges exacted by trust companies and banks;
i. The character of the work done in the course of administration, whether routine or involving skill and judgment;
j. Any estimate which the trustee has given of the value of his own services; and
k. Payments made by the cestuis to the trustee and intended to be applied toward his compensation.

10. The Trustees argued, and their experts opined, that based on the *West Coast* factors, a fee between $51,000,000.00 to $55,000,000.00 was reasonable.

Foundation's Argument

11. The Foundation argued that the federal lodestar method should be used to determine the reasonable fee for the Trustees. See Florida Patient's Compensation Fund v. Rowe, 472 So. 2d 1145 (Fla. 1985). The Foundation's experts opined that under this analysis, the Trustees would be entitled to a total of $375,000.00 for all three Trustees.

. . .

Analysis

West Coast versus Lodestar Analysis

12. The lodestar method has been used for attorneys' fees and fees in bankruptcy cases. The Foundation argued that recent case law held that the lodestar method could be used to determine reasonable fees for guardians or personal representatives, and thus should also be applied to other fiduciaries such as trustees. However, no authority was presented to the Court which applied the lodestar standard to trustee fees. The Court finds that there is no precedent for use of the lodestar analysis to determine a reasonable fee for trustees, and further finds that use of the lodestar analysis would be unreasonable under the particular facts and circumstances of this case. The Court respectfully declines to apply the lodestar standard in this case.

. . .

Compensation

21. "If the terms of a trust do not specify the trustee's compensation, a trustee is entitled to compensation that is reasonable under the circumstances." §736.0708(1), Fla. Stat. (2007). The evidence established that the Trust provides only that the Trustees are entitled to a reasonable fee for their services.

22. The witnesses at trial testified that the Trustees rendered many services during administration. Upon Rauschenberg's death, the Trustees planned, advertised, and managed several exhibitions and memorials. The Trustees developed a strategic plan to withdraw Rauschenberg's art from the market, in order to prevent a decline in value from speculators or collectors flooding the market with his art. Mr. Grutman testified that this decline in value had occurred following the death of other famous artists, such as Andy Warhol. The Trustees contacted all galleries holding art on consignment, and directed that the art be returned. They contacted insurance agents regarding insurance on all assets. The Trustees moved all artwork to the Mount Vernon warehouse in New York for inventory and appraisals. They hired an art advisor. They then interviewed companies regarding a formal appraisal of all artwork, and hired Christie's to perform the appraisal. The Trustees reviewed the collection to determine which pieces should remain in the Foundation's permanent collection. The Trustees oversaw security, maintenance and conservation of the art and properties. The Trustees handled litigation of employment and intellectual property issues, and managed authentication requests. The Trustees managed placement of art in museums and galleries for exhibitions when the time was right to re-introduce the art on the market. They interviewed galleries and selected the Gagosian Gallery to hold exhibitions worldwide. The Trustees curated, set prices, negotiated with the galleries and museums, and were involved in all aspects of each exhibition, such as advertisements and catalogs.

23. With respect to the *West Coast* factors, the Court makes the following findings:

a. The amount of capital and income received and disbursed: The value of the assets upon Rauschenberg's death was $605,645,595.00. Upon disbursement to the

Foundation, the value was estimated to be approximately $2,179,000,000.00, which is approximately three and one-half (3 1/2) times the original value of the estate. While the majority of assets were artwork, there was also significant real property including his home and 20 acres on Captiva Island, houses in California and New York, and an art warehouse.

b. The wages or salary customarily granted for like service in the community: Both Mr. Ranson and Mr. Ruttenberg [expert witnesses for the Trustees] testified that this was a unique case, and neither could find anyone who had handled such a complex trust.
c. The success or failure of the administration: The Court finds that the performance of the Trustees contributed to the increased value of the assets during their administration. Mr. Ranson testified that "this was a pretty significant administration, and I've never seen anything like it." Rauschenberg's artistry was recognized in the marketplace, and some of that recognition is attributable to the Trustees' management of his "brand." It should be noted, however, that the talent of Robert Rauschenberg and favorable market conditions were also contributing factors towards the increased value of the estate assets.
d. Any unusual skill or experience held by trustee: Mr. Ranson testified that the Trustees were an extraordinary selection by Rauschenberg, since they had knowledge of him, his art, his businesses, and they had experience with the estates of other artists and the art world. The record reflects that the Trustees were close friends and business associates of Rauschenberg. Mr. Pottorf was an artist who lived and worked with Rauschenberg for over 25 years, collaborating on pieces of art. Mr. Grutman was Rauschenberg's accountant for 18 years, assisting him with business, investments, tax and estate planning, as well acquisition and disposition of property. Mr. Grutman had experience in the art world, and had served as trustee for the estates of other artists. Mr. Goldston operated a fine art publishing company and was Rauschenberg's business partner. He collaborated with Rauschenberg on several pieces of art, and was experienced with the art market. The Court finds that Rauschenberg made a wise and deliberate decision, and picked the best possible Trustees for the estate.
e. The fidelity or disloyalty displayed by the trustee: The Court finds that the Trustees were loyal to Rauschenberg and his vision. Mr. Grutman testified that the focus of the Trustees was always on maximizing benefits to the Foundation, as Rauschenberg would have wanted. The success of the administration reflects that this was true.
f. The amount of risk and responsibility assumed: The evidence established that the Trust contained exculpation clauses, insulating the Trustees from financial risk. However, both Mr. Ranson and Mr. Ruttenberg testified that the Trustees shouldered enormous responsibility. Neither witness believed that a bank or trust company would have been willing to handle this estate. Mr. Ruttenberg also testified that the Trustees put their reputations on the line.
g. The time consumed in carrying out the trust: There was some dispute as to whether four years was a reasonable or lengthy period for administration. Based on the testimony and evidence presented that the Foundation was not set up and

prepared for turnover for a few years, this Court finds the time was reasonable under the unique circumstances of this estate.

h. The custom in the community as to allowances to trustees, and charges exacted by trust companies and banks: This Court was presented with expert testimony from a number of witnesses as to fees. Mr. Ranson and Mr. Ruttenberg testified that if a bank or trust company had accepted this case, it would have charged 1% to 2% of the trust assets per year, plus 40 to 60 basis points in fees for extraordinary services. As trier of fact, this Court finds that an application of the percentage plus basis points formula to be unreasonably high. These fee estimates are based on trust company or bank practices that recognize the issue of profit to the company, as well as overhead and salaries for employees. Moreover, these standards were not intended for multi-billion dollar estates. The Court considered these rates, but finds they would be unreasonable in this case, considering the testimony that there are sliding fee scales for fees charged by banks and trust companies for large estates. The Court also considered basis points, both as a stand-alone application in a range depending on the circumstances and as an additional application along with a percentage consideration. The testimony was that additional basis points could be considered for the performance of extraordinary services. The Court finds that the Trustees made very good decisions and rendered very good service. It should be noted, however, that they rendered the services Rauschenberg selected them to perform and requested they perform. Their services were those expected of them by Rauschenberg.

i. The character of the work done in the course of the administration: The evidence at trial supports a finding that the Trustees did an exemplary job.

j. Any estimate which the trustee has given of the value of his services: The evidence established that the Trustees had informed the Foundation prior to turnover that the estimate of their fees was between $36,000,000.00 and $54,000,000.00. The Trustees originally requested $60,000,000.00 in fees during this proceeding. At trial, the Trustees requested $51,000,000.00 to $55,000,000.00. The Court notes that the Foundation has maintained throughout these proceedings that a total amount of $375,000.00 was a reasonable fee for all three Trustees.

k. Payments made to trustee to apply towards compensation: The Trustees received $8,035,199.00 during administration.

Conclusion

24. Having reviewed the testimony and evidence admitted at trial, the arguments by the parties, and the *West Coast* factors, the Court finds that a reasonable fee for the services of the Trustees under the particular facts and circumstances of this case is $24,600,000.00.

Accordingly, it is

Ordered and Adjudged that the Trustees are entitled to $24,600,000.00 in total trustees' fees to be divided among all three Trustees, less the $8,035,199.00 already received by the Trustees.

Robert Rauschenberg, Canyon, 1959
© The Estate of Robert Rauschenberg
Photo: Metropolitan Museum of Art

Robert Rauschenberg, *Canyon*, 1959. Combine: oil, pencil, paper, fabric, metal, cardboard box, printed paper, printed reproductions, photograph, wood, paint tube, and mirror on canvas with oil on bald eagle, string, and pillow. 81 3/4 x 70 x 24 inches (207.6 x 177.8 x 61 cm). The Museum of Modern Art, New York. Photo: Metropolitan Museum of Art. *Copyright © by Robert Rauschenberg Foundation / Licensed by VAGA, New York, NY.*

QUESTIONS

9. The Trustees, who devoted approximately 1,500 hours to administering the Trust, initially argued that compensation of $60 million was reasonable. On an hourly basis, the Trustees' compensation would produce a fee arrangement of $40,000 per hour. The court found the Trustees' request unreasonable and, instead, ordered disbursement of $24,600,000 in fees. On an hourly basis, the court's award produced an hourly rate of $16,400 assuming 1,500 hours of administration work. Do you agree with the court's finding on the reasonableness of the fee award?

   ANSWER. The Trustees' compensation ordered by the court, although reduced by more than half of what they initially requested, still strikes us as unreasonably high absent prior consent from the settlor. The fee award corresponds to more than 4 percent of the value of the inception assets and more than 1.1 percent of the value of the assets upon distribution to the Foundation. Many corporate fiduciaries would charge significantly lower fees as a percentage of the value of the trust corpus for a trust of this size.

10. The Trustees argued that their work had caused the trust corpus to appreciate by more than 3.5 times the value of the inception assets. Assuming for the sake of argument that the Trustees were responsible for the increase in value, does the capital appreciation of the trust corpus warrant a corresponding increase in trustee compensation?

    ANSWER. We believe that capital appreciation obtained by trustees does not provide a basis for a significant increase in trustee compensation. Trustees are required to perform the duties of trusteeship in compliance with fiduciary duties including care and loyalty (see Chapter 11). Failure to manage the trust assets in a manner that preserves their value would constitute a breach of those duties, not a basis for additional reward.

11. What is the drafting lesson for estate planning attorneys who want to insulate trust-making clients from costly litigation over trustee compensation? What, if anything, can be written into the trust to prevent trustees from exaggerating the value of their services in court and introducing expert testimony on trustee compensation that a court may nonetheless find persuasive?

    ANSWER. The matter of trustee compensation should be addressed explicitly in the trust instrument. In the *Rauschenberg* case, the trust's silence on trustee compensation invoked the default standard of reasonableness, which, as demonstrated by this case, can produce a wide range of possible interpretations. By expressly limiting trustee compensation in the trust instrument, the settlor retains control over the amounts paid for trust administration rather than delegating the decision to a court.

By default, under state law, the powers of trustees are broad and generally include all rights to conduct transactions with, and otherwise manage, the trust property. A settlor of a trust generally may augment or limit the default powers in the trust instrument.[41] Trustees' powers are often described as general or specific.

Uniform Trust Code
§815 General Powers of Trustees

(a) A trustee, without authorization by the court, may exercise:

(1) powers conferred by the terms of the trust; and

(2) except as limited by the terms of the trust:

(A) all powers over the trust property which an unmarried competent owner has over individually owned property;

41. Often, the trust instrument's sections enumerating setting out the trustees' powers is extensive. Trustee powers also frequently appear in a smaller font and with a narrower line spacing than other terms of the trust document.

(B) any other powers appropriate to achieve the proper investment, management, and distribution of the trust property; and

(C) any other powers conferred by this [Code].

. . .

UTC §815's comment emphasizes the breadth of these default general powers: "This section is intended to grant trustees the broadest possible powers, but to be exercised always in accordance with the duties of the trustee and any limitations stated in the terms of the trust." The UTC's standard for defining these general powers align with "all powers that an unmarried competent owner has over individually owned property." UTC §815(a)(2)(A).

In addition, UTC §816 ("Specific Powers of Trustee") sets out twenty-six specifically defined powers carried over from the earlier Uniform Trustees' Powers Act of 1964. For example, the first three enumerated powers in UTC §816 are as follows:

> (1) to collect, hold, and retain trust assets received from a trustor until, in the judgment of the trustee, disposition of the assets should be made . . . ;
>
> (2) to receive additions to the assets of the trust;
>
> (3) to continue or participate in the operation of any business or other enterprise, and to effect incorporation, dissolution, or other change in the form of the organization of the business or enterprise[.]

A competently drafted trust instrument will have an extended section granting specific powers to the trustees. Although the "powers section" of a trust document is mostly boilerplate (and, in any event, most of the specified powers are already supplied by state law), unusual circumstances regarding trust property, the trust purposes, and other factors sometimes require the drafting attorney to customize the trustees' powers. An express grant of specific powers, however, should be drafted in a way that does not unintentionally deprive the trustee of broad statutory powers applicable by default.

Trustees hold their powers and serve as trustees subject to fiduciary duties.[42] Indeed, the term "fiduciary" derives from the Latin verb "fidere," to trust. A fiduciary is a person or entity who has accepted a position of trust, such as an agent under an agency agreement, an attorney-in-fact under a power of attorney, a personal representative (an executor or an administrator) of a decedent's estate, or a trustee of a trust. The primary fiduciary duties are a duty of loyalty, a duty of care, and a duty of obedience. The duty of loyalty requires a trustee to avoid all conflicts of interest and always to make decisions solely in the beneficiaries' best interests. The duty of care requires a trustee to act in accordance with objective standards of prudence. The duty of obedience requires trustees to be faithful to the settlor's purposes.

Trustees' fiduciary duties generally are strictly applied. In one of the most frequently quoted observations in judicial opinions, Benjamin Cardozo, then serving as Chief Judge of New York's Court of Appeals, observed:

---

42. The comment to UTC §815 reminds us of the distinction between a power and a duty: "A power differs from a duty. A duty imposes an obligation or a mandatory prohibition. A power, on the other hand, is a discretion, the exercise of which is not obligatory."

> Many forms of conduct permissible in a workaday world for those acting at arm's length, are forbidden to those bound by fiduciary ties. A trustee is held to something stricter than the morals of the market place. Not honesty alone, but the punctilio of an honor the most sensitive, is then the standard of behavior. As to this there has developed a tradition that is unbending and inveterate. Uncompromising rigidity has been the attitude of courts of equity when petitioned to undermine the rule of undivided loyalty by the "disintegrating erosion" of particular exceptions. Only thus has the level of conduct for fiduciaries been kept at a level higher than that trodden by the crowd. It will not consciously be lowered by any judgment of this court.

Meinhard v. Salmon, 164 N.E. 545, 546 (N.Y. Ct. App. 1928). Trustees' duties, and remedies for the breach of trustees' duties, are discussed in detail in Chapter 11.

8.4 TYPES OF PRIVATE TRUSTS

Trusts may be formed for virtually any legal purpose or for any purpose that is not contrary to public policy.[43]

Uniform Trust Code
§404 Trust Purposes

> A trust may be created only to the extent its purposes are lawful, not contrary to public policy, and possible to achieve. A trust and its terms must be for the benefit of its beneficiaries.

Trusts are typically described by their purposes (private or charitable), the time of their creation (inter vivos or testamentary), whether they are revocable or irrevocable, and their duration (perpetual, for a term of years, or for a period terminating upon the happening of an event (or the failure of the event to occur)). Settlors create private trusts for myriad reasons but in all cases the key motivation is a settlor's desire to benefit family members or friends, but to confer such a benefit while exercising control over the transfer or use of the gifted property.[44]

The idiosyncratic purposes served by a particular private trust are often indicated in the title of the trust. For example, a predeceasing spouse may create a testamentary "marital trust" for the benefit of a surviving spouse. An "exemption trust" holds assets exempt from federal estate taxation in the settlor's estate. A "spendthrift" trust shelters the trust property from beneficiaries' creditors. A "descendants' trust" generally accumulates trust income for so long as the trust can exist under any applicable Rule Against Perpetuities; when that period ends, the trust terminates, and the trust property is distributed to the settlor's then-living descendants. "Minority trusts" hold assets set aside (for any number of reasons) for individuals who have not achieved the age of

---

43. The ubiquitous use of business trusts for commercial purposes is not addressed in this text, which is limited to the law of donative transfers.

44. For private trusts that benefit pets or that serve other purposes, see the section on Honorary Trusts, below in Chapter 9. Until recently, the common law tradition limited the duration of private trusts, and consequently, the duration of the settlor's control over property held in trust, to a period governed by the Rule Against Perpetuities ("lives in being plus 21 years," which effectively meant approximately 100 years). Statutory development over the past thirty years of perpetual private trusts (sometimes referred to as "dynasty trusts") is described below.

majority. There are "beach-bum trusts," so called because settlors use them to limit a beneficiary's access to trust property to an amount measured by a multiple of the beneficiary's earned income reported on the beneficiary's tax returns, thus creating an incentive for the beneficiary to work: the more the beneficiary earns, the more the beneficiary receives from trust distributions. "Special needs" trusts are created to benefit individuals with disabilities; they are written to provide funds to supplement, rather than replace, governmental assistance programs for which the beneficiary is otherwise eligible. The examples could continue. The point is this: The purposes for which a private trust can be created are essentially infinite, provided the trust and its purposes create a benefit for the trust beneficiaries and are lawful, not contrary to public policy, and achievable.

8.4.1 Inter Vivos and Testamentary Trusts

Inter vivos trusts are created and intended to take effect during the settlor's lifetime. Creation of an inter vivos trust constitutes a present disposition of property. Testamentary trusts, by contrast, are created by will and come into being upon the settlor's death.

Restatement (Third) of Trusts
§17 Creation of Testamentary Trusts

(1) A testamentary trust is one created by a valid will.

(2) Except as provided in §19, a trust is created by a will if the intention to create the trust and other elements essential to the creation of a testamentary trust (ordinarily, identification of the trust property, the beneficiaries, and the purposes of the trust) can be ascertained from

(a) the will itself; or

(b) an existing instrument properly incorporated by reference into the will; or

(c) facts referred to in the will that have significance apart from their effect upon the disposition of the property bequeathed or devised by the will.

Although an inter vivos trust may provide for the creation of one or more continuing trusts when the settlor dies, those trusts are not "testamentary" trusts: They are not created under the terms of a testator's will but, rather, under the terms of a valid inter vivos instrument. Although inter vivos trusts typically are revocable during the settlor's lifetime, dispositions in continuing trust when the settlor dies are irrevocable.

8.4.2 Revocable and Irrevocable Trusts

At common law, trusts were presumed *irrevocable* unless the settlor specifically reserved powers to revoke or modify the trust. Thus, trusts were treated similarly to gifts — once a donor delivered possession of property to a donee, the donor lost all dominion and control over the gifted property, including the ability to revoke the gift. The Uniform

Trust Code, however, takes the opposite position, creating a presumption of revocability unless otherwise stated.

Uniform Trust Code
§602 Revocation or Amendment of Revocable Trust

(a) Unless the terms of a trust expressly provide that the trust is irrevocable, the settlor may revoke or amend the trust. This subsection does not apply to a trust created under an instrument executed before [the effective date of this Code]. . . .

. . .

(c) The settlor may revoke or amend a revocable trust:

(1) by substantial compliance with a method provided in the terms of the trust; or

2) if the terms of the trust do not provide a method or the method provided in the terms [of the trust] is not expressly made exclusive, by:

(A) a later will or codicil that expressly refers to the trust or specifically devises property that would otherwise have passed according to the terms of the trust; or

(B) any other method manifesting clear and convincing evidence of the settlor's intent.

(d) Upon revocation of a revocable trust, the trustee shall deliver the trust property as the settlor directs. . . .

The distinction between the common law rule and the provisions of the UTC should make little practical difference for trusts drafted by a competent attorney, who will state clearly in the instrument whether the trust is revocable or irrevocable. See, e.g., John Langbein, The Uniform Trust Code: Codification of the Law of Trusts in the United States, 15 Tr. L. Int'l 66, 70 (2001).

8.4.3 Perpetual Trusts

A recent development in trust law has been the adoption of legislation permitting private trusts to last, at least theoretically, in perpetuity (or for some other period that would be longer than allowed under the Rule Against Perpetuities). These "perpetual" or "dynasty" trusts have been codified in jurisdictions that have either repealed or otherwise abrogated the Rule Against Perpetuities or permitted the creation, under specific statutory requirements, of perpetual trusts:

> For centuries, Anglo-American law [imposed] a Rule Against Perpetuities that curtailed dead hand control by limiting the permissible duration of restrictions governing the use or enjoyment of property transferred to a private, noncharitable donee. Originating in seventeenth-century England, the Rule invalidates contingent future interests in property that are uncertain to vest (or fail to vest) "not later than twenty-one years after some life in being at the creation of the interest." Under the Rule, the interest of a person unborn or unascertained at the time of conveyance is contingent upon that person being born or ascertained. For property held in trust, the Rule limits the number of successive generations the settlor may include as beneficiaries because, at the time of the trust's creation, remote

> generations are unborn or unascertained and, therefore, their interests are not certain to vest within a life in being plus twenty-one years. The Rule has been incorporated expressly into the law of trusts, which requires the settlor to select beneficiaries who can be identified or ascertained "within the period and terms of the rule against perpetuities." As Professor Ray Madoff explains, "[t]he theory of the Rule is that a person should be able to impose restrictions only on people whom he or she knows plus the period of minority for the next immediate generation." Over the last thirty years, however, most jurisdictions in the United States abrogated or repealed the Rule Against Perpetuities by statute to permit perpetual or near-perpetual trusts.

Reid K. Weisbord, Trust Term Extension, 67 Fla. L. Rev. 73, 80-81 (2015).

8.5 CHARITABLE TRUSTS

Charitable and private trusts share many characteristics: Similarly to private trusts, charitable trusts may be testamentary or inter vivos, created under a deed or declaration of trust, and need not be in writing although, for tax reasons, invariably they are. Nevertheless, charitable trusts differ from private trusts in important ways, including who their beneficiaries can be, what their purposes are, how long they can exist, and who has the power to enforce their terms. Charitable trusts are one legal form by which individuals accomplish philanthropic goals. Another, the charitable nonprofit corporation, is far more common today than charitable trusts. Still, trusts continue to form a significant part of the charitable sector of our economy, and a unique body of statutory and common law has developed to address their unique nature.[45]

8.5.1 Charitable Beneficiaries

Beneficiaries of *private* trusts must be ascertainable. The opposite rule distinguishes charitable trusts: Beneficiaries of *charitable* trusts must be the general public or an *un*ascertainable segment of the general public constituting a class of charitable beneficiaries: for example, "residents of the city of Omaha, Nebraska," "students enrolled in XYZ Law School," "visual artists." In defending the validity of Benjamin Franklin's testamentary charitable trust (one hundred years after it had been established),[46] a Pennsylvania court emphasized the differences between beneficiaries of private and charitable trusts:

> The essential part of the definition of a charity is that the persons who are to receive it must be indefinite and uncertain; in other words, they must be of a class; for if a gift be made to

---

45. This section addresses fully charitable trusts. So-called split interest trusts such as charitable lead and charitable remainder trusts (in which charitable and noncharitable beneficiaries hold successive interests) are beyond the scope of our discussion.

46. "At the expiration of the first 100 years, Dr. Franklin directed that of the £131,000, which he expected the fund would then reach, "£100,000 should be donated to the City of Philadelphia to be laid out in public works, such as fortifications, bridges, aqueducts, baths, pavements, or whatever will make living in a town more convenient to its people, and render it more agreeable to strangers resorting thither for health or a temporary residence." And he recommended that a part of the money be employed in bringing, by pipes, the water of Wissahickon creek into the town so as to supply the inhabitants." Case of Apprentices' Fund, 2 Pa. D. 435, 438 (Pa. C.P. 1893).

individuals by name or description, so that they may be selected and set apart, although they are of a class, the gift is not a charity, but a [noncharitable] legacy.[47]

Accordingly, the beneficiaries of charitable trusts are the general public or a described segment of the general public; in no circumstances may a valid charitable trust be formed if the beneficiaries are, as with private trusts, ascertainable by name or description.

8.5.2 Charitable Purposes

Today, following a long history of common law development, the permissible purposes for charitable trusts are generally defined by state statutes. Those purposes almost always echo the first codification of charitable purposes in the English Statute of Charitable Uses 43 Eliz. I, c. 4 (1601):

> . . . the relief of aged, impotent, and poor people; the maintenance of sick and maimed soldiers and mariners; schools of learning; free schools and scholars in universities; the repair of bridges, ports, havens, causeways, churches, sea banks, and highways; the education and preferment of orphans; the relief, stock, or maintenance of houses of correction; marriages of poor maids; support, aid, and help of young tradesmen, handicraftsmen and persons decayed; the relief or redemption of prisoners or captives; and the aid or ease of any poor inhabitants. . . .

UTC §405(a), the modern statutory equivalent, states that "[a] charitable trust may be created for the relief of poverty, the advancement of education or religion, the promotion of health, governmental or municipal purposes, or other purposes the achievement of which is beneficial to the community." See also Restatement (Third) of Trusts §28.

Today, settlors invariably create charitable trusts with language that will secure Internal Revenue Service (IRS) recognition of the trusts as charitable, tax-exempt entities described in Internal Revenue Code (Code) §501(c)(3).[48] Such recognition permits charitable trusts to qualify for tax exemption on their income, and allows settlors' contributions to the trusts to be deductible for settlors' income, gift, and estate tax purposes. Code §501(c)(3) describes the purposes for which a charitable entity must be organized and operated to qualify for these tax benefits:

> [To qualify as tax-exempt, charitable trusts and charitable nonprofit corporations must be] . . . organized and operated exclusively for religious, charitable, scientific, testing for public safety, literary, or educational purposes, or to foster national or international amateur sports competition . . . or for the prevention of cruelty to children or animals. . . .

Although the Code does not define "charitable," IRS Regulations do:

---

47. *Id.* at 437.

48. IRC §501(c)(3) applies not only to charitable trusts but also—and more commonly—to charitable, nonprofit corporations. Thus, a charitable entity may be formed under state law either as a charitable trust or a charitable nonprofit corporation and receive similar beneficial tax treatment. Federal recognition as charitable entity described in IRC §501(c)(3) generally produces additional beneficial tax treatment at state and local levels.

> The term charitable is used in section 501(c)(3) in its generally accepted legal sense. . . . [The term "charitable"] includes: Relief of the poor and distressed or of the underprivileged; advancement of religion; advancement of education or science; erection or maintenance of public buildings, monuments, or works; lessening of the burdens of Government; and promotion of social welfare by organizations designed to accomplish any of the above purposes, or (i) to lessen neighborhood tensions; (ii) to eliminate prejudice and discrimination; (iii) to defend human and civil rights secured by law; or (iv) to combat community deterioration and juvenile delinquency. . . .

26 C.F.R. 1.501(c)(3)-1(d)(2). Again, parallels with the English Statute of Charitable Uses are clear.

Uniform Trust Code
§405 Charitable Purposes; Enforcement

> (a) A charitable trust may be created for the relief of poverty, the advancement of education or religion, the promotion of health, governmental or municipal purposes, or other purposes the achievement of which is beneficial to the community.
>
> (b) If the terms of a charitable trust do not indicate a particular charitable purpose or beneficiary, the court may select one or more charitable purposes or beneficiaries. The selection must be consistent with the settlor's intention to the extent it can be ascertained.
>
> (c) The settlor of a charitable trust, among others, may maintain a proceeding to enforce the trust.

Notwithstanding the special purposes set out in UTC §405, charitable trusts share with private trusts the limitations imposed by UTC §404: "A trust may be created only to the extent its purposes are lawful, not contrary to public policy, and possible to achieve."

PROBLEM V

A Silicon Valley billionaire seeks your law firm's representation to establish a charitable trust to "build, endow, manage, and maintain a state-of-the-art, tuition-free, secondary school to provide quality education for poor, orphaned, white girls of the Christian faith, so they may take their rightful places in the technology industries." The client is willing to fund the trust with sufficient assets so that the school—even without future contributions—should be financially independent in perpetuity. What is your advice to the client?

8.5.3 Duration and Modification of Charitable Trusts

Although settlors of charitable trusts might require a shorter duration, charitable trusts can, theoretically at least, last forever because they are exempt from the Rule Against

Perpetuities. Thus, settlors may establish charitable trusts for a period of years or for a period measured by the accomplishment of a specific charitable purpose, but more frequently, charitable trust documents either explicitly state that they are to continue "forever" or "in perpetuity" or are silent on the issue, with the assumption that perpetual duration is intended.

Forever, of course, is a long time. Circumstances change with time, and the worthwhile charitable cause of one generation may well be a purpose that no longer requires philanthropic support by a later generation. Accordingly, the law has adopted two doctrines permitting a court to address changing circumstances in the context of charitable trusts.

First, the *doctrine of cy pres* permits a court to change the *purposes* of a charitable trust if the settlor's stated purposes are (or become) illegal, impossible, or impracticable to accomplish or if accomplishing the settlor's purposes would waste charitable assets. Under such circumstances, the court may alter the trust's charitable purposes to other purposes as close to (assez près = cy pres) the donor's stated purposes as possible. A cy pres proceeding addresses a change in charitable purposes.

Second, under the *doctrine of equitable deviation*, if, because of circumstances unforeseen by the settlor, the *means* by which a settlor's charitable purposes are to be accomplished are (or become) illegal, impossible, or impracticable the court may alter the administrative terms of the trust to facilitate accomplishment of the donor's charitable purposes by other means. The alternate terms must be the least possible variation from the settlor's in light of the changed circumstances. An equitable deviation proceeding results not in changed charitable purposes but in alterations to how the charitable purposes are accomplished.[49]

These doctrines are often confused by courts and legal commentators. That confusion stems from the difficulty in determining whether a given instruction in a charitable trust states a charitable purpose or the means of accomplishing a charitable purpose.

8.5.4 Enforcement of Charitable Trusts

Until recent statutory changes, the sole party with standing to enforce the terms of charitable trusts was the state attorney general.[50] Traditionally, not even the settlor of an inter vivos charitable trust had standing to bring suit to assure that the trust was fulfilling its intended charitable purposes or that the trustees were not in breach of their fiduciary duties. The reasoning behind this limitation was two-fold. First, the general rule applicable to private trusts — that beneficiaries are the proper parties to enforce fiduciary duties and therefore have standing to sue the trustees to enforce the terms of the trust — is unproblematic when the trust beneficiaries are ascertainable. When, however, the beneficiaries comprise the entire public (or a defined segment of the public), the number of potential plaintiffs is daunting and the collective action problem

49. We discuss the *cy pres* and equitable deviation doctrines again in Chapter 9, when we cover trust modification and termination more generally.

50. Additionally, most jurisdictions granted standing also to individuals with a "special interest" in a charitable trust. The special interest was interpreted to mean a direct financial interest in the trust.

precludes effective enforcement by private parties. Focusing the enforcement power in a government office that already represents the public's interest as parens patriae (parent of the fatherland) — the states' attorneys general's offices — made logical, good sense. Second, there was a fear that trustees of charitable trusts would face many, vexatious, and unfounded lawsuits if any potential beneficiary of a charitable trust (i.e., a member of the general public) had standing to enforce the trust. Unpopular decisions by trustees, it was thought, would trigger second-guessing and expensive, distracting lawsuits. By limiting the potential plaintiffs to a state's attorney general, the expectation was that only legitimate cases of trustees' breaches of their fiduciary duties would be pursued.

Two problems with this reasoning stimulated the recent expansion of donor standing by statute and common law. First, states that initiated the trend to relax the prohibition on private party standing for certain parties, such as donors, did not observe a flood of hectoring lawsuits, so the concern about waves of vexatious litigation may have been overblown. Second, state attorneys general tend to have limited staff and budgets, and the enforcement of charitable trusts often slips to a low priority, leading many to observe (correctly) that enforcement is weak.[51]

Granting charitable settlors with standing to enforce the terms of a charitable trust, however, is not without its own potential perils:

> There is little evidence supporting the claim that donor standing provides social benefits, but the social costs that accompany enforcement rights create cause for concern. Donor enforcement litigation can waste vast sums of charitable assets on litigation costs and consume scarce judicial resources to adjudicate gift disputes. In *Robertson v. Princeton University*, for example, the parties settled when Princeton [University], having spent $40 million to defend itself, agreed to reimburse $40 million of the plaintiffs' litigation costs from funds that would otherwise have flowed to charitable beneficiaries (after the court issued hundreds of pages of judicial opinions deciding cross-motions for summary judgment). The creation of donor enforcement rights can also frustrate efforts by nonprofit organizations to serve the community when donors pursue personal objectives contrary to the public interest. In *Howard v. Administrators of the Tulane Education Fund*, for example, the plaintiffs attempted to unravel Tulane's post-Katrina recovery plan, undermining the public's substantial stake in an educational institution of critical importance to a community plagued by natural disaster.

Reid K. Weisbord & Peter DeScioli, The Effects of Donor Standing on Philanthropy: Insights from the Psychology of Gift-Giving, 45 Gonz. L. Rev. 225, 288 (2010). Thus, the policy question of how best to enforce and regulate charitable assets held in trust by private trustees remains the subject of debate.

51. See, e.g., Evelyn Brody, Whose Public? Parochialism and Paternalism in State Charity Law Enforcement, 79 Ind. L.J. 937 (2004) ("[A]s a practical matter, few state attorneys general have the funding and inclination to engage in aggressive charity enforcement. Indeed, the very lack of state involvement with the organization and operation of nonprofit entities might explain how legislatures, attorneys general, and even courts can misconstrue their proper roles in the regulation of charities and other nonprofits.").

9 Trust Distributions and Modification; Implied Trusts

9.1 DISTRIBUTIONS: RIGHTS OF BENEFICIARIES AND CREDITORS IN PRIVATE TRUSTS

This section will discuss arguably the most critical function of a private trust — the distribution of trust assets. We will focus on two stakeholders: trust beneficiaries and creditors of trust beneficiaries.

First, with regard to *beneficiaries*, we will examine the circumstances under which a trustee may or must distribute trust assets to a beneficiary or, alternatively, to a third party at the beneficiary's direction. The beneficiary's right to receive or assign distributions from the trust is determined, in the first instance, by the nature of the trust interest the settlor created. Trust interests may be mandatory, discretionary, support, spendthrift, or a hybrid of these options.

Second, with regard to *creditors* of beneficiaries, we will examine ways in which settlors can use trusts to protect assets from collection by creditors seeking repayment of a beneficiary's debts. Some trust interests, such as discretionary and support trusts, contain natural asset protection features because the nature of the interest limits the beneficiary's right to compel a distribution. If the beneficiary cannot compel a distribution, then there is nothing for a beneficiary's creditor to attach. Another asset protection technique is the use of spendthrift trusts, which expressly prohibit the trustee from making distributions directly to a beneficiary's creditors.

9.1.1 Beneficiaries

A beneficiary's right to compel a distribution of trust assets is determined, in the first instance, by the settlor. The trustee's failure to distribute trust assets upon a beneficiary's entitlement to a distribution constitutes a breach of trust and subjects the trustee to damages for both the unpaid distribution (payable from the trust) and for injuries arising from the trustee's failure to make a timely distribution (payable personally by the trustee).

Beneficiaries sometimes use (or attempt to use) an assignment or transfer of their trust interest as a form of consideration or payment in their dealings with other third parties. Upon assignment, the third party, now standing in the shoes of the beneficiary, will seek a distribution of trust assets directly from the trustee. However, a beneficiary's right to compel payment of a trust distribution to herself is not always the same as the right to voluntarily alienate (i.e., assign, transfer, pledge, encumber, etc.) the beneficiary's interest in favor of someone else. Trust interests are generally assignable by the beneficiary unless the nature of the trust interest imposes a restraint on voluntary alienation.[1]

A trust interest may exhibit one or more of the following characteristics:

A. Mandatory. A mandatory trust interest expressly requires the distribution of trust assets, either periodically at defined intervals (e.g., "the trustee shall pay the beneficiary monthly distributions of $5,000 from the trust corpus"; "the trustee shall distribute all interest earned by the trust quarterly") or on a one-time basis (e.g., "the trustee shall distribute $250,000 to the beneficiary upon her 25th birthday"; "upon the death of Beneficiary A, the trust shall terminate and the trustee shall distribute the remainder to Beneficiary B"). Once the preconditions of a mandatory trust interest have been met, the beneficiary has an absolute right to receive the distribution.[2] Upon the trustee's failure to comply, the beneficiary may bring suit against the trustee to compel the distribution.

A mandatory interest is voluntarily assignable, which means that the beneficiary may direct the trustee to distribute the interest to a third party and the trustee must comply with that instruction.

B. Discretionary. In a discretionary trust interest, a settlor grants the trustee discretion regarding the distribution of trust assets. A discretionary trust interest allows the settlor to delegate to the trustee decisions about the amount, timing, and allocation of trust distributions among the beneficiaries. A beneficiary has no right to receive a distribution unless the trustee has exercised discretion in favor of making a distribution. Thus, the settlor's gift in trust to the beneficiary is conditioned upon the trustee's discretionary review and approval of the distribution.

The settlor's repose of discretion may be broad (e.g., "the trustee shall have absolute discretion to make distributions of principal and income to and among the beneficiaries"), or narrow (e.g., "the trustee shall have discretion to make distributions limited to the following purposes: . . ."; "the trustee shall consider the following factors when exercising discretion to distribute trust assets: . . ."). A popular form of discretionary trust is known as a "sprinkle trust," in which the trustee has discretion to

---

1. See Restatement (Third) of Trusts §51 ("Except as provided in Chapter 12 [Spendthrift Trusts and Other Restraints on Voluntary and Involuntary Alienation], a beneficiary of a trust can transfer his or her beneficial interest during life to the same extent as a similar legal interest.").

2. A properly drafted trust instrument will make special provisions for the possibility that the trust beneficiary is a minor at the time of the compulsory distribution.

distribute income or principal and, if so, to which beneficiaries and in what amounts. A "spray trust," a variation on this concept, requires the trustee to distribute all income but vests the trustee with discretion in allocating the income among the beneficiaries.

The trustee's power to exercise discretion properly is constrained by the fiduciary duties generally imposed upon all trustees.[3] Upon the trustee's failure to exercise discretion properly, a beneficiary may seek judicial review of whether the trustee's discretion was properly exercised in light of the terms and purposes of the trust. In most cases, judicial review of the trustee's decision under the abuse of discretion standard is typically quite deferential to the trustee. Some courts have applied this standard by determining whether the trustee acted in the state of mind contemplated by the settlor.[4] Note, however, that regardless of the purportedly broad scope of discretion reposed by the trust in the office of the trustee, the trustee's conduct still remains subject to judicial review.

A beneficiary may alienate her interest in a discretionary trust and direct the trustee to remit the beneficiary's distribution from the trust directly to a third party. However, such an assignment is entirely contingent upon the trustee's exercise of discretion in favor of making a distribution because the beneficiary of a purely discretionary trust is not entitled to receive income or principal in any particular amount or at any particular time. The trustee, furthermore, may take into consideration the beneficiary's voluntary alienation of the trust interest when exercising discretion to decide whether to make a distribution.

Restatement (Third) of Trusts
§50 Enforcement and Construction of Discretionary Interests

(1) A discretionary power conferred upon the trustee to determine the benefits of a trust beneficiary is subject to judicial control only to prevent misinterpretation or abuse of the discretion by the trustee.

(2) The benefits to which a beneficiary of a discretionary interest is entitled, and what may constitute an abuse of discretion by the trustee, depend on the terms of the discretion, including the proper construction of any accompanying standards, and on the settlor's purposes in granting the discretionary power and in creating the trust.

C. Support. Support trust interests, previously categorized as a distinct species of trust, are now generally understood as a subcategory of discretionary trusts in which the settlor imposes a support standard governing the trustee's exercise of discretion. A support standard generally restricts trust distributions to living expenses (e.g., housing, food, clothing, health care, education, etc.) incurred by the beneficiary and

---

3. Repose of discretion in a trust, however, does not create a power of appointment. See Restatement (Third) of Trusts §50, comment a ("A trustee's discretionary power with respect to trust benefits is to be distinguished from a power of appointment. The latter is not subject to fiduciary obligations and may be exercised arbitrarily within the scope of the power.").

4. See, e.g., Conlin v. Murdock, 43 A.2d 218, 220 (N.J. Ch. 1945) ("I do not believe that the executor-trustees are acting in that state of mind in which it was contemplated by the testator that they should act.") (citing 2 Scott on Trusts §187, at 987).

members of the beneficiary's household.[5] Thus, the trustee's exercise of discretion serves to evaluate the reasonableness of living expenses covered by the trust. In the absence of an express provision and to the extent of the availability of trust resources, most courts construe a support trust to imply a standard of living consistent with the beneficiary's accustomed lifestyle. Like other discretionary trusts, a beneficiary may enforce a support standard by seeking judicial review of the trustee's exercise of discretion. Unlike other discretionary trusts, however, support trust interests are unassignable because the beneficiary's alienation would preclude the trust from carrying out the settlor's intent to provide a lifelong resource for the beneficiary's living expenses.

D. Spendthrift. Spendthrift provisions, which are usually imposed to protect trust assets against creditor claims (see Section 9.1.2.3, below), generally disable both voluntary alienation (i.e., assignment) and involuntary alienation (i.e., creditor collection) of the beneficial interest. By disabling the voluntary alienation, a spendthrift provision prevents the trust beneficiary from assigning the trust interest to third parties before its distribution by the trustee. A beneficiary may disclaim her interest in a spendthrift trust, but she may not direct the transfer of the disclaimed interest to someone else.

In re JP Morgan Chase Bank, N.A.
956 N.Y.S.2d 856 (Surr. Ct. 2012)

KRISTIN BOOTH GLEN, S.

This case raises important questions about the obligations of fiduciaries, including institutional trustees, to beneficiaries, with disabilities, of trusts that seek to provide for the welfare of those beneficiaries. A review of the history of this trust and related proceedings places the issue in sharp perspective.

This history reveals a severely disabled, vulnerable, institutionalized young man, wholly dependent on Medicaid, unvisited and virtually abandoned, despite a multimillion dollar trust left for his care by his deceased mother. It reveals two cotrustees, one who was personally involved with the deceased and who holds himself out as an expert in planning for children with intellectual disabilities, and one which is a major banking institution, neither visiting or inquiring after the beneficiary's needs nor spending a single penny on him.

The history turns brighter after a serendipitous SCPA article 17-A proceeding,[6] where the cotrustees were called to task, educated about available services, and hired

5. For estate tax reasons, support trusts sometimes limit distributions to the "health, education, maintenance, and support of" the beneficiary. (That standard is often referred to by an acronym, HEMS.) For example, a settlor may wish to create a support trust for his surviving spouse and, upon his surviving spouse's death, to distribute the balance of the trust to another beneficiary. To give the surviving spouse greater control over the support trust, the settlor may appoint the surviving spouse the trustee during her life. Under 26 U.S.C. §2041(b)(1)(A), so long as the surviving spouse's power to consume, invade, or appropriate property for her own benefit "is limited by an ascertainable standard relating to the health, education, support, or maintenance," the power is not deemed to be a general power of appointment in her hands and, all else equal, will not be included in her gross estate at her death.

6. [Article 17-A of the New York Surrogate's Court Procedure Act provides procedures and protections concerning "guardians of mentally retarded and developmentally disabled persons." — EDS.]

a certified care manager to attend to the beneficiary's needs. That intervention, now after almost four years, has dramatically improved the beneficiary's quality of life and his functional capacity to enjoy what is now a near "normal" existence in the community.

This history, and the legal consequences that flow from it, discussed below, should provide a clarion call for all fiduciaries of trusts whose beneficiaries are known to have disabilities to fulfill their "unwavering duty of complete loyalty to the beneficiary" (106 NY Jur 2d, Trusts §247) or be subject to the remedies available for breach of their fiduciary obligation.

HISTORY

Will and Trusts

Marie H. died on March 20, 2005 at the age of 85, survived by two adopted children, Charles A.H., and Mark C.H., then 16 years old. Prior to her death, upon learning of her terminal cancer, Marie searched for an appropriate residential setting for Mark, and ultimately placed him in the Anderson School in Straatsburg, New York.[7] Mark's disabilities are described more fully below.

In her will, Marie left her entire estate to the Marie H. Revocable Trust of 1995, created by trust agreement dated March 23, 1995 (the Revocable Trust). The Revocable Trust provided that, upon Marie's death, after dividing her tangible property between her two children, the balance was to be divided into two equal shares, one for Mark's trust, and one for Charles's trust. The will, also dated March 23, 1995, named her sister Betty as executor and guardian of the person and property of her minor children. Marie's attorney, H.J.P., was named the successor executor.

The will was admitted to probate on July 5, 2005. Because Betty predeceased Marie, letters testamentary issued to H.J.P.[8] The federal estate tax return (the 706) indicated a gross estate of approximately $12 million, of which $2,575,000 was the date of death valuation of Marie's co-op apartment, and $8,973,653.79 was the date of death value of her stocks and bonds. Other miscellaneous property was valued at $471,439.77. According to the 706, the only assets that were transferred to the Revocable Trust during Marie's lifetime were two Citibank accounts totaling $1,390.41.

The 706 estimated the executor's commission at $133,000 and attorney fees at $300,000, with other administration expenses shown as $462,717.45 [primarily related to the sale of the co-op apartment]. Federal estate taxes were shown as $3,479,561.55.

7. Charles is Mark's biological brother, and is one year older. He had no contact with Mark from the time Mark was placed at the Anderson School.

8. According to the guardian ad litem's report, H.J.P. reported that he specializes in estate planning and trusts and estates, and has long been involved in issues around people with intellectual disabilities, having served, inter alia, as co-chairperson of the New York State Association for Retarded Children Trust and on the Board of the Association for the Help of Retarded Children (AHRC). He has lectured on planning for families who have children with intellectual disabilities, and, in fact, met Marie H. after one such lecture.

On the same day that she executed her will and the Revocable Trust, March 23, 1995, Marie entered into two irrevocable trust agreements, one for Charles and one for Mark, the Mark C.H. Discretionary Trust of 1995 (the Mark Trust), with herself and Betty as trustees. H.J.P. was named successor trustee if either of the two named trustees should cease to serve, and, upon Marie's death, the Chase Manhattan Bank, N.A. (Chase) was designated as additional trustee "to serve with the other Trustees in office." The Mark Trust was funded with an initial contribution of $18.

It is clear that the Mark Trust is for the benefit of a person with disabilities. Article 2.1 provides for distributions of income and principal to Mark for his "care, comfort, support and maintenance," in the trustees' discretion, and further provides:

> "(ii) In the event such net income shall in any year be insufficient to provide for the support, maintenance, care and comfort of the beneficiary or for necessary medical expenses as determined by the Trustees, in their sole and absolute discretion, the said trustees shall expend out of the principal of said fund such sums as they deem necessary for any such purposes. Before expending any amounts from the net income and/or principal of this trust, the Trustees may wish to consider the availability of any benefits from government or private assistance programs for which the [grantee] may be eligible and that where appropriate and to the extent possible, the Trustees may endeavor to maximize the collection of such benefits and to facilitate the distribution of such benefits for the benefit of the beneficiary."

In article 2.1, section (iii) continues, authorizing the trustees "to pay or apply . . . to any facility [the beneficiary] may be residing in and/or to any organization where he may be a client or a participant in any program(s) sponsored by them, as the Trustees shall determine, for the general uses of such facility and/or organization."[9]

Article 2.1, §(v) gives the trustees the right to terminate the trust "as if the beneficiary were deceased" if the existence of the trust causes the beneficiary to be excluded from government benefits.

The Account

After probate of Marie's will, in the SCPA article 17-A proceeding, described below, this court, sua sponte, ordered H.J.P. and Chase to account as trustees of the Mark Trust, noting, "questions having arisen as to whether the funds intended by Marie H. to benefit Mark . . . had been duly applied by [sic] for such purposes by her chosen fiduciaries." The court appointed a guardian ad litem (GAL) for Mark in this accounting proceeding (SCPA 403[2]).

On December 7, 2010, the trustees filed an amended accounting covering the period of March 23, 1995 through March 31, 2010. Schedule A of that accounting showed the total amount of principal received as $1,420,343.28. In objections filed by the GAL, he noted his belief that, with a net estate of approximately $10 million, the Mark Trust should have been funded with $5 million. After meeting with Chase's

9. Notably, these provisions do not appear in the trust for Mark's brother, Charles, established on the same day.

attorney, he concluded, based on her statements to him, that estate taxes of $3,479,561.55 accounted for the diminution of the amount with which the Trust was funded. This, of course, was clearly not the case, as the estate tax would have been paid before distribution of the residuary estate, first to the Revocable Trust, and from there, in equal shares to the Mark Trust and the trust for Charles. If, in fact, all the estate taxes were somehow allocated to Mark's share, a major error would have occurred.

Schedule G, "the Statement of Principal Assets on Hand," as of March 31, 2010, showed a market value of $2,733,094.49. The substantial increase over the amount shown as principal received in 2005 is, however, not due to investment strategies but rather, according to a subsequent communication from Chase, the result of underreporting the initial principal received with many securities incorrectly listed at a $0 inventory value on schedule A.

Schedule C shows commissions paid to the trustees in amounts of $17,622.53 to H.J.P. and $34,914.61 to Chase. Significantly, schedule G-1 shows income on hand of $248,881.36, while schedule E-1, distribution of income, shows $0. The statement of administration expenses chargeable to income, schedule C-2, totals $29,493.49, of which the largest items are the commissions paid to the trustees. Of the total administrative expenses and taxes shown on schedule C, New York State income taxes (after substantial refunds) constituted $7,158.54; federal income taxes (after substantial refund) were $6,367.70; commissions were, as already noted, to Chase ($34,914.61) and H.J.P. ($17,622.53); H.J.P.'s firm's legal fees were $11,500; the fees of the guardian ad litem were $7,375; and the fees of Staver Eldercare Services (the care manager hired for Mark as a result of the article 17-A proceeding) were only $3,525.

The almost negligible amount paid to Staver, beginning in February 2009, is the only money paid out for the benefit of Mark, the disabled beneficiary, in five years. That is 1.4% of the income on hand at the end of the accounting period and 3.6% of all expenses. On an almost $3 million trust, the money spent on the beneficiary, over a five-year period — and only because of the court's intervention — was approximately 0.1%.

The Article 17-A Proceeding

In October 2006, H.J.P. brought a proceeding pursuant to article 17-A to be appointed as guardian of the person of Mark. In support of his petition, he submitted affirmations from two health care providers. One, Robert C. Williams, Ph.D., described Mark as "[p]rofound[ly] mentally retarded, suffering from autism," as well as "non-verbal and engag[ing] in numerous repetitive and self stimulating behaviors." Dr. Lynn Liptay provided a diagnosis of autism and mental retardation, noting that Mark was "nonverbal and requires constant supervision and assistance with all ADL's,"[10] and, as well, that he "engaged in frequent aggressive behaviors including spitting, throwing objects and hitting his own head."

10. ADL's are activities of daily living and include bathing, feeding oneself, toileting, dressing, etc. Mark was, according to Anderson's records, unable to perform any of these activities.

Because Mark was living in an institution, he was represented by Mental Hygiene Legal Services (MHLS) (Mental Hygiene Law §81.07[g][1][vii]). The report of the principal attorney for MHLS in the Second Department, who visited him there, notes that, according to the Anderson School records, Mark "has the receptive communication skills of someone less than two years old and the expressive skills of a three month old." The attorney described her visit to Anderson and her observation of Mark: "[E]ffective communication was not possible, [Mark's] only responses were facial grimaces and attempts to return to his classroom chair. He remained nonverbal, did not make eye contact, and appeared to be responding to internal stimuli."

At the initial hearing, on September 18, 2007, where Mark's presence was excused, H.J.P. revealed that, although he was applying for guardianship as a result of a promise to Mark's mother on her death bed, he had not seen Mark since Mark was six years old, when Marie brought him and Charles to H.J.P.'s law office. H.J.P. had never visited Anderson to ascertain Mark's condition nor, more critically, his needs,[11] nor had he inquired of the staff about any unmet needs. Also revealing the existence of Mark's trust and his position as cotrustee, H.J.P. admitted that he had not expended a single dollar on Mark's behalf in almost three years.

I adjourned the hearing to permit the other cotrustee to appear. Subsequently, a representative of Chase came to court with H.J.P. in response to my instruction; Chase's "excuse" for inaction was its lack of institutional capacity to ascertain or meet the needs of this severely disabled, institutionalized young man. If the bank lacked such expertise, I noted, they should obtain the services of someone who could assess Mark's situation and ascertain his needs. After some initial missteps, H.J.P. and Chase retained the services of a certified care manager with extensive experience with people with intellectual disabilities, Robin Staver, M.S., Ed., CMC.

First contacting, and then visiting Anderson, she learned of a list of items the professionals there believed would enhance Mark's quality of life and assist his learning and development. Over the past four years she has, as a representative of the trustees, been actively involved in Mark's life and care, attending meetings, in person or by phone, planning meetings, arranging medical and other consultations, purchasing equipment, including assistive communication devices, recreational materials, clothing, etc., and providing for Mark's first forays into the community. What follows is a brief snapshot of the extraordinary — and heartwarming — progress Mark has made since the funds his mother left for his care have been well and thoughtfully used for that purpose. The detail included, what anthropologists call a "thick description," is important in understanding how apparently trivial expenditures and interventions can have a huge impact on the progress and quality of life of a person with intellectual disabilities.

---

11. According to the guardian ad litem, the director of corporate compliance at Anderson, Linda Geraci, "stated that she is concerned that [H.J.P.] has not inquired into Mark's needs nor has he purchased anything for him — [despite the fact] that Mark's residence manager has recommended purchasing the following for Mark's benefit: an acoustic synthesizer and other musical equipment, furniture, clothing, adult swings, slides, climbing equipment, a stereo system and a computer with game software."

[The opinion provides a detailed account of Mark's progression under Staver's care from December 2008 to September 2012. During that period, the trustees distributed funds to cover a wide range of expenses necessary for Mark's care and comfort including: (1) medication not covered by Medicaid to reduce side effects caused by Mark's other prescription drugs; (2) personal computing devices, an iPad, and electronic game systems; (3) an electronic keyboard; (4) a playground system with outdoor chairs; (5) "an augmentative communication device . . . [to] enhance Mark's communication skills"; (6) gift certificates for restaurants and clothing for use by Mark's caretakers on his behalf; (7) a portable DVD player with wireless headphones; (10) a reclining chair with massage capabilities; (11) installation of sensory items in the van used to transport Mark for the purpose of calming his behavior during van rides; (12) a new mattress and box spring, with headboard and footboard; and (13) a trampoline with rubber mats for safety. The result of these purchases and additional care was marked improvement in Mark's mental and physical abilities.]

. . .

Finally, as a truly happy ending, Staver reports that she "facilitated a visit and accompanied Mark's older brother Charles to see Mark at his residence on September 22, 2012. . . . [Charles] stated that he was amazed at the progress Mark made in the last 8 years. He also said he felt reassured by the staff's caring, sensitivity and commitment to their clients. He said he knows Mark thrives because of the environment he's in and looks forward to bringing his family to meet Mark in the near future."

DISCUSSION

As this history demonstrates, once the trustees were required to make themselves knowledgeable about Mark's condition and his needs, and the availability of services that would enable them to provide for those needs, they began, and continue to use funds from his trust for the purposes his deceased mother anticipated and so deeply desired.

The history brings into sharp focus the obligations of trustees, both individual and institutional, to the beneficiaries of trusts they administer when they know,[12] or should know,[13] that those beneficiaries have disabilities, and have medical, educational or quality of life needs that can and should be met from trust income.

It is fundamental that a fiduciary takes on obligations beyond those imposed by ordinary relationships or transactions; in the oft-quoted works of Judge Cardozo, her responsibility is "something stricter than the [mere] morals of the market place . . .

12. Through his 10 years of work with her, and the planning he did, H.J.P. unquestionably knew of Mark's severe disability, and the circumstances which had caused Marie to institutionalize him. Further, H.J.P. holds himself out as an expert in the legal needs of children with disabilities, and, in fact, first met Marie after giving a lecture on the subject at AHRC.

13. Presumably Chase had conversations with its cotrustee H.J.P. But the language of the Mark Trust itself, quoted, supra, was more than enough to put them on notice that this was, as H.J.P. characterized it, an *Escher* trust for a person with disabilities.

but the punctilio of an honor the most sensitive" (Meinhard v. Salmon, 249 NY 458, 464 [1928]). This is no less the case for trustees, who have "an unwavering duty of complete loyalty to the beneficiary of the trust to the exclusion of the interests of all other parties" (106 NY Jur 2d, Trusts §247).

The Mark Trust empowers the trustees with "absolute discretion," gives them latitude to withhold or pay out income, and, in the event of an income shortfall, to invade the principal, for the "care, comfort, support and maintenance" of Mark and his descendants. However, the words "absolute discretion" do not insulate the trustees, even trustees of lifetime trusts, as here, from liability.

Article 6.1 purports to absolve the trustees from a duty to account (except for a final account). That violates public policy and cannot be enforced where, as here, the beneficiary is a person under a disability, and no one is protecting the beneficiary's interests. In an accounting, the court can assess the trustees' failure to take reasonable interest in and action on behalf of Mark.

The trustees left Mark to languish for several years with inadequate care, despite the fact that the Mark Trust had abundant assets. In so doing, the trustees failed to exhibit a reasonable degree of diligence toward Mark. Courts will intervene not only when the trustee behaves recklessly, but also when the trustee fails to exercise judgment altogether ("even where a trustee has discretion whether or not to make any payments to a particular beneficiary, the court will interpose if the trustee, arbitrarily or without knowledge of or inquiry into relevant circumstances, fails to exercise the discretion") (Restatement [Third] of Trusts §50, Comment b). That is, sadly, precisely what occurred here.

The plain language of the Mark Trust elucidates Marie's intent in its creation. Article 2.1, §(iii) authorizes the trustees to pay any income not applied for Mark's benefit "to any facility he may be residing in and/or to any organization where he may be a client or a participant in any program(s)." This provision reflects both the importance of Mark's quality of life to Marie and the minimum knowledge that Marie expected her trustees to have about Mark and his situation. In order to exercise their discretionary power of expenditure, at the very least they are required to take steps necessary to keep themselves fully informed of Mark's residential situation and ancillary services. It is not sufficient for the trustees to simply safeguard the Mark Trust's assets; instead, the trustees have a duty to Mark to inquire into his condition and to apply trust income to improving it. The trustees abused their discretion by failing to exercise it. H.J.P.'s complicity is exacerbated by the fact that as drafter of the Mark Trust, as well as the drafter of Marie's will, he was aware of Mark's incapacity for years before serving as trustee.

. . .

. . . [I]t was not sufficient for the trustees merely to prudently invest the trust corpus and to safeguard its assets. The trustees here were affirmatively charged with applying trust assets to Mark's benefit and given the discretionary power to apply additional income to Mark's service providers. Both case law and basic principles of trust administration and fiduciary obligation require the trustees to take appropriate steps to keep abreast of Mark's condition, needs, and quality of life, and to utilize trust assets for his actual benefit.

While the accounting in this trust is not yet complete, their failure to fulfill their fiduciary obligations should result in denial or reduction of their commissions for the period of their inaction.

NEXT STEPS

The current accounting leaves many questions unanswered, particularly since an accurate statement of the opening principal received depends on the administration under both Marie's will and the somewhat inexplicable[14] Revocable Trust. Without expressing a view, or making any negative assumption, whether or not the estate and Revocable Trust were appropriately administered affects the amount of assets the Mark Trust should rightfully have received.

. . .

Accordingly, H.J.P. is ordered to account as executor of the will of Marie H., and he and Chase are ordered to account as cotrustees of the Marie H. Revocable Trust of 1995 within 90 days of the order to be entered following this decision. Further, the cotrustees of the Mark Trust are ordered to file and serve a supplemented and revised accounting herein for proceedings through December 31, 2012, reflecting the proper values of the assets with which the trust was funded, by that same deadline.

QUESTIONS

1. Using the taxonomy above (i.e., mandatory, discretionary, support, etc.), how would you categorize the Mark Trust? Did Mark have a right to compel the trustees to make distributions from the trust?

   ANSWER. The Mark Trust is a discretionary support trust because, under Article 2.1, the trust combines the repose of discretion ("sole and absolute discretion") with a support standard ("care, comfort, support and maintenance"). Because the trust did not mandate the distribution of principal, Mark, through his guardians, could not directly compel the trustees to make distributions of income or corpus. Rather, his recourse was limited to judicial review of the trustees' conduct for abuse of discretion. Beneficiaries rarely prevail against trustees under the abuse of discretion standard, but the trustees' deficiencies in this case are so stark and apparent that Mark was able to establish an abuse of discretion.

2. Before the Surrogate's Court intervened, the trustees in this case had not received any communication from Mark or his caretakers indicating a need for trust

14. It is difficult to understand the use of this Revocable Trust, created on the same day as the execution of Marie's will and as the Mark and Charles trusts, and like the latter, only nominally funded, as a planning device. Marie's estate could, as easily and without any negative tax consequences, simply have poured directly into the Mark and Charles trusts. Without an accounting, it is impossible to know if commissions, appropriate or otherwise, were taken, or what expenses, if any, were charged to the Revocable Trust.

distributions to cover Mark's living expenses. Given that Mark was unable to communicate or otherwise capable of articulating his needs because of his disability, why could not the trustees rely on Mark's caretakers to request distributions from the trust? Aside from communication with Mark's caretakers, how else could the trustees of ascertained Mark's needs?

ANSWER. Perhaps Mark's caretakers should have reached out to the trustees, but they were not trustees and therefore had no obligation under trust law to contact the trustees. It is also possible that Mark's caretakers did not know of his trust's existence. The trustees, by contrast, had actual knowledge of Mark's incapacity from either the language of the trust or their interaction with the settlor (or both). The trustees' knowledge of Mark's incapacity meant that they could not comply with the discretionary support standard simply by waiting for Mark to request trust distributions. The trustees could have discharged their obligation to comply with the discretionary support standard by ascertaining Mark's needs in the same manner that the court did: hiring a certified care manager experienced in the care of disabled persons like Mark. The costs of engaging the care manager would properly have been paid out of trust assets.

3. Article 2.1(iii) of the Mark Trust authorized the trustees "to pay or apply . . . to any facility [the beneficiary] may be residing in and/or to any organization where he may be a client or a participant in any program(s) sponsored by them, as the Trustees shall determine, for the general uses of such facility and/or organization." Suppose that, prior to the Surrogate's Court's intervention, the trustees had consistently made monthly payments to Mark's in-patient facility for his care but otherwise took no action to ascertain Mark's needs. Would the trustees have complied with the standard of distribution imposed by the trust?

   ANSWER. No, likely not. The trustees had an affirmative obligation to ascertain the beneficiary's needs. Although such distributions were authorized by the trust, in the absence of a reasonable attempt to determine Mark's needs, distributing monthly payments for his in-patient care reflects little more than speculative guesswork. In fact, such payments would likely be inconsistent with the trust's purpose to ensure that Mark received and remained eligible for government benefits.[15] Mark's residential in-patient facility expenses were covered by Medicaid, so if the trustees distributed trust assets to cover costs already paid for by the State, then such payments might constitute a further breach of fiduciary duty. See, e.g., Liranzo v. LI Jewish Education/Research, No. 28863/1996 (N.Y. Sup. Ct. Kings Cty. June 25, 2013) (imposing surcharge on corporate fiduciary for distributing trust assets for services that would have been covered by Medicaid).

4. The trust reposed the trustees with "sole and absolute discretion." If, as here, the trustees assert their belief that they exercised discretion properly, would not the

15. The opinion describes one such provision of the trust: "Article 2.1, section (v) gives the trustees the right to terminate the trust 'as if the beneficiary were deceased' if the existence of the trust causes the beneficiary to be excluded from government benefits."

terms of the trust require the court to defer to the trustees' evaluation of their own conduct?

ANSWER. No. Discretionary trusts often purport to vest trustees with broad discretion using language such as "sole," "absolute," and "uncontrolled" discretion. This level of discretion requires deference to the trustees, but courts, as here, have consistently held that, regardless of the purported scope of discretion, the trustee's conduct still remains subject to judicial review.

PROBLEM I

Claire and Buddy were married in 1951. They had four children and eight grandchildren. In 1996, Claire established a marital trust providing that all income would be distributed to Buddy during his life and the following:

> Whenever in the sole judgment of the trustee the income being paid to Buddy, together with any other income or periodic payments known to the trustee that are being received by Buddy shall be insufficient for his proper support, maintenance, or to enable him to meet any difficulty produced by sickness, accident, or similar cause, such portion of the corpus of this trust estate as in the discretion of the trustee is deemed appropriate shall be paid to him or for his benefit.

Upon Buddy's death, the trust provided that the balance of the corpus would be distributed to Claire's and Buddy's descendants.

When Claire died in 1997, the value of the trust was $2 million and Reliance Bank & Trust Company accepted the trust's appointment as trustee.

After Claire's death, Buddy's annual living expenses routinely and significantly exceeded his income distributions from the trust. Buddy remained in constant communication with Reliance and he submitted dozens of requests to invade the trust corpus each year to pay for his expenses not covered by the income distributions.

Over the years, Reliance made significant distributions of trust corpus, but the distributions were made in an inconsistent manner. Sometimes, though not always, Reliance required Buddy to submit bills or invoices for the claimed expenses. Sometimes, though not always, Reliance invaded principal to pay for the mortgage and maintenance on Buddy's out-of-state vacation home. Sometimes, though not always, Reliance distributed funds from the trust corpus to pay for Buddy's attorneys' fees. Concerned about the depletion of the trust corpus, Reliance eventually placed Buddy on an annual budget for invasions of principal. Sometimes, however, Reliance made exceptions to the annual budget and allowed distributions of principal above the allotted amount.

After Buddy died last year, his children and grandchildren (the remainder beneficiaries) discovered that the invasions of principal over the years had depleted the trust corpus to $800,000. The remainder beneficiaries claim that Reliance failed to comply with the standard of distribution set forth in the trust and should be liable for making excessive distributions of principal. Reliance counters that Claire's trust vested the trustee with broad discretion and reposed the decision to invade principal in the "sole judgment of the trustee." Reliance argues, further, that if it had neglected to cover as much of Buddy's living expenses as possible, Buddy could have brought suit for failing to ascertain his needs and meet his living expenses. Who should prevail and why?

PROBLEM II

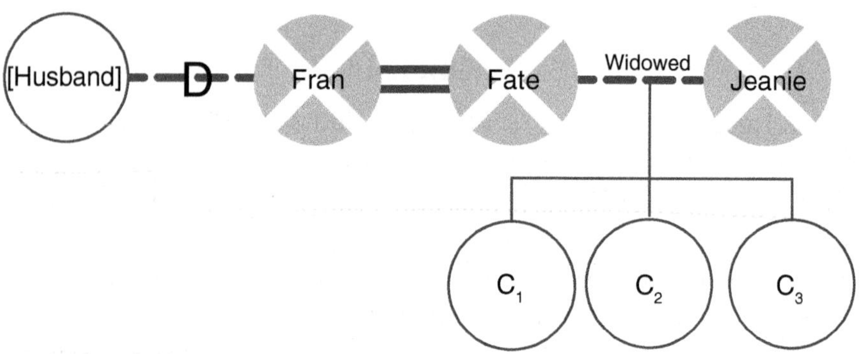

Fate and Fran were married three years ago in a second marriage for both. Fate had three adult children from his prior marriage to Jeanie, who died four years ago. Fran had no children of her own. At the time of their marriage, Fate owned assets worth $1.3 million, including a house in Lubbock and a cabin in the woods. Fran came into the marriage with assets worth $300,000, including a house in Wichita Falls. Fate and Fran signed a prenuptial agreement in which Fate agreed to support their high standard of living, grant Fran a life estate in Fate's cabin, and pay for the monthly mortgage, property taxes, and maintenance of Fran's house in Wichita Falls.

At Fate's request, Fran retired from her job as an interior decorator, which paid an annual salary of $70,000, so that the couple could share their golden years together and travel. Indeed, the couple maintained a high standard of living, with three homes and five cars, and frequent trips including cruises to Panama and Alaska. On average, their standard of living generated expenses of $5,600 per month.

Fate's will devised his entire estate in trust to Fran and his children as follows:

> The primary purpose of "THE FATE FAMILY TRUST" shall be to provide for the support, maintenance, and health of my wife in the standard of living to which she is accustomed at my death. If my wife's own income and other financial resources from sources other than from this trust are not sufficient to so maintain her in such standard of living, the Trustee shall distribute, from time to time, as much of the current trust net income, or accumulated trust net income, as shall be necessary to so maintain her. If my wife's own income and other financial resources, together with distributions of current and accumulated trust net income from this trust, are not sufficient to maintain her in such standard of living, then the Trustee shall distribute as much of the trust corpus as shall be necessary to so maintain her. After my wife has been provided for in the manner described

> above, and if in the Trustee's judgment, it will not endanger my wife's present or reasonably foreseeable future support, the Trustee may distribute to my descendants, from time to time, such amounts of the current or accumulated trust net income and as much of the trust corpus, as shall be necessary for their respective support, maintenance, health, and education. Upon Fran's death, the Trustee shall distribute the balance of the trust corpus to my descendants, per capita at each generation.

The trust appointed Fate's friend, Lynn, as trustee. Lynn was a longtime friend of Fate and Jeanie.

Fate died earlier this year. Fran has requested several disbursements from the trust to cover her living expenses, which significantly exceed her monthly social security income of $1,100. Lynn, however, refuses to make any distributions of income or principle to Fran. Lynn argues that the trust requires a distribution of trust income only if Fran's "own income and other financial resources from sources other than from this trust are not sufficient to so maintain her in such standard of living" (with a similar provision governing distribution of principal). Lynn contends that, because Fran's own financial resources include $300,000 in assets she brought with her into the marriage, Fran is not entitled to distributions from the trust until she exhausts her assets down to one car and one house.

A. What is the nature of Fran's interest in the Fate Testamentary Trust?

B. What standard of review governs the trustee's decisions regarding trust distributions?

C. Should Fran be required to deplete her assets before receiving distributions from the trust?

D. If and when Fran becomes eligible for distributions from the trust, how should the trustee determine the amount to distribute?

E. Given the trustee's close friendship with Fate and his first wife, Jeanie, was he able to act impartially when exercising discretion regarding the allocation of trust assets between Fran and the descendants of Fran and Jeanie?

F. Could the conflict between Fran and the trustee been avoided by more careful draftsmanship of the trust? If so, how would you revise the trust instrument?

9.1.2 Creditors

A trust beneficiary's unpaid creditors are not party to the trust, but they are stakeholders who have an interest in compelling the distribution of trust assets. When a trust beneficiary defaults on a payment obligation, such as a credit card bill, mortgage payment, or child support decree, the unpaid creditor will often search far and wide for assets owned by or available to the defaulting beneficiary to pursue collection on the unsatisfied debt. Upon discovering the debtor's beneficial interest in a donative trust, the creditor may seek to attach trust assets to the extent necessary to satisfy the outstanding debt and compel the trustee to distribute the assets directly to the creditor instead of the beneficiary. As a general rule, Uniform Trust Code §501 authorizes a creditor or assignee to attach a trust beneficiary's interest.

Uniform Trust Code
§501 Rights of Beneficiary's Creditor or Assignee

To the extent a beneficiary's interest is not subject to a spendthrift provision, the court may authorize a creditor or assignee of the beneficiary to reach the beneficiary's interest by attachment of present or future distributions to or for the benefit of the beneficiary or other means. The court may limit the award to such relief as is appropriate under the circumstances.

Several significant exceptions to this general rule, however, provide for the insulation of trust assets against collection by a beneficiary's unpaid creditors. This section will consider three such features: (1) the effect of a discretionary standard; (2) spendthrift trusts; and (3) self-settled asset protection trusts.

9.1.2.1 Effect of Discretionary Standard

Recall that, in a discretionary trust, the nature of the beneficiary's interest is conditioned entirely upon the trustee's exercise of discretion in favor of making a distribution. The effect of the settlor's delegation of discretion to the trustee is that the beneficiary has no right to receive any particular amount at any particular time. Thus, in a dispute between a beneficiary and trustee regarding distributions from a discretionary trust, the beneficiary's only legal recourse is the right to seek judicial review of the trustee's exercise of discretion and the standard of judicial review is typically deferential to the trustee.

When a creditor obtains a court order under UTC §501 attaching a discretionary trust interest, the trustee must comply with the attachment.[16] An attachment order functions by imposing a requirement on the trustee to pay the creditor upon a vesting of the beneficiary's right to receive a trust distribution. In a discretionary trust, however, a beneficiary has no vested right to receive trust assets until the trustee exercises discretion in favor of making a distribution. The attachment order does not require the trustee to exercise discretion one way or the other, so, in the exercise of discretion and upon consideration of the attachment's adverse effect on the beneficiary's enjoyment, the trustee may decide to indefinitely postpone all distributions of trust assets to the defaulted beneficiary.

Under UTC §504(b), the discretionary standard further insulates trust assets from creditor collection by precluding creditors from seeking judicial review of the trustee's decision making. The fiduciary duties of trusteeship, including the duty to act in good faith when exercising a discretionary power, are owed solely to the trust beneficiaries.[17] A trustee owes no such duty to a creditor who, unlike a beneficiary, lacks standing to enforce the

---

16. A trustee must comply with an attachment order unless the trust contains a spendthrift provision, as discussed below.

17. See UTC §814(a) ("Notwithstanding the breadth of discretion granted to a trustee in the terms of the trust, including the use of such terms as 'absolute,' 'sole,' or 'uncontrolled,' the trustee shall exercise a discretionary power in good faith and in accordance with the terms and purposes of the trust and the interests of the beneficiaries.").

trustee's obligations of trusteeship. Thus, under UTC §504(b), a creditor may not compel a discretionary distribution *even if the trustee's refusal constitutes an abuse of discretion*. The creditor may obtain a court order prohibiting further disbursements to the beneficiary until the creditor has been repaid,[18] but the creditor's right to collect from the trust remains contingent upon the trustee's unconstrained discretion to decide whether to make a distribution. The attachment procedure authorized under UTC §501 may confer a marginal benefit on creditors because the beneficiary's ineligibility to receive trust distributions creates an incentive to repay the outstanding debt. But the creditor's inability to challenge the trustee's exercise of discretion forecloses the more potent form of relief that creditors would overwhelmingly prefer: direct collection of trust assets over the trustee's objection.

The creditor's inability to challenge a trustee's abuse of discretion under UTC §504(b), however, is subject to an important exception for a narrow category of creditors entitled to special protection: family support claimants. Under UTC §504(c), a family support claimant holding an unpaid judgment for spousal support, alimony, or child support may challenge a trustee's refusal to make a distribution and, upon a finding of abuse of discretion, the court may compel a distribution directly to the unpaid family support claimant. UTC §504(c)(2), however, limits the amount of compulsory distributions to that which "the trustee would have been required to distribute to or for the benefit of the beneficiary had the trustee complied with the standard or not abused the discretion." Thus, a family support claimant is not necessarily entitled to a discretionary distribution in full satisfaction of the outstanding support claim; rather, the relief is limited to the amount that should have been distributed to the beneficiary had the trustee properly exercised discretion.

Uniform Trust Code
§504 Discretionary Trusts; Effect of Standard

. . .

(b) Except as otherwise provided in subsection (c), whether or not a trust contains a spendthrift provision, a creditor of a beneficiary may not compel a distribution that is subject to the trustee's discretion, even if:

(1) the discretion is expressed in the form of a standard of distribution; or

(2) the trustee has abused the discretion.

(c) To the extent a trustee has not complied with a standard of distribution or has abused a discretion:

(1) a distribution may be ordered by the court to satisfy a judgment or court order against the beneficiary for support or maintenance of the beneficiary's child, spouse, or former spouse; and

(2) the court shall direct the trustee to pay to the child, spouse, or former spouse such amount as is equitable under the circumstances but not more than the amount the trustee would have been required to distribute to or for the benefit of the beneficiary had the trustee complied with the standard or not abused the discretion.

except

18. This procedure was applied in Hamilton v. Drogo, 150 N.E. 496 (N.Y. 1926), and is authorized by UTC §501.

(d) This section does not limit the right of a beneficiary to maintain a judicial proceeding against a trustee for an abuse of discretion or failure to comply with a standard for distribution.

. . .

The Restatement (Third) of Trusts §60 adopts a contrary minority view that creditors may both attach a discretionary interest *and* compel its distribution by enforcing the trustee's proper exercise of discretion:

> [I]f the terms of a trust provide for a beneficiary to receive distributions in the trustee's discretion, a transferee or creditor of the beneficiary is entitled to receive or attach any distributions the trustee makes or is required to make in the exercise of that discretion after the trustee has knowledge of the transfer or attachment.

The Restatement's comment explains that when a trustee's abuse of discretion interferes with creditor collection, the trust corpus is unjustly enriched. This, in turn, produces a result presumably (according to the Restatement) in conflict with the settlor's intended repose of discretion. Most jurisdictions do not follow the Restatement's approach.

9.1.2.2 Effect of Support Standard

Support trusts also provide a form of asset protection arising from the nature of the beneficial interest. Recall that a beneficiary cannot alienate her interest in a support trust because alienation would be inconsistent with the trust's purpose to provide for the beneficiary's living expenses. Most creditors cannot attach a beneficiary's interest in a support trust for the same reason that a beneficiary cannot alienate her interest: the settlor's intent to create a trust for the beneficiary's support implies a restraint on voluntary and involuntary alienation for other purposes. A support trust is, in effect, a conditional gift authorizing distributions solely for the beneficiary's support. Courts, however, have recognized narrow exceptions for creditor claims by family support claimants and suppliers of necessities because payment of such claims is consistent with the trust's purpose to support the beneficiary's living expenses.

9.1.2.3 Spendthrift Trusts

Spendthrift trusts provide a powerful form of asset protection under a venerable doctrine dating to the nineteenth century.[19] The salient feature of spendthrift trusts imposes a categorical restraint on distributions to creditors of the beneficiary. Spendthrift trusts, therefore, carve out a significant exception to the general rule under UTC §501 permitting creditors to attach a beneficiary's interest. Because a spendthrift trust is not subject to attachment, the law permits the trustee to disregard collection claims against the trust and to distribute assets directly into the hands of the beneficiary. Spendthrift protection, however, applies only to *future* payments from the trust, so unpaid creditors and assignees may attach and collect against trust assets after they have been distributed to the beneficiary.

---

19. The origins of spendthrift trusts in the United States can be traced to dicta in Nichols v. Eaton, 91 U.S. 716 (1875), and the express recognition of the validity of spendthrift protection in Broadway National Bank v. Adams, 133 Mass. 170 (1882).

Spendthrift trusts are so named because the distribution restraint insulates trust assets against a beneficiary's liability-generating conduct. (A *spendthrift* is a person who behaves irresponsibly with money or engages in profligate spending.)

Actress Farrah Fawcett, one of the original Charlie's Angels, died in 2009 and reportedly left a spendthrift trust for the benefit of her son, Redmond, who has served time in prison for drug-related offenses.

Under traditional law, a spendthrift trust must disable both voluntary and involuntary alienation such that a beneficiary can neither voluntarily pledge trust assets as a form of payment nor expose trust assets to involuntary collection for liabilities arising from the beneficiary's conduct. Some interpretations of the spendthrift doctrine validate a trust provision that imposes an automatic forfeiture of the beneficiary's interest effective upon either a beneficiary's attempt to alienate the trust or a creditor's attempt to collect against trust assets.[20] Spendthrift protection arises under state trust law but is generally enforceable under federal bankruptcy law, which expressly respects a

20. See Restatement (Third) of Trusts §57 ("Except with respect to an interest retained by the settlor, the terms of a trust may validly provide that an interest shall terminate or become discretionary upon an attempt by the beneficiary to transfer it or by the beneficiary's creditors to reach it, or upon the bankruptcy of the beneficiary."). Although enforceable under state trust law, such a provision may not be enforceable under federal bankruptcy law, which defines the debtor's bankruptcy estate to include interests "conditioned on the solvency or financial condition of the debtor." 11 U.S.C. §541(c)(1)(B).

"restriction on the transfer of a beneficial interest of a debtor in a trust that is enforceable under applicable nonbankruptcy law." 11 U.S.C. §541(c)(2).

Uniform Trust Code
§502 Spendthrift Provisions

(a) A spendthrift provision is valid only if it restrains both voluntary and involuntary transfer of a beneficiary's interest.

(b) A term of a trust providing that the interest of a beneficiary is held subject to a "spendthrift trust," or words of similar import, is sufficient to restrain both voluntary and involuntary transfer of the beneficiary's interest.

(c) A beneficiary may not transfer an interest in a trust in violation of a valid spendthrift provision and, except as otherwise provided in this [article], a creditor or assignee of the beneficiary may not reach the interest or a distribution by the trustee before its receipt by the beneficiary.

Spendthrift trusts are not recognized in England and were sharply criticized in the United States when courts began to validate them in the late 1800s. The central criticism of spendthrift trusts is that their preferential treatment of debtors frustrates legitimate interests of creditors to collect on debt and impairs the value of creditor claims. Spendthrift trusts, therefore, seemed to undermine a fundamental tenet of civil liability limiting enforcement of judgments to collection of the debtor's property rather than incarceration or other methods of coercing payment. Peonage and debt slavery practices have long been prohibited in the United States, so a debtor who cannot satisfy a liability claim is generally not subjected to further sanction aside from collection of assets. But by preventing attachment of trust distributions, spendthrift protection precludes creditors from exercising their only civil enforcement remedy (collection of property) against the beneficiary's interest in the trust.

Despite these concerns, almost all U.S. jurisdictions recognize the validity of spendthrift trusts. The justification for tolerating spendthrift protection, however, is not based on a policy of special protection for trust beneficiaries or preferential treatment for debtors. Rather, the policy of validating spendthrift trusts is justified by the animating principle of wealth transfer law: facilitation of the *donor's* freedom of disposition.[21] Spendthrift trusts, therefore, exist for the benefit of the settlor rather than the beneficiary.

To better understand this rationale, consider the following two hypotheticals:

Case A

Martha is a wealthy business owner who is planning to make a significant gift of money to her grandchild, Albert, who recently graduated from college with significant student debt. In addition to Albert's federal student loans ($100,000), he graduated with the following outstanding liabilities: (1) $8,000 in unpaid rent owed to a private landlord; (2) $12,000 in credit card debt; and (3) $14,000 in private student loans from a local bank. Albert now works as a junior software

21. See, e.g., Estate of Morgan, 72 A. 498, 499 (1909) ("[C]onsideration for the beneficiary does not even in the remotest way enter into the policy of the law; it has regard solely to the rights of the donor. Spendthrift trusts can have no other justification than is to be found in considerations affecting the donor alone.").

developer making a salary of $50,000 and, to the extent he has any disposable income after paying for basic expenses (rent at a new apartment, food, clothing, health insurance, etc.), he applies it toward repayment of his federal student loans. Martha is aware of Albert's financial situation and is worried that if she gives him a large gift as a lump sum payment, his creditors will attach it and prevent him from using it for his enjoyment. Therefore, Martha hand delivers Albert an unmarked envelope containing $1,000 in cash each month and verbally instructs him to use it for "fun." Albert accepts the monthly payments and obeys Martha's direction to use it for his enjoyment. He typically spends the money on nice restaurants, fine clothes, and travel. If Albert's creditors remain unpaid and discover what Martha is doing, they could not attach future cash payments from Martha to Albert. Martha's refusal to deliver the monthly payments to Albert's creditors has an indirect effect on the creditors who cannot use the funds to satisfy their unpaid claims. But Martha may give or withhold inter vivos donative transfers with absolute impunity because she has no legal obligation to indemnify Albert's debts.

Case B

Now, suppose that Martha dies before learning of Albert's financial situation and she devises her entire estate in trust for the benefit of Albert. The trust provides for monthly cash payments of $1,000 to Albert until he reaches the age of 30, whereupon he may invade the trust principal. The trust expressly states Martha's wish that Albert use the $1,000 monthly payments for "fun and enjoyment, not living expenses or essentials." Absent spendthrift protection, Albert's creditors may attach his interest in the trust and, because the monthly distributions are mandatory, the creditors may compel the trustee to distribute the attached funds as they become due. And when Albert turns 30, because the trust allows him to invade the trust principal, the creditors may attach the trust corpus to satisfy any outstanding claims and compel distribution from the trustee. The creditors' attachment, however, would frustrate the purpose of Martha's gift to Albert, which was for his personal enjoyment. Spendthrift protection, which prevents attachment by creditors, allows Martha to carry out her intent, which she was permitted to do during life, by delegating these distributions to a trustee after her death.

Thus, a spendthrift trust extends the donor's freedom to give or withhold inter vivos donative transfers to gifts that take place after the donor's death. After the donor's death, spendthrift protection authorizes the trustee to perform the same act that the settlor could have performed during life: remit trust distributions directly to the beneficiary without legal interference or attachment by the beneficiary's creditors.[22] Spendthrift trusts are now valid throughout the United States and, in some

22. In Nichols v. Eaton, 91 U.S. 716, 727 (1875), Justice Miller observed in dicta, "Why a parent . . . who . . . wishes to use his own property in securing [his child] . . . from the ills of life, the vicissitudes of fortune, and even his own improvidence, or incapacity for self-protection, should not be permitted to do so, is not readily perceived." For additional literature on spendthrift trusts, see Robert T. Danforth, Article Five of the UTC and the Future of Creditors' Rights in Trusts, 27 Cardozo L. Rev. 2551 (2006); Jeffrey A. Schoenblum, In Search of a Unifying Principle for Article V of the Uniform Trust Code: A Response to Professor Danforth, 27 Cardozo L. Rev. 2609 (2006); Adam J. Hirsch, Spendthrift Trusts and Public Policy: Economic and Cognitive Perspectives, 73 Wash. U. L.Q. 1 (1995).

jurisdictions, spendthrift protection is presumed in the absence of express language in the trust.[23] UTC §502, above, adopts the majority rule that applies spendthrift protection against a general creditor's attachment of the beneficiary's entire interest. However, some states have softened the rule by allowing creditors to attach a portion of a beneficiary's interest in a spendthrift trust.[24]

In the illustrations presented above, even though Albert's creditors remain unpaid, their initial decision to extend credit was voluntary. For example, the former landlord chose to lease the college apartment to Albert notwithstanding Albert's insufficient income to cover the monthly rent and lack of credit history. The landlord voluntarily assumed the risk of Albert's default in exchange for a year's worth of potential rental income. The landlord, therefore, is a voluntary creditor. What about involuntary creditor claimants who did not choose to enter into a defaulted relationship with a spendthrift beneficiary?

Scheffel v. Krueger
146 N.H. 669 (2001)

DUGGAN, J.

The plaintiff, Lorie Scheffel, individually and as mother and next friend of Cory C., appeals a Superior Court (Hollman, J.) order dismissing her trustee process action against Citizens Bank NH, the trustee defendant. *See* RSA 512:9-b (1997). We affirm.

In 1998, the plaintiff filed suit in superior court asserting tort claims against the defendant, Kyle Krueger. In her suit, the plaintiff alleged that the defendant sexually assaulted her minor child, videotaped the act and later broadcasted the videotape over the Internet. The same conduct that the plaintiff alleged in the tort claims also formed the basis for criminal charges against the defendant. *See* State v. Krueger, 146 N.H. 541, 542 (2001). The court entered a default judgment against the defendant and ordered him to pay $551,286.25 in damages. To satisfy the judgment against the defendant, the plaintiff sought an attachment of the defendant's beneficial interest in the Kyle Krueger Irrevocable Trust (trust).

The defendant's grandmother established the trust in 1985 for the defendant's benefit. Its terms direct the trustee to pay all of the net income from the trust to the beneficiary, at least quarterly, or more frequently if the beneficiary in writing so requests. The trustee is further authorized to pay any of the principal to the beneficiary if in the trustee's sole discretion the funds are necessary for the maintenance, support and education of the beneficiary. The beneficiary may not invade the principal until he reaches the age of fifty, which will not occur until April 6, 2016.

23. In New York, for example, the income interest of an express trust is presumptively construed as protected by a spendthrift provision. N.Y. EST. POWERS & TRUSTS LAW §7-1.5 (McKinney).

24. See, e.g., CAL. PROB. CODE §15306.5 (West) (limiting the attachment of spendthrift interest "in satisfaction of the judgment [to] an amount [not] exceeding 25 percent of the payment that otherwise would be made to, or for the benefit of, the beneficiary"); N.Y. EST. POWERS & TRUSTS LAW §7-3.4 (McKinney) ("Where a trust is created to receive the income from property and no valid direction for accumulation is given, the income in excess of the sum necessary for the education and support of the beneficiary is subject to the claims of his creditors in the same manner as other property which cannot be reached by execution.").

The beneficiary is prohibited from making any voluntary or involuntary transfers of his interest in the trust. Article VII of the trust instrument specifically provides:

> No principal or income payable or to become payable under any of the trusts created by this instrument shall be subject to anticipation or assignment by any beneficiary thereof, or to the interference or control of any creditors of such beneficiary or to be taken or reached by any legal or equitable process in satisfaction of any debt or liability of such beneficiary prior to its receipt by the beneficiary.

Asserting that this so-called spendthrift provision barred the plaintiff's claim against the trust, the trustee defendant moved to release the attachment and dismiss the trustee defendant. The trial court ruled that under RSA 564:23 (1997), this spendthrift provision is enforceable against the plaintiff's claim and dismissed the trustee process action.

We first address the plaintiff's argument that the legislature did not intend RSA 564:23 to shield the trust assets from tort creditors, especially when the beneficiary's conduct constituted a criminal act. The plaintiff's claim presents a question of law involving the interpretation of a statute, which we review *de novo*. *See* Appeal of Rainville, 143 N.H. 624, 631 (1999). "We interpret legislative intent from the statute as written, and therefore, we will not consider what the legislature might have said or add words that the legislature did not include." Rye Beach Country Club v. Town of Rye, 143 N.H. 122, 125 (1998).

We begin by examining the language found in the statute. RSA 564:23, I, provides:

> In the event the governing instrument so provides, a beneficiary of a trust shall not be able to transfer his or her right to future payments of income and principal, and a creditor of a beneficiary shall not be able to subject the beneficiary's interest to the payment of its claim.

The statute provides two exceptions to the enforceability of spendthrift provisions. The provisions "shall not apply to a beneficiary's interest in a trust to the extent that the beneficiary is the settlor and the trust is not a special needs trust established for a person with disabilities," RSA 564:23, II, and "shall not be construed to prevent the application of RSA 545-A or a similar law of another state [regarding fraudulent transfers]," RSA 564:23, III. Thus, under the plain language of the statute, a spendthrift provision is enforceable unless the beneficiary is also the settlor or the assets were fraudulently transferred to the trust. The plaintiff does not argue that either exception applies.

Faced with this language, the plaintiff argues that the legislature did not intend for the statute to shield the trust assets from tort creditors. The statute, however, plainly states that "a creditor of a beneficiary shall not be able to subject the beneficiary's interest to the payment of its claim." RSA 564:23, I. Nothing in this language suggests that the legislature intended that a tort creditor should be exempted from a spendthrift provision. Two exemptions are enumerated in sections II and III. Where the legislature has made specific exemptions, we must presume no others were intended. *See* Brahmey v. Rollins, 87 N.H. 290, 299 (1935). "If this is an omission, the courts cannot supply it. That is for the Legislature to do." *Id.* (quotation omitted).

The plaintiff argues public policy requires us to create a tort creditor exception to the statute. The cases the plaintiff relies upon, however, both involve judicially created spendthrift law. *See* Sligh v. First Nat. Bank of Holmes County, 704 So. 2d 1020, 1024 (Miss. 1997); Elec. Workers v. IBEW-NECA Holiday Trust, 583 S.W.2d 154, 162 (Mo. 1979). In this State, the legislature has enacted a statute repudiating the public policy exception sought by the plaintiff. *Compare* RSA 564:23, I, *with* Athorne v. Athorne, 100 N.H. 413, 416 (1957). This statutory enactment cannot be overruled, because "[i]t is axiomatic that courts do not question the wisdom or expediency of a statute." *Brahmey*, 87 N.H. at 298. Therefore, "[n]o rule of public policy is available to overcome [this] statutory rule." *Id.*

The plaintiff next argues that the trust does not qualify as a spendthrift trust under RSA 564:23 because the trust document allows the beneficiary to determine the frequency of payments, to demand principal and interest after his fiftieth birthday, and to dispose of the trust assets by will. These rights, the plaintiff asserts, allow the beneficiary too much control over the trust to be recognized as a trust under RSA 564:23. Beyond the exclusion of trusts settled by the beneficiary, *see* RSA 564:23, II, the statute does not place any limitation on the rights a beneficiary is granted under the trust instrument. Rather, by its plain language the statute applies where a trust's "governing instrument . . . provides, a beneficiary . . . shall not be able to transfer his or her right to future payments of income and principal, and a creditor of a beneficiary shall not be able to subject the beneficiary's interest to the payment of its claim." RSA 564:23, I. In this case, the trust instrument contains such a provision. Because the settlor of this trust is not the beneficiary, the spendthrift provision is enforceable. The legislature did not see fit to pronounce further limitations and we will not presume others were intended. *See Brahmey*, 87 N.H. at 299.

Finally, the plaintiff asserts that the trial court erred in denying her request that the trust be terminated because the purpose of the trust can no longer be satisfied. The plaintiff argues that the trust's purpose to provide for the defendant's support, maintenance and education can no longer be fulfilled because the defendant will likely remain incarcerated for a period of years. The trial court, however, found that the trust's purpose "may still be fulfilled while the defendant is incarcerated and after he is released." *See, e.g.*, RSA 622:55 (Supp. 2000). The record before us supports this finding.

Affirmed.

QUESTIONS

5. In a few (but significant) contexts, the organizing principle of wealth transfer law— that the law should facilitate, not regulate, the donor's freedom of disposition— yields to public policy considerations that override the law's reluctance to displace donative intent (e.g., spousal elective share, unenforceability of unreasonable restraints on the donee's marriage, unenforceability of charitable trusts that

discriminate on the basis of race). Under the spendthrift doctrine described in *Scheffel*, which represents the majority rule, how do the interests of tort creditors compare with the interests of other stakeholders who are protected on public policy grounds (e.g., disinherited surviving spouses, donees whose marital freedoms are unreasonably constrained by a restricted gift, and individuals subject to discrimination under a charitable trust)?

ANSWER. The interests of stakeholders protected in other wealth transfer law contexts on public policy grounds are difficult to distinguish from the interests of tort creditors who are generally not entitled to a special exception from the enforcement of a spendthrift trust. Perhaps one distinction, however, is that the spousal elective share, the unenforceability of unreasonable restraints on the donee's marriage, and the unenforceability of charitable trusts that discriminate on the basis of race all impose limitations in contexts where the donor's conduct is harmful or contrary to public policy. By contrast, a public policy exception for spendthrift trusts would impose a limitation on a context where the donee's conduct is responsible for the tort victim's harm. Is this distinction significant?

6. The opinion states that the trust allowed Mr. Krueger to invade principal on his fiftieth birthday, which occurred on April 6, 2016. According to the New Hampshire Department of Corrections' inmate locator, Mr. Krueger was eligible for parole on January 8, 2016 and released from prison on or near that date. Suppose Mr. Krueger asked the trustee for a distribution of $100,000 on his fiftieth birthday for the purpose of buying a new house. Could the trustee refuse to make a distribution? What, if anything, could Ms. Scheffel do to attach or collect the distribution? Would the trustee be permitted to notify Ms. Scheffel upon making a distribution?

ANSWER. The opinion does not reproduce the exact language of the trust provision allowing Mr. Krueger to invade principal upon reaching the age of 50, but the court's description implies that the trustee's discretion regarding distributions terminates at that time, at least to the extent of any request from Mr. Krueger. Thus, a request from Mr. Krueger would impose a mandatory obligation on the trustee to comply with the requested distribution. Ms. Scheffel, however, could not attach or collect upon the distribution until the assets reached Mr. Krueger's hands. If he used the trust distribution to purchase a house, then Ms. Scheffel could attach his interest in the house. The trustee, however, would most likely not be permitted to notify Ms. Scheffel of the distribution. A trustee generally owes a fiduciary duty to furnish information to beneficiaries, not creditors of beneficiaries. Cf. Restatement (Third) of Trusts §82.

Most jurisdictions and UTC §503 follow the rule in *Scheffel*: They do not recognize a public policy exception exempting tort creditors from enforcement of a spendthrift provision. There are, however, a few notable categories of creditors who *are* entitled to an exemption from the enforcement of a spendthrift provision: claimants for unpaid family support obligations, services provided for the protection of the beneficiary's interest in the trust, and government claims against the beneficiary.

Uniform Trust Code
§503 Exceptions to Spendthrift Provision

(a) In this section, "child" includes any person for whom an order or judgment for child support has been entered in this or another State.

(b) A spendthrift provision is unenforceable against:

(1) a beneficiary's child, spouse, or former spouse who has a judgment or court order against the beneficiary for support or maintenance;

(2) a judgment creditor who has provided services for the protection of a beneficiary's interest in the trust; and

(3) a claim of this State or the United States to the extent a statute of this State or federal law so provides.

(c) A claimant against which a spendthrift provision cannot be enforced may obtain from a court an order attaching present or future distributions to or for the benefit of the beneficiary. The court may limit the award to such relief as is appropriate under the circumstances.

PROBLEM III

Frank is in his late 70s and made his fortune in show business as a film director and producer. Frank's closest relative is his nephew, Nick, who also made a fortune in the motion picture business. Nick has had significant difficulty managing his finances. In recent years, Nick has spent beyond his means and purchased multiple personal residences, a Gulfstream jet, several Rolls Royces, a yacht, and rare dinosaur fossils. Frank is aware of Nick's spending habits, and would like to find some way of providing Nick with a safety net of financial support and stability.

A. Suppose Nick asks Frank for an inter vivos gift of $1 million so that he can purchase the LaLaurie Mansion, a historic property in New Orleans that is believed to be the most haunted house in America. Frank refuses to give Nick the money and explains, "If you can't afford the property, then don't buy it. This is not the type of financial support I want to provide for you." If Nick sues Frank for $1 million on grounds that Frank promised to provide Nick with financial support, what result?

B. Now suppose Frank died earlier this year and his will includes a substantial testamentary trust for Nick's benefit.

   1. The trust vests the trustee with "absolute, uncontrolled, sole discretion" regarding distributions from the trust. Nick asks the trustee for a distribution of $1 million so that he can purchase the LaLaurie Mansion and the trustee refuses. If Nick sues the trustee for $1 million on grounds that the trustee abused his discretion, what result?
   2. After being turned down for a distribution by the trustee, Nick asks his ex-wife, Lisa Marie, for a loan of $1 million. As collateral for the loan, Nick assigns his interest in the trust to Lisa Marie to the extent of $1 million in principal and $150,000 in interest. Lisa Marie agrees, and gives Nick the $1 million. When Nick defaults on the loan, the trustee refuses to distribute anything to Lisa Marie. If Lisa Marie sues the trustee to enforce Nick's assignment, what result?

The LaLaurie Mansion, New Orleans

C. Now suppose Frank died earlier this year and his will includes a substantial testamentary trust for Nick's benefit. The trust directs the trustee to make distributions for the health, education, maintenance, and support of Nick for the duration of his lifetime. Nick defaults on his payment of health insurance premiums and asks the trustee for a distribution of $30,000 to cover the balance.

   1. The trustee refuses to make a distribution and explains that he will not distribute any funds from the trust until Nick sells at least one of his many residences. If Nick sues the trustee for $30,000 to cover his health insurance premiums, what result?
   2. Nick then asks Lisa Marie for a loan of $30,000 and promises to assign his interest in the trust to repay her. Lisa Marie agrees, but when Lisa Marie asks the trustee to make good on Nick's promise, the trustee refuses to make a distribution to her. If Lisa Marie sues the trustee for $30,000 to enforce Nick's assignment, what result?
   3. Would your answer to Question B.2 change if Nick owed Lisa Marie alimony, and she sued the trustee for back payments?

D. Suppose Frank died earlier this year and his will includes a substantial testamentary trust for Nick's benefit. The trust vests the trustee with "absolute, uncontrolled, sole discretion" regarding distributions from the trust and contains the following spendthrift provision: "To the maximum extent permitted by law, no interest of the beneficiary shall be subject to claims for the repayment of debt, alimony, maintenance, support, or any other form of involuntary transfer. Nor shall the beneficiary have the right to alienate his right to distributions from this trust."

1. Nick asks the trustee for a distribution of $1 million so that he can purchase the LaLaurie Mansion and the trustee refuses. Nick then enters into a contract with a subprime lender who accepts Nick's pledge of his interest in the trust as collateral for a $1 million loan. Nick defaults and the trustee refuses to make a distribution to either Nick or the lender. If the lender sues the trustee for $1 million based on Nick's pledge of collateral, what result?
2. Lisa Marie learns about the trust and asks the trustee for a distribution of $1 million to cover Nick's unpaid alimony obligations. If the trustee refuses to make a distribution to Lisa Marie, what result?
3. The trustee hires an attorney to defend the trust assets from claims asserted by Nick's creditors. Following the attorney's successful representation, however, the trustee refuses to distribute assets from the trust to pay the attorney's fees. What result if the attorney sues the trustee for a distribution to pay for the attorney's fees?
4. The Internal Revenue Service obtains federal tax lien against Nick in the amount of $6.2 million for unpaid income taxes. The IRS demands that the trustee make a distribution from the trust to satisfy the outstanding tax lien, but the trustee refuses. What result if the IRS sues the trustee to compel a distribution of $6.2 million for Nick's tax delinquency?

9.1.2.4 Self-Settled Asset Protection Trusts

Under traditional trust law and UTC §505, below, a spendthrift provision is not valid if it disables the alienation of an interest retained by the settlor. See Restatement (Third) of Trusts §58(2) ("A restraint on the voluntary and involuntary alienation of a beneficial interest retained by the settlor of a trust is invalid."). The rationale for allowing spendthrift trusts — to give effect to the donor's intent to protect trust assets against the beneficiary's improvidence — is much more difficult to justify on policy grounds when the donor is also a beneficiary. Recall that trust law tolerates third-party spendthrift trusts to protect the donor's intentions. A settlor, therefore, may create a spendthrift trust to protect trust assets from creditor claims asserted against the beneficiary because a donor's manifestation of intent to make a gift does not obligate the donor to indemnify the donee's outstanding debt obligations at the time of the gift. By contrast, self-settled spendthrift trusts, also known as asset protection trusts, do not serve the similar purpose of implementing donative intent. Rather, self-settled spendthrift trusts prevent creditors from attaching the settlor's *own* assets to satisfy the settlor's *own* debt obligations. Put another way, traditionally the law has prevented settlors from placing their own assets beyond the reach of their own creditors.

Uniform Trust Code
§505 Creditor's Claims Against Settlor

(a) Whether or not the terms of a trust contain a spendthrift provision, the following rules apply:

(1) During the lifetime of the settlor, the property of a revocable trust is subject to claims of the settlor's creditors.

(2) With respect to an irrevocable trust, a creditor or assignee of the settlor may reach the maximum amount that can be distributed to or for the settlor's benefit. If a trust has more than one settlor, the amount the creditor or assignee of a particular settlor may reach may not exceed the settlor's interest in the portion of the trust attributable to that settlor's contribution.

The modern trend of trust law, however, has gradually begun to abandon this traditional prohibition on self-settled spendthrift trusts. In the 1990s, recognition of self-settled spendthrift trusts began in foreign countries seeking to stimulate their local economies by attracting an inflow of trust assets from abroad. This inflow of assets, in turn, produced a lucrative cottage industry of trust companies employing local residents. For U.S. citizens seeking to protect assets against various forms of personal liability, offshore havens such as the Cook Islands presented an appealing alternative to domestic trusts. They authorized self-settled spendthrift trusts that effectively allowed the settlor to retain access to trust assets as a beneficiary,[25] but if a U.S. creditor pursued collection against the trust, the spendthrift provision would bar attachment, and the jurisdiction's foreign sovereignty would place the trust assets beyond the jurisdictional reach of U.S. courts seeking to invalidate the trust. Offshore self-settled spendthrift trusts are rarely tested in court, but a settlor's attempt to enforce a spendthrift provision to avoid repatriating assets necessary to repay domestic creditors can lead to a finding of civil contempt and imprisonment. See Federal Trade Commission v. Affordable Media, LLC, 179 F.3d 1228 (9th Cir. 1999).

Self-settled spendthrift trusts remain invalid in most U.S. jurisdictions, but at least sixteen states have authorized some form of asset protection trust. One of the challenges presented by such trusts is how to distinguish a facially legitimate self-settled spendthrift trust authorized by law from a fraudulent transfer established by the settlor for the purpose of hindering creditor collection. A fraudulent transfer creates the appearance of a real conveyance of property, but, in fact, the transfer is a sham designed to protect the transferred property against creditor claims. The fraudulent transfer doctrine, recognized under both state and federal law, sets aside such transfers and treats them as voidable as to creditors. See, e.g., Uniform Voidable Transfers Act §4 (Transfer or Obligation Voidable as to Present or Future Creditor); 11 U.S.C. §548 (fraudulent transfer provision under the federal Bankruptcy Code).

25. Self-settled spendthrift trusts are typically irrevocable and confer the trustee with absolute discretion regarding distributions. However, in practice, the trustee would generally exercise discretion in favor of making a distribution upon receiving a request from the settlor.

Under the Bankruptcy Code, the fraudulent transfer doctrine generally allows a bankruptcy court to set aside conveyances by the debtor within two years of the filing date of the bankruptcy petition. 11 U.S.C. §548(a)(1). In 2005, Congress sought to prevent the abuse of self-settled spendthrift trusts by extending the fraudulent transfer look-back period to ten years for self-settled trusts in which the debtor is a beneficiary. 11 U.S.C. §548(e)(1).

In re Mortensen
Bankruptcy Court Docket No. A09-90036-DMD (Bankr. D. Alaska May 26, 2011)

DONALD MACDONALD, IV, Bankruptcy Judge.

Kenneth Battley, chapter 7 trustee, has brought this adversary proceeding to set aside a transfer of real property as a fraudulent conveyance. It is a core proceeding under 28 U.S.C. §157(b)(2)(H). Jurisdiction arises under 28 U.S.C. §1334(b) and the district court's order of reference. Trial was held on March 21-23, 2012. I find for the plaintiff.

FACTUAL BACKGROUND

Thomas Mortensen, the debtor and one of the defendants herein, is a self-employed project manager. He has a master's degree in geology but has not worked in that field for 20 years. He manages the environmental aspects of construction projects. Mortensen has contracted with major oil companies for work in the past.

In 1994, Mortensen and his former wife purchased 1.25 acres of remote, unimproved real property located near Seldovia, Alaska. They paid $50,000.00 cash for the purchase. The parties divorced in 1998. Mortensen received his former wife's interest in the property. Subsequently, improvements were made to the property. A small shed was placed on the parcel in 2000 and some other small structures were built on it from 2001 through 2004. There is power to the property along with a well and septic system. The debtor transferred the property to a self-settled trust on February 1, 2005. The transfer of this property is the focal point of the current dispute.

Mortensen's divorce was a contested proceeding. . . . In total, Mortensen received assets of $164,402.00 in the divorce. [The divorce litigation, however, caused Mortensen's financial situation to deteriorate substantially.]

. . .

Prior to the divorce, Mortensen had averaged $50,000.00 to $60,000.00 a year in net income. [After the divorce, however, his income declined to $32,822 in 2000, $16,985 in 2001, $3,236 in 2002, and $13,185 in 2003.]

Mortensen didn't reveal his interest in establishing an asset protection trust at the [divorce] hearing in December of 2004. Mortensen had heard about Alaska's asset protection trust scheme in casual conversation. He researched the topic and, using a template he had found, drafted a document called the "Mortensen Seldovia Trust (An Alaska Asset Preservation Trust)." Mortensen then had the trust document reviewed by an attorney. He said only minor changes were suggested by the attorney.

The express purpose of the trust was "to maximize the protection of the trust estate or estates from creditors' claims of the Grantor or any beneficiary and to minimize all wealth transfer taxes." The trust beneficiaries were Mortensen and his descendants. Mortensen had three children at the time the trust was created.

Mortensen designated two individuals, his brother and a personal friend, to serve as trustees. His mother was named as a "trust protector," and had the power to remove and appoint successor trustees and designate a successor trust protector. She could not designate herself as a trustee, however. The trustees and Mortensen's mother are named defendants in this adversary proceeding.

The trust was registered on February 1, 2005. As required by AS 34.40.110(j), Mortensen also submitted an affidavit which stated that: 1) he was the owner of the property being placed into the trust, 2) he was financially solvent, 3) he had no intent to defraud creditors by creating the trust, 4) no court actions or administrative proceedings were pending or threatened against him, 5) he was not required to pay child support and was not in default on any child support obligation, 6) he was not contemplating filing for bankruptcy relief, and 7) the trust property was not derived from unlawful activities.

On February 1, 2005, Mortensen quitclaimed the Seldovia property to the trust, as contemplated in the trust document. Per the trust, this realty was "considered by the Grantor and the Grantor's children to be a special family place that should not be sold and should remain in the family." To facilitate this purpose, the trustees of the trust were requested, but not directed, to maintain and improve the Seldovia property "in the trust for the benefit, use and enjoyment of the Grantor's descendants and beneficiaries."

The Seldovia property was worth roughly $60,000.00 when it was transferred to the trust in 2005. Mortensen's mother sent him checks totaling $100,000.00 after the transfer. Mortensen claims this was part of the deal in his creation of the trust; his mother was paying him to transfer the property to the trust because she wanted to preserve it for her grandchildren. This desire is corroborated by notes his mother included with the two $50,000.00 checks she sent to him.

. . .

Mortensen says he used the money his mother sent him to pay some existing debts and also put about $80,000.00 of the funds into the trust's brokerage account as "seed money" to get the trust going and to pay trust-related expenses, such as income and property taxes. There was no promissory note for the money he lent to the trust. Mortensen said these funds were invested, some profits were made, and he was repaid "pretty much" all of the loan within about a year's time.

Mortensen says the Seldovia property is recreational property. It was used primarily by him and his three children, but other family members also used it. Before the trust was created, Mortensen had lived on the property the majority of the time, and he says he could have exempted it from creditors' claims as an Alaska homestead if he had retained it rather than placing it in the trust. In support of this contention, he has provided copies of his 2004 Alaska voter registration application, his 2003 fishing certificate, his 2004 Alaska PFD application (filed in 2005), a January, 2005, jury summons, and his Alaska driver's license, which all indicate that he resided in Seldovia when the trust was created.

Mortensen's financial condition has deteriorated since the establishment of the trust.

. . .

Mortensen filed his chapter 7 [i.e., bankruptcy] petition on August 18, 2009. He owned no real property at the time of filing, but his Schedule B itemized personal property with a value of $26,421.00. . . . His interest in the Seldovia Trust was not scheduled, but Mortensen disclosed the creation of the trust on his statement of financial affairs. . . .

ANALYSIS

The trustee alleges that Mortensen failed to establish a valid asset protection trust under Alaska's governing statutes because Mortensen was insolvent when the trust was created on February 1, 2005. Under A.S. 34.40.110(j)(2), the settlor of an Alaskan asset protection trust must file an affidavit stating that "the transfer of the assets to the trust will not render the settlor insolvent." "Insolvent" is not defined in Alaska's asset protection trust statute or in any cases arising thereafter. . . .

. . . I conclude that insolvency is established for purposes of Alaska's asset protection trust law if the debtor's liabilities exceed its assets, excluding the value of fraudulent conveyances and exemptions. Here, the applicable exemptions will be determined under state rather than federal law, because this court is applying Alaska law to determine if the trust was correctly established. The federal exemption statutes have no role in making that determination.

[To determine whether Mortensen was solvent at the time of the trust's creation on February 1, 2005, the court admitted evidence reconstructing his balancing sheet (assets and liabilities) as of that date. Mortensen's assets, less deductions for exemptions, were $143,914. Mortensen listed liabilities of $49,711, but he testified that he owed an additional $85,000 in credit card debt at the time.] Using either figure, however, Mortensen was solvent at the time he created the trust. The trust was created in accordance with Alaska law.[26]

Battley [the bankruptcy trustee] seeks judgment against Mortensen under 11 U.S.C. §548(e), which contains a ten-year limitation period for setting aside a fraudulent transfer. Section 548(e) provides:

---

26. [For the purpose of determining whether Mortensen was solvent on February 1, 2005, the date of the trust's creation, the court found that Mortensen's mother's promise to pay him $100,000 if he transferred the Seldovia property into a trust for himself and his children should be treated as an asset (specifically, a contract right) on his balance sheet on the date of the trust's creation. He did not receive the $100,000 payment until after February 1, but the promise was made before that date. Thus, when Mortensen conveyed the property into the trust on February 1, he had a contractual right to receive $100,000, which he did, in fact, receive shortly thereafter. But for the inclusion of this contract right, valued at $100,000, Mortensen would have been insolvent on the date of the trust's creation, so the trust would have been deemed invalid *ab initio*. — EDS.]

(e)(1) In addition to any transfer that the trustee may otherwise avoid, the trustee may avoid any transfer of an interest of the debtor in property that was made on or within 10 years before the date of the filing of the petition, if—

(A) such transfer was made to a self-settled trust or similar device;

(B) such transfer was by the debtor;

(C) the debtor is a beneficiary of such trust or similar device; and

(D) the debtor made such transfer with actual intent to hinder, delay, or defraud any entity to which the debtor was or became, on or after the date that such transfer was made, indebted.

Section 548(e) was added to the Bankruptcy Code in 2005, as part of the Bankruptcy Abuse Prevention and Consumer Protection Act. Section 548(e) "closes the self-settled trusts loophole" and was directed at the five states that permitted such trusts, including Alaska. Its main function "is to provide the estate representative with an extended reachback period for certain types of transfers." However, the "actual intent" requirement found in §548(e)(1)(D) is identical to the standard found in §548(a)(1)(A) for setting aside other fraudulent transfers and obligations.

Mortensen's trust, established under AS 34.40.110, satisfies the first three subsections of §548(e) — the Seldovia property was transferred to a self-settled trust, Mortensen made the transfer, and he is a beneficiary of the trust. The determinative issue here is whether Mortensen transferred the Seldovia property to the trust "with actual intent to hinder, delay, or defraud" his creditors.

Mortensen says he did not have this intent when he created the trust and that he simply wanted to preserve the property for his children. Battley counters that Mortensen's intent is clear from the trust language itself. The trust's stated purpose was "to maximize the protection of the trust estate or estates from creditors' claims of the Grantor or any beneficiary and to minimize all wealth transfer taxes." Mortensen argues that the trust language cannot be used to determine intent because Alaska law expressly prohibits it. Under Alaska law, "a settlor's expressed intention to protect trust assets from a beneficiary's potential future creditors is not evidence of an intent to defraud." But is this state statutory provision determinative when applying §548(e)(1)(D) of the Bankruptcy Code?

Ordinarily, it is state law, rather than the Bankruptcy Code, which creates and defines a debtor's interest in property.

. . .

Here, Congress has codified a federal interest which requires a different result. Only five states allow their citizens to establish self-settled trusts. Section 548(e) was enacted to close this "self-settled trust loophole."

. . .

It would be a very odd result for a court interpreting a federal statute aimed at closing a loophole to apply the state law that permits it. I conclude that a settlor's expressed intention to protect assets placed into a self-settled trust from a beneficiary's potential future creditors can be evidence of an intent to defraud. In this bankruptcy proceeding, AS 34.40.110(b)(1) cannot compel a different conclusion.

To establish an avoidable transfer under §548(e), the trustee must show that the debtor made the transfer with the actual intent to hinder, delay and defraud present or future creditors by a preponderance of the evidence. Here, the trust's express purpose was to hinder, delay and defraud present and future creditors. However, there is additional evidence which demonstrates that Mortensen's transfer of the Seldovia property to the trust was made with the intent to hinder, delay and defraud present and future creditors.

First, Mortensen was coming off some very lean years at the time he created the trust in 2005. [The court cites additional evidence.]

. . .

The bottom line for Mr. Mortensen is that he attempted a clever but fundamentally flawed scheme to avoid exposure to his creditors. When he created the trust in 2005, he failed to recognize the danger posed by the Bankruptcy Abuse Protection and Consumer Protection Act, which was enacted later that year. Mortensen will now pay the price for his actions. His transfer of the Seldovia property to the Mortensen Seldovia Trust will be avoided.

. . .

CONCLUSION

The transfer of the Seldovia property from Thomas Mortensen to the Mortensen Seldovia trust will be avoided, pursuant to 11 U.S.C. §548(e). The trustee will be awarded his costs but denied attorney's fees. An order and judgment will be entered consistent with this memorandum.

QUESTIONS

7. Why do you think the Alaska legislature included the following provision in its asset protection trust statute: "[A] settlor's expressed intention to protect trust assets from a beneficiary's potential future creditors is not evidence of an intent to defraud," ALASKA STAT. §34.40.110(b)(1)?

   ANSWER. This provision protects settlors by explicitly declaring that, under Alaska state law, asset protection is a legitimate reason for establishing a self-settled spendthrift trust and, therefore, self-settled trusts that articulate this objective expressly should not be automatically deemed to be a fraudulent transfer. Another portion of the same subsection protects settlors further by imposing a high evidentiary standard on creditors seeking to set aside the spendthrift protection: "[T]he creditor [must] establish[] by clear and convincing evidence that the settlor's transfer of property in trust was made with the intent to defraud that creditor." ALASKA STAT. §34.40.110(b)(1).

8. The bankruptcy court held that the above provision, Alaska Stat. §34.40.110(b)(1), was preempted by 11 U.S.C. §548(e), the fraudulent transfer provisions of the Bankruptcy Code governing self-settled trusts. The court then found that Mortensen created the trust with the intent to defraud creditors. Might

the court have reached a different outcome if the trust did not contain an express statement of purpose "to maximize the protection of the trust estate or estates from creditors' claims of the Grantor"?

ANSWER. Probably not. In addition to considering the trust's express statement of purpose, the court considered the circumstances surrounding the creation of the trust. Although Mortensen was not insolvent when he created the trust, he was heavily in debt, a fact that the court found to support the bankruptcy trustee's claim that Mortensen was using the trust to shield assets from known creditors. The court also considered Mortensen's use of the trust to engage in speculative investments, which generated profits that were not available to creditors for collection.

9. The bankruptcy court concluded that, when Mortensen "created the trust in 2005, he failed to recognize the danger posed by the Bankruptcy Abuse Prevention and Consumer Protection Act, which was enacted later that year." But how could Mortensen have anticipated a change in the law that would be applied in the future to invalidate his trust? Why wasn't Mortensen entitled to rely on 11 U.S.C. §548(a)(1), imposing a two-year look-back period for fraudulent transfers, in effect on the date he created the trust?

ANSWER. Although the court's discussion does not develop this point in full, the Bankruptcy Abuse Prevention and Consumer Protection Act of 2005 §1501(b)(1) provides that "the amendments made by this Act shall not apply with respect to cases commenced under title 11, United States Code, before the effective date of this Act." Here, although the trust was established before the effective date of the Act, the debtor's bankruptcy petition was filed years after the enactment of the provision.

10. Given that Mortensen was solvent when he established the trust, what, if anything, could he have done to ensure the trust would be enforceable in court and not deemed to be a fraudulent conveyance?

ANSWER. Perhaps Mortensen's claim would have been stronger if he had no outstanding debt when he established the trust because he could argue that, in the absence of known creditors, there was no one to defraud. But the entire purpose of self-settled spendthrift protection is to place a debtor's assets out of the reach of legitimate creditor claims, whether known or anticipated, so this structure is inherently vulnerable to challenge under the fraudulent transfer doctrine.

There is simply not enough case law on which to base predictions or recommendations regarding the enforceability of self-settled spendthrift protection. Despite reports that billions of dollars have poured into domestic asset protection trusts in the United States, as states have raced to authorize them, only a tiny handful of cases challenging the enforceability of self-settled spendthrift protection have been litigated in court. And, so far, most decisions have rejected self-settled spendthrift protection as a defense to creditor claims asserted against the settlor.

Professor Ronald Mann, who concludes that such trusts do not provide a reliable form of asset protection, offers the following observations:

> The real question is what to make of the paucity of cases. We could read the small number of cases as flowing from a consensus that the plain ineffectiveness of the trusts makes it futile to litigate their validity. On this reading, *Mortensen* is instructive because it suggests that in a relatively small consumer bankruptcy with no substantial debts owed other than to credit card issuers, the trustee nevertheless readily found the resources to overcome the obstacles of the Alaska APT.
>
> On the other hand, we might read the small number of cases as proof that the costs of litigation are so high (as compared to the potential assets to be reached) as to make litigation fruitless. On this reading, the ability of strongly motivated debtors to combine the use of an APT with other strategies means that creditors will routinely find themselves stymied by the costs of fighting through the entire matrix of asset-protection strategies, whatever the ultimate legal penetrability of any single strategy.
>
> The discussion above suggests yet another example of how ineffective it is to "purchase" legislation for the benefit of a particular interest. The analysis in this Article suggests that the onshore APT statutes are providing little or no formal legal benefit to the settlors that use them. They presumably provide considerable benefits to the attorneys and investment professionals that recommend and implement them. But that seems a far cry from the "build it and they will come" expectations that an APT statute could turn a state into a haven for incoming financial investment.

Ronald J. Mann, A Fresh Look at State Asset Protection Trust Statutes, 67 Vand. L. Rev. 1741, 1764-66 (2014).

9.1.3 Special Needs Trusts for Disabled Beneficiaries

Special asset protection considerations apply when planning for the needs of disabled persons, particularly those who require expensive long-term care or medical treatment. Some of the most significant costs of caring for disabled persons may be covered by Medicaid, a federally created social benefit program administered by states to provide health coverage for low-income individuals. For example, in Pennsylvania, a permanently disabled person living alone will qualify for full Medicaid coverage if her monthly income does not exceed $981 ($11,772 annually) and other resources or assets do not exceed $2,000.[27] All property owned by the individual counts as other resources for purposes of determining Medicaid eligibility unless the category of property is specifically excluded or the particular Medicaid program does not take into account other resources. Categorical exclusions generally cover a personal residence,

27. See, e.g., http://www.phlp.org/wp-content/uploads/2015/02/2015-Monthly-Income-and-Resource-Limits-for-Medicaid-and-Other-Health-Programs.pdf.

one car, household goods and furnishings, and other miscellaneous interests, such as the value of a burial plot and life insurance with no cash value. Thus, an individual need not be wealthy to exceed either the maximum income or resource criteria for Medicaid eligibility.

A disabled person with resources exceeding the Medicaid eligibility limit cannot qualify by artificially impoverishing herself through an inter vivos transmission of her estate. Gratuitous transfers of property within sixty months of application for Medicaid assistance count as resources owned by the applicant for eligibility purposes and can result in denial of coverage. 42 U.S.C. §1396p(c)(1)(B)(i). There are, however, two estate planning techniques available to disabled persons[28] seeking to preserve Medicaid eligibility:

1. *Self-settled*[29] *special needs trusts.* A special needs trust may be funded by the disabled person's own assets (e.g., from a tort judgment award or a significant lump sum liability insurance payment) for her own benefit if it is established by a parent, grandparent, legal guardian of the individual, or a court, and "if the State will receive all amounts remaining in the trust upon the death of such individual up to an amount equal to the total medical assistance paid on behalf of the individual under a State plan." 42 U.S.C. §1396p(d)(4)(A). Federal law expressly authorizes self-settled trusts to facilitate a disabled person's use of her own assets for special needs not covered by Medicaid without causing the assets held in trust to disqualify the person from Medicaid eligibility (so long as the state is a remainder beneficiary).[30] Such trusts must be carefully structured in compliance with the statutory requirements, or the settlor's beneficial interest will count against Medicaid eligibility.
2. *Third-party trusts.* A third-party trust created by a donor for the benefit of a disabled person is not subject to the state remainder beneficiary requirement imposed on self-settled trusts. However, trust distributions that are paid or entitled to be paid to a disabled beneficiary count as available resources for Medicaid eligibility. Trusts that provide for mandatory payments to the beneficiary or impose a support standard for trust distributions, therefore, may be considered in determining Medicaid eligibility. To avoid disqualifying the disabled beneficiary from state aid, third-party special needs trusts should be

28. "[A]n individual shall be considered to be disabled for purposes of this subchapter if he is unable to engage in any substantial gainful activity by reason of any medically determinable physical or mental impairment which can be expected to result in death or which has lasted or can be expected to last for a continuous period of not less than twelve months." 42 U.S.C. §1382c(a)(3)(A).

29. Note that the term "self-settled" here differs slightly from the use of the same term in the context of asset protection trusts, described above. Here, the assets are the beneficiary's but the settlor must be a third party—the disabled person cannot be, although that person may be functionally treated as the settlor. There, the settlor can be the beneficiary and place his/her own assets in the trust.

30. "These [supplemental] expenses—books, television, Internet, travel, and even such necessities as clothing and toiletries—[are not covered by Medicaid and] would rarely be considered extravagant. [Other expenses] may include medical expenses, dental expenses, nursing and custodial care, psychiatric/psychological services, recreational therapy, occupational therapy, physical therapy, vocational therapy, durable medical needs, prosthetic devices, special rehabilitative services or equipment, disability-related training, education, transportation and travel expenses, dietary needs and supplements, related insurance and other goods and services specified by the department." Lewis v. Alexander, 685 F.3d 325, 333-35 (3d Cir. 2012).

purely discretionary,[31] subject to spendthrift protection, and requires that distributions be made in the form of direct payment to those providing goods or services to the beneficiary.

Attorneys who counsel clients regarding asset protection in the Medicaid planning context must do so with a comprehensive understanding of this highly complex area of the law. An attorney can be subject to serious consequences, including criminal liability, for providing bad advice. For example, a federal felony prohibits making a "statement, representation, concealment, failure, or conversion" in connection with a Medicaid applicant's attempt to qualify for medical assistance where the advisor, "for a fee[,] knowingly and willfully counsels or assists [a Medicaid applicant] to dispose of assets (including by any transfer in trust) in order for the individual to become eligible for medical assistance . . . if disposing of the assets results in the imposition of a period of ineligibility for such assistance. . . ." 42 U.S.C. §1320a-7b(a)(6).

In 2014, Congress enacted a new program under the Achieving a Better Life Experience Act. Under 26 U.S.C. §529A, individuals may make contributions to tax-free savings accounts "established for the purpose of meeting the qualified disability expenses of the designated beneficiary of the account." 26 U.S.C. §529A(b)(1)(A).

PROBLEM IV

Mary, a widow, died last week at the age of 80. She is survived by two adult children, Andrew and Betsy, both of whom suffer from a severe developmental disability. Each child receives Medicaid and other public support to cover health care expenses and resides at a state-run nursing home.

A. Mary's will contains an outright devise of $400,000 to Andrew. Would Andrew remain eligible for Medicaid if his guardian disclaimed the devise thereby allowing the $400,000 to pass to Andrew's minor child, Anita?

B. Mary's will contains a devise of $400,000 to Betsy accompanied by the following provision:

> I devise Betsy the sum of $400,000 to my Trustee to administer for Betsy's benefit by paying to or applying for her benefit so much of the income and/or principal of such trust as the Trustee, in her sole discretion, thinks necessary or advisable to provide for the proper care, maintenance, support, and education of Betsy, provided that the Trustee must make at least an annual or more frequent distribution of the Trust income in the trustee's sole discretion.

31. Any mention of a support standard may cause a third-party trust to be treated as an asset of the beneficiary because the beneficiary has a right to compel the trustee to make distributions for living expenses. See, e.g., N.D. Admin. Code §75-02-02.1-31(3) ("For purposes of this subsection, 'support trust' means a trust which has, as a purpose, the provision of support or care to a beneficiary. The purpose of a support trust is indicated by language such as 'to provide for the care, support, and maintenance of . . . '; 'to provide as necessary for the support of . . . '; or 'as my trustee may deem necessary for the support, maintenance, medical expenses, care, comfort, and general welfare.' No particular language is necessary, but words such as 'care,' 'maintenance,' 'medical needs,' or 'support' are usually present. The term includes trusts which may also be called 'discretionary support trusts' or 'discretionary trusts,' so long as support is a trust purpose.").

Would Betsy remain eligible for Medicaid upon creation of the trust described in Mary's will?

PROBLEM V

Last year, Ann established an irrevocable trust for her own lifetime benefit and, upon her death, the benefit of her descendants. She funded the trust with $500,000. The trust contains the following provision:

> The Trustees may, from time to time and at any time, distribute to or expend for the benefit of the beneficiary, so much of the principal and current or accumulated net income as the Trustees may in their sole discretion, determine. The Trustees, however, shall have no authority whatsoever to make any payments to or for the benefit of any Beneficiary hereunder when the making of such payments shall result in the Beneficiary losing her eligibility for any public assistance or entitlement program of any kind whatever. It is the specific intent of the Grantor hereof that this Trust be used to supplement all such public assistance or entitlement programs and not defeat or destroy their availability to any beneficiary hereunder.

Last month, Ann entered a nursing home and applied for Medicaid benefits to pay for her care.

A. What result if Ann discloses the existence of the irrevocable trust?

B. What result if Ann does not disclose the existence of the irrevocable trust?

9.2 MODIFICATION AND TERMINATION OF PRIVATE TRUSTS

The rules governing modification and termination of a settled trust take into account several factors including the identity of the party seeking relief (i.e., settlor, beneficiary, or trustee); the type of trust (i.e., revocable or irrevocable, private or charitable); the material purposes of the trust; and the circumstances of the parties at the time of the requested relief.

A settlor may modify or terminate a trust generally under two circumstances: (1) the trust remains revocable at the time of the requested relief,[32] or (2) the trust is noncharitable, irrevocable, and all beneficiaries consent.[33] The settlor's consent may be exercised under a power of attorney or by a guardian or conservator on the settlor's behalf, but (at the risk of saying the obvious) consent from the settlor cannot be obtained after the settlor's death.

There are several doctrines that provide for modification or termination upon request of a beneficiary (or, in some cases, a trustee) in the absence of settlor consent.

---

32. UTC §602(a) ("Unless the terms of a trust expressly provide that the trust is irrevocable, the settlor may revoke or amend the trust.").

33. UTC §411(a) ("A noncharitable irrevocable trust may be modified or terminated upon consent of the settlor and all beneficiaries, even if the modification or termination is inconsistent with a material purpose of the trust."). In 2004, the UTC Drafting Committee recommended the additional requirement of court approval to prevent potentially adverse federal estate tax consequences.

Although these doctrines permit a beneficiary to displace the express terms of a settled trust over the settlor's objection or lack of consent, the UTC's primary purpose for authorizing such relief is to preserve the settlor's manifested donative intent: "The purpose . . . is not to disregard the settlor's intent but to modify inopportune details to effectuate better the settlor's broader purposes." UTC §412, comment. Thus, under the UTC, these doctrines generally require the party seeking relief to show that the requested modification or termination would not be inconsistent with the trust's purposes. The Restatement (Third) of Trusts, by contrast, adopts a minority rule authorizing beneficiaries to compel modification or termination where the relief "would be inconsistent with a material purpose of the trust, [but] the court . . . determines that the reason(s) for termination or modification outweigh the material purpose."[34]

We will focus on the UTC doctrines because they have been enacted in most jurisdictions. The fidelity of the UTC approach to the material trust purposes established by the settlor is often described as the *Claflin* doctrine.

Claflin v. Claflin
20 N.E. 454 (Mass. 1889)

FIELD, J.

By the eleventh article of his will, as modified by a codicil, Wilbur F. Claflin gave all the residue of his personal estate to trustees, "to sell and dispose of the same, and to pay to my wife, Mary A. Claflin, one-third part of the proceeds thereof, and to pay to my son Clarence A. Claflin, one-third part of the proceeds thereof, and to pay the remaining one-third part thereof to my son Adelbert E. Claflin, in the manner following, viz.: Ten thousand dollars when he is of the age of twenty-one years, ten thousand dollars when he is of the age of twenty-five years, and the balance when he is of the age of thirty years." Apparently, Adelbert E. Claflin was not quite 21 years old when his father died, but he some time ago reached that age, and received $10,000 from the trust. He has not yet reached the age of 25 years, and he brings this bill to compel the trustees to pay to him the remainder of the trust fund. His contention is, in effect, that the provisions of the will postponing the payment of the money beyond the time when he is 21 years old are void. There is no doubt that his interest in the trust fund is vested and absolute, and that no other person has any interest in it; and the authority is undisputed that the provisions postponing payment to him until some time after he reaches the age of 21 years would be treated as void by those courts which hold that restrictions against the alienation of absolute interests in the income of trust property are void. There has indeed, been no decision of this question in England by the house of lords, and but one by a chancellor, but there are several decisions to this effect by masters of the rolls, and by vice-chancellors. . . . These decisions do not proceed on the ground that it was

34. Restatement (Third) of Trusts §65(2). For support of its minority rule, the Restatement, in comment d, explains that the rule was enacted in California in 1990 and "has apparently proved useful and noncontroversial." See Cal. Prob. Code §15403(b) (if the "court, in its discretion, determines that the reasons for [modification or termination] under the circumstances outweigh the interest in accomplishing a material purpose . . .").

the intention of the testator that the property should be conveyed to the beneficiary on his reaching the age of 21 years, because in each case it was clear that such was not his intention, but on the ground that the direction to withhold the possession of the property from the beneficiary after he reached his majority was inconsistent with the absolute rights of property given him by the will. This court has ordered trust property conveyed by the trustee to the beneficiary when there was a dry trust,[35] or when the purposes of the trust had been accomplished, or when no good reason was shown why the trust should continue, and all the persons interested in it were sui juris, and desired that it be terminated; but we have found no expression of any opinion in our reports that provisions requiring a trustee to hold and manage the trust property until the beneficiary reached an age beyond that of 21 years are void if the interest of the beneficiary is vested and absolute. This is not a dry trust, nor have the purposes of the trust been accomplished, if the intention of the testator is to be carried out.

In Sears v. Choate[, 146 Mass. 395 (1888),] it is said: "Where property is given to certain persons for their benefit, and in such a manner that no other person has or can have any interest in it, they are in effect the absolute owners of it; and it is reasonable and just that they should have the control and disposal of it, unless some good cause appears to the contrary." In that case the plaintiff was the absolute owner of the whole property, subject to an annuity of $10,000, payable to himself. The whole of the principal of the trust fund, and all of the income not expressly made payable to the plaintiff, had become vested in him when he reached the age of 21 years by way of resulting trust as property undisposed of by the will. Apparently the testator had not contemplated such a result, and had made no provision for it, and the court saw no reason why the trust should not be terminated, and the property conveyed to the plaintiff. In the case at bar nothing has happened which the testator did not anticipate, and for which he has not made provision. It is plainly his will that neither the income nor any part of the principal should now be paid to the plaintiff. It is true that the plaintiff's interest is alienable by him, and can be taken by his creditors to pay his debts, but it does not follow because the testator has not imposed all possible restrictions that the restrictions which he has imposed should not be carried into effect. The decision in Bank v. Adams, 133 Mass. 170, rests upon the doctrine that a testator has a right to dispose of his own property with such restrictions and limitations, not repugnant to law, as he sees fit, and that his intentions ought to be carried out, unless they contravene some positive rule of law, or are against public policy. The rule contended for by the plaintiff in that case was founded upon the same considerations as that contended for by the plaintiff in this, and the grounds on which this court declined to follow the English rule in that case are applicable to this; and for the reasons there given we are unable to see that the directions of the testator to the trustees to pay the money to the plaintiff when he reached the ages of 25 and 30 years are against public policy, or are so far inconsistent with the rights of property given to the plaintiff, that they should not be carried into effect. It cannot be said that these restrictions upon the plaintiff's possession and control of the property are altogether useless, for there is not the same danger that he will spend the property while it is in the hands of the trustees as there would be if it were in his own.

35. [A dry trust is a passive trust that imposes no active duties upon the trustee. — Eds.]

The strict execution of the trust has not become impossible; the restriction upon the plaintiff's possession and control is, we think, one that the testator had a right to make; other provisions for the plaintiff are contained in the will, apparently sufficient for his support; and we see no good reason why the intention of the testator should not be carried out. . . .

Decree affirmed.

SAYS FATHER DESERTED BOY.

Adelbert E. Claflin Locked Up in Default of Bail.

On the charge that he had abandoned his son, Adelbert E. Claflin of 179 Park Place, Brooklyn, was committed to the West Side Court Prison yesterday by Magistrate Flammer in default of $312 bail. Mrs. Alma Banta of 240 West Forty-sixth Street, a niece of Claflin, appeared as complainant.

Mrs. Banta said that she and her mother, who is dead, had cared for William Claflin, the son, ever since he was two years old. He is now fourteeen. She said that the father had contributed only $45 to the lad's support, although he had a bank account of $30,000.

Claflin declared that he had had trouble with his niece, and wanted to take charge of his son himself. Mrs. Edith Dees, with whom Mrs. Banta is living, said that in all the time that she had known Claflin to call at her house he had not once asked for his son.

After saying that he would leave the boy with Mrs. Banta, Magistrate Flammer ordered the father to pay her $6 a week toward the son's support and placed Claflin under $312 bonds to secure the payment.

Claflin asked to be paroled for a day to give him time to get the money for the bond, but on Mrs. Banta's request the Magistrate would not permit it, and he was committed to the prison.

Case Epilogue: In 1904, the *New York Times* reported that Adelbert E. Claflin had "deserted [his] boy," who was then 14 years old, and had been "locked up in default of bail." Adelbert E. Claflin Locked Up in Default of Bail, N.Y. Times, July 2, 1904. Adelbert's niece, who had taken care of Claflin's son from the age of 2 to 14, sued for child support. "She said that the father had contributed only $45 to the lad's support, although he had a bank account of $30,000." *Id.* Does this anecdote lend support to the exceptions to spendthrift protection for family support claimants? (See discussion of those exceptions later in this chapter.)

In *Claflin*, the court enforced the settlor's instruction to postpone full distribution of the beneficiary's interest until he reached the age of 30. The court distinguished its holding from the English rule, which generally allows a beneficiary to terminate a trust after the settlor's death. Professor Daniel Kelly examines this divergence between the American rule (the *Claflin* doctrine) and the English rule (the *Saunders* doctrine) from the perspective of ex ante and ex post considerations:

> Ex post analysis looks at an event or dispute after the fact. [Professor Lawrence] Solum explains it this way: "The ex post perspective is backward looking. From the ex post point of view, we ask questions like: Who acted badly and who acted well? Whose rights were violated?" By contrast, ex ante analysis looks at an event or dispute before the fact. We might ask: "What [e]ffect will this rule have on the future? Will deci[ding] . . . a case in this way produce good or bad consequences?" Thus, "[e]x post analysis tends to focus on fairness and distributional concerns, whereas ex ante analysis is more likely to consider incentives for future conduct."
>
> . . .
>
> It may be true that English law disregards the donor's intention, while American law privileges intention as the controlling consideration. It also may be true that English law considers the trust to be the beneficiaries' property, while American law considers it to be, functionally, the settlor's property. But what explains these underlying differences? Is there any divergence in the mode of legal reasoning or policy analysis that might result in such disparate outcomes on the same issue? My hypothesis is that, in attempting to explain these differences, the distinction between ex ante and ex post considerations is relevant. Specifically, the competing approaches to the issue of trust modification and termination may stem from a failure to identify and distinguish between the ex ante and ex post perspective.
>
> Ex post, the English view (Saunders [v. Vautier, (1841) 49 Eng. Rep. 282 (Ch.),]) has a certain degree of plausibility. Once a settlor is dead, it seems as if the beneficiary or beneficiaries, assuming they all agree, should be permitted to terminate the trust and utilize the property in whatever manner they deem best. Not permitting modification or termination would mean the property would not be devoted to its highest valued use. The extension of this approach in the Variation of Trusts Act, which allows English courts to consent on behalf of incompetent, minor, or unborn beneficiaries, might be beneficial as well. Again, under these circumstances, without modification or termination, the beneficiaries would not be able to use the property in the manner they deem best, meaning the property may not be devoted to its highest use.

> Yet, once ex ante considerations are incorporated into the analysis, the American view (*Claflin*) arguably has some merit. If a settlor knows the beneficiaries can easily convince a court to modify or terminate the trust once the settlor has died, the settlor may receive less satisfaction during life or have less incentive to accumulate property. Moreover, the settlor may anticipate the possibility of a court's modifying or terminating the trust and alter the structure or timing of the gift. Or the settlor may decide not to give the gift at all. Indeed, once ex ante considerations are incorporated, beneficiaries may themselves favor the American rule for precisely this reason. [Professor Robert] Sitkoff points out that "though a particular beneficiary might prefer the power to terminate the trust once it is established, the *Claflin* doctrine is advantageous to potential beneficiaries as a class because it increases the willingness of grantors to create a trust in the first place."

Daniel B. Kelly, Restricting Testamentary Freedom: Ex Ante Versus Ex Post Justifications, 82 Fordham L. Rev. 1125, 1141, 1178-79 (2013).

Uniform Trust Code
§411 Modification or Termination of Noncharitable Irrevocable Trust by Consent

[(a) [A noncharitable irrevocable trust may be modified or terminated upon consent of the settlor and all beneficiaries, even if the modification or termination is inconsistent with a material purpose of the trust. . . .]

(b) A noncharitable irrevocable trust may be terminated upon consent of all of the beneficiaries if the court concludes that continuance of the trust is not necessary to achieve any material purpose of the trust. A noncharitable irrevocable trust may be modified upon consent of all of the beneficiaries if the court concludes that modification is not inconsistent with a material purpose of the trust.

[(c) A spendthrift provision in the terms of the trust is not presumed to constitute a material purpose of the trust.]

(d) Upon termination of a trust under subsection (a) or (b), the trustee shall distribute the trust property as agreed by the beneficiaries.

(e) If not all of the beneficiaries consent to a proposed modification or termination of the trust under subsection (a) or (b), the modification or termination may be approved by the court if the court is satisfied that:

(1) if all of the beneficiaries had consented, the trust could have been modified or terminated under this section; and

(2) the interests of a beneficiary who does not consent will be adequately protected.

UTC §§411(b)-(e) govern the modification and termination of irrevocable noncharitable trusts by consent of the beneficiaries. Subsection (b) articulates a general rule that incorporates the *Claflin* doctrine. It does so by conditioning the court's approval of a beneficiary's petition for modification or termination upon the requested relief being consistent with the material trust purposes. Subsection (c) states a rule of construction that presumes the inclusion of a spendthrift provision does not constitute a material trust purpose. However, after several jurisdictions enacted Section 411 without subsection or with a provision that reversed the presumption, the UTC's drafting committee concluded that uniformity could not be achieved; it therefore placed the provision in brackets to indicate adoption of the subsection is optional.

Uniform Trust Code
§412 Modification or Termination Because of Unanticipated Circumstances or Inability to Administer Trust Effectively

(a) The court may modify the administrative or dispositive terms of a trust or terminate the trust if, because of circumstances not anticipated by the settlor, modification or termination will further the purposes of the trust. To the extent practicable, the modification must be made in accordance with the settlor's probable intention.

(b) The court may modify the administrative terms of a trust if continuation of the trust on its existing terms would be impracticable or wasteful or impair the trust's administration.

(c) Upon termination of a trust under this section, the trustee shall distribute the trust property in a manner consistent with the purposes of the trust.

Under the common law doctrine of equitable deviation, a court may permit deviation from the trust where strict compliance with the trust's administrative provisions would frustrate accomplishment of the settlor's trust purposes. UTC §412(a) liberalizes this doctrine by explicitly permitting deviation from an administrative *or* dispositive term where the proposed modification or termination would further the trust purposes. UTC §412(b) limits a settlor's ability to impose unreasonable restrictions on trust property by permitting modification of an administrative term where compliance would be impracticable, wasteful, or impair the trust's administration.

Other related modification doctrines include: (1) cy pres, which permits modification of a charitable trust where the particular charitable purpose selected by the settlor becomes unlawful, impracticable, impossible to achieve, or wasteful (UTC §413); (2) modification or termination of uneconomic trusts (UTC §414); (3) reformation to correct mistakes (UTC §415); (4) modification to achieve the settlor's tax objectives (UTC §416); and (5) combination and division of trusts where the modification does not adversely affect accomplishment of the trust purposes.

PROBLEM VI

Determine whether the following irrevocable trusts may be modified or terminated by request and consent of the beneficiaries:

a. The trust provides for the lifelong support of B and, upon B's death, for the trust corpus to be distributed among B's descendants. B seeks termination of the trust and outright distribution of the trust corpus on grounds that she is self-sufficient, she could survive solely on her own resources without any future distributions from the trustee, and that she needs the trust corpus now in order to invest in a lucrative business opportunity.

b. The trust provides for the lifelong support of B and, upon B's death, for the trust corpus to be distributed among B's descendants. After the settlor's death, B sustained catastrophic injuries in an automobile accident and is now paralyzed below the neck. B has applied for Medicaid but her interest in the trust disqualifies her from receiving public assistance. B seeks to modify the trust's distributive provision such that the trust will qualify as a special needs trust. The requested modifications would make distributions purely discretionary, subject to spendthrift protection, and would be limited to paying for expenses not covered by Medicaid.

c. The trust provides for the monthly payment of $100 to her grandchild Betty for life, subject to a spendthrift provision, and the remainder to Children's Hospital, a local charity. The trust was established forty years ago with an initial trust corpus of $120,000, which has since increased in value to $3,500,000. Betty and Children's Hospital reach an agreement to seek termination of the trust and, if approved by the court, Children's Hospital will continue to pay Betty $100 per month for life plus a one-time lump sum payment of $300,000.

d. The testator's will devises his entire estate, in charitable trust, for the benefit of Memorial University for the purpose of providing financial aid to local students pursuing higher education. On the date of the testator's death, however, Memorial University was no longer in operation. H, the testator's sole heir, argues that the trust fails and that a resulting trust should be imposed in favor of H. The trustee of the charitable trust seeks to modify the trust to provide financial aid to students at Green State University, another local school.

PROBLEM VII

In 1973, philanthropist Avery Fisher donated $10.5 million ($56 million in 2016 dollars, adjusting for inflation) to the New York Philharmonic and Lincoln Center in New York City on the condition that the Philharmonic's performance hall be renamed Avery Fisher Hall. According to the condition, the name Avery Fisher Hall was required to "appear on tickets, brochures, program announcements and advertisements and the like [in perpetuity]" in connection with all performances inside the hall. The New York Philharmonic and Lincoln Center accepted the gift. Avery Fisher died in 1994.

In 2015, the hall was in need of extensive renovations to modernize the facility. Movie mogul and philanthropist David Geffen offered to donate $100 million toward a $300 million renovation of Avery Fisher Hall. Geffen, however, conditioned his gift on the venue being renamed David Geffen Hall.

Suppose Avery Fisher's restricted gift were construed to form a charitable trust and, upon the beneficiary's failure to comply with the condition, the gift would revert back to Avery Fisher's heirs. Suppose further that the New York Philharmonic and Lincoln Center seek modification of the trust to permit renaming the hall and the state attorney general does not object.

A. Would Avery Fisher's heirs have standing to object?

B. If granted standing to object, what would be the heirs' best argument?

C. How might the New York Philharmonic and Lincoln Center respond to the heirs' objection?

D. How should a court rule on this dispute?

9.3 IMPLIED TRUSTS AND "NON-TRUSTS"

The prior section examined the typology of *express* trusts. You may have noticed that each type of express trust exhibited at least one common trait of legal significance: the donor's intent to separate beneficial enjoyment from legal ownership of gifted property. This section, by contrast, examines *implied* trusts that are judicially imposed or arise by operation of law when the parties' conduct or surrounding circumstances justify equitable relief from the express terms of a transfer.

Implied trusts are not actually trusts, nor are they regulated by the full range of trustee fiduciary duties.[36] Rather, implied trusts are remedial doctrines that selectively borrow concepts and terminology from trust law, and are more aptly described as equitable principles that prevent transferred property from landing in the wrong hands. When an implied trust is imposed or arises by default, the transferee is said to hold property as a nominal trustee whose sole obligation is to surrender title to the rightful owner. Because implied trusts are only superficially related to actual trusts, they are sometimes described as *non-trusts.*

Implied trusts typically supply equitable remedies in contexts where the express terms of the original transfer are ineffective, fail, or convey property in a manner that is objectively unjust or presumptively contrary to the transferor's intent. Because the reasons for imposing an implied trust are usually based on the parties' conduct or the surrounding circumstances, implied trusts are almost always established by extrinsic evidence.

This section will discuss four types of implied trusts: (1) resulting trusts; (2) constructive trusts; (3) secret and semi-secret trusts; and (4) honorary trusts.

9.3.1 Resulting Trusts

A resulting trust[37] requires the transferee to return property when the parties' conduct or surrounding circumstances reveal that the donor, in fact, intended to retain ownership of the transferred property. A resulting trust imposes an implied reversion: It divests the transferee of legal title which then reverts back to the original transferor (or, if deceased, the original transferor's successors in interest). A resulting trust supplies a

36. Cf. UTC §102, comment e ("Excluded from the Code's coverage are resulting and constructive trusts, which are not express trusts but remedial devices imposed by law.").

37. "Resulting" in this context derives from the Latin verb *resultare,* meaning to jump or spring back.

potent equitable remedy because it effectively reverses the express terms of the donor's original transfer of legal title. To minimize the potential for overuse, which would harmfully undermine legitimate expectations of finality and certainty throughout property law, courts generally limit the imposition of resulting trusts to three discrete applications: (1) the failure of an express trust (in whole or in part); (2) the failure of an express trust to exhaust the entire trust corpus; and (3) purchase-money trusts. See generally Restatement (Third) of Trusts §§7-9.

The first two applications are straightforward. When a settlor creates an express trust that makes an incomplete or ineffective disposition of the entire trust corpus, a resulting trust reverts any property remaining in the trustee's possession to the settlor. This situation can occur for several reasons: All of the trust beneficiaries could die before all of the trust property is consumed; the trust's terms could be found to violate public policy; or the trust could have been created through fraud or coercion. To do otherwise, and leave the remaining undisposed trust property in the hands of the trustee, would unjustly enrich the trustee at the expense of the settlor or the settlor's successors in interest. The presumption is that by settling a trust and conveying legal title to the trustee, the settlor intended the trustee to function as a fiduciary, not as a beneficiary.

The third application, purchase-money trusts, applies when a transaction creates the outward appearance of a gratuitous transfer but, in reality, the transfer was never intended as a gift. A purchase-money trust arises when a person pays some or all of the purchase price to acquire property, but directs the seller to issue title in the name of someone else (other than the purchaser). On its face, this type of transaction creates the appearance of a gift from the purchaser to the resulting titleholder, but courts generally infer from the surrounding circumstances that the purchaser did not intend to confer a beneficial interest (except when title is issued to a close relative of the purchaser, such as a spouse or child). Rather, courts generally presume that the purchaser's intent was to convey nominal legal title subject to the purchaser's reversionary interest.

Consider the following example of a purchase-money trust: A well-known real estate developer would like to acquire land for a major commercial development but is concerned that disclosing her identity would cause the seller to increase the asking price. If, instead of buying the land in her own name, the developer secretly supplies the purchase money and directs title to be issued in her lawyer's name, the transaction creates a purchase-money trust. The lawyer is, in effect, a strawman holding legal title subject to the developer's reversionary interest. If the lawyer refused to surrender title, the developer could petition the court to impose a resulting trust to enforce her reversionary interest.

In the example above, the developer had a legitimate reason for purchasing the property through a strawman. In other contexts, however, strawman purchases are commonly used to conceal illegal transactions, such as money laundering and tax evasion. Thus, resulting trusts cannot be used to enforce an implied reversionary interest when "the transfer is made to accomplish an unlawful purpose." Restatement (Third) of Trusts §9(1)(b).

The purpose for imposing a resulting trust is to carry out the donor's presumed intent, but in most jurisdictions, the party seeking to impose a resulting trust must meet a high evidentiary burden:

> While an implied or resulting trust may be established by parol evidence, yet both upon reason and authority the courts will not enforce it, unless it be established by the most convincing and irrefragable evidence. In other words, it must be sustained by proof of the clearest and most convincing character. To sustain a resulting trust upon parol evidence in the teeth of the terms of the written instrument, it is not essential that the evidence be of a character to remove all reasonable doubt, but only that it be so clear, cogent and convincing as to overcome the opposing evidence, coupled with the presumption that obtains in favor of the written instrument.

In re Estate of Nichols, 856 S.W.2d 397, 402-03 (Tenn. 1993) (internal citations omitted). In his influential trust law treatise, Professor George Bogert explained, "If the evidence is doubtful or capable of reasonable explanation upon a theory other than the existence of the [resulting] trust, it is not sufficient to support a decree declaring and enforcing the trust." 10 Bogert, Trusts and Trustees §472, at 44-49 (2d rev. ed. 1978).

PROBLEM VIII

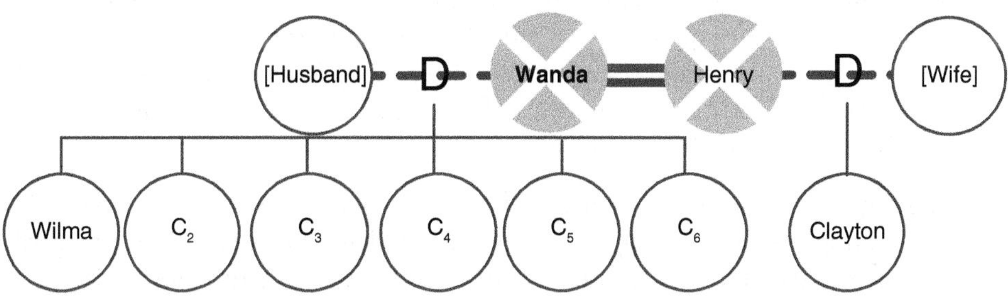

Wanda and Henry were married sixteen years ago in a second marriage for both. Wanda had six children with her first husband and Henry had one son (Clayton) with his first wife, but Wanda and Henry had no joint children between them. Ten years ago, Wanda and Henry executed reciprocal wills: Each was the sole beneficiary of the other's estate and the children were named as contingent beneficiaries, with each of the seven children receiving one-seventh of the estate.

Henry died three years ago. His will left everything to Wanda and, additionally, Wanda became the sole owner of their residence titled in joint tenancy with right of survivorship.

Two years ago, Wanda conveyed title to the residence by deed to Clayton. Wanda drafted the deed without the help of a lawyer, but copied most of the language from another deed provided by her friend. The deed contains the following recital: "*the true and actual consideration paid for this transfer is $-0-; estate planning.*"

Wanda died earlier this year and her eldest child, Wilma, was appointed executor of the estate. Wilma claims that Clayton holds title to the residence subject to a resulting trust in favor of Wanda's estate, which would give each child a one-seventh interest in the property. Wilma testified that she discussed the deed with Wanda, who said the purpose of transferring the property Clayton was to avoid probate. Wilma argues that the deed's mention of "estate planning" renders the instrument ambiguous and that the court should construe "estate planning" to mean that Wanda intended to divide the property according to the terms of her will.

The trial court agreed with Wilma and imposed a resulting trust on the residence in favor of the estate. The trial court explained, "It appears that the decedent was concerned that she wanted to avoid the expense of probate, wanted to make things easy on everyone, and she expected that by putting the property into Clayton's name that he would then follow the instruction of the will and divide the property equally among her children and himself."

Clayton appeals the imposition of a resulting trust. Should the appellate court affirm? Consider the following questions in your analysis:

A. Why might Wanda have transferred the residence to Clayton, to the exclusion of her own six children, when her will devises an equal share of her estate to each of her children and stepson? Was the deed conveyance sufficient to avoid her stated goal of avoiding probate?

B. Recall that courts generally limit resulting trusts to three discrete applications: (1) failure of an express trust; (2) the failure of an express trust to exhaust the entire trust corpus; and (3) purchase-money trusts. Which theory best supports Wilma's argument that the court should impose a resulting trust requiring Clayton to surrender title to the estate?

C. How would you evaluate the evidence proffered by Wilma in support of a resulting trust? Assume that the appellate standard of review is de novo regarding matters of law and abuse of discretion regarding findings of fact and credibility.

D. What evidentiary standard should govern whether to impose a resulting trust and why?

PROBLEM IX

Three years ago, Jack McMichael retained his longtime attorney, William Johnson, to draft his estate planning documents. William prepared the following two documents for Jack's review and signature: (1) a pour-over will devising the entire probate estate to the trustee of an inter vivos trust; and (2) an inter vivos trust containing a series of specific gifts of money and property but no residuary clause. The trust appointed William as trustee. Jack executed both documents and left them on file at William's law firm.

Two years ago, Jack opened a savings account at the Cape May Savings Bank with an initial deposit of $150,000. The account allowed Jack to designate a payable-on-death beneficiary and, when asked for a death beneficiary by the bank officer, Jack said he wanted to designate the trustee of his trust. The bank officer, however, advised against designating a trustee without having the trust document in hand to verify the existence of the trust and confirm the exact wording necessary to identify the trust. Jack followed the bank officer's advice and signed a death beneficiary form reciting the following designation: "William Johnson Atty."

Jack died earlier this year. The trust, funded by the pour-over will, contains a corpus of $500,000, but the aggregate value of specific gifts of money and property conveyed by the trust is only $300,000. Jack's heirs argue that the undistributed trust corpus of $200,000 should revert to Jack's estate and pass by intestacy. William disagrees and argues that the $200,000 balance should be divided *pro rata* among the trust beneficiaries.

Jack's intestate heirs also recently discovered the savings account at Cape May Savings Bank. They ask William to distribute the remaining account balance of $155,000 to Jack's estate for distribution to the intestate heirs. William disagrees and states the following: "I have no idea why this account was established. It was established approximately six weeks after Jack executed his will in my office, which leads me to believe the intent of this account was clearly to take it outside the estate itself. I have no idea what motivated this action. I was completely unaware that this had occurred. I had not seen nor talked with Jack since the day he left my office. I can only surmise that something happened on his way to Florida or after he got to Florida for him to take this action. I have looked at this situation from various points of view seeking to fathom the intent of this account. I come back to the only conclusion that I can draw, which is — for whatever reason — he wanted me to have this money."

A. Should a court impose a resulting trust on the undistributed funds remaining in the trust corpus? Why or why not? If a resulting trust is imposed, to whom and how should the $200,000 be distributed?

B. Should a court impose a resulting trust on the $155,000 balance remaining in Jack's savings account? Why or why not? If a resulting trust is imposed, to whom and how should the $155,000 be distributed?

9.3.2 Constructive Trusts

A constructive trust imposes a nominal obligation of trusteeship on the titleholder of property when the interests of equity require the title holder to convey the property to someone else. Like a resulting trust, a constructive trust is an equitable remedial doctrine rather than an actual trust,[38] so the constructive trustee's sole obligation of trusteeship is to turn over the property to its rightful owner. Constructive trusts, however, differ from resulting trusts in three significant respects: First, whereas resulting trusts are often imposed on innocent transferees who came upon ownership of title without committing any misconduct, constructive trusts are generally imposed to prevent unjust enrichment by transferees who have engaged in wrongful or unfair

38. Indeed, for the most part, "[c]onstructive trusts are not dealt with in the Restatement of Trusts, except in so far as they arise out of express trusts or attempts to create express trusts." Restatement (Third) of Trusts §1, comment e. See also UTC §102, comment e.

conduct concerning the property.[39] Second, whereas resulting trusts provide a limited form of relief—an implied reversionary interest in favor of the transferor, the remedial scope of constructive trusts is broader and may require the transferee to surrender title to any aggrieved claimant, not necessarily the transferor, when necessary to achieve equity. Third, whereas resulting trusts are generally imposed for the purpose of carrying out the transferor's presumed intent, constructive trusts are imposed in the interests of justice and equity (which may or may not correspond with the transferor's presumed intent).

Restatement (Third) of Restitution and Unjust Enrichment §55 Constructive Trust

(1) If a defendant is unjustly enriched by the acquisition of title to identifiable property at the expense of the claimant or in violation of the claimant's rights, the defendant may be declared a constructive trustee, for the benefit of the claimant, of the property in question and its traceable product.

(2) The obligation of a constructive trustee is to surrender the constructive trust property to the claimant, on such conditions as the court may direct.

Notice that the standard for imposing a constructive trust under Restatement §55(1), above, requires a claimant to establish two elements: (1) unjust enrichment *by the acquisition of title*; and (2) *identifiable property*. These related prerequisites set the doctrine of constructive trusts apart from other more general remedial doctrines, such as rescission and restitution, which are not limited to wrongful conduct related to the acquisition of title to identifiable property. Thus, constructive trusts provide an equitable remedy to recover specific property from a party in wrongful possession of legal title. The party seeking a constructive trust must also generally assert a legal claim challenging the titleholder's acquisition, such as fraud, mistake, or wrongful interference with the claimant's legally protected interests. *Id.*, comment f.[40]

39. Examples of inequitable conduct warranting a constructive trust include:

1) a person procures the legal title to property in violation of a duty to the actual owner;
2) the title to property is obtained by some inequitable means;
3) a person makes use of some influence in order to obtain title on better terms than it otherwise would have been obtained;
4) a person acquires property with notice that someone else is entitled to its benefits.

Estate of Queener v. Helton, 119 S.W.3d 682, 687 (Tenn. Ct. App. 2003).

40. For further discussion of the role and development of constructive trusts as a venerable and distinct theory of equitable relief, see Lionel Smith, Legal Epistemology in the Restatement (Third) of Restitution and Unjust Enrichment, 92 B.U. L. Rev. 899, 907-16 (2012) (discussing the history of constructive trusts in the context of legal realism); Emily Sherwin, Unjust Enrichment and Creditors, 27 Rev. Litig. 141 (2007) (discussing the priority of claimants over other creditors); and H. Jefferson Powell, "Cardozo's Foot": The Chancellor's Conscience and Constructive Trusts, 56 Law & Contemp. Probs. 7 (1993) (tracing the history of constructive trusts in the United States through Benjamin Cardozo).

PROBLEM X

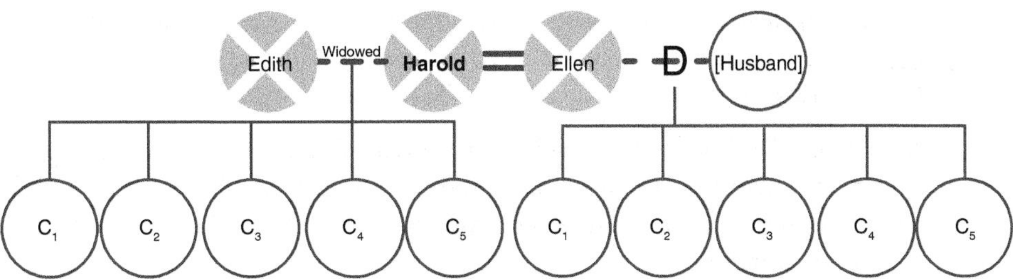

Harold and Edith were married with five children and, until Edith's death, they resided in a house on Canyon Road that they purchased as joint tenants with rights of survivorship. After Edith's death, Harold married Ellen, who had five adult children from her first marriage. Harold and Ellen had no joint children of their own and they resided together in the Canyon Road residence, which remained titled solely in Harold's name.

After Harold died intestate, Harold's children met with Ellen to discuss the handling of his estate as well as Ellen's plans for her own estate. They reached an oral agreement consisting of the following terms: (1) Harold's children agreed to indefinitely postpone their right to inherit from Harold's estate and to grant Ellen's request to continue residing in the Canyon Road house; (2) Ellen agreed to discharge all debts owed by Harold's children to their father's estate; and (3) the parties agreed that, upon Ellen's death, Harold's children would receive the balance of Harold's estate including the Canyon Road residence, and that Ellen's children would receive property attributed to her estate.

Ellen retained an attorney, who drafted a trust that mostly gave effect to the parties' agreement. The trust provided for an equal division of property between Harold's children and Ellen's children, but did not specify that Harold's children would receive the Canyon Road house. Ellen executed the trust instrument but did not provide a copy to Harold's children. Two years after executing the trust, however, Ellen executed an amendment that entirely removed Harold's children as trust beneficiaries. Under the amended trust, Ellen's children were the sole beneficiaries.

Ellen died approximately ten years later, but her children neither published an obituary nor notified Harold's children of Ellen's death. When Harold's children eventually obtained a copy of Ellen's amended trust, they brought suit seeking title to the Canyon Road property.

A. Should the court impose a constructive trust and, if so, what should the constructive trust require?

B. Was Ellen's conduct legal? What aspects of her conduct are relevant to the imposition of a constructive trust? What about Ellen's children? Did they act lawfully? How, if at all, is their conduct relevant to the imposition of a constructive trust?

C. The oral agreement between Ellen and Harold's children concerned the transfer of title to real property. Does the Statute of Frauds, which requires contracts concerning real property to be in writing, prevent a court from imposing a constructive trust to enforce the unwritten agreement and convey title to the Canyon Road property?

D. After Harold's death, while residing at Canyon Road, Ellen assumed responsibility for paying the monthly mortgage payments on the house. Ellen's children now argue that a constructive trust in favor of Harold's children would confer a windfall benefit unless Harold's children reimburse Ellen's estate for the mortgage payments. Does the fact that Ellen continued to pay the monthly mortgage payments on the house alter your analysis of whether to impose a constructive trust? If so, how?

PROBLEM XI

In each of the following hypotheticals, determine whether a court should impose a resulting trust, a constructive trust, or neither:

a. Ruby had one adult child, Jerald, and two grandchildren (Jerald's children). Ruby's will devised half of her estate to Jerald and a quarter to each of her grandchildren. After executing her will, Ruby purchased Certificates of Deposit worth $165,000 and took title in the name of herself and Jerald as joint tenants with right of survivorship. However, Ruby orally instructed Jerald to share the CDs equally with his two children after Ruby's death. Ruby's attorney, however, advised her that such an oral instruction would not be legally enforceable. In response, Ruby told her attorney, "I trust Jerald to do it." When Ruby died, Jerald refused to share the CDs with his children.

b. For much of his later life, Mr. Keener did not maintain close relations with his family but he surrounded himself with numerous friends who provided help and personal services around the house. On numerous occasions, Mr. Keener stated that he would draft a will containing generous gifts for several of his helpful friends. Mr. Keener drafted a will containing the promised testamentary gifts, but he died intestate before executing it. Now, the putative beneficiaries of Mr. Keener's unexecuted will argue that a court should impose a resulting or constructive trust giving effect to the provisions contained in the draft will.

9.3.3 Secret and Semi-Secret Trusts

In Chapter 4, we discussed contracts concerning succession in which a decedent breaches a promise to make a will or devise, not revoke a will or devise, or die intestate. Recall that UPC §2-514 requires contracts concerning succession to be memorialized in writing and signed by the decedent, but if a decedent breaches an oral contract by failing to include the promised testamentary disposition, the injured party may seek equitable remedies against the estate including a constructive trust. In this section, we consider the reverse situation in which the breaching party is a will beneficiary who made an oral promise to the testator concerning the devised property. Secret trusts and semi-secret trusts are non-trust doctrines that provide equitable remedies when a beneficiary accepts a testamentary gift subject to an oral promise made to the testator and then fails to abide by the promise.

A secret trust arises when a beneficiary makes an oral promise to the testator concerning inherited property and the testator's will fails to disclose both the existence and terms of the agreement. A secret trust may also arise when a decedent dies intestate in reliance on an oral promise made by an heir concerning property inherited by intestacy. Likewise, a secret trust may be implied when a decedent has designated a party as the beneficiary of a life insurance policy based on the beneficiary's promise to distribute the proceeds in accordance with the decedent's instructions.

The beneficiary's oral promise concerning the devised property is said to create a secret trust because its existence cannot be discerned from the face of the will. If the beneficiary accepts the devise and refuses to comply with the oral agreement, courts will impose a constructive trust on the devised property to carry out the decedent's intent and to prevent the beneficiary's unjust enrichment. The terms of the constructive trust will exact compliance with the oral agreement and require the beneficiary to convey any wrongfully retained property obtained from the estate to the testator's intended donees.

A semi-secret trust arises when a beneficiary makes an oral promise to the testator concerning inherited property and the testator's will manifests the existence of the promise but does not reveal its essential terms or particulars (e.g., identity of the intended beneficiaries). The promise is said to create a semi-secret trust because its existence can be discerned from the face of the will but the undisclosed particulars remain secret. In most jurisdictions, the equitable remedy for a semi-secret trust is a resulting trust, not a constructive trust, because partial disclosure of the oral agreement manifests intent to create an express trust but the will's inadequate specificity of terms causes the express trust to fail.[41] Courts that impose a resulting trust as the remedy for breach of a semi-secret trust reason that the undisclosed terms of the secret agreement cannot be established by extrinsic evidence because oral expressions of intent do not comply with Wills Act formalities. See, e.g., Pickelner v. Adler, 229 S.W.3d 516, 529 (Tex. App. 2007).

Secret and semi-secret trusts are relatively uncommon and, almost always, they are ill advised. The oral nature of secret promises in this context tends to breed conflicting, unverifiable testimony and creates incentives for unscrupulous promisors to engage in inequitable conduct after the testator's death. Secret and semi-secret trusts are also difficult to enforce because the claimant seeking to impose a constructive or resulting trust must establish proof of the alleged promise by clear and convincing evidence. See Restatement (Third) of Trusts §18, comment h. And lastly, litigation to enforce the terms of a secret or semi-secret trust almost always has the effect of disclosing and publicizing the secret oral instructions omitted from the face of the testator's will, so

41. By contrast, the Restatement (Third) of Restitution and Unjust Enrichment §46, comment g recommends imposing a constructive trust in favor of the intended donee for both secret trusts and semi-secret trusts. The commentary explains that, by imposing a resulting trust in cases of semi-secret trusts, the remedy unjustly enriches the testator's successors in interest at the expense of the intended donee.

these doctrines should not be viewed as a reliable technique for maintaining sensitive confidences.

Restatement (Third) of Trusts
§18 Secret Trusts

(1) Where a testator devises or bequeaths property to a person in reliance on the devisee's or legatee's expressed or implied agreement to hold the property upon a particular trust, no express trust is created, but the devisee or legatee holds the property upon a constructive trust for the agreed purposes and persons.

(2) Where a property owner dies intestate relying upon the expressed or implied agreement of an intestate successor to hold upon a particular trust the property acquired by intestate succession, no express trust is created, but the intestate successor holds the property upon a constructive trust for the agreed purposes and persons.

PROBLEM XII

Tiger is married to Angela but is having a secret affair with Becca. Tiger has succeeded in keeping his affair secret for several years by allowing Becca to live rent-free at his lake house, which Angela dislikes and never visits. Angela assumes (incorrectly) that Tiger's frequent weekend trips to the lake house are spent fishing with friends.

Tiger would like to execute a will leaving the bulk of his estate to Angela and the lake house to Becca, but he does not want to alert Angela of his relationship with Becca or otherwise publicize his affair. Tiger knows that Angela will see his will while he is still alive and that his will becomes a matter of public record once probated.

A. Suppose Tiger executes a will containing the following bequest: "I give, devise and bequeath my lake house, titled solely in my name, to my dear friend Jack"; Tiger's will leaves his residuary estate to Angela. After executing the will, Tiger orally instructs Jack that when he inherits the lake house, he must immediately and gratuitously convey title to Becca. Tiger also tells Becca about the bequest and his discussion with Jack. What result if, upon Tiger's death, Jack accepts the devise but refuses to convey the lake house to Becca?

B. Suppose Tiger executes a will leaving his residuary estate to Angela and containing the following provision: "I give, devise, and bequeath my lake house, titled solely in my name, to my dear friend Jack, who shall use the property solely for the purposes I explained to him in private conversation." After executing the will, Tiger orally instructs Jack that when he inherits the lake house, he must immediately and gratuitously convey title to Becca. What result if, upon Tiger's death, Jack accepts the devise but refuses to convey the lake house to Becca?

9.3.4 Honorary Trusts

In most cases, private donative trusts are established for the benefit of one or more identifiable human beings. Indeed, to create a valid private trust, the law *requires* the settlor to designate at least one human beneficiary whose identity can be ascertained within the applicable perpetuities period.[42] This requirement of a definite beneficiary ensures that at least one person always has standing to enforce the trustee's fiduciary duties. Sometimes, however, donors wish to convey property in trust for other non-charitable purposes, such as the maintenance of a relative's gravesite or the care of a beloved pet after its owner's death. Such transfers are unenforceable as trusts because they violate the definite beneficiary requirement, but so long as the donor does not impose a capricious purpose,[43] the law gives effect to the donor's intent by imposing an *honorary trust.*

Restatement (Third) of Trusts
§47 Trusts for Noncharitable Purposes

(1) If the owner of property transfers it in trust for indefinite or general purposes, not limited to charitable purposes, the transferee holds the property as trustee with the power but not the duty to distribute or apply the property for such purposes; if and to whatever extent the power (presumptively personal) is not exercised, the trustee holds the property for distribution to reversionary beneficiaries implied by law.

(2) If the owner of property transfers it in trust for a specific noncharitable purpose and no definite or ascertainable beneficiary is designated, unless the purpose is capricious, the transferee holds the property as trustee with power, exercisable for a specified or reasonable period of time normally not to exceed 21 years, to apply the property to the designated purpose; to whatever extent the power is not exercised (although this power is not presumptively personal), or the property exceeds what reasonably may be needed for the purpose, the trustee holds the property, or the excess, for distribution to reversionary beneficiaries implied by law.

A transferee holding property subject to an honorary trust has the power, but not a legal obligation, to carry out the donor's stated purposes. The exercise of this power is entirely optional and at the transferee's election. The transferee's failure to apply the property according to the donor's stated purpose is not a breach of fiduciary duty because an honorary trust is not an actual trust and the traditional duties of trusteeship do not regulate the transferee's conduct. Instead, the transferee's failure to comply with the donor's request effects a reversion by operation of law. The honorary trustee must then surrender the property back to the donor or, if deceased, to the donor's successors in interest. The donor's successors, therefore, have an incentive to monitor the

42. See Restatement (Third) of Trusts §44 ("A trust is not created, or if created will not continue, unless the terms of the trust provide a beneficiary who is ascertainable at the time or who may later become ascertainable within the period and terms of the rule against perpetuities.").

43. The Restatement (Third) of Trusts describes the following examples of capricious purposes:

> [I]t is capricious to provide that money shall be thrown into the sea, that a field shall be sowed with salt, that a house shall be boarded up and remain unoccupied, or that a wasteful undertaking or activity shall be continued. Also, an intended trust for the progeny of particular pets, or for the maintenance of a menagerie under circumstances that are inhumane or not of reasonably widespread interest to others . . . may be invalidated as capricious even within the "reasonable time" limit allowed [by law].

Restatement (Third) of Trusts §47, comment e.

honorary trust and seek enforcement of the reversion if the honorary trustee fails to carry out the intended purpose.

Perhaps the most popular type of honorary trust is for the care of a pet after the owner's death. The UTC and a majority of states have enacted statutes specifically authorizing pet trusts. UTC §408, for example, authorizes trusts for the care of "an animal alive during the settlor's lifetime," but imposes limitations on the duration and value of the trust. Careful attention in this context should be paid to the application of the Rule Against Perpetuities, which invalidates contingent interests not certain to vest within the lifespan plus twenty-one years of a measuring life. Under the traditional interpretation of the Rule, "measuring lives must be human lives," so animal species that enjoy great longevity may pose special concerns. Adam J. Hirsch, Trusts for Purposes: Policy, Ambiguity, and Anomaly in the Uniform Laws, 26 Fla. St. U. L. Rev. 913, 942 (1999). Professor Hirsch cautions that "courts have usually held invalid trusts to provide support for the lives of pet animals because they might continue too long, unless expressly limited to some human life or lives and/or twenty-one years." *Id.* at 935.

Uniform Trust Code
§408 Trust for Care of Animal

(a) A trust may be created to provide for the care of an animal alive during the settlor's lifetime. The trust terminates upon the death of the animal or, if the trust was created to provide for the care of more than one animal alive during the settlor's lifetime, upon the death of the last surviving animal.

(b) A trust authorized by this section may be enforced by a person appointed in the terms of the trust or, if no person is so appointed, by a person appointed by the court. A person having an interest in the welfare of the animal may request the court to appoint a person to enforce the trust or to remove a person appointed.

(c) Property of a trust authorized by this section may be applied only to its intended use, except to the extent the court determines that the value of the trust property exceeds the amount required for the intended use. Except as otherwise provided in the terms of the trust, property not required for the intended use must be distributed to the settlor, if then living, otherwise to the settlor's successors in interest.

10 | Nonprobate Transfers at Death and Will Substitutes

10.1 INTRODUCTION

This chapter discusses *nonprobate transfers*, a broad term that describes the many methods of transferring property at death other than by will. Often called *will substitutes*, nonprobate transfers generally pass outside the decedent's probate estate and are not controlled by the terms of the decedent's will. The most common examples of nonprobate transfers include the titling of property in a joint tenancy with right of survivorship, the creation of a payable-on-death (POD) account, and the execution of a death beneficiary designation on a retirement account or life insurance policy. Under modern wealth transfer law, assets such as these pass at death outside probate even if the underlying instruments do not satisfy Wills Act formalities.

Financial institutions have come to dominate the field of nonprobate transfers because most financial products, such as consumer bank accounts, stock brokerage investment accounts, and so on, now include death beneficiary designations to be completed by the account holder. The ubiquity of contractual death beneficiary designations means that financial services institutions (and their beneficiary forms) not only often play a vital role in the estate planning process, but they also serve important functions after the account holder's death, such as overseeing the disposition of assets at death outside the probate system.

10.2 WILL SUBSTITUTES

The concept of "will substitutes" is relatively new because, with the exception of joint tenancies, the law historically disfavored the transfer of property at death by means other than a will. As noted in Chapter 4, the English Wills Act of 1837, widely adopted in the United States, established the formal requirements necessary for disposing of real and personal property at death: a properly executed will. Probate courts strictly applied Wills Act formalities even in cases where rejection of the defective instrument frustrated the decedent's clear intent. This doctrine of strict compliance with Wills Act formalities was, in part, the judiciary's prophylactic response to concerns about fraud, coercion, and undue influence against elderly victims in the execution of wills. The earliest will substitutes, such as payable-on-death contracts, were therefore treated with great suspicion unless executed with all the formalities required of a valid will. Courts treated will substitutes as "attempted testamentary transfers," ineffective to pass property at death. Indeed, throughout much of the twentieth century, courts struggled to make sense of countless types of new will substitutes devised by attorneys and financial institutions in the relentless pursuit of probate avoidance. These innovations spawned volumes of litigation and judicial opinions that we mention but, thankfully, can otherwise omit from this book.[1]

Today, by contrast, Uniform Probate Code §6-101 recognizes a wide range of postmortem transfers as valid even if they are "nontestamentary." In this context, "nontestamentary" means that these transfers may be effected at the decedent's death even if the documents — deeds, beneficiary designation forms, etc. — do not comply with Wills Act formalities. Such instruments do not have to be probated and the property governed by such instruments are not under the power of the estate's personal representative. As the comment to UPC §6-101 puts it: "The sole purpose of this section is to prevent the transfers authorized here from being treated as testamentary."

Uniform Probate Code
§6-101 Nonprobate Transfers on Death

A provision for a nonprobate transfer on death in an insurance policy, contract of employment, bond, mortgage, promissory note, certificated or uncertificated security, account agreement, custodial agreement, deposit agreement, compensation plan, pension plan, individual retirement plan, employee benefit plan, trust, conveyance, deed of gift, marital property agreement, or other written instrument of a similar nature is nontestamentary. This subsection includes a written provision that:

(1) money or other benefits due to, controlled by, or owned by a decedent before death must be paid after the decedent's death to a person whom the decedent designates either in the instrument or in a separate writing, including a will, executed either before or at the same time as the instrument, or later;

(2) money due or to become due under the instrument ceases to be payable in the event of death of the promisee or the promisor before payment or demand; or

(3) any property controlled by or owned by the decedent before death which is the subject of the instrument passes to a person the decedent designates either in the instrument or in a separate writing, including a will, executed either before or at the same time as the instrument, or later.

---

1. For a notable example, see Farkas v. Williams, 125 N.E.2d 600 (Ill. 1955), in which the decedent held stock "as trustee" for his named beneficiary, who had no real ownership rights until the owner's death because the owner reserved the right, among others, to revoke the trust. The trust certificate was not executed in compliance with Wills Act formalities but appeared to dispose of a property interest at death. The court sought to determine "(1) whether upon execution of the so-called trust instruments [the beneficiary] acquired an interest in the subject matter of the trusts, the stock of defendant Investors Mutual, Inc., [and] (2) whether [the stockholder], as settlor-trustee, retained such control over the subject matter of the trusts as to render said trust instruments attempted testamentary dispositions."

Widespread acceptance and use of nonprobate transfers, such as those enumerated in UPC §6-101, reflects what has been described by Professor John H. Langbein as a "nonprobate revolution." See John H. Langbein, The Nonprobate Revolution and the Future of the Law of Succession, 97 Harv. L. Rev. 1108 (1984). By the mid-1980s, Langbein estimated that the majority of property transferred at death passed outside of probate. As Langbein explained:

> Over the course of the twentieth century, persistent tides of change have been lapping at the once-quiet shores of the law of succession. Probate, our court-operated system for transferring wealth at death, is declining in importance. Institutions that administer noncourt modes of transfer are displacing the probate system. Life insurance companies, pension plan operators, commercial banks, savings banks, investment companies, brokerage houses, stock transfer agents, and a variety of other financial intermediaries are functioning as free-market competitors of the probate system and enabling property to pass on death without probate and without will. The law of wills and the rules of descent no longer govern succession to most of the property of most decedents. Increasingly, probate bears to the actual practice of succession about the relation that bankruptcy bears to enterprise: it is an indispensable institution, but hardly one that everybody need use.

Id. That trend continues, and Article VI of the UPC, which governs nonprobate transfers, reflects this enormous shift in emphasis away from probate as the dominant process for transferring property at death.

The Restatement now defines the term "will substitute" as "an arrangement respecting property or contract rights that is established during the donor's life, under which (1) the right to possession or enjoyment of the property or to a contractual payment shifts outside of probate to the donee at the donor's death; and (2) substantial lifetime rights of dominion, control, possession, or enjoyment are retained by the donor." Restatement (Third) of Property: Wills & Other Donative Transfers §7.1(a). Professor Langbein, however, draws a distinction between will substitutes that are "pure" and "imperfect." Pure will substitutes — payable-on-death accounts and revocable trusts, for instance — effectively function as do wills: "[E]ach [pure will substitute] reserves to the owner complete lifetime dominion, including the power to name and to change beneficiaries until death." Langbein, 97 Harv. L. Rev. at 1108. Importantly, pure will substitutes never give the beneficiary any current possessory or other interest during the owner's life, and the owner may change beneficiaries as often (and as secretly) as he or she wishes. Imperfect will substitutes, unlike wills, affect the ownership control over or enjoyment of property during life. Joint tenancies (in real property and, under some circumstances, in personalty), for example, are imperfect will substitutes because they allow the owner to retain substantial control but create a present possessory interest in the joint tenant, including the right to sever the joint tenancy, during the owner's life.

Although now expressly validated by the UPC, many legal aspects of nonprobate transfers remain unsettled because the courts have not yet had a chance to fully develop a body of interpretive rules and doctrines in this area. And, in some cases where the law of nonprobate transfers has begun to form, different legal rules and doctrines sometimes apply to functionally similar transfers, with one treatment under the law of wills and another treatment under the law of nonprobate transfer. For example, the probate process subjects the decedent's estate to creditor claims under a shortened statute of limitations, and the personal representative represents the estate in defending or satisfying creditor claims. However, the rules concerning creditor collection against nonprobate transfers are, in several ways, quite unsettled: Can the owner of property avoid creditor claims at death by using nonprobate transfers rather than a will? Is there a duty to notify creditors of the existence of nonprobate transfers? Who is responsible for dealing with the decedent's creditors asserting claims against nonprobate transfers? Must creditors assert claims against the probate estate before proceeding against nonprobate transfers? Which nonprobate transfers abate first?

Courts have answered some of these questions, but not others, so the journey is far from complete. For now, we will note that the modern trend in the law governing nonprobate transfers has generally favored applying the corresponding rules applicable to wills (except in the case of execution formalities). This approach helps to achieve consistency in the disposition of property at death regardless of the decedent's chosen form of transfer.

10.2.1 Revocable Trusts as Will Substitutes and Pour-Over Wills

In recent decades, the inter vivos revocable trust, in conjunction with a pour-over will, has become a common estate planning technique and, if properly structured, can serve as a pure will substitute. Revocable inter vivos trusts permit settlors to arrange for the disposition of property at death *and* for management of their property while they are alive (most importantly, during any period of a settlor's physical or mental incapacity) without surrendering control over their property until death. To do so, the settlor establishes an inter vivos trust for use as the primary instrument for conveying assets both during life and at death. The settlor, then, channels all property into the trust: All nonprobate transfers, such as POD accounts and life insurance policies, designate the trustee as the death beneficiary. All probate property in the estate is devised through the residuary clause of the decedent's will to the trustee as well. This type of will is known as a *pour-over will* because its sole purpose is to pour over all remaining property in the decedent's estate into the trust. The trust instrument then controls the ultimate disposition of the property to the decedent's chosen beneficiaries.

Restatement (Third) of Property: Wills & Other Donative Transfers §3.8 Pour-Over Devises

(a) A "pour-over" devise is a provision in a will that (i) adds property to an inter vivos trust or (ii) funds a trust that was not funded during the testator's lifetime but whose terms are in a trust instrument that was executed during the testator's lifetime.

(b) A pour-over devise may be validated by statute, by incorporation by reference, or by independent significance.

Subsection (a)(ii) of this section of the Restatement authorizes a will to distribute property even to an inter vivos trust that was not funded during the settlor's lifetime, creating a rare exception to the rule that a valid trust requires trust property. The Uniform Testamentary Additions to Trusts Act of 1991 (integrated into the UPC as UPC §2-511) sets out the parameters within which a pour-over will may operate.

Uniform Probate Code
§2-511 Uniform Testamentary Additions to Trusts Act

(a) A will may validly devise property to the trustee of a trust established or to be established

(i) during the testator's lifetime by the testator, by the testator and some other person, or by some other person, including a funded or unfunded life insurance trust, although the settlor has reserved any or all rights of ownership of the insurance contracts, or

(ii) at the testator's death by the testator's devise to the trustee, if the trust is identified in the testator's will and its terms are set forth in a written instrument, other than a will, executed before, concurrently with, or after the execution of the testator's will or in another individual's will if that other individual has predeceased the testator, regardless of the existence, size, or character of the corpus of the trust. The devise is not invalid because the trust is amendable or revocable, or because the trust was amended after the execution of the will or the testator's death.

(b) Unless the testator's will provides otherwise, property devised to a trust described in subsection (a) is not held under a testamentary trust of the testator, but it becomes a part of the trust to which it is devised, and must be administered and disposed of in accordance with the provisions of the governing instrument setting forth the terms of the trust, including any amendments thereto made before or after the testator's death.

(c) Unless the testator's will provides otherwise, a revocation or termination of the trust before the testator's death causes the devise [to the trustee of a trust described in section (a)] to lapse.

If the settlor of a revocable inter vivos trust has successfully transferred title to all assets to the trustees, the settlor will die owning no property subject to probate administration. The trustees will distribute the trust property to the settlor's beneficiaries as provided in the trust instrument. If there are no concerns about actual or potential creditor claims, probate may be unnecessary. Unless there are unusual circumstances, the terms of the trust will not become part of the public record. Revocable trusts serving as will substitutes are treated in some jurisdictions similarly to wills in important ways, including revocability, ademption, and antilapse.[2]

PROBLEM I

Mary Dooley is a successful attorney in Miami. She was widowed several years ago, and her three adult children have busy lives in Baltimore, St. Louis, and San Diego. Mary, though not wealthy, has significant assets including homes in Miami and Southampton, New York, and a well-diversified portfolio of investments that she manages herself. Mary is concerned about her recent health problems. To assure that her assets are managed for

---

2. See Restatement (Third) of Property: Wills & Other Donative Transfers §7.2; Uniform Trust Code §602(c) (revocability); Restatement (Third) of Property: Wills & Other Donative Transfers §5.2, comment i (ademption); *id.* §5.5, comment p (antilapse).

her benefit during her lifetime and to establish a plan to distribute her property after she dies, Mary creates an inter vivos, revocable trust for which Mary and one of her law partners serve as co-trustees. Mary transfers property to the trustee by retitling the deeds to her houses from herself individually to the "Trustees of the Mary Dooley Revocable Trust"; all of her investment accounts in the name of the trustees of the trust; and her tangible personal property by executing a general assignment of her title in that property to the trustees. Mary maintains a checking account in her own name, and each month the trustees transfer funds from a trust account into Mary's checking account.

A. During Mary's life, what rights has she retained in the trust property?

B. How would the trust be administered if Mary became incapacitated?

C. What happens to the trust property when Mary dies?

10.3 JOINT TENANCIES

A joint tenancy, in use since at least the thirteenth century, is a form of concurrent co-ownership that includes the right of survivorship, or *jus accrescendi*, which entitles the surviving joint tenant(s) to the complete interest of the predeceasing joint tenant. The basic principles of joint tenancies have not changed much over the centuries, and most jurisdictions still rely on the four "unities"—interest, title, time, and possession—described by Sir William Blackstone:

> The properties of a joint-estate are derived from its unity, which is fourfold; the unity of *interest*, the unity of *title*, the unity of *time*, and the unity of *possession*; or, in other words, joint-tenants have one and the same interest, accruing by one and the same conveyance, commencing at one and the same time, and held by one and the same undivided possession.

2 Sir William Blackstone, Commentaries on the Laws of England 180 (1765-1769).

Under the common law, forms of co-ownership satisfying these four unities were presumed to be joint tenancies with right of survivorship. Today, in some jurisdictions, survivorship language must be expressly included in the property title to assure a right of survivorship, and in all jurisdictions it is the better practice to state expressly that intention. Thus, a deed conveying real property in a joint tenancy would read, "*To Co-owner X and Co-owner Y as joint tenants with right of survivorship.*" In some jurisdictions, a simple statement such as, "*To Co-owner X and Co-owner Y as joint tenants*" or "*To Co-owner X and Co-owner Y,*" would be deemed to form a tenancy in common, which has no right of survivorship. See FLA. PROB. CODE §689.15. Importantly, unlike pure will substitutes such as revocable inter vivos trusts, joint tenancies (at least in real property) convey a *current, irrevocable, actionable interest* in the property during the owner's life.

10.3.1 Joint Tenancies—Real Property

Joint tenancies are used frequently in the titling of real property, which is immovable, is typically an individual's most valuable asset, and tends to change hands less frequently than personal property. The personal residence of married or partnered couples is usually held in joint tenancy so that a surviving spouse or partner obtains full ownership of the property upon the death of the first spouse or partner without a probate proceeding. As a will substitute, however, the joint tenancy is "imperfect" because joint tenants have a vested proprietary interest in the property held in joint tenancy as soon as the joint tenancy is created. A relatively recent new alternative form of real property ownership, the transfer-on-death (TOD) deed, by contrast provides a more pure nonprobate substitute for transfer by will. Under the Uniform Real Property Transfer on Death Act (URPTODA), added to the UPC in 2009 (UPC §6-401 *et seq.*), an owner of real property may designate a beneficiary to receive the property upon the owner's death outside probate. Unlike a joint tenant, the beneficiary of a TOD deed has *no* vested interest in the property before the owner's death, and the owner is free to transfer the property, revoke the deed, or change the named beneficiary on the deed. Eight states and the District of Columbia have enacted URPTODA.[3]

PROBLEM II

Questions A-D below refer to the following facts: Ten years into their relationship, Juan and Sean decided to purchase a condominium as joint tenants with right of survivorship. Each of them contributed one-half of the purchase price in cash.

Juan and Sean continued to live at the condominium together as a couple. In 2014, Juan was diagnosed with an untreatable cancer. To prevent Sean from dealing with probate issues, Juan created a revocable inter vivos trust and transferred all of his personal property to himself and Sean as co-trustees of the trust. Juan was the sole beneficiary of the trust during his lifetime and Sean was named as the sole beneficiary of the trust assets after Juan's death.

Juan was particularly concerned about the well-being of his sister, Maria, a single mother with three children who had been unemployed for many years. After talking the situation over with Sean, Juan changed the beneficiary of his life insurance policy from Sean to Maria. Although Juan believed he had transferred all of his assets to the revocable trust, he signed a will to be certain he did not die intestate as to any portion of his estate. Juan's will states in its entirety:

> I leave everything I own, including my interest in any property I own in joint tenancy, to my sister, Maria.

After Juan dies, one of his creditors asserts a claim against Juan's interest in the condominium, seeking repayment of a $10,000 unsecured and unpaid loan. The creditor had obtained a judgment while Juan was alive but never collected or sought to attach Juan's property.

A. When Juan died, what happened to his interest in the condominium?

B. Did Juan's will effectively transfer his interest in the condominium to Maria?

---

3. For a good discussion of the advantages and disadvantages of using TOD deeds, see Susan N. Gary, Transfer-on-Death Deeds: The Nonprobate Revolution Continues, 41 Real Prop. Prob. & Tr. J. 529 (2006).

C. Can Juan's creditor successfully assert the claim against Juan's interest in the condominium?

D. Is Juan's joint property interest in the condominium included in calculating his federal estate tax liability?

Questions E-H refer to the following facts. Assume that Daniel and Leah live in a separate, rather than a community, property state: After three years of marriage, Daniel and Leah had saved enough money to purchase a small house for $100,000. They each contributed $25,000 from their own savings for the down payment of $50,000 and borrowed $50,000 from a bank, securing that loan with a mortgage on the house. Daniel and Leah took title to the house as joint tenants with right of survivorship.

Soon after purchasing the house, their marriage began to deteriorate. They decided to separate and seek a divorce. Leah moved in with her mother, and Daniel continued to live in the house.

At the time of their separation, Leah's only assets were her interest in the house and a checking account solely in her name with a balance of $10,000. Daniel's assets consisted of his interest in the house, a $50,000 certificate of deposit from a local bank, and a savings account with a $20,000 balance, both held in his name only. They also had a checking account as joint tenants with right of survivorship with a balance of $1,000.

Just after they separated, Leah met with a lawyer. She instructed the lawyer to convey her interest in the house to herself as a tenant in common. She also executed a new will leaving everything she owned to her mother. Daniel also met with a lawyer. He executed a codicil giving the CD and his one-half interest in the house to his mother; however, Leah remained the beneficiary of the remainder of Daniel's estate under the unrevoked residuary provision of his prior will. Daniel's will required his executor to pay all "just debts."

E. At the time of purchase, what options did Leah and Daniel have for taking title to their house? What are the advantages of each option?

F. If Leah died after signing her new will, survived by Daniel and her mother, what would happen to her interest in the house?

G. If Daniel died after signing the codicil, survived by Leah and his mother, what would happen to his interest in the house?

H. Would Daniel's estate be responsible for paying off the remainder of the loan secured by the mortgage on the house?

10.3.2 Joint Tenancies in Tangible Personal Property

Joint tenancies with right of survivorship can provide a useful form of nonprobate transfer for tangible personal property (sometimes abbreviated as "TPP"). Most joint tenancies involving personalty are typically created in the context of multiple-party bank or investment accounts (i.e., *intangible* personal property, discussed below at Section 10.3.3), but individuals can also own *tangible* personal property as joint tenants.

With the exception of automobiles (and, in some jurisdictions, boats), for which state departments of motor vehicles issue title certificates, the law provides no general mechanism to establish or trace title for tangible personal property. Although subject to fewer formalities for establishing title, tangible items such as art, rare books, and jewelry can nevertheless be quite valuable yet, at the same time, are small enough to be easily transported and concealed. Accordingly, proof of title and the right to possess TPP can present unique problems, not just in trusts and estates law, but also in the fields of commercial law and art law.

The next case demonstrates some of the difficulties of proving title held as joint tenants in TPP. It also illustrates the confusion resulting from the lack of careful coordination among multiple probate and nonprobate instruments.

Funerary Sculpture of a Horse and Rider; China, Tang dynasty, 618-906; Sculpture, Mold-built earthenware with white slip painted; 21 1/2 × 7 × 18 1/4 in. (54.61 × 17.78 × 46.36 cm). *Los Angeles County Museum of Art; Gift of Nasli M. Heeramaneck (M.73.48.119).*

Robinson v. Robinson
651 So. 2d 1271 (Fla. Dist. Ct. App. 1995)

Opinion

PER CURIAM.

[Marvin Robinson ("Decedent") was survived by his wife Marilyn and brother David, both of whom Marvin appointed as co-personal representatives of his probate estate. This opinion refers to David as "Personal Representative" and Marilyn as "Wife." Marvin also appointed David as co-trustee of his Amended and Restated Declaration of Trust ("Trust"). David appeals the trial court's order that] all household furnishings and art vested by operation of law [rather than by will or trust] in Wife [because Decedent and Wife held the property as tenants by the entireties]; and because Wife agreed to abide by Decedent's wishes, the "Tang Horse and Rider" and "Neiman sailboat print" were held estate assets. We affirm.

This case arises from a family dispute over the ownership of 112 pieces of art (Art) and household furnishings (Household Goods). Two of the pieces of Art were devised in Decedent's will. Wife petitioned for a declaration as to her ownership rights in all of the Art and Household Goods. Personal Representative, Decedent's brother, claimed that all of the items were estate assets. He planned to utilize proceeds from the sale of same to satisfy estate tax liability on the $9.8 million gross estate. Conversely, Wife, also a co-personal representative of Decedent's estate, claimed that she was the sole owner of the property by reason of either an inter vivos gift made at the time of purchase of the personal property or by operation of the right of survivorship incident to tenancy by the entirety. There was conflict between the Will, First Codicil, Letter, Trust, testimony and other evidence as to the ownership and disposition of the Art and Household Goods.

Decedent and Wife were married in 1974 and it was conceded that the 18-year marriage, a second marriage for both, was a happy one. Decedent has two daughters from a prior marriage, Shirley and Jill. There was no prenuptial agreement.

Decedent's Last Will and Testament, executed on February 13, 1987, provided in Item 4 that Decedent may leave a written statement or list disposing of certain items of tangible personal property and that all personal property not so listed would be disposed of as provided in Item 5 of the Will. Item 5 provided that except as provided in Item 4, all remaining tangible property was bequeathed to Wife. Item 6 provided that the residue of Decedent's personal and real property was bequeathed to the Trust established on June 3, 1976 and restated on February 3, 1987.

The First Codicil amended Item 4 of the Will and made specific bequests of personal property. The "Tang Horse and Rider" and "Neiman sailboat print" were devised to Decedent's daughter, Shirley, and "my large Tang Camel" was devised to Wife if she displays it in her home; otherwise, it was to be auctioned and the proceeds added to the Trust. Decedent also bequeathed any three items of personal property except the Chinese Art, paintings and antiques to his daughter, Jill.

Decedent's July 31, 1990, Letter directed that Shirley receive the Horse and Rider, Neiman sailboat print and the "three colored Tang." It also directed that Wife display the Camel or auction it [as provided in First Codicil].

The Third Amendment to the Trust provided that the trustees shall distribute all of the grantor's works of art used by grantor at his personal residence and household furniture and furnishings outright to Wife free and discharged from the Trust, as grantor did not intend to claim any interest in any such property which may already belong to his wife. The trustees were authorized to honor, in their discretion, any such ownership.

Wife conceded that the property in issue was purchased with Decedent's money — not from a joint account, and that some of the purchase invoices were in Decedent's name. Wife was not employed during the marriage, but volunteered, painted and took classes. All of the property was located in the home where the Decedent and Wife lived when Decedent expired.

The doctrine of tenancy by the entirety with respect to personal property was expressly recognized in Bailey v. Smith, 89 Fla. 303, 103 So. 833 (1925) (savings bank deposit and mortgage). Adhering to *Bailey*, in a case where a judgment creditor, Hector Supply, brought a garnishment proceeding against the bank as garnishee for collection against the bank account held by the judgment debtor and his wife, our supreme court expounded on the doctrine and set forth the test for determining whether such an estate in personalty has been created in First National Bank of Leesburg v. Hector Supply Co., 254 So. 2d 777 (Fla. 1971):

> In *realty* matters, where property is acquired specifically in the name of husband and wife, we consider it to be a rule of construction that a tenancy by the entireties is created, although fraud may be proven. . . . [I]n personalty matters, a different standard obtains: *not only must the form of the estate be consistent with entirety requirements, but the intention of the parties must be proven.* The reason for this double standard is easily understood. Realty matters are matters of record which occur infrequently, and which generally involve formal transactions necessarily requiring consent of both spouses. Personalty, on the other hand, is generally not under mandate of record; it may easily be passed by either spouse without mutual consent or without knowledge of the other spouse; finally, it may change hands with great frequency, as in the case of the checking account. Another reason for the distinction is that the application of entireties concepts to personalty becomes exceedingly complex as the nature of the personalty increases in sophistication, and the judicial mind seeks to require greater safeguards lest the tenancy be abused.

Leesburg articulates that in addition to proof of intent:

> A viable tenancy by the entirety, with regard to either *realty or personalty*, must possess always and at the same time the following characteristics of form: unity of possession (joint ownership and control); unity of interest (the interests must be the same); unity of title (the interests must originate in the same instrument); unity of time (the interests must commence simultaneously); and, the unity of marriage.

The Personal Representative argued that we should reverse because the trial court utilized a presumption that a tenancy by entirety was established, when such a presumption does not exist in regard to personal property. As the court explained in

In re Marchini, 45 B.R. 187 (Bankr. S.D. Fla. 1984), there is no presumption that the personal property is held as an estate by the entirety, rather than as tenancy in common, merely from the character or use of the personal property. The court elaborated that personal property is not under mandate of record, changes hands frequently without knowledge and consent of the other spouse and is a ready and tempting shelter for creditors' claims, which require greater safeguards lest the tenancy be abused. The problem with the Personal Representative's argument is that the trial court did not utilize the presumption.

Here, the trial court found that the evidence presented indicated that: (1) the property was purchased with Decedent's funds and certain purchase invoices were in Decedent's name; (2) a homeowner's insurance policy and the policies insuring the art work named both the Decedent and Wife as co-insureds; (3) the decision to purchase the property and what property was selected for purchase were made jointly by Decedent and Wife; (4) the Decedent and Wife maintained a binder in which all paperwork for the items of art work was contained and in which an itemized inventory of the art work was kept; (5) the Decedent affixed a label upon each item of art work containing a number corresponding to the number assigned to the item in the inventory and on which the words "M & M Robinson Collection" were written, which signified that Decedent and Wife were the owners of these items; (6) the items of art work were not segregated or otherwise set aside for the exclusive use of the Decedent, but instead were displayed throughout the home of Wife and Decedent; and (7) the Decedent and Wife transported the art work to each new home they purchased and displayed it throughout each home.

Although the order being appealed did not expressly articulate which items of evidence established each of the five unities and the requisite intent for the creation of a tenancy by the entireties estate, neither did it rely on a presumption that the property was owned as tenants by the entirety merely because it was acquired during the marriage. The evidence in the record clearly supports the trial court's conclusion — absent any presumption — that the subject property was held as tenants by the entireties.

Affirmed.

QUESTIONS

1. Contests involving the titling of property in the form of tenancy by the entirety often arise in the context of an action by creditors to attach the property (see *Hector Supply*, discussed in the case above). Why is the titling of property as tenancy by the entirety significant to creditors?

ANSWER. When property is held jointly by spouses as tenants by the entirety, a non-joint creditor of one spouse cannot attach property held jointly within the tenancy. Although this feature of protection against creditor claims does not directly concern the transfer of property rights at death, it is often a significant consideration by owners who decide to create a tenancy by the entirety.

2. Under Item 5 of the Will, the Decedent left Wife all tangible personal property not otherwise disposed of under Item 4. Under Item 6 of the Will, the Decedent left the residue of his estate to his Trust, which instructed "the trustees [to] distribute all of the grantor's works of art used by grantor at his personal residence and household furniture and furnishings outright to Wife free and discharged from the Trust, as grantor did not intend to claim any interest in any such property which may already belong to his wife." If Item 5 of the Will gave all of Decedent's remaining tangible personal property to Wife, then why did the Trust also distribute Decedent's works of art to Wife? Was the Trust redundant?

   ANSWER. The Trust provision likely served two functions. First, the Trust clarified Decedent's intentions regarding the ownership of art after his death. Second, Decedent may have transferred title to certain artwork to the Trust during his lifetime; if so, the provision would not simply repeat instructions contained in his Will.

3. The court noted that "because Wife agreed to abide by Decedent's wishes, the 'Tang Horse and Rider' and 'Neiman sailboat print' were held estate assets." Had Wife not voluntarily relinquished ownership of those two items to Decedent's daughter, how would they have been distributed? Stated otherwise, would Item 4 of the Codicil or the 1990 Letter control the disposition of these items?

   ANSWER. Wife would have received the Tang Horse and Rider and Neiman sailboat print because the court found the property held in tenancy by the entirety. When property is held jointly as tenants by the entirety, the death of one spouse confers the surviving spouse with sole ownership of the property by operation of law. Property held jointly by tenants by the entirety cannot be transferred at death by will.

PROBLEM III

One of the difficulties with joint tenancies in personalty is that title is not only unrecorded, but often unwritten. In this case, there was written documentation of intent, but typically there isn't. What advice would you have for a married couple who sought advice about their large collection of contemporary art, a collection they acquired during thirty-five years of marriage? What kind of documentation would you want to see? If the couple had not kept good records of their acquisitions, what would you suggest they do?

PROBLEM IV

While attending law school, Jose purchased a condominium apartment and recorded title to the property as "Jose Jimenez, a Single Man." Shortly after his first semester, Jose met Susie, a medical resident. Following a brief courtship, Jose and Susie were engaged.

As a sign of commitment to his new fiancée, Jose transferred ownership of his condominium under a new deed recording title to the property as "Jose Jimenez and Susie Blair as Joint Tenants with Right of Survivorship."

A few days later, Jose purchased a small sculpture at an auction at Christie's in New York. When he brought it home, Jose placed it on Susie's bedside table, telling her, "This is the first piece in our new collection." Over the next two years, Jose and Susie continued to collect: Jose purchased sculptures and antiquities, while Susie focused on collecting artwork and photographs.

Jose and Susie both executed wills soon after they moved in together. Both wills contained a provision stating that if either of them predeceased the other, the survivor would take "the joint art collection."

Following graduation, Jose was studying for the bar exam when Susie and he had a huge fight. Jose ordered Susie to "get out." Jose told her that she was trespassing, and that if she did not leave, he would call the police. Susie declared that she had as much right to be there as Jose did. Nevertheless, reluctantly, Susie left.

A few weeks later, while Jose was sitting for the bar, Susie returned to the condominium and removed all of the artwork and photographs she had purchased. When Jose returned home and discovered that several items were missing, he angrily called Susie. Jose then tried to intimidate Susie into returning the items by asserting legal theories he had recently reviewed while preparing for the bar exam. First, Jose told Susie that she had committed a burglary by unlawfully entering the condominium and removing items of value without permission. Second, he claimed that, since they purchased the collection together, it was held in joint tenancy and Susie had no right to take jointly held property without his permission.

Susie coolly responded that (1) Jose had put the condominium in both of their names as joint tenants, so she had a present possessory interest in the property; and (2) there was no way that, by merely purchasing artwork contemporaneously and in coordination, they had established a joint tenancy in the collection. Susie laughed and said, "I know more about property law than you do. You probably didn't even pass the bar!" Jose became enraged and shouted, "I know one sure way to get my home and my collection back. I'll kill you dead!" Susie didn't believe Jose's bluster, but she wants to change her estate plan and learn about her legal rights, so she comes to see you.

A. What are Susie's rights with regard to the condominium?

B. Did Jose and Susie establish a joint tenancy in the art collection?

C. Could Susie remove the artwork she purchased and keep it for herself?

D. Susie did not take Jose's threat to kill her seriously. Nevertheless, she wants to prevent Jose from taking her interest in the condominium or the artwork should something happen to her. What steps could Susie take to assure that Jose would not receive Susie's interest in the condominium or the art if she predeceased him?

10.3.3 Joint Tenancies — Intangible Personal Property: Multiple-Party Accounts

An issue of particular complexity, but also importance, concerns what the UPC calls "multiple-party accounts with financial institutions," typically, joint tenancy bank accounts and POD accounts. A typical situation involves an account holder who names a family member or close friend as a joint tenant or as the POD beneficiary without an express statement of reasons for creating such accounts. Because individuals create these accounts for many different reasons, joint tenancy and POD accounts have generated a large body of (often conflicting) case law addressing rights of the parties during the lifetime of the account holder and at the account holder's death. Among the many questions these situations raise are the following:

- In creating a joint account, did the original depositor intend
    - to make a *current* gift of some or all of the account's assets?
    - for the joint tenant merely to have the ability to write checks on the account to assist the account holder in managing his or her affairs, but not for the purpose of giving the joint tenant a personal interest in the account?
    - for the joint tenant to use the account's assets primarily for the benefit of the account holder and secondarily as a back-up fund if the joint tenant needed money; and, if so, did the account holder intend for the joint tenant's withdrawal to be a loan or a gift?
    - for the joint tenant to have only a survivorship right and no right to access the account's assets while the account holder was alive?
    - to create an irrevocable right of survivorship?
- In naming a POD beneficiary, did the account holder intend
    - for the beneficiary to have access to the account's assets during the account holder's lifetime?
    - to create an irrevocable right to succeed to the account's assets upon the account holder's death?

The account holder's failure to articulate and memorialize his or her intent at the outset of establishing a joint or POD account can lead to misunderstandings and conflict later on. And even when the depositor completes all of the bank's required forms properly, it is common for heirs and beneficiaries (who would inherit the account proceeds through the probate estate but for the joint or POD titling) to contest the nonprobate status of the account. These challenges pit issues of documentary formalities — typically an objective test to ascertain the facial validity of the account — against arguments predicated on the decedent's intent — often a highly subjective excursion into the decedent's reasons for creating the account. In other words, should the nonprobate status of jointly held accounts be determined solely by written manifestations in the instrument creating the account or by extrinsic evidence of the account holder's intentions? The following case demonstrates how the Rhode Island Supreme Court dispatched with intent-based determinations and firmly stated its position favoring reliance on formalities to determine the ownership of multi-party account.

Robinson v. Delfino
710 A.2d 154 (R.I. 1998)

Opinion

BOURCIER, Justice.

This case came before us on the appeal of the defendants, Elisa Delfino (Delfino), Delfino's husband, Paul, and Donald C. Rich (Rich), from the order of a trial justice, rendered after a nonjury trial in the Superior Court. The trial justice, relying primarily upon our opinion in Nocera v. Lembo, 121 R.I. 216, 397 A.2d 524 (1979), ordered the defendants to return [to the estate] the monetary funds previously contained in joint bank accounts that Delfino and Rich individually maintained with Florence A. Izzi [because, although the decedent established the accounts as "joint accounts," she did not intend to transfer ownership of funds to the joint account holders during life or at death. As a result, the trial justice held that the contents of the accounts belonged to the probate estate].

I. FACTS AND CASE TRAVEL

On December 27, 1993, Florence A. Izzi (decedent) died intestate. At the time of her death, she had two living siblings, her brother, John Izzi (Izzi), and her sister, Delfino. Prior to her death, on August 27, 1987, the decedent had opened a joint certificate of deposit in the names of Izzi and herself. That account was funded entirely with the decedent's own money, and her Social Security number appeared on the account. Both Izzi and the decedent signed signature cards for that account. No other deposits to or withdrawals from that account were ever made.

The decedent also maintained a safe-deposit box, as a joint tenant, with Delfino, for which they both signed signature cards, and with Rich as a joint tenant, for which they also both signed signature cards.

On October 16, 1984, and April 21, 1992, Rich, who lived for many years in the decedent's home prior to and at the time of the decedent's death, had opened with his own funds two joint bank accounts in his and the decedent's names. Rich's Social Security number appeared on both of those accounts.

The decedent, on February 5, 1993, had opened three joint bank accounts in her and Rich's names with funds taken entirely from joint bank accounts the decedent maintained with her sister, Delfino.[4] The decedent's Social Security number appeared on all those accounts, and both Rich and the decedent signed account signature cards for the accounts. The signature cards all contained the statement "Joint Tenancy Account with Right of Survivorship." During the decedent's lifetime, Rich never had occasion to make any deposits into or withdrawals from those accounts. After the decedent's death, however, Rich withdrew the entire balance of the funds remaining in those accounts. In addition to those joint accounts with Rich, the decedent had also opened three other joint bank accounts with Rich

4. Prior to transferring those funds, the decedent discussed her plans with Delfino, she was fully aware of and, in fact, approved of the decedent's withdrawal of those funds for deposit into joint accounts maintained with the decedent's long-time friend, Rich.

on January 28, 1991, February 24, 1992, and April 6, 1992, which were all entirely funded with her own funds and on all of which the decedent's Social Security number appeared. Rich also withdrew the entire balance of those accounts after the decedent's death.

The decedent also maintained seven joint bank accounts with her sister, Delfino. All the accounts were funded entirely with money from the decedent, and the decedent's Social Security number also appeared on all those accounts. After the decedent's death, Delfino withdrew the balances remaining in four of those accounts and placed those funds into joint accounts that Delfino maintained with her husband, Paul.

Neither Rich nor Delfino had ever had possession of any of the passbooks, bank statements, or certificates of deposit for any of the above accounts. In addition to the joint bank accounts referenced above, the decedent also maintained a separate personal checking account in her own name.

While the decedent was in a nursing home during her last illness, she requested her sister to retain an attorney for her. Delfino discussed with Izzi, brother to both the decedent and Delfino, the decedent's request, and Izzi recommended his own personal attorney, John Vallone (Vallone). Vallone was contacted, and he went to visit the decedent at the nursing home on December 23, 1993, a few days before she died. During that visit the decedent told Vallone that she wanted to give Delfino and Izzi a power of attorney so that they could handle her affairs. However, she said that she was not yet ready to make a will. According to Vallone, the decedent also said that she did not know what she wanted to do with her money or what she wanted to do with some of the other assets in her estate. It is unclear whether the decedent, when referring to her "money," was referring to her personal bank account or to her joint accounts. Vallone apparently assumed that she was referring to the joint accounts because he then asked her if she had given the money in the joint bank accounts to other people during her lifetime. She responded that she had not. Vallone therefore personally concluded that those joint accounts would be part of the decedent's estate when she died.

In the trial justice's decision he relied in great part upon our holding in Nocera v. Lembo, 121 R.I. 216, 397 A.2d 524 (1979), and believed it to be applicable to the facts before him. In so doing, he attempted to determine whether the decedent had intended to make an inter vivos gift of the funds contained in the joint accounts effective at the time of her death. In *Nocera* we said that the form of a joint bank account constituted only prima facie evidence that the creator of the account intended an inter vivos gift. That presumption of an inter vivos gift we held could then be rebutted by "evidence tending to show that the name of the survivor was added to the account by the original owner for his [or her] convenience and not with the intention of making a gift of an interest therein to the survivor or [by evidence tending to show] that the original owner's intention was to vest an interest in the survivor only after the owner's death."

The trial justice found controlling the trial evidence indicating that the decedent "retained dominion and control of the passbook or certificate of deposit at all times prior to her death; [that] there was no commingling of . . . money with Decedent's money in said accounts; [and that] the interest earned [on the joint accounts] was paid to Decedent and she paid any income taxes on it." Relying on that evidence, the trial justice found that there was no clear and satisfactory proof that the decedent "added the respective survivor's name to the joint accounts in dispute here with the intention of making and fully executing a present and immediate gift." The trial justice concluded that the decedent intended a testamentary transfer of her money and that as a result the funds in the joint bank accounts were not the property of the surviving joint owner but were instead the property of the decedent's estate. Accordingly, the trial justice ordered Rich and Delfino "to return any funds removed by them from any of the joint bank accounts that Decedent had opened in her name and in the name of a Defendant, plus interest earned thereon." Delfino, Rich, and Delfino's husband, the joint owner of the account into which Delfino deposited the funds she withdrew from her joint accounts with the decedent, appeal from that decision.

II. NEW LAW

We conclude that the law heretofore applied to joint bank accounts both in this jurisdiction and elsewhere has been both unpredictable and inconsistent, often frustrating the public's common understanding of what it always believed that a joint bank account was intended to accomplish.[5] Accordingly, the time has now arrived for us to revisit our previous holdings in contested joint bank account cases, some of which date back into the last century.

. . .

The most recent trend among courts confronted with the ownership issue in joint bank accounts, however, and the trend that we conclude is most in conformity with the way the majority of the public actually perceive joint bank accounts, is that which finally recognizes that joint bank accounts cannot be uniformly understood or analyzed under any of the pre-existing common law methods. "Slowly and unevenly, through various gradations of evolution, courts have moved toward the inevitable realization that the joint and survivorship bank account has its own identity unconforming to any hitherto recognized common-law methods of transferring property." Wright v. Bloom, 635 N.E.2d 31, 37 (Ohio 1994). As a result of that recognition courts have begun to treat joint bank accounts differently from gifts, trusts, joint tenancies, or contracts and have concluded that the form of the joint bank account is itself the conclusive proof of the depositor's intent to transfer a vested possessory interest in the ownership of the joint account money.

In an attempt to make the effect of joint bank accounts more predictable and the law surrounding joint bank accounts less ambiguous and inconsistent, the *Wright* court concluded that "the depositor's intent to transfer a present interest in a joint and survivorship account to be irrelevant in a controversy involving the rights of a surviving party to the sums remaining in such account at the death of the depositor."

---

5. It has been facetiously noted that there are two ways to start a civil action in this state. The first is pursuant to Super. R. Civ. P. 3, and the second is by opening a joint bank account with right of survivorship.

The court further explained the reasoning behind its new joint bank account analysis:

> If there is one thing that is clear from reviewing the foregoing cases, it is that our efforts to determine survivorship rights by a post-mortem evaluation of extrinsic evidence of depositor intent are flawed to the point of offering no predictability. Regardless of the depositor's true motivation in opening a joint and survivorship account, he or she simply cannot be certain of how his or her lifetime actions will be construed in regard to transferring survivorship rights. Only when the depositor knows that the terms of the contract will be conclusive of his or her intent to transfer a survivorship interest will the depositor be able to make an informed choice as to whether to utilize the joint and survivorship account.

Thus, the court determined that "the need for uniformity is essential," and that to permit extrinsic proof of the depositor's intent only served to perpetuate confusion and to sanction "the use of joint and survivorship accounts by those who do not intend to transfer survivorship rights," thereby "encouraging the very evils of misinformation and litigation sought to be avoided" by the previous court practice of examining the depositor's intent.

. . . The Ohio court in *Wright* then proceeded to hold that

> the opening of an account in joint and survivorship form shall, in the absence of fraud, duress, undue influence or lack of mental capacity on the part of the depositor, be conclusive evidence of the depositor's intention to transfer to the survivor the balance remaining in the account at the depositor's death.

The court further held that

> The opening of the account in joint or alternative form without a provision for survivorship shall be conclusive evidence, in the absence of fraud or mistake, of the depositor's intention not to transfer a survivorship interest to the joint party in the balance of funds contributed by the depositor remaining in the account at the depositor's death. Such funds shall belong exclusively to the depositor's estate. . . .

After carefully considering the troublesome and often inconsistent results coming from the annals of our joint bank account litigated cases, we conclude, as did the Ohio court in *Wright* . . . that

> It would seem that when a depositor opens a joint and survivorship account and executes signature cards which recite that the account is to be paid to either during the depositors' joint lives and to the survivor upon the death of either, a rebuttable presumption of an intent to make a gift of a joint interest should arise. After the depositor's death only evidence of fraud, undue influence or lack of capacity should be admissible to rebut the presumption. It serves no useful social purpose to encourage litigation concerning the disposition of the balance of the joint account upon the death of the depositor, when in most instances he [or she] intended, in his [or her] unlearned manner, to make a testamentary disposition of his [or her] property. If the joint account is sound, as a means of transferring property, it should be uniformly administered.

. . .

To persist in clinging to ancient fictions created in most part to avoid the pitfalls emanating from the statute of wills to justify in some cases and to deny in others what the joint account with right of survivorship was truly intended to accomplish will simply perpetuate needless confusion. We should not subvert what is common understanding by wandering in bypaths of ancient logic. A surviving named joint account holder should be entitled to obtain funds remaining on deposit in a joint account without the necessity of first having to travel through several court systems and to have lawyers, trial judges, juries, and appellate judges perform post mortem cerebral autopsies and examinations in order to determine and second-guess what the subjective intent of the deceased joint owner of the account was at the time the account was created. In enacting §19-9-14, the General Assembly in 1995 commendably acted to rescue banks and financial institutions from the chaos rampant in the uncertainties of joint bank account problems by permitting those institutions, without any fear of penalty or liability, to pay out any funds remaining in a joint bank account to any named survivor on the particular joint account. We today rescue the remaining parties, the named account holders, from that same chaotic setting. As Justice Cardozo once said, "Precedents drawn from the days of travel by stage coach do not fit the conditions of travel today." It is now time to adapt our law to the common understanding of those who establish joint bank accounts and to make the law predictable and reliable for those people. Accordingly, we conclude that the opening of a joint bank account wherein survivorship rights are specifically provided for is conclusive evidence of the intention to transfer to the survivor an immediate *in praesenti* joint beneficial possessory ownership right in the balance of the account remaining after the death of the depositor, absent evidence of fraud, undue influence, duress, or lack of mental capacity. Likewise, if a joint bank account does not provide for survivorship rights, that absence will be conclusive evidence of an intent not to transfer any right of ownership to the survivor, absent evidence of mistake or fraud.

Returning to the facts of this case, we find it clear that all of the accounts in question were joint accounts with a right of survivorship in whoever survived. On the basis of the record facts before us, our opinion today clearly establishes the right of each of the surviving persons named on those accounts to the funds remaining in them upon the death of Florence A. Izzi on December 27, 1993.

. . .

For all the foregoing reasons the defendants' appeals are sustained and the order of the trial justice is reversed. The papers in this case are remanded to the Superior Court for entry of judgment in accordance with this opinion.

QUESTIONS

4. The *Delfino* court promulgated a clear, objective test for determining whether a surviving joint tenant succeeded to the balance in an account upon the account

holder's death. The determination is based entirely on what the account title says. Or, as the court put it:

> Accordingly, we conclude that the opening of a joint bank account wherein survivorship rights are specifically provided for is conclusive evidence of the intention to transfer to the survivor an immediate *in praesenti* joint beneficial possessory ownership right in the balance of the account remaining after the death of the depositor, absent evidence of fraud, undue influence, duress, or lack of mental capacity. Likewise, if a joint bank account does not provide for survivorship rights, that absence will be conclusive evidence of an intent not to transfer any right of ownership to the survivor, absent evidence of mistake or fraud.

ANSWER. The court is attempting to make the law "predictable and reliable" for those who establish joint bank accounts. The possessory interest of the non-depositing joint account holder does not vest upon the creation of the account. Rather, the creation of a joint account with rights of survivorship is conclusive proof that the depositor *intended* for the surviving joint account holder to obtain a possessory interest upon the depositor's death. Unless the depositor changes the terms of the account — or if there is evidence of fraud, undue influence, duress, or lack of capacity — the survivor gains a future interest, created upon the establishment of the account, in the balance upon the death of the depositor.

5. What did the court mean when it said that the opening of a bank account in joint tenancy with right of survivorship transferred to the surviving joint tenant "an immediate *in praesenti* joint beneficial possessory ownership right in the balance of the account remaining after the death of the depositor"? If the survivorship right vests at the moment the account is open, what happens if the account holder changes his or her mind and wants to name a different individual to succeed to the account?

   ANSWER. The survivorship right does not vest at the moment the account is opened. Rather, the survivorship right vests only upon the death of the depositor. Until then, the depositor is free to change the nature of the account or name a different individual or individuals to succeed to the account. Once the depositor has died, however, a third party cannot deny the survivor possession of the balance of the account by arguing that the depositor intended to change the name or nature of the account. If the account has not been changed by the depositor before the depositor dies, the survivor is entitled to the balance of the account.

6. Does the "*in praesenti* joint beneficial possessory ownership right in the balance of the account" mean that a current gift of the assets in the account may be withdrawn by the joint tenant during the account holder's lifetime?

   ANSWER. No. The "*in praesenti* joint beneficial possessory ownership right in the balance of the account" does not vest until after the death of the depositor. Until that time, the joint tenant does not have a possessory interest in any funds that the joint tenant did not deposit in the account personally. The joint tenant may also withdraw funds if the funds are for the benefit of the depositor and the depositor has given the joint tenant permission or if the account is established as a joint account specifically for the convenience of the parties. See Bielecki v. Boissel, 715 A.2d 571 (R.I. 1998).

In *Bielecki*, decided by the same court shortly after *Delfino*, the court held that the ruling in *Delfino* was inapplicable to joint bank accounts established for the purposes of convenience only. *Id.* at 574. The depositor in *Bielecki* made it clear that the joint accounts were created for convenience purposes only and included a clause in his will stating:

> [T]hose names on the aforementioned accounts were placed on those accounts for convenience only and I did not intend to give those accounts as a gift to any person other than the gifts and bequests contained in this my estate and further declare that those names on the aforementioned accounts were placed on those accounts for convenience only and I did not intend to give those accounts as a gift to any person other than the gifts and bequests contained in this my last will and testament.

The depositor's daughter, aware of this provision in the will, closed the accounts she held jointly with her father shortly after he went into a coma. After he died, the court ordered her to return the withdrawn funds to the decedent's estate, but allowed her to keep the money she contributed (plus interest) and held that she was not required to reimburse the estate for money expended from the accounts for renovations to the family home made for the benefit of her father with his tacit approval.

Like the *Delfino* court, UPC §6-212 adopts a simple, objective test for determining the rights of joint and POD account holders upon the death of a party: The surviving party (or parties) to a joint account owns the contents. "[O]n death of a party[6] sums on deposit in a multiple-party account belong to the surviving party or parties." UPC §6-212(a). The court does not inquire into the deceased account holder's subjective intent. Rather, the decedent's intent to create survivorship rights is discerned solely from the status of the account as joint or POD.[7]

The UPC also brings greater certainty to a related question involving joint and POD accounts: What are the parties' rights during the respective lifetimes of joint and POD account holders? For example, suppose the original depositor of a savings account adds second account holder (thereby creating a joint account) with the intention that the latter have access to the funds after the original depositor's death. What if the new joint account holder, who deposited nothing into the account, withdraws funds while the original depositor is still alive? Does that withdrawal constitute a conversion of the depositor's property or a gift from the depositor to the joint account holder? UPC §6-211 sets out relatively simple tests to resolve such conflicts.[8]

---

6. UPC §6-201(6) defines the term "party" as "a person who, by the terms of an account, has a present right, subject to request, to payment from the account other than as a beneficiary or agent."

7. Under UPC §6-213, death beneficiary designations are revocable and amendable during life by a party.

8. The UPC now incorporates the Uniform Multiple-Person Accounts Act, first promulgated in 1989. The provisions addressing ownership among multiple parties to financial accounts is set out in UPC §§6-211–6-216.

Uniform Probate Code
§6-211 Ownership [of Multiple-Person Accounts] During Lifetime

(a) In this section, "net contribution" of a party means the sum of all deposits to an account made by or for the party, less all payments from the account made to or for the party which have not been paid to or applied to the use of another party and a proportionate share of any charges deducted from the account, plus a proportionate share of any interest or dividends earned, whether or not included in the current balance. The term includes deposit life insurance proceeds added to the account by reason of death of the party whose net contribution is in question.

(b) During the lifetime of all parties, an account belongs to the parties in proportion to the net contribution of each to the sums on deposit, unless there is clear and convincing evidence of a different intent. As between parties married to each other, in the absence of proof otherwise, the net contribution of each is presumed to be an equal amount.

(c) A beneficiary in an account having a POD designation has no right to sums on deposit during the lifetime of any party.

(d) An agent in an account with an agency designation has no beneficial right to sums on deposit.

The UPC's approach to governing multiple-party accounts during life flows from the "assumption that a person who deposits funds in an account normally does not intend to make an irrevocable gift of all or any part of the funds represented by the deposit." UPC §6-211, comment. Thus, UPC §6-211 provides as a general rule that, *during the lifetime of parties to a multiple-party account, a party owns only the amounts he or she has deposited into the account* (§6-211(b)). The section also states that a designated beneficiary of a POD account has no right to any amount on deposit during the lifetime of the account holder (§6-211(c)); and an individual named as an agent in an account with an agency designation has no beneficial interests in the account (§6-211(d)).

PROBLEM V

Roy and Michelle met a year ago at a speed-dating event. They recently married and moved into a house they purchased, taking title as "Joint Tenants with Rights of Survivorship." Each of them contributed one-half of the purchase price, which they paid in cash. Roy's payment on the house depleted his savings, and he now lives month to month on his salary as a public defender.

Michelle, an orthopedic surgeon, set up a new checking account titled in her and Roy's names as "Joint Tenants with Rights of Survivorship." Michelle told Roy that if he needed money, he should just write a check from the joint account. Michelle deposited $100,000 into the account.

A few months later, Roy met Katerina and was smitten. Without telling Michelle, Roy wrote himself a check for $30,000 from the joint checking account and deposited that amount into his own checking account, of which he is sole owner, at another bank. Roy then left Michelle and moved in with Katerina.

What potential causes of action would Michelle have against Roy? Against the bank? What defenses might Roy assert? Does Michelle have cause of action against the bank?

10.4 PAYABLE-ON-DEATH ACCOUNTS

Similar to joint tenancy accounts, payable-on-death accounts create a right of survivorship. However, unlike joint tenants, the beneficiary of a POD account has no interest in the funds during the account holder's lifetime. UPC §6-211(c). The account holder is free to change the beneficiary at any time and free to dispose of the account funds in part or in whole as desired. A POD beneficiary has absolutely no say in the matter during the account holder's life. Thus, in In re Guardianship and Conservatorship of Anderson, 353 Mont. 139 (2009), the Supreme Court of Montana held that a POD beneficiary was not considered an "interested person" during the account holder's lifetime and was not entitled to notice of the hearing to consider removing her as beneficiary. Because she had no present possessory interest in the account before the account holder's death, she had no standing to be heard or to object to the change in beneficiary designation that was made by the account holder's conservator. By extension, *a fortiori*, such a beneficiary would have no standing to object to a change in beneficiary designation made by the account holder personally. However, although an account holder is at liberty to change beneficiary designations at will, a conservator or guardian generally may do so only with a court order. See Grahl v. Davis, 971 S.W.2d 373, 377-78 (Tenn. 1998).

Creating an effective POD account requires compliance with the financial institution's instructions and procedures set forth in the governing contract. Those requirements and the forms institutions use for POD accounts vary and easily can create confusion, as the following case indicates. UPC §6-204 provides a standard form for establishing a single-party or multiple-party account with a POD provision or right of survivorship. The Uniform Multiple-Person Accounts Act, UPC §6-201 *et seq*., seeks to encourage banks and credit unions to offer POD options by standardizing the applicable law.[9]

Newman v. Thomas
264 Neb. 801 (2002)

CONNOLLY, J.

In this case, we must decide whether the Nebraska Probate Code requires the owner of a non-pay-on-death, single-party account to give his or her financial institution signed written notice to add a pay-on-death (POD) beneficiary to the account. Before his death, John Henry M. Chamberlin opened a single-party certificate of deposit account (CD) with no POD beneficiary at American National Bank (American National). Although there is some evidence that Chamberlin attempted to add the appellant, Alfred Thomas, as a POD beneficiary, it is

9. For a discussion of the problems of "accidental inheritance" that arise when account holders lack complete understanding of the forms used by financial institutions for the designation of death beneficiaries, see Stewart E. Sterk & Melanie B. Leslie, Accidental Inheritance: Retirement Accounts and the Hidden Law of Succession, 89 N.Y.U. L. Rev. 165 (2014).

undisputed that Chamberlin did not give American National signed written notice. The district court ruled that Chamberlin's signed written notice was required and entered summary judgment for Ivorie Pearl Newman, the personal representative of Chamberlin's estate. We affirm.

I. BACKGROUND

In May 1997, Chamberlin opened a non-POD, single-party CD with American National. A standard form was used to open the CD. Consistent with its normal practice, American National gave Chamberlin the original form and retained two copies for its records.

Chamberlin died on April 16, 1999. His will named his sister, Newman, as the personal representative. On August 31, Newman requested American National to deposit the proceeds of the CD into an estate checking account at American National. American National then deposited about $50,000, the proceeds of the CD, into the estate checking account. At the time the funds were deposited, Newman was not aware of any other claims on the CD.

Thomas had been Chamberlin's friend and had helped Chamberlin with errands and household chores. After Chamberlin's death, Thomas arrived at an American National branch and claimed that before Chamberlin's death, he had made Thomas a POD beneficiary to the CD. When Thomas arrived at American National, he presented the original form issued to Chamberlin when he opened the CD. On the area of the form designated for the names of POD beneficiaries, someone had typed "POD ALFORD THOMAS [sic]." Someone had also placed a handwritten "x" in the box labeled "Single Party Account with Pay on Death." Notably, next to this box is a space for the owner's initials. This space is blank.

As noted above, American National retained two copies of the form used when Chamberlin opened the CD. "POD ALFORD THOMAS" and the handwritten "x" do not appear on either of these copies. No one at American National knows who made the changes. In addition, American National has no other document or record indicating that Chamberlin requested that Thomas be made a POD beneficiary to the CD.

Thomas claims that an American National employee, Patrice Smith, was responsible for making the handwritten "x" and typing "POD ALFORD THOMAS." According to Thomas' deposition testimony, in January or February 1998, he drove Chamberlin to an American National branch so that Chamberlin could withdraw interest from the CD. While there, Chamberlin met with Smith. Thomas claims he was present throughout this meeting and that during the meeting, Chamberlin orally requested that Thomas be added as the POD beneficiary to the CD. Thomas stated that Chamberlin then handed Smith the original form used to open the CD and that she "typed something" on it. Thomas also claimed that Chamberlin signed at least one and perhaps two documents during the meeting. Thomas admitted, however, that he did not notice what Chamberlin was signing.

Chamberlin's signature appears three times on the original form used to open the CD. Two of these signatures were clearly made when the account was opened.

The third signature is under a notation made on the second page. The notation refers to a withdrawal of interest made on January 7, 1998. The notation contains no reference to the addition of Thomas as a POD beneficiary.

In her deposition, Smith said that she does not remember the January 1998 meeting with Chamberlin. She also testified that she does not know if she made the handwritten "x" or typed "POD ALFORD THOMAS."

After Thomas attempted to claim the CD, American National froze the estate checking account into which it had previously deposited the proceeds from the CD. Newman then filed this declaratory judgment action against American National and Thomas. American National filed a motion seeking leave to deposit the disputed funds into court. The court granted the motion and dismissed American National.

Newman moved for summary judgment. At the summary judgment hearing, Thomas filed an affidavit under Neb. Rev. Stat. §25-1335 (Reissue 1995) seeking a continuance so that Thomas could have an expert analyze whether Smith's typewriter had been used to type "POD ALFORD THOMAS." The court treated the affidavit as a motion to resist summary judgment.

The court entered summary judgment for Newman. It held that to change Chamberlin's CD to a POD account, the Nebraska Probate Code required him to give signed written notice to American National requesting that the bank add Thomas as a POD beneficiary. Because there was no evidence that Chamberlin had given signed written notice to American National, the court granted Newman summary judgment. Thomas appealed.

II. ASSIGNMENTS OF ERROR

Thomas assigns, rephrased and reordered, that the district court erred in (1) interpreting and applying the applicable provisions of the Nebraska Probate Code, (2) granting Newman's motion for summary judgment, and (3) failing to order a continuance of the summary judgment hearing.

. . .

IV. ANALYSIS

1. Interpretation of Applicable Provisions of Nebraska Probate Code

Article 27 of the Nebraska Probate Code governs nonprobate transfers, including POD accounts. See Neb. Rev. Stat. §§30-2715 through 30-2746 (Reissue 1995). In 1993, the Legislature repealed the previous version of article 27 and replaced it with a version based on the revised article VI of the Uniform Probate Code. The revised version of article 27 governs this case.

Under the revised article 27, when the owner of a POD, single-party account dies, the sums on deposit belong to the surviving beneficiary or beneficiaries. §30-2723(b)(2). A non-POD, single-party account, however, is not affected by the death of the owner. Instead, the amount the owner was beneficially entitled to immediately before death is transferred to the estate. §30-2723(c). If Chamberlin's CD was a POD, single-party account with Thomas as the beneficiary, Thomas is entitled to the proceeds from the CD. But, if Chamberlin never successfully added Thomas as the CD's POD beneficiary, then Chamberlin's estate is entitled to the proceeds.

The district court determined that §30-2724 governs changing a non-POD, single-party account into a POD account. Section 30-2724 provides:

> Rights at death under section 30–2723 are determined by the type of account at the death of a party. *The type of account may be altered by written notice given by a party to the financial institution to change the type of account or to stop or vary payment under the terms of the account. The notice must be signed by a party and received by the financial institution during the party's lifetime.*

(Emphasis supplied.) The court interpreted the emphasized language as making the signed written notice of a party to the account a mandatory requirement for changing the type of account.

Thomas claims that the court made two errors in interpreting §30-2724. First, he claims that the language sets out a permissive rather than a mandatory method for changing the type of account. Second, he argues that even if the language of §30-2724 is mandatory, the section applies only to the modification of an existing multiparty or POD account and not to the creation of a multiparty or POD account. We disagree with both of these arguments.

(a) Is Language of §30-2724 Mandatory?

Thomas argues that the use of the word "may" in §30-2724 sets out a permissive rather than a mandatory method for altering the type of account. Newman counters that "may" in §30-2724 refers only to the ability of a party to alter the form of his or her account. She argues that §30-2724 is permissive in the sense that a party may choose to change his or her account from one form to another. But, to put the change into effect, the party must give his or her financial institution signed written notice.

In the absence of anything to the contrary, statutory language is to be given its plain and ordinary meaning; an appellate court will not resort to interpretation to ascertain the meaning of statutory words which are plain, direct, and unambiguous. Neither Thomas' nor Newman's construction of §30-2724 is facially unreasonable. We note that other courts are split on whether similar statutory language is permissive or mandatory. Compare Linehan v. First Nat. Bank of Gordon, 7 Neb. App. 54, 579 N.W.2d 157 (1998) (construing predecessor to §30-2724 as mandatory), Conservatorship of Milbrath, 508 N.W.2d 360 (N.D. 1993), and Estate of Wolfinger v. Wolfinger, 793 P.2d 393 (Utah App. 1990), with Jampol v. Farmer, 259 Va. 53, 524 S.E.2d 436 (2000). We thus resort to statutory interpretation.

Initially, we note that the Legislature has instructed us to construe the provisions of article 27 so as "to effectuate their general purpose to make uniform the law of those states which enact them." §30-2746. Section 30-2724 corresponds to §6-213 of the revised article VI of the Uniform Probate Code. (We note that there has been a technical amendment to §6-213, which Nebraska has not adopted.) Nine other jurisdictions have adopted §6-213. Unif. Multiple Person Accounts Act, Table of

Jurisdictions Wherein Act Has Been Adopted, 8B U.L.A. 1 (Supp. 2002) (listing jurisdictions which have enacted Multiple Person Accounts Act portion of revised article VI). None of these jurisdictions appear to have addressed whether the method set out for altering the type of account in §6-213 is mandatory.

However, §6-105 of the prerevision version of article VI, the predecessor of §6-213, contained the same "may be altered" language that appears in §§6-213 and 30-2724:

> [The form of the account] *may be altered* by written order given by a party to the financial institution to change the form of the account. . . . The order or request must be signed by a party, received by the financial institution during the party's lifetime, and not countermanded by other written order of the same party during his lifetime.

(Emphasis supplied.) Unif. Probate Code §6-105, 8 U.L.A. 474 (1998). Because of the similarity between §§6-105 and 6-213, the manner in which courts have interpreted §6-105 is persuasive in predicting how courts will interpret §6-213. The majority of courts interpreting provisions based on §6-105, including the Nebraska Court of Appeals, have determined that the language in §6-105 sets out a mandatory method for altering the form of an account.

. . .

To construe §30-2724 as permissive would be to render the statute meaningless. It would neither create new rights nor limit existing ones. Any other method for modifying a contract would remain available to alter the form of an account. Signed written notice would simply be a nonbinding legislative suggestion.

By contrast, to read §30-2724 as setting out a mandatory method for altering the type of an account gives the statute a purpose consistent with the rest of article 27. Article 27 is designed to provide simple nonprobate alternatives for the disposition of assets upon death of a party to a multiparty or POD account. Requiring signed written notice to alter the type of account furthers this purpose by ensuring clear evidence of the account owner's intent, thus preventing fraud and adding certainty to nonprobate transfers.

We conclude that the use of the word "may" in §30-2724(a) grants a party the right to alter the type of account the party owns. To exercise that right, however, a party must give his or her financial institution signed written notice.

(b) Does §30-2724 Apply to Transforming Non-POD, Single-Party Account into POD Account?

Thomas argues that even if §30-2724 sets out a mandatory method for altering the type of account, it applies only to altering an existing multiparty or POD account, not to transforming a non-POD, single-party account into a POD account.

. . .

The court finds that signed written notice is now required for transforming a non-POD, single party account into a multiparty or POD account.

. . .

V. CONCLUSION

We determine that to add a POD beneficiary to a non-POD, single-party account, the owner of the account must give signed written notice to his or her financial institution. Because Thomas has failed to present any evidence showing that Chamberlin gave signed written notice to American National requesting the bank to add Thomas as a POD beneficiary to Chamberlin's CD, Newman was entitled to summary judgment.

Affirmed.

QUESTIONS

7. In Chapter 4, we discussed the UPC's adoption of the harmless error rule applicable to defects in the execution or revocation of wills. See UPC §2-503. Article VI of the UPC, however, does not provide a curative doctrine for harmless error in the execution of death beneficiary designation forms. Did the court in this case apply a doctrine of strict compliance to the execution of nonprobate transfers?

   ANSWER. The court most likely applied a doctrine of strict compliance for nonprobate transfers. The court decided the matter on a motion for summary judgment upon finding that Mr. Thomas's testimony about the decedent's attempt to create a POD account did not create a genuine issue of disputed fact. Thus, as a matter of law, because the decedent failed to provide the bank with written notice of the POD designation, the account passed into the probate estate. Because evidence tending to prove that the decedent attempted but failed to create a POD account was insufficient to create a genuine issue of disputed fact, we understand the court to have applied a doctrine of strict compliance, which turns solely on proof of compliance with required formalities, not the decedent's intent or attempt to comply with required formalities.

8. What alternatives to strict compliance are available in jurisdictions that do not extend the harmless error rule to nonprobate transfers?

   ANSWER. This area of the law remains somewhat underdeveloped, but perhaps a court sympathetic to carrying out the depositor's intentions might resort to a doctrine of substantial compliance, whereby the proponent would have to prove the decedent's donative intent to create a POD and that the formalities observed fulfill the underlying purposes of the formalities required.

9. If the court were to have credited Thomas's testimony that an officer of the bank supervised and directed the decedent's execution of the POD account forms, should the bank be liable to Thomas for failing to implement the decedent's intent? How is this situation different from an estate planning lawyer who provides misinformation to the testator and attesting witnesses resulting in a defectively

executed will? Would not the lawyer be liable for malpractice to the intended beneficiaries who did not inherit but for the lawyer's misinformation?

ANSWER. The two scenarios appear to be substantively indistinguishable, but financial institutions are protected under the law from liability arising from this set of facts. The law places the burden of compliance on the account holder, whose assumes the risk and all costs of failing to comply.

PROBLEM VI

What policy function is served by requiring formalities with regard to beneficiary designations? For whose protection do they exist: banks, the donor, the beneficiary? Is there a policy reason why curative doctrines should or should not apply to nonprobate transfers?

10.5 PENSION PLANS AND RETIREMENT ACCOUNTS

Retirement accounts, which in almost all cases are accompanied by a death beneficiary provision, feature prominently in this area of the law because they store vast amounts of accumulated wealth, at least some of which is often left over upon the retiree's death. There are many ways of saving for retirement, with the most common form being pensions and retirement plans sponsored by the account holder's employer as a fringe benefit.

For more than a half century, employer-sponsored retirement plans were largely structured as *defined-benefit* pension plans, which guaranteed private sector workers a predictable income following retirement. Under these plans, employers acted as the guarantor of retirement benefits and assumed the obligation of making payments long into the future, typically for the retired employee's and spouse's lifetimes. Defined-benefit plans, however, have proven financially too risky for modern corporations, which prefer not to carry such long-term liabilities. Accordingly, defined-benefit plans have been in rapid decline in the United States:

> In 1975, 88 percent of workers with workplace retirement plans had defined-benefit pensions. . . . Today, [however,] more than half of U.S. workers have no workplace retirement plan. Of those who do, just 35 percent still have defined-benefit pensions.[10]

The great exception is, of course, public sector workers at federal, state, and local levels, most of whom still provide defined-benefit plans. Most private sector employers,

10. Harold Meyerson, Steering America Toward a More Secure Retirement, Wash. Post, Mar. 6, 2013, at http://www.washingtonpost.com/opinions/harold-meyerson-steering-america-toward-a-more-secure-retirement/2013/03/06/65e777d0-85d8-11e2-98a3-b3db6b9ac586_story.html.

by contrast, to the extent they provide any form of retirement benefit, now do so in the form of a *defined-contribution* plan.

Defined-contribution plans expressly set forth the employer's contribution to the employee's retirement account. Some employers contribute a fixed percentage of the employee's base salary; other employers match the contribution of employees up to a maximum amount; other employers sponsor retirement plans that allow employees to save for retirement without any contribution by the employer. Employer-sponsored retirement benefit plans, such as "401(k) plans," receive preferential income tax treatment under the Internal Revenue Code because they allow the employee to amass savings for retirement on a pre-tax basis. Contributions to these plans are made before the employee pays an income tax and, if well invested, appreciate in value free of income taxation. The employee pays income tax on the plan's assets only when making withdrawals from the account, presumably after the employee has retired and is in a lower income tax bracket.

Virtually all private sector pension plans, whether defined-benefit or defined-contribution, are governed by the federal Employee Retirement Income Security Act of 1979, 29 U.S.C. §1001 *et seq.* (ERISA). ERISA also created individual retirement accounts (IRAs), a tax-advantaged savings mechanism designed to provide post-retirement income either as a supplement to defined-contribution plans or for individuals without access to employer-sponsored plans. Approximately 40 percent of Americans have an IRA. Unlike most forms of nonprobate transfers, which are governed by state law, employee pension plans and individual retirement accounts are regulated by ERISA, a federal law, which preempts state law to the extent of any conflict.

Under ERISA, the administrator of a retirement plan has a fiduciary duty to "discharge his duties with respect to a plan solely in the interest of the participants and beneficiaries and . . . in accordance with the documents and instruments governing the plan. . . ." 29 U.S.C. §1104(a)(1). Thus, the terms governing the retirement plan, and the forms used to administer the plan, play a critical role in determining the rights of account holders and beneficiaries.

Because most plans provide for "survivor benefits," that is, for payment of remaining principal in a defined-contribution plan or for a portion of the income stream from a defined-benefit plan, an individual may designate a beneficiary to receive such post-mortem benefits. Under ERISA, plan administrators are obligated to distribute death benefits to the beneficiary properly designated by the account holder. Thus, individuals must comply precisely with the specific rules applicable to their plan to designate or modify a beneficiary designation. IRAs, typically offered by financial institutions or investment companies, also permit death beneficiary designations to dispose of any funds remaining in the account upon the depositor's death. If an individual fails to designate a beneficiary, all proceeds become payable to the individual's estate and will be distributed either under applicable intestacy statutes for individuals who die without a valid will or under the terms of a testate decedent's will.

As the cases in this chapter illustrate, problems often arise when an individual executes multiple estate planning documents but fails to ensure that the directives into those various instruments are consistent and well coordinated. One example of this problem occurs when there is a discrepancy between a decedent's will and an ERISA-governed retirement plan beneficiary designation. Suppose an individual names her brother as the death beneficiary of her ERISA retirement plan but states in her will, "I give any remaining balance of my retirement plan to my sister." Who takes the balance of the retirement account? The brother or sister of the decedent? Because federal law preempts state law,[11] ERISA prevails over state wills law to the extent of any conflict. Here, the retirement account beneficiary designation overrides the inconsistent devise in the decedent's will. The Supreme Court has clarified how ERISA operates in relation to state law in three decisions that illustrate the broad scope of ERISA's preemption power:

First, in Boggs v. Boggs, 520 U.S. 833 (1997), the Court was presented with a conflict between Louisiana's community property law and ERISA's requirement that the proceeds of a joint and survivor annuity be paid to the pensioner's surviving spouse. 29 U.S.C. §1055(a). The pensioner's first wife predeceased him and, in her will, she attempted to devise her marital interest in her husband's annuity to her sons, as permitted under Louisiana state law. After the death of his first wife, the pensioner remarried and remained married to his second wife until his death. The second wife, now the pensioner's surviving spouse, claimed that ERISA mandated that she receive the annuity proceeds and that ERISA overrides any state law to the contrary. The Supreme Court agreed with the second wife and held that ERISA preempted Louisiana community property law. Thus, the first wife's devise to her sons was not enforceable because it interfered with ERISA's protection for the surviving spouse of deceased retirees.

Second, in Egelhoff v. Egelhoff, 532 U.S. 141 (2001), Mr. Egelhoff designated his spouse, Mrs. Egelhoff, as the death beneficiary of his retirement accounts and employer-sponsored life insurance policy. The couple subsequently divorced, but Mr. Egelhoff but failed to update his death beneficiary designations to remove Mrs. Egelhoff as the beneficiary. Mr. Egelhoff was killed in a car crash shortly after the divorce and died intestate. Here, unlike in *Boggs*, ERISA did not mandate any distribution to Mrs. Egelhoff as the surviving spouse because the divorce rendered her a former spouse. But Mr. Egelhoff's death beneficiary designation forms clearly and unequivocally stated that Mrs. Egelhoff was the death beneficiary, so she claimed that the proceeds should be payable to her. Mr. Egelhoff's estate claimed that Washington state's revocation-on-divorce statute applied, thereby revoking all designations in favor of a former spouse and entitling the estate to all proceeds. The Court, siding with Mrs. Egelhoff, held that ERISA preempted any state law that had "an impermissible connection with ERISA plans," *id.* at 147, and held that ERISA prevailed over Washington's revocation-on-divorce statute. The Court held that state law statutes that required ERISA plan administrators to comply with anything other than the ERISA plan itself interfered "with nationally uniform plan administration[,] one of the principal goals of ERISA" legislation. *Id.* at 148.

---

11. See 29 U.S.C. §1144(a) (ERISA "shall supersede any and all State laws insofar as they may now or hereafter relate to any employee benefit plan" covered by ERISA).

Third, in Kennedy v. Plan Adm'r for DuPont Sav. and Inv. Plan, 555 U.S. 285 (2009), the Supreme Court once again clarified that ERISA preempts claims arising under state law that would direct the ERISA plan administrator to distribute proceeds contrary to the terms of the ERISA plan documents. Like in *Egelhoff*, the retirement account holder in *Kennedy* named his spouse as the death beneficiary, subsequently divorced, and later died without having revoked or updated the death beneficiary designations in favor of his former spouse. In *Kennedy*, however, the terms of the couple's divorce decree made clear that Mrs. Kennedy waived all rights in Mr. Kennedy's retirement account. But because the divorce decree arose under state law, the Court held that ERISA's requirement to pay the beneficiary listed on the plan's death beneficiary designation form prevailed over claims that Mrs. Kennedy waived her rights to such proceeds as part of the divorce settlement.

Thus, sometimes ERISA not only operates quite clearly against the decedent's intent regarding the disposition of retirement assets at death, but ERISA can also displace state law rules enacted for the very purpose of giving effect to the decedent's probable intent. In most contexts, such intent-defeating results are most likely attributable to shortcomings in the original ERISA legislation. When Congress enacted ERISA, it was primarily concerned with the administration of employee and retirement benefits during the employee's life, not upon the employee's death. Consequently, Congress did not attempt to enumerate the many rules and doctrines governing the disposition of retirement assets at death and the Supreme Court's extremely broad application of preemption in this context has swept away many of the state law inheritance rules that would have filled in the gaps left behind by this legislative oversight. At bottom, ERISA plan administrators are legally obligated to pay death benefits to named beneficiaries as determined by the ERISA plan document even if such distributions are at odds with compelling evidence of the decedent's contrary intent.[12]

Outside the ERISA context, state courts have also demonstrated rigid adherence to payment of the designated beneficiary and reluctance to modify nonprobate death beneficiary designations in the face of compelling evidence of contrary intent.[13] For example, in the following case, the Delaware Court of Chancery refused to reform a beneficiary designation to carry out the testator's intent as expressed in his will.

12. In Schmidt v. Sheet Metal Workers' National Pension Fund, 128 F.3d 541 (7th Cir. 1997), Allen Schmidt was informed by doctors that he had pancreatic cancer and had only a few months to live. Schmidt was unmarried and wished to designate his son as the beneficiary on the pension benefit that would be payable on his death. Schmidt requested the necessary paperwork from his ERISA-governed plan administrator, filled it out, and mailed it back. He died a little more than a month later. The plan administrator, however, had sent Mr. Schmidt the wrong forms to effectuate a change in the beneficiary and the plan administrator refused to recognize the improper form. The Seventh Circuit agreed that the pension should be distributed according to the last official designated beneficiary; since there was no designated beneficiary, the proceeds were split, under the terms of the plan, evenly between Schmidt's son and daughter.

13. See Jones v. State Employees' Retirement Bd., 830 A.2d 607 (Pa. Commw. Ct. 2003). In *Jones*, the decedent named his wife as beneficiary and their two children as contingent beneficiaries, but did not provide for his mistress and their two minor children. Denying benefits to the decedent's secret family, the court stated, "The member's written nomination controls no matter how seemingly harsh the result." *Id.* at 609.

Emmert v. Prade
711 A.2d 1217 (Del. Ch. 1997)

CHANDLER, Chancellor.

Plaintiff requests this Court to reform the beneficiary designations of a decedent's life insurance policy and pension plan to mirror the disposition of assets in the decedent's will. Plaintiff does not allege ambiguity of language or flawed execution of the beneficiary designation forms. Plaintiff bases the reformation request on his belief that payment of the death benefits to the named beneficiary would be contrary to the wishes of the decedent. Concluding that plaintiff has not stated a proper claim for reformation of contract, even taking as true all facts pleaded by plaintiff, I find that defendant is entitled to judgment as a matter of law and, thus, grant defendant's motion for summary judgment.

I. BACKGROUND

The decedent, Karl Franz, executed a will in June 1964 in which he left his residuary estate to his parents. In the event his parents should predecease him, decedent's will provided that Michael A. Prade would receive the residuary estate. In August 1985, decedent executed beneficiary designation forms for a Savings and Investment Plan ("Pension Plan") and Group Life Insurance Policy ("Insurance Policy") administered by his employer, E.I. du Pont de Nemours & Co. ("DuPont"), expressly naming Michael A. Prade as the sole beneficiary of both plans. There are no allegations in the complaint that decedent was mentally impaired or subject to undue influence or deception when he made these beneficiary designations.

In August 1993, decedent consulted with attorney Edmund F. Lynch about modifying his estate plan. Decedent allegedly indicated to Mr. Lynch that he wished to completely disinherit Mr. Prade. Mr. Lynch has experience in the area of estate planning and is aware that the disposition of nonprobate assets, such as the Pension Plan and Insurance Policy, normally is not governed by the terms of one's will. Mr. Lynch's handwritten notes from his consultation with decedent indicate that he broached the subject of nonprobate assets during their meeting. Although Mr. Lynch's notes do not indicate what advice he gave to decedent regarding his Pension Plan or Insurance Policy, Mr. Lynch has testified that he typically explains to clients that pension plan and insurance policy beneficiary designations are not affected by changes made to one's will.

Following the consultation with Mr. Lynch, decedent executed a new will on August 24, 1993, in which he "disinherited" Mr. Prade and named several relatives as beneficiaries. It is undisputed, however, that decedent took no steps to change the beneficiary designations for the Pension Plan or Insurance Policy. He died a little over a year later, on September 4, 1994.

Included among the residuary beneficiaries of the 1993 will — which is uncontested as decedent's last will and testament — is plaintiff Mack Emmert, executor of decedent's estate. On February 16, 1995, plaintiff filed a Verified Petition against

Mr. Prade and DuPont seeking to reform decedent's Insurance Policy and Pension Plan to change the beneficiary designations from Mr. Prade to the estate of Mr. Franz.

On January 30, 1996, Mr. Prade answered the Verified Petition and brought a cross-claim against DuPont seeking an Order directing DuPont to distribute to Mr. Prade the death benefits under the Insurance Policy and Pension Plan. DuPont filed an answer to the cross-claim on February 16, 1996.

On May 21, 1997, Mr. Prade (hereinafter "defendant") moved for summary judgment on plaintiff's claims in the Verified Petition and his own cross-claim against DuPont on the basis of the clear and unambiguous language of the beneficiary designation forms naming defendant as the sole beneficiary. This is my decision on defendant's motion for summary judgment.

Plaintiff contends that the beneficiary designations of the Insurance Policy and Pension Plan should be reformed to conform to the decedent's expressed wish to "disinherit" defendant. Plaintiff lists nineteen witnesses who are prepared to testify that the decedent wanted to leave defendant no assets upon his death. Plaintiff also offers the testimony of attorney Lynch that during their consultation, the decedent indicated that he wished to "cut someone out" of his will. Because, plaintiff asserts, the decedent "through inadvertent error or mistake, failed to change the designated beneficiary," plaintiff calls upon the equitable powers of this Court to reform the documents so as to implement the decedent's "true" wishes.

Defendant argues that because the language on the beneficiary designation forms is clear and unambiguous, this Court should not interpret the language, but rather should enforce the contract as written and order DuPont to pay out the death benefits to defendant, the undisputed beneficiary designated on those forms. Defendant notes that plaintiff has not alleged any legal basis, such as incompetence, undue influence or fraud in the execution, for attacking those designations. Further, defendant argues that it is settled Delaware law that the proceeds of insurance policies and pension plans pass to the beneficiary named therein, and do not go to the decedent's estate unless they are expressly made payable to the estate. Based on established Delaware law, defendant argues that plaintiff has not articulated a cognizable legal theory supporting reformation in this case and, thus, defendant is entitled to judgment as a matter of law.

II. LEGAL STANDARD

The function of summary judgment is the avoidance of a useless trial where there is no genuine issue as to any material fact. After reviewing the complete record and drawing all inferences in favor of the non-moving party, the Court must find that there is no genuine issue of material fact and that the moving party is entitled to judgment as a matter of law.

III. ANALYSIS

As a preliminary matter, I note that it is undisputed that the beneficiary designations on the Insurance Policy and Pension Plan are clear and unambiguous.

Plaintiff concedes that "[t]here are no ambiguous terms in any of these documents, and the court does not need to interpret their terms." Thus, the issue before this Court is not one of contract interpretation, but rather one of contract reformation.

A. Grounds for Reformation

It is a basic principle of equity that the Court of Chancery may reform a document to make it conform to the original intent of the parties. But reformation is appropriate "only when the contract does not represent the parties' intent because of fraud, mutual mistake or, in exceptional cases, a unilateral mistake coupled with the other parties' knowing silence."

Plaintiff here requests reformation of the Insurance Policy and Pension Plan to bring their 1985 beneficiary designations into conformity with the distribution plan embodied in the decedent's final will executed in 1993. The basis for plaintiff's petition is the fact that decedent's 1993 will altered an earlier disposition scheme from 1964 and that decedent purportedly made numerous statements that he wished to disinherit defendant. For the reasons stated below, neither circumstance, taking all facts pleaded as true, warrants the relief sought by plaintiff.

First, the beneficiary designations at issue *do* express the original intent of the parties. It is undisputed that decedent competently and knowingly designated the defendant as the sole beneficiary of his Insurance Policy and Pension Plan. Thus, the 1985 beneficiary designations reflect decedent's intent *at that time* to make defendant his beneficiary. Plaintiff seeks reformation in order to bring the documents into conformity with an intention that arose (if at all) several years *after* the original contracts were executed. This is not the purpose of reformation.

Second, assuming *arguendo* that plaintiff did seek reformation for a proper purpose (*i.e.*, to conform the documents to the parties' original intent), plaintiff pleads none of the established grounds for reformation. Plaintiff asserts no misrepresentation, mistake, duress, undue influence or lack of competence that might make reformation appropriate. Instead, plaintiff's sole ground for requesting this relief is a belief "that to pay over to Defendant, Michael A. Prade, the proceeds of [the plans] would be contrary to the express wishes of Decedent" — at the time of his death.

Even assuming, obliged as I am to draw all inferences in favor of the non-moving party, that the decedent's intention when he executed a new will in 1993 was to prevent defendant from receiving any benefits at his death, plaintiff's basis for seeking reformation — "[decedent's] wish to disinherit" — does not satisfy the legal requirements. "It is undisputed that Mr. Franz took no steps to change the beneficiary designation forms for the pension plan or insurance policy." Decedent executed a new will in 1993. Plaintiff asserts that "through inadvertent error or mistake [decedent] failed to change" the beneficiary designations for the Insurance Policy and Pension Plan at the same time. Failure to change the beneficiary designations, however, does not constitute the sort of "mistake" justifying reformation.

Plaintiff asks whether a decedent's "wish to disinherit will allow this Court to change the named beneficiary of a Savings and Investment Plan and separate Insurance Policy." The answer, without more, is "no."

B. Summary Judgment

. . .

In conclusion, plaintiff has not stated a proper legal basis for the relief sought. Assuming all facts alleged are true and drawing all inferences in favor of plaintiff, the non-moving party, I find that there is no genuine issue of material fact and that defendant, Mr. Prade, is entitled to judgment as a matter of law.

For all of these reasons, I grant defendant's motion for summary judgment.

It is so ordered.

Emmert illustrates a critically important cautionary tale: When executing, revoking, or modifying a nonprobate death beneficiary designation form, one must comply strictly with the requirements of the custodian of the account, plan, or policy. In many, if not most cases, nonprobate death beneficiary designation forms cannot be modified by executing a will naming a new beneficiary. Courts have been quite protective of account custodians who lack notice of the account holder's intent to modify and therefore risk liability for paying the wrong beneficiary.

QUESTIONS

10. Was the decedent mistaken as to the legal significance of the will's disinheritance of Michael?

ANSWER. Possibly. From the facts of the case, it is clear that Karl Franz had some kind of relationship with Michael Prade from 1964 (when Franz named Prade the alternate residuary legatee if Franz's parents did not survive Franz) through 1985 (when Franz named Prade as the beneficiary of Franz's pension plan and life insurance policy). In 1993, Franz is alleged to have told his attorney that he wanted to disinherit Prade. Franz then executed a new will. It is not clear whether Franz's 1993 will included an explicit disinheritance provision or if it simply eliminated Prade as a named beneficiary. The court says, "[Franz] . . . executed a new will on August 24, 1993, in which he 'disinherited' Mr. Prade and named several relatives as beneficiaries." Notwithstanding that Franz's lawyer may have given Franz advice to change the beneficiary designation forms on the pension plan and life insurance policy, Franz never did so. Prade remained the named beneficiary on those forms when Franz died in 1994.

It may well have been that Franz misunderstood the significance of the residuary clause of his will and assumed it would have the effect of altering the beneficiary designation forms. Indeed, as the nineteen witnesses were prepared to testify, it may well have been that Franz had said and even meant that he wanted Prade to receive nothing on account of Franz's death. However, the fact remains that Franz, apparently a person of sufficient sophistication to have made two wills, never changed the beneficiary designation forms.

That simple fact may tell a larger story than the one reflected in the court's opinion. What are the possibilities? Were Franz and Prade a couple? Did they part ways, triggering Franz to rewrite his will? Did Franz subsequently have regrets about disinheriting Prade? If so, is that why Franz never changed the beneficiary designation forms? Or, did Franz assume that the residuary clause of his will would work to cut Prade out entirely — not just from Franz's probate assets but also from his nonprobate assets?

The point is, the only person who could answer these questions is no longer alive. The proffered witnesses may well have heard Franz say he wanted to disinherit Prade, but was Franz telling them the truth? The court has only Franz's documents to rely on as a means of discerning Franz's intentions. And under applicable law, the court found no grounds to reform the contractual pension plan and insurance policy documents.

11. How would this case have been decided under the UPC's reformation provision, §2-805?

ANSWER. UPC §2-805 states:

> The court may reform the terms of a governing instrument, even if unambiguous, to conform the terms to the transferor's intention if it is proved by clear and convincing evidence what the transferor's intention was and that the terms of the governing instrument were affected by a mistake of fact or law, whether in expression or inducement.

Elsewhere the UPC defines "governing instrument" to include a pension plan or an insurance policy (see UPC §1-201(18)). Thus, the doctrine of reformation would be available to the beneficiary designation forms at the center of this lawsuit. However, the UPC's reformation provision is not broad enough to encompass changes in intentions *after* the date of execution of a document.

UPC §2-805 is based on similar provisions in UTC §415 and the Restatement (Third) of Property: Wills & Other Donative Transfers §12.1. While the UPC provision does not have substantive comments, it cites the comments provided in the Restatement. There, in comment h, we read:

> *h. Limitations on the scope of reformation.* Reformation is a rule governing mistakes in the content of a donative document, in a case in which the donative document does not say what the transferor meant it to say. Accordingly, reformation is not available . . . to modify a document in order to give effect to the donor's post-execution change of mind (Illustration 2). . . .
>
> **Illustrations:**
>
> . . .
>
> 2. G validly executed a will that devised his estate to his sister, A. After execution, G formed an intent to alter the disposition in favor of A's daughter, X, in the mistaken belief that he could substitute his new intent by communicating it to X orally. G's oral communication to X does not support a reformation remedy. Although a donative

> document exists that could be reformed by substituting "X" for "A," the remedy does not lie because G's will was not the product of mistake. The will when executed stated G's intent accurately. G's mistake was his subsequent failure to execute a codicil or a new will to carry out his new intent. This is a mistake of the same sort that G made in Illustration 1 in not making a valid will in the first place.
>
> . . .
>
> Accordingly, given the facts of this case, the outcome should be the same under the UPC's reformation provision: A post-execution change in intent is not susceptible to reformation.

ERISA mandates that a surviving spouse receives the remainder of a covered benefit plan unless the surviving spouse consents by signing a waiver, witnessed by a notary or a plan representative. 29 U.S.C. §1055(c)(2)(A). Thus, for divorcing couples, ERISA may cause significant problems if the divorce is not finalized before one of the spouses dies. Even if the decedent did everything possible to prevent a soon-to-be-ex-spouse from receiving death benefits, the law operates to pass the benefits to the decedent's surviving spouse. In Groh v. Groh, 288 N.J. Super. 321 (1995), the decedent, who was in the middle of divorce proceedings with his estranged wife, became concerned that he would die before his divorce became final. He filed a motion to sequester his pension benefits should he die during the pendency of the divorce and sought to expedite the proceedings. His motion was denied, and he died before the court entered a divorce decree. ERISA operated to award the survivor benefits to his wife.

ERISA applies to private sector plans; it does not apply to plans sponsored by state or local governments. 29 U.S.C. §1003(b)(1). In Pennsylvania, for example, members of the State Employees' Retirement Systems are free to designate any person as beneficiary or to change beneficiaries at any time. There is no requirement that a surviving spouse receive post-mortem benefits, and the Pennsylvania courts have held that named beneficiaries receive those benefits free from encumbrances by the surviving spouse.[14] Unconstrained by ERISA's strict compliance rules, courts applying state law in cases involving state and local government retirement plans sometimes permit substantial rather than strict compliance where necessary to carry out the decedent's intent.[15]

10.6 LIFE INSURANCE

Life insurance is a special type of contract in which the insurer (the life insurance company) is obligated to pay a promised benefit upon the death of the insured (in

14. Titler v. State Employees' Retirement Bd., 768 A.2d 899 (Pa. Commw. Ct. 2001); Hoffman v. Pennsylvania State Employees' Retirement Bd., 743 A.2d 1014 (Pa. Commw. Ct. 2000).

15. See, e.g., Westmoreland ex rel. Westmoreland v. Westmoreland, 280 Ga. 33 (2005) (finding city retirement plan participant substantially complied with procedure by going to the human resource department and filling out all forms given to him to change the beneficiary, even though the human resources employee mistakenly omitted a critical form).

most cases, the person who purchased the life insurance policy) to beneficiaries named under the policy. Life insurance policies are governed strictly by their terms. Life insurance policies obtained as part of an employee benefit program generally are also subject to ERISA. Language in a will purporting to change a beneficiary designation in a life insurance policy are almost always ineffective. Instead, to name or modify a beneficiary, the policy holder must comply with the policy, which usually requires that the insurance company receive all beneficiary designations, modifications, and revocations before the insured's death. Instructions in a will to pay the death benefit of a life insurance policy are generally insufficient to override a clear beneficiary designation to the contrary.

Life insurance policies operate upon the decedent's death, before which the policy holder may change beneficiaries as often as he or she wishes. Life insurance is sometimes described as a "pure" will substitute because it grants no present possessory or other interest in the designated beneficiary so long as the policy holder is alive. Life insurance, however, differs in several respects from the transfer of property by will. First, life insurance requires the payment of premiums whereas a testamentary disposition does not. Second, life insurances policies are often concerned with *how* and *when* the decedent died whereas wills are generally effective regardless of when or how the decedent dies (except in cases implicating the slayer inheritance bar). Likewise, whereas pension plans and POD accounts are payable on death no matter the cause, life insurance policies are payable on death only if that death comes about in a manner covered under the terms of the policy. Third, life insurance policies differ with regard to what the beneficiary gets. Many life insurance policies balloon in value upon the insured's death because the death benefit is much larger than the sum of insurance premiums paid on the policy. In a transfer by will, conversely, the beneficiaries receive the net probate estate, nothing more and nothing less.

Life insurance policies are often coupled with accidental death benefits. Such policies are commonly referred to as double indemnity policies because the insurance company will pay double if the policy holder dies accidentally, but these policies typically exclude coverage for deaths from suicide or drug overdose. Of course, what constitutes an accidental death is not always clear. The following excerpt discusses some of the challenges of determining what constitutes an accidental death.

Drugs, Sex, and Accidental Death Insurance

Douglas R. Richmond
45 Tort Trial & Ins. Prac. L.J. 57 (2009)

I. INTRODUCTION

Americans engage in a wide variety of activities in the pursuit of pleasure or personal need or satisfaction that are unlawful or simply unwise and that can lead to calamity in any event. In the case of unlawful conduct, consider the premature demise of Paul Phillips, who died from a heroin overdose. Phillips was not a heroin addict but, rather, was a repeat recreational user of the illegal drug. Regardless, he certainly did not expect his fatal injection to be his last. Abusers of prescription medications are also vulnerable to terminal overdoses or lethal drug combinations, as with James Adair, who died from an overdose of valium and methadone. A doctor had prescribed both medications for him. Adair apparently exceeded the prescribed doses of his medications, not pursuing pleasure but desperately attempting to alleviate chronic pain caused by Guillain-Barré syndrome. Like many people who die from prescription drug overdoses, he presumably believed that he could tolerate higher doses of his medications than his physician prescribed. Finally, and further into the realm of legal but terribly unwise behavior, consider the sad case of Gerald Padfield, who died naked from the waist down, hanged by his necktie in the backseat of his family's van. Was his death a suicide or the result of foul play? No, Padfield died from the oddly common practice of autoerotic asphyxiation. He had a long history of such self-gratification and surely expected to survive his final episode as he had enjoyed and survived the practice numerous times before.

A recurring question in cases such as those of Phillips, Adair, and Padfield is not whether their deaths were senseless or tragic but whether they were accidents. This is an issue of considerable economic significance because millions of people hold insurance policies providing accidental death benefits to their loved ones. Unfortunately, the term *accident* lends itself to differing interpretations. Indeed, few issues so confound courts as determining when deaths are to be considered accidents for purposes of insurance policies affording accidental death coverage. Insurers commonly resist paying accidental death benefits to the spouses, children, and other beneficiaries of policyholders killed by illicit and prescription drug overdoses or strangled during autoerotic episodes on the grounds that the policyholders' deaths are not accidental or are intentionally self-inflicted injuries. Yet, these same insurance companies would never employ those justifications to deny coverage to innocent beneficiaries of insureds who died in skydiving, rappelling, or rock-climbing mishaps. Insurers' rationale seems to be that extreme sports are controlled risks while drug use and autoerotic asphyxiation are not, but this distinction is illusory. The vast majority of people who engage in activities with any measure of physical risk believe that they have those risks under control.

Courts' widespread acceptance of insurers' arguments that deaths attributable to drug overdoses and autoerotic asphyxiation gone wrong are not accidental or are the product of self-inflicted injuries is to some extent understandable. Substance abuse is widely condemned regardless of whether users' drugs of choice are illicit or therapeutic, with the latter being only somewhat more acceptable to many people than the former. Autoerotic asphyxiation is poorly understood and stigmatized. Neither substance abuse nor extraordinary sexual behavior is sympathetic or consistent with the public's conception of accidents, and it is easy for courts to deny benefits in such cases on the rationale that the decedents voluntarily rode the thunderbolts that killed them.

On the other hand, many accidents are attributable to the actors' lapses in judgment or major miscalculations. The fact that a person's death was senseless or the product of foolhardy behavior or recklessness does not mean that it was nonaccidental. Resolving accident questions for insurance purposes by reference to societal norms or to advance the public policy of deterring undesirable or illegal behaviors leads to inconsistent, and often unfair, results. This conclusion especially resonates with the beneficiaries of accident insurance policies, who may be denied needed recovery despite disapproving of or disliking the insured's fatal habit or practice or being unaware of it.

. . .

V. A REASONABLE APPROACH TO EVALUATING DRUG ABUSE AND AUTOEROTIC ASPHYXIATION DEATHS AS INSURANCE ACCIDENTS

The many disparate decisions concerning drug overdose deaths of all types and autoerotic asphyxiations as insurance "accidents" are largely irreconcilable. Different courts often reach very different results on quite similar facts. This inconsistency is perhaps to be expected in light of courts' historical struggle to define and recognize "accidents" and "accidental" deaths for insurance purposes, but it is nonetheless confusing. To avoid still more uneven results in the future, courts presented with these cases should carefully apply the analytical framework from Wickman [v. Nw. Nat'l Ins. Co., 908 F.2d 1077 (1st Cir. 1990)]. The First Circuit in *Wickman* crafted a balanced analytical approach that, if conscientiously applied, properly focuses the accidental death inquiry on the facts of the particular case rather than allowing controversies to be decided based on moral judgments, behavioral assumptions, or artificial distinctions between accidental means and accidental results.

A. Applying the Wickman *Test*

Under *Wickman*, a court first analyzes the insured's reasonable expectations. If the insured did not expect to suffer an injury similar to that suffered, the court must "examine whether the suppositions which underlay that expectation were reasonable." If the insured's suppositions are judged to be unreasonable, then the injuries will be deemed nonaccidental. In determining the reasonableness of the insured's suppositions, the court should view matters from the insured's perspective and take into account the insured's personal characteristics and experiences. The first prong, therefore, is essentially subjective. Second, if the court cannot ascertain the insured's subjective expectations because of insufficient evidence, then it should objectively analyze the insured's expectations. "In this analysis, one must ask whether a reasonable person, with background and characteristics similar to the insured, would have viewed the injury as highly likely to occur as a result of the insured's intentional conduct." . . .

Using a drug overdose case as an example, a variety of evidence may support the conclusion that the insured did not subjectively expect to be injured or killed by her habit and that those expectations were reasonable. For example, before taking the fatal dose, did the insured make future plans? Did she tell people that she would see them the next day? Did she communicate with anyone after taking her final dose and indicate future plans or otherwise reveal her intention of living? Was she looking forward to some upcoming event? Did she generally seem to be in good spirits? Had she been using the drug for a long time? Were her prior experiences with the drug uneventful from a health standpoint? Did she know that her friends used the same drug without harmful incident? Affirmative answers to these questions and others like them indicate that the insured did not subjectively intend to be injured or die as a result of her drug use.

Other questions may also be relevant in determining an insured's subjective intent. For example, how large a dose did she ingest? What are the properties of the subject drug? In the case of a prescription drug, for example, is the insured unlikely to appreciate or understand the line between a therapeutic dose and a fatal one? In the case of an illicit drug, did the insured obtain the fatal dose from the same supplier to whom she always turned, thus diminishing the chance of obtaining a dose that was somehow contaminated or tainted?

. . .

In many cases, the insured's death, coupled with the privacy of its occurrence, makes the insured's subjective intent impossible to determine. The analysis then shifts to *Wickman*'s objective prong, which requires the court to assess whether a reasonable person with the insured's background and characteristics would have viewed death from a drug overdose as "highly likely to occur." A court may not apply an objective analysis to override sufficient evidence of an insured's subjective intent. Objective analysis is appropriate only if the court lacks sufficient evidence to determine the insured's subjective expectations.

For an event to be highly likely to occur, it must be more than reasonably foreseeable. The occurrence must be more than possible; in other words, it must be probable or, perhaps, substantially probable. There is nothing to suggest that is the case with respect to autoerotic asphyxiation. Indeed, a powerful argument can be made that all of the literature supports the opposite conclusion. With respect to drug abuse, consider that in 2007, an estimated 19.9 million Americans aged twelve or older used illicit drugs (including nonmedical uses of therapeutic drugs). That estimate represents 8 percent of that age group population. In other words, many, many more Americans are using illicit drugs than are reportedly dying from their use or being seriously injured thereby. The latest national estimates of the ten leading causes of death by age group and the ten leading causes of nonfatal injuries treated in hospital emergency departments published by the Centers for Disease Control do not include drug overdoses. These are not the only relevant statistics, of course, but they do suggest that the risk of overdosing on drugs is not the equivalent of, say, Russian roulette, as courts are fond of suggesting when denying accidental death benefits.

On the other side of the coin, there are several conceivable facts or sets of facts that might indicate that an insured's subjective expectation of survival was unreasonable or that the insured's death was highly likely to occur when objectively analyzed. If, for example, an insured previously overdosed on the same drug or a similar one and had to be hospitalized, revived by medical personnel, or resuscitated as a result, any expectation of survival by the insured is unreasonable. In terms of autoerotic asphyxiation, if an insured dies using a technique or mechanism that previously claimed another practitioner's life and the insured knew of the other death, it may be fair to say that the insured's subjective expectation of survival was unreasonable or that the insured's death was highly likely to occur when viewed objectively.

. . .

VI. CONCLUSION

Illicit drug use is potentially dangerous and unquestionably irresponsible, as are the abuse of therapeutic medications and autoerotic asphyxiation. A person's participation in any of these activities reflects seriously poor judgment. But many injuries and fatalities are attributable to the actors' wretched judgment, seriously flawed reasoning, or recklessness. As foolhardy, irresponsible, or reckless as illicit drug use, prescription drug abuse, and autoerotic asphyxiation clearly are, it is unreasonable to conclude that any significant number of their practitioners expect or intend to die or be seriously injured as a result of their behavior or that these outcomes are highly likely. The fact that these behaviors are risky does not render their participants' deaths nonaccidental for insurance purposes.

Actor David Carradine (who reportedly died from autoerotic asphyxiation)

Courts have split on whether death caused by driving under the influence of alcohol should be considered accidental. A majority of courts agree that such deaths are not accidents because they are a foreseeable consequence of drinking and driving.[16] However, other courts have concluded that coverage exceptions for self-inflicted deaths do *not* apply to DWI cases because the death was unintended, even if the decedent was engaging in risky behavior voluntarily.[17]

Courts have generally agreed that deaths resulting from "Russian roulette" are not accidental. In the traditional form of this dangerous game, a player puts live ammunition into one chamber of a revolver, spins the chamber, places the gun against his or her head, and pulls the trigger. In a standard revolver that holds six bullets, the player has a 16.3 percent of shooting him- or herself. Nevertheless, for life insurance purposes, decedents are presumed to assume the risk of death when placing a loaded gun to the head and pulling the trigger.[18]

10.7 "SUPERWILLS"

As seen throughout this chapter, testamentary dispositions in a will generally do not control the disposition of nonprobate assets or override a nonprobate death beneficiary designation made outside the will. Although some courts have allowed the testator's intent in a will to win the day when disposing of the testator's nonprobate assets, courts typically defer to the terms of the nonprobate account, plan, or policy rather than the testator's will. Some commentators, however, believe that a testator who wants to modify nonprobate death beneficiary designations by will should be able to do so. In 1998, to this end, Washington state enacted a so-called superwill statute, which allows testators to alter beneficiary designations on certain nonprobate assets by addressing them in a will. Under this statute, a will provision governing the disposition of covered nonprobate transfers prevails over a previously completed beneficiary designation form expressing a contrary preference.

The Washington state legislature, however, was willing to extend the reach of the superwill only so far. The Washington statute does not apply to real property held in joint tenancy; TOD deeds; conveyances, rights, or interests under community property agreements; or individual retirement accounts or bonds. WASH. REV. CODE §11.11.010(7)(a) (2008). Thus, the statute seems to cover joint bank accounts with right of survivorship and revocable living trusts. See Cynthia J. Artura, Superwill to the Rescue? How Washington's Statute Falls Short of Being a Hero in the Field of Trust and Probate Law, 74 Wash. L. Rev. 799, 819 (1999). Furthermore, if the owner designates a death beneficiary for a nonprobate asset after the will has been executed, the will no longer governs the disposition of that asset, even if the designation is later

16. See Lennon v. Metro. Life Ins. Co., 504 F.3d 617 (6th Cir. 2007); Eckelberry v. Reliastar Life Ins. Co., 469 F.3d 340 (4th Cir. 2006); Cozzie v. Metro. Life Ins. Co., 140 F.3d 1104 (7th Cir. 1998).

17. See King v. Hartford Life and Acc. Ins. Co., 414 F.3d 994 (8th Cir. 2005); Harrell v. Metro. Life Ins. Co, 401 F. Supp. 2d 802 (E.D. Mich. 2005). For a breakdown of the conflicting views, see Gary Schuman, Dying Under the Influence: Drunk Driving and Accidental Death Insurance, 44 Tort Trial & Ins. Prac. L.J. 1 (2008).

18. See Arnold v. Metro. Life Ins. Co., 970 F.2d 360 (7th Cir. 1992); see also Adam F. Scales, Man, God and the Serbonian Bog: The Evolution of Accidental Death Insurance, 86 Iowa L. Rev. 173 (2000).

revoked. WASH. REV. CODE §11.11.020(4) (2006). Nevertheless, some testators have effectively used the superwill statute to control the disposition of nonprobate assets by will. See Manary v. Anderson, 176 Wash. 2d 342 (2013) (en banc).

Do you like the idea of a superwill? If so, what do you see as its primary advantages? If not, why do you suppose the concept has not caught on in other states?

11 | Fiduciary Duties

11.1 INTRODUCTION

Legal title to trust property resides in trustees who are authorized to exercise broad powers over trust property.[1] The trustees' powers include all rights of a legal owner and, to the extent granted by the settlor, authority to exercise subjective discretion in decisions regarding administration and distribution.As we discussed in Chapter 9, vesting such broad power and authority in trustees provides flexibility: For instance, by delegating to trustees discretion concerning distributions, the settlor enables trustees to adapt to events and changed circumstances that may not be foreseeable at the time of the trust's creation. However, to ensure that trustees exercise their broad powers properly and refrain from abusing their control over trust property, trust law subjects trustees' performance to judicial review by imposing strict fiduciary duties.

Fiduciary duties regulate trustee performance by specifying certain obligations and prohibitions of trusteeship and by establishing legal standards of care governing trustees' actions. Fiduciary duties help to assure settlors that the trust purposes will be accomplished according to the settlor's intent. Fiduciary duties also provide trust beneficiaries with a legal mechanism to enforce their rights to enjoy trust property. Modern fiduciary law reflects almost a thousand years of common law and statutory development. In England, the earliest fiduciary duties were enforced by ecclesiastical courts.[2] Today, fiduciary law is generally enforced and adjudicated by courts of equity, and, of

1. Uniform Trust Code §815(a) ("A trustee . . . may exercise powers conferred by the terms of the trust and, except as limited by . . . the trust: (A) all powers over the trust property which an unmarried competent owner has over individually owned property; (B) any other powers appropriate to achieve the proper investment, management, and distribution of the trust property; and (C) any other powers conferred by this [Code]."). Additionally, UTC §816 enumerates twenty-six specific powers of trusteeship.

2. Professor R.H. Helmholz recounts one such illustration under English common law:

> For example, in 1375 the feoffees [trustees] to uses [trusts] of a certain John Roger were cited to appear before the court at Canterbury for violating the directions given to them by their feoffor [settlor]. Upon interrogation, they confessed that they had received ten and three quarters of an acre of land, a windmill, and a grange under Roger's instructions that they convey it to his wife Margery after his death. They admitted violation of this instruction by alienating half the land to a certain Hugh Pryor, but maintained that they had only done so out of compulsion and fear of Hugh. The judge, apparently after a brief hearing, held that the alleged fear had been "empty and insufficient to move a constant man," and that the feoffees must suffer the canonical penalties for failing to carry out their duty.

R.H. Helmholz, The Early Enforcement of Uses, 79 Colum. L. Rev. 1503, 1505 (1979).

course, the canonical penalties imposed by the church have been replaced with civil remedies ordered by secular courts.

For the most part, trust law fiduciary duties are default rules and are variable according to a settlor's preference to modify or, in the case of certain duties, opt out altogether.[3] Thus, any evaluation of trustee performance must account for not only the statutory and common law fiduciary duties but also the standards for trustee conduct established by the settlor's terms in the deed or declaration of trust.

Recall that in Chapter 5 we noted that the fiduciary duties imposed on personal representatives of a decedent's estate are generally the same as the fiduciary duties imposed upon trustees.[4] The duties discussed in this chapter, therefore, generally apply not just to trustees administering a trust but equally to personal representatives of a decedent's estate.

In this chapter, we will focus on the core duties of loyalty and prudence. We will then survey some of the subsidiary fiduciary rules, including duties of impartiality, to inform, and to account. Lastly, we will discuss remedies for breach of fiduciary duties and the settlor's right to exculpate the trustee from liability in the event of breach.

Uniform Trust Code
§801 Duty to Administer Trust

Upon acceptance of a trusteeship, the trustee shall administer the trust in good faith, in accordance with its terms and purposes and the interests of the beneficiaries, and in accordance with this [Code].

11.2 DUTY OF LOYALTY

The duty of loyalty, a polestar of fiduciary law, imposes a strict obligation on trustees to act solely in the best interests of the beneficiaries. Trustees are typically given extensive powers over trust property, so the law imposes upon them a duty to exercise those broad powers with undivided loyalty to the beneficiaries. Professor Karen Boxx explains:

> One reason that loyalty is so highly valued is that it is impossible to guarantee and impossible to buy. The trust law concept of the duty of loyalty acknowledges that human nature will cause any person to favor his or her personal interests over the interests of another, and it is this assumption of disloyalty that gives rise to the strict prohibitions of trustee conflicts of interest required under the label of "duty of loyalty."

Karen E. Boxx, Of Punctilios and Paybacks: The Duty of Loyalty Under the Uniform Trust Code, 67 Mo. L. Rev. 279 (2002). Thus, the duty of loyalty, subject to exceptions, categorically prohibits two forms of disloyalty: (1) self-dealing and (2) conflicted

---

3. UTC §105(a) provides, "Except as otherwise provided in the terms of the trust, this [Code] governs the duties and powers of a trustee. . . ." However, "the duty of a trustee to act in good faith and in accordance with the terms and purposes of the trust and the interests of the beneficiaries" is mandatory and prevails over any contrary trust provision. UTC §105(b)(2).

4. See, e.g., Uniform Probate Code §3-703(a) ("A personal representative is a fiduciary who shall observe the standards of care applicable to trustees as described by Section 7-302.").

transactions. Under UTC §802(b), both types of transactions are voidable by a beneficiary without regard to the fairness of the transaction or the purported good faith of the trustee. Thus, this prohibition is sometimes called the "no further inquiry" rule.

Self-dealing occurs when a trustee transacts with trust property in a personal capacity, such as a trustee's purchase of trust property for her own account. Likewise, a trustee may not borrow assets from the trust corpus even if the trustee later repays all of the borrowed funds. The prohibition on self-dealing also prohibits a trust company serving as a corporate fiduciary from investing trust assets in its own corporate stock. Such a transaction implicates the bar on self-dealing because it involves the trustee's sale of an equity interest in its own corporate entity to the trust.

A conflicted transaction occurs when a trustee's personal interest affects or conflicts with a transaction involving trust property. Suppose, for example, a real estate developer offered to purchase real property from the trust and, in addition to paying the purchase price, the developer offered the trustee a highly remunerated seat on its corporate board of directors. Such a transaction is conflicted because the trustee's decision to sell real property owned by the trust is affected by the purchaser's lucrative offer to the trustee in her personal capacity.

A trustee's direct personal interest in a transaction involving trust property is deemed presumptively disloyal because most self-dealing and conflicted transactions are harmful (or pose an unreasonable risk of harm) to beneficiaries. Since human behavior is almost always motivated by self-interest, it is unrealistic to expect a trustee to faithfully protect the interests of beneficiaries when she has a personal stake in the transaction. Thus, the automatic voidability of self-dealing and conflicted transactions reflects a policy choice to deter such conduct altogether. The influential Bogert trust law treatise explains:

> The public policy reasons underlying the duty of loyalty are several. A trustee is expected to act on behalf of the beneficiary with an independent and disinterested judgment. If his individual interest is injected into trust matters he cannot remain independent or disinterested. It is not possible for any person to act fairly in the same transaction on behalf of himself and in the interest of the trust beneficiary. It is only human that he will tend to favor his individual interest, whether consciously or unconsciously, over that of the beneficiary. Furthermore, the confidential nature of the trust relationship lends itself to secrecy and concealment on the part of a trustee who may be tempted to exploit the trust. In addition, even though the trustee may render accounts to the beneficiary or to the court, the beneficiary's chance of discovering the disloyal act is remote; thus, as a practical matter, the beneficiary may have no opportunity to object or to obtain relief.

George Gleason Bogert, George Taylor Bogert & Amy Morris Hess, The Law of Trusts and Trustees §543 (2015). A transaction prohibited by the duty of loyalty is also voidable if made by a party related to the trustee, such as a spouse, close family member, personal attorney, agent, and other person or enterprise controlled by the trustee.

The "no further inquiry" rule is tempered by several exceptions, such as transactions authorized by the trust terms or approved by a court. UTC §802(b). Other routine, but technically self-dealing, transactions are permitted if fair to the beneficiaries. Examples include the payment of reasonable compensation to the trustee from the trust corpus and "a deposit of trust money in a regulated financial-service institution operated by the trustee." UTC §802(h). The latter exception would allow a bank serving as a corporate fiduciary to deposit the trust assets in a savings account operated by the bank.

The duty of loyalty prohibits other conflicts of interest beyond a trustee's personal transaction with trust property. For example, suppose a trustee retains a professional asset management firm to invest the trust assets. If the asset manager informs the trustee of a promising investment and the trustee takes the business opportunity for herself rather than investing the trust assets, the trustee's decision is tainted by a conflict of interest even though she has not directly transacted with trust property for her own account. Rather, the trustee has taken for herself a business opportunity that properly belonged to the trust because she learned of the investment while discharging the duties of trusteeship. UTC §802(e).

Uniform Trust Code
§802 Duty of Loyalty

(a) A trustee shall administer the trust solely in the interests of the beneficiaries.

(b) Subject to the rights of persons dealing with or assisting the trustee as provided in Section 1012, a sale, encumbrance, or other transaction involving the investment or management of trust property entered into by the trustee for the trustee's own personal account or which is otherwise affected by a conflict between the trustee's fiduciary and personal interests is voidable by a beneficiary affected by the transaction unless:

(1) the transaction was authorized by the terms of the trust;

(2) the transaction was approved by the court;

(3) the beneficiary did not commence a judicial proceeding within the time allowed by Section 1005;

(4) the beneficiary consented to the trustee's conduct, ratified the transaction, or released the trustee in compliance with Section 1009; or

(5) the transaction involves a contract entered into or claim acquired by the trustee before the person became or contemplated becoming trustee.

(c) sale, encumbrance, or other transaction involving the investment or management of trust property is presumed to be affected by a conflict between personal and fiduciary interests if it is entered into by the trustee with:

(1) the trustee's spouse;

(2) the trustee's descendants, siblings, parents, or their spouses;

(3) an agent or attorney of the trustee; or

(4) a corporation or other person or enterprise in which the trustee, or a person that owns a significant interest in the trustee, has an interest that might affect the trustee's best judgment. . . .

Restatement (Third) of Trusts
§78 Duty of Loyalty

(1) Except as otherwise provided in the terms of the trust, a trustee has a duty to administer the trust solely in the interest of the beneficiaries, or solely in furtherance of its charitable purpose.

(2) Except in discrete circumstances, the trustee is strictly prohibited from engaging in transactions that involve self-dealing or that otherwise involve or create a conflict between the trustee's fiduciary duties and personal interests.

(3) Whether acting in a fiduciary or personal capacity, a trustee has a duty in dealing with a beneficiary to deal fairly and to communicate to the beneficiary all material facts the trustee knows or should know in connection with the matter.

The duty of loyalty imposed by trust law upon trustees is far more stringent than the duty of fair dealing imposed by corporate law upon a corporation's board of directors. Under corporate law, when a corporation enters into a transaction with a director in her personal capacity or a transaction in which a director has a personal interest apart from that of the corporation, further inquiry is expressly authorized rather than prohibited. A conflicted transaction between a corporation and one of its directors is generally permissible if (1) the conflicted director fully discloses the conflict in all material respects; (2) the transaction is approved by nonconflicted directors; and (3) the conflicted transaction is, in fact, fair to the corporation.[5] Under trust law, by contrast, conflicted transactions are generally voidable even if the trustee fully discloses the conflict, the transaction is approved by nonconflicted co-trustees, and the transaction is fair to the beneficiaries at the time of performance.

The duty of undivided loyalty and "no inquiry rule" apply with special force to licensed attorneys, who are governed by state law provisions that typically require the deposit of client funds into strictly regulated trust accounts. The Rules of Professional Conduct categorically prohibit — and severely punish — self-dealing transactions between an attorney and a trust account that contains client funds.[6]

In re Blumenstyk
704 A.2d 1 (N.J. 1997)

Per Curiam.

. . .

Upon a *de novo* review of the record, the Court is satisfied by clear and convincing evidence that respondent was guilty of unethical conduct involving the knowing misappropriation of clients' funds in violation of RPC 1.15[7] and RPC 8.4(c).[8]

---

5. See, e.g., American Law Institute, Principles of Corp. Governance: Analysis and Recommendations §5.02(a) (1994).

6. The assumption of fiduciary duties as trustee of a private trust is always voluntary: "Upon acceptance of a trusteeship, the trustee shall. . . ." UTC §801. However, when an attorney accepts funds from a client, a fiduciary relationship arises as a matter of law: The acceptance of those funds suffices to place the attorney in a trust relationship and to assume the duties and obligations of a trustee. In some jurisdictions, the relevant statutory provision or rule of professional conduct explicitly uses "hold in trust" language. In others (as in New Jersey — see the next footnote) and in the American Bar Association's Model Rules of Professional Conduct that language is implied:

> A lawyer shall hold property of clients or third persons that is in a lawyer's possession in connection with a representation separate from the lawyer's own property. Funds shall be kept in a separate account maintained in the state where the lawyer's office is situated, or elsewhere with the consent of the client or third person.

Rule 1.15 Safekeeping Property. Recall that words such as "in trust" are not necessary to create a valid trust relationship.

7. [New Jersey Rule of Professional Conduct 1.15(a) provides, "A lawyer shall hold property of clients or third persons that is in a lawyer's possession in connection with a representation separate from the lawyer's own property. Funds shall be kept in a separate account maintained in a financial institution in New Jersey. . . . Complete records of such account funds and other property shall be kept by the lawyer and shall be preserved for a period of seven years after the event that they record." — Eds.]

8. [New Jersey Rule of Professional Conduct 8.4(c) provides, "It is professional misconduct for a lawyer to . . . engage in conduct involving dishonesty, fraud, deceit or misrepresentation. . . ." — Eds.]

The facts, as recapitulated by the [Disciplinary Review Board (DRB or Board)], disclose that respondent, who was admitted to the New Jersey bar in 1977 and is engaged in the practice of law in Morristown, Morris County, misappropriated from the trust account of a client Donald Cresitello, *viz*:

> Respondent represented Donald Cresitello in a real estate matter. On December 2, 1994, respondent deposited into his trust account $65,000 received from Cresitello. The entire $65,000 should have been held intact from the date of deposit until January 27, 1995, when respondent paid the funds over to the proper recipient. However, on December 19, 1994 and January 16, 1995, respondent invaded client trust funds held in behalf of Cresitello, in the amounts of $10,000 and $5,412.55, respectively. Respondent did not have his client's authorization to withdraw the funds.

The facts further reveal knowing misappropriation of trust funds belonging to another client, Edith Messler, *viz*:

> Respondent represented Edith Messler in a personal injury matter. The case settled for $115,000. . . . However, between November 3, 1994 and May 3, 1995, respondent drew ten checks payable to himself, totaling $95,412.55. Respondent was entitled to a legal fee of $25,412.55 for the Messler matter. Therefore, he utilized $70,000 ($95,412.55 minus $25,412.55) of the Messler funds for his own purposes. Respondent did not have his client's authorization to withdraw the funds. Respondent misappropriated the following amounts from Messler on the following days:

January 27, 1995	$ 4,587.45
February 7, 1995	$ 5,412.55
March 20, 1995	$ 5,000.00
April 24, 1995	$30,000.00
April 28, 1995	$10,000.00
May 3, 1995	$15,000.00

Noting that respondent was well aware of the state of his attorney trust and business accounts during the time period in question, the DRB found that respondent's misappropriations were knowing. Thus, as respondent stated, "I knew what I was doing when I was taking the Messler money. It is hard to think back on what a bizarre thing I did. But I certainly—I wrote the check with my hand and I knew. I hated it and I did it all the same time." The DRB further concluded that on several occasions respondent transferred misappropriated funds from his trust account to his business account to avoid overdrafts in the business account and that respondent's records revealed that he had taken loans from family members.

Respondent cites the fact that he borrowed the funds only temporarily and his restitution of the funds as mitigating factors.

We are fully cognizant, as was the DRB, of respondent's explanation for his misconduct. He stated that he had made financial commitments with the expectation that he would receive, in March 1994, a distribution from personal trust funds established by his parents in the amount of approximately $100,000. He used the funds to defray personal expenses solely for his own convenience, including a family vacation to Israel in December 1994 (approximately $15,000), his son's Bar Mitzvah in April 1995 (approximately $30,000), and tax payments to the Internal Revenue Service in April 1995 ($21,199). Because of his parents' physical and marital difficulties, the anticipated distribution was not made until June 1995. On June 9, 1995, almost three months before he was notified that he would be the subject of a random audit, respondent deposited $100,046.99 of his personal funds into the trust account, and thereby fully restored the amounts that had been improperly withdrawn from the respective accounts. Respondent stated that although he could have borrowed the money he needed from other sources, he chose not to do so because he could not bring himself to discuss his finances with his wife or parents. Respondent acknowledges that he now realizes that not telling his wife about his finances was "absolutely stupid."

Respondent's restitution of the funds prior to notification of the random audit of his records indicates that he did intend only to "borrow" funds in the sense that he planned to use the funds for his own purposes only temporarily before restoring them. Nevertheless, restitution does not alter the character of knowing misappropriation and misuse of clients' funds.

> Intent to deprive permanently a client of [his or her] funds . . . is not an element of knowing misappropriation. Nor is the intent to repay funds or otherwise make restitution a defense to the charge of knowing misappropriation. A lawyer who uses funds, knowing that the funds belong to a client and that the client has not given permission to invade them, is guilty of knowing misappropriation. The sanction is disbarment.

In re Barlow, 140 N.J. 191, 198-99 (1995).

The restitution of misappropriated funds does not alter or obscure the fact that

> [w]hen restitution is used to support the contention that the lawyer intended to "borrow" rather than steal, it simply cloaks the mistaken premise that the unauthorized use of clients' funds is excusable when accompanied by an intent to return them. The act is no less a crime. Lawyers who "borrow" may, it is true, be less culpable than those who had no intent to repay, but the difference is negligible in this connection.

In re Wilson, 81 N.J. 451, 458 (1979).

Respondent apparently contends that his motives in using the funds were not nefarious because he sought merely to use these funds only temporarily for his own convenience. He maintains that his motives should militate against the gravity of the misappropriation. But in [In re Noonan, 102 N.J. 157 (1986),] the Court underscored the irrelevance of an attorney's intent and motives:

> It makes no difference whether the money is used for a good purpose or a bad purpose, for the benefit of the lawyer or for the benefit of others, or whether the lawyer intended to return the money when he took it, or whether in fact he ultimately did reimburse the client; nor does it matter that the pressures on the lawyer to take the money were great or

minimal. The essence of *Wilson* is that the relative moral quality of the act, measured by these many circumstances that may surround both it and the attorney's state of mind, is irrelevant: it is the mere act of taking your client's money knowing that you have no authority to do so that requires disbarment.

The misuse of clients' money as a matter of convenience to defray personal expenses, such as for a vacation and a party, does not ameliorate the ethical misconduct. Family financial pressures cannot excuse an attorney's ethical dereliction.

Respondent also cites his unblemished record as a mitigating factor. The Court has made it clear that a satisfactory or distinguished career does not lessen the enormity of the knowing misappropriation of a client's funds[.]

. . .

We determine that respondent's knowing misappropriation violated RPC 1.15 and RPC 8.4(c). We conclude, as we stated in *Wilson* . . . that "disbarment is the only appropriate discipline" for knowing misappropriation of client funds. We, therefore, disbar respondent. Respondent shall reimburse the Disciplinary Oversight Committee for the appropriate administrative costs.

So ordered.

QUESTIONS

1. When the attorney in this matter borrowed $85,000 in client funds from the trust account, he was expecting to receive a gift from his parents of $100,000. The attorney did, in fact, receive the $100,000 gift, which he used to fully repay the trust account. Why did the court impose the sanction of disbarment even though all funds were restored and there was no delay in distributing client funds?

ANSWER. Self-dealing in a client trust fund is such a gravely disloyal act that it is functionally indistinguishable from theft, a crime of dishonesty that disqualifies an attorney from practicing law by reason of unfit moral character. In an earlier case, the New Jersey Supreme Court explained that restitution, while relevant to making the client whole, is insufficient to rehabilitate the problem of an attorney's character unfitness to practice law:

> We do not attach very much importance, as a rule, to the matter of restitution, because that may depend more upon financial ability or other favoring circumstances than repentance or reformation. A thoroughly bad man may make restitution, if he is able, in order to rehabilitate himself and regain his position in the community; and a thoroughly good man may be unable to make any restitution at all. Without underestimating the importance of restitution, a moment's reflection must convince one that of all the factors that enter into the question of moral fitness, the mere circumstance of restitution is the one most likely to be fortuitous and to depend upon conditions and circumstances that afford no reliable test of moral qualities. The money may have come from wealthy relatives, or from a lucky speculation, or from engaging in some alien

> business venture, or it may have been borrowed, in which case the old liability is apparently extinguished by the creation of a new one. Taken in connection with other circumstances, restitution may be of the utmost significance, but this, oftener than not, is due to such other circumstances rather than to the mere fact of non-restitution; as, for instance, if the former attorney became possessed of sufficient money with which to make restitution but refused so to apply it.

In re Harris, 95 A. 761, 762 (N.J. 1915) (en banc).

2. What action could be taken against a non-lawyer trustee for borrowing funds from a testamentary trust for the trustee's personal use? What if the trustee, like the attorney above, restores all borrowed funds without delaying or otherwise affecting distributions to the trust beneficiaries?

ANSWER. Under UTC §1001, the remedies for a breach of trust include "(1) compel[ling] the trustee to perform the trustee's duties; (2) enjoin[ing] the trustee from committing a breach of trust; (3) compel[ling] the trustee to redress a breach of trust by paying money, restoring property, or other means; (4) order[ing] a trustee to account; (5) appoint[ing] a special fiduciary to take possession of the trust property and administer the trust; (6) suspend[ing] the trustee; (7) remov[ing] the trustee as provided in Section 706; (8) reduc[ing] or deny[ing] compensation to the trustee; (9) subject to Section 1012, void[ing] an act of the trustee, impos[ing] a lien or a constructive trust on trust property, or trac[ing] trust property wrongfully disposed of and recover[ing] the property or its proceeds; or (10) order[ing] any other appropriate relief."

UTC §1002 imposes personal liability on a breaching trustee "for the greater of: (1) the amount required to restore the value of the trust property and trust distributions to what they would have been had the breach not occurred; or (2) the profit the trustee made by reason of the breach."

The trustee may also be criminally prosecuted for theft, embezzlement, and other financial misappropriation offenses.

Some commentators have questioned whether the absolute and unforgiving nature of the "no inquiry rule" tends to over-deter self-dealing or conflicted transactions that actually serve to *benefit* the trust beneficiaries. Professor John Langbein explains:

> The rule against self-dealing with trust property is said to respond to the danger that a trustee transacting on his or her own account may subordinate the interest of the trust when valuing the property or setting other terms of the transaction. Yet even in a case in which the trustee consigns trust property for sale at a public auction open to all bidders, and hence cannot control the price or alter the terms, the sole interest rule will invalidate the trustee's purchase.
>
> Thus, for example, supposing the trust in question to own a Monet that must be sold to pay taxes, and I as trustee place it for sale at Sotheby's annual spring auction of Impressionist paintings, I cannot safely bid on the picture. Even though my bid, in

> order to be successful, would have to be higher and thus more beneficial to the trust than any other, the sole interest rule would apply to my purchase. In consequence, were I to resell the painting a few years later at a profit, the trust beneficiary would be able to invoke the rule and capture the gain for the trust. Or, if I held the painting and a beneficiary later determined to reacquire it, I could be ordered to rescind the purchase. Knowing that my title would be infirm in this way, I would be, as the rule intends, deterred from purchasing the painting. This outcome is value impairing; it harms the beneficiary by successfully deterring what would have been the high bid.

John H. Langbein, Questioning the Trust Law Duty of Loyalty: Sole Interest or Best Interest?, 114 Yale L.J. 929, 952 (2005). Professor Langbein argues that the duty of loyalty should not categorically prohibit conflicted transactions by entirely foreclosing judicial review of the surrounding circumstances. Instead, he suggests that the duty of loyalty should impose a rebuttable presumption of invalidity for conflicted and self-dealing transactions, which would be permitted if the trustee can prove the transaction was undertaken with prudence and served the beneficiary's best interests. *Id.* at 981.

However, Professor Melanie Leslie disagrees and contends that the "no further inquiry" rule serves an important protective purpose:

> The flaw in Professor Langbein's argument is that he fails to appreciate the ways in which trusts differ from relationships between family members, between service providers and customers, and between corporate fiduciaries and shareholders. These latter relationships are characterized by features that curb exploitative behavior—factors that are weak or nonexistent in the trust context. Although Professor Langbein's article occasionally acknowledges these differences, he fails to account for them in his analysis.
>
> Specifically, in the relationships that Professor Langbein cites as analogous to the trust, parties have strong abilities to monitor the other's behavior, and to exit if the other party proves untrustworthy. In addition, external pressures, such as social disapproval and market forces, induce parties to the relationship to act in a trustworthy manner. In the trust context, however, beneficiaries' monitoring ability is poor, there is little opportunity to exit, and there are few, if any, market forces that pressure trustees to be loyal. The no further inquiry rule compensates for these deficiencies by reducing monitoring costs, expressing and enforcing the loyalty norm, and imposing unusually harsh penalties so that the threat of liability supplies the pressure that external forces do not. Abolishing the rule and replacing it with a rule that allows a "best-interest defense" would increase monitoring costs and weaken the social norm of loyalty. Compared to the no further inquiry rule, the best interest defense would significantly underdeter opportunistic behavior by trustees.

Melanie B. Leslie, In Defense of the No Further Inquiry Rule: A Response to Professor John Langbein, 47 Wm. & Mary L. Rev. 541, 554-55 (2005).

As you read the following case and work through Problem I, below, think about the debate between Professors Langbein and Leslie over how to calibrate the duty of loyalty in various contexts.

Stegemeier v. Magness
728 A.2d 557 (Del. 1999)

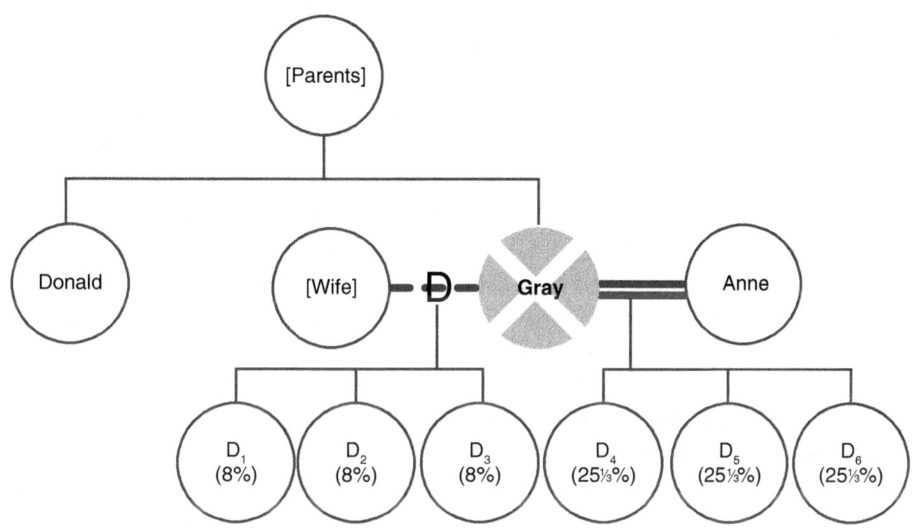

Opinion

Before VEASEY, Chief Justice, WALSH, HOLLAND, and HARTNETT, Justices, and BABIARZ, Judge (sitting pursuant to Del. Const. Art. IV 13(2)), constituting the Court en Banc.

HARTNETT, Justice, for the majority.

. . .

I. FACTS AND PROCEDURAL HISTORY

Gray Magness died testate on December 17, 1980. In his will he named his brother, Donald Magness, to be the trustee of two testamentary trusts established under the will. [This case concerns the residuary trust.] Anne [Magness, the decedent's widow,] was named the income beneficiary of the residuary trust for life. Upon Anne's death the remainder . . . is to be divided among [Mr.] Magness' six daughters. Three of the beneficiaries are the daughters of Mr. Magness and Anne and each have a 25⅓% interest in the residuary trust. Mr. Magness' other three daughters, from a previous marriage, are each entitled to a[n] 8% interest. Charles Allmond, III, Esquire and Anne Magness were appointed as co-administrators c.t.a. of Mr. Magness' will. The will made certain specific bequests and the balance of the assets was to be divided into equal portions to fund the . . . trust. . . .

. . . Mr. Magness owned, at his death, 171 lots and approximately 74 acres of adjacent undivided land in a New Castle County real estate development known as Harmony Crest and 83% of the stock of Magness Construction Company[, which was later used to fund the residuary trust]. Donald Magness owned the other 17% of the stock in the company. Upon the death of A. Gray Magness, title to the real estate vested in Donald Magness as the trustee of the [testamentary] trusts, subject, however, to a power of sale granted in the will to the administrators.

. . .

On November 4, 1982, Anne Magness and Donald Magness formed a new corporation, Magness Builders, Inc., after one of the banks, Colonial Mortgage, suggested that the possibility of financing new home construction would be increased if a new debt-free corporation was formed specifically to apply for and carry construction loans. Donald was issued 51% and Anne 49% of the corporation's stock. Donald proposed that the estate sell the Harmony Crest property to the new corporation at the price he offered. Shortly after the formation of the new corporation, Charles Allmond, III and Anne Magness, as co-administrators of the estate, accepted the offer and contracted to sell some of the lots to Magness Builders, Inc., and over the next six years, the co-administrators sold all of the land to the company. The purchase price of each sale was secured by a purchase money mortgage to the estate. Although, Magness Builders, Inc. made payments on the principal debt, it did not make any interest payments required by the financing agreements until 1988 when it paid a lump sum.

In five separate transactions, the estate sold approximately 409 lots to Magness Builders, Inc. for approximately $2,062,500. Magness Builders, Inc. built homes on the lots which it had purchased from the estate and sold the homes to third-party purchasers. Neither Stegemeier or Mulrooney, two of the three residuary beneficiaries who are each entitled to an 8% interest in the residuary trust created under the will, was advised of the sales nor given the opportunity to consent to the transactions.[9]

In January 1993, Stegemeier and Mulrooney brought this action in the Court of Chancery alleging that Anne M. Magness and Charles M. Allmond, III, as co-administrators of the estate, and Donald L. Magness, as testamentary trustee, breached their fiduciary duties to the beneficiaries. . . . The court dismissed Charles M. Allmond, III from the suit because Stegemeier and Mulrooney did not seek to impose any liability against him. . . .

Also challenged are the Court of Chancery's holdings after trial. The court . . . held that Stegemeier and Mulrooney's request for damages or rescission was denied and found that neither Anne nor Donald had engaged in self-dealing. The Court of Chancery also held that no beneficiary could have suffered any financial loss because the real estate was sold for a fair price.

II. CLAIMS OF APPELLANTS

Stegemeier and Mulrooney, plaintiffs below-appellants, assert error on four issues. First, they claim that the appropriate method to determine the existence of self-dealing by a trustee is whether the fiduciary had a personal interest in the

9. The residuary and marital trusts were not funded until 1989. Each trust received a portion of the stock in Magness Construction Company. Upon its funding, the marital trust was immediately disbursed to Anne Magness. The residuary trust was funded, in part, by the outstanding purchase money mortgages for the real estate sales to Magness Builders, Inc.

transaction. They, therefore, argue that the trial court erred in finding that Donald L. Magness did not commit a breach of fiduciary duty because he was not on both sides of the transaction. Second, they argue that the trial court improperly applied the fiduciary principles of corporate law instead of the principles of trust law in finding that Anne Magness as co-administrator did not engage in self-dealing because the co-administrator, Mr. Allmond, who joined in the deed, was disinterested in the transaction. Third, they argue that even if corporate fiduciary principles apply, the court incorrectly found that Mr. Allmond was a disinterested co-fiduciary because he represented the estate and Magness Builders, Inc. in the real estate transactions. . . .

III. STANDARD AND SCOPE OF REVIEW

In an appeal from a decision in the Court of Chancery, we review conclusions of law *de novo*. The trial court's factual findings, however, will be accepted "[i]f they are sufficiently supported by the record and are the product of an orderly and logical deductive process." When reviewing decisions based on the live testimony of witnesses, determinations of credibility, and expert witness presentations, this Court affords the trial court's decision substantial deference.

IV. THE FIDUCIARY DUTY OF A TRUSTEE NOT TO PURCHASE TRUST PROPERTY

The trial court held "[t]o be found culpable of self-dealing, a defendant fiduciary must have had the ability to cause the challenged transaction to occur." In making that finding it relied on the law relating to corporate fiduciaries. The Court of Chancery found that Donald Magness did not breach his fiduciary duty because he did not have the power to cause the sale of the land[10] and therefore did not stand on both sides of the transaction. The trial court, again relying on corporate law, further concluded that Anne Magness could not be held culpable of self-dealing because she, as one co-administrator, could not have unilaterally caused the sale of the land and Mr. Allmond, the other co-administrator, was disinterested and independent. Because the court's finding that Mr. Allmond was disinterested and independent is sufficiently supported by the record and is the product of an orderly and logical deductive process, we will not disturb that finding. Because, however, we decline to extend corporate fiduciary legal principles to a claim of breach of fiduciary duty as to a trust or estate, we find that Mr. Allmond's disinterest in the transaction to be irrelevant to Donald or Anne Magness' culpability.

V. THE CORRECT STANDARD TO BE APPLIED TO A CLAIM OF BREACH OF FIDUCIARY DUTY

The trial court incorrectly equated the standard of fiduciary duty of a corporate director with that of a trustee of a trust. The absolute prohibition under common law

10. [Recall that Donald, in his capacity as trustee of the residuary trusts, exercised power over the Magness Construction Company's real estate holdings subject to a power of sale held by the administrators of the will. — Eds.]

against self-dealing by a trustee has been modified in the corporate setting to offer a safe harbor for the directors of a corporation if the transaction is approved by a majority of disinterested directors. Transactions approved by the directors are therefore not voidable because there are interested directors, if a committee of disinterested directors approves the transaction. In such a case the directors are protected by the business judgment rule. If, however, the transaction is not approved by the requisite number of disinterested directors, the directors must prove that the transaction was entirely fair. Defendants argue that there is no distinction between the law of self-dealing whether corporate law or trust law is involved because the type of the transaction does not change the nature of the act. That argument is not persuasive.

In *Oberly v. Kirby*, this Court made it clear that in conducting a review of allegations of self-dealing, the standards of trust law and corporation law are different. In that decision, this Court refused to apply the stricter standards of trust law to the decision of the directors of a nonstock, charitable corporation to engage in a transaction where the directors had a personal interest. Because the grantor chose the form of a charitable corporation over a charitable trust, this Court applied the less stringent restrictions of corporate law. Which standard will apply, therefore, is governed by the legal format the grantor chose to accomplish his purposes. Because A. Gray Magness chose a trust to carry out his testamentary intent, the stricter principles of trust law must apply to the challenged transaction.

Unlike corporate law, "[u]nder trust law, self-dealing on the part of a trustee is virtually prohibited." Originally under Delaware law "a trustee [was] prohibited absolutely from purchasing the property entrusted to his care." Under current Delaware law:

> [a]n interested transaction is not void but is voidable, and a court will uphold such a transaction against a beneficiary challenge only if the trustee can show that the transaction was fair and that the beneficiaries consented to the transaction after receiving full disclosure of its terms. However, a court of equity has the power to approve a transaction on behalf of the trust's beneficiaries if they are not *sui juris* and if it finds the transaction to be in their best interest.

Although a sale by an interested trustee is no longer automatically void, even under the more relaxed rule, a court will carefully scrutinize all the attendant circumstances before it can find that the sale is not detrimental to the trust. Courts have recognized that a sale by a trustee with a personal interest is not voidable, if there is a before-the-fact approval by the grantor, the court, or the beneficiaries. None of these exceptions is present here, however, and the transaction would be voidable at the instance of the beneficiaries, if the land had not been sold to bona fide purchasers.

Some authorities have held that good faith and the payment of full consideration is irrelevant as a trustee's defense. Under those authorities, the evidence of a fair price is not even admissible on the issue of whether the transaction is voidable. In any case, the burden of persuasion to justify the upholding of a transaction by an interested trustee rests on the fiduciary, not the beneficiary.

. . .

Defendants assert that because Donald Magness did not stand on both sides of the challenged transaction he did not engage in self-dealing and under the rule applied [to corporate fiduciaries], he therefore did not breach his fiduciary duty to the beneficiaries. The principles of trust law, however, impose a higher standard. Under trust law, self-dealing occurs when the fiduciary has a "personal interest in the subject transaction of such a substantial nature that it might have affected his judgment in material connection."

Under trust law, it is irrelevant that Donald and Anne did not have the exclusive power to sell the land. Even if a sale of trust property is conducted by someone else, a trustee can not purchase the trust property. Defendants assert that because Donald Magness never had the "power to sell," he had no obligation to refrain from purchasing trust property. The non-existence of a power of sale is not the test, however. The rule is well established that a person acting in a fiduciary capacity cannot also act for himself where he has duties to perform for another, "[s]pecifically [that] one who is acting in such a position of trust cannot be a purchaser from the estate for which he is trustee, however fair the terms of sale or however honest the circumstances of an individual transaction may be."

. . .

This principle was established not only "to prevent fraud in the management of the sale, but to the broader object of relieving trustees from any possible conflict between duty and self interest." There are considerations other than unfairness of the actual sale, such as the trustee may have obtained important information regarding the value of the property that he has kept to himself. Although Donald may not have been both the buyer and the seller of the property, he, as the trustee of the residuary trust, had a fiduciary duty not to purchase trust property regardless of whether he executed the deed to the property.

Defendants assert that because Charles Almond was disinterested in the sale, his executing the deed cured any breach of fiduciary duty. This premise is without merit because it is again predicated on fiduciary principles of corporate law, not trust law. . . . Therefore, execution of the deed by Mr. Allmond did not cure the breach of fiduciary duty.

A trustee is under a duty to "participate in the administration of the trust and to use reasonable care to prevent a co-trustee from committing a breach of trust." Although Mr. Allmond was disinterested in the transaction, he knew of Anne and Donald's interest in the corporation that purchased the property and he should have refused to enter into the sale without prior notice to the beneficiaries or court approval.

. . .

Defendants also assert that this sale was necessary to save trust assets because of the decline in the real estate market and the heavy financial debt of Magness Construction Company. While this reasoning may offer an explanation for the need to sell the land and may affect any remedy, it does not excuse a breach of fiduciary duty. The co-administrators should have resigned, requested court approval, or sought the beneficiaries' consent.

VI. THE REMEDY

Although we hold that the challenged transaction would ordinarily be voidable by the beneficiaries (at least if they all sought to invalidate it), it is clear that the transaction can not be rescinded because Magness Builders, Inc. has built homes on the land and sold all of it to third parties. Therefore the issue is whether Stegemeier and Mulrooney could be entitled to any rescissory damages.

Stegemeier and Mulrooney assert that they are entitled to the profits made by Magness Builders Inc. Their position is legally well founded:

> The beneficiary is entitled to any profit made by the trustee [who is guilty of a breach of fiduciary duty], and may recover from the trustee the amount for which he sold the property to another, less the expenses of the trustee incurred in the resale or in perfecting title and the amount of taxes paid by the trustee after his purchase of the property. The rule that a fiduciary cannot profit personally from dealings with the trust property and will be held accountable for all profits from such dealings applies although the fiduciary acquiring the property for himself is only one of two or more fiduciaries and although the co-fiduciaries fixed or consented to the purchase price.

It is clear that if Magness Builders, Inc. had resold the land without making any improvements, the trust would be entitled to any profit it made from the sale. The Court of Chancery, however, held that Magness Builders, Inc. purchased the lots for their true fair value and then made improvements to the land, including erecting houses. If this is correct, any profit from the sale of the improved lots to the third parties was due to the improvements made by Magness Builders, Inc. and not from the profit on the sale of the land alone.

If it had been shown at trial that the land was sold for less than fair market value the trust would be entitled to receive the difference between the fair market value and the purchase price. The Court of Chancery found, however, that Magness Builders, Inc. paid the fair market value for the land.

VII. BURDEN OF PERSUASION AS TO THE VALUE OF THE LAND

The Court of Chancery found that because Stegemeier and Mulrooney had not proven self-dealing that it was their burden to show that the estate did not receive the fair market value for the sale of the land. Because we find that the trial court erred in finding there was no breach of fiduciary duty, we conclude that it was error for the Court of Chancery to have placed the burden of persuasion on Stegemeier and Mulrooney to establish the fair market value of the land.

Although the Court of Chancery erred in placing the burden of persuasion to show that the sale prices were not fair upon Stegemeier and Mulrooney, this error might not change the result. The evidence on fair market value consisted of an expert for each side. In reviewing the opinion of an expert witness as to the value of real estate the most significant factor is the value of the comparable sales. This factor is not dependent on which party has the burden of persuasion but rather is on other factors, such as the validity of the comparable sales examples presented. We, therefore, remand this matter to the Court of Chancery for it to reconsider whether the real estate at issue was sold for a fair price. If the Court of Chancery again determines that the real estate was sold for its fair market value, any errors of the Court of Chancery may be harmless because the rescissory damages might be zero.

. . .

IX. CONCLUSION

We find that Court of Chancery erred in finding that trustee Donald Magness and co-administrator Anne Magness did not breach their fiduciary duties of loyalty and in applying corporate principles of self-dealing to non-corporate trust law. We also find that the trial court improperly assigned to Stegemeier and Mulrooney the burden of persuasion to show that the sales price of the lands was unfair. We therefore REVERSE in part and REMAND to the Court of Chancery to redetermine whether the real estate in question was sold for a fair price to Magness Builders Inc. We leave to the Vice Chancellor's discretion whether additional evidence would be helpful to his reconsideration on remand of the value of the property.[11]

QUESTIONS

3. How was Donald Magness, the decedent's brother, conflicted in his role as trustee of the residuary trust? How, if at all, did Donald benefit from this conflict?

ANSWER. Donald was conflicted because he had a personal interest in a transaction involving trust property. As sole trustee of the residuary trust, Donald owed a duty of undivided loyalty to the trust beneficiaries, Anne and the decedent's six daughters. Donald's duty, as trustee, required him to protect and maximize the value of trust property. As a principal of Magness Builders, Inc., by contrast, Donald's personal interests in the Harmony Crest transaction were threefold: (1) to obtain the lowest purchase price possible, (2) shift the risk of mortgage default to the trust, and (3) obtain credit from the trust at the lowest possible interest rate. Although Donald did not have the power to approve the Harmony Crest transaction (because the power of sale was reserved for the administrators of the will, Anne and Charles), he had a 51 percent stake in Magness Builders, Inc., which purchased 409 lots of real property in the Harmony Crest development owned by the residuary trust.

On remand, the Chancery Court found that Magness Builders, Inc., paid the fair market value of the real estate, but Donald benefitted from two aspects of the transaction aside from the purchase price. First, Magness Builders, Inc., received

11. [On remand to the Court of Chancery, the Vice Chancellor considered evidence of market valuation for the real property sold by the residuary trust to Magness Builders, Inc. The Vice Chancellor concluded that Magness Builders, Inc. paid fair market value as proven by clear and convincing evidence. Stegemeier v. Magness, Civil Action No. 12845 (Del. Ch. Nov. 23, 1999.)—Eds.]

access to working capital that was otherwise unavailable from traditional credit markets. Magness Builders, Inc., purchased the real property from the residuary trust on credit after banks had turned down the business for traditional construction loans. Query whether the residuary trust's acceptance of a mortgage note as consideration for the sale of real property represented an appropriate credit risk of the trust if the business was having trouble obtaining construction financing from traditional banks. Second, Donald, in his capacity as trustee, did not enforce the residuary trust's right to collect interest on the purchase money mortgage debt owed by Magness Builders, Inc., to the trust between 1982 and 1988.

4. How was Anne Magness, the decedent's widow, conflicted in her role as co-administrator of the probate estate? How, if at all, did Anne benefit from this conflict?

ANSWER. Anne was conflicted because she had a personal interest in a transaction that directly affected the interests of estate beneficiaries. As a co-administrator of the probate estate, Anne owed a fiduciary duty to the estate beneficiaries to act solely in their best interests concerning the administration of Gray's probate estate. This duty required Anne to pursue the highest possible sale price for any estate property disposed of during the administration. Gray's will provided that, as a co-administrator, she also had the power to approve the sale of real property that passed to the residuary trust. As a principal of Magness Builders, Inc., by contrast, Anne's personal interests in the Harmony Crest transaction were the same as Donald's. As a 49 percent owner of Magness Builders, Inc., Anne derived the same benefits as Donald from approving the sale of the Harmony Crest real estate from the trust to Magness Builders, Inc.

PROBLEM I

In each of the following hypotheticals, determine whether the trustee's conduct has breached the duty of loyalty and whether the "no further inquiry" rule should apply.

A. Alpha Bankcorp is a large financial services company. One of Alpha Bankcorp's business units, the Alpha Trust Company, is a trust department that provides corporate fiduciary services for trusts settled by high net worth clients. The Alpha Trust Company generates income by charging an annual percentage-based commission on the value of each trust for which it serves as trustee. Another business unit, Alpha Mutual Funds, sponsors and underwrites a popular selection of mutual funds.[12] Alpha Mutual Funds generates income by charging a commission on the sale of each mutual fund (a "load") and an annual fee assessed as a percentage of the value of each fund.

12. A mutual fund is a diversified portfolio of investments that allows investors to diversify their holdings without owning individual stocks or bonds. For the duty to diversify trust assets, see section 11.3 below.

Suppose Alpha Trust Company invests trust assets in mutual funds sponsored by Alpha Mutual Funds. May Alpha Trust Company and Alpha Mutual Funds deduct their commissions and fees directly from the corpus of each trust?

B. The Alpha Trust Company typically invests 5 percent of each trust in shares of Alpha Bankcorp's corporate stock, which is publicly traded on the New York Stock Exchange (NYSE). Last year, the share price of Alpha Bankcorp declined 15 percent even though, on average, the share price of companies traded on the NYSE increased 7 percent over the same time period. A trust beneficiary has sued Alpha Trust Company alleging breach of the duty of loyalty.

1. What result if the trust instrument expressly authorizes the trustee to "retain or purchase shares of a corporate trustee"?
2. What result if the trust instrument does not expressly address the trust's ownership of shares of a corporate trustee and, two years ago, Alpha Trust sent the beneficiary a report in which it first disclosed its investment of trust assets in Alpha Bankcorp corporate stock?

C. Dotty's will left her estate of $10 million to the trustee of a testamentary support trust for the benefit of her daughter, Sandra. The trust provides for Sandra's support until she reaches the age of 50, at which time the trustee may, in the trustee's discretion, invade trust principal for Sandra's health needs as she grows older. Tommy, the trustee, would like to borrow $250,000 from the trust to purchase a house. Tommy is willing to pay interest on the loan at the prevailing market rate and repay the principal over a ten-year amortization schedule. Tommy sends Sandra a letter summarizing his request. Sandra writes "OK" at the bottom of the letter, signs her name below, and mails the document back to Tommy.

1. What result if Tommy defaults on the mortgage and Sandra sues him for breach of the duty of loyalty?
2. Suppose that, instead of borrowing funds from the trust for his mortgage, Tommy asks Sandra for a personal loan from her own account. Sandra agrees to give Tommy a mortgage on the terms described above and the transaction is kept entirely separate from the trust. What result if Tommy defaults on the mortgage and Sandra sues him for breach of the duty of loyalty?

D. Esther, in her personal capacity, owns a 40 percent interest in the outstanding shares of PaperMax, a publicly traded company. Esther is a passive owner of PaperMax stock and is not in any way involved in the management of the company. PaperMax has promising growth potential, but Esther has long thought that the company could generate higher profits if the shareholders voted to replace its longtime chief executive officer.

Esther is also the trustee of a trust established by her sister for the benefit of Esther's nieces and nephews. Acting as trustee, Esther acquires an 11 percent interest in PaperMax on behalf of the trust. Esther, having acquired a majority of voting shares, then votes both her personal shares and the trust's shares to remove the incumbent CEO, who is replaced by a new chief executive.

1. Suppose shares of PaperMax increase by 20 percent the following year. What result if Esther is sued by one of the trust beneficiaries for breach of the duty of loyalty?
2. Suppose shares of PaperMax decline by 20 percent the following year. What result if Esther is sued by one of the trust beneficiaries for breach of the duty of loyalty?

11.3 DUTY OF PRUDENCE

The duty of prudence, also known as the duty of care, imposes an obligation upon trustees to exercise a reasonable degree of diligence, caution, skill, effort, and care with regard to the trust's administration. The duty of care is typically expressed as a generalized standard of conduct rather than an enumeration of specific mandates or directives because of the comprehensive and all-encompassing nature of the obligation.[13] Perhaps more hindsight-oriented than any of the other trustee duties, most aspects of the duty of care are usually invoked to evaluate the reasonableness of a trustee's past performance in the context of trust litigation, not as a prospective guide for proper trust administration. Nevertheless, most commentators would agree that, at a minimum, the duty of care requires trustees to (1) familiarize themselves with all terms set forth in the trust instrument; (2) understand the settlor's purposes, objectives, restrictions, and prohibitions, as articulated in the trust instrument; (3) ascertain all facts, including information about the needs and circumstances of trust beneficiaries, necessary to carry out the trust terms and exercise discretion in an informed and intelligent manner; (4) administer all aspects of the trust with competence, attention, diligence, organization, and care; and (5) avoid delegation of duties (with limited exceptions).

Uniform Trust Code
§804 Prudent Administration

A trustee shall administer the trust as a prudent person would, by considering the purposes, terms, distributional requirements, and other circumstances of the trust. In satisfying this standard, the trustee shall exercise reasonable care, skill, and caution.

Restatement (Third) of Trusts
§77 Duty of Prudence

(1) The trustee has a duty to administer the trust as a prudent person would, in light of the purposes, terms, and other circumstances of the trust.

(2) The duty of prudence requires the exercise of reasonable care, skill, and caution.

(3) If the trustee possesses, or procured appointment by purporting to possess, special facilities or greater skill than that of a person of ordinary prudence, the trustee has a duty to use such facilities or skill.

---

13. See, e.g., Restatement (Third) of Trusts §77, comment b(1) ("It is not possible to state all of the factors that are necessary or appropriate for a trustee to take into account in making decisions or taking action in the many diverse aspects of the investment, management, protection, and distribution of trust property.").

In re Will of Crabtree
865 N.E.2d 1119 (Mass. 2007)

MARSHALL, Chief Justice.

[A court-appointed guardian ad litem, alleging breach of fiduciary duties, petitioned for the removal of Francis J. Harney and Robert G. Naughton as trustees of several related charitable trusts. The Probate and Family Court ordered the trustees removed and the intermediate appellate court affirmed. The trustees now appeal the removal order to the Supreme Judicial Court.]

. . .

2. FACTUAL BACKGROUND

a. The Will

On September 25, 1924, [Lotta M.] Crabtree, a well-known vaudeville star and stage actress, died.[14] In her will, dated October 5, 1922, she created eight testamentary charitable trusts. Seven are currently active. Each of the Crabtree trusts is a separate entity with a distinct charitable purpose, requiring separate administration and the filing of separate probate accounts. The stated purpose of the largest trust, the agricultural fund trust, is to provide loans to graduates of what is now the University of Massachusetts, as well as financial assistance to needy and meritorious students for their studies at the university. As of December 31, 1999, the assets of the agricultural fund trust had a market value of $4,082,766.05. The other six trusts have fewer assets, with market values as of December 31, 1999, ranging between $159,120.02 and $1,050,052.34. The combined market value of the other six trusts as of December 31, 1999, was $3,806,730.26.

b. Operation of the Crabtree Trusts

The [Probate and Family Court] judge made detailed findings concerning the operation of the seven trusts. Although the trustees argue otherwise, the judge found that the administration of the Crabtree trusts, particularly the smaller trusts, was not particularly onerous. Having available to him records including minutes of trustee meetings and lawyers' diaries, the judge found that the trustees met weekly for less

14. [Lotta Crabtree, reportedly the richest stage actress of the late nineteenth century, entered show business at age 6. "At the head of her own company, at the age of 7, 'La Petite Lotta' played one-night stands throughout the mining region [of California] and in those days scored her biggest night at a rough Nevada camp, where, after a rather hostile reception, she finally so won the hearts of the miners that they pitched bags of gold-dust and nuggets at her feet." Lotta Crabtree, Actress, Is Dead, N.Y. Times, Sept. 26, 1924, at A21. In 1873, at the height of her acting career, Crabtree was reportedly engaged to a Philadelphia gentleman who was "not inherited from the main trunk of the family," so Crabtree "gave him entire charge of her finances." Lotta's Many Conquests, N.Y. Times, June 19, 1883, at A2. But Crabtree's fiancé was not a good steward of her property: "The temptation was too strong, and one night while she was playing in Niblo's Garden in New York he took $13,000 of her money and gambled it away. That broke off the match." *Id.* Crabtree was a shrewd business woman who invested her earnings in real estate, eventually acquiring ownership of several hotels and theaters across the United States. She retired from acting in 1891 with an estimated fortune of $2 million and, at the time of her death in 1924, she was survived by no close family relatives. Crabtree left her entire estate to charity. — EDS.]

than one and one-half hours, on average, to discuss grant making and other trust matters, and that they rarely engaged in trust activities at other times.

In addition to making loans to farmers, the judge found that the trustees had distributed income of the agricultural fund trust to the Lotta M. Crabtree Endowment Fund (endowment). The endowment was established by the trustees in 1987 at the suggestion of officials at the university. Under the arrangement, rather than making direct grants or loans from trust income to eligible students, income from the agricultural fund trust was disbursed to the University of Massachusetts Foundation, Inc., which administers the endowment. The endowment, in turn, used some, but not all, of the funds to make scholarship grants to undergraduate and graduate students at the university. From 1987 until 1999, the trustees paid $631,751 of income from the agricultural fund trust into the endowment, and as of 2003, only $301,500 had been paid out. The trustees also agreed that ten per cent of the annual income of the endowment itself would be added to the endowment principal.

c. General Accounting, Fees, and Expenses

Trustees' fees formed the bulk of trust expenditures. Both [trustees] Naughton and Harney submitted affidavits averring that they did not keep itemized records of the time they spent on trust business, and that their compensation was not based on the time spent, "but rather on the basis customary to Boston trustees, i.e., law firms and banks managing trust assets, a percentage of principal under management and of income periodically." Under the formula adopted by the trustees, each trustee was paid a flat fee of "$3,500 per month which in total is approximately one-half of one percent of the principal assets, plus about $1,000.00 per quarter, which represents approximately one-third of [three] trustees' share of 6% of earned income." The percentage fee was paid on a quarterly basis. The trusts also generated administrative expenses, primarily for rent, accounting services, and a part-time secretary.

The assets of the seven trusts were held in seven separate investment accounts at the brokerage firm Salomon Smith Barney, where each trust also had its own checking account. However, the trustees' practice was to pay the administrative expenses for all seven trusts, as well as the flat monthly portion of the trustees' fee, from the agricultural fund trust account alone. At the end of the year, the six other trusts reimbursed the agricultural fund trust, without interest, for their respective share of administrative expenses incurred. The six trusts did not reimburse the agricultural fund trust for their respective portion of the flat monthly trustees' fee. The accounts of each respective trust indicated that the administrative expenses were paid on a pro rata basis by the separate trusts, with no indication in the accounts that the payments were actually reimbursements.

Against this factual background, we consider the merits of this appeal. We turn first to the issue of removal.

3. REMOVAL OF THE TRUSTEES

The law controlling trustees' actions is well developed. The trustee of a testamentary trust acts, in effect, as the instrumentality of the decedent to promote the well-being of the trust beneficiaries in a specific manner, dictated by the terms of the trust. Where the trustee is a professional trustee, as in this case, the fiduciary duty is higher than that imposed on a lay trustee. This court has also held that "[t]he law does not look with special favor upon attempts to impair the breadth and strength of the safeguards which experience has erected for the protection of those whose property has been confided to the good faith and sound judgment of trustees. And certainly this general attitude should not be softened first for the benefit of trust companies and professional trustees who hold themselves out as fully conversant with the duties of trustees and fully competent to perform them." New England Trust Co. v. Paine, 317 Mass. 542, 550 (1945).

"It is fundamental that a trust instrument must be construed to give effect to the intention of the donor as ascertained from the language of the whole instrument considered in the light of circumstances known to the donor at the time of its execution." Watson v. Baker, 444 Mass. 487, 491 (2005). Where trustees are shown to act in disregard of the settlor's intent, they breach their fiduciary duties in a manner that may justify their removal. Dismissal of a trustee need not be predicated on the trustee's dishonest or selfish actions. Rather, the "question in each case is whether the circumstances are such that allowing the trustee to continue would be detrimental to the trust." 2 A.W. Scott & M.L. Ascher, Trusts §11.10, at 656 (5th ed. 2006). If challenged, a trustee has "the burden of showing that he ha[s] discharged the duties of trustee with reasonable skill, prudence, and judgment." Rugo v. Rugo, 325 Mass. 612, 617 (1950). We review the decision of a judge to remove a trustee to determine whether the judge's findings are clearly erroneous, or whether there has been an abuse of discretion, or other error of law.

In ordering removal of the trustees, the judge appropriately applied these standards. He listed eighteen separate breaches of fiduciary duty by the trustees, the bases for each of which are fully laid out in the judge's detailed factual findings, which we see no reason to dispute. The trustees counter that, even were we to accept the judge's findings, the documented infractions are, at most, minor and easily remediable, and do not justify removal. The severe sanction of removal, they argue, is reserved for cases such as those where a breach of duty evidences a palpable adversity to the interest of the beneficiaries or has improperly benefited the trustees. While some breaches of fiduciary duty found by the judge are less significant than others, we agree with the judge that together they document a history of, in the judge's words, the trustees' "basic lack of understanding" of their obligations as fiduciaries. Two of the breaches of fiduciary duty found by the judge, alone or in combination, are sufficient to justify removal: the breach of fiduciary duty inherent in the misuse of the agricultural fund trust (both by using the agricultural fund trust account to pay trustees' fees for all of the trusts, and by using that account as an operating account for the other trusts), and the breach of fiduciary duty inherent in the unauthorized and undisclosed creation and maintenance of an endowment, the operation of which was not countenanced by the will. We address each of these in turn.

a. The Use of the Agricultural Fund Trust

The trustees admit that neither the will nor any subsequent order modifying the terms of the agricultural fund trust authorized them to use the agricultural fund trust as an operating fund for all seven trusts. They claim that the practice was nevertheless appropriate and certainly not so egregious as to warrant removal. We disagree.

The trustees make three main claims in defense of their actions generally. First, they argue that they utilized this particular accounting method because it had been the practice of previous Crabtree trustees (and previous Crabtree accountants) to do so. They also note that the Probate and Family Court and the Attorney General had approved previous accounts for the trusts in which the same accounting method was employed.

We recognize that a successor trustee is not strictly liable for the acts of a predecessor. However, "the successor trustee has a positive duty, upon taking over the trust estate, to see that the predecessor has properly accounted for the whole of it." Loring, A Trustee's Handbook §7.2.4, at 500 (C.E. Rounds ed. 2007). . . . Historical practice does not excuse a present failure of diligence. Nor can we say that the Attorney General had no objection to the trustees' method of accounting where the judge found that these impermissible accounting practices are not obvious from the accounts filed and not disclosed until the present litigation.

Second, relying on Hutchinson v. King, 339 Mass. 41, 44 (1959), the trustees claim that, because G. L. c. 206, §2, does not require any specific method of accounting, using the agricultural fund trust to pay trustees' fees for services rendered to the other trusts was not a breach of fiduciary duty. However, we emphasized that, in whatever form presented to the court, the statements of accounts must be "consistent with the facts . . . [and] with applicable substantive rules of law." Here, they were neither. The use of the agricultural fund trust as an operating fund for all seven trusts was not "consistent with the facts," as this practice was not disclosed in the accounts.

Moreover, such unauthorized and undocumented cross-usage of funds contravenes "substantive rules of law." "It is ordinarily the duty of the trustee not to mingle property held upon one trust with property held upon another trust, whether the two trusts are created by separate settlors or by the same settlor." Restatement (Second) of Trusts §179 comment c (1959). The judge found that by using the agricultural fund trust as an operating account to pay the expenses for the other six trusts, they deprived the agricultural fund trust of substantial income available for its beneficiaries. The trustees' actions in this regard illustrate the reason for the commingling prohibition: to avoid the negative consequences for beneficiaries that resulted here.

Finally, the trustees claim that the error, if any, of paying monthly trustees' fees for all seven trusts from the agricultural fund trust alone was de minimis and easily correctable. The trustees note that the "practice" of paying their flat monthly fee from the agricultural fund trust arose because they spent the majority of their time in the administration of that trust. But if at any point the trustees deemed the independent operation of the seven trusts impractical or impossible, they could have filed a complaint for instruction. What was not appropriate was for the trustees to alter the terms of the Crabtree will of their own accord and without disclosure to the court. As the judge rightly noted, the effect of the trustees' actions was to create an annual "gift of income" from the agricultural fund trust to the smaller funds that "add[ed] up to thousands of dollars each year that should have been going [under the agricultural fund trust] to the students," as Crabtree intended. Such damage to the intended beneficiaries of the agricultural fund trust can hardly be deemed de minimis.

b. The Creation of a Separate Endowment

Another basis for removal cited by the judge concerns the creation of a separate endowment at, and its subsequent administration by, the [University of Massachusetts]. Without seeking prior court approval, the trustees created the endowment in 1987 using funds from the agricultural fund trust that were allocated for a farm loan that was not consummated. The endowment was then supplemented with additional contributions of income from the agricultural fund trust, in amounts ranging from a high of $157,751 in 1994 to no contribution in 2002. The trustees claim that both the will and the terms of a 1971 court order (1971 order) permit the establishment of the endowment. Alternatively, they argue that the language of the will and the 1971 order create enough ambiguity about the matter so that reasonable minds could differ. Neither argument has merit.

The will established the agricultural fund trust to provide loans, from trust income, to graduates of the Massachusetts Agricultural College in Amherst who wished "to follow agricultural pursuits." Any remaining income is to be distributed semiannually "to assist needy and meritorious students in completing their courses of study in said Massachusetts Agricultural College." The 1971 order, issued on a complaint for instruction brought by predecessor trustees, authorizes the trustees to offer grants or loans to any graduate student or undergraduate student at the university should there be an insufficient number of loan applicants. The 1971 order also authorizes the trustees to seek the assistance of university financial aid staff when making these grants and loans, and specifically directs that loan repayments be added to agricultural fund trust income for subsequent disbursement as a grant or loan.

We discern in neither the will nor any subsequent order any permission either to create an entirely new vehicle for dispensing the income of the agricultural fund trust or to assign management of that vehicle to a third party. The trustees did not seek direction from the court for the creation of the endowment, or disclose in their accounts the existence of, balance in, or grants made from the endowment. The trustees were required by the terms of the will to distribute the income earned from the agricultural fund trust semiannually. By establishing the endowment, the trustees essentially converted trust income into a parallel pool of principal, only a small part of which was actually paid out to needy students. Whether or not this approach was "a good idea," as the trustees claim, it was not countenanced under the Crabtree will. In the absence of a court order, it is the terms set out by Crabtree that must dictate the distribution of income from her estate. Having concluded that the trustees breached their fiduciary duty as to the agricultural fund trust, such a finding justifies their removal as trustees from the other involved trusts. . . .

c. Excessive Trustees' Fees

The judge concluded that the two breaches of fiduciary duty discussed above, "coupled with [the trustees'] payment to themselves of excessive compensation," warranted removal of the trustees. We therefore consider the trustees' challenge to the judge's finding that the fees charged were excessive.

. . .

The judge carefully examined the range of fees that other entities would have charged for all services (except tax preparation and grant making) for managing accounts similar in size to the accounts at issue here. He determined that the fees those entities would have charged to the fifth accounts[15] of all the trusts would have ranged from a low of $39,849.89 to a high of $58,184.35. In contrast, the total fee actually charged by the trustees to the fifth accounts was $149,223. The judge's reliance on the fee schedules in evidence, and his determination of a fee in the amount of $41,000 — a figure that, while at the low end of the range, was not unreasonable — does not evidence an abuse of discretion.

. . .

8. CONCLUSION

The orders of the Probate and Family Court removing the trustees are affirmed. The orders concerning the trustees' fees are affirmed. . . .

So ordered.

Lotta Crabtree

15. [In a portion of the case not reproduced here, the court discusses the "fifth accounts," which the trustees filed on May 25, 2000 for calendar year 1999. See 865 N.E.2d at 1123. — Eds.]

QUESTIONS

5. The guardian ad litem challenged the trustees' continued practice of prior trustees in paying the administrative expenses and trustee fees incurred by all seven trusts from the agricultural fund trust. However, given that (1) the $4 million value of the agricultural fund trust exceeded the $3.8 million value of the other six trusts combined; (2) most of the trustees' work was attributed to the agricultural trust; and (3) the record-keeping necessary to accurately account for and allocate such costs among the other six trusts would have required the trustees to perform additional billable work, why wasn't the trustees' accounting practice a reasonable one?

   ANSWER. The duty of care imposes upon trustees an obligation to carry out the terms of trust as established by the settlor. If the trustees believe that modification of the settlor's chosen terms is necessary to prevent impairment of or otherwise further the material trust purposes, then the trustees must petition a court for relief. Only a court can invoke a modification doctrine to permit deviation from an administrative or distributive term, consolidate or terminate trusts that are too small to be administered economically, or otherwise alter the terms of a trust.

   Here, the comparatively higher value of the agricultural trust provided no basis for the trustees to deduct from it administrative expenses incurred by entirely separate trusts created by the settlor. If the other trusts were too small to be administered separately in economical manner, then the trustees should have petitioned the court for consolidation or termination of the trusts. The additional record-keeping necessary to accurately account for expenses incurred by the other six trusts probably would not have generated additional billable work for the trustees. The trustees were not charging an hourly fee for their work, but rather, a fixed fee assessed both monthly and quarterly.

   The court was also troubled by the trustees' record-keeping that not only failed to document the agricultural fund's payment of expenses for the other trusts, but also appeared to affirmatively represent that the other trusts were, in fact, paying a *pro rata* share of the administrative expenses and trustee fees.

6. The trustees argued that they applied the same method for calculating their fees as other local professional trustees. Each of the three trustees charged an annual fee of approximately $46,000 for administering charitable trusts worth roughly $8 million. Why, then, did the court find the trustees' fees to be unreasonably high?

   ANSWER. The trial court evaluated the reasonableness of the trustees' fees in comparison to the fee schedules issued by eight other local corporate fiduciary firms and concluded that the Crabtree trustees' fee structure generated fees that were approximately three times higher than comparable firms. Thus, the Supreme Judicial Court affirmed the trial court's surcharge against the trustees for excessive fees.

7. The agricultural fund trust authorized distributions for the purpose of providing financial assistance to students at the University of Massachusetts. The Lotta M.

Crabtree Endowment created by the trustees in 1987 also provided financial assistance to students at the University of Massachusetts. Why, then, did the court find that the trustees' creation and operation of the endowment was a breach of trust?

ANSWER. The primary purpose of the agricultural fund trust was "to provide loans, from trust income, to graduates of the Massachusetts Agricultural College in Amherst who wished 'to follow agricultural pursuits.'" 865 N.E.2d at 1131. The secondary purpose of the trust was, to the extent the income was not exhausted for the primary purpose, to provide financial assistance for needy students at the university. The trust required distributions of income semiannually for these purposes.

Both the creation and operation of the Lotta M. Crabtree Endowment were contrary to the trust instrument's express terms. The trustees established the endowment with funds that were allocated for a farm loan approved by the trust but never actually issued. The trustees then repurposed the unused funds, not by making another farm loan or providing direct financial aid to students, but by transferring the funds to the University of Massachusetts to create an endowment with terms that were similar but not identical to the agricultural fund trust. The trustees then distributed additional trust income to the endowment over the following twelve years.

The Lotta M. Crabtree Endowment's terms differed from those of Crabtree's trust because the endowment did not require semiannual distribution of income for either farm loans or student financial aid. For the twelve years in question, the trustees paid $631,751 into the endowment, but the university only distributed $301,500. The endowment, therefore, was less beneficial to the charitable beneficiary class than the original testamentary trust.

PROBLEM II

Yolanda died ten years ago and left her entire estate of $4 million in trust. Her testamentary trust provided for discretionary distributions of income and principal for the comfort and support of her surviving spouse, Thomas, for life. Upon Thomas's death, the trust provided for outright distribution of the remainder to Yolanda's three children from a prior marriage. Yolanda appointed the attorney who drafted the trust, Adam, as trustee.

Thomas, who was 79 years old at the time of Yolanda's death, has no savings of his own and his sole source of income is his monthly Social Security retirement benefit. Thomas lives in the house he shared with Yolanda. Title to the house is now owned by the trustee and the trust grants Thomas a life estate so that he can continue residing there. The trustee pays all property taxes directly to the local tax assessor, but the house has fallen into disrepair.

Thomas died in the house earlier this year. His cause of death was malnutrition and hypertension. Thomas is survived by his daughter, Dolly, from a prior marriage.

A. Suppose that, several years ago, Thomas contacted Adam and requested money from the trust because he was having trouble paying for routine expenses (e.g., food, medical, etc.) and providing for basic upkeep of the house. In response, Adam sent a check for $500 with a note explaining that if Thomas needed additional funds, he should submit each request in writing with a short explanation. Thomas never replied and Adam never made another distribution from the trust. What result if Dolly sues Adam for breach of trust?

B. Suppose that every year since Yolanda's death, Adam contacted Thomas and asked if he was in need of distributions from the trust.
   1. Thomas declined each offer even though he, in fact, could have used additional support to pay for food, medical expenses, and upkeep of the house. What result if Dolly sues Adam for breach of trust?
   2. Instead, Thomas did not respond to any of Adam's letters even though he, in fact, could have used additional support to pay for food, medical expenses, and upkeep of the house. What result if Dolly sues Adam for breach of trust? Now suppose that, after noticing that Thomas had not responded to the first two letters, Adam sought the advice of legal counsel regarding his duty. The attorney advised that sending a letter every year was sufficient to discharge the duty of care whether or not Thomas responded. What result if Dolly sues Adam for breach of trust? Would this result change if, unbeknownst to Adam, Thomas had long suffered from dementia and was not capable of managing his own affairs?

The duty of prudence described above applies generally to all aspects of trust administration, but a more detailed set of subsidiary rules governs a critical function of trust administration: the investment of trust assets.

Before the 1990s, fiduciary duties regulated the trustee's selection of trust investments by establishing "legal lists," which were bright-line distinctions between permissible and impermissible asset types. Permissible investments, such as United States bonds, were presumptively safe because they pose a low risk of default while providing a reliable source of modest income. Impermissible investments, such as equities, were presumptively unsafe and speculative because they are more volatile and pose a higher risk of default or loss of capital. The legal list system's concept of prudence, which rewarded trustee compliance with a safe harbor from personal liability, sought to ensure each individual investment owned by the trust belonged to a category of assets presumed by law to minimize default risk. This policy preference for preserving capital had the effect of stabilizing the value of trust principal over time in absolute dollar terms.

The legal list system's exclusive concern for default risk, however, had the adverse effect of skewing trust investments away from capital markets that, in the aggregate, tend to outperform "safe" assets and appreciate more in value over time. In addition to the lost opportunity for capital appreciation, after accounting for inflation, the legal list restrictions caused the value of permissible trust investments to decline over time in real dollar terms (as measured by purchasing power) because, although the principal remained intact, overall investment performance did not keep apace with the rising cost of goods and services in the economy.

A mechanical binary distinction between presumptively safe and unsafe asset classes also overlooked the return-enhancing opportunities presented by diversification and portfolio asset management. Modern Portfolio Theory, a paradigm-shifting theory of finance first published in the 1950s, identified two patterns of economic behavior exhibited by assets invested in an efficient market: (1) risk is inversely correlated with expected returns, such that the market compensates investors for most types of risk by yielding higher expected returns; and (2) an important exception to the risk/return corollary holds that an investor assumes uncompensated risk by failing to diversify. Taken together, the teachings of Modern Portfolio Theory revealed two compelling reasons to invest in a diversified portfolio of assets:

First, diversification enables investors to maximize total expected returns within the parameters of their unique combination of investment goals and level of risk tolerance. Investors with long-term investment goals and a higher tolerance for risk might choose a diversified portfolio of equities, which can be volatile in the short term but, on average, generate higher long-term returns than traditional bonds. Investors with short-term investment goals and a lower tolerance for risk might opt for a diversified portfolio of bonds and other fixed income investments,[16] which pose a low risk of default but do not typically appreciate in value over the long term. Further, it would not be unreasonable for both long-term and short-term investors to incorporate some mixture of both stocks and bonds in their diversified portfolios, even if the portfolio's overall concentration is weighted more heavily to one asset class or the other.

Second, diversification enables investors to reduce or greatly eliminate the uncompensated default risk for any specific investment. The market does not compensate investors for the risk created by putting all of one's eggs in a single basket. Diversification eliminates this risk by allocating small shares of the portfolio to a large number of different investments. If one investment defaults or loses capital, the portfolio's loss exposure is limited to the share allocated to the bad investment.

Modern Portfolio Theory had a profound influence on trust law's regulation of the investment function under the duty of prudence. Whereas legal lists focused exclusively on capital preservation and examined each investment without regard to the trust's other investments, portfolio investing presented a radical new approach: It sought to maximize the aggregate performance of a portfolio of trust investments subject to an appropriately tailored balance between risk and return. Trust law reformers soon realized that prudent investing required the trustee to evaluate the suitability of each investment, not in isolation, but in relation to the overall portfolio of trust assets.

Promulgated in 1994, the Uniform Prudent Investor Act (UPIA), or some variation of it, has been adopted all states and is incorporated by reference into the Uniform Trust Code as Article 9. The UPIA codifies several important aspects of the Prudent Investor Rule: (1) prudent investing requires consideration of the trust's purposes, terms, distribution requirements, and other relevant circumstances (§2(a), (c)); (2) consideration of any individual investment must be evaluated, not in isolation, but in relation to its suitability for the trust's overall portfolio of assets (§2(b)); (3) prudent

16. A fixed income investment, such as a government bond, generates returns according to an interest rate, coupon payment, or other predetermined structure.

investing *requires* diversification of trust assets unless special circumstances weigh against the presumed benefits of diversifying (§3); (4) a trustee must evaluate the prudence of existing trust assets within a reasonable time after accepting a trusteeship (§4); (5) a trustee's compliance with the Prudent Investor Rule is evaluated, not in hindsight, but as of the time of the trustee's investment decision (§8); and (6) the Prudent Investor Rule's standard of care is a set of default rules subject to modification by the trust (§1(b)).

GLASBERGEN

"Yes, our investments are diversified: 20% out the window, 65% down the drain, and 15% gone with the wind."

Uniform Prudent Investor Act

SECTION 1. PRUDENT INVESTOR RULE

(a) Except as otherwise provided in subsection (b), a trustee who invests and manages trust assets owes a duty to the beneficiaries of the trust to comply with the prudent investor rule set forth in this [Act].

(b) The prudent investor rule, a default rule, may be expanded, restricted, eliminated, or otherwise altered by the provisions of a trust. A trustee is not liable to a beneficiary to the extent that the trustee acted in reasonable reliance on the provisions of the trust.

SECTION 2. STANDARD OF CARE; PORTFOLIO STRATEGY; RISK AND RETURN OBJECTIVES

(a) A trustee shall invest and manage trust assets as a prudent investor would, by considering the purposes, terms, distribution requirements, and other circumstances of the trust. In satisfying this standard, the trustee shall exercise reasonable care, skill, and caution.

(b) A trustee's investment and management decisions respecting individual assets must be evaluated not in isolation but in the context of the trust portfolio as a whole and as a part of an overall investment strategy having risk and return objectives reasonably suited to the trust.

(c) Among circumstances that a trustee shall consider in investing and managing trust assets are such of the following as are relevant to the trust or its beneficiaries:

(1) general economic conditions;

(2) the possible effect of inflation or deflation;

(3) the expected tax consequences of investment decisions or strategies;

(4) the role that each investment or course of action plays within the overall trust portfolio, which may include financial assets, interests in closely held enterprises, tangible and intangible personal property, and real property;

(5) the expected total return from income and the appreciation of capital;

(6) other resources of the beneficiaries;

(7) needs for liquidity, regularity of income, and preservation or appreciation of capital; and

(8) an asset's special relationship or special value, if any, to the purposes of the trust or to one or more of the beneficiaries.

(d) A trustee shall make a reasonable effort to verify facts relevant to the investment and management of trust assets.

(e) A trustee may invest in any kind of property or type of investment consistent with the standards of this [Act].

(f) A trustee who has special skills or expertise, or is named trustee in reliance upon the trustee's representation that the trustee has special skills or expertise, has a duty to use those special skills or expertise.

SECTION 3. DIVERSIFICATION

A trustee shall diversify the investments of the trust unless the trustee reasonably determines that, because of special circumstances, the purposes of the trust are better served without diversifying.

SECTION 4. DUTIES AT INCEPTION OF TRUSTEESHIP

Within a reasonable time after accepting a trusteeship or receiving trust assets, a trustee shall review the trust assets and make and implement decisions concerning the retention and disposition of assets, in order to bring the trust portfolio into compliance with the purposes, terms, distribution requirements, and other circumstances of the trust, and with the requirements of this [Act].

. . .

SECTION 7. INVESTMENT COSTS

In investing and managing trust assets, a trustee may only incur costs that are appropriate and reasonable in relation to the assets, the purposes of the trust, and the skills of the trustee.

SECTION 8. REVIEWING COMPLIANCE

Compliance with the prudent investor rule is determined in light of the facts and circumstances existing at the time of a trustee's decision or action and not by hindsight.

In re HSBC Bank USA (formerly Marine Midland Bank) (Ely)
2012 N.Y. Slip Op. 22284 (Surr. Ct. Sept. 25, 2012)

HOWE, J.

This is a proceeding for judicial settlement of the final account of HSBC Bank USA [(HSBC)], as corporate trustee of the testamentary trust of James S. Ely ["Ely"]. The testamentary trust was established by Ely in his Last Will and Testament dated September 28, 1959, for the benefit of his son, James S. Ely, Jr. ["James, Jr."].

[Ely's testamentary trust was initially funded in 1968 and appointed Marine Midland Bank as a co-trustee. HSBC later became a successor trustee after acquiring Marine Midland Bank.]

James, Jr. died on December 21, 2004. His Will was admitted to probate by the Monroe County Surrogate's Court, and his surviving spouse, Michele T.K. Ely ["Michele"], was issued Letters Testamentary. Pursuant to his Last Will and Testament, James, Jr. exercised a power of appointment and directed that the remaining trust funds be paid over into a new trust for the benefit of his surviving spouse, and he named the Genesee Valley Trust Company ["Genesee Valley"], as trustee.

[Michele and Genesee Valley object to HSBC's accounting for the period of July 10, 2000 to September 7, 2006.]

Objectants allege that HSBC violated the Prudent Investor Rule and the Prudent Investor Act under EPTL[17] §11-2.2(a) and §11.2.3, and they allege that HSBC imprudently and negligently managed the trust assets. Objectants urge that HSBC should be surcharged for damages to the trust resulting from its negligence. HSBC denies the allegations, and has filed a motion for summary judgment seeking dismissal of the objections on the ground that HSBC met its fiduciary obligations to the trust. Michele opposes HSBC's motion, and has cross-moved for partial summary judgment on the issue of liability with respect to her objections.

I now find and decide as follows.

---

17. [EPTL is the abbreviation for New York's Estates, Powers and Trusts Law. — EDS.]

(A)

(i) The Objections

. . .

What objectants' contentions come down to in the end is succinctly set forth [in their brief]:

> . . . HSBC Bank ("the Bank") acted imprudently in its conduct as Trustee . . . for the period of July 10, 2000, to September 7, 2006. During this period, approximately 60% of the total market value of the Trust consisted of stock in the closely held, family-owned Soper Company ("Soper"). As a closely held, family-owned company, there was virtually no market for Soper stock, and thus, only 40% of the Trust's assets were marketable. But despite holding nearly 60% of the Trust's assets in unmarketable stock, the Bank invested nearly 30% of the Trust's total assets in the stock of just four companies: Pfizer, Merck, Microsoft, and General Electric. The heightened prudence standard imposed on the Bank required further diversification of the non-Soper assets to minimize risk. The Bank's failure to diversify the non-Soper assets was imprudent, and thus, the Bank violated it[s] fiduciary duties causing loss to the Trust of which the Bank should be surcharged.

On July 10, 2000, the trust was valued at approximately $4.6 million, with $2.7 million of the value (approximately 60% of the total trust assets) attributed to the Soper stock. The remaining 40% of the trust assets were held in 25 various stock holdings. The four stocks at issue General Electric, Merck, Microsoft, and Pfizer constituted approximately $1.3 million of the trust value, or approximately 70% of the 40% of the non-Soper stock.

The value of the trust principal, as of September 7, 2006, as listed in the accounting, is $3,772,413.82.

(ii) Law

On January 1, 1995, the Prudent Investor Act [EPTL 11-2.3] became the governing standard for fiduciaries, and it imposes an affirmative duty on a fiduciary "to invest and manage property held in a fiduciary capacity in accordance with the prudent investor standard defined by this section" (EPTL 11-2.3[a]). The standard of conduct under this role is ***not*** defined by "outcome"; rather, compliance "is determined in light of facts and circumstances prevailing at the time of the decision or action of the trustee" (EPTL 11-2.3[b][1]).

The rule expressly requires that a "trustee shall exercise reasonable care, skill and caution to make and implement investment and management decisions as a prudent investor would *for the entire portfolio*, taking into account the purposes and terms and provisions of the governing instrument" (EPTL 11-2.3[b][2], emphasis added). When evaluating a fiduciary's decisions, "it is not sufficient that hindsight might suggest that another course would have been more beneficial; nor does a mere error of investment judgment mandate a surcharge" (Matter of Bank of N.Y., 35 N.Y.2d 512, 519 [1974]).

. . .

Furthermore, HSBC's expert has pointed out *why* "the entire portfolio" has to be taken into consideration:

. . .

"Of particular importance is the [the legislative history's discussion of] 'Modern Portfolio Theory,' where the [Legislative Advisory] Committee states:

> 'According to so-called modern portfolio theory, systematic risk cannot be avoided.[18] The marketplace compensates the buyer only for systematic risk but not for specific risk.[19] This is because specific risk can be eliminated by diversification. For example, a properly diversified portfolio of common stocks will greatly reduce specific risk associated with these securities taken individually. *Indeed, the foundation of modern portfolio theory rests on the mathematically derived conclusion that a security which is itself highly volatile, when combined with one or more other securities to create a portfolio, can actually reduce overall portfolio volatility to levels below those associated with individual securities.* . . .
>
> 'The traditional prudent man rule may not sanction investment strategies based on modern theory. For example, [an evaluation that] focus[es] on each separate investment as prudent or imprudent does not sufficiently recognize *that a prudence standard should be applied to an entire portfolio.* . . .
>
> 'To summarize, the modern prudent investor assesses *total portfolio* return; balances the level of current income with its expected growth relative to inflation; considers the proportions allocated among various categories of assets to assure that the overall portfolio structure is appropriate for the client circumstances; weighs the tax consequences of portfolio changes and makes the trade-offs necessary to improve the portfolio's characteristics going forward on an after-tax basis; sees the portfolio as a whole and diversifies investments to limit specific risks; assesses the acceptable risk and seeks to maximize return at that risk level; and hires professional help where needed.'"

(B) ANALYSIS

It is undisputed, as objectants note, that the trust's main holding was stock in a family-owned, closely held company known as "The Soper Company." When the trust was funded in 1968, it was the understanding of the co-trustees . . . that the trust would hold an overweight position, or concentration, of stock in The Soper Company, in which the Ely family had significant ownership interests. James, Jr., the trust beneficiary did not then, and objectants do not now, urge that retention of the Soper stock was imprudent. Rather, objectants ask this Court to focus solely on the remaining trust assets as if the Soper stock were not a part of the portfolio.

I reject objectants' argument that the actions of HSBC must be examined in isolation from the Soper stock. Neither the statutes nor the case law permit a Court to review a fiduciary's actions and, in that process, ignore a critical aspect of the overall trust strategy and investment decision-making. In determining whether a trustee has met the standard of conduct required by the Prudent Investor Act, the "investment and management decisions" for "the entire portfolio" must be

18. [Systematic risk, sometimes called market risk, refers to the unavoidable possibility of loss associated with investing in the marketplace. The only way to avoid systemic risk is to not invest. — EDS.]

19. [Specific risk is the risk of default or loss of capital for a specific firm. — EDS.]

considered (EPTL 11-2.3[b][2]). The prudent investor standard requires that a trustee must consider:

> "to the extent relevant to the decision or action, the size of the portfolio, the nature and estimated duration of the fiduciary relationship, the liquidity and distribution requirements of the governing instrument, general economic conditions, the possible effect of inflation or deflation, *the expected tax consequences of investment decisions or strategies and of distributions of income and principal, the role that each investment or course of action plays within the overall portfolio*, the expected total return of the portfolio (including both income and appreciation of capital), and the needs of beneficiaries (to the extent reasonably known to the trustee) for present and future distributions authorized or required by the governing instrument" (EPTL 11-2.3[b][3][B]) [emphasis added].

Objectants argue that HSBC should have diversified the stock holdings, other than Soper, because "the market value" of General Electric, Merck, Microsoft, and Pfizer, "caused the market value of all such shares held by the Trust to exceed five percent of the total market value of the assets held in the Trust." However, the decisions related to HSBC's acquisition and/or retention of the General Electric, Merck, Microsoft, and Pfizer stocks cannot be evaluated in a vacuum and without consideration of 60% of the trust assets [represented by the Soper stock].

There is no blanket prohibition to retaining stocks in a concentrated manner, provided the decision to do so was made with "reasonable care, skill and caution" (EPTL 11-2.3[b][2]).

> "Compliance with the prudent investor rule is determined in light of facts and circumstances prevailing at the time of the decision or action of a trustee. A trustee is not liable to a beneficiary to the extent that the trustee acted in substantial compliance with the prudent investor standard or in reasonable reliance on the express terms and provisions of the governing instrument" (EPTL 11-2.3[b][1]).

A trustee need not diversify assets if "*the trustee reasonably determines that it is in the interests of the beneficiaries not to diversify*, taking into account the purposes and terms and provisions of the governing instrument" (EPTL 11-2.3[b][3][c], emphasis added). Our Court of Appeals has held that the prudent investor standard "dictates against any absolute rule that a fiduciary's failure to diversify, in and of itself, constitutes imprudence.". . .

I find that HSBC complied with the prudent investor standards when it determined to retain the General Electric, Merck, Microsoft, and Pfizer stocks. The evidence establishes that these stocks were on HSBC['s] list of approved stocks which could be held in its investment portfolios. The four stocks were selected to comply with trust beneficiary James, Jr.'s direction that the focus of the trust's investments be on long-term growth rather than on current income-generating assets. This strategy was consented to by co-trustee Franklin Ely, and was reflected in the accounting settled by release from James, Jr. in the year 2000. The accounting and the evidence submitted in support of its motion also demonstrate that HSBC complied fully with its internal policies regarding acceptable equity holdings in relation to these four stocks within the entire portfolio.

The trust assets were managed by both a trust administrator and an investment manager, and the trust's performance and investment strategy was reviewed at least annually. When funded in 1968, the trust was valued at $172,618.45, and it grew to over $3.6 million in 2006. And, the 2006 net portfolio value takes into account approximately $1.9 million paid out to James, Jr., in trust distributions, including dividends from the four stocks at issue, during his lifetime. This was hardly an underperforming portfolio.

The General Electric, Merck, Microsoft, and Pfizer stocks all did exceptionally well until the year 2001, when the record reflects that the entire market experienced an overall decline. At that time, the four stocks were reviewed, and it was determined, in light of the goal of long-term growth, that it was appropriate to retain the majority of those stock holdings because, given the overall market decline, it would not have been prudent to sell all of the stocks in a declining market. Further, the trustee also determined that, if substantial stock shares were sold, the trust would have to pay significant capital gains taxes. Even if one were to disagree with the strategy [—] and I express no opinion in that regard — the record demonstrates a thoughtful, well-considered evaluation by the trustee of the portfolio and the stocks it held, and the trustee came to a balanced approach to managing the assets under all the circumstances.

I find that HSBC has established its entitlement to judgment as a matter of law, and I further find that objectants have failed to raise any issues of material fact that HSBC violated its fiduciary duty in any way in carrying out its management of the trust assets.

Accordingly, I hereby grant HSBC's motion in its entirety, and dismiss all objections to the amended accounting, and I hereby deny objectants' cross-motion. Finally, I direct that HSBC shall file a proposed decree for judicial settlement of its account within 30 days from the date hereof.

QUESTIONS

8. There are differing views about how much diversification is necessary to achieve the benefits of portfolio investing, but most would agree that a portfolio allocating 60 percent to a single investment is not diversified. Why, then, didn't the trust beneficiaries object to the trustees' 60 percent allocation of trust assets to Soper stock?

   ANSWER. The Uniform Prudent Investor Act imposes upon trustees an affirmative duty to diversify trust assets (and to do so within a reasonable time after accepting the trusteeship) "unless the trustee reasonably determines that, because of special circumstances, the purposes of the trust are better served without diversifying." UPIA §3. Here, the Soper stock represented the Ely family's significant ownership interest in a closely held family business. Because Soper stock was not publicly traded, the trustees might not have been able to realize the true value of the stock by selling it in a private placement. Thus, the Soper stock and any income it generated might have been more valuable if retained by the trust than if sold for the purpose of diversification. Given that the shares of Soper stock were part of the trust corpus at inception in 1968, the settlor appears to have consented to the trust's high concentration of this single investment. These considerations would support the trustees' decision to retain Soper stock notwithstanding the general affirmative duty to diversify trust assets.

9. Suppose you were appointed as the new trustee of the Ely trust. Assuming all of the trust assets could be sold at a loss for tax purposes, how, if at all, would you change the allocation of trust investments and why?

   ANSWER. Setting aside the high concentration of Soper stock, which should probably be left in place (see above), the allocation of more than 5 percent of trust assets to each of four single stocks, Merck, Pfizer, General Electric, and Microsoft, may not provide enough diversification to realize the benefits of portfolio investing. Furthermore, this particular selection of stocks contains a high concentration in a single industry: Merck and Pfizer are both pharmaceutical companies exposed to similar risks affecting all manufacturers of prescription drugs (e.g., possibility of government price controls, structural changes in the health insurance industry, which typically purchases prescription drugs on behalf of patients, costs of complying with product safety regulations, possibility of the government imposing more rigorous drug approval processes and standards). If the investment objective for this trust is focused on long-term growth, a low-fee no-load growth stock mutual fund might provide better higher returns and better diversification.

10. The objections in this case relate to an accounting period beginning on July 10, 2000 and ending on September 7, 2006. In July 2000, the stock market was near the peak of all-time record highs generated by the "dot com" bubble. Global stock markets crashed in 2001 and had recovered partially by September 2006. Could the trustees have avoided the unrealized losses sustained by the trust through better diversified portfolio of stocks?

    ANSWER. Probably not. The steep losses sustained by most, if not all, investments following the "dot com" crash reflect systematic risk that cannot be avoided other than by not investing in the stock market at all. Thus, a well-diversified portfolio of stocks most likely would have sustained similar losses during this period because the market crash affected stocks as an asset class. The trustees could have preserved capital by investing in government bonds, which did not default as a result of the "dot com" crash, but the beneficiary directed the trustees to adopt an investment strategy of long-term capital appreciation that could not be achieved with fixed income investments.

PROBLEM III

A. Walter is a wealthy attorney who maintains a moderately successful law practice, but the bulk of his vast fortune came from profitable investments in the stock market. Walter started investing twenty-five years ago when, as a junior in college, he received a small inheritance. Walter majored in finance, so he used the techniques he learned in school to select a portfolio of three stocks that went on to generate annual returns of 35 percent over the last twenty-five years. These returns far outperformed the stock market as a whole and made Walter very rich. Recently, as part of his law practice, Walter accepted the trusteeship of a testamentary trust settled by one of his firm's estate planning clients. Upon taking control of the trust assets, Walter invests the corpus in the three stocks he chose for his own investments twenty-five years ago. Has Walter satisfied his fiduciary duties concerning the investment of trust assets?

B. Sandra is one of the original employees of Tesla Motors. As part of her compensation package, Sandra received 3,000 shares of Tesla in 2010, when the company completed its initial public offering and began trading shares on the Nasdaq stock exchange. On the date of Tesla's IPO, shares were valued at $20/share, so Sandra's stake in Tesla was worth $60,000 at that time. Since its IPO, the value of Tesla shares has increased ten-fold; the stock now trades for $200/share. Sandra decides to place her Tesla stock in an irrevocable trust for the benefit of her children and appoints Walter (see Question A, above) as trustee. Upon assuming control as trustee, should Walter diversify the trust corpus?

11.4 SUBSIDIARY DUTIES

The fiduciary duties of loyalty and prudence are core fundamental principles of trusteeship, but trust law regulates other aspects of trust administration by imposing an array of subsidiary duties. In this section, we will focus on two subsidiary duties in particular: the duty of impartiality and the duty to inform and report.

Other subsidiary duties require the trustee to (1) control, collect, and protect trust property, UTC §§809, 812; (2) maintain adequate records of trust administration, UTC §810; (3) maintain trust property separately from the trustee's personal property, UTC §§802, 810(b); and (4) enforce claims belonging to the trust and defend claims against the trust, UTC §811.

11.4.1 Impartiality

The duty of impartiality applies to trusts with multiple beneficiaries and prohibits the trustee from improperly favoring some beneficiaries at the expense of others. The duty of impartiality is a default rule and does not require that all beneficiaries receive equal treatment. Thus, the settlor may expressly instruct the trustee to prioritize the interests of certain beneficiaries over others or structure the trust in a manner that provides an unequal distribution of trust benefits. The duty of impartiality simply requires that the trustee act impartially and give due regard to the interests of each beneficiary as those interests are defined in the trust.

Uniform Trust Code
§803 Impartiality

If a trust has two or more beneficiaries, the trustee shall act impartially in investing, managing, and distributing the trust property, giving due regard to the beneficiaries' respective interests.

Restatement (Third) of Trusts
§79 Duty of Impartiality; Income Productivity

(1) A trustee has a duty to administer the trust in a manner that is impartial with respect to the various beneficiaries of the trust, requiring that:

(a) in investing, protecting, and distributing the trust estate, and in other administrative functions, the trustee must act impartially and with due regard for the diverse beneficial interests created by the terms of the trust; and

(b) in consulting and otherwise communicating with beneficiaries, the trustee must proceed in a manner that fairly reflects the diversity of their concerns and beneficial interests.

(2) If a trust is created for two or more beneficiaries or purposes in succession and if the rights of any beneficiary or the expenditures for a charitable purpose are defined with reference to trust income, the trustee's duty of impartiality includes a duty to so invest and administer the trust, or to so account for principal and income, that the trust estate will produce income that is reasonably appropriate to the purposes of the trust and to the diverse present and future interests of its beneficiaries.

Sometimes, a trust may selectively appoint one or more beneficiaries to serve as trustee without extending the trusteeship to all beneficiaries. For example, a settlor who creates a trust for the lifetime benefit of his or her surviving spouse, with the remainder to the settlor's children, might appoint the surviving spouse as trustee but not the children. The duty of loyalty generally forbids a trustee from making personal use of trust property, but not so when the trustee is also a beneficiary. The prohibition on self-dealing does not apply because the conflict of interest is a structural one created and implicitly authorized by the settlor. Thus, to the extent permitted by the trust, the trustee may distribute trust property to herself as a beneficiary and, indeed, may favor her own interests over those of other beneficiaries. In this context, the trustee's conduct is regulated by the duty of impartiality rather than the duty of loyalty.

The duty of impartiality is frequently implicated by trusts with successive beneficial interests, such as a lifetime income interest followed by a remainder interest. Beneficiaries of income and remainder interests are often in conflict on the issue of how to invest the trust assets. For example, settlors often name their spouse as income beneficiaries, followed by their children as remainder beneficiaries. In second marriages, where the spouse's children are not also the settlor's children, this arrangement can exacerbate existing conflict in the blended family.

Under the Uniform Principal and Income Act, the character of receipts determines whether property received by the trustee is allocated to income or principal. UPIA §401 (Character of Receipts). Receipts allocated to income include money received from bond interest payments, cash dividends, rents, and royalties. Receipts allocated to principal include proceeds from the sale of trust assets, including assets that appreciate in value. Income beneficiaries therefore prefer investments that generate the maximum amount of income, such as bonds and high-dividend stocks, even though income-producing assets typically do not appreciate in value in the long term. By contrast, remainder beneficiaries prefer investments that cause the principal to appreciate in value over the long term, such as growth stocks, even though such assets typically do not generate income in the form of dividends or coupon payments.

The duty of impartiality generally prohibits the trustee from managing trust investments in a manner that favors one class of beneficiaries over another unless the trust provides otherwise. However, the traditional standards of prudent trust investment favored income beneficiaries by prescribing legal lists and a liability safe harbor for presumptively "safe" assets that preserve capital and generate moderate income but typically do not appreciate in value over time. By contrast, the UPIA's prudent investor standard, which incorporates Modern Portfolio Theory, allows the trustee to invest in a diversified portfolio of assets that include a mixture of income and growth investments.

The UPIA's prudent investor standard and diversification rules enable the trustee to balance the portfolio of trust investments impartially between income and remainder interests. But a portfolio selection influenced by the character of receipts generated by each individual asset as income or principal can undermine the more important goal of maximizing overall portfolio returns. UPIA §104 solves this problem by granting the trustee power to adjust the allocation of trust assets between income and principal:

> The purpose of Section 104 is to enable a trustee to select investments using the standards of a prudent investor without having to realize a particular portion of the portfolio's total return in the form of traditional trust accounting income such as interest, dividends, and rents. Section 104(a) authorizes a trustee to make adjustments between principal and income if three conditions are met: (1) the trustee must be managing the trust assets under the prudent investor rule; (2) the terms of the trust must express the income beneficiary's distribution rights in terms of the right to receive "income" in the sense of traditional trust accounting income; and (3) the trustee must determine, after applying the rules in Section 103(a) [general principles governing allocation of receipts and disbursements], that he is unable to comply with Section 103(b) [duty of impartiality]. In deciding whether and to what extent to exercise the power to adjust, the trustee is required to consider the factors described in Section 104(b), but the trustee may not make an adjustment in circumstances described in Section 104(c).

UPIA §104, comment.

To prevent abuse of the adjustment power, the trustee is prohibited from adjusting between income and principal when the trustee is also a beneficiary of the trust or would benefit directly or indirectly from the adjustment.[20]

11.4.2 Duty to Inform and Report

The duty to inform and report requires trustees to furnish beneficiaries with all material information necessary to protect their interests in the trust and enforce

20. UPIA §104(c)(7)-(8). Subsection c enumerates a total of eight circumstances in which a trustee is prohibited from invoking the adjustment power.

the other fiduciary duties of trusteeship. Material information includes the existence of the beneficiary's interest in the trust, a copy of the trust instrument, the trustees' appointment and contact information, the trustees' method for determining their compensation, and an annual report summarizing the cash flow and balance sheet of the trust.

Uniform Trust Code
§813 Duty to Inform and Report

(a) A trustee shall keep the qualified beneficiaries of the trust reasonably informed about the administration of the trust and of the material facts necessary for them to protect their interests. Unless unreasonable under the circumstances, a trustee shall promptly respond to a beneficiary's request for information related to the administration of the trust.

(b) A trustee:

(1) upon request of a beneficiary, shall promptly furnish to the beneficiary a copy of the trust instrument;

(2) within 60 days after accepting a trusteeship, shall notify the qualified beneficiaries of the acceptance and of the trustee's name, address, and telephone number;

(3) within 60 days after the date the trustee acquires knowledge of the creation of an irrevocable trust, or the date the trustee acquires knowledge that a formerly revocable trust has become irrevocable, whether by the death of the settlor or otherwise, shall notify the qualified beneficiaries of the trust's existence, of the identity of the settlor or settlors, of the right to request a copy of the trust instrument, and of the right to a trustee's report as provided in subsection (c); and

(4) shall notify the qualified beneficiaries in advance of any change in the method or rate of the trustee's compensation.

(c) A trustee shall send to the distributees or permissible distributees of trust income or principal, and to other qualified or nonqualified beneficiaries who request it, at least annually and at the termination of the trust, a report of the trust property, liabilities, receipts, and disbursements, including the source and amount of the trustee's compensation, a listing of the trust assets and, if feasible, their respective market values. Upon a vacancy in a trusteeship, unless a cotrustee remains in office, a report must be sent to the qualified beneficiaries by the former trustee. A personal representative, [conservator], or [guardian] may send the qualified beneficiaries a report on behalf of a deceased or incapacitated trustee.

(d) A beneficiary may waive the right to a trustee's report or other information otherwise required to be furnished under this section. A beneficiary, with respect to future reports and other information, may withdraw a waiver previously given. . . .

The settlor may waive or modify the duty to inform and report. The Uniform Trust Code initially limited the settlor's ability to waive the affirmative notice requirements for beneficiaries ages 25 and older, UTC §§105(b)(8); 813(b)(2)-(3), in response "to the desire of some settlors that younger beneficiaries not know of the trust's bounty until they have reached an age of maturity and self-sufficiency." UTC §105, comment. The Code also initially prohibited the settlor from waiving the trustee's obligation under §813(a) to furnish a copy of the trust instrument upon the beneficiary's request. UTC §105(b)(9). In 2004, however, the Uniform Law Commissioners designated both waiver restrictions as optional provisions. Thus, in some UTC states, a settlor may entirely waive the beneficiary's right to information about the existence and administration of the trust so long as some party, such as a trust protector, has standing to enforce the fiduciary duties.

11.5 REMEDIES FOR BREACH AND EXCULPATORY CLAUSES

Trust law provides a variety of remedies for a trustee's breach of fiduciary duty. The range of available remedies includes a court order to file an accounting, an injunction against committing a breach of trust, suspension or removal of the trustee, denial of trustee compensation, imposition of a constructive trust on property wrongfully transferred from the trust, and monetary damages for which the trustee is personally liable. UTC §1001. Monetary damages assessed against a trustee for breach of trust, often referred to as a "surcharge," are "the greater of: (1) the amount required to restore the value of the trust property and trust distributions to what they would have been had the breach not occurred; or (2) the profit the trustee made by reason of the breach." UTC §1002(a).

A settlor may opt out of the default rule imposing personal liability on the trustee for damages arising from a breach of trust. An exculpatory clause relieving the trustee of personal liability is enforceable unless the trustee has acted recklessly or in bad faith, or the trustee abused her relationship with the settlor in seeking inclusion of the exculpatory provision. These limitations on the enforcement of exculpatory clauses prevent trustees from profiting from an unconscionable abuse of the settlor's reliance and trust. Professor David Horton explains:

> Exculpatory clauses became common in the early twentieth century, as trust companies emerged and the nature of the trust shifted from a mechanism for the conveyance of land to one for holding and investing financial assets. Corporate trustees began to draft instruments or refer the settlor to a law firm that would do so, and trusts began to feature terms that exonerated the trustee from liability for poor decisions. At first, courts were unsure how to treat an exculpatory term in instruments that the trustee or its associates had drafted. The Restatement of Trusts set forth six factors for courts to gauge the validity of such a provision:
>
> > (1) whether the trustee prior to the creation of the trust had been in a fiduciary relationship to the settlor, as where the trustee had been guardian of the settlor; (2) whether the trust instrument was drawn by the trustee or by a person acting wholly or partially on his behalf; (3) whether the settlor has taken independent advice as to the provisions of the trust instrument; (4) whether the settlor is a person of experience and judgment or is a person who is unfamiliar with business affairs or is not a person of

> much judgment or understanding; (5) whether the insertion of the provision was due to undue influence or other improper conduct on the part of the trustee; (6) the extent and reasonableness of the provision.

For example, in *Rutanen v. Ballard*, the Massachusetts Supreme Judicial Court voided [an exculpatory] clause, reasoning that "the settlor received no independent advice, . . . was seventy years old, had had a stroke and was 'in questionable health.'" Conversely, in *Americans for the Arts v. Ruth Lilly Charitable Remainder Annuity Trust*, an Indiana appellate court rejected the claim that an exculpatory clause was invalid because the trustee had "buried" it in the instrument:

> No party was naïve, unrepresented, or taken advantage of in this situation. Moreover, paragraph 10(b) is neither buried nor misleadingly labeled. Indeed, it takes up one-half of one page in a ten-page document. The language is signaled with a double-spaced lead-in indicating that the provisions to follow encompass all of the powers and rights of the trustee in administering the document.

David Horton, Unconscionability in the Law of Trusts, 84 Notre Dame L. Rev. 1675, 1728-29 (2009).

Uniform Trust Code
§1008 Exculpation of Trustee

(a) A term of a trust relieving a trustee of liability for breach of trust is unenforceable to the extent that it:

(1) relieves the trustee of liability for breach of trust committed in bad faith or with reckless indifference to the purposes of the trust or the interests of the beneficiaries; or

(2) was inserted as the result of an abuse by the trustee of a fiduciary or confidential relationship to the settlor.

(b) An exculpatory term drafted or caused to be drafted by the trustee is invalid as an abuse of a fiduciary or confidential relationship unless the trustee proves that the exculpatory term is fair under the circumstances and that its existence and contents were adequately communicated to the settlor.

12 | Federal Transfer Taxes: An Introduction

By Jay A. Soled

12.1 INTRODUCTION

Welcome to the world of the federal transfer tax system. Often bemoaned by taxpayers and practitioners alike, this regime has important implications for how wills are crafted, trusts are arranged, and estates are administered. Accordingly, it is important that trusts and estates students have a basic understanding of the gift tax, estate tax, and generation-skipping transfer tax.

Students who never had any affinity for numbers or the federal income tax, fear not. The numerical operations this chapter presents are rudimentary and, as a practical matter, never go beyond simple arithmetic. Also, the transfer tax system bears virtually no resemblance to the income tax; the former explores overall wealth accumulation and disposition, and the latter involves an examination of annual wealth accretions. Thus, knowledge of the federal income tax is not a prerequisite for understanding federal transfer taxes.

But the journey to transfer tax comprehension is not easy. To simplify the task, we have segmented the journey into manageable steps. If you stumble along the way, retrace your steps and regain your footing. At the journey's end, while we cannot promise the proverbial pot of gold, we can instead offer something far better and longer-lasting: knowledge that we hope will well serve you and, by extension, your clients. So, let's get started.

Maps are useful for any journey and this one is no exception. Our first map presents a high level view: a basic introduction to the federal transfer tax system. We will then zoom in for a closer look at the three taxes that constitute the pillars of the federal transfer tax system: (1) the gift tax, (2) the estate tax, and (3) the generation-skipping transfer tax (GST tax). We will describe the fundamentals of each tax and then explore common tax-minimization strategies that have received tacit congressional approval or explicit judicial endorsement. Our discussion of these tax-planning strategies will introduce some of the basic techniques used in contemporary estate planning practice.

12.2 THE BASICS OF FEDERAL WEALTH TRANSFER TAXATION

The federal transfer taxes are imposed on the privilege of transferring property during lifetime or at death. In addition to the traditional goal of generating tax revenue for the federal government, a fundamental policy underlying the federal wealth transfer tax system is to curtail the political and commercial power associated with family dynasties that would otherwise pass down wealth from one generation to the next. The estate tax, which taxes the transfer of property at death, was the first of the three federal transfer taxes enacted by Congress in 1916. Professor James Repetti explains the policy rationale:

> President Theodore Roosevelt proposed an estate tax in 1906 to prevent "the owner of one of these enormous fortunes to hand more than [a] certain amount to any one individual." One major concern about dynastic wealth was its impact on democracy. In 1916, the economist Irving Fisher favored the adoption of an estate tax to help curb the "danger of an hereditary plutocracy" to "democratic ideals." In 1935, President Franklin D. Roosevelt proposed expanding transfer taxes because he felt that large accumulations of wealth "amount to the perpetuation of great and undesirable concentration of control in a relatively few individuals over the employment and welfare of many, many others."

James R. Repetti, Should We Tax the Gratuitous Transfer of Wealth? An Introduction, 57 B.C. L. Rev. 815, 816 (2016).

The history of the gift tax begins in 1924, when Congress decided that it was a necessary complement to the existing estate tax, which had been in place since 1916. Without a gift tax, taxpayers could circumvent the estate tax by making lifetime transfers because the estate tax applied only to transfers at death. When first instituted, the gift tax and estate tax operated as two, separate tax regimes, with their own tax rates and exemptions. In 1976, recognizing that both taxes share a common policy goal, namely, the curtailment of family-wealth dynasties, Congress combined the gift and estate tax regimes, thereby instituting the unified gift and estate tax system in place today.

Unification of the gift and estate taxes is reflected principally in two ways. First, the gift and estate tax rates are unified, meaning that they impose identical rates of taxation. As of 2017, the unified rate is 40 percent. Second, the gift and estate taxes are imposed cumulatively on wealth transfers, such that lifetime transfers subject to the gift tax are taken into account when computing transfers at death subject to the estate tax. The mechanism for this cumulative computation is the "unified credit," which gives each taxpayer a set dollar-for-dollar reduction against tax liability for wealth transfers subject to either the gift tax or estate tax. In 2017, the unified credit amount was $2,141,800, which had the effect of exempting $5,490,000 from gift or estate tax liability. Put another way, in 2017, individuals could make tax-free lifetime or testamentary transfers totaling $5,490,000. Cumulative transfers in excess of this amount, unless covered by another deduction or exemption provision, are subject to a 40 percent gift or estate tax. Additionally, since 1981, married individuals may make unlimited tax-free transfers during life or at death to their spouse.

In 1976, Congress imposed a new GST tax as an additional tax on the transfer of property to individuals two or more generations younger than the transferor (e.g., the transferor's grandchildren). The purpose of the GST tax was to close loopholes that sometimes prevented wealth from being taxed at each generation.

Federal transfer taxes are to be distinguished from "inheritance" taxes, which are imposed on the privilege of *receiving* property from a decedent. Still in effect in six states (Iowa, Kentucky, Maryland, Nebraska, New Jersey, and Pennsylvania), inheritance taxes are progressive, with lower tax rates applied to individuals more closely related to the decedent (e.g., siblings compared to first cousins). Fifteen states and the District of Columbia impose a state-level estate tax.

"Death taxes," a term coined for political purposes, has no legal definition: It may refer to an estate tax, to an inheritance tax, or to both.

12.3 GIFT TAX

The gift tax is generally imposed on the gratuitous transfer of property during the donor's lifetime.

12.3.1 What Is a "Taxable Gift"?

Anything of value that a taxpayer transfers to another person or entity, absent adequate consideration, is potentially subject to the federal gift tax. Code §2511 provides that the gift tax applies broadly "whether the transfer is in trust or otherwise, whether the gift is direct or indirect, and whether the property is real or personal, tangible or intangible. . . ." Some gifts are obvious (e.g., a graduation present); others are less so (e.g., forgiving a loan made to one's child). The Treasury Regulations state that donative intent is "not an essential element in the application of the gift tax to the transfer." Treas. Reg. §25.2511-1(g)(1).[1] Thus, in forgiving a loan to one's child, the intent may be to alleviate a financial burden rather than to make a gift. Nevertheless, forgiving the loan constitutes a taxable gift because, in the example above, the father gratuitously relinquished an interest in property: his legal claim against the child for repayment of the loan. As the Treasury Regulation explains:

> Transfers reached by the gift tax are not confined to those only which, being without a valuable consideration, accord with the common law concept of gifts, but embrace as well sales, exchanges, and other dispositions of property for a consideration to the extent that the value of the property transferred by the donor exceeds the value in money or money's worth of the consideration given therefor.

Treas. Reg. §25.2512-8.

---

1. By contrast, recall the discussion above in Chapter 8: Under the common law and the Restatement (Third) of Property: Wills & Other Donative Transfers, a finding of donative intent is essential for determining whether a donor has made a gift: "To be a gift, a transfer must be made with donative intent. The requirement of donative intent is the essence of a gift." Restatement §6.1, comment b.

Aside from an actual transfer of property, there is another avenue through which a taxpayer can generate a taxable gift: the exercise or release of a *general* power of appointment. The Code defines *general power of appointment* as a power that its possessor can exercise "in favor of the individual possessing the power . . . , his estate, his creditors, or the creditors of his estate." 26 U.S.C. §2514(c). All other powers are known as special powers of appointment, the exercise of which does not give rise to gift tax exposure.[2] Congress treats the broad latitude held by the possessor of a *general* power of appointment as tantamount to outright ownership of the property subject to the power. In contrast, the more restrictive right held by the possessor of a *special* power of appointment falls short of outright ownership, so the exercise of a special power of appointment is not considered a taxable gift under the Code.

Illustrated below are examples of general and special powers of appointment, commonplace in trust instruments.

Sample General Power of Appointment

LIFETIME GENERAL POWER OF APPOINTMENT. During the lifetime of a child of mine for whom a trust was established pursuant to this Paragraph, any such child may, in his or her absolute discretion, pursuant to an instrument in writing delivered to my Trustee acknowledged in the same manner as is then required to record deeds of real estate in the State of New Jersey, appoint all or any part of the then remaining principal and undistributed income of his or her trust established pursuant to this Paragraph to or **for the benefit of himself or herself, his or her estate, his or her creditors, or the creditors of his or her estate**, in such portions or amounts, and upon such estates, whether in trust or otherwise, as he or she may, appoint to receive same, and, if so appointed, my Trustee shall pay over, transfer, and distribute such property to or for the beneficiary's benefit, as so appointed by such child of mine. (Emphasis added.)

In the example above, the settlor's children hold general powers of appointment because they have the power to appoint principal and undistributed income to themselves, their creditors, their estate, or creditors of their estate. By exercising this power to appoint property from the trust, a child will make a taxable gift.[3]

Sample Special Power of Appointment (Limited in Scope to Donee's Issue)

LIFETIME SPECIAL POWER OF APPOINTMENT. During the lifetime of a child of mine for whom a trust was established pursuant to this Paragraph, any such child may, in his or her absolute discretion, pursuant to an instrument in writing delivered to my Trustee acknowledged in the same manner as is then required to record deeds of real estate in the State of New Jersey, appoint all or any part of the then remaining principal and undistributed income of his or her

2. See the discussion of powers of appointment in Chapter 5.

3. If the trust beneficiary dies without having exercised the power, the trust property will nevertheless be included in the trust beneficiary's taxable estate. 26 U.S.C. §2041(a)(2).

trust established pursuant to this Paragraph to or **for the benefit of his or her issue**, and, if so appointed, my Trustee shall pay over, transfer, and distribute such property to or for the benefit of the issue of such child of mine, as so appointed by such child of mine. (Emphasis added.)

In the example above, the settlor's children hold special powers of appointment because their power to appoint principal and undistributed income is limited to their issue. By exercising this special power which is limited in scope, beneficiary child will not make a taxable gift.[4]

Example of Special Power of Appointment (Broad in Scope)

LIFETIME SPECIAL POWER OF APPOINTMENT. During the lifetime of a child of mine for whom a trust was established pursuant to this Paragraph, any such child may, in his or her absolute discretion, pursuant to an instrument in writing delivered to my Trustee acknowledged in the same manner as is then required to record deeds of real estate in the State of New Jersey, appoint all or any part of the then remaining principal and undistributed income of his or her trust established pursuant to this Paragraph to or **for the benefit of anyone other than himself or herself, his or her estate, his or her creditors, or the creditors of his or her estate**, and, if so appointed, my Trustee shall pay over, transfer, and distribute such property to or for the benefit of the aforesaid beneficiary(ies), as so appointed by such child of mine. (Emphasis added.)

In the example above, the settlor's children hold special powers of appointment because their power to appoint principal and undistributed income is limited to anyone *other than* themselves, their estate, their creditors, or the creditors of their estate, making this power of appointment a special one. By exercising this special power, which is broad in scope, the child will not make a taxable gift.[5]

12.3.2 Valuation of a Gift

Once a transfer is identified as taxable, the taxpayer must determine the transferred property's value as of the date of the gift. Code §2512. The Treasury Regulations define the term *value* to mean "the price at which the property would change hands between a willing buyer and a willing seller, neither being under any compulsion to buy or to sell, and both having reasonable knowledge of relevant facts." Treas. Reg. §25.2512-1. Sometimes determining the value of a gift is straightforward (e.g., a $1 million cash gift); other times, valuation requires a more sophisticated appraisal (e.g., a gift of a

4. If the trust beneficiary dies without having exercised the power, because the power is limited in nature (i.e., not a general power), the trust property is not included in the beneficiary's taxable estate. 26 U.S.C. §2041(b)(1)(A).

5. If the trust beneficiary dies without exercising this power of appointment, because the power is limited in nature (i.e., it remains a special power of appointment despite its broad breadth), the trust property is nevertheless not includable in the beneficiary's estate. 26 U.S.C. §2041(b)(1)(A).

minority interest in a closely held business).[6] Gifts of tangible personal property such as works of art also raise complex valuation issues. To minimize transfer tax liability, which is based on the value of property transferred, taxpayers often attempt to understate the value of the property for gift tax purposes, but overstate the value for purposes of a charitable gift, estate, or income tax deduction.[7]

12.3.3 Deductions and Exclusions

Once a transfer is identified as a taxable gift and its value determined, the next question is whether the transfer qualifies for a gift tax deduction or is excluded from the gift tax base altogether. Elaborated below are the most commonly used gift tax deductions, namely, (1) the marital deduction and (2) the charitable deduction, and gift tax exclusions, namely, (3) the annual exclusion and (4) medical and educational exclusions.

12.3.3.1 The Marital Deduction

Gifts passing outright to a spouse generally qualify for the unlimited gift tax marital deduction. Code §2523(a). The policy underlying the unlimited marital deduction reflects Congress's treatment of a married couple as a single economic unit.[8] Therefore, if a wife transfers $1 million to her husband, she has made a gift that would be valued for gift tax purposes at $1 million; but the Code provides a marital deduction of an equivalent dollar amount, and thus no gift tax would be due or owing. Assuming the donee spouse (here, the husband) subsequently dies owning the gifted property, the property would be included in his estate for estate tax purposes when passing to his beneficiaries. Thus, the integrity of the transfer tax system is preserved because the property is taxed upon its transfer to persons outside the marriage. It does not matter that the husband might consume the gift, say, on lavish vacations, and thereby prevent its inclusion in his estate at death because the wife could have presumably consumed the property as well without making a taxable transfer.

Not all transfers between spouses qualify for the gift tax deduction, however. More specifically, transfers between spouses will generally not qualify for the gift tax marital deduction in those instances when, upon the death of the surviving spouse, the property will pass to a third party without being subject to the estate tax. For example, a gift of a

---

6. Over the last several decades, the Tax Court's docket has been beset with IRS challenges of taxpayers who, in attempts to reduce their gift tax liability, have taken aggressive marketability and minority valuation discounts with respect to closely held business interests. Sometimes the IRS has prevailed, and the valuation discounts have been disallowed (e.g., Estate of Murphy v. Commissioner, T.C. Memo. 1992-472 (1992) (minority discount disallowed for transfer made eighteen days before the decedent's death for the sole purpose of securing a valuation discount)); other times taxpayers have prevailed and secured steep valuation discounts (e.g., Estate of Bailey v. Commissioner, T.C. Memo. 2002-152 (2002) (Tax Court sanctioning a 50 percent combined minority and marketability discount)). The IRS has promulgated proposed Treasury Regulations that seek to eliminate minority discounts (e.g., Treas. Reg. §25.2704); whether these proposed regulations are adopted and will withstand judicial scrutiny remain open issues.

7. To constrain taxpayer abuse in this area, the Code requires that taxpayers secure a "qualified appraisal" for any charitable gift of more than $5,000 that does not consist of easily valued assets such as cash and marketable securities. Code §170(f)(11)(C).

8. For discussion of the partnership theory of marriage, see Chapter 7.

terminable interest, that is, an interest that lapses after a certain length of time or event (such as remarriage), does *not* qualify for the gift tax marital deduction because the estate tax does not capture terminable interests. Denial of the gift tax marital deduction is thus appropriate to prevent married individuals from circumventing their transfer tax obligations. For example, suppose a wife places $10 million in trust for the benefit of her husband and, after the earlier of ten years or his death, the trust property to pass to the couple's children. This transfer creates a terminable interest because the husband's trust terminates upon the earlier of ten years or his death. If the husband does, in fact, die during this term, two things happen: first, the trust property would pass to the couple's children, and second, because the husband could not dictate the disposition of the trust property (i.e., he lacked direct or indirect indicia of control), it would not be included in the husband's taxable estate. Congress, therefore, decided that the initial transfer (namely, the terminable interest gift to the husband) should not qualify for the gift tax marital deduction. Code §2523(b).

There is an important and commonly utilized exception to the rule disallowing the marital deduction for terminal interests. The donor spouse can elect to treat an intra-marital gift of a life estate as "qualified" terminable interest property (QTIP), and, therefore, deductible under the gift tax marital deduction. Code §2523(f). To do so, the donor spouse must be the transferor and "the donee spouse [must have] a qualifying income interest for life." Code §2523(f)(2). The surviving donee spouse has a qualifying income interest if he or she is entitled to all income from the property and "no person has a power to appoint any part of the property to any person other than the surviving spouse." Code §2056(b)(7)(B). If these conditions are met, assuming the donor spouse wishes the transfer to qualify for the unlimited gift tax marital deduction, the donor must then make a QTIP election on his gift tax return. This election enables the donor spouse to qualify for the unlimited marital gift tax deduction while providing a lifetime source of income in trust for the donee spouse and, upon the donee spouse's death, to control the disposition of the remaining trust corpus. The quid pro quo of this arrangement is that if the donee spouse makes an inter vivos transfer of her qualifying income interest, that transfer results in a taxable gift payable by the donee spouse. Code §2519. Alternatively, if the donee spouse dies as a beneficiary of the interest, the balance of the original transfer is includable in her gross estate for estate tax purposes.[9] Code §2044.

The advantage of a QTIP arrangement can be readily summed up in two words: tax deferral. Upon transfer, no immediate transfer tax is paid, with one only being levied upon the surviving spouse's demise.[10]

---

9. In addition, there is an infrequently utilized exception to the terminable interest rule under Code §2523(e), which permits a spouse to transfer to another spouse a life estate (another form of a terminable interest) and still have it qualify for the gift tax marital deduction. As a quid pro quo for permitting this deduction, Congress requires that the donee spouse have either a lifetime or testamentary general power to transfer the trust property to whomever she wishes. By instituting this requirement, in the hands of the transferee spouse, the value of the trust property remains part of the transfer tax base.

10. The downside is borne by the donee spouse, who assumes the burden of all federal transfer taxes (i.e., taxable gift treatment for transfers of QTIP property during life and gross estate inclusion of the QTIP property balance at death) and may lack control over disposition of the remaining corpus at death.

The following provides an example of the salient provisions of a lifetime QTIP trust:

> **ADMINISTRATION OF TRUST A.** Any property passing into TRUST A shall be administered by my Trustee (hereinafter named in Article 7 of this Will) in accordance with the following terms and conditions:
>
> **(i) PAYMENT OF INCOME.** During the life of my spouse, **ELAINE**, my Trustee shall pay to or apply for the benefit of my spouse all of the net income of TRUST A, in convenient installments, but not less frequently than quarter-annually.
>
> **(ii) PAYMENT OF PRINCIPAL.** During the life of my spouse, **ELAINE**, my Trustee shall pay to or apply for the benefit of my spouse such amounts from the principal of TRUST A as my Trustee deems necessary or desirable for the health, education, support, and maintenance of my spouse.
>
> **(iii) TERMINATION OF TRUST A.**
>
> **(a) Distribution of Income and Principal.** Upon the death of my spouse, **ELAINE**, any accrued and undistributed income of TRUST A and any part of the principal of TRUST A remaining upon the death of my spouse shall be distributed to my then living issue, *per stirpes*.
>
> **(b) Taxes Attributable to QTIP Property.** Prior to the termination of TRUST A, my Trustee shall pay, either directly to the appropriate taxing authority or to the executors or personal representatives of the estate of my spouse, as my Trustee deems advisable, the amount requested and certified by such executors or personal representatives as being equal to the amount by which the estate and inheritance taxes assessed by reason of the death of my spouse are increased as a result of the inclusion of the principal and undistributed income of TRUST A in the estate of my spouse for such tax purposes.

The settlor's creation of the above inter vivos trust for the lifetime benefit of his wife, Elaine, qualifies for the unlimited gift tax marital deduction because the settlor/transferor is Elaine's spouse and Elaine has a qualifying income for life ("my Trustee shall pay to or apply for the benefit of my spouse all of the net income of TRUST A, in convenient installments, but not less frequently than quarter-annually"). However, a gift tax would be imposed on transfers (if any) by Elaine of her QTIP income interest during life and, upon Elaine's death, any remaining principal will be includable in her estate for estate tax purposes before passing to the settlor's living issue, per stirpes. By directing the trustee to pay any associated estate and inheritance taxes attributable to the inclusion of the QTIP property in Elaine's estate, it mitigates Elaine's ultimate estate tax burden.

12.3.3.2 The Gift Tax Charitable Deduction

The value of any gift passing to either a public enterprise (e.g., federal or state government) "for exclusively public purposes" or an organization "organized and operated exclusively for religious, charitable, scientific, literary, or educational purposes, or to foster national or international amateur sports competition" (Code §501(c)(3)) will qualify for the unlimited gift tax charitable deduction. Code §2522(a). Therefore, if a taxpayer makes a gift to his or her city government to support the refurbishment of a public park, makes a contribution to the American Red Cross, or gifts a work of art to a nonprofit art museum, those gifts qualify for the gift tax charitable deduction, meaning that no gift tax liability arises from the making of the gift.

12.3.3.3 The Annual Exclusion

To "obviate the necessity of keeping an account of and reporting numerous small gifts," Congress enacted the annual gift tax exclusion, Code §2503(b), which allows taxpayers to make gifts of relatively small value that are excluded from the gift tax base. S. Rep. No. 665, 72d Cong., 1st Sess. (1932), reprinted in 1931-1 (Part 2) C.B. 496, 525. The value of this gift tax exclusion is adjusted annually for inflation and, therefore, has risen over time. Code §2503(b)(1), (2). In 2017, the "annual exclusion amount" was $14,000 per donee. A donor in 2017 could make gifts of up to $14,000 to an unlimited number of donees without incurring any federal gift tax liability.[11] Thus, in addition to excluding the multitude of small gifts given by taxpayers each year, the annual exclusion amount is now significantly large enough to exclude more substantial gifts as well. In contemporary practice, the gift tax annual exclusion provides a vehicle for wealthy taxpayers to reduce the size of their taxable estates through lifetime gifts without exhausting their lifetime applicable exclusion amount (see below).

The annual gift tax exclusion is limited, however, to gifts of a present interest, defined as a transfer to the donee of an "unrestricted right to the immediate use, possession, or enjoyment of property or the income from property." Treas. Reg. §25.2503-3(b). Gifts of future interests — essentially, gifts that do not immediately vest with the donee (or as the Treasury Regulations put it, are "limited to commence in use, possession, or enjoyment at some future date or time," Treas. Reg. §25.2503-3(a)) do not qualify for the exclusion. Code §2503(b)(1). However, Code §2503(c) provides an important exception to the future interest rule when three conditions are met: (1) the gifted property can be expended solely for the donee's benefit; (2) if the donee dies before attaining age 21, the property is payable to the donee's estate; and (3) the property vests in the donee when the donee reaches age 21. Upon meeting these conditions, which are commonplace features of Uniform Transfers to Minors Act (UTMA) accounts, the transfer is treated as a present interest and qualifies for the annual exclusion. This exception allows a donor to make UTMA gifts to minor children that would otherwise constitute a future interest while qualifying for the annual gift tax exclusion.

11. Through the mechanism of "gift-splitting," a married couple may transfer up to $28,000 to an unlimited number of donees even if the entirety of such gifts is given by one spouse.

QUESTIONS

In testing your skills, consider three scenarios involving Taxpayer A, who has an 18-year-old daughter, Taxpayer B. In each scenario, determine whether the gift qualifies for the annual exclusion.

1. Taxpayer A gives a $14,000 check to Taxpayer B.

   ANSWER. Since Taxpayer B is at immediate liberty to cash the check and use the money, the transfer qualifies as a present-interest gift and is excluded from the donor's gift tax base.

2. Taxpayer A places $14,000 into a trust for the benefit of Taxpayer B, but the trust is to be held for a ten-year term before making any distributions of income or principal to B.

   ANSWER. Since Taxpayer B lacks immediate access to these funds and the ultimate beneficiary of the trust money is unknown (e.g., what happens to the trust property if Taxpayer B dies before the ten-year term expires?), the trust contribution constitutes a future interest gift and therefore does not qualify for the gift tax annual exclusion.

3. Taxpayer A places $14,000 into a Uniform Transfers to Minors account for the benefit of Taxpayer B.

   ANSWER. Since these funds vest with Taxpayer B at age 21 or are includable in Taxpayer's estate should she die before attaining age 21, this transfer qualifies for the annual exclusion under Code §2503(c).

12.3.3.4 Medical and Education Exclusions

Taxpayers are at liberty to pay the medical and educational expenses of anyone they wish, and such payments, if made directly to the medical provider or the educational institution, do not constitute taxable gifts. Code §2503(e). Under Code §2503(e), the exclusions for medical and education expenses are in addition to the annual exclusion under Code §2503(b). Thus, in any year, a taxpayer could make an outright gift to an individual of the annual exclusion amount (as of 2017, $14,000) and also pay that individual's medical and tuition bills without incurring a gift tax liability. Together, the annual gift tax exclusion and the exclusions for medical and education expenses provide opportunities for wealthy individuals to reduce the size of their taxable estates by making significant lifetime transfers that are not subject to the gift tax.

QUESTIONS

4. Once again, test your skills: In each of the two scenarios below, determine whether a donor's payment of the described expense qualifies for a gift tax exclusion under Code §2503(e) (exclusion for certain transfers for educational or medical expenses).

a. The taxpayer's friend, a male model, wants a complete $30,000 surgical makeover (i.e., a face-lift, tummy tuck, and buttock lift). The taxpayer pays for his friend's elective surgical procedures.
b. The taxpayer's godson, a high school senior, has been accepted to a private four-year college with annual tuition costs of $45,000. The taxpayer pays the tuition for his godson's freshman year of college.

ANSWER. If the taxpayer pays for the model's medical expenses or the student's tuition bill, the payments are excluded from the donor's gift tax base as long as (1) in the first case, the payment is made directly to the medical providers (i.e., the hospital and physicians rendering the treatment), and (2) in the second case, the tuition payment is made directly to the educational institution. Code §2503(e).[12]

12.3.4 Computation of the Gift Tax

There are four other salient features of the gift tax that every trusts and estates student must understand before attempting to compute the gift tax.

First, Congress has been magnanimous in the amount taxpayers can give away before any gift tax must be paid. In addition to gifts excluded by the annual, medical, and educational exclusions, the cumulative amount taxpayers can transfer tax-free during their lifetimes or at death (known as "the applicable exclusion amount") is $5,490,000 in 2017. Code §2505. Given the available exclusions and the value of the applicable exclusion amount, it is no surprise that so few taxpayers actually pay any gift tax. Most taxpayers never amass enough wealth to reach the applicable exclusion amount. In 2014, a meager 2,977 taxpayers — .009% of the U.S. population of 319 million — paid a gift tax. This small number of annual gift tax payments, however, does not include the many reportable taxable gifts that reduce the exclusion amount applied toward the estate tax at the time of a taxpayer's death. For example, if a widow makes a $4 million taxable gift to her son and dies later that same year, assuming the $4 million gift was her only taxable lifetime transfer, the widow's remaining applicable exclusion amount would only shield the first $1,490,000 (i.e., $5,490,000 less $4 million) of transfers at death from the estate tax.

Second, the current gift tax rate is a flat 40 percent. Code §2502. By historical standards, this tax rate is fairly low (it has been as high as 70 percent). The good news for donors is that the gift tax is tax-exclusive, meaning that taxpayers do not have to pay gift tax on the dollars they use to pay the gift tax; by contrast, the estate tax, as we will learn, is tax-inclusive, meaning that taxpayers pay estate tax on the dollars they use to pay the

12. Note, however, that the costs of books, supplies, room, and board are not within the unlimited exclusion for educational expenses. Treas. Reg. §25.2503-6(b)(ii)(2). The taxpayer could apply her annual exclusion amount under Code §2503(b) toward those expenses.

estate tax. To illustrate the difference between the gift and estate tax computations, consider the following examples:

Case A

Suppose a taxpayer previously exhausted his applicable exclusion amount by making substantial taxable gifts to his children and his remaining assets are now worth $1.4 million. If the taxpayer gives $1 million to his granddaughter, the entire gift is taxable, so he must pay a gift tax of $400,000 (i.e., $1,000,000 × .4). Thus, the total cost of the gift borne by the taxpayer is $1.4 million (i.e., the $1 million gift plus the $400,000 gift tax), but the gift tax liability is based on the gift amount received by the donee ($1 million) rather than the total cost of the transfer ($1.4 million).

Case B

Now, suppose instead that, rather than giving $1 million to his granddaughter, the taxpayer dies owning assets worth $1.4 million *devised* to his granddaughter. Because the taxpayer exhausted his applicable exclusion amount during life, the estate tax rate of 40 percent is imposed on the taxpayer's entire estate of $1.4 million, thereby producing an estate tax liability of $560,000 (i.e., $1,400,000 × .4). After payment of the estate tax, the decedent taxpayer's granddaughter receives a net devise of $840,000 (i.e., $1,400,000 – $560,000).

In comparing Case A and Case B, notice that, although the estate in Case B ($1.4 million) was more valuable than the gift in Case A ($1 million), the granddaughter received a larger net transfer by gift in Case A than by devise in Case B. This is because the estate tax is tax-inclusive, meaning that it is imposed on estate assets used to pay the tax, which, in turn, increases the estate tax base. By contrast, the gift tax is tax-exclusive, meaning that it is imposed on only the amount received by the donee, thereby lowering the gift tax base. Because of these different computational approaches, the granddaughter receives $160,000 (i.e., $1 million versus $840,000) more by gift subject to the gift tax rather than a bequest subject to the estate tax.

Third, to ensure that taxpayers in community property states and non–community property states are treated equally, Code §2513 permits married taxpayers to split their gifts (i.e., they can elect to treat the value of any gift as being made one-half by each spouse). To illustrate, if a mother in a non–community property state makes a $100,000 gift to her daughter, her husband can elect to treat one-half of the gift, or $50,000, as if he made it.

Fourth, in terms of filing requirements, those taxpayers who make taxable gifts are required to file Form 709 (U.S. Gift (and Generation-Skipping Transfer) Tax). This tax return is due the fifteenth day of the fourth month following the close of the taxpayer's year, which is automatically extended if the taxpayer secures an income tax return extension. Code §6075. However, similar to the nation's income tax regime, gift tax *payment* extensions are impermissible.

PROBLEM I

A. A taxpayer makes the following transfers. What are the gift tax consequences, if any, imposed on the taxpayer?
   1. Out of affection, a taxpayer gives a $200,000 diamond ring to his wife.
   2. Out of passion, a taxpayer gives a $200,000 diamond ring to his girlfriend.
   3. Out of pride, a taxpayer gives a $200,000 diamond ring to his daughter.
   4. Out of frustration, a taxpayer pays his son's $200,000 delinquent mortgage.

B. What are the gift tax–filing obligations associated with the following transfers, all of which are made in 2017 (when the lifetime gift tax exemption amount equaled $5,490,000 and the annual exclusion equaled $14,000)?
   1. Mother A gifts $10,000 in trust for the benefit of her 10-year-old daughter, the terms of which provide that the income and principal will vest with the daughter upon reaching age 30.
   2. Mother B gifts $10,000 into a UTMA account for the benefit of her 10-year-old daughter, the terms of which provide that the account balance will vest with the daughter upon attaining age 21.
   3. Mother C gifts $10,000 directly to her 30-year-old daughter.
   4. Mother D gifts $5 million to her 30-year-old daughter.
   5. Mother E gifts $10 million to her 30-year-old daughter.

C. During his lifetime, a husband seeks to establish a trust for the benefit of his wife. He decides to fund the trust with $5 million. Which of the following trust terms, if any, would disqualify the trust from qualifying for the unlimited gift tax marital deduction?
   1. The trust terms provide the wife with a lifetime special power of appointment limited to her children.
   2. The trust terms provide the wife with a testamentary general power of appointment to appoint the trust principal to her estate.
   3. The trust terms provide that if the husband and wife divorce, the wife's income interest ceases and instead is paid to their only child.
   4. The trust terms provide the wife with a lifetime income interest; and upon her demise, she has a testamentary special power of appointment.

12.3.5 Trusts in Contemporary Gift Tax Practice

In contemporary practice, estate planners often use trusts to minimize transfer taxes for their clients. Below we explore the three most common inter vivos trusts for reducing gift tax liability: (1) the Crummey trust, (2) the Grantor Retained Annuity Trust, and (3) the Qualified Personal Residence Trust.

12.3.5.1 Crummey Trust

A common reason for establishing a trust is to postpone the trust beneficiary's enjoyment of the trust property. In such trusts, the timing of when the beneficiary receives trust funds is dictated by the trust terms and, if applicable, the trustee's discretion. In a trust that postpones the distribution of either principal or income, the beneficiary's interest is, for gift tax purposes, a future interest that does not qualify for the present-interest gift tax annual exclusion under Code §2503(b). Thus, when the settlor transfers property into the trust, those transfers should be treated as taxable gifts that exhaust part or all of the settlor's lifetime applicable exemption amount (i.e., every trust contribution should reduce dollar for dollar the taxpayer's unused applicable exemption amount and, if this amount is fully utilized, trigger gift tax).

But then along came Mr. and Mrs. Crummey, who created a trust for the benefit of their children. The Crummeys (presumably along with their advisor) devised the following creative idea: Upon each transfer into the trust, the trust beneficiaries would have a fixed number of days within which to withdraw the contributed amount. If a trust beneficiary exercised this right, the amount would be distributed from the trust corpus; on the other hand, if a trust beneficiary failed to exercise this right during the available withdrawal window, the transferred amount would become part of the trust corpus, which postponed distribution of funds until the beneficiaries reached the age of 21. What was the purpose of this withdrawal window? To transform what otherwise was a future interest (i.e., a right to receive the transferred amount upon reaching the age of 21) into a present-interest trust contribution that qualified for the gift tax annual exclusion.

In *Crummey v. Commissioner*, despite the IRS's challenge, the taxpayers' position prevailed and the Crummeys' transfers into the trust qualified for the present-interest annual exclusion.

Crummey v. Commissioner
397 F.2d 82 (9th Cir. 1968)

BYRNE, District Judge: . . .

On February 12, 1962, the petitioners executed, as grantors, an irrevocable living trust for the benefit of their four children. The beneficiaries and their ages at relevant times are as follows:

	Age 12/31/62	Age 12/31/63
John Knowles Crummey	22	23
Janet Sheldon Crummey	20	21
David Clarke Crummey	15	16
Mark Clifford Crummey	11	12

Originally the sum of $50 was contributed to the trust. Thereafter, additional contributions were made by each of the petitioners in the following amounts and on the following dates:

$ 4,267.77	6/20/62
49,550.00	12/15/62
12,797.81	12/19/63

The dispute revolves around the tax years of 1962 and 1963. Each of the petitioners filed a gift tax return for each year. Each petitioner claimed a $3,000 per beneficiary tax exclusion under the provisions of 26 U.S.C. 2503(b).[13] The total claimed exclusions were as follows:

D.C. Crummey	1962 - $12,000	1963 - $12,000
E.E. Crummey	1962 - $12,000	1963 - $12,000

The Commissioner of Internal Revenue determined that each of the petitioners was entitled to only one $3,000 exclusion for each year. This determination was based upon the Commissioner's belief that the portion of the gifts in trust for the children under the age of 21 were "future interests" which are disallowed under §2503(b). The taxpayers contested the determination of a deficiency in the Tax Court. The Commissioner conceded by stipulation in that proceeding that each petitioner was entitled to an additional $3,000 exclusion for the year 1963 by reason of Janet Crummey having reached the age of 21.

The Tax Court followed the Commissioner's interpretation as to gifts in trust to David and Mark, but determined that the 1962 gift in trust to Janet qualified as a gift of a present interest because of certain additional rights accorded to persons 18 and over by California law. Thus, the Tax Court held that each petitioner was entitled to an additional $3,000 exclusion for the year 1962.

The key provision of the trust agreement is the "demand" provision which states:

> "THREE. *Additions. . . . With respect to [trust] additions, each child of the Trustors may demand at any time (up to and including December 31 of the year in which a transfer to his or her Trust has been made) the sum of Four Thousand Dollars ($4,000.00) or the amount of the transfer from each donor, whichever is less, payable in cash immediately upon receipt by the Trustee of the demand in writing and in any event, not later than December 31 in the year in which such transfer was made. Such payment shall be made from the gift of that donor for that year. If a child is a minor at the time of such gift of that donor for that year, or fails in legal capacity for any reason, the child's guardian may make such demand on behalf of the child. The property received pursuant to the demand shall be held by the guardian for the benefit and use of the child.*"

13. [$3,000 was the maximum amount that qualified for the gift tax annual exclusion in 1962 and 1963.—Eds.]

The whole question on this appeal is whether or not a present interest was given by the petitioners to their minor children so as to qualify as an exclusion under §2503(b). The petitioners on appeal contend that each minor beneficiary has the right under California law to demand partial distribution from the Trustee. In the alternative they urge that a parent as natural guardian of the person of his minor children could make such a demand. As a third alternative, they assert that under California law a minor over the age of 14 has the right to have a legal guardian appointed who can make the necessary demand. The Commissioner, as cross petitioner, alleges as error the Tax Court's ruling that the 1962 gifts in trust to Janet (then age 20) were present interests.

It was stipulated before the Tax Court in regard to the trust and the parties thereto that at all times relevant all the minor children lived with the petitioners and no legal guardian had been appointed for them. In addition, it was agreed that all the children were supported by petitioners and none of them had made a demand against the trust funds or received any distribution from them.

The tax regulations define a "future interest" for the purposes of §2503(b) as follows:

> "'Future interests' is a legal term, and includes reversions, remainder, and other interests or estates, whether vested or contingent, and whether or not supported by a particular interest or estate, which are limited to commence in use, possession or enjoyment at some future date or time." Treasury Regulations of Gift Tax, §25.2503-3.

This definition has been adopted by the Supreme Court. Fondren v. Commissioner of Internal Revenue, 324 U.S. 18 . . . (1945); Commissioner of Internal Revenue v. Disston, 325 U.S. 442 . . . (1945). In *Fondren* the court stated that the important question is when enjoyment begins. There the court held that gifts to an irrevocable trust for the grantor's minor grandchildren were "future interests" where income was to be accumulated and the corpus and the accumulations were not to be paid until designated times commencing with each grandchild's 25th birthday. The trustee was authorized to spend the income or invade the corpus during the minority of the beneficiaries only if need were shown. The facts demonstrated that need had not occurred and was not likely to occur.

Neither of the parties nor the Tax Court has any disagreement with the above summarization of the basic tests. The dispute comes in attempting to narrow the definition of a future interest down to a more specific and useful form.

The Commissioner and the Tax Court both placed primary reliance on the case of Stifel v. Commissioner of Internal Revenue, 197 F.2d 107 (2nd Cir. 1952). In that case an irrevocable trust was involved which provided that the beneficiary, a minor, could demand any part of the funds not expended by the Trustee and, subject to such demand, the Trustee was to accumulate. The trust also provided that it could be terminated by the beneficiary or by her guardian during minority. The court held that gifts to this trust were gifts of "future interests." They relied upon *Fondren* for the proposition that they could look at circumstances as well as the trust agreement and under such circumstances it was clear that the minor could not make the demand and that no guardian had ever been appointed who could make such a demand.

The leading case relied upon by the petitioners is Kieckhefer v. Commissioner of Internal Revenue, 189 F.2d 118 (7th Cir. 1951). In that case the donor set up a trust with his newly born grandson as the beneficiary. The trustee was to hold the funds unless the beneficiary or his legally appointed guardian demanded that the trust be terminated. The Commissioner urged that the grandson could not effectively make such a demand and that no guardian had been appointed. The court disregarded these factors and held that where any restrictions on use were caused by disabilities of a minor rather than by the terms of the trust, the gift was a "present interest." The court further stated that the important thing was the right to enjoy rather than the actual enjoyment of the property. . . .

Although there are certainly factual distinctions between the *Stifel* and *Kieckhefer* cases, it seems clear that the two courts took opposing positions on the way the problem of defining "future interests" should be resolved. As we read the *Stifel* case, it says that the court should look at the trust instrument, the law as to minors, and the financial and other circumstances of the parties. From this examination it is up to the court to determine whether it is likely that the minor beneficiary is to receive any present enjoyment of the property. If it is not likely, then the gift is a "future interest." At the other extreme is the holding in *Kieckhefer* which says that a gift to a minor is not a "future interest" if the only reason for a delay in enjoyment is the minority status of the donee and his consequent disabilities. The *Kieckhefer* court noted that under the terms there present, a gift to an adult would have qualified for the exclusion and they refused to discriminate against a minor. The court equated a present interest with a present right to possess, use or enjoy. The facts of the case and the court's reasoning, however, indicate that it was really equating a present interest with a present right to possess, use or enjoy except for the fact that the beneficiary was a minor. In between these two positions there is a third possibility. That possibility is that the court should determine whether the donee is legally and technically capable of immediately enjoying the property. Basically this is the test relied on by the petitioners. Under this theory, the question would be whether the donee could possibly gain immediate enjoyment and the emphasis would be on the trust instrument and the laws of the jurisdiction as to minors. It was primarily on this basis that the Tax Court decided the present case, although some examination of surrounding circumstances was apparently made. This theory appears to be the basis of the decision in George W. Perkins, 27 T.C. 601 (1956). There the Tax Court stated that where the parents were capable of making the demand and there was no showing that the demand could be resisted, the gift was of a present interest. This approach also seems to be the basis of the "right to enjoy" language in both *Kieckhefer* and *Gilmore*. . . .

There is very little dispute between the parties as to the rights and disabilities of a minor accorded by the California statutes and cases. The problem comes in attempting to ascertain from these rights and disabilities the answer to the question of whether a minor may make a demand upon the trustee for a portion of the trust as provided in the trust instrument. . . .

Given the trust, the California law, and the circumstances in our case, it can be seen that very different results may well be achieved, depending upon the test used.

Under a strict interpretation of the *Stifel* test of examining everything and determining whether there is any likelihood of present enjoyment, the gifts to minors in our case would seem to be "future interests." Although under our interpretation neither the trust nor the law technically forbid a demand by the minor, the practical difficulties of a child going through the procedures seem substantial. In addition, the surrounding facts indicate the children were well cared for and the obvious intention of the trustors was to create a long term trust. No guardian had been appointed and, except for the tax difficulties, probably never would be appointed. As a practical matter, it is likely that some, if not all, of the beneficiaries did not even know that they had any right to demand funds from the trust. They probably did not know when contributions were made to the trust or in what amounts. Even had they known, the substantial contributions were made toward the end of the year so that the time to make a demand was severely limited. Nobody had made a demand under the provision, and no distributions had been made. We think it unlikely that any demand ever would have been made. . . .

Under the general language of *Kieckhefer* which talked of the "right to enjoy," all exclusions in our case would seem to be allowable. The broader *Kieckhefer* rule, which we have discussed is inapplicable on the facts of this case. That rule, as we interpret it, is that postponed enjoyment is not equivalent to a "future interest" if the postponement is solely caused by the minority of the beneficiary. In *Kieckhefer*, the income was accumulated and added to the corpus until the beneficiary reached the age of 21. At that time everything was to be turned over to him. This is all that happened unless a demand was made. In our case, on the contrary, if no demand is made in any particular year, the additions are forever removed from the uncontrolled reach of the beneficiary since, with the exception of the yearly demand provision, the only way the corpus can ever be tapped by a beneficiary, is through a distribution at the discretion of the trustee.

We decline to follow a strict reading of the *Stifel* case in our situation because we feel that the solution suggested by that case is inconsistent and unfair. It becomes arbitrary for the I.R.S. to step in and decide who is likely to make an effective demand. Under the circumstances suggested in our case, it is doubtful that any demands will be made against the trust—yet the Commissioner always allowed the exclusion as to adult beneficiaries. There is nothing to indicate that it is any more likely that John will demand funds than that any other beneficiary will do so. The only distinction is that it might be easier for him to make such a demand. Since we conclude that the demand can be made by the others, it follows that the exclusion should also apply to them. In another case we might follow the broader *Kieckhefer* rule, since it seems least arbitrary and establishes a clear standard. However, if the minors have no way of making the demand in our case, then there is more than just a postponement involved, since John could demand his share of yearly additions while the others would never have the opportunity at their shares of those additions but would be limited to taking part of any additions added subsequent to their 21st birthdays.

We conclude that the result under the *Perkins* or "right to enjoy" tests is preferable in our case. The petitioners should be allowed all of the exclusions claimed for the two year period.

The decision of the Tax Court denying the taxpayers' exclusions on the gifts to David and Mark Crummey is reversed. The decision of the Tax Court allowing the taxpayers' exclusions on the 1962 gift to Janet Crummey is affirmed.

Eponymously named after this case, so-called Crummey withdrawal rights are now ubiquitously used in the estate planning practice and embedded in the majority of inter vivos irrevocable trusts. In practice, most tax practitioners will tell you that they have gone through their entire careers and never once seen a trust beneficiary actually exercise his withdrawal right, making this right more fiction than reality. Nevertheless, over the last several decades, the power of the *Crummey* decision remains fully intact, as tax advisors constantly seek to stretch its limits further and further.[14]

Consider the plight of a husband who wants to make a Crummey trust contribution in which his wife and three children are beneficiaries. Assuming that the trust terms are properly drafted (i.e., Crummey withdrawal rights are operative), in 2017, the husband can contribute $98,000 free of any gift tax (i.e., the $14,000 Crummey withdrawal right granted to his wife that she can exercise and the $28,000 Crummey withdrawal rights granted to each of his three children (with the underlying assumption that the husband and his wife will make a "split gift" election with respect to the trust contribution that is directed toward each of their three children, respectively, on their gift tax returns)).

While Crummey trusts can be funded with virtually anything of value (e.g., real estate), the most common mode of trust funding is with life insurance on the life of the trust settlor. Consider the following facts: A husband establishes an irrevocable trust that has Crummey withdrawal rights, and the couple has one child. The trustee of the trust (who, in this case, is the husband's wife) decides the trust should secure a $1 million whole-life insurance policy on her husband's life, the annual premiums of which are $42,000 annually. The husband contributes $42,000 to the trust; in return, the wife, as trustee, issues written notices to herself and her son declaring that trust beneficiaries each have a thirty-day period to exercise their right to withdraw the trust contribution (i.e., in the wife's case, she can withdraw $14,000; in the son's case, he can withdraw $28,000; the reason for these Crummey withdrawal rights is simple: they transform the trust contribution from a future into a present interest and thereby qualify it for the gift tax annual exclusion). After thirty days, assuming no withdrawal has been made, the trustee (namely, the wife) is at liberty to write a check from the trust's bank account to the underwriting insurance company to pay the annual insurance premium.

14. See, e.g., Estate of Cristofani v. Commissioner, 97 T.C. 74 (1991) (holding that even if trust beneficiaries were contingent remaindermen (in this case, the settlor's child had to predecease the settlor's grandchildren before any financial benefit would inure to the latter), these trust beneficiaries could still have a legitimate withdrawal right qualifying the trust contribution for the gift tax annual exclusion).

Over the next several years, suppose the process described in the prior paragraph continues, and then the husband subsequently dies. The trust will then have $1 million in life insurance proceeds that will be used in accordance with the trust terms. If the trust was properly drafted, the $1 million of life insurance proceeds will *not* be includable in the husband's gross estate because he did not possess "any of the incidents of ownership" at death. Code §2042(2). Furthermore, upon the wife's demise, assuming that she has no indicia of ownership over the trust assets (i.e., her power to invade trust principal is limited by a so-called ascertainable standard as delineated in Code §2041(b)(1)(A) for her "health, education, maintenance, and support"), for purposes of the federal estate tax, the remaining trust income and principal will not be in her gross estate, either.

Among estate planners, Crummey trusts are ubiquitous, but their terms vary tremendously. Some taxpayers establish them for the benefit of their spouse, others for the benefit of their children, others for the benefit of both their spouse and children, and still others for the benefit of more distant relations or friends. The common denominator of these trusts, though, is that the provisions for the withdrawal period have been repeatedly challenged by the IRS, and the courts have universally rejected the IRS's challenges with the same frequency.

Appendix 1 provides a sample life insurance trust.

12.3.5.2 Grantor Retained Annuity Trust

In this section, we discuss the Grantor Retained Annuity Trust (GRAT). However, by way of background, we first examine a predecessor of the GRAT, the Grantor Retained Income Trust (GRIT). For years, as a transfer-tax-savings device, taxpayers established trusts in which they would retain an income interest for a term of years with the remainder passing to designated trust beneficiaries. This technique proved to be a boon to taxpayers and a bust to the government, enabling billions of dollars to pass free of transfer tax.

Here is how GRITs were used to reduce transfers taxes: Taxpayers would contribute assets into a GRIT; over its term, the trust assets were invested to grow the value of the trust corpus rather than to generate income. For gift tax valuation purposes, however, in valuing the trust remainder interest, the Code instructed taxpayers to use IRS valuation tables that presumed moderate income generation; this mandate, therefore, greatly diminished the deemed value of the remainder interest passing to trust beneficiaries and, correspondingly, the reportable value of the taxable gift.

Lost by the jargon in the last two paragraphs? You're probably not alone, but an example should help lift the veil of confusion. Suppose a taxpayer contributed $1 million of highly appreciating closely held stock to a GRIT with a twenty-year term that paid a mere 1 percent annual dividend (or $10,000). At the time of GRIT contribution, suppose further that the applicable federal rate under Code §7520 was 8 percent (theoretically producing $80,000 in annual trust income). Given this set of assumptions, according to the statutory valuation table, the value of the trust remainder interest (and the value of the taxpayer's taxable gift) would be $164,470.[15] The settlor's retained interest was not subject to the gift tax because the settlor was presumed to have kept that portion of the trust for herself without transferring it gratuitously to others. However, if the taxpayer was truly able to achieve an 8 percent return on the trust investments, over the course of twenty years these investments would grow to $4,660,957 and would pass as the remainder to the trust beneficiaries. The GRIT in this example would have thus allowed $4,496,487 ($4,660,957 – $164,470) to pass free of transfer tax to the designated trust remainder beneficiaries.

Frustrated by this transfer tax technique and other valuation ploys, Congress took decisive action in 1990 and enacted Chapter 14, entitled "Special Valuation Rules." Consisting of a mere four Code sections, this chapter's foremost objective was to ensure that, in the transfer tax context, asset valuations (and the presumptions on which they were based) were more accurate.

Targeted at GRIT valuation abuses, Code §2702 found in Chapter 14 had sweeping implications for irrevocable inter vivos trusts. Entitled "Special Valuation Rules in Case of Transfers of Interests in Trusts," this section sets forth specific valuation rules related to those trusts that taxpayers establish in which they retain either an interest spanning a lifetime or a term of years, fundamentally changing the trust-formation landscape.

Going forward, if a trust beneficiary is a member of the transferor's family (defined in Code §2701(e)(2)), any interest that the trust settlor retains that is not "qualified" is deemed to be zero. Under Code §2702, a taxpayer's retention of an income interest is not deemed a qualified interest (see below); therefore, in the prior example in which the transferor contributed $1 million to a trust and retained a twenty-year income interest, the amount of the taxable gift would be $1 million (rather than $164,470) because, in the donor taxpayer's hands, the value of the retained trust income interest would be deemed to be zero; the value of the remainder trust interest would therefore be $1 million.

Code §2702(b) defines those interests that are *qualified*.[16] From this definition of qualified interests came the genesis of two newly minted trust forms known in the estate planning vernacular as GRATs (i.e., Grantor Retained Annuity Trusts) and GRUTs (Grantor Retained Unitrusts). The salient features of each are as follows:

GRATs:

- They are set up for a term of years that is generally fewer years than the actuarial life span of the trust settlor; this strategy minimizes the possibility of the trust settlor dying prior to the end of the trust term with a retained interest and thereby triggering estate tax inclusion of the trust principal.

---

15. This amount essentially is the actuarial value of $1 million to be received twenty years from now, discounted at an 8 percent assumed interest rate.

16. Code §2702(b) specifies that the following interests are qualified:

(1) any interest which consists of the right to receive fixed amounts payable not less frequently than annually;

(2) any interest which consists of the right to receive amounts which are payable not less frequently than annually and are a fixed percentage of the fair market value of the property in the trust (determined annually); and

(3) any noncontingent remainder interest if all of the other interests in the trust consist of interests described in paragraph (1) or (2).

- They require the use of the so-called Code §7520 interest rate to compute the value of the trust remainder interest.
- They feature annual or more frequent payments of a fixed annuity sum.
- At the end of the trust term, the balance of the trust income and principal (if any) passes transfer tax–free to the designated trust remainder beneficiaries.
- Once established, no additional trust contributions may be made.

GRUTs:

- They are set up for a term of years that is generally fewer years than the actuarial life span of the trust settlor; this strategy minimizes the possibility of the trust settlor dying prior to the end of the trust term with a retained interest and thereby triggering estate tax inclusion of the trust principal.
- They require the use of the so-called Code §7520 interest rate to compute the value of the trust remainder interest.
- They feature annual or more frequent payment of a fixed percentage of the fair market value of trust assets (determined on an annual basis).
- At the end of the trust term, the balance of the trust income and principal (if any) passes transfer tax–free to the trust beneficiaries.
- Additional trust contributions can be made.

Over the ensuing two and a half decades in the estate planning world, GRUTs never gained traction. One of the primary reasons for the lack of GRUT popularity is that GRATs yield far superior transfer tax outcomes, often resulting in little or no transfer tax burden. Another GRUT shortcoming is that, depending upon its funding mechanism (e.g., real estate or closely held stock), fulfillment of its terms (i.e., the payment of a fixed percentage of the trust assets valued on a current basis) often necessitates costly annual valuation appraisals.

Compared to their GRUT counterpart, GRATs have enjoyed immense popularity. The reason for such popularity is that their usage offers a tremendous upside transfer tax potential with virtually no downside risk. You rightfully might ask how this seemingly magical feat is possible. After all, once a trust contribution is made, don't trust investment returns dictate whether or not transfer tax savings can actually be achieved? Nonetheless, short-term GRATs afford taxpayers the following unique luxury: When taxpayers get it "right" and their invested trust assets outperform the Code §7520 rate, they achieve tremendous transfer tax savings; and when they get it "wrong" and their invested trust assets underperform the Code §7520 rate, they lose nothing.

An example of how GRATs operate illustrates their allure. Suppose a taxpayer contributes $1 million into a GRAT, the term of which is two years. After the two-year trust term, the trust assets (if any) that remain will be distributed to the taxpayer's daughter. Suppose further that the Code §7520 rate in the month of trust contribution is 5 percent; the amount of the retained annuity is $537,808; and even if the taxpayer settlor dies during the two-year term, the remaining annuity payments will continue to be made to his estate. Under this set of assumptions, the deemed value of the trust remainder interest passing to the taxpayer's daughter is zero. (By the way, within milliseconds of making a few keystroke entries of the Code §7520 rate and the trust term, tax software programs supply the exact annuity amount to achieve this zero transfer tax outcome.) The estate planning industry commonly refers to this sort of trust as a zeroed-out GRAT (in which the trust remainder interest and, by extension, the value of the taxable gift is deemed to be zero). Walton v. Commissioner, 115 T.C. 41 (2000) (sanctioning the use of this technique).

Zeroed-out GRATs are every estate planner's dream. Consider what happens if the trust experiences hefty 30 percent annual returns. After year 1, the trust grows in value to $1.3 million ($1 million + ($1 million × .3)) and, pursuant to its terms, then must distribute $537,808 to the trust settlor, leaving assets worth $762,192 ($1,300,000 – $537,808) in trust. After year 2, the trust would have $990,850 ($762,192 + ($762,192 × .3)) but would then have to distribute another $537,808, leaving assets worth $453,042 ($990,850 – $537,808) in trust. This sum could then be distributed to the taxpayer's daughter transfer tax–free. Suppose instead that the GRAT experiences poor or lackluster investment returns and at the end of the two-year period, nothing remains in the trust. Aside from the administrative expense of establishing the trust, the taxpayer has neither endured a financial downside nor used a single dollar of his lifetime applicable exclusion amount; instead, the taxpayer is perfectly poised to establish another two-year GRAT and hope for a better investment return on the new go-round. (Another reason for tax practitioners' preference for short-term GRATs is to avoid the increased mortality risk of the taxpayer settlor dying during the trust term (e.g., if the stated GRAT term was ten or twenty years) and the trust assets thereby included in the transferor taxpayer's estate.)

Appendix 2 provides a sample two-year GRAT.

12.3.5.3 Qualified Personal Residence Trust

As reflected in the nation's income tax laws, Congress has always harbored a deep-seated affection for home ownership. Reflected in Code §2702, the depth of this affection extends into the transfer tax realm as well. This Code section permits a taxpayer to convey title to a personal residence into trust that delays possession until a later date, thereby minimizing gift tax exposure. Taxpayers can avail themselves of the "old" GRIT rules and capitalize on potential transfer tax savings. While taxpayers can establish either a basic personal residence trust or a so-called Qualified Personal Residence Trust (QPRT), the vast majority choose the latter because it provides far more flexibility (i.e., the trust can hold title to a broader range of assets, including cash reserves). That being the case, QPRTs are the focal point of our discussion.

True to its name, a QPRT involves transferring title to a personal residence into a trust. Akin to GRATs and GRUTs, a QPRT involves the trust settlor retaining a term interest in the trust, but rather than retaining an annual fixed payment or percentage of the trust assets, he retains the annual right to reside in the personal residence. Along with this right, the settlor bears the obligation to pay the costs associated with the personal residence's upkeep, including annual real estate taxes, insurance, and general maintenance expenses. At the end of the trust term, ownership of the personal residence inures to the benefit of the trust's remainder beneficiaries, who can then enter into an arm's-length lease agreement with the settlor so that he may remain on the premises, or force him to leave.

Some other practice points to consider are as follows. Generally, the length of the trust term is set to be shorter than the settlor's actuarial life span. Once again, this strategy minimizes the risk of the settlor dying during the trust term and the then value of the personal residence being includable in the settlor's gross estate, negating its effectiveness for transfer tax purposes. Practitioners also generally prefer that the contributed personal residence be free of any liabilities (e.g., a mortgage); otherwise, each future liability payment constitutes an additional trust contribution with concomitant gift tax implications. Finally, if the personal residence is sold during the trust term, the Treasury Regulations require that within two years of the sale the sale proceeds be reinvested in another personal residence or, alternatively, that the trust be converted into a GRAT.

An example illustrates the attractive transfer tax outcomes associated with QPRT use. Suppose a taxpayer who was born on July 17, 1963, owns a $1 million personal residence and that on June 17, 2017, he transfers title to this residence to a twenty-year QPRT when the Code §7520 rate was 5 percent. Based upon this set of assumptions, the value of the remainder interest would be $288,910 and constitute the value of the taxable gift (because this remainder interest is a future interest, no portion of it would qualify for the gift tax annual exclusion). Over the twenty-year trust term, if the value of the $1 million personal residence appreciates to $2,653,298 (representing a 5 percent annual growth rate), the taxpayer, by utilizing the QPRT, would have been able to shed this $2,653,298 of wealth at a meager gift tax cost of only $288,910.

To help keep QPRT practice somewhat standardized, the IRS has published a prototype of this trust. While tax practitioners may add a few ancillary features to this prototype (e.g., grafting a clause that, should the need arise, enables the last-named trustee to name a successor trustee), they rarely seek to stray too far from the substantive terms provided.

Appendix 3 provides a sample Qualified Personal Residence Trust.

12.4 ESTATE TAX

In 1916, as the United States was on the verge of entering World War I, Congress passed the Revenue Act of 1916, increasing the federal income tax rates and establishing the federal estate tax. The purpose of the estate tax was twofold: to raise revenue and to militate against the perpetuation of family-wealth dynasties. Over the last century, however, it has neither raised a tremendous amount of revenue nor, as many commentators would argue, done much to curtail inherited wealth. Notwithstanding these shortcomings, and despite many politicians' entreaties to repeal it, the estate tax has remained a stalwart feature of the nation's tax system.

In the subsections below, we will explore (1) estate tax fundamentals and (2) planning devices that practitioners commonly use to minimize their clients' estate tax exposure.

12.4.1 Estate Tax Fundamentals

When exploring estate tax fundamentals, there are three basic considerations: (1) determining what items are *includable* in the decedent's gross estate, (2) determining what items are *deductible* from the decedent's gross estate, and (3) computing estate tax liability and filing the decedent's estate tax return.

12.4.1.1 Items Included in the Decedent's Gross Estate

The decedent's gross estate includes both property owned by the decedent directly and assets over which the decedent could exercise dominion and control. Congress adopted a sweepingly inclusive definition of the gross estate to prevent taxpayers from avoiding the tax by titling property in ways (e.g., nonprobate transfers and outright gifts shortly before death) that might otherwise conceal or mask indicia of property control.

Here, as with the gift tax, fair market value of property included in the gross estate is defined as "the price at which the property would change hands between a willing buyer and a willing seller, neither being under any compulsion to buy or sell and both having reasonable knowledge of relevant facts." Treas. Reg. §20.2031-1(b). The valuation of assets in the gross estate is generally determined either on the date of the decedent's death or six months after the decedent's death.[17]

The first component of estate tax inclusion — that is, direct ownership — is usually easy to identify. See Code §2033 (requiring inclusion of "all property to the extent of the interest therein of the decedent at the time of death"). It includes the fair market value of assets titled or held in the decedent's name, such as automobiles and investment portfolios. Harder to identify are those items that fall within the scope of the second component of estate tax inclusion, namely, assets over which the decedent could exercise sufficient incidents of ownership to bring them within the gross estate. The following are among the more salient items in this category:

Certain Transfers Within Three Years of Death (Code §2035). Certain interests in property that the decedent has transferred within three years of death are brought back into the decedent's gross estate. These include transfers of ownership in a life insurance policy on the decedent's life; gift taxes paid; and relinquishment of any of the rights specified in Code §§2036, 2037, and 2038 (described below).

> **Example:** A taxpayer transfers the ownership of a $1 million life insurance policy on her life two years before she dies to her son (i.e., she completes a change of ownership that the underwriting insurance company provides, submits the completed form to the company, and the company thereafter effectuates the ownership change). The full $1 million of life insurance proceeds are includable in her gross estate. 26 U.S.C. §2035(a).

> **Example:** In 2017, a taxpayer transfers $6 million to her daughter and pays $204,000 of gift tax (i.e., 40 percent gift tax rate × ($6,000,000 – $5,490,000

17. In those instances when there would be an overall reduction in the amount of estate tax due, the Code permits executors to elect the so-called alternate valuation date. If this election is made, executors assess the fair market value of a decedent's assets six months after the decedent's death. Code §2032(a).

lifetime applicable exclusion)) two years before she dies. The $204,000 of gift tax paid is includable in her gross estate. However, the $6 million gift itself is not included in the gross estate because that transfer was already subject to the gift tax. 26 U.S.C. §2035(b).

Example: A taxpayer establishes a trust, funding it with $1 million and retaining an income interest therein. Two years before the taxpayer dies, she relinquishes her right to income from the trust; the actuarial value of the right to income from the trust is includable in her gross estate. 26 U.S.C. §2035(a).

Transfers with Retained Life Estates (Code §2036(a)). When a taxpayer transfers property for inadequate consideration in trust or otherwise and retains a life interest or can control beneficial enjoyment of such property, the full fair market value of the property is includable in the taxpayer's gross estate at death.

Example: A taxpayer makes a transfer into trust and retains a lifetime income interest. Upon death, the full fair market value of the trust assets would be includable in the taxpayer's gross estate.

Example: A taxpayer makes a transfer into trust and retains the right to select who will receive the trust property when the taxpayer dies. Upon death, the full fair market value of the trust assets would be includable in the taxpayer's gross estate.

Transfers Taking Effect at Death (Code §2037). When a taxpayer transfers property for inadequate consideration in trust or otherwise, and if the taxpayer retains a reversionary interest that immediately before his death exceeds 5 percent of the value of such property, the fair market value of the trust property is includable in the taxpayer's gross estate at death if the transferee's possession can only be obtained by surviving the decedent. Such interests are included in the gross estate because, had the taxpayer lived just long enough to receive the reversionary interest, the taxpayer would have died owning the reverted property.

Example: A taxpayer transfers property into a trust that pays income to her husband (of equivalent age) for life and, upon her husband's death, the remainder to the taxpayer or, if she is not then living, to their daughter. The taxpayer predeceases her husband, so the reversionary interest that would have reverted to the taxpayer instead will pass as a remainder interest to the daughter (who will receive possession when the husband dies). Assuming the value of the taxpayer's reversionary interest immediately before death exceeds 5 percent, the fair market value of the trust property (less the value of the husband's outstanding life estate) is includable in the taxpayer's gross estate.

Revocable Transfers (Code §2038). When a taxpayer transfers property for inadequate consideration in trust or otherwise and retains the right to alter, amend, revoke, or terminate such transfer, the transferred property is includable in the decedent's gross estate.

> **Example:** A taxpayer establishes a revocable trust, the terms of which he can change up to the moment of death. Because the taxpayer retained the power to revoke the trust, the full value of the trust assets is includable in the taxpayer's gross estate.

Annuities (Code §2039). When a taxpayer dies owning an annuity that is then payable to another beneficiary by reason of surviving the taxpayer, the value of the annuity receivable by the beneficiary is included in the taxpayer's gross estate.

> **Example:** A taxpayer purchases a lifetime annuity that, after the taxpayer's death, pays the same annuity amount to her husband. Assuming the husband survives the taxpayer, the actuarial fair market value of the remaining annuity payments is includable in the taxpayer's gross estate.

Jointly Owned Property (Code §2040). The general rule is that the entire value of jointly owned property is includable in the decedent taxpayer's gross estate except to the extent that the estate can prove that another taxpayer contributed to the purchase price of the property. In the latter case, only the portion attributable to the decedent taxpayer's contribution (an amount equal to the consideration paid by the decedent divided by the total consideration paid times the fair market value of the property) is included in the decedent taxpayer's gross estate. The Code, however, provides an exception for married couples: It presumes a one-half contribution by each spouse. Therefore, only one-half of the fair market value of such jointly held property by married persons is includable in the decedent's estate.

> **Example:** Two people, Taxpayer A and Taxpayer B, purchase a farm for $100,000. Taxpayer A contributes $60,000, and Taxpayer B contributes $40,000. They purchased the farm together and took title in their joint names with right of survivorship. Ten years later, Taxpayer A dies. The farm has appreciated in value to $1 million. Because Taxpayer A contributed 60 percent of the purchase price ($60,000 of $100,000), 60 percent of the fair market value—$600,000—would be includable in Taxpayer A's estate. If Taxpayer A and Taxpayer B were married, by contrast, then only $500,000 would have been includable in Taxpayer A's estate because Taxpayer A's contribution would be presumed one-half.

General Power of Appointment (Code §2041). Property over which the decedent possessed a general power of appointment (i.e., any power over property that is exercisable in favor of "the decedent, his estate, his creditors, or the creditors of his estate") is includable in the decedent's gross estate whether or not the decedent exercised the power. By default, all other powers of appointment are known by the estate tax vernacular as special powers of appointment, the most common of which are those limited to the health, education, maintenance, and support of the appointee.

Example: A father establishes a trust for the benefit of his daughter. The terms of the trust give the daughter a testamentary general power of appointment over the trust's assets, meaning that she can appoint the remaining trust corpus at her death by will to her estate, her creditors, or the creditors of her estate. The existence of this power causes the trust assets to be included in the daughter's gross estate. If, instead, the trust gave the daughter a power to make periodic withdrawals for her health, education, maintenance, and support, the existence of this limited power would not cause estate tax inclusion in the daughter's gross estate.

Life Insurance (Code §2042). When life insurance proceeds are payable to a taxpayer's estate or, alternatively, the taxpayer has any indicia of ownership in the life insurance policy, the life insurance proceeds are includable in the taxpayer's gross estate. Indicia of ownership of a life insurance policy include "the power to change the beneficiary, to surrender or cancel the policy, to assign the policy, to revoke an assignment, to pledge the policy for a loan, or to obtain from the insurer a loan against the surrender value of the policy, etc." Treas. Reg. §20.2042-1(c).

Example: A taxpayer owns a life insurance policy, the proceeds of which are payable to her estate. In such a case, upon the taxpayer's death, the life insurance proceeds would be includable in the taxpayer's gross estate.

Example: A taxpayer owns a life insurance policy, the proceeds of which are payable to her daughter. The taxpayer has the power to change the beneficiary. Upon the taxpayer's death, the life insurance proceeds would be includable in the taxpayer's gross estate.

Estate Tax Marital Deduction Property (Code §2044). When a taxpayer has received property from the estate of a deceased spouse and dies owning property that previously qualified for the estate tax marital deduction (see below), the value of that property is includable in the taxpayer's gross estate.

Example: A husband establishes a testamentary trust for the benefit of his wife, the terms of which qualify for the unlimited estate tax marital deduction. The husband dies and his executor makes a QTIP election (see below) with respect to the trust property received by the wife. This trust qualifies for the estate tax marital deduction and, as a result, passes through the husband's estate tax-free. Upon the wife's subsequent death, the fair market value of the trust's assets is includable in her gross estate because the trust was previously deducted from the husband's gross estate.

This long list of inclusion items reflects congressional intent to broaden the estate tax base and ensure that each taxpayer's gross estate captures his or her true net worth at death. Items included in the gross estate may, however, be offset by deductions that reduce the value of property subject to the estate tax.

12.4.1.2 Items Deducted from the Gross Estate

In contrast to the sweeping nature of the estate tax inclusion provisions, there are only five Code sections that set forth the estate tax deductions, which reduce the value of the gross estate dollar for dollar:

General Administrative Expenses and Indebtedness (Code §2053). Deductible expenses include funeral expenses, administrative expenses (e.g., legal and accounting fees associated with estate administration), claims against the estate, and any indebtedness with respect to property in the estate.

Casualty and Theft Losses (Code §2054). During the estate administration process, if an estate incurs casualty and theft losses, such expenditures are deductible.

Charitable Bequests (Code §2055). Bequests made to organizations "organized and operated exclusively for religious, charitable, scientific, literary, or educational purposes, including the encouragement of art, or to foster national or international amateur sports competition (but only if no part of its activities involve the provision of athletic facilities or equipment), and the prevention of cruelty to children or animals" are deductible.

Marital Bequests (Code §2056). Property passing from the estate to the decedent's surviving spouse is generally deductible, but as explained below, there are exceptions and limitations.

On one level, the estate tax marital deduction is simple: The fair market value of any property passing to a surviving spouse (assuming he or she is a U.S. citizen) is deductible, and the amount of the deduction is unlimited. Essentially, married couples are treated as a single economic unit, so the imposition of the estate tax is deferred until both spouses die. On another level, the estate tax marital deduction is much more complex because it prohibits the deductibility of a so-called *terminable interest*. Technically defined, a terminable interest is one that terminates with respect to the surviving spouse "on the lapse of time, on the occurrence of an event or contingency, or on the failure of an event or contingency to occur," and then passes to someone other than the surviving spouse. Code §2056(b)(1). As a general rule, terminable interests do not qualify for the marital deduction because the termination of the surviving spouse's interest means that nothing is includable in the surviving spouse's gross estate when the interest passes to the next person.

> **Example:** A husband dies leaving a will that establishes a testamentary trust for his wife's benefit. Under the trust, when the wife dies, the trust assets pass to the husband's children from his first marriage. The wife's interest in this trust is a terminable interest because it terminates upon the occurrence of an event — her death — and passes to persons other than the surviving spouse — the decedent's children from a prior marriage. As such, the fair market value of assets passing into this trust would not qualify for the estate tax marital deduction.

However, a terminable interest *does* qualify for the estate tax marital deduction if the surviving spouse has a lifetime income interest and holds a *general power of appointment*:

- *General Power of Appointment.* If a surviving spouse has both (1) a lifetime income interest in all the assets *and* (2) an inter vivos or testamentary general power of appointment over such property exercisable in her favor or in favor of her estate, a terminable interest passing to the surviving spouse will qualify for the estate tax marital deduction. Code §2056(b)(5).

Example: A husband dies leaving a will that establishes a testamentary trust for his wife's benefit. The terms of this trust grant the wife an income interest in all of the trust property for life and permit her to appoint any trust assets remaining in the corpus at her death to her own estate. Because the wife has both a lifetime income interest in the trust and a testamentary general power of appointment in the remaining corpus, the fair market value of the trust assets would qualify for the estate tax marital deduction.

Another way in which a terminable interest may qualify for the estate tax marital deduction is by satisfying the requirements with respect to *qualified terminable interest property* (QTIP). If these requirements are satisfied, the executor may make a *QTIP election*:

- *QTIP Election.* If the following three conditions are met, a terminable interest will qualify for the estate tax marital deduction: (1) a surviving spouse has a lifetime income interest in the assets, (2) with respect to this lifetime income interest, "no person has a power to appoint any part of the property to any person other than the surviving spouse," and (3) the executor of the first decedent spouse estate elects to allow such property to be includable in the surviving spouse's gross estate. Code §2056(b)(7).

Example: A husband dies with a will that establishes a testamentary trust for his wife's benefit. The trust terms provide the wife an income interest (payable at least annually) for life and, upon the wife's death, that the principal be distributed to the husband's children from a prior marriage. The husband's executors make a QTIP election on his estate tax return. Under these circumstances, the fair market value of the trust assets would qualify for the estate tax marital deduction.[18]

Example: A husband dies with a will that establishes a testamentary trust for his wife's benefit. The trust terms provide the wife an income interest (payable at least annually) for life so long as she remains unmarried and, upon the wife's death or remarriage, that the principal be distributed to the husband's children from a prior marriage. Under these circumstances, the trust does not qualify for the marital

18. And recall that, under Code §2044, when the wife later dies, this property will be included in her gross estate because it previously qualified for the estate tax marital deduction.

deduction (and, as a result, the husband's executor could not make a QTIP election) because the wife's income interest is not for the duration of her life, but rather, terminable upon her remarriage.

State Death Taxes Paid (Code §2058). Several states (e.g., New York and Pennsylvania) levy estate and inheritance taxes. For purposes of computing the federal estate tax, these state death taxes are fully deductible.

12.4.1.3 Computation of the Estate Tax and Preparation of the Estate Tax Return

As discussed in Chapter 1, one of the foremost state law duties of the executor is to pay all taxes imposed on the estate. This duty to pay estate taxes is reaffirmed by the Code, which mandates that the estate tax "shall be paid by the executor." Code §2002. This mandate has teeth: If the executor pays other debts of the estate before satisfying unpaid claims of the federal government, the executor is personally liable for the unpaid government claims. 31 U.S.C. §3713(b). The executor must therefore understand precisely how to compute the estate tax, prepare the estate tax return (Form 706), and file it within nine months of the decedent's death. The executor may request a six-month extension for filing the return, but the Code does not permit an extension for payment of the estate tax.

An executor must file an estate tax return when the value of the taxable estate — the gross estate minus deductions — exceeds the decedent's applicable exclusion amount. Under Code §2010(c)(3), the basic exclusion amount is $5 million, adjusted annually for inflation. As of 2017, the applicable exclusion amount equaled $5,490,000. The applicable exclusion amount, however, is reduced by the amount of taxable gifts made during the decedent's lifetime. The estate tax rate applicable to estates whose values exceed this threshold is, as of 2017, a flat 40 percent. Code §2001(c).

> **Example:** Suppose a husband dies in 2017 with $6 million of assets in his name. Because the fair market value of the assets in the husband's estate exceeds the applicable exclusion amount (i.e., $6 million > $5,490,000), his executor must file an estate tax return.

> **Example:** Suppose a husband makes $3 million of taxable gifts during his lifetime and then dies in 2017 with $3 million of assets in his name. Because the fair market value of the assets in the husband's estate (i.e., $3 million) exceeds his remaining applicable exclusion amount (i.e., $2,490,000, or $5,490,000 – $3,000,000), his executor must file an estate tax return.

The one other situation when an executor needs to file an estate tax return is when a surviving spouse seeks to use the so-called Deceased Spousal Unused Exclusion (DSUE) amount. The Code permits the "portability" of the unused applicable exclusion amount between spouses. If the first spouse to die has not made lifetime and death-time taxable transfers, the aggregate of which do not exceed the applicable exclusion amount, the unused amount can be transferred to the surviving spouse for use upon his or her subsequent death. The executor of the estate of the first spouse must file Form 706 and elect to have the unused applicable exclusion amount transferred to the surviving spouse. Code §2010(c)(4), (5).

> **Example:** Suppose a husband makes a $4 million taxable gift in 2014 and subsequently dies in 2017 with no assets in his name. That being the case, the DSUE amount would be $1.49 million (i.e., $5,490,000 – $4,000,000). The executor of the husband's estate can elect to transfer the husband's DSUE amount to the decedent's wife. After the election is made, the decedent's wife is at liberty to transfer during her life or upon her death $6.98 million (i.e., $5,490,000 + $1,490,000) free of federal gift or estate taxes.

The estate tax is computed on Form 706 as follows:

(Gross Estate) – (Allowable Deductions)	= **Tentative Taxable Estate**
(Tentative Taxable Estate) – (State Death Tax Deduction)	= **Taxable Estate**
(Taxable Estate) + (Adjusted Taxable Gifts)	= **Estate Tax Base**
(Estate Tax Base) × (Estate Tax Rate)	= **Tentative Estate Tax**
(Tentative Estate Tax) – (Gift Tax Paid or Payable)	= **Gross Estate Tax**
(Gross Estate Tax) – (Applicable Credit Amount & Other Credits)	= **Net Estate Tax**

Upon completion and filing of Form 706 with the IRS, the executor awaits word from the agency that either the estate will be audited or, alternatively, the IRS accepts the executor's computations and agrees to close the estate. If the IRS closes the estate, the executor may then proceed with the next steps of estate administration (payment of other creditor claims, distribution of property beneficiaries, etc.) in accordance with state law. Prior to making any distributions, however, best practices mandate that the executor secure a Release and Refunding Bond from each beneficiary. True to their name, these instruments serve a dual role: first, they release executors from liability regarding any putative defalcations that they may have committed; and, second, each estate beneficiary agrees to refund the estate should a subsequent estate liability or debt come to light.

PROBLEM II

A taxpayer dies owing an interest in Blackacre, real property worth $1 million on the date of the taxpayer's death. For purposes of the federal estate tax, what amount, if any, should be included in the taxpayer's gross estate in the following four cases?

a. Title held in taxpayer's name alone
b. Title held jointly with his wife
c. Title held jointly with his friend
d. Title in which the taxpayer held a life estate

PROBLEM III

Which of the following estate expenses and payments, if any, are deductible from the decedent's gross estate?

a. $100,000 gold-plated casket
b. $100,000 of legal fees
c. $100,000 bequest to a longtime significant other
d. $100,000 bequest to the surviving spouse
e. $100,000 in trust for the benefit of the surviving spouse, the terms of which grant discretion to the trustee to make income and principal distributions to her
f. $100,000 in trust for the benefit of the surviving spouse, the terms of which provide lifetime income interest and grant discretion to the trustee to make principal distributions to her

PROBLEM IV

A widow taxpayer dies in 2017 with a $6 million estate.

A. Would a federal estate tax return need to be filed?

B. Would federal estate tax be due? Describe those circumstances in which no tax would be due.

C. If the widow instead died with a $1 million estate in 2017, describe those circumstances, if any, when an estate tax return would need to be filed.

D. If a decedent died on December 31, 2017, what is the exact estate tax return due date?

E. If a decedent died on December 31, 2017, and the executor secured an estate tax return extension, what is the exact estate tax return due date?

F. Suppose instead that the taxpayer were not a widow but married, and suppose further that she died in 2017 with a taxable estate of $1 million. Are there circumstances that might require her executor to file an estate tax return?

12.4.2 Estate Tax Application

Taxpayers often establish testamentary trusts as part of their estate plan. Such trusts, which come into effect upon death, are ordinarily designed to mitigate estate tax liability and serve other agendas (e.g., keeping assets within family bloodlines). While the nature of these trusts spans the gamut, the three most common testamentary trusts are (1) bypass trusts, (2) QTIP trusts, and (3) minors' trusts. Their salient features are enumerated below.

12.4.2.1 Bypass Trusts

Before the era of portability (when executors were precluded from using the DSUE amount), the applicable exclusion amount had to be used at the death of the first spouse or else be forfeited. For example, if a husband died in 2003 (when the applicable exclusion amount was $1 million) and he left his entire estate of $1 million to his wife, there would have been no estate tax due because of the marital deduction. Suppose that the surviving spouse had $1 million in assets in addition to the inheritance from her late husband. Upon her death, she could only utilize her own $1 million applicable exclusion amount, reflective of the fact that her decedent husband's applicable exclusion amount of $1 million was forever lost. Thus, as a married couple, the husband and wife had a combined applicable exclusion amount of $2 million, but because the husband's estate passed to the wife tax-free under the marital deduction, his applicable exclusion amount was wasted.

Frustrated at the prospects of losing estate tax–sheltering benefits, estate planning attorneys devised what has commonly become known as the *bypass trust.* This trust is designed to absorb the first decedent spouse's unused applicable exclusion amount. It does so by passing trust assets to at least one beneficiary other than the surviving spouse, exhausting all or a portion of the applicable exclusion amount rather than qualifying for the estate tax marital deduction. Consider, in the prior example, if the husband dies and leaves his $1 million estate to a bypass trust rather than outright to his wife. The bypass trust provides a lifetime benefit for his wife and, at her death, for distribution of the balance to their children. Suppose that over the next ten years, the bypass trust makes annual income payments and periodic distributions of principal to his wife. Upon his wife's death in year 10, suppose further that the trust assets have grown in value to $2 million. All assets owned by the wife (including distributions of income and principal from the bypass trust) would, of course, be includable in her taxable estate — to be sheltered, if possible, by her own applicable exclusion amount. Whatever assets that remain in the bypass trust, however, would not be includable in her taxable estate — thus earning this trust the "bypass" moniker.[19]

For the past several decades, at the first spouse's death, bypass trusts were a central feature in the estate plans of most married couples. In contrast to the terms of marital trusts that qualify for QTIP treatment (see below), the terms of bypass trusts are far less regimented, varying across the board.

The following example provides model terms of a simple bypass trust:

> **ADMINISTRATION OF TRUST B.** Any property passing into TRUST B shall be administered by my Trustee (named in Article X of this Will), in accordance with the following terms and conditions:
>
> **(i) PAYMENT OF INCOME AND PRINCIPAL.** During the life of my spouse, **CANDI**, my Trustee shall pay to or apply for the benefit of my spouse such amounts from the net income and

19. Recall that the assets that initially passed into the bypass trust at the husband's death were includable in his estate, enabling him to capitalize upon the full use of his applicable exclusion amount of $1 million.

principal of TRUST B as my Trustee deems necessary or desirable for the health, education, support and maintenance of my spouse.

(ii) TERMINATION OF TRUST B. Upon the death of my spouse, **CANDI**, any accrued and undistributed income of TRUST B and any part of the principal of TRUST B remaining upon the death of my spouse shall be distributed to my then living issue, per stirpes. If no issue of mine is then living, such property shall be distributed to those persons who would have taken, and in such shares as they would have taken, my property if I had died intestate a resident of the State of New Jersey, as of the date of such distribution.

Now that the applicable exclusion amount is portable between spouses and, as such, its utilization is not necessary at the first spouse's demise, bypass trust use has been called into question. Yet, many estate planners still employ bypass trusts for the following three reasons: First, in states that have retained their estate taxes, there is no portability of state estate tax exemptions; that being the case, the "use it or lose" problem remains prevalent and, left unaddressed (i.e., failure to establish a bypass trust at the first spouse's demise), can cause a married couple to forfeit a state estate tax exemption for the first spouse to die. Second, DSUE amounts do not grow in the surviving spouse's hands, whereas assets passing into the bypass trust that appreciate in value remain sheltered from future estate tax imposition. Finally, the generation-skipping transfer (GST) tax exemption, detailed below, is not portable between spouses; bypass trusts thus afford the opportunity for the first decedent spouse to utilize the GST exemption amount in an effective manner. The bottom line: Bypass trusts remain a potentially potent tool in the hands of a well-versed estate planning attorney.

12.4.2.2 QTIP Trusts

For a whole host of reasons, many married taxpayers do not want to leave all or a portion of their estates outright to their surviving spouse. Sometimes they fear that their surviving spouse will remarry and pass along any inherited wealth to the new family; other are concerned that their spouse is a spendthrift and, if left unchecked, inherited assets could be quickly dissipated; and still others want to retain dead hand control of their estate. As a common vehicle to achieve these objectives, taxpayers use trusts to provide for, but do not cede full control to, their surviving spouse.

To qualify for the estate tax marital deduction, the Code imposes several technical requirements. A QTIP trust, for example, must provide the surviving spouse a qualifying income interest for life, be exclusively for his benefit, and not grant him (or anyone else) a lifetime special power of appointment. Assuming that these conditions are met, the decedent spouse's executor can make a QTIP election on Form 706 and choose to have the assets passing into this trust qualify for the estate tax marital deduction.

So long as the trust complies with the QTIP requirements, taxpayers retain the ability to decide how much discretion to give their trustees for making distributions of principal from the trust corpus. For example, some taxpayers grant "absolute discretion" to their trustees; others restrict fiduciary authority to an ascertainable standard (i.e., for the surviving spouse's health, education, maintenance, and support); and still others preclude any principal distributions. What's more, the continued availability of *principal* distributions can be conditioned on the spouse not remarrying or on some other condition, even though the *income* interest cannot be so conditioned if it is going to be a qualifying income interest for life.

The following example provides model terms of a simple QTIP trust:

> **ADMINISTRATION OF TRUST A.** Any property passing into TRUST A shall be administered by my Trustees (hereinafter named in Article 7 of this Will) in accordance with the following terms and conditions:
>
> **(i) PAYMENT OF INCOME.** During the life of my spouse, **RICHARD**, my Trustees shall pay to or apply for the benefit of my spouse all of the net income of TRUST A, in convenient installments, but not less frequently than quarter-annually.
>
> **(ii) PAYMENT OF PRINCIPAL.** During the life of my spouse, **RICHARD**, my Trustees shall pay to or apply for the benefit of my spouse such amounts from the principal of TRUST A as my Trustees deem necessary or desirable for the health, education, support and maintenance of my spouse.
>
> **(iii) TESTAMENTARY SPECIAL POWER OF APPOINTMENT.** Upon the death of my spouse, **RICHARD**, my spouse may, by his Last Will and Testament, appoint the then remaining principal of TRUST A to or for the benefit of my issue, equally or unequally and to or for the benefit of any one or more of them to the exclusion of the others, in such portions or amounts, and upon such estates, whether in trust or otherwise, as my said spouse shall so indicate; and if the then remaining principal of TRUST A is so appointed, my Trustees shall pay over, transfer and distribute such property to or for the benefit of my issue, as so indicated by my said spouse; *provided, however,* that my spouse, **RICHARD**, shall not be deemed to have exercised this testamentary special power of appointment unless he specifically refers to this power in his Last Will and Testament.
>
> **(iv) TERMINATION OF TRUST A.**
>
> > **(a) Distribution of Income and Principal.** Upon the death of my spouse, **RICHARD**, any accrued and undistributed income of TRUST A and any part of the principal of TRUST A remaining upon the death of my spouse, to the extent not appointed by my spouse, **RICHARD**, pursuant to the provisions of Subparagraph (iii), shall be distributed to my then living issue, per stirpes. If no issue of mine is then living, such property shall be distributed to those persons who would have taken, and in such shares as they would have taken, my property if I had died intestate a resident of the State of New Jersey, as of the date of such distribution.
> >
> > **(b) Taxes Attributable to QTIP Property.** Notwithstanding anything to the contrary in this Article 3, prior to the termination of TRUST A, my Trustees shall pay, either directly to the appropriate taxing authority or to the executors or personal representatives of the estate of my spouse, as my Trustees deem advisable, the amount requested and certified by such executors or personal representatives as being equal to the amount by which the estate and inheritance taxes assessed by reason of the death of my spouse are increased as a result of the inclusion of the principal and undistributed income of TRUST A in the estate of my spouse for such tax purposes. If neither my spouse nor the executors or personal representatives of the estate of my spouse waives the right of recovery pursuant to Section 2207A of the Code, the estate of my spouse shall be entitled to all rights provided by such Section.

As a practical matter, now that the federal estate tax affects only the smallest slice of the taxpaying public — far less than 1 percent — some people predict that QTIP trust usage might fall by the wayside. However, because families tend to be protective of their wealth and trust use is one way of exercising enduring control, we predict that QTIP trust usage will remain a vibrant feature of the contemporary estate planning practice.

12.4.2.3 Minors' Trust

When it comes to athletics and free-spiritedness, youth is a wonderful attribute. It knows few bounds. Yet, when it comes to astute financial management and planning, youth is rarely a blessing. Indeed, it regularly results in ruinous mistakes. Taxpayers and their estate planners know this and plan accordingly. Taxpayers planning a substantial gift to a young (or, sometimes, a young at heart) beneficiary commonly use minors' trusts (also known as minority trusts) to manage property for a minor beneficiary or protect an adult beneficiary from financial indiscretion.

A key virtue of trusts is that they enable the settlor to exercise long-term, and even post-mortem, control over the trust property. Some donors trust their children to manage their own affairs, and, accordingly, they limit the duration of their trust to the beneficiary's minority or mandate trust distributions at a fairly young adult age (e.g., age 21). Other taxpayers are much more circumspect and postpone trust distributions until the beneficiary is more mature (e.g., age 35). A common feature of minors' trusts is to establish three different age distribution dates (e.g., one-third of the trust principal at age 30, one-half of the trust principal at age 35, and the undistributed trust income and remaining trust principal at age 40). A reason for using staggered age distributions is that, if trust beneficiaries quickly dissipate the first or even second trust distribution amounts, they can hopefully learn from their financial mistakes and plan to use future distributions more productively.

Appendix 4 provides a sample testamentary minor's trust.

Notwithstanding possible future changes in the federal estate tax laws, the use of minors' trusts is likely to endure. Taxpayers know that youth rarely appreciate the hard work, effort, and energy required to accumulate significant wealth. So, handing such wealth to a young person on a proverbial silver platter is rarely advised; in contrast, a long-term plan minor's trust can form a protective barrier around accumulated wealth until the beneficiary has reached financial maturity.

PROBLEM V

Seeking professional estate planning advice, a married couple — first marriage for both — visits your office. Regarding the terms of their wills, do you recommend outright bequests or bequests in trust? What considerations might dictate your recommendations?

PROBLEM VI

Seeking professional estate planning advice, a married couple — second marriage for both — visits your office. Regarding the terms of their wills, do you recommend outright bequests or bequests in trust? What considerations might dictate your recommendations?

PROBLEM VII

Seeking professional estate planning advice, a married couple visits your office. The couple expresses misgivings regarding the financial acumen of their children. Regarding the terms of their wills, what do you recommend and why?

12.5 GENERATION-SKIPPING TRANSFER TAX

When it comes to tax planning, taxpayers and their advisors have historically proven to be quite savvy, devising tax-saving stratagems that successfully circumvent even some of the most well-crafted and comprehensive tax statutes. And so has been the case with the federal estate tax.

Decades ago, taxpayers, along with their advisors, developed a formidable strategy to keep the federal estate tax at bay: Wealthy taxpayers would establish a lifetime trust for each of their children; and upon each child's death, the undistributed income and trust principal would pass to the deceased child's children (namely, the initial taxpayer's grandchildren). While these lifetime trusts for the benefit of the taxpayer's children had their own virtues (e.g., asset protection), their true benefit was the fact that the trust assets escaped estate tax inclusion at each child's death. More specifically, upon the termination of a child's lifetime interest, the deceased child had no property interest in the trust to be included in his or her gross estate. This strategy of using cascading lifetime trusts (i.e., trusts whose terms provide for the benefit of lineal descendants until the trust principal is ultimately exhausted) forestalled estate tax application for generations of trust beneficiaries. Consistent with the general axiom that taxes deferred constitute taxes saved, so-called generation-skipping trusts grew rapidly in popularity. Indeed, the only obstacle preventing these trusts from avoiding the federal estate tax in perpetuity was the Rule Against Perpetuities established under state law. A common law restriction on dead hand control, the Rule Against Perpetuities applies to contingent future interests and generally requires that an interest vest (or fail to vest) within twenty-one years of a life in being.

Because generation-skipping transfers gravely threatened the federal estate tax base, Congress felt compelled to take action. While its first legislative attempt to address this problem proved disastrous and had to be retroactively repealed, in 1986, Congress devised a viable generation-skipping transfer (GST) tax targeted to close the cascading lifetime interest trust loophole.[20] This section of the chapter summarizes the salient attributes of these legislative efforts.

In the two subsections below, we explore (1) GST tax fundamentals and (2) planning devices that seasoned practitioners commonly employ to minimize their clients' GST tax burdens.

12.5.1 Generation-Skipping Transfer Tax Fundamentals

12.5.1.1 Determination of a GST Taxable Event

When it comes to mastering the GST tax, there are five terms of art that every practitioner (and, by extension, trusts and estates student) should know:

- **Skip Person.** "[A] *natural person* assigned to a generation which is 2 or more generations below the generation assignment of the transferor, or . . . a trust (A) if all interests in such trust are held by skip persons, or (B) if— (i) there is no person holding an interest in such trust, and (ii) at no time after such transfer may a distribution (including distributions on termination) be made from such trust to a nonskip person." Code §2613(a) (emphasis added).
- **Non-Skip Person.** "[A]ny person who is not a skip person." Code §2613(b).
- **Direct Skip.** "[A] transfer subject to [gift or estate tax] of an interest in property to a skip person." Code §2612(c).
- **Taxable Distribution.** "[A]ny distribution from a trust to a skip person (other than a taxable termination or a direct skip)." Code §2612(b).
- **Taxable Termination.** "[T]he termination (by death, lapse of time, release of power, or otherwise) of an interest in property held in trust unless—(A) immediately after such termination, a non-skip person has an interest in such property, or (B) at no time after such termination may a distribution (including distributions on termination) be made from such trust to a skip person." Code §2612(a).

These definitions are not self-explanatory; each requires further explication and examples that reflect their intent and import.

We start with skip and non-skip persons, which are statutorily defined and distinguished to ensure that a transfer tax is levied at least once every generational level. Code §2651 provides intricate definitions for generational assignments, but we will try to keep things simple and straightforward:

- **Skip Person.** A lineal descendant of the transferor is a skip person if the descendant is a grandchild or more remote descendant (e.g., great-grandchild).

20. Since 1986, however, most states have either repealed or modified the Rule Against Perpetuities. These legislative repeals and modifications enable trust settlors to take advantage of a loophole in the GST tax insofar as once the GST exemption is allocated, the trust is forever safeguarded from GST application no matter how many future generations it skips. See, e.g., Reid K. Weisbord, A Catharsis for U.S. Trust Law: American Reflections on the Panama Papers, 116 Colum. L. Rev. Online 93, 102-03 (2016).

A person other than a lineal descendant is a skip person if he or she is more than 37.5 years younger than the transferor.

- **Non-Skip Person.** Older transferees (e.g., ancestors, contemporaries, and children of the transferor), by contrast, are non-skip persons.

There are three events that trigger GST tax: direct skips, taxable distributions, and taxable terminations.

- **Direct Skip.** A *direct skip* is a gift or bequest made to a skip person (e.g., a taxpayer makes a $100,000 gift to his granddaughter or a bequest of the same amount to his grandson). Recall that a skip person may also include a trust; that being the case, if a taxpayer makes a gift or bequest to a trust in which all of the beneficiaries are skip persons (and hence the trust itself constitutes a skip person), then the transfer will trigger application of the GST tax.
- **Taxable Distribution.** A *taxable distribution* is exactly what it purports to be: a transfer by the trust to a skip person (e.g., a taxpayer establishes a trust for the benefit of his children and grandchildren; and during the term of trust administration, the trustee distributes $100,000 to one of the taxpayer's granddaughters).
- **Taxable Termination.** Finally, a *taxable termination* occurs when a trust term ends and some or all of its assets inure to one or more skip persons (e.g., at the death of the transferor's last surviving child, a trust terminates and its undistributed income and principal are distributed to the transferor's then-living grandchildren in equal shares).

These three GST tax triggering–events are subject to two important exceptions: First, in cases of lineal generational assignments, if a parent of the recipient has died, under the so-called predeceased parent rule, the recipient moves up a generational level. To illustrate, suppose a grandparent has a daughter who has a son (i.e., the grandparent's grandson); if the daughter predeceases the grandparent, the Code moves the grandson up one generational level, causing him to shed his skip person status and deeming him to be a non-skip person. Code §2651(e). Second, if a transfer is excluded from the gift tax base insofar as it is (1) a present-interest gift that does not exceed the annual exclusion, or (2) a medical or tuition expense payment made on another's behalf, it will likewise be excluded from the GST tax base. Code §2642(c)(3)(A), (B).

12.5.1.2 Computation of the GST Tax

Assuming that a GST taxable event has occurred (i.e., a direct skip, taxable distribution, or taxable termination), the next step is to compute the GST tax. To compute this tax, multiply the taxable amount by the applicable rate. Code §2602.

12.5.1.2.1 Taxable Amount

The nature of the GST taxable event determines the taxable amount.

- For *direct skips*, the taxable amount is the value of property received by the transferee. Code §2623.

- For *taxable distributions*, the taxable amount is the value of property received by the transferee, reduced by any expense incurred by the transferee in connection with the determination, collection, or refund of the tax imposed by application of the GST tax. Code §2621.
- For *taxable terminations*, the taxable amount includes all property held in the trust reduced by defined trust administration expenses. Code §2622.

12.5.1.2.2 Applicable Rate

Computation of the applicable rate requires the introduction of two new terms, namely, *GST exemption* and *inclusion ratio.*

The *GST exemption* is the amount that taxpayers can exclude from the GST tax base. Congress determined that this amount should equal the estate tax's applicable exclusion amount ($5,490,000 as of 2017). Taxpayers are at liberty to allocate this exemption amount (Code §2632(a)); and, as a prophylactic measure, sometimes this allocation is made automatically to certain transfers (Code §2632(b), (c)).

The *inclusion ratio* is computed by subtracting from the number 1 the "applicable fraction." The applicable fraction's numerator is equal to the GST exemption being allocated, and its denominator is equal to the fair market value of the property being transferred (reduced by (1) federal and state estate taxes, if any, and (2) charitable deductions, if any). For example, if a taxpayer makes a $100,000 transfer to her granddaughter and allocates an equivalent amount of GST exemption, the inclusion ratio would be 0 (i.e., 1 – $100,000/$100,000); in contrast, if the taxpayer makes the identical transfer to her granddaughter but only has $25,000 of remaining GST exemption available, the inclusion ratio would be .75 (i.e., 1 – $25,000/$100,000).

The applicable rate requires that the taxpayer multiply the maximum federal estate tax rate (currently, 40 percent) by the inclusion ratio with respect to such transfer. Code §2641. In the two examples cited in the prior paragraph in which the inclusion ratio was 0 and .75, respectively, the applicable rate would be 0 percent (i.e., .4 × 0) and 30 percent (.4 × .75). Given the $100,000 taxable amount, the first transfer would have generated no GST tax ($100,000 × .4 × 0), and the second transfer would have generated a GST tax of $30,000 ($100,000 × .4 × .3).

There are two remaining odds and ends pertaining to the GST tax that warrant attention. First, just as married taxpayers are at liberty to treat a gift made by one spouse as if made in equal shares by both spouses, the same latitude extends to the GST tax (i.e., married couples have the ability to "split" their gifts for purposes of allocating their GST exemptions). Code §2652(a)(2). Second, for purposes of applying the GST tax, a transferor is normally the donor or decedent whose transfer or death generates gift or estate tax. Code §2652(a). Consistent with this rule, when a donor or decedent's estate makes a QTIP election qualifying a gift or bequest for the unlimited marital deduction, such property is subsequently included in the surviving spouse's estate (Code §2044); as such, the surviving spouse's estate is deemed the transferor of such property for purposes of applying the GST tax. However, the Code provides the opportunity to make what is known as a "reverse QTIP election." Code §2652(a)(3). This election retains the original taxpayer who made the gift or bequest as the transferor, enabling him to allocate his GST exemption amount to the value of the gift or bequest that initially qualified for the estate tax marital deduction. The reason for this allocation is important: It obviates the need to utilize the surviving spouse's GST exemption to safeguard the trust assets from future GST tax exposure; and, furthermore, even if the trust assets grow in value, the inclusion ratio will remain set in place.

> **Example:** A husband dies and establishes a $5 million QTIP trust for the benefit of his wife. In addition to making a QTIP election to qualify the assets of this trust for the estate tax marital deduction, his executors also make a so-called reverse QTIP election. The latter election enables them to allocate GST exemption amounts to this trust and thereby safeguard it from potential future GST tax imposition. Upon the wife's subsequent demise, notwithstanding the fact that the value of the trust assets will be included in her gross estate, her husband will remain the deemed transferor for purposes of applying the GST tax.

Finally, consider what taxpayers must do to fulfill their GST tax obligations under the Code. Administrative requirements vary depending on the nature of the transfer. In the case of direct skips, administrative compliance burdens fall upon the transferor's shoulders; in the case of inter vivos direct skips, the transferor must file Form 709 on or before April 15 of the year following the transfer, unless an extension of time is granted; and in the case of testamentary direct skips, the transferor (namely, the decedent's estate) must file Form 706 reporting the transfer, due nine months after the transferor's death, unless an extension of time is granted. In the case of taxable distributions, the administrative compliance burden is bifurcated: The trustee must file an informational Form 706-GS(D-1) by April 15 of the year following the calendar year in which the distribution was made and provide a copy to each distributee; once in hand, each distributee must file Form 706-GS(D) by the fifteenth day of the fourth month after the close of the taxable year of the taxable distribution. Finally, in the case of taxable terminations, the administrative compliance burden falls on the shoulders of the trustee, who must file Form 706-GS(T) by the fifteenth day of the fourth month after the close of the trust's taxable year, unless an extension is granted.

PROBLEM VIII

A taxpayer makes several transfers. Which of the following ones are subject to GST tax?

a. The taxpayer transfers $1 million to his wife, who is forty years his junior.
b. The taxpayer transfers $1 million to his mistress, who is forty years his junior.
c. The taxpayer transfers $1 million into a trust for his granddaughter's education.
d. The taxpayer transfers $1 million into a trust in which his granddaughter and the American Red Cross are named as discretionary beneficiaries.

PROBLEM IX

Classify each of the following transfers as direct skip, taxable distribution, or taxable termination.

a. A taxpayer establishes a trust for the benefit of his children and grandchildren. During the administration of the trust, the trustee distributes $100,000 to one of the taxpayer's grandchildren.
b. A taxpayer establishes a trust for the lifetime benefit of his children and grandchildren. Many years later, during the administration of the trust, the taxpayer's last child passes away.
c. A taxpayer dies and bequeaths the sum of $10 million to his favorite granddaughter.

PROBLEM X

In 2017, for the first time in a taxpayer's life, she makes a taxable gift, transferring $10 million to her granddaughter. How much tax would be owed, when is it due, and on what tax return form would the taxpayer report it?

12.5.2 Generation-Skipping Transfer Tax Application

Taxpayers seek to avoid GST tax application and, in a strategic fashion, utilize their GST exemption to achieve this objective. Three kinds of trusts are emblematic of this strategy's utilization: (1) inter vivos dynasty trusts, (2) testamentary dynasty trusts, and (3) grandchildren trusts that contain a general power of appointment.

12.5.2.1 Inter Vivos Dynasty Trusts

With the intent to have their wealth cascade down multiple generations, taxpayers establish dynasty trusts. In the absence of the Rule Against Perpetuities (or in those states that have attenuated this rule), this is a successful strategy.

To avoid the GST tax (the application of which would significantly deplete the trust corpus), taxpayers strategically allocate their GST exemption to their trust contributions. By making these strategic allocations, taxpayers secure trusts that have a zero inclusion ratio and, as such, are immune to GST tax exposure — now and forevermore.

When it comes to dynasty trusts, a question that taxpayers often raise is whom they should designate as their initial trustees and successor trustees. After all, naming contemporaries or children is a short-term solution for a trust that is supposed to extend decades and centuries to come. A common practice is to have a provision in the trust instrument that allows the last serving trustee to name his or her own successor(s). The addition of such a provision adds flexibility to the trust instrument, helping to ensure long-term preservation of the trust corpus. The following is a model "last acting trustee" provision:

> **LAST ACTING TRUSTEE.** The last acting sole individual Trustee for whom the Settlor has not named a successor in this Article or otherwise, but for whom a successor would be necessary if he or she ceases to act, may, by an instrument in writing, executed by him or her during his or her lifetime (which he or she may alter from time to time) acknowledged in the same manner as is then required to record deeds of real estate in the State of California, or by his or her Last Will and Testament duly admitted to probate, designate any individual, individuals and/or corporate banking institutions (and may fix the order in which such individuals and/or corporate banking institutions shall serve) as (1) co-Trustees or co-Trustee, to serve with such individual sole Trustee; and/or (2) successor Trustees or successor Trustee, to succeed such individual sole Trustee in the event that he or she shall cease to act as Trustee hereunder for any reason whatsoever.

12.5.2.2 Testamentary Dynasty Trusts

Since death usually strikes taxpayers unexpectedly, they ordinarily cannot plan with any precision how much wealth they will have or the exact amount of their remaining GST exemption. That being the case, taxpayers usually direct that a portion or all of their residuary estate equal to their remaining GST exemption goes into a trust with a zero inclusion ratio and immediately or ultimately inures to skip persons, and the balance of their residuary estate (if any) goes either outright or into another trust that has an inclusion ratio of 1 and that inures immediately or in the not-too-distant future to non-skip persons.

Below is sample formulaic bequest language that bifurcates a taxpayer's residuary estate into GST-tax-exempt trusts (designed for the ultimate benefit of the taxpayer's grandchildren) and non-GST-tax-exempt trusts (designed for the benefit of the taxpayer's children):

> **BEQUEST TO CHILDREN.** Whenever any interest of a child of mine is to be distributed subject to the directions set forth in this Paragraph, such interest shall be divided into two (2) separate portions: one such portion to be referred to as the "GST EXEMPT PORTION" and the other such portion as the "NON–GST EXEMPT PORTION." The GST EXEMPT PORTION allocable to a child of mine shall be equal in value to the result of dividing the amount of my unused GST exemption, if any, as provided by Section 2631(a) of the Internal Revenue Code of 1986, as amended (the "Code"), by the number of children of mine who survive me. The GST EXEMPT PORTION shall be held in trust and be administered for the benefit of such child subject to the directions hereinafter set forth in Paragraph C of this Article 3. The NON–GST EXEMPT PORTION allocable to a child of mine shall consist of the balance, if any, of the interest passing to such child subject to the provisions of this Paragraph B, after the allocation of all or a portion of such

interest to the GST EXEMPT PORTION as provided in this Paragraph B. The NON–GST EXEMPT PORTION allocable to a child of mine shall be distributed subject to the directions hereinafter set forth in Paragraph D of this Article 3.

Because GST-tax-exempt trusts are designed to span decades and centuries to come, taxpayers often grant lifetime and testamentary special powers of appointment to trust beneficiaries. These special powers of appointment enhance the flexibility of the trust instrument, enabling trust beneficiaries to experience something more akin to direct ownership. In contrast, with respect to non-GST-tax-exempt trusts, taxpayers often grant non-skip trust beneficiaries a testamentary general power of appointment. The addition of this power causes the trust property to be included in the trust beneficiary's estate, making the trust beneficiary the new transferor and thereby voiding GST tax exposure in the form of a taxable termination.

12.5.2.3 Grandchildren Trusts with General Power of Appointment

As a general axiom, taxpayers relish their grandchildren and, if they are able, love showering them with financial gifts. What these same taxpayers don't enjoy is making taxable gifts that utilize part of their lifetime exemption amount; instead, they prefer to avail themselves of the gift tax annual exclusion. If, however, taxpayers make gifts directly to a grandchild or into a UTMA account, the grandchild will have immediate access to such funds or gain access at age 21. For many grandparents, giving their grandchildren large sums of wealth at such impressionable ages is simply not acceptable.

Congress has presented these taxpayers with a viable option to satisfy their needs. As long as these taxpayers establish trusts that have only one skip person (usually, a grandchild) as a beneficiary and this skip person has a testamentary general power of appointment over the trust corpus, contributions to it will qualify for the gift tax annual exclusion (assuming the trust beneficiary has a present interest in the contribution vis-à-vis a Crummey power) and will simultaneously be exempt from GST tax. Code §2642(c). This option gives the opportunity to grandparents to defer the financial gratification of their grandchildren to much later in life, say, when the latter attain ages 30, 40, or 50.

PROBLEM XI

A taxpayer wants his wealth to cascade down the generations. Insofar as the GST tax is concerned, what should be the taxpayer's paramount tactic to achieve his goal?

PROBLEM XII

What kind of provision can be added to any trust instrument to protect against GST tax imposition?

PROBLEM XIII

A taxpayer wants to secure a $10 million life insurance policy, the annual premiums of which are $100,000. Assuming that the policy will be owned by an irrevocable trust from inception, what do you instruct the taxpayer to do as premium payments are made?

12.6 CONCLUSION

Over the course of the last two decades, the federal transfer tax regime has fallen out of political favor. Labeled by many politicians as the "death tax," federal transfer taxes have struggled for their very existence, on many occasions narrowly avoiding outright repeal. While outright repeal has been avoided, Congress has significantly weakened the transfer tax regime by raising the monetary amounts that are sheltered from the gift, estate, and generation-skipping transfer taxes. During his 2016 campaign, President Donald Trump promised to repeal the estate tax in its entirety.

As a practical matter, an emasculated federal transfer tax regime means that the number of taxpayers faced with transfer tax exposure has dwindled. Indeed, current statistics indicate that each year only a few thousand taxpayers annually pay any gift, estate, or GST tax. In light of anemic revenue collections, the viability of the entire transfer tax regime has been called into question.

What this chapter indicates is that the federal transfer tax regime has played a pivotal role in shaping salient trust terms and how estates are administered. But as the federal transfer tax regime wanes in importance, taxpayers and practitioners alike should anticipate two important trends. First, in the absence of a meaningful federal transfer tax regime, there will be fewer inter vivos and testamentary trusts established. Second, because complex estate tax returns will often no longer need to be prepared and filed, the estate administration process should be simplified.

Nevertheless, we do not want to conclude this chapter with the notion that the economic prospects for a talented trusts and estates student are dim. Those students with an acumen and zest for trust and estate law will find plenty of opportunities for gainful employment. Why? Because there will always be taxpayers who have entered into multiple marriages, have offspring or other objects of their bounty who lack maturity, or have other issues or concerns that necessitate trust usage. Moreover, until the fountain of youth is discovered, people will die, and their estates will require administration. The opportunity for legal services thus abounds for those with sharp minds who have mastered the material in this textbook and who are enthusiastically willing to employ their newly developed skills.

While you have reached your immediate destination (i.e., the end of this book), an even more rewarding and enriching journey awaits those who choose to practice in the trusts and estates area of the law. For those choosing this option, you are embarking on a professional path filled with intense intellectual challenges and immeasurable excitement in which no two days at the office will ever be the same — two virtues that few other career options can bestow.

Appendix 1 | Life Insurance Trust[21]

Prepared by:

___________________,
an Attorney at Law of the
State of New Jersey

THE JOHN DOE FAMILY TRUST

THIS AGREEMENT, made and executed this ____________ day of ____________, 20____________, by and among JOHN DOE, currently residing in ____________, New Jersey, hereinafter called the "Grantor", and JANE DOE, currently residing in ____________, New Jersey, and MARY DOE, currently residing in ____________, New Jersey, hereinafter called the "Trustees."

W I T N E S S E T H:

WHEREAS, the Grantor desires to create a trust of the property described in Schedule "A" annexed hereto and made a part hereof, for the benefit of the beneficiaries hereinafter named, which trust shall be known as "THE JOHN DOE FAMILY TRUST," and for the uses and purposes and upon the terms and conditions as hereinafter more fully set forth; and

WHEREAS, the Trustees have agreed to accept this trust and to be bound by the terms and provisions of this Agreement;

N O W   T H E R E F O R E:

In consideration of the premises, the mutual promises herein contained, the love and affection which the Grantor has for the respective beneficiaries hereof, and other good and valuable consideration, the receipt of which is hereby acknowledged, the parties hereto agree as follows:

FIRST: The Grantor has assigned to the Trustees the property set forth on Schedule "A" for the benefit of the beneficiaries hereinafter named to have and to hold the same, in trust, for and upon the uses and purposes, and subject to the terms and conditions hereinafter set forth.

SECOND: The Grantor or any other person may hereafter, and from time to time, grant, convey, transfer, bequeath, set over and assign to the Trustees additional property, including cash, securities, policies of life insurance, annuity contracts, accident policies, and any writing evidencing an interest in any retirement plan, profit sharing plan or contract under which death benefits can be made payable to the Trustees. Any such properties shall be held and received by the Trustees under the same terms and conditions, and subject to all the provisions of this Agreement. The Trustees agree and are empowered to accept distributions from any other person, including but not limited to the estate of the Grantor or the Grantor's spouse or from any trust created under the Will of the Grantor or the Grantor's spouse and/or from any living trust established during the life of the Grantor or the Grantor's spouse, and to hold such property under the same terms and conditions, and subject to all the provisions of this Agreement. The property administered pursuant to the provisions of this Agreement is designated as the "Trust Estate."

THIRD: (A) During each calendar year prior to the Grantor's death, (i) the Grantor's spouse, JANE DOE, if said spouse is then living, and (ii) each then-living child (such children presently being DAVID DOE, JOSHUA DOE, and JENNIFER DOE) and grandchild of the Grantor, in this order of priority (each such person hereinafter called "beneficiary" or, collectively, "beneficiaries"), shall have the right, following any contribution to the Trust Estate, to make withdrawals from the trust in accordance with the following provisions:

> (1) First, the Grantor's spouse may withdraw the lesser of: (a) the amount of the initial contribution or addition, or (b) the amount of the annual exclusion from the Federal Gift Tax under Internal Revenue Code Section 2503(b), as amended from time to time, or any section of like import, [limited, however, to the greater of FIVE (5%) PERCENT of the value of the trust corpus or FIVE THOUSAND ($5,000.00) DOLLARS].

COMMENT 1: The bracketed language in Subparagraph (1), above, and Subparagraph (2), below, only applies where the demand power is limited to a "5/5" power. If the use of a "hanging" power is desired, the bracketed language should be omitted.

> (2) Then, any then-living child and grandchild of the Grantor may withdraw an amount determined by subtracting from the amount of the initial contribution or addition the amount, if any, which the Grantor's spouse is entitled to withdraw with respect to such contribution or

addition under Subparagraph (1) above, and by dividing the result by the number of the Grantor's then-living children and grandchildren; provided, however, that the aggregate amount of such withdrawals by any one child or grandchild of the Grantor during any calendar year shall not exceed the amount of the annual exclusion from the Federal Gift Tax under Internal Revenue Code Section 2503(b), as amended from time to time, or any section of like import, [limited, however, to the greater of FIVE (5%) PERCENT of the value of the trust corpus or FIVE THOUSAND ($5,000.00) DOLLARS].

COMMENT 2: See Comment 1 as to bracketed language. The language of an alternate hanging power follows, taking into account that the insured's spouse may split the gift and double the amount of the exclusion available for contributions:

(2) . . . ; provided, however, that the aggregate amount of such withdrawals by any one child or grandchild during any calendar year shall not exceed twice the amount of the annual exclusion from the Federal Gift Tax under Internal Revenue Code Section 2503(b), as amended from time to time, or any section of like import, if the donor shall be married at the time of such contribution or addition, or the amount of the aforementioned annual exclusion if the donor shall not be married at the time of such contribution or addition.

(3) The Trustees shall notify each beneficiary who is entitled to withdraw, within seven (7) days of receipt of the initial contribution into trust, of the details concerning the property so contributed or added to the trust. Each such beneficiary shall then have the unrestricted right, subject to the provisions of Subparagraph (4) below, from the date of the notice of the Trustees to demand and undeniably receive from the trust the amount he or she is entitled to under Subparagraphs (1) or (2) hereunder. Each beneficiary shall have a similar right of withdrawal after each subsequent addition into the trust.

(4) Each beneficiary shall have the unrestricted right for a period of thirty (30) days from the date of contribution or addition to demand and undeniably receive from the trust the amount he or she is entitled to under Subparagraphs (1) or (2) hereunder. If no such demand is made within the thirty (30) day period designated, this right of withdrawal shall lapse, and shall not cumulate to any future years.

COMMENT 3: [Deleted.]

COMMENT 4: The use of this Subparagraph (4) is appropriate when the demand power is limited to a "5/5" power. If a "hanging" power is used, Subparagraph (4) should be replaced with the following alternative language:

(4) Such rights of withdrawal shall continue and cumulate to subsequent years to the extent such rights have not been exercised or terminated as hereinafter provided. On December 31 of each year, the cumulative amount which may be withdrawn by each beneficiary shall be reduced by the greater of FIVE THOUSAND ($5,000.00) DOLLARS or FIVE (5%) PERCENT of the value of the Trust Estate on such date; provided, however, such termination shall not occur prior to thirty (30) days from the date of contribution or addition unless the Trustees are notified in writing by a beneficiary prior to such time that he or she intends to waive his or her right to withdraw.

(5) In the event a beneficiary herein shall be under the age of eighteen (18) years, the guardian for the beneficiary may exercise this right of withdrawal on behalf of such

beneficiary, and the guardian shall receive all notices required under Subparagraph (3) hereunder.

> **COMMENT 5:** This provision allows a present interest to be created in a minor beneficiary.

(B) The Trustees may satisfy the exercise of any right of withdrawal by distributing, to the person making the withdrawal, cash or other assets, including insurance policies (or interests therein).

> **COMMENT 6:** This provision allows a present interest to be created in a trust holding only an unmatured life insurance policy.

(C)(1) For purposes of this paragraph, the term "contribution" or "addition" shall mean any cash or other assets, including life insurance policies (or interests therein), which are transferred to the Trustees to be held as part of the Trust Estate, and shall also include any premiums on policies of life insurance (or any interests therein) owned by the Trustees, which are paid by the Grantor or any other person, directly to the insurance companies issuing such policies, rather than first being paid to the Trustees.

> **COMMENT 7:** This provision accounts for the possibility that the insured will pay the premiums directly to the insurance company.

(2) In the case of any such premium which is paid directly to any insurance company, the date of the contribution or addition for purposes of this agreement shall be deemed to be the date on which such premium payment is transmitted to the insurance company issuing the policy.

(3) The amount of any contribution or addition to the Trust Estate shall be the value of such contribution for Federal gift tax purposes.

FOURTH: The Trustees shall hold the initial trust contribution and all subsequent contributions or additions in trust, nonetheless, upon the following terms and conditions:

(A) The Trustees shall invest and reinvest the same, and shall collect and receive the income and profits therefrom.

(B) The Trustee other than the Grantor's spouse (hereinafter called "disinterested Trustee") shall pay or apply so much or all of the net income and principal thereof to or for the benefit of any one or more of the members of a class consisting of the Grantor's spouse, JANE DOE, and the Grantor's then-living children and grandchildren from time to time as the disinterested Trustee shall, in the disinterested Trustee's sole discretion, deem necessary or desirable for the support, maintenance, health, and education (including college, professional, and/or graduate school) of the members of such class, or any of them. Any income not so paid or applied shall be added to the principal annually. No payment or application of income or principal shall be deemed an advancement of any share to which any person may be entitled upon the termination of this trust.

COMMENT 8: As discussed in the article, this "spray" provision permits the trustee to distribute the policy held by the trust to the insured's spouse during the insured's lifetime, to enable the insured to establish a new trust with different provisions.

(C)(1) The disinterested Trustee is authorized to make such payments or applications to or among the members of such class to the exclusion of any one or more of them in such proportions and at such time or times as the disinterested Trustee, in the exercise of the discretion hereinabove conferred, may determine to be in the best interests of the members of such class, or any of them.

(2) In exercising such discretion, the disinterested Trustee may, but shall not be required to, to the extent practical, inquire into or take into consideration any other property or sources of income or support the members of such class, or any of them, may have, together with any other factors which the disinterested Trustee may deem pertinent. In this connection, the Grantor directs that the disinterested Trustee take into consideration that, during the lifetime of the Grantor's spouse, the Grantor's spouse shall be considered the primary beneficiary of the trust assets, and that said spouse's needs of health, maintenance, and support are to be considered paramount.

(3) The disinterested Trustee's decision in the exercise of such discretion shall be binding upon all interested persons, including the Grantor's spouse.

(D) No Trustee hereunder shall exercise the discretion herein conferred for his or her own benefit or to discharge his or her respective obligation to support a beneficiary hereunder.

COMMENT 9: This provision aims to protect a trustee from being considered to have a general power of appointment over trust property merely due to his powers to make distributions of trust property. To be effective, there should be two trustees serving at all times, so that the second trustee can make distributions for the benefit of the first trustee (or his minor children).

(E) Upon the death of the Grantor, the property then remaining in trust shall be distributed, paid, or applied as follows:

(1) In the event the Grantor's spouse shall then be surviving, the property shall remain in further trust, nonetheless, upon the following terms and conditions:

(a) The Trustees shall invest and reinvest the same and shall collect and receive the income and profits therefrom, and pay over and distribute all of the net income to the Grantor's spouse in quarter-annual or more frequent intervals, as the Trustees shall determine.

(b) The Trustee other than the Grantor's spouse ("disinterested Trustee") shall pay or apply so much or all of the principal of this trust to and for the benefit of the Grantor's spouse, from time to time and in such amounts as the disinterested Trustee, in his sole discretion, shall deem necessary to meet the Grantor's spouse's needs of health, maintenance, and support.

(c) The Trustees, upon written request of the Grantor's spouse, shall pay to the Grantor's spouse out of the principal of this trust, in each calendar year (during the period December 15 through December 31 only), during the Grantor's spouse's lifetime, the greater of (i) the sum of FIVE THOUSAND ($5,000.00) DOLLARS, or (ii) FIVE (5%) PERCENT of the aggregate value of such principal at the time of such request. The power to withdraw shall be exercised by written instrument, shall expire on the last day of each calendar year, and shall be non-cumulative.

(d) At any time or times during the lifetime of the Grantor's spouse and upon the death of the Grantor's spouse, the Trustees shall pay over, transfer, convey, assign and administer upon such estates, in trust or otherwise in such amounts or shares, any part or all of the property then held in trust to, among, or on behalf of the Grantor's descendants, as the Grantor's spouse shall from time to time direct and appoint, by an instrument executed during the spouse's lifetime and acknowledged as in the case of Deeds of real estate in the State of New Jersey, or under the Last Will and Testament of the Grantor's spouse; the exercise of such special power of appointment, whether by instrument as aforesaid executed during the Grantor's spouse's lifetime, or by the spouse's Will, shall refer specifically to the special power of appointment herein granted.

COMMENT 10: The granting of a special power of appointment to the spouse provides certain flexibility to redirect the distribution of trust property among their children, based on circumstances that may arise after the death of the insured.

(e) Upon the death of the Grantor's spouse, the property then remaining in trust, if any, shall pass pursuant to the terms and conditions of [Sub]Paragraph (2).

(2) In the event the Grantor's spouse shall have predeceased the Grantor, or upon the death of the Grantor's spouse, as the case may be, the property then remaining in trust shall be divided into as many equal shares as there are the Grantor's children then surviving, such children presently being DAVID DOE, JOSHUA DOE, and JENNIFER DOE, and one such share for the then-living descendants, if any, collectively, of each of the Grantor's children who is then deceased, and such shares shall be distributed as follows:

(a) A share set apart for a child of the Grantor then surviving shall be held and administered as follows:

(i) The Trustees shall hold, manage, invest, and reinvest the property held in each such child's trust; receive and collect the income, rents, and profits arising therefrom or incident thereto; and accumulate and add to principal any portion of such income not used, applied, or paid as hereinafter directed.

(ii) The Trustees shall use and apply such part or all of the net income and principal in each child's respective trust on behalf of or pay such part thereof to each such child at such time or times and in such amounts as the Trustees, in the Trustees' absolute discretion, shall deem necessary, to meet each such child's respective needs of health, maintenance, support, and education (including college, professional, and/or graduate school); provided, however, that when such child attains the age of twenty-one (21) years old, or upon creation of such share if the child has then reached such age, the Trustees shall pay to or apply for the benefit of such child all of the net income from such child's trust in quarter-annual or more frequent intervals, as the Trustees shall determine.

(iii) The Trustees shall distribute, pay over, and transfer to each such child all of the property then remaining in his or her respective trust as follows:

(a) One-half (1/2) thereof, when he or she attains the age of twenty-five (25) years old; and

(b) The balance thereof, when he or she attains the age of thirty (30) years old; provided, however, that if at the time the aforesaid trusts are established any of the

Grantor's children has already attained an age at which partial or full distribution is directed to be made, the Trustees shall distribute, pay over, and transfer to each said child such portion of his or her trust as he or she would have received, had the trust been in existence when such an age was attained.

COMMENT 11: It is unclear whether the trust as originally written (with distribution by age thirty (30)) is a [generation-skipping transfer] (GST) trust for the purposes of the deemed allocation rules of Section 2632(c). Since the trust distribution may not occur before the specified age if the spouse survives the grantor, technically the trust would not satisfy any of the exceptions, and deemed allocation would occur. This may result in a waste of a portion of the grantor's GST exemption. In this situation, the grantor may elect out of the deemed allocation for transfer to this trust for post-2000 transfers.

Alternative 1:

(iii) The Trustee shall distribute, pay over, and transfer to each such child all of the property then remaining in his or her respective trust when he or she attains the age of fifty (50) years old.

COMMENT 12: Delaying the age of distribution past forty-six (46) will clearly cause this to be a "GST trust" for purposes of the new deemed allocation rules.

Alternative 2:

(iii) Upon the death of the child, all of the property then remaining in his or her respective trust shall be paid over and distributed to such child's descendants.

COMMENT 13: This is clearly a GST trust for deemed allocation purposes. In this situation, the grantor's intention is to create a GST trust, and the deemed allocation rules are helpful to avoid the failure to affirmatively allocate exemption for post-2000 transfers.

(iv) In the event any of the Grantor's children shall die prior to full distribution of his or her trust, as above directed, then and in such event, subject to the provisions of Paragraph SIXTH of this Trust Agreement, the Trustees shall pay over and distribute the full principal and undistributed income then remaining in such deceased child's trust to the then-surviving descendants of such deceased child, in equal shares, *per stirpes*, and if there be no descendants surviving, to his or her brothers or sisters, in equal shares, otherwise to the Grantor's surviving descendants, in equal shares, *per stirpes*; provided, however, that the share passing to any person for whose benefit a trust has been created under this Trust Agreement shall be added to the trust created for such person's benefit, to be held and administered as a part thereof.

(b) A share set apart for the descendants of a deceased child of the Grantor shall be paid over and distributed to such descendants, in equal shares, *per stirpes*, subject to the provisions of Paragraph SIXTH.

FIFTH: In making any payment or application of income or principal to or for the benefit of any beneficiary pursuant to the discretion hereinabove conferred, the Trustees may make payment directly to such beneficiary if the Trustees deem that said beneficiary is of reasonable age and competence (even if such beneficiary is a minor) or may make application directly or by payment to a parent of such beneficiary, to a guardian or committee of such beneficiary appointed in the State of New Jersey or in any other jurisdiction, to a custodian (including the Trustees) for the beneficiary under the Uniform Transfers to Minors Act of New Jersey or any jurisdiction (whether appointed by the Trustees or any other person), or to an adult person with whom such beneficiary resides or who has the care or custody of such beneficiary temporarily or permanently. Evidence of any such payment or application or the receipt therefor executed by such beneficiary, parent, guardian, committee, custodian or adult person shall discharge the Trustees with respect to such payment or application of such income or principal to such beneficiary, parent, guardian, committee, custodian or adult person.

SIXTH: If any legatee or distributee designated under this Trust has not attained the age of thirty (30) years at the time herein specified for the outright distribution of his or her share, then and in such event, notwithstanding such direction, the distribution of such beneficiary's share shall be postponed, and the Trustees shall hold the same in trust until such beneficiary shall have attained the age of thirty (30) years; and until such time the Trustees shall apply so much or all of the net income, and if that is insufficient, so much or all of the principal thereof, as the Trustees shall deem to be necessary to meet such beneficiary's needs of health, maintenance, support, and education (including college, professional, and/or graduate school), and shall accumulate any income not so applied. The principal and accumulated income, if any, so held in trust as provided in this Paragraph SIXTH, shall nevertheless vest in interest in such beneficiary and shall be distributed to such beneficiary upon his or her attaining the age of thirty (30) years; or in the event of his or her death prior thereto, shall be distributed to his or her surviving descendants, in equal shares, *per stirpes*, and if there be no such descendants, to his or her surviving brothers and/or sisters in equal shares, otherwise to the Grantor's surviving descendants, in equal shares, *per stirpes*; provided, however, that in any event, the share passing to any person for whose benefit property is being administered under this Paragraph SIXTH shall be added to the property otherwise being held for such person's benefit, and shall be administered as a part thereof.

SEVENTH: (A) The Grantor, and/or any other person, from time to time, may assign to the Trustees all of the incidents of ownership in any policy or policies of insurance on the life of the Grantor, and/or may transfer to the Trustees a portion thereof on a split-ownership basis, and/or may cause all or part of the proceeds thereof, or other death benefits, to be made payable to the Trustees, pursuant to a revocable or irrevocable designation of beneficiary, or otherwise. Any such policies and death benefits, and/or the proceeds or portion of the proceeds thereof transferred to or made payable to the Trustees, shall be subject to all of the terms and conditions of this Trust Agreement in the same manner as if they had been included herein at the time of the making and execution hereof. All references in this Trust Agreement to insurance policies shall be deemed to include policies of insurance procured by the Trustees, contributed by the Grantor, and/or the portion of any other policy or policies which shall hereafter be transferred to or procured by the Trustees on a split-ownership basis and/or the proceeds of any other policy or policies which are hereafter made payable to the Trustees primarily or upon the occurrence of certain contingencies.

(B) As used in this Trust Agreement, the term "split-ownership" shall refer to any policy or policies of insurance, whereunder the right to receive the portion of the death proceeds in excess of the cash value is vested in the Trustees, and the cash value, including the right to receive the portion of the death proceeds equal to the cash value, is obligated to any person or corporation other than the Trustees, whether such rights shall have arisen by virtue of assignment from the Grantor or any other person or by endorsement to such policy or policies, or otherwise.

(C) The Trustees shall not be personally liable for the payment of premiums on any life insurance policies and shall be under no other duty in that regard. The Trustees may surrender the policies or any of them or secure a loan thereon, using the proceeds to pay premiums, or if the trust property is exhausted, the Trustees may convert any policy into a paid up policy.

(D) Upon the death of the Grantor, the Trustees shall collect and receive such sums and proceeds as may be paid to said Trustees by the company or companies that have issued policies of insurance upon the life of the deceased Grantor that are payable to said Trustees as Trustees hereunder, and the Trustees shall also receive and collect such proceeds as may be paid to the Trustees under the Last Will and Testament of the Grantor or any other person, or as may be paid to the Trustees under the terms of any other trust or document, and all such sums and proceeds, together with any other property then held by the Trustees, shall be held by the Trustees in trust pursuant to the terms of this Trust Agreement.

EIGHTH: With respect to all property, real or personal, at any time held in trust under this Agreement, the Trustees shall be authorized, empowered, and granted the powers and authority, permitted by state law.

NINTH: [(A) With respect to any trust established hereunder, the Grantor shall have the right, at any time exercisable in a non-fiduciary capacity, without the approval or consent of any person acting in a fiduciary capacity, to acquire any property then held in such trust by substituting other property of an equivalent value on the date of substitution, pursuant to Code Section 675(4)(C), provided that, in the event of the exercise of this power of substitution, the Grantor shall certify in writing to the Trustee that any substituted property is of equivalent value to the property previously held in such trust for which it is substituted, and the Trustee may, in such Trustee's discretion, independently verify such determination of value and any dispute regarding such determination of value may be resolved in an appropriate judicial forum.]

COMMENT 14: If more than reliance on Section 677(a)(3) is desired, this substitution power can be used to invoke grantor trust status. See Rev. Rul. 2008-22 and 2011-28.

(B) Notwithstanding anything hereinabove to the contrary, in the event any of the proceeds of the life insurance assigned to this trust shall be included in the gross estate of the Grantor for Federal estate tax purposes, whether by virtue of the provisions of Section 2035 of the Internal Revenue Code or otherwise, and in the event the Grantor's spouse, JANE DOE, shall survive the Grantor, the Trustees shall pay over and distribute to the Grantor's spouse so much of the life insurance proceeds so that no Federal estate tax will be payable in the Grantor's estate after allowing for all allowable credits, including the maximum unified credit in effect on the date of the Grantor's death. The remaining proceeds of the insurance so included shall be held by the Trustees hereunder, to be administered under the provisions of this Trust Agreement.

COMMENT 15: This provision eliminates the adverse tax consequences, which would otherwise occur in the event of the insured's death within three years of the transfer of an existing policy, by creating a disposition that will qualify for the marital deduction, to the extent necessary.

TENTH: Neither the income nor the principal of any trust created hereunder shall be liable for the debts, undertakings, or engagements of any beneficiary thereof, nor shall the same be assigned, pledged, alienated, or anticipated; any endeavor by any beneficiary to circumvent this direction in any manner shall be wholly disregarded by the Trustees and shall be null and void.

ELEVENTH: The Trustees may, but shall not be required to, render an accounting from time to time and upon termination of any of the trusts established hereunder, setting forth the receipts and disbursements of principal and income and the assets on hand at the commencement and expiration of the accounting period. The written approval of such accounting by the then-living adult income beneficiaries shall be final and binding upon all who are then or may thereafter become entitled to any part of the assets, as to all matters and transactions shown on said account, notwithstanding that an approving beneficiary may also be a Trustee hereunder. Nothing contained herein shall preclude the Trustees from submitting an accounting to a court for settlement.

TWELFTH: The Grantor has been fully advised as to the legal effects of the execution of this Agreement and informed as to the character and amount of the property hereby transferred and conveyed, and has given consideration to the question whether the settlement herein contained shall be revocable or irrevocable, and now declares that it shall be irrevocable and the Grantor shall hereafter stand without the power at any time to revoke, change, alter, amend, or annul any of the provisions contained herein.

COMMENT 16: Insofar as irrevocable instruments such as insurance trusts are not covered by the automatic revocation upon divorce provisions of most state laws (which only apply to revocable instruments and appointments), some practitioners insert the following additional language to deal with the possibility of a divorce between the insured and the spouse following creation of the trust:If, at the date of the Grantor's death, the Grantor is divorced from the Grantor's spouse, JANE DOE, the marriage has been annulled, or the Grantor is not cohabitating with said spouse, any dispositions or appointment of property made by this Trust to said spouse, any provision conferring a general or special power of appointment on said spouse, and any nomination of said spouse as trustee shall be revoked. Any property prevented from passing to said spouse because of revocation by divorce, annulment, or failure to cohabitate shall pass as if said spouse failed to survive the Grantor, and other provisions conferring some power or office on said spouse shall be interpreted as if said spouse failed to survive the Grantor.

THIRTEENTH: (A) All powers granted to the Trustees hereunder shall be exercised jointly or severally by the Trustees, except as specifically set forth herein. The signature of any one Trustee shall be sufficient to bind the trust.

(B) Notwithstanding the foregoing, no Trustee hereunder may exercise any power granted herein for his or her benefit or to satisfy any legal obligation of support he or she may have to a beneficiary hereunder.

FOURTEENTH: (A) In the event either Trustee named herein is unable or unwilling, for any reason, to serve as Trustee, then the Grantor's son, DAVID DOE, currently residing in ___________, ___________, is hereby appointed as Successor Co-Trustee.

(B) In the event the Grantor's son, DAVID DOE, is unable or unwilling, for any reason, to serve as Successor Co-Trustee, then the Grantor's son, JOSHUA DOE, currently residing in ___________, ___________, is hereby appointed as Successor Co-Trustee.

(C) It is the Grantor's intent that there shall be two Trustees serving hereunder at all times. Accordingly, the last serving Trustee herein, other than the Grantor's spouse, shall have the right to appoint an individual, or a bank or trust company qualified to do business in the State of New Jersey, to serve as a Co-Trustee or a Successor Trustee hereunder. Any such appointment during lifetime shall be in writing duly acknowledged as in the case of Deeds in the State of New Jersey, or at death by the deceased Trustee's Last Will and Testament duly admitted to probate in a court of competent jurisdiction.

(D) Any Co-Trustee may, by an instrument filed with the trust records, resign as trustee of any trust, such resignation to become effective when the individual resigning ceases to act. A Successor Co-Trustee shall qualify by filing his consent to act with the trust records.

FIFTEENTH: The Trustees shall be relieved from all responsibility or liability for any loss to the trust properties which may occur because of errors of judgment, and shall not be liable to any beneficiary hereunder for any discretionary action taken pursuant to the terms of this Trust Agreement and shall be liable for failure to act in good faith only.

SIXTEENTH: No bond or security shall be required of any Trustee in the faithful performance of his or her duties in such capacity.

SEVENTEENTH: It is agreed that these presents shall extend to and be obligatory upon the heirs, executors, administrators, legal representatives, and successors of the parties hereto or beneficiaries hereof.

EIGHTEENTH: As used herein, each of the masculine, feminine, and neuter genders shall include the other genders; the singular shall include the plural and the plural shall include the singular wherever appropriate to the context.

IN WITNESS WHEREOF, the parties hereto have set their respective hands and seals the day and year first above written.

WITNESS:	GRANTOR:
____________________	____________________
	JOHN DOE

WITNESS: TRUSTEE:

________________________ ________________________

JANE DOE

WITNESS: TRUSTEE:

________________________ ________________________

MARY DOE

STATE OF NEW JERSEY)
) SS.:
COUNTY OF __________)

BE IT REMEMBERED, that on this __________ day of __________, 20__________, before me, __________, personally appeared JOHN DOE, who I am satisfied is the person named in and who executed the within Instrument, and thereupon he acknowledged that he signed, sealed, and delivered the same as his act and deed, for the uses and purposes therein expressed.

____

STATE OF NEW JERSEY)
) SS.:
COUNTY OF __________)

BE IT REMEMBERED, that on this __________ day of __________, 20__________, before me, __________, personally appeared JANE DOE, who I am satisfied is the person named in and who executed the within Instrument, and thereupon she acknowledged that she signed, sealed, and delivered the same as her act and deed, for the uses and purposes therein expressed.

____

STATE OF NEW JERSEY)
) SS.:
COUNTY OF __________)

BE IT REMEMBERED, that on this __________ day of __________, 20__________, before me, __________, personally appeared MARY DOE, who I am satisfied is the person named in and who executed the within Instrument, and thereupon she acknowledged that she signed, sealed and delivered the same as her act and deed, for the uses and purposes therein expressed.

____

SCHEDULE "A"

Property assigned to THE JOHN DOE FAMILY TRUST under Trust Agreement dated the __________ day of __________, 20__________ by and among JOHN DOE, as Grantor, and JANE DOE and MARY DOE, as Trustees.

DATE	PROPERTY	
____/____/____	__________	Life Policy #__________

Appendix 2 | Sample GRAT[22]

Prepared by:

__________________________,
an Attorney at Law of the
State of New Jersey

THE FATHER TWO YEAR ANNUITY TRUST

THIS TRUST, made and executed as of the day of, 20, by and between FATHER, residing in Anywhere, New Jersey, hereinafter called the "Grantor", and the said FATHER and JOHN, residing in Somewhere, New Jersey, hereinafter called the "Trustees";

> **COMMENT 1:** The Grantor of a GRAT may serve as the sole trustee. In that case, the trust may be drafted as a Declaration of Trust.

WITNESSETH:

WHEREAS, the Grantor desires to create an irrevocable Grantor Retained Annuity Trust, the retained interest of which is intended to constitute a qualified interest within the meaning of Section 2702(b)(1) of the Internal Revenue Code (hereinafter referred to as the "Code"), of the property described in Schedule "A" annexed hereto and made a part hereof, for the benefit of the beneficiaries hereinafter named, and for the uses and purposes and upon the terms and conditions as hereinafter more fully set forth; and

WHEREAS, the Trustees have agreed to accept this trust and to be bound by the terms and provisions of this Trust Indenture;

NOW THEREFORE:

The Trustees shall hold in trust and shall administer, use, and dispose of the property set forth on Schedule "A" exclusively for the uses and purposes and upon the terms and conditions, set forth herein, as follows:

FIRST: The Grantor has irrevocably assigned to this Trust the property set forth on Schedule "A" (hereinafter sometimes called "Trust Estate") for the benefit of the beneficiaries hereinafter named, to have and to hold the same, in trust, for and upon the uses and purposes, and subject to the terms and conditions, hereinafter set forth.

SECOND: (A) The Grantor reserves the right in each taxable year of the Trust during the two (2) years following the date of this Trust Indenture (the "Trust Term") to receive an annuity amount equal to __________% percent of the initial net fair market value of the assets constituting the trust (the "Annuity Amount"), valued as of the date of the transfer of such assets to the Trust.

COMMENT 2: The annuity amount must be fixed; that is, an amount must be fixed in the trust instrument, either as a fixed dollar amount or a fixed percentage of the initial fair market value of the property transferred to the trust. Treas. Reg. §25.2702-3(b)(2)(ii). The regulations do not require that the fixed amount be the same for each year. The only requirement imposed on variations from year to year is the requirement that an amount payable in one year not be more than 20 percent higher than the amount payable in the prior year. Treas. Reg. §25.2702-3(b)(1)(ii).

The Trustee is not prohibited from distributing amounts in excess of the annuity amount to the annuitant. Treas. Reg. §25.2702-3(b)(1)(iii). Such distributions may be made from income or principal. The value, however, of any right to receive payments in addition to the qualified annuity interest has a zero value for gift tax purposes so that, tax-wise, such excess distributions would accomplish little and would actually be detrimental since [they] would have the effect of building up the Grantor's estate.

(B) The Annuity Amount shall be paid in a single annual installment in such manner and by such time as may be mandated by the Code and applicable Treasury Regulations, including any requirement for proration of payments for a short taxable year or a final short period; however, if permitted, the Annuity Amount shall be paid in a single annual installment from income and, to the extent income is not sufficient, from principal, using the anniversary date of this Agreement as the time for payment and including extensions permitted by Regulations. Any income of the trust in excess of the Annuity Amount shall be added to principal. The Annuity Amount may be paid in money, securities or other assets of the Trust. The Annuity Amount shall not be satisfied by the use of a note, other debt instrument, option or similar financial arrangement.

COMMENT 3: The Treasury Regulations permit an annuity payment to be made after the close of the taxable year, so long as the annuity is paid by the due date for filing the GRAT's Form 1041. See Treas. Reg. §25.2702-3(b)(1)(i). In the case of an annuity payable on the trust's anniversary date, this is 105 days after the anniversary date. The advantage of the deferral is to give the trust assets additional time to possibly appreciate, thereby enhancing the value of the GRAT.

(C) If the net fair market value of the Trust assets is incorrectly determined, then within a reasonable period after the value is finally determined for Federal tax purposes, the Grantor shall receive from the Trust (in the case of an undervaluation) or shall pay to the Trust (in the case of a overvaluation) an amount equal to the difference between the Annuity Amount(s) properly payable and the Annuity Amount(s) actually paid.

COMMENT 4: If the annuity amount has been defined as a percentage of or as a fraction of the value of the trust assets, the trust instrument must allow for adjusting annuity amounts previously paid if an error was made by the trustee in determining such value. This provision is beneficial in the case of a GRAT funded with closely held stock, real property, or interests in a family limited partnership. If the Service determines on audit that the underlying assets and/or the closely held interest has been undervalued, the payout can be modified prospectively to redetermine the annuity amount to eliminate any potential adverse tax consequences. See Treas. Reg. §25.2702-3(b)(2). In addition, any underpayments of prior annuity amounts must also be paid after such determination.

(D) In the event the Grantor shall die prior to the expiration of the Trust Term, the Successor Trustee shall pay the remaining Annuity Amount(s) to the legal representatives of the Grantor's estate until the expiration of the Trust Term, at which time the Successor Trustee shall pay over and distribute all of the then principal and income of the Trust in accordance with Paragraph THIRD.

THIRD: Upon the expiration of the Trust Term, the then-serving Trustees shall distribute all of the then principal and income of the Trust (the "Remaining Trust Estate") in equal shares to then surviving children of the Grantor, such children presently being JOHN and JACK, or to the estate of any predeceased child.

COMMENT 5: Trust corpus should not be directed to pass to grandchildren since the valuation rules of Code §2702 are inapplicable for generation-skipping transfer tax purposes. Upon termination of a GRAT, if a grandchild is the remainderman, the full value of the trust corpus will be treated as a generation-skipping transfer.

FOURTH: (A) No additional contributions shall be made to the trust after the initial contribution.

COMMENT 6: See Treas. Reg. §25.2702-3(b)(4).

(B) During the Trust Term, no distributions shall be made to or for the benefit of any person other than the Grantor, so long as the Grantor is living, or to or for the benefit of any person other than the Grantor's personal representative as provided herein, after the Grantor's death during the Trust Term.

COMMENT 7: See Treas. Reg. §25.2702-3(d)(3).

(C) The interest of the Grantor shall not be subject to commutation.

COMMENT 8: The trust instrument must prohibit "commutation"; that is, a trust may not allow for the prepayment by the trustee of the annuitant's annuity interest. Although the regulations prohibit commutation of the trust by the trustee, in New Jersey, the grantor and all remainder beneficiaries may consent to terminate the trust and accomplish a similar result, so long as all parties are identifiable adults. Therefore, rather than the trust remainder passing to the issue of a predeceased child, it is directed to pass to the estate of the last surviving child.

(D) During the Trust Term, the Grantor shall have the right, at any time, exercisable in a non-fiduciary capacity, without the approval or consent of any person acting in a fiduciary capacity, to acquire any property then held in the Trust by substituting other property of an equivalent value on the date of substitution.

COMMENT 9: To obtain maximum benefit from a GRAT, the trust must be designed to be a grantor trust under Code Sections 671 et seq. If a trust is wholly a grantor trust, all income and losses pass through to the grantor; thus, a distribution from the trust will not itself be taxable. Furthermore, all transactions between the grantor and the trust itself are ignored for income tax purposes. See, for example, PLR 9057011. In addition, a grantor trust is a qualified stockholder for S Corporation purposes. Therefore, a GRAT that qualifies as a grantor trust will not destroy the S Corporation election.

FIFTH: In making any payment or application of income or principal to or for the benefit of any beneficiary pursuant to the discretion hereinabove conferred, the Trustees may make payment directly to such beneficiary if the Trustees deem such beneficiary to be of reasonable age and competence (even if such beneficiary is a minor) or may make application directly or by payment to a parent of such beneficiary, to a guardian or committee of such beneficiary appointed in the State of New Jersey or in any other jurisdiction, to a custodian (including the Trustees) for the beneficiary under the Uniform Transfers to Minors Act of New Jersey, or to an adult person with whom such beneficiary resides or who has the care or custody of such beneficiary temporarily or permanently. Evidence of any such payment or application or the receipt therefore executed by such beneficiary, parent, guardian, committee, custodian, or adult person shall discharge the Trustees with respect to such payment or application of such income or principal to such beneficiary, parent, guardian, committee, custodian, or adult person.

SIXTH: With respect to all property, real or personal, at any time held in trust under this Trust Indenture, the Trustees are authorized, empowered, and granted the privileges, powers, and authority [as] permitted by state law, provided, however, that such powers shall not be exercised in such manner and to such extent that the exercise would result in the disqualification of the retained interest as a qualified interest under Code Section 2702(b)(1) and Sections 25.2702-3(b) and (d) of the Treasury Regulations.

COMMENT 10: This provision is intended as a savings clause to preserve the GRAT status should the trust be inadvertently administered in a manner that would jeopardize the GRAT from achieving its intended tax benefits.

SEVENTH: The Trustees shall keep records showing all receipts and disbursements of income and principal and all changes in investments. Upon request, but not more often than once each year, the Trustees shall render to each beneficiary, or a duly authorized representative of them, a full and complete statement of receipts and disbursements of income and principal, together with such changes of investment as may have occurred since the last statement. Such statement shall be in lieu of any statutory requirement for the Trustees to file a judicial accounting under the laws of any jurisdiction.

EIGHTH: No purchaser at any sale made by the Trustees shall be bound to inquire into the expediency, propriety, validity, or necessity of such sale or to see to or be liable for the application of the purchase monies arising therefrom; nor shall any person who, during the administration of the trust, shall pay over to or transfer any money or other property to the Trustees, be bound to inquire into or see to or be liable for the application of such funds or monies so transferred or paid over to the Trustees.

NINTH: The Grantor has been fully advised as to the legal effects of the execution of this Trust Indenture and informed as to the character and amount of the property hereby transferred and conveyed and has given consideration to the question of whether the settlement herein contained shall be revocable or irrevocable, and now declares that it shall be irrevocable and the Grantor shall hereafter stand without power at any time to revoke, change, alter, amend, or annul any of the provisions contained herein. However, any Trustee other than the Grantor shall have the power, acting alone, to amend the Trust Indenture in any manner required for the sole purpose of ensuring that the Grantor's retained interest qualifies and continues to qualify as a "qualified interest" within the meaning of Section 2702(b)(1) of the Code.

COMMENT 11: See Comment 10.

TENTH: The validity, construction, effect, and administration of this Trust Indenture and the trust created hereunder shall be governed and determined by and under the laws of the State of New Jersey. It is the Grantor's intention that the Grantor's retained interest shall constitute a "qualified interest," as that term is defined under the provisions of Code Section 2702 and the regulations promulgated thereunder. To the extent any provision of this Trust Indenture is inconsistent with the Grantor's retained interest constituting a qualified interest, such provision shall be deemed void and of no consequence. Furthermore, no power or discretion conferred in this Trust Indenture shall be exercisable by any Trustee, including the Grantor, except in a manner so that the Grantor's retained interest constitutes a qualified interest.

ELEVENTH: In the event either Trustee named herein shall be unable or unwilling, for any reason, to serve as Trustee hereunder, then the remaining Trustee will serve as sole Trustee. In the event the remaining Trustee is unable or unwilling, for any reason, to serve as sole Trustee hereunder, the Grantor nominates and appoints the Grantor's son, JACK, as Successor Trustee. The sole remaining Trustee named hereunder shall have the right to nominate and appoint an individual, or a bank or trust company qualified to do business in the applicable jurisdiction, to serve in said Trustee's place and stead as Successor Trustee. Any such appointment shall, during lifetime, be in writing, duly acknowledged as in the case of Deeds in the applicable jurisdiction, or at death by such Trustee's Last Will and Testament duly admitted to probate in a court of competent jurisdiction. The rights, duties, privileges, obligations, powers, and immunities given and granted to the Trustees herein named shall fully extend to any Successor Trustee appointed hereunder.

TWELFTH: The Trustees, or any Successor Trustee, shall be relieved from all responsibility or liability for any loss to the trust properties which may occur because of errors of judgment and shall be liable only for failure to act in good faith.

THIRTEENTH: No bond or security shall be required of any Trustee, including a Successor, in the faithful performance of his or her duties in such capacity.

FOURTEENTH: Any Successor Trustee shall signify acceptance of the terms of this Trust by a writing attached hereto.

FIFTEENTH: It is agreed that these presents shall extend to and be obligatory upon the heirs, executors, administrators, legal representatives, and successors of the parties hereto or beneficiaries hereof.

SIXTEENTH: Nothing in this Trust Indenture shall be construed to restrict the Trustees from investing the trust assets in a manner that could result in the annual realization of a reasonable amount of income or gain from the sale or disposition of trust assets.

SEVENTEENTH: As used herein, each of the masculine, feminine, or neuter genders shall include the other genders, the singular shall include the plural and the plural shall include the singular, wherever appropriate to the context. The term Trustee, when used throughout this Trust Indenture, shall include, where relevant, any Successor Trustee appointed herein.

IN WITNESS WHEREOF, the parties hereto set their respective hands and seals.

WITNESS:	GRANTOR:
______________________	______________________
	FATHER
WITNESS:	TRUSTEE:
______________________	______________________
	FATHER
WITNESS:	
	TRUSTEE:
______________________	______________________
	JOHN

STATE OF NEW JERSEY)
) SS.:
COUNTY OF BERGEN)

BE IT REMEMBERED, that on the day of, 20__________, before me, a notary public, personally appeared FATHER, who, I am satisfied, is the person named in and who executed the within Instrument, and thereupon he acknowledged that he signed, sealed, and delivered the same as his act and deed, for the uses and purposes therein expressed.

____

STATE OF NEW JERSEY)
) SS.:
COUNTY OF BERGEN)

BE IT REMEMBERED, that on the day of, 20__________, before me, a notary public, personally appeared JOHN, who, I am satisfied, is the person named in and who executed the within Instrument, and thereupon he acknowledged that he signed, sealed, and delivered the same as his act and deed, for the uses and purposes therein expressed.

____

SCHEDULE "A"

Property assigned to THE FATHER TWO-YEAR ANNUITY TRUST dated __________, 20, by and between FATHER, as Grantor, and FATHER and JOHN, as Trustees:

Date

Description

Appendix 3 | Sample QPRT with Subsequent Grantor Trust[23]

Prepared by:

___________________________,
an Attorney at Law of the
State of New Jersey

ALICE TEN YEAR TRUST

THIS DECLARATION OF TRUST, made and executed on the ____________ day of ____________, 2014, by ALICE, residing at, Ramsey, New Jersey, hereinafter called the "Grantor" and ALICE, hereinafter called the "Trustee";

> **COMMENT 1:** The Grantor of a QPRT may serve as the sole trustee, in which case, the trust is drafted as a Declaration of Trust. However, an advantage to having at least one trustee besides the Grantor arises where the residence is subject to a mortgage. In that event, the argument can be advanced that the trustee other than the Grantor will not serve as such unless the Grantor retains responsibility for payment of the mortgage. See discussion in COMMENT 2. Additionally, having an independent trustee may enhance the position for obtaining a discount for lack of marketability of a 50 percent tenant-in-common interest. If there are 2 or more trustees, the document should be drafted as an Agreement.

WITNESSETH:

WHEREAS, the Grantor desires to create an irrevocable trust of the property described in Schedule "A" annexed hereto and made a part hereof, for the benefit of the beneficiaries hereinafter named, and for the uses and purposes and upon the terms and conditions as hereinafter more fully set forth;

WHEREAS, the Grantor intends this trust to be a qualified personal residence trust within the meaning of Section 2702 of the Internal Revenue Code of 1986, as amended from time to time, and the Treasury Regulations thereunder (for purposes of this Declaration of Trust, the Internal Revenue Code of 1986 is referred to as "Code" and the Treasury Regulations thereunder are referred to as "Treasury Regulations") and Revenue Procedure 2003-42; and

WHEREAS, the within Declaration of Trust shall be known as the ALICE TEN YEAR TRUST;

[WHEREAS, the Trustees have agreed to accept this Trust and to be bound by the terms and provisions of this Indenture only if the Trustees will not be liable, in their capacity as Trustees, for payment of any mortgage obligation or other indebtedness relating to the Trust property for the term of the Trust;]

COMMENT 2: The bracketed language is only applicable in the event the residence is subject to a mortgage or other indebtedness. As noted in the article, it is preferable to fully satisfy any outstanding mortgage prior to transferring the residence to the trust. However, if that is not practical, the residence may be transferred to the trust, but the grantor should retain responsibility for payment of the mortgage principal, and the other trustee should only accept responsibility to act as fiduciary on that condition. Although this strategy has not been authorized by any regulation or ruling, it has been recommended as a possible means to avoid an additional gift each time mortgage principal is paid. See Richard B. Covey, Practical Drafting (2013), at 3371-72.

NOW THEREFORE:

The Grantor hereby declares as follows:

FIRST: The Grantor hereby declares that the Grantor, as Trustee, and all Successor Trustees hereinafter named, shall hold, manage and distribute the property set forth on Schedule "A" for the benefit of the beneficiaries hereinafter named, in trust, nevertheless, for and upon the uses and purposes, and subject to the terms and conditions hereinafter set forth. The property administered pursuant to the provisions of this Declaration of Trust is designated as the "Trust Estate".

[(B) The Grantor represents that the property located at _____________, is secured by indebtedness with a principal balance on _____________ 2014, of approximately $_____________. The Grantor hereby agrees (1) to continue to be responsible for the Grantor's payments (of interest and principal) under the indebtedness for the balance of the term of the Trust, and (2) to indemnify and hold harmless the Trustees from any damages, loss, or liability arising from such indebtedness. In consideration of the provisions of this Subparagraph (B), the Trustees have agreed to accept the responsibility of acting as Trustees pursuant to the terms of this Trust Indenture.]

> **COMMENT 3:** See COMMENT 2 as to bracketed language.

SECOND: The Grantor intends to create a qualified personal residence trust ("QPRT") within the meaning of the Treasury Regulations under Code Section 2702 and this Declaration of Trust shall be so interpreted and amended, if necessary, by the Trustee, solely for this purpose.

THIRD: During the ten (10) year period beginning with the date of this Declaration of Trust (the "Initial Trust Term"):

(A) The Grantor reserves the use and occupancy of the personal residence (as defined in Paragraph SIXTH), which shall be held and administered as part of the Trust Estate.

(B) The trust shall not hold any property other than one residence, or a tenant-in-common interest in a residence, to be used or held for use by the Grantor as a personal residence, as defined in Paragraph SIXTH, except as otherwise provided in Paragraphs SEVENTH, EIGHTH and NINTH.

(C) Any income of the trust shall be distributed to the Grantor not less frequently than annually.

(D) No distribution of principal shall be made to any person other than the Grantor prior to termination of the Initial Trust Term.

(E) In the event the trust shall cease to be a QPRT, the provisions of Paragraph NINTH shall apply.

(F) All of the requirements set forth or incorporated by reference in this Paragraph THIRD and in Paragraphs SIXTH, SEVENTH, EIGHTH and NINTH shall continue in effect during the entire Trust Term.

(G) The interest of the Grantor shall not be subject to commutation.

> **COMMENT 4:** This sentence is required under Reg. §25.2702-5(c)(6). However, if all adults who are vested in interest consent to early termination, a significant savings can result in the case where the grantor becomes terminally ill and is not expected to survive the trust term.

(H) Notwithstanding anything herein to the contrary, in the event the Grantor shall die prior to expiration of the Initial Trust Term, the Successor Trustee shall pay over and distribute the entire Trust Estate to the Grantor's estate.

> **COMMENT 5:** This paragraph permits use of the marital deduction if the grantor's spouse is surviving. Furthermore, this paragraph will further reduce the value of the gift since the grantor has retained a contingent interest in addition to the use of the residence.

(I) The Trustees shall not sell or otherwise transfer the personal residence in a manner that conflicts with the provisions of Treasury Regulation Section 25.2702-5(c)(9).

[FOURTH: Upon expiration of the Trust Term, if the Grantor is then surviving, the Trustees shall distribute and pay over the property passing hereunder, outright and free of trust, in equal shares to those of the Grantor's children then surviving, said children currently being SON and DAUGHTER. If none of the Grantor's children are then surviving, the Trustees shall distribute and pay over the property to the estate of the last surviving child of the Grantor.]

COMMENT 6: The bracketed language should be used when no subsequent term trust is desired, and the trust should be revised accordingly to delete references to Initial Trust Term and Subsequent Trust. Although the regulations prohibit commutation of the trust by the trustee, the grantor and all remainder beneficiaries may consent to terminate the trust and accomplish a similar result as long as all parties are identifiable adults. Therefore, rather than the trust remainder passing to the issue of a predeceased child, it is directed to pass to the estate of the last surviving child. This disposition also avoids a generation-skipping transfer tax (GST) problem that would arise if the portion of the trust remainder payable to a predeceased child were instead payable to the issue of such child. The problem would arise because no GST exemption may be allocated to this trust so long as the property could still be included in the grantor's estate, under the GST estate tax inclusion period rules. Code §2642(f). Therefore, if the corpus were directed to pass to the issue of a deceased child, the trust could generate GST upon termination of the trust term.

FOURTH: Upon expiration of the Initial Trust Term, if the Grantor is then surviving, the Trust Estate shall continue to be held in further trust (the "Subsequent Term Trust") by the Trustees hereinafter named (the "Subsequent Trustees") as Trustees of the Subsequent Term Trust, upon the following terms and conditions:

(A) The Subsequent Trustees shall hold, manage, invest and reinvest the property held in the Subsequent Term Trust and receive and collect the income, rents and profits arising therefrom or incident thereto, and shall accumulate and add to principal any portion of such income not used, applied or paid as hereinafter directed.

(B) The Subsequent Trustees shall use and apply such part or all of the net income and principal in the Subsequent Term Trust on behalf of or to pay such part thereof to the Grantor's children, MARK, TODD and KARIN (all of whom are hereinafter referred to individually as the Grantor's "Child" or collectively as the Grantor's "Children"), at such time or times and in such amounts as the Subsequent Trustees, in their absolute discretion, shall deem necessary, even to the point of exhaustion of the trust.

(C) The Subsequent Trustees of the Subsequent Term Trust established under this Paragraph FOURTH shall have the power, within their sole discretion, to loan the principal or income of any such trust to the Grantor, directly or indirectly, without adequate security.

FIFTH: (A) Upon the earliest to occur of (i) the tenth (10th) Anniversary of the establishment of the Subsequent Term Trust created under Paragraph FOURTH, or (ii) the death of the Grantor, the Subsequent Trustees shall distribute and pay over the property then remaining in the Subsequent Term Trust, outright and free of trust, in equal shares to those of the Grantor's Children who are then surviving and to the respective estate of any Child who is not then surviving.

(B) Notwithstanding the foregoing, during the Subsequent Term or upon the termination of the Subsequent Term (as described above), the Subsequent Trustee shall have the authority to contribute the Trust property to an entity, such as a limited liability company or partnership, in which the Grantor's Children (or the respective estate of any Child who is not then surviving) are owners, to facilitate the maintenance and management of the Trust property.

SIXTH: For purposes of this Declaration of Trust, "personal residence" shall mean any fee interest, condominium, or shares in a cooperative (or an undivided fractional interest therein) which is either:

(A)(1) the principal residence of the Grantor (within the meaning of Code Section 1034); or

(2) one other residence of the Grantor (within the meaning of Code Section 280A(d)(1) but without regard to Code Section 280A(d)(2)).

(B) The term "personal residence" may include appurtenant structures used by the Grantor for residential purposes and adjacent land not in excess of that which is reasonably appropriate for residential purposes (taking into account the size and location of the residence), but does not include any personal property, such as household furnishings.

(C) A residence is a personal residence only if its primary use is as a legal residence of the Grantor when occupied by the Grantor. A residence is not a personal residence if, during any period not occupied by the Grantor, its primary use is other than as a residence.

SEVENTH: During the Initial Trust Term:

(A) The trust may hold the following assets (in addition to the personal residence) in the following amounts and in the following manner:

(1) cash, and additions of cash, in a separate account, in an amount which, when added to the cash already held in the account for such purposes, does not exceed the amount required:

(a) for payment of trust expenses (including mortgage payments) already incurred or reasonably expected to be paid by the trust within six (6) months from the date the addition is made;

(b) for improvements to the personal residence to be paid by the trust within six (6) months from the date the addition is made;

(c) for purchase by the trust of the initial personal residence, if applicable, within three (3) months of the date the trust is created, provided that no addition may be made for this purpose, and the trust may not hold any such addition, unless the Trustee has previously entered into a contract to purchase that residence; and

(d) for purchase by the trust of a personal residence to replace another personal residence, within three (3) months of the date the addition is made, provided that no addition may be made for this purpose, and the trust may not hold any such addition, unless the Trustee has previously entered into a contract to purchase that residence;

(2) improvements to the personal residence, which may be added to the trust, provided that the personal residence, as improved, satisfies the requirements of a personal residence, as hereinbefore defined;

(3) proceeds from any sale of the personal residence, in a separate account; and

(4) one or more policies of insurance on the personal residence, and, in a separate account, proceeds of insurance received as a result of damage to or destruction of the personal residence, subject to the provisions of Paragraph EIGHTH. For purposes of this Subparagraph (A)(4), amounts received as a result of the involuntary conversion (within the meaning of Code Section 1033) of the personal residence are treated as proceeds of insurance.

(B)(1) The Trustee shall determine, not less frequently than quarterly, the amount of cash held in the trust in excess of the amount permitted by Subparagraph (A)(1) above and shall distribute such excess to the Grantor immediately thereafter.

(2) Any cash, held in the trust for the purposes permitted by Subparagraph (A)(1) above, that is not used to pay trust expenses due and payable upon the termination of the trust (including expenses directly related to termination) shall be distributed to the Grantor within thirty (30) days of termination.

COMMENT 7: Although the regulations permit the trust to hold cash in certain circumstances, the recommendation is to avoid holding cash in the trust in most cases. Normally, the grantor will pay the required expenses directly.

EIGHTH: During the Initial Trust Term:

(A) The trust will cease to be a QPRT if the residence ceases to be used or held for use as a personal residence of the Grantor. The residence will be held for use as a personal residence of the Grantor so long as the residence is not occupied by any other person (other than the spouse or a dependent of the Grantor) and is available at all times for use by the Grantor as a personal residence.

(B) The trust will cease to be a QPRT with respect to all proceeds of sale held by the trust not later than the earlier of:

(1) the date that is two (2) years after the date of sale;

(2) the termination of the Grantor's interest in the trust; or

(3) the date on which a new residence is acquired by the trust.

(C) The trust will cease to be a QPRT if damage or destruction renders the residence unusable as a residence, on the date that is two (2) years after the date of damage or destruction (or the date of termination of the Grantor's interest in the trust, if earlier) unless, prior to such date:

(1) replacement of or repairs to the residence are completed; or

(2) a new residence is acquired by the trust.

(D) The trust will cease to be a QPRT with respect to all proceeds of insurance received as a result of damage to or destruction of the residence not later than the earlier of:

(1) the date that is two (2) years after the date of damage or destruction;

(2) the termination of the Grantor's interest in the trust; or

(3) the date on which replacement of or repairs to the residence are completed, or a new residence is acquired by the trust.

(E) Within thirty (30) days after the date on which the trust has ceased to be a QPRT with respect to certain assets in accordance with Subparagraphs (A)-(D) above, those assets shall be converted to and held for the balance of the Initial Trust Term in a separate share of the trust to be referred to and administered as a grantor retained annuity trust ("GRAT") in accordance with Paragraph NINTH below, meeting the requirements of a qualified annuity interest (as defined by

Treasury Regulation Section 25.2702-3) in accordance with Treasury Regulation Section 25.2702-5(c)(8)(ii).

NINTH: During the Initial Trust Term, each GRAT administered as a separate share under this Paragraph NINTH (each of which is referred to as "the GRAT" with regard to that separate share) is intended to provide for the payment of a qualified annuity interest as defined in Treasury Regulation Section 25.2702-3 for the benefit of the Grantor. No amount of the qualified annuity interest shall be paid before the termination of the Initial Term of this trust other than to or for the Grantor's benefit.

(A) In each taxable year of the GRAT, beginning with the year beginning on the Cessation Date (as defined below), the Trustee shall pay to the Grantor an annuity, the amount of which shall be determined in accordance with Subparagraph (D) of this Article NINTH.

(B) The annuity amount shall be paid in equal monthly installments. The annuity amount shall be paid first from the net income of the GRAT and, to the extent net income is not sufficient, from principal.

(C) The right of the Grantor to receive the annuity amount begins on the date of the sale of the residence, the date of damage to or destruction of the residence, or the date on which the residence ceases to be used or held for use as a personal residence, as the case may be (the "Cessation Date"). Notwithstanding the preceding sentence, the Trustee may defer payment of any annuity amount otherwise payable after the Cessation Date until the date that is thirty (30) days after the assets are converted to a qualified annuity interest (the "Conversion Date"); provided that any deferred payment must bear interest from the Cessation Date at a rate not less than the Code Section 7520 rate in effect on the Cessation Date. The Trustee may reduce the aggregate deferred annuity payments by the amount of income actually distributed by the trust to the Grantor during the deferral period.

(D) The amount of the annuity payable to the Grantor shall be determined as follows:

(1) If, on the Conversion Date, the assets of the trust do not include a residence used or held for use as a personal residence of the Grantor, the annuity shall be the amount determined by dividing the lesser of (a) the value of the interest retained by the Grantor (as of the date of the original transfer) or (b) the value of all the trust assets (as of the Conversion Date) by the annuity factor determined (i) for the original term of the Grantor's interest and (ii) at the rate used in valuing the retained interest at the time of the original transfer to the QPRT.

(2) If, on the Conversion Date, the assets of the trust include a residence used or held for use as a personal residence of the Grantor, the annuity shall be the amount determined under subparagraph (1) of this Paragraph (D) multiplied by a fraction. The numerator of the fraction is the excess of the fair market value of the assets of the trust on the Conversion Date over the fair market value of the assets as to which the trust continues as a QPRT, and the denominator of the fraction is the fair market value of the trust assets on the Conversion Date.

(3) In computing the annuity amount for any second or subsequent GRAT to be administered under this Paragraph NINTH, the Trustee shall make appropriate adjustments to the formulas above in this Subparagraph (D) that are consistent with the applicable provisions of the Code and Treasury Regulations and with the Grantor's intent to maintain qualification of each of the trust shares hereunder as a QPRT or a GRAT.

(4) If there is an error in the determination of the annuity amount, then, within a reasonable period after the error is discovered, the difference between the annuity amount payable and the amounts actually paid shall be paid to or for the use of the Grantor by the Trustee in the event of any underpayment, or shall be repaid by the Grantor to the Trustee in the event of any overpayment.

(5) In no event shall the annuity amount hereunder be less than the amount determined under Treasury Regulation Section 25.2702-5(c)(8)(ii)(C).

(E) Notwithstanding the preceding subparagraphs of this Paragraph NINTH, in determining the annuity amount for a short taxable year, the Trustee shall prorate the annuity amount on a daily basis. In determining the annuity amount for the taxable year of the termination of the GRAT, the Trustee shall prorate the annuity amount for the final period of the annuity interest on a daily basis.

(F) No additional contributions shall be made to the GRAT after its creation hereunder.

(G) The GRAT shall terminate on the first to occur of (1) the death of the Grantor and (2) the termination of the Initial Trust Term. Upon termination of the GRAT, the Trustee shall distribute all of the GRAT trust property pursuant to the terms of this Declaration of Trust as if the GRAT trust property had been part of the QPRT.

TENTH: In making any payment or application of income or principal to or for the benefit of any beneficiary pursuant to the discretion hereinabove conferred, the Trustee may make payment directly to such beneficiary if the Trustee shall deem him or her to be of reasonable age and competence or may make application directly or by payment to a guardian or committee of such beneficiary appointed in the State of New Jersey or in any other jurisdiction, to a custodian (including the Trustee) for the beneficiary under the Uniform Transfers to Minors Act of New Jersey or any other jurisdiction, or to an adult person with whom such beneficiary resides or who has the care or custody of such beneficiary temporarily or permanently. Evidence of any such payment or application or the receipt therefor executed by such beneficiary, guardian, committee, custodian or adult person shall discharge the Trustee with respect to such payment or application of such income or principal to such beneficiary, guardian, committee, custodian or adult person.

ELEVENTH: With respect to all property, real or personal, at any time held in trust under this Declaration of Trust, the Trustee is particularly authorized, empowered and granted the following privileges, powers and authority in addition to, and not in limitation of, any powers heretofore granted or otherwise permitted by law, provided, however, that such powers shall not be exercised in such manner and to such extent that the exercise would result in the disqualification of this QPRT under the Regulations, as described in this Declaration of Trust:

(A) To hold and retain all or any part of the trust property in the form in which such property may be at the time it is received, without liability for decrease in the value of such property.

(B) To sell, convey, exchange, lease, mortgage, loan, borrow, hypothecate, or encumber, all or any part of the property, real or personal, or any interest therein, at such time or times, in such manner, and upon such terms as the Trustee, in the Trustee's absolute judgment and discretion, shall deem to be for the best interest of each beneficiary of the trust, and to execute and deliver good and sufficient deeds or other instruments and documents requisite therefor; to invest and reinvest the trust property or the proceeds arising from the sale, exchange, or mortgage thereof in such securities and properties as may be deemed suitable, including, but not by way of limitation, common or preferred stocks of any kind or description, undivided interests and common trust funds without regard to whether such securities or properties so retained, taken, exchanged or purchased are authorized as legal investments for fiduciaries under the laws of any state; *and to sell to anyone, including the Grantor, any portion or all of the trust corpus at the then determined fair market value of such property*, subject to the provisions of Subparagraph (I) of Paragraph THIRD.

COMMENT 8: The emphasized language achieves grantor trust status under Section 675(4)(C). Rev. Rul. 2008-22, 2008 I.R.B. 796.

(C) To vote in person or by proxy, all stocks or other securities having voting privileges; to exercise or refrain from exercising, any right or privilege with respect to stock or other securities, including rights or privileges to subscribe for or otherwise to acquire additional stock or other securities, or to sell the same.

(D) To invest in real property or personal property or both including improved and unimproved real estate.

(E) To liquidate, settle, compromise, set-off, forgive, or otherwise discharge all claims, inclusive of taxes, which are either due from or payable to each trust, in such manner and upon such term or terms and at such time or times as the Trustee, in the Trustee's absolute discretion, deems advisable.

(F) To manage any real property at any time held in the trusts created hereunder and to make all ordinary repairs and any extraordinary repairs, alterations or improvements as the Trustee, in the Trustee's absolute discretion, may deem advisable; to insure for any and all risks and to deal with any such property in all other lawful ways.

(G) To divide or distribute all or any part of the trust property in cash or in kind, or partly in each, and to fix the value of any distribution in kind even though such distribution may differ in kind from property allocated to any other beneficiary, and in making such division or distribution or fixation of values, the judgment of the Trustee shall be binding and conclusive upon all persons interested therein.

(H) To determine whether money and property earned or received hereunder shall be principal or income, and to allocate administrative expenses either to principal or income in accordance with uniform trust accounting principles.

(I) To engage such attorneys, investment counsel, clerks, employees, agents, accountants, brokers, officers, architects, contractors, subcontractors, surveyors, and such other persons, firms or corporations, as the Trustee shall deem necessary or helpful in connection with the administration of the trust created hereunder, at such wages, fees, compensation, remuneration, commission rates, prices, consideration or otherwise, as the Trustee shall deem proper; to employ a custodian and to acquire, hold, register, or dispose of property in the name of such custodian, or its agent or nominee, without designation of fiduciary capacity; to employ investment counsel or other agents and to pay out of principal or income or both the charges and expenses of any such other agent; and to delegate investment discretion to a registered investment advisor; provided, however, that all powers, rights, privileges and discretions granted to each Trustee under this Agreement shall be exercised by such Trustees in a fiduciary capacity for the exclusive benefit and in the best interests of the beneficiaries.

TWELFTH: The Trustee shall keep records showing all receipts and disbursements of income and principal and all changes in investments. Upon request, but not more often than once each year, the Trustee shall render to each beneficiary, or a duly authorized representative of each beneficiary, a full and complete statement of receipts and disbursements of income and principal, together with such changes of investment as may have occurred since the last statement. Such statement shall be in lieu of any statutory requirement for the Trustee to file a judicial accounting under the laws of any jurisdiction.

THIRTEENTH: No purchaser at any sale made by the Trustee shall be bound to inquire into the expediency, propriety, validity or necessity of such sale or to see to or be liable for the application of the purchase monies arising therefrom; nor shall any person who, during the administration of the trusts, shall pay over to or transfer any money or other property to the Trustee, be bound to inquire into or see to or be liable for the application of such funds or monies so transferred or paid over to the Trustee.

FOURTEENTH: The Grantor has been fully advised as to the legal effects of the execution of this Declaration of Trust and informed as to the character and amount of the property hereby transferred and conveyed; and has given consideration to the question of whether the settlement herein contained shall be revocable or irrevocable, and now declares that it shall be irrevocable and the Grantor shall hereafter stand without power at any time to revoke, change, alter, amend or annul any of the provisions contained herein. However, at any time during the Initial Trust Term, the Subsequent Trustee named herein shall have the power (at any time and prior to serving hereunder), acting alone, to amend the Declaration of Trust in any manner required for the sole purpose of ensuring that the trust qualifies and continues to qualify as a QPRT within the meaning of the Treasury Regulations under Code Section 2702, as amended.

FIFTEENTH: (A)(1) During the Initial Trust Term, in the event the Grantor shall be unable or unwilling to serve as Trustee hereunder, for any reason, including "disability" as defined in Subparagraph (C) below, the Grantor nominates and appoints the Grantor's son TODD, residing in, New Jersey, to serve as Successor Trustee hereunder.

(2) Upon expiration of the Initial Trust Term, the Grantor nominates and appoints the Grantor's son, MARK, residing in, New Jersey, as Subsequent Trustee.

(3) In the event that MARK shall be unable or unwilling, for any reason, to serve as Trustee, then TODD is nominated as Successor Subsequent Trustee, to serve hereunder. At any time that more than one (1) Trustee is serving hereunder, any action may be taken on the agreement of at least two (2) Trustees then serving; provided, however, that the signature of any one (1) Trustee shall be sufficient to bind the Trust in any matter.

(B) The last surviving Trustee shall have the right to appoint an individual, or bank or trust company qualified to do business in the applicable jurisdiction, to serve as Successor or Co-Trustee or Subsequent Trustee hereunder. Any such appointment shall be made during lifetime in writing duly acknowledged as in the case of Deeds in the applicable jurisdiction, or at death by his or her Last Will and Testament duly admitted to probate in a court of competent jurisdiction.

(C) The term "disability" shall be defined as a condition wherein the physician who is regularly treating the Grantor certifies that the Grantor is unable to administer the trust based upon either a mental or physical condition.

(D) The rights, duties, privileges, obligations, powers and immunities given and granted to the Trustee herein named shall fully extend to any substitute or Successor Trustee or Subsequent Trustee appointed hereunder.

SIXTEENTH: The Trustee, or any Successor Trustee or Subsequent Trustee, shall be relieved from all responsibility or liability for any loss to the trust properties which may occur because of errors of judgment, and shall be liable only for failure to act in good faith or for acts of gross negligence.

SEVENTEENTH: No bond or security shall be required of the Trustee, including a Successor or Subsequent, in the faithful performance of his or her duties in such capacity.

EIGHTEENTH: The Trustee, by signing this Declaration of Trust, signifies acceptance of the terms hereof, and any Successor Trustee or Subsequent Trustee shall signify acceptance of the terms of this Declaration of Trust in writing.

NINETEENTH: This Declaration of Trust shall be governed and construed in accordance with the laws of the State of New Jersey.

TWENTIETH: It is agreed that these presents shall extend to and be obligatory upon the heirs, executors, administrators, legal representatives, successors and assigns of the parties hereto or beneficiaries hereof.

TWENTY-FIRST: As used herein, each of the masculine, feminine or neuter genders shall include the other genders, the singular shall include the plural and the plural shall include the singular wherever appropriate to the context.

IN WITNESS WHEREOF, the parties hereto set their respective hands and seals.

WITNESS:	GRANTOR and TRUSTEE:
____________________	____________________
	ALICE

STATE OF NEW JERSEY)
) SS.:
COUNTY OF BERGEN)

BE IT REMEMBERED, that on the day of, 20__, before me, the subscriber, a notary public of the State of New Jersey, personally appeared ALICE who, I am satisfied, is the person named in and who executed the within Instrument, and thereupon she acknowledged that she signed, sealed and delivered the same as her act and deed, for the uses and purposes therein expressed.

____

SCHEDULE "A"

Property assigned to the ALICE TEN YEAR TRUST dated ___________, 20__, by ALICE, as Grantor and Trustee:

Date	Property
/ /20__	50% tenant-in-common interest in residence and lot located at: Ramsey, New Jersey

> **COMMENT 9:** This form of trust may be useful when husband and wife jointly own the residence. Their interest can be severed into 50 percent tenant-in-common interests, and each spouse may transfer the respective interest to a separate QPRT. Alternatively, a single Grantor may contribute 50 percent to each of two trusts, each for a different term of years.

Appendix 4 | Sample Testamentary Minor's Trust[24]

ADMINISTRATION OF CONTINGENT TRUST(S) FOR ISSUE. Whenever any interest in property is to be distributed to a person subject to the directions set forth in this Paragraph, that interest shall be distributed as follows:

(1) If the person is at least forty (40) years old at the time for distribution, the entire interest shall be distributed to him or her outright and free of trust.

(2) If the person is at least thirty-five (35) years old but not yet forty (40) years old at the time for distribution, two-thirds (2/3) of the interest shall be distributed to him or her outright and free of trust.

(3) If the person is at least thirty (30) years old but not yet thirty-five (35) years old at the time for distribution, one-third (1/3) of the interest shall be distributed to him or her outright and free of trust.

The balance of the person's interest, if any, shall be held by my Trustee in a separate trust for the benefit of the person in accordance with the following terms and conditions:

(i) PAYMENT OF INCOME.

(a) Prior to Age 21. My Trustee shall pay to, or apply for the benefit of, any person for whom a trust was established pursuant to this Paragraph and who has not reached the age of twenty-one (21) years such amounts from the net income of his or her trust as my Trustee deems necessary or desirable for such person's health, education, support and maintenance, adding any excess income to principal at the discretion of my Trustee.

(b) After Attaining Age 21. My Trustee shall pay to, or apply for the benefit of, any person for whom a trust was established pursuant to this Paragraph and who has attained the age of twenty-one (21) years all of the net income of his or her trust, in convenient installments, but not less frequently than quarter-annually.

(ii) PAYMENT OF PRINCIPAL. My Trustee shall pay to, or apply for the benefit of, any person for whom a trust was established pursuant to this Paragraph such amounts from the principal

24.

of his or her trust as my Trustee deems necessary or desirable for such person's health, education, support and maintenance.

(iii) DISTRIBUTIONS. When a person for whom a trust was established pursuant to this Paragraph attains the age of thirty (30) years during the term of such trust, on or as soon as practicable after such birthday, my Trustee shall distribute to the person, outright and free of trust, one-third (1/3) of the balance of such trust as of that birthday. When a person for whom a trust was established pursuant to this Paragraph attains the age of thirty-five (35) years during the term of such trust, on or as soon as practicable after such birthday, my Trustee shall distribute to the person, outright and free of trust, one-half (1/2) of the balance of such trust as of that birthday. When a person for whom a trust was established pursuant to this Paragraph attains the age of forty (40) years during the term of such trust, on or as soon as practicable after such birthday, my Trustee shall distribute to the person, outright and free of trust, the entire balance of such trust. Such trust shall then terminate.

(iv) DEATH OF PERSON PRIOR TO DISTRIBUTION OF ENTIRE TRUST. If a person for whom a trust was established pursuant to this Paragraph dies before his or her respective trust is completely distributed, the remainder of such person's trust shall be paid to such person's then living issue, *per stirpes*, and, if none, in equal shares to his or her then living brothers and sisters, with an equal share passing to the then living issue, *per stirpes*, of any brother or sister not then living (including only persons who are my issue), if any, and, if none, then to my then living issue, *per stirpes*; *provided, however*, that each portion otherwise payable to any issue of mine who is under forty (40) years of age shall be retained in trust, subject to the directions set forth above in this Paragraph. If no issue of mine is then living, such trust property shall be distributed to those persons who would have taken, and in such shares as they would have taken, my property if I had died intestate a resident of the State of New Jersey, as of the date of such distribution.

Table of Cases

Principal cases are italicized.

A

Aldrich v. Basile, 201

Anderson, In re Guardianship & Conservatorship of, 470

Apprentices' Fund, Case of, 384

Arnold v. Metro. Life Ins. Co., 491

B

Bailey, Estate of, v. Commissioner, 542

Baker v. Wood, Ris & Hames, Prof'l Corp., 40

Bartolovich, In re Estate of, 35

Bell v. Estate of Bell, 332

Benavides v. Mathis, 325

Bielecki v. Boissel, 468

Blumenstyk, In re, 497

Boggs v. Boggs, 478

Boyer, In re Estate of, 371

Branigan, In re Estate of, 305

Breeden v. Stone, 92

Broadway Nat'l Bank v. Adams, 406

C

Carpenter v. Miller, 244, 247, 248

Castro v. Ballesteros-Suarez, 32

Cate-Schweyen v. Cate, 362, 370

Claflin v. Claflin, 428, 431

Clark v. Greenhalge, 193

Cohen v. Guardianship of Cohen, 27

Condon, Estate of, 276

Conley, In re Estate of, 172, 175, 176

Conlin v. Murdock, 391

Cook v. Estate of Seeman, 237

Covert, In re Estate of, 31

Cozzie v. Metro. Life Ins. Co., 491

Crabtree, In re Will of, 513, 518, 520

Cristofani, Estate of, v. Commissioner, 555

Crummey v. Commissioner, 550, 555

D

Diep v. Rivas, 31

E

Eckelberry v. Reliastar Life Ins. Co., 491

Edwards, In re, 262, 263, 264

Egelhoff v. Egelhoff, 478, 479

Ehrlich, Estate of, 150

Ellis v. Vespoint, 369

Emmert v. Prade, 480, 483

Estate of. *See name of decedent*

Eyerman v. Mercantile Trust Co., 6

F

Farkas v. Williams, 448

Federal Trade Comm'n v. Affordable Media, LLC, 417

Feinberg, In re Probate Proceeding, Will of, 90

Ferree, In re Will of, 148

First Nat'l Bank of Leesburg v. Hector Supply Co., 458

Flohl, In re Estate of, 100

Fournier, In re Estate of (902 A.2d 852), 369

Fournier, In re Estate of (966 A.2d 855), 369

Fox v. Lincoln Fin. Grp., 330

Foxley, Estate of, 158

G

Gardner, In re Estate of, 38

Gassmann, In re Estate of, 94

Gates, In re Estate of, 369

Gifford v. Gifford, 193

Grahl v. Davis, 470

Griffith, Estate of, 126, 132, 133

Groh v. Groh, 485

Guardianship & Conservatorship of. *See name of ward/conservatee*

Gushwa, Estate of, 162, 170

H

Hamilton v. Drogo, 405

Hand, Estate of, 80, 81

Hargrove v. Rich, 212

Harrell v. Metro. Life Ins. Co., 491

Harris, In re, 501

Henneghan, In re Estate of, 116, 118, 119

Herceg, Estate of, 300, 303

Herron, In re Estate of, 304

Hodel v. Irving, 10, 13

Hoffman v. Pennsylvania State Emps.' Ret. Bd., 485

HSBC Bank USA (formerly Marine Midland Bank) (Ely), In re, 525

I

Irving Trust Co. v. Day, 9

J

Jones v. State Emps.' Ret. Bd., 479
Jones, In re Estate of, 216
JP Morgan Chase Bank, N.A., In re, 392

K

Kaplan v. Fair (In re Estate of Herron), 304
Kaufman's Will, In re, 78
Kennedy v. Plan Adm'r for DuPont Sav. & Inv. Plan, 479
King v. Hartford Life & Acc. Ins. Co., 491
Kurrle, In re Estate of, 100, 103, 104

L

Last Will & Testament & Trust Agreement of Moor, In re, 197
Leete Estate, In re, 252
Lennon v. Metro. Life Ins. Co., 491
Lewis v. Alexander, 425
Lincoln Benefit Life Co. v. Guerrero, 308
Liranzo v. LI Jewish Educ./Research, 400
Lorenzo v. Medina, 260
Lung, In re Estate of, 273

M

Maher, Estate of, v. Iglikova, 339
Mahoney v. Grainger, 287
Malleiro v. Mori, 203
Manary v. Anderson, 492
Mannara, In re Estate of, 357, 359
Martelle, In re Estate of, 330
McCay v. State, 98
Mebust, Estate of, 60
Meinhard v. Salmon, 381
Milbank Ins. Co. v. Indiana Ins. Co., 345
Moor, In re Last Will & Testament & Trust Agreement of, 197
Morgan, Estate of, 408
Morris, In re Will of, 140, 144
Mortensen, In re, 418
Muchemore, In re Estate of, 207, 211
Mueller, In re Estate of, 31
Mull, In re Guardianship of, 159
Murphy, Estate of, v. Commissioner, 542
Mustapher; United States v., 35

N

Nalaschi, Estate of, 86
Nale Estate, In re, 35
New York Trust Co. v. Eisner, 9
Newman v. Thomas, 470
Nicholas v. Kershner, 83
Nichols v. Eaton, 406, 409
Nichols, In re Estate of, 437

O

Olsen v. Comm'n for Lawyer Discipline, 98

P

Patch v. White, 290
Paul v. Patton, 41
Payne, In re Estate of, 304-305
Peterson v. Peck, 346, *348,* 351
Pickelner v. Adler, 443
Polson v. Craig, 282

Q

Quattlebaum v. Simmons Nat'l Bank, 239
Queener, Estate of, v. Helton, 440
Quill v. Koppell, 20

R

Ranney, In re Will of, 148
Rauschenberg, In re Estate of, 373, 379
Raynolds' Estate, In re, 3
R.M.S., In re, 227
Robinson v. Delfino, 462, 466, 468
Robinson v. Robinson, 456
Rosasco, In re Estate of, 105
Rosenberg's Will, In re, 159
Ruso, Estate of, 123

S

Sagel, In re Estate of, 270, 272
Saunders v. Vautier, 431
Scheffel v. Krueger, 410, 413
Schmidt v. Sheet Metal Workers' Nat'l Pension Fund, 479
Schumacher, In re Estate of, 177, 181
Shapira v. Union Nat'l Bank, 4, 8
Sheldon, In re Estate of, 281
Shumway, In re Estate of, 222
Standard Oil Co. of N.J. v. United States, 284
Steen & Berg Co. v. Berg, 200
Stegemeier v. Magness, 503, 509
Stephens v. Beard, 256
Sterling v. Sterling, 22
Strittmater, In re, 77, 78
Sturdivant v. Birchett, 146-147
Swain v. Estate of Tyre ex rel. Reilly, 31

T

Thiemann, In re Estate of, 66, 70
Titler v. State Emps.' Ret. Bd., 485
Tulsa Prof'l Collection Servs. v. Pope, 16

U
United States v. See name of opposing party
University of Southern Indiana Foundation v. Baker, 292

V
Vacco v. Quill, 20
Vincent, In re Estate of, 233, 235

W
Walton v. Commissioner, 559
Westmoreland ex rel. Westmoreland v. Westmoreland, 485

Z
Zielinski, Estate of, 94
Zukerman, In re Estate of, 362, 370

Table of Authorities

Uniform Laws

Revised Uniform Fiduciary Access to Digital Assets Act (RUFADAA)
§2(22) . . . 24
§4 . . . 24
§4(a) . . . 24
§4(c) . . . 24

Uniform Commercial Code
§2-403(2) . . . 345

Uniform Health Care Decisions Act
§5(b) . . . 21

Uniform Multiple-Person Accounts Act. See UPC §6-201 *et seq.*

Uniform Power of Attorney Act
§104 . . . 22
§201(a) . . . 22

Uniform Principal and Income Act (UPIA)
§104 . . . 533
§104, comment . . . 533
§104(c)(7)-(8) . . . 533
§401 . . . 532

Uniform Probate Code (UPC)
art. III . . . 15
art. VI . . . 449, 475
pt. 2 . . . 316
§1-201 . . . 260
§1-201(18) . . . 308, 484
§2-101 . . . 43, 236-237
§2-101, comment . . . 237
§2-101(b) . . . 236-237
§2-102 . . . 50-51, 55, 337, 341
§2-102(1)(b) . . . 338
§2-103 . . . 52-53, 55, 70, 71
§2-103(a)(1) . . . 53
§2-103(a)(2) . . . 53
§2-103(a)(3) . . . 53
§2-103(a)(4)-(5) . . . 53
§2-103(b) . . . 53, 54
§2-104 . . . 55, 243, 251
§2-105 . . . 55
§2-107 . . . 66
§2-109 . . . 75, 276
§2-116 . . . 71
§2-118 . . . 71, 72
§2-119 . . . 71-72
§2-119(b) . . . 72, 73
§2-119(c) . . . 73
§2-119(d) . . . 73, 74
§2-201 . . . 318
§2-202 . . . 318-319, 322
§2-202, comment (1969) . . . 317
§2-202(b) (1990) . . . 321
§2-203 . . . 322-323
§2-203(b) . . . 321, 322
§2-207 . . . 319
§2-209 . . . 323
§2-209(a) . . . 322
§2-213 . . . 50
§2-301 . . . 331
§2-301, comment . . . 331
§2-302 . . . 337, 338-339
§2-402 . . . 330
§2-403 . . . 330
§§2-404 to 2-405 . . . 330
§2-501 . . . 82
§2-502 . . . 115
§2-502, comment c . . . 158
§2-502, comment o . . . 122
§2-502(a) . . . 120, 121
§2-502(a)(1) . . . 122
§2-502(a)(2) . . . 122
§2-502(a)(3)(A) . . . 116
§2-502(a)(3)(B) . . . 119
§2-502(b) . . . 138, 140, 144, 146
§2-502(b), comment . . . 140

§2-502(c) . . . 140
§2-503 . . . 149, 170, 171, 196, 205, 299, 475
§2-504 . . . 124-125
§2-504(a) . . . 124
§2-504(b) . . . 124
§2-505(a) . . . 122
§2-505(b) . . . 123
§2-507 . . . 157, 174, 176, 179
§2-507, comment . . . 162
§2-507(a)(2) . . . 162
§2-507(c) . . . 159, 162
§2-508 . . . 181
§2-509 . . . 187-188
§2-509(a) . . . 187
§2-509(b) . . . 187
§2-509(c) . . . 187
§2-510 . . . 192, 194, 195
§2-511 . . . 369, 450-451
§2-512 . . . 137
§2-513 . . . 196, 198, 199, 200
§2-514 . . . 188-189, 442
§2-517 . . . 221
§2-603 . . . 242
§2-603, comment . . . 259
§2-603(a)(8) . . . 258
§2-603(b) . . . 257
§2-603(b)(1) . . . 257
§2-603(b)(3) . . . 259, 265
§2-604 . . . 243
§2-605 . . . 281-282
§2-605, comment . . . 282
§2-606(a)(3) . . . 272
§2-606(a)(6) . . . 270
§2-606(b) . . . 275
§2-607 . . . 232
§2-609(a) . . . 276, 278
§2-702 . . . 243, 251, 258
§2-702(d) . . . 243
§2-705(f) . . . 71
§2-706 . . . 260
§2-707 . . . 260
§2-802 . . . 308
§2-803 . . . 30-31
§2-803(b) . . . 30
§2-803(c)(1)-(2) . . . 30
§2-803(g) . . . 31
§2-804 . . . 182-183, 308
§2-804, comment . . . 308
§2-804(e) . . . 307
§2-805 . . . 299, 484
§2-806 . . . 300
§2-1102(3) . . . 36
§2-1105 . . . 37
§2-1105(e) . . . 36
§2-1106(b)(3) . . . 36
§§2-1107 to 2-1111 . . . 36
§2-1113 . . . 37
§2-1113, comment . . . 37
§3-101 . . . 36
§3-108(a) . . . 15
§3-303(c) . . . 87
§3-401 . . . 15
§3-407 . . . 97
§3-502 . . . 15
§3-603 . . . 220
§3-605 . . . 220
§3-611 . . . 216, 219
§3-703(a) . . . 215, 494
§3-711 . . . 220
§3-801 . . . 16
§3-803 . . . 16
§3-902 . . . 279-280, 281
§5-202 . . . 226-227, 231
§5-203 . . . 227, 231
§5-204 . . . 227
§6-101 . . . 448
§6-101, comment . . . 448
§6-201 *et seq.* . . . 470
§6-201(6) . . . 468
§6-204 . . . 470
§§6-211 to 6-216 . . . 468
§6-211 . . . 468, 469
§6-211, comment . . . 469
§6-211(b) . . . 469
§6-211(c) . . . 469, 470
§6-211(d) . . . 469
§6-212 . . . 468
§6-212(a) . . . 468
§6-213 . . . 468
§6-401 *et seq.* . . . 453
§7-302 . . . 215

Uniform Prudent Investor Act (UPIA)
§1 . . . 523
§1(b) . . . 523
§2 . . . 524

§2(a) . . . 522
§2(b) . . . 522
§2(c) . . . 522
§3 . . . 523, 524, 529
§4 . . . 523, 524
§7 . . . 525
§8 . . . 523, 525

Uniform Real Property Transfer on Death Act (URPTODA). See UPC §6-401 *et seq.*

Uniform Testamentary Additions to Trusts Act. See UPC §2-511

Uniform Trust Code (UTC)
art. 7 . . . 372
art. 9 . . . 522. *See also* Uniform Prudent Investor Act (UPIA)
§102, comment e . . . 435, 439
§103 . . . 361
§105, comment . . . 535
§105(a) . . . 494
§105(b)(2) . . . 494
§105(b)(8) . . . 534
§105(b)(9) . . . 535
§112 . . . 260
§401 . . . 352, 353
§401(1) . . . 353
§401(2) . . . 353
§401(3) . . . 353
§402 . . . 353, 354
§402(b) . . . 371
§404 . . . 343, 370, 381, 386
§405 . . . 386
§405(a) . . . 385
§407 . . . 353, 369
§408 . . . 446
§411 . . . 432
§411(a) . . . 427
§411(b)-(e) . . . 432
§411(b) . . . 432
§411(c) . . . 432
§412 . . . 433
§412, comment . . . 428
§412(a) . . . 433
§412(b) . . . 433
§413 . . . 433
§414 . . . 433
§415 . . . 299, 433, 484
§416 . . . 300, 433
§501 . . . 404, 405, 406
§502 . . . 408, 410
§503 . . . 413, 414
§504 . . . 405-406
§504(b) . . . 404-405
§504(c) . . . 405
§504(c)(2) . . . 405
§505 . . . 416, 417
§601 . . . 354, 355
§602 . . . 383
§602(a) . . . 427
§602(c) . . . 451
§704(b) . . . 372
§704(c) . . . 372
§801 . . . 372, 494, 497
§802 . . . 496, 531
§802(b) . . . 495
§802(e) . . . 496
§802(h) . . . 495
§803 . . . 532
§804 . . . 512
§809 . . . 531
§810 . . . 531
§810(b) . . . 531
§811 . . . 531
§812 . . . 531
§813 . . . 534
§813(a) . . . 535
§813(b)(2)-(3) . . . 534
§814(a) . . . 404
§815 . . . 379-380
§815, comment . . . 380
§815(a) . . . 493
§815(a)(2)(A) . . . 380
§816 . . . 380, 493
§1001 . . . 501, 535
§1002 . . . 501
§1002(a) . . . 535
§1008 . . . 536

Uniform Voidable Transfers Act
§4 . . . 417

Restatements

Restatement (Third) of Law Governing Lawyers
§51(3)(a) . . . 40

Restatement (Third) of Property: Wills & Other Donative Transfers
§1.1 . . . 15
§1.1(a) . . . 44
§2.7 . . . 237
§3.2, comment a . . . 138
§3.4, comment b . . . 159
§3.5 . . . 191-192
§3.8 . . . 369, 450
§3.8(a)(ii) . . . 450
§4.1, comment j . . . 176
§4.3 . . . 184
§5.1 . . . 268
§5.2, comment b . . . 270
§5.2, comment d . . . 274
§5.2, comment i . . . 451
§5.2(c) . . . 270
§5.3 . . . 282
§5.4 . . . 276
§5.5, comment p . . . 451
§6.1 . . . 346
§6.1, comment b . . . 345, 539
§7.1(a) . . . 449
§7.2 . . . 451
§8.1 . . . 82, 355
§8.1, comment c . . . 83, 84, 157
§8.1, comment f . . . 85
§8.1, comment m . . . 90
§8.1, comment s . . . 94
§8.3 . . . 97, 104
§8.3, comment b . . . 98
§8.3, comment d . . . 98, 100
§8.3, comment e . . . 99, 104
§8.3, comment f . . . 99
§8.3, comment g . . . 99
§8.3, comment h . . . 99-100
§8.3, comment j . . . 110
§8.4 . . . 30
§10.1 . . . 3
§10.1, comment a . . . 2
§10.2, comment c . . . 288
§11.1 . . . 291
§11.2 . . . 292
§11.2, comments n-q . . . 289
§11.2(b)(3), comment . . . 290
§12.1 . . . 299
§12.1, comment h . . . 484-485
§12.2 . . . 300
§13.1 . . . 267
§17.1 . . . 205
§17.3 . . . 206
§19.1 . . . 212
§19.21 . . . 206
§26.1, comment b . . . 242
§41 . . . 361

Restatement (Third) of Restitution and Unjust Enrichment
§45 . . . 30
§46, comment g . . . 443
§55 . . . 440
§55, comment f . . . 440
§55(1) . . . 440

Restatement (Third) of Trusts
§1, comment e . . . 439
§2, comment i . . . 361
§§7-9 . . . 436
§9(1)(b) . . . 436
§10 . . . 352
§11 . . . 355
§13 . . . 355
§13, comment d . . . 357
§16 . . . 362
§17 . . . 382
§18 . . . 444
§18, comment h . . . 443
§19 . . . 369
§19, comment a(3) . . . 369
§20 . . . 369
§22(1) . . . 361
§28 . . . 385
§31 . . . 372
§32 . . . 372
§33, comment b . . . 372
§35 . . . 372
§36 . . . 372
§40 . . . 361
§43, comment a . . . 370
§44 . . . 371, 445
§44, comment d . . . 370
§47 . . . 445
§47, comment e . . . 445
§50 . . . 391
§50, comment a . . . 391
§51 . . . 390

§57 . . . 407
§58(2) . . . 416
§60 . . . 406
§65(2) . . . 428
§65(2), comment d . . . 428
§77 . . . 512
§77, comment b(1) . . . 512
§78 . . . 496
§79 . . . 532

Federal Statutes

Achieving a Better Life Experience Act
26 U.S.C. §529A . . . 426
§529A(b)(1)(A) . . . 426

Bankruptcy Abuse Prevention and Consumer Protection Act
§1501(b)(1) . . . 423

Bankruptcy Code
11 U.S.C. §541(c)(1)(B) . . . 407
§541(c)(2) . . . 408
§548 . . . 417
§548(a)(1) . . . 418, 423
§548(e) . . . 422
§548(e)(1) . . . 418

Electronic Communications Privacy Act of 1986
Pub. L. No. 99-508, 100 Stat. 1848 . . . 24

Employee Retirement Income Security Act of 1979 (ERISA)
29 U.S.C. §1001 *et seq.* . . . 477
§1003(b)(1) . . . 485
§1055(a) . . . 478
§1055(c)(2)(A) . . . 485
§1104(a)(1) . . . 477
§1144(a) . . . 478

Indian Land Consolidation Act
§207 . . . 13

Internal Revenue Code (IRC)
26 U.S.C. §170(f)(11)(C) . . . 542
§401(k) . . . 477
§501(c)(3) . . . 385-386, 544
§529A . . . 426
§529A(b)(1)(A) . . . 426
§671 *et seq.* . . . 599
§1014 . . . 189
§2001(c) . . . 567
§2002 . . . 567
§2010(c)(3) . . . 567
§2010(c)(4) . . . 568
§2010(c)(5) . . . 568
§2032(a) . . . 561
§2033 . . . 561
§2035 . . . 561, 591
§2035(a) . . . 561, 562
§2035(b) . . . 562
§2036 . . . 561
§2036(a) . . . 562
§2037 . . . 561, 562
§2038 . . . 561, 562
§2039 . . . 563
§2040 . . . 563
§2041 . . . 563
§2041(a)(2) . . . 540
§2041(b)(1)(A) . . . 392, 541, 556
§2042 . . . 564
§2042(2) . . . 556
§2044 . . . 543, 564, 566, 577
§2053 . . . 565
§2054 . . . 565
§2055 . . . 565
§2056 . . . 565
§2056(b)(1) . . . 565
§2056(b)(5) . . . 566
§2056(b)(7) . . . 566
§2056(b)(7)(B) . . . 543
§2058 . . . 567
§2502 . . . 547
§2503(b) . . . 545, 546, 547, 550
§2503(b)(1) . . . 545
§2503(b)(2) . . . 545
§2503(c) . . . 545, 546
§2503(e) . . . 546, 547
§2505 . . . 547
§2511 . . . 539
§2512 . . . 541
§2513 . . . 548
§2514(c) . . . 540
§2518 . . . 37
§2519 . . . 543
§2522(a) . . . 544
§2523(a) . . . 542
§2523(b) . . . 543

§2523(e) . . . 543
§2523(f) . . . 543
§2523(f)(2) . . . 543
§2602 . . . 576
§2612(a) . . . 575
§2612(b) . . . 575
§2612(c) . . . 575
§2613(a) . . . 575
§2613(b) . . . 575
§2621 . . . 577
§2622 . . . 577
§2623 . . . 576
§2631(a) . . . 580
§2632(a) . . . 577
§2632(b) . . . 577
§2632(c) . . . 577
§2641 . . . 577
§2642(c) . . . 581
§2642(c)(3)(A) . . . 576
§2642(c)(3)(B) . . . 576
§2651 . . . 575
§2651(e) . . . 576
§2652(a) . . . 577
§2652(a)(2) . . . 577
§2652(a)(3) . . . 577
§2701(e)(2) . . . 557
§2702 . . . 557, 559
§2702(b) . . . 557
§6075 . . . 548
§7520 . . . 556, 558, 560

Medicaid Act
42 U.S.C. §1396p(c)(1)(B)(i) . . . 425
§1396p(d)(4)(A) . . . 425

Medicare Act
42 U.S.C. §1395cc(f)(1)(A)(i) . . . 20

Social Security Act
42 U.S.C. §1382c(a)(3)(A) . . . 425

Stored Communications Act (SCA)
18 U.S.C. §2702 . . . 24
§2702(a)(1) . . . 24
§2702(b)(3) . . . 24

Other Federal Statutes
31 U.S.C. §3713(b) . . . 567
42 U.S.C. §1320a-7b(a)(6) . . . 426
49 U.S.C. §44101(a) . . . 352
Pub. L. No. 109-3, 119 Stat. 15 (Mar. 21, 2005) . . . 19

State Statutes

Alaska
Alaska Stat. §34.40.110(b)(1) . . . 422

Arizona
Ariz. Rev. Stat. Ann. §32-1365.01 . . . 26

Arkansas
Ark. Code Ann. §28-39-407 . . . 337

California
Cal. Com. Code §9102(42) . . . 200
Cal. Health & Safety Code §7100 . . . 26
Cal. Prob. Code §101 . . . 325
Cal. Prob. Code §6240 . . . 139
Cal. Prob. Code §8461 . . . 215
Cal. Prob. Code §15306.5 . . . 410
Cal. Prob. Code §15403(b) . . . 428
Cal. Prob. Code §21110(b) . . . 259
Cal. Prob. Code §21110(c) . . . 257

Colorado
Colo. Stat. Ann. §15-14-202 . . . 231
Colo. Stat. Ann. §15-14-203 . . . 231

District of Columbia
D.C. Code §18-103 . . . 118
D.C. Code §20-312(b) . . . 119

Florida
Fla. Prob. Code §689.15 . . . 452
Fla. Stat. Ann. §732.517 . . . 221

Georgia
Ga. Code Ann. §53-12-20(a) . . . 370

Indiana
Ind. Code Ann. §29-1-6-2 . . . 221

Missouri
Mo. Rev. Stat. §474.040 . . . 69

Montana
Mont. Code Ann. §72-2-203(4) . . . 64

Nevada
Nev. Rev. Stat. §133.170 . . . 337

New Hampshire
N.H. Rev. Stat. Ann. §551:10 . . . 337

New Jersey
N.J. Stat. §26:6A-2 . . . 18
N.J. Stat. §26:6A-3 . . . 18
N.J. Stat. §3B:27-1(a) . . . 19
N.J. Stat. §3B:31-18 . . . 353, 370
N.J. Stat. Ann. §3B:12-27 . . . 90
N.J. Stat. Ann. §3B:3-33.1(a) . . . 304

New York
N.Y. Est. Powers & Trusts Law §3-2.1(a)(1) . . . 116
N.Y. Est. Powers & Trusts Law §3-3.3(a)(2) . . . 263
N.Y. Est. Powers & Trusts Law §7-1.5 . . . 410
N.Y. Est. Powers & Trusts Law §7-1.17 . . . 353, 370
N.Y. Est. Powers & Trusts Law §7-3.4 . . . 410
N.Y. Surr. Ct. Proc. Act Law art. 17-A . . . 392
N.Y. Surr. Ct. Proc. Act Law §1811 . . . 232

Pennsylvania
20 Pa. Cons. Stat. §2514 . . . 270
20 Pa. Cons. Stat. Ann. §2514(18) . . . 273
20 Pa. Cons. Stat. Ann. §2514(18)(iii) . . . 271
20 Pa. Cons. Stat. ch. 33, subch. B . . . 219-220

South Dakota
S.D. Codified Laws §55-1-3 . . . 344

Tennessee
Tenn. Code §1-3-105(31) . . . 135
Tenn. Code §32-1-104 . . . 135
Tenn. Code §32-2-110 . . . 135

Texas
Tex. Trusts & Est. Code §304.001 . . . 215

Virginia
Va. Code §64.1-49 . . . 144
Va. Code §64.2-403 . . . 144

Washington
Wash. Rev. Code §11.11.010(7)(a) . . . 491
Wash. Rev. Code §11.11.020(4) . . . 492
Wash. Rev. Code §11.28.250 . . . 219

Table of Authors

A
Albee, Edward, 5
American Law Institute, 14, 497
Artura, Cynthia J., 491
Ascher, Mark L., 260
Atkinson, Thomas E., 158, 176, 269

B
Banta, Natalie M., 24
Blackstone, Sir William, 452
Bogert, George G., 437, 495
Bogert, George T., 495
Boni-Saenz, Alexander A., 21, 146
Boxx, Karen E., 494
Brody, Evelyn, 388

C
Chandrasekher, Andrea Cann, 54
Coscarelli, Joe, 22
Cott, Nancy F., 2

D
Danforth, Robert T., 409
Daughtery, Greg, 5
DeScioli, Peter, 388
Dressler, Rebecca, 20-21
Duncan, Gregory J., 330

E
Eliot, T.S., 286

F
Foster, Frances H., 26
Friedan, Betty, 77, 78

G
Gallanis, Thomas, 189
Gary, Susan N., 453
Geisel, Theodor Seuss (Dr. Seuss), 305
Gittler, Josephine, 189
Glover, Mark, 79-80

H
Halbach, Edward C., 257
Hamburger, Philip, 114
Helmholz, R.H., 493
Hernandez, Tanya K., 26
Hess, Amy Morris, 495
Hirsch, Adam J., 2, 37, 48, 330, 409, 446
Horton, David, 17, 54, 215, 264, 535-536
Houppert, Karen, 3

K
Kafka, Franz, 9
Kelly, Daniel B., 431-432
Kornstein, Daniel J., 10
Kossow, Julian R., 93
Kovaleski, Serge F., 22
Kübler-Ross, Elisabeth, 18

L
Langbein, John H., 17, 113, 147-148, 299-300, 383, 448-449, 501-502
LaPiana, William P., 37
Leslie, Melanie B., 77, 470, 502
Lindgren, James, 114

M
Madoff, Ray D., 3, 25, 384
Maitland, F., 343
Mann, Bruce H., 124
Mann, Ronald J., 424
Mellinkoff, David, 187
Meyerson, Harold, 476

N
Nir, Sarah Maslin, 149
Nuland, Sherwin B., 18

P
Paulson, Michael, 5
Powell, H. Jefferson, 440
Primack, Dan, 320

R
Repetti, James R., 538
Richmond, Douglas R., 486-490
Rosenbury, Laura A., 316

S
Sax, Joseph L., 5
Scales, Adam F., 491
Schoenblum, Jeffrey A., 409
Schuman, Gary, 491

Scott, Austin W., 391
Sendak, Maurice, 9
Seuss, Dr. (Theodor Seuss Geisel), 305
Shakespeare, William, 111
Sherwin, Emily, 440
Sitkoff, Robert, 432
Smith, Lionel, 440
Soled, Jay A., 537
Solum, Lawrence, 431
Spivack, Carla, 31
Sterk, Stewart E., 470
Strahilevitz, Lior Jacob, 5
Strand, Palma Joy, 46-47

T

Tate, Joshua C., 2, 189
Turano, Margaret V., 14

W

Waggoner, Lawrence W., 115, 257, 266-267, 307
Wang, William K.S., 2
Weisbord, Reid K., 44-46, 264, 384, 388, 575
Wiggins, Raley L., 273

Z

Zaritsky, Howard M., 343

Index

A
Abatement, 241, 279-281
  classification of bequests and, 201
  defined, 279
  order of, 279-280
Accession, 241, 281-285
Accidental death
  benefits, 486-491
  DWI cases, 490-491
  "Russian roulette" cases, 491
"Accidental inheritance," 470
Achieving a Better Life Experience Act, 426
Acknowledgment, 115. *See also* Attested wills
ACTEC. *See* American College of Trusts and Estates Counsel (ACTEC)
Acts of independent significance, 136-138
Ademption, 241
  defined, 269
  by extinction, 201, 269-275
    identity theory, 269
    intent theory, 269
  by satisfaction, 275-279
    partial satisfaction, 278
Administrator cum testament annexo, 357. *See also* Personal representative
Adoption and intestacy, 70-75
  adult adoption, 71
  child of assisted reproduction who is subsequently adopted, 72
  death of both genetic parents, adoption after, 72, 73-74
  gestational child who is subsequently adopted, 72
  parent-child relationship, 71-72
    adoptee and adoptee's adoptive parent or parents, 71
    adoptee and adoptee's genetic parents, 71-72
  relative of genetic parent, adoption by, 72, 73
  stepchild adopted by stepparent, 72
  "stranger to the adoption" rule, 71
Advance directives, 20-21
Advancements
  intestate share, effect on, 75-76, 276
  testamentary devise, effect on, 276-279
Age requirement
  emancipation from parental control, 77
  valid will, making of, 77, 82
Alaska
  asset protection trust, 418-424
  fraudulent conveyance, 418-422
  intestacy under UPC provisions, 43
Alienation of trust interest, 390, 391
Ambiguity, 242, 288-298
  extrinsic evidence and, 288, 290, 291-298
  inter vivos trust, 292-297
  latent, 288-289, 290-291
  patent, 288, 289
  "personal usage" exception, 290
  resolution of, 291-298
American College of Trusts and Estates Counsel (ACTEC)
  cognitive status of client, 85
  diminished capacity, determining extent of, 85
  safeguarding client documents, 136
  testamentary capacity, 85
Ancestors, 49
Ancillary administration, 16
Animal, trust for care of, 446
Animus testandi, 79
Annual exclusion, 545-546. *See also* Gift tax
  "annual exclusion amount," 545
  future interest, gift of, 545, 546
  gift splitting, 545
Annuities, estate tax, 563
Antilapse, 257-265. *See also* Wills
Appointment
  of agent under durable power of attorney, 22
  of executor, 144
  of fiduciary, 215-219
  of guardian, 226-227
  of personal representative, 15
  of trustee, 358, 372
Appointment, powers of. *See* Powers of appointment
Arizona
  community property, 324
  disclaimers, 38-40
  in terrorem clause, 222-225
  intestacy under UPC provisions, 43
  slayer statute, 32-34

Arkansas
  children omitted from will, 337
  incorporation by reference, 193-195
  lapse, 244-247
  negative wills, non-recognition of, 237-239
  tangible personal property, inter vivos gift of, 348-350
Ascertainable beneficiary, 360, 371
Assignment of trust interest, 390
Attachment of trust beneficiary's interest, 404-405
Attestation clauses, 123-136
Attestation not required, private trust, 370
Attested wills, 115-138
  acknowledgment, 115
  acts of independent significance, 136-138
  attest, defined, 115
  attestation clauses, 123-136
  doctrine of independent significance, 136-138
  execution of wills, 115
  interested witnesses, 122-123
  notarization, 115
  procedural requirements, 115
  "purging" statutes, 122-123
  safeguarding the will, 136
  self-proving affidavits, 123-136
  signature requirements, 115
  simultaneous presence requirement, 116
  witness competency, 122-123
  writing requirement, 115
Attorney-client privilege, 288
Australia, substantial compliance in, 148
Authentication
  attested will, 115
  holographic will, 138

B

Bailment, defined, 345
Bankruptcy Abuse Prevention and Consumer Protection Act, 423
Bankruptcy Code, fraudulent transfer under, 417-418, 422
Bankruptcy law, 407-408, 417-418, 418-423
Beach-bum trusts, 382
Beneficiaries
  charitable trusts, 371, 384-385
  designation in nonprobate assets. *See* Beneficiary designation
  private trusts, 370-371, 389-403
  probate system, 14
  trust, 344
Beneficiary designation
  life insurance, 480-483
  nonprobate transfers, 478, 479, 480-483
  pension plan, 478, 479
  retirement account, 478, 479
  superwill, 491-492
Blended families, 51, 532
Breach of trust, 389-390. *See also* Fiduciary duties
Business trusts, 381
Bypass trusts
  as common testamentary trusts, 569
  features of, 570-571
  model terms, 570-571

C

California
  antilapse rule, 257, 259
  community property, 324
  executor, selection of, 215
  intangible personal property, 200
  modification of trust, 428
  quasi-community property, 325
  spendthrift interest, attachment of, 410
  statutory will, 139
  termination of trust, 428
Cancellation, revocatory act of, 176. *See also* Revocation of will
Capacity requirements
  of testator making, amending, or revoking will, 77, 79, 82, 83, 156, 157, 354
  of trust settlor, 354-360
    revocable vs. irrevocable trusts, 354-355
Cardozo, Benjamin, 380, 440
Casualty and theft losses, deductibility of, 565. *See also* Estate tax
Cestui que trust, 344, 370
Charitable bequests, deductibility of, 565. *See also* Estate tax
Charitable deduction, gift tax, 544-545
Charitable lead trusts, 384
Charitable remainder trusts, 384
Charitable trusts, 384-388. *See also* Private trusts; Trusts
  beneficiaries, 371, 384-385
  charitable, defined, 385-386
  charitable lead trusts, 384
  charitable remainder trusts, 384
  cy pres, doctrine of, 387, 433
  donor standing, 388
  duration of, 386-387
  enforcement of, 386, 387-388
  equitable deviation, doctrine of, 387
  illegal, impossible, or impracticable means or purposes, 387
  modification of, 386-387

purposes
charitable, 385-386
illegal, impossible, or impracticable, 387
"special interest" in, standing of individuals with, 387
standing for enforcement of, 387-388
Children. *See also* Minor children
adopted. *See* Adoption and intestacy
emancipation, 77
intestacy and. *See* Intestacy
omitted from will, 183, 337-342
Civil law countries, limitation on testamentary freedom in, 2-3
Claflin doctrine, 428-432
Class gifts, 241, 266-267
antilapse, interplay with, 266
defined, 267
how created, 267
Clinton, Bill, 74
Codicils, 157-160
defined, 157-158
holographic, 158
partial revocation by inconsistency, 159
republication by codicil, 159
Collateral relatives, 49, 50. *See also* Intestacy
first line collaterals, 50
second line collaterals, 50
Colorado
intestacy under UPC provisions, 43
minor children, judicial appointment of guardian for, 227-231
partial revocation of will by physical act, 177-181
"Common disaster" provisions in wills, 250, 255-256
Community property, 324-329
commingling separate property with, 325, 328
contracting to change status of property, 324-325
gift tax, 548
moving from separate to community property jurisdiction and vice versa, 325
quasi-community property, 325
separate property, earnings from, 324
separate property vs., 324
states, 316, 324
Compensation
"just compensation" for takings, 13
of trustees, 359, 372-379, 495, 513-518, 534, 535
Confidentiality of information, 41, 42. *See also* Model Rules of Professional Conduct (MRPC); Professional responsibility
Conflicted transactions
attorneys, 41-42. *See also* Model Rules of Professional Conduct (MRPC); Professional responsibility
trustees, 494-497, 502, 509, 510. *See also* Duty of loyalty
Conflicts of interest. *See* Conflicted transactions
Consanguinity, table of, 49
Conservator, 359
Conservatorships, 21
Construction, rules of. *See* Rules of construction
Constructive trusts, 188, 344, 439-442
identifiable property, 440
inequitable conduct, 440
unjust enrichment, 440
Contract Clause, 9
Corporate merger, 281
Corporation as trustee, 372
Corpus of trust, 344
Credit shelter trusts, 207-210
Creditors' rights, 389, 403-424
attachment of trust beneficiary's interest, 404-405
discretionary standard, effect of, 404-406
family support claimants, 405, 406
fraudulent transfers and, 417-418, 418-423
government claims, 413, 414
necessities, suppliers of, 406
nonprobate transfers, collection against, 450
self-settled asset protection trusts, 416-424
settlor, claims against, 416-424
spendthrift provision, exceptions to, 414
spendthrift trusts, 392, 406-416
support standard, effect of, 406
tenants by the entirety, 458
tort creditors, 410-413
trustee abuse of discretion and, 405-406
Crummey power, 550-556, 581
Cy pres doctrine, 387, 433

D

Dead hand control, 3, 383, 571, 574
Dead Man's statutes, 288
Death
determination of, 18-20
planning for, 18, 20-23
presumptive declaration of, 19
"Death taxes," 539, 582

Deceased Spousal Unused Exclusion (DSUE) amount, 567-568, 570
Declaration of trust, 344, 353, 362, 369-370, 384, 494
Deed of gift, 346
Deed of trust, 344, 346, 353, 369-370, 384, 494
Defined-benefit pension plan, 476
Defined-contribution pension plan, 477
Definitions
- abatement, 279
- ademption, 269
- ambiguity, 291
- attest, 115
- bailment, 345
- charitable, 385-386
- class gift, 267
- codicil, 157-158
- direct skip, 575, 576
- disabled individual, 425
- disclaimer, 36
- executor, 14, 15
- governing instrument, 308, 484
- heirs, 14
- intestate estate, 43
- mutual fund, 510
- non-skip person, 575, 576
- personal representative, 14
- powers of appointment, 205, 206-211
- property not disposed of by will, 279
- property under UTC, 361
- self-settled, 425
- settlor, 2
- "signature" or "signed," 135
- skip person, 575-576
- spendthrift, 407
- tangible personal property, 200
- taxable gift, 539-541
- testator, 2
- value, 541

Degree of relationship, 50. *See also* Intestacy
Delaware
- beneficiary designation, 479, 480-483
- duty of loyalty, 503-510
- personal property memorandum referenced in will, 197-199, 200
- self-dealing by trustee, 503-510

Delivery of gift, 346
- actual, 346
- constructive, 346
- symbolic, 346

Demonstrative devises, 201, 268, 273
Dependent relative revocation (DRR), 183-186
Descendants' trust, 381
Descent and distribution, statutes of, 43. *See also* Intestacy
Destruction of will, 172-176
Devises
- classification of, 201-205, 268
- demonstrative, 201, 268, 273
- general, 201, 268
- residuary, 201, 268
- specific, 201, 268

Digital assets, 23-25
- accessing a decedent's electronic accounts, 23-24
- inheritability of, 2, 18

Diminished capacity, 85
Disabled beneficiaries
- disabled individual, defined, 425
- discretionary support trusts for, 392-401
- Medicaid eligibility, 424-427
- special needs trusts for, 424-427
  - self-settled special needs trusts, 425
  - third-party special needs trusts, 425-426

Disclaimers, 18, 36-40
- of assets, 36
- barred, 37
- defined, 36
- of fiduciary duties, 36
- ineffective, 37
- limited, 37
- power to disclaim, 37
- of powers of appointment, 36
- prohibited, 37
- qualified, 37
- relation-back doctrine, 36
- of survivorship rights, 36

Discretionary support trusts for disabled beneficiaries, 392-401
Dispensing power, 149
District of Columbia
- abbreviated probate procedure, 119
- attesting witness in, 116-118, 118-119
- execution of will, 116-118, 119
- notarization in, 118-119
- state-level estate tax, 539
- URPTODA enactment, 453

Diversification of investments, 510, 522-523, 525-530, 533
Double indemnity life insurance policies, 486
DRR. *See* Dependent relative revocation (DRR)
Dry trust, 361, 368-369, 429

DSUE. *See* Deceased Spousal Unused Exclusion (DSUE) amount
Due Process Clause, 9
Durable powers of attorney, 21, 22, 275
Duress, 97-98, 104-109. *See also* Testamentary intent
Duty of care, 380. *See also* Duty of prudence; Fiduciary duties
Duty of loyalty, 380, 494-512
  conflicted transactions, 494-497, 502, 509, 510
  "no further inquiry" rule, 495, 497, 502, 510
  self-dealing transactions, 494-495, 497
Duty of obedience, 380
Duty of prudence, 494, 502, 512-531
  investments. *See* Investments
  objective standards of prudence, 380
Dynasty trusts, 381, 383-384
  inter vivos, 579-580
  "last acting trustee" provision, 579-580
  powers of appointment, special, 581
  testamentary, 580-581

E

Education exclusion from gift tax, 546-547. *See also* Gift tax
Elective share, 9, 317-324
  amount of, 322
  calculation of, 322, 331
  charging spouse with gifts received, 319
  liability of others for balance of, 319
  right of, 318
  satisfaction of, 322, 323-324
  separate property states, 316
  sources from which payable, 323-324
"Elective share" statutes, 9, 315, 316, 317, 319, 320, 321, 331
Electronic communications, 24
Electronic Communications Privacy Act of 1986, 24
Emails, inheritability of, 2, 18. *See also* Digital assets
Employee Retirement Income Security Act of 1979. *See* ERISA
End-of-life decisions, 18
England
  family maintenance statute, 3
  fiduciary duties, enforcement of, 493
  Great Fire of London (1666), 114
  Great Plague of London (1665-1666), 114
  Inheritance (Provisions for Family and Dependents) Act (1975), 3
  Statute of Charitable Uses (1601), 385, 386
  Statute of Frauds (1677), 113-114
  Statute of Wills (1540), 113
  Wills Act (1937), 113, 447-448
Equitable conversion, doctrine of, 269
Equitable deviation, doctrine of, 387, 433
ERISA, 477-479, 485
Estate tax, 537, 560-574
  administrative expenses, deductibility of, 565
  annuities, 563
  application, 569-574
  bypass trusts, 570-571
  casualty losses, deductibility of, 565
  charitable bequests, deductibility of, 565
  computation of, 567-569
  constitutionality of, 9
  credit shelter trusts, 207-210
  Deceased Spousal Unused Exclusion (DSUE) amount, 567-568, 570
  deductible items, 565-567
  exclusion amount, 567-568, 570, 571
  fair market value of property, 561
  fundamentals, 560-569
  gross estate, 561-567
  includable items, 561-564
  indebtedness, deductibility of, 565
  jointly owned property, 563
  life insurance proceeds, 564
  marital bequests, deductibility of, 565-567
  marital deduction, 565-567
  marital deduction property, 564
  marital deduction trusts, 207-210
  minors' trust, 573-574
  powers of appointment
    general, 563-564, 566
    special, 563, 564
  preparation of return, 567-569
  QTIP election, 566-567
  QTIP trusts, 570, 571-573
  Release and Refunding Bond, 568
  retained life estates, transfers with, 562
  revocable transfers, 562-563
  state death taxes paid, deductibility of, 567
  support trusts, 392
  terminable interests, 565-566
  theft losses, deductibility of, 565
  transfers taking effect at death, 562
  transfers within three years of death, 561-562
Exculpatory clauses, 236, 240, 535-536
Execution of wills, 115

Executor
  defined, 14, 15
  priority list for selection of, 16
  refusal to serve, 16
Exemption trust, 381
Exoneration doctrine, 232-236
Extrinsic evidence
  ambiguity, resolution of, 288, 290, 291-298
  integration, doctrine of, 192
  testamentary intent, 140
  wills, 286

F
Facebook, decedent's electronic accounts on, 23, 24. *See also* Digital assets; Social media accounts
Family allowance, 330
Family protection, 315-330
  accidental omission, protection against, 330-342. *See also* Omission
  additional protections, 329-330
  community property. *See* Community property
  elective share. *See* Elective share
  family allowance, 330
  homestead allowance, 330
  separate property. *See* Elective share
  tangible property set-aside, 330
  UPC (1969), 317-320
  UPC (1990), 320-324
Family status, changes in, 307-315
Federal Aviation Administration, 352
Fiduciaries, appointment of, 215-219
Fiduciary duties, 380-381, 391, 404, 493-536
  administration of trust, 494
  care, duty of. *See* Duty of prudence
  diversification of trust assets. *See* Diversification of investments
  enforcement of, 493-494
  exculpatory clauses, 535-536
  impartiality, 531-533
  inform, duty to, 533-535
  loyalty, duty of. *See* Duty of loyalty
  prudence, duty of. *See* Duty of prudence
  remedies for breach, 535-536
  report, duty to, 533-535
  subsidiary duties, 531-535
Fifth Amendment, 13
First line collaterals, 50. *See also* Intestacy
Florida
  children omitted from will, 339-341
  circuit court's handling of probate matters, 14
  devises, 201-205
  half-blood, inheritance by, 65
  holographic wills not recognized, 185, 203
  joint tenancy in tangible personal property, 456-458
  lapse, 260-261
  no contest clauses, 221
  personal property memorandum referenced in will, 197-199, 200
  remains of deceased, disposition of, 27-29
  republication by codicil, 159
  suspicious circumstances, 100
  tenancy in common, 452
  trustees' fees, 373-379
Form 706, 568, 571, 578
Form 706-GS(D), 578
Form 706-GS(D-1), 578
Form 706-GS(T), 578
Form 709 (U.S. Gift (and Generation-Skipping Transfer) Tax), 548
Fourteenth Amendment, 9
France, limitation on testamentary freedom in, 2-3
Franklin, Benjamin, 1, 356, 384
Fraud
  in conveyancing. *See* Fraudulent transfer doctrine
  in execution, 110
  in inducement, 110
  in will transfers, 97-98, 110-111
Fraudulent transfer doctrine, 417-418, 418-423
Freedom of disposition. *See* Testamentary freedom
Future interests, gift of, 347, 545, 546

G
Generation-skipping transfer (GST) tax, 537, 574-582
  administrative requirements, 578
  applicable rate, 577-579
  application of, 579-582
  avoidance of, 579-582
  computation of, 576-579
  determination of taxable event, 575-576
  direct skip, 575, 576, 578
  exclusion from tax base, 576, 577
  exemption, 571, 577, 579, 580
  fundamentals, 575-579
  gift splitting, 577
  grandchildren trusts with general power of appointment, 581-582
  historical background, 574-575
  inclusion ratio, 577, 578
  inter vivos dynasty trusts and, 579-580

non-skip person, 575, 576
portability of exemption between spouses, 571
predeceased parent rule, 576
reverse QTIP election, 577-578
skip person, 575-576
taxable amount, 576-577
taxable distribution, 575, 576, 577
taxable termination, 575, 576, 577
testamentary dynasty trusts and, 580-581

Georgia
powers of appointment, 212-214
written trust requirement, 370

Germany, limitation on testamentary freedom in, 2-3

Gift splitting, 545, 548, 555, 577

Gift tax, 537, 539-560
annual exclusion, 545-546
"annual exclusion amount," 545
"applicable exclusion amount," 547
charitable deduction, 544-545
community property states, 548
computation of, 547-549
deductions and exclusions, 542-547
donative intent, 539
education exclusion, 546-547
estate tax computation vs., 548
filing requirements, 548
future interests, gifts of, 545
general power of appointment and, 540
"gift-splitting," 545, 548, 555
history of, 538
marital deduction, 542-544
medical exclusion, 546-547
minor children, gifts to, 545
rate, 547
"taxable gift," defined, 539-541
trusts used to reduce tax liability, 549-560
Crummey trust, 550-556
Grantor Retained Annuity Trust, 556-559, 560, 596-602
life insurance trust, 555-556, 583-595
Qualified Personal Residence Trust, 559-560, 603-613
valuation of gift, 541-542
value, defined, 541

Gifts, 345-346
acceptance, 346
aircraft, 352
automobiles, 352
boats, 352
constructive delivery, 346
deed of gift, 346
delivery, 346
donative intent, 346
future interests, 347
lifetime gifts, outright or in trust, 355
real property, 346
registration certificates and, 352
symbolic delivery, 346
tangible personal property, 346, 348-352
tax on. *See* Gift tax

Google, decedent's electronic account on, 23, 24. *See also* Digital assets

Grandchildren trusts with general power of appointment, 581-582

Grantor Retained Annuity Trust (GRAT), 556-559, 560
sample GRAT, 596-602

Grantor Retained Income Trust (GRIT), 556-557, 559

Grantor Retained Unitrust (GRUT), 557, 558, 559

Grantor trust, 343
sample QPRT with subsequent grantor trust, 603-613

GST tax. *See* Generation-skipping transfer (GST) tax

Guardian, 359

Guardian ad litem, 359

Guardian for minor children, 226-232
appointment of, 226-227
conditions for appointment, 227
judicial appointment, 227
objection by minor or others to appointment, 227

H

Half-blood
intestacy and, 65-70
kindred of, 66

Harmless error, 149-156. *See also* Will formalities

Hawaii, intestacy in, 43

Hearsay, 288

Heir hunting, 54

Heirs, 43, 287. *See also* Intestacy
ancestors, 49
collateral relatives, 49, 50
defined, 14
descendants, 49
exclusion of intestate heirs, 236-240
heir hunting, 54
laughing, 53-54
surviving spouse, 49, 50-51

Heirs apparent, 48, 287
HEMS (health, education, maintenance, and support) standard, 392, 415, 556, 563, 564, 571, 572. *See also* Private trusts; Trusts
Holographic codicils, 158
Holographic wills, 82, 91-92, 138-146
  authentication, 138
  extrinsic evidence to establish testamentary intent, 140
  preprinted forms, 139
  typewritten language in, 138-140
  validity of, 115
Homestead allowance, 330
Honorary trusts, 344, 444-446
  animal, trust for care of, 446
  definite beneficiary requirement and, 445
  noncharitable, indefinite or general purposes, trusts for, 445
  pet trusts, 446

I

Idaho
  community property, 324
  intestacy under UPC provisions, 43
Impartiality, 531-533. *See also* Fiduciary duties
Implied trusts, 344, 435-446
  constructive trusts, 344, 439-442
  honorary trusts, 344, 444-446
  resulting trusts, 344, 435-439, 439-440
  secret trusts, 442-444
  semi-secret trusts, 442-444
In terrorem clause, 220-226
Incapacity, planning for, 18, 20-23
  advance directives, 20-21
  conservatorships, 21
  durable powers of attorney, 21, 22
  sexual advance directives, 21
  trusts, 21, 22. *See also* Private trusts; Trusts
Incorporation by reference, 137, 192-196
Independent significance, doctrine of, 136-138
Indian Land Consolidation Act, 10-13
Indiana
  ambiguity in inter vivos trust, 292-297
  no contest clauses, 221
Individual retirement accounts (IRAs), 16, 477
Inform and report, duty to, 533-535. *See also* Fiduciary duties
"Inheritance" taxes vs. federal transfer taxes, 539. *See also* Taxation
Insane delusion, 92, 93-97
Intangible personal property
  joint tenancy in, 454-455, 461-469
  stock certificates, 200
Integration, 191-192, 193
Interested witnesses, 122-123
Internal Revenue Code, 37, 385, 477. *See also* Table of Authorities
Interpretation, rules of. *See* Rules of construction
Intestacy, 43-76
  adoption, 70-75
  adult adoption, 71
  advancements, effect of, 75-76
  blended families, 51
  consanguinity, table of, 49
  default rules, 48
  disadvantages of dying intestate, 45-46
  divorce proceeding, effect of, 50
  expectancy, 48
  familial relationships, 49
  former spouse and, 50
  half-blood, 65-70
  heirs. *See* Heirs
  high rate of, 44-45
  laughing heirs, 53-54
  lifetime gifts, effect of, 75-76
  modes of distribution, 55-59
  no taker, 55
  nontraditional families, 46
  parent-child relationship, effect of, 71-72
  partial, 33
  per capita at each generation, 56, 59-60, 63, 64, 65
  per stirpes
    English ("strict"), 56, 57-58, 62-63
    modern (per capita with representation), 56, 58-59, 63
  personal property, 43
  priority in, 50, 53
  real property in another state, 43
  representation, 55-59
  shares, 48-55
  simultaneous death, 55
  spouse, share of, 50-51
  state, intestate estate passing to, 55
  statutes, 43
  survival requirement, 55
  table of consanguinity, 49
  takers, 48-55
  widespread, 44-45
Investments
  diversification, 510, 522-523, 525-530, 533
  fixed income investment, 522
  "legal lists," 521
  Modern Portfolio Theory, 522, 533
  portfolio asset management, 522

Prudent Investor Rule, 522-525, 533
selection of, 521, 533
specific risk, 527
systematic risk, 527
Involuntary manslaughter, 31
Iowa
ademption by satisfaction, 276-279
inheritance taxes, 539
IRAs. *See* Individual retirement accounts (IRAs)
Italy, limitation on testamentary freedom in, 2-3

J
Joint representation, 41. *See also* Model Rules of Professional Conduct (MRPC); Professional responsibility
Joint tenancies, 17, 449, 452-469
in intangible personal property, 454-455, 461-469
multiple-party accounts, 461-469
in real property, 452-454
in tangible personal property, 454-460
unities, 452
with rights of survivorship, 16-17
Jurisdiction, probate, 16
Jus accrescendi, 452
Just compensation, 13. *See also* Takings
"Just debts," payment of, 232-236

K
Kentucky, inheritance taxes in, 539

L
Lapse, 241, 242-249
"Last acting trustee" provision, 579-580
Last will and testament, 187
Latent ambiguity, 288-289, 290-291
extrinsic evidence and, 288-289, 290-291
mistake vs., 304
Laughing heirs, 53-54
Letters of administration, 15
Letters testamentary, 15, 217
Life insurance, 16, 17, 450, 485-491
accidental death benefits and, 486-491
beneficiary designation, 480-483
double indemnity policies, 486
estate tax and, 564
Life insurance trust, 555-556
sample trust, 583-595
Lincoln, Abraham, intestacy of, 48
Lost wills, 155, 172-176
presumption of revocation and, 172-176
probating a lost will, 155
reliable duplicate copy, 172
Louisiana
community property law, 324, 478
LaLaurie Mansion in New Orleans, 415
Lucid intervals, 89-93. *See also* Testamentary capacity

M
Maine, intestacy in, 43
Malpractice liability, 40-41. *See also* Professional responsibility
Marital bequests, deductibility of, 565-567. *See also* Estate tax
Marital deduction
estate tax, 565-567
gift tax, 542-544
marital deduction property, 564
"qualified" terminable interest property, 543-544
terminable interest, gift of, 543-544
Marital deduction trusts, 207-210
Marriage
community property states, 316
partnership theory of, 315, 316, 320-321, 324, 542
same-sex, 46
separate property states, 315-316
support theory of, 315, 321
Maryland, inheritance taxes in, 539
Massachusetts
Claflin doctrine, 428-432
duty of prudence, 513-520
intestacy under UPC provisions, 43
Medicaid eligibility, 37, 424-427. *See also* Disabled beneficiaries
Medical exclusion, 546-547. *See also* Gift tax
Merger doctrine, 344
Michigan
intestacy under UPC provisions, 43
simultaneous death, 252-255
undue influence, 100-103
Minnesota, intestacy in, 43
Minor children
gifts to, 545
guardian for. *See* Guardian for minor children
transfers to. *See* Uniform Transfers to Minors Act
trusts for. *See* Minors' trusts
Minority trusts. *See* Minors' trusts
Minors' trusts, 381-382, 390, 573-574
sample testamentary trust, 614-615
staggered age distributions, 573

Mississippi, attesting witnesses in, 126-133
Missouri
half-blood, inheritance by, 65, 66-69
Kingsbury Place in St. Louis, 5
testamentary freedom, 5, 6-9
Mistakes, 242, 287, 298-305
correction of, 299-304, 433
latent ambiguity vs., 304
probable intent, doctrine of, 304-305
reformation to correct, 299-305
scrivener's error, 287
by testator, 287
Model Rules of Professional Conduct (MRCP)
confidentiality of information, 41
conflict of interest, current clients, 41-42
diminished capacity of client, 85
Rule 1.6, 41
Rule 1.7, 41-42
Rule 1.14(b), 85
Rule 1.15, 497
Rule 1.15(a), 136
safeguarding of client property, 136
testamentary capacity, lack of, 85
Modern Portfolio Theory, 522, 533. *See also* Investments
Modification and termination of trust, 427-435
beneficiary, request of, 427-428
Claflin doctrine, 428-432
combination and division of trusts, 433
by consent, 432
cy pres, 387, 433
equitable deviation, doctrine of, 433
inability to administer trust effectively, 433
material purposes of trust, 428
mistakes, correction of, 433
reformation to correct mistakes, 433
by settlor, 427
tax objectives, 433
unanticipated circumstances, 433
uneconomic trusts, 433
Montana
intestacy under UPC provisions, 43
trust property requirement, 362-368
Mortgage on property, 232-236
MRPC. *See* Model Rules of Professional Conduct (MRPC)
Multiple-party accounts, 461-469
Mutual fund, defined, 510

N

National Conference of Commissioners on Uniform State Laws, 14. *See also* Uniform Law Commission
Natural objects of one's bounty, 83
Nebraska
inheritance taxes, 539
intestacy under UPC provisions, 43
POD accounts, 470-475
powers of appointment, 207-210
Negative wills, 236-240
Negligent homicide, 31. *See also* Slayer rule
Nemo est haeres viventis, 48
Nevada
children omitted from will, 337
community property, 324
New Hampshire
children omitted from will, 337
spendthrift interest, attachment of, 410-412
New Jersey
duty of loyalty, 497-501
harmless error rule, 150-155, 155-156
holographic wills, 185
inheritance taxes, 539
intestacy under UPC provisions, 43
lucid interval, 89-90
misappropriation of client funds from trust account, 497-501
notarized wills, 151
probable intent, doctrine of, 304-305
strict compliance, 148
substantial compliance, 148
written trust requirement, 353, 370
New Mexico
ascertainable beneficiaries, 371
community property, 324
intestacy under UPC provisions, 43
revocation of will, 162-170
revocation-on-divorce statute, 308-315
spouse omitted from will, 332-335
strict compliance, 170-171
New York
antilapse statute, 262-263
death taxes, 567
debts of decedent, 232
duress, 105-109
elective share statute, 9, 317
fiduciaries of trusts for disabled beneficiaries, 392-401
insane delusion, 94-97
lapse, 264
lucid interval, 90
Mt. Zion Cemetery in Brooklyn, 26
prudent investor rule, 525-530
reformation doctrine, 300-303
republication by codicil, 159
spendthrift interest, attachment of, 410

spendthrift protection, 410
strict compliance, 149
subscription, 116
Surrogate's Court as probate court, 300
testamentary capacity, 85, 97
trust, creation of, 357-358
undue influence, 105-109
written trust requirement, 353, 370
New Zealand, family maintenance statute in, 3
No contest clause, 220-226
"No extrinsic evidence" rule, 287
"No further inquiry" rule, 495, 497, 502, 510
No reformation rule, 287
Nonclaim statutes, 16
Nonprobate property, 16-18. *See also* Nonprobate transfers
Nonprobate transfers, 13, 16-18, 447-492
antilapse, 260
beneficiary designation, 478, 479, 480-483
joint tenancies. *See* Joint tenancies
life insurance. *See* Life insurance
pension plans. *See* Pension plans
POD accounts. *See* Payable-on-death (POD) accounts
"poor person's will," 17
probate, avoidance of, 17-18
retirement accounts, 16, 17, 476-485
strict compliance, 475
substantial compliance, 475
"superwills," 491-492
transfer-on-death deed, 17
"Non-trusts," 435-446
No-residue-of-a-residue rule, 201, 243, 247, 264
North Dakota
intestacy under UPC provisions, 43
lost will, 172-175
support trust, 426
Notarization, 115
Nuncupative will, 115

O
Ohio, testamentary intent in, 80-81
Omission
accidental, 330-342
child omitted, 183, 337-342
spouse omitted, 183, 331-337
Oral trusts, 353, 369-370
Oral wills, 115
Orphans' court, 14

P
Parens patriae, 388
Partnership theory of marriage, 315, 316, 320-321, 324, 542
Patent ambiguity, 288, 289
Payable-on-death (POD) accounts, 17, 470-476
creation of, 447, 470
death beneficiary, designation of, 450
multiple-party accounts, 461, 468
as will substitute, 448
Pennsylvania
ademption by extinction, identity theory of, 270-273
death taxes, 567
designated beneficiary, pension plan, 485
elective share statute, 317
inheritance taxes, 539
personal representative powers, 219-220
testamentary capacity, 86-88
Pension plans, 16, 17, 476-485
beneficiary designation, 478, 479, 485
conflict between ERISA and state law, 478-479
defined-benefit, 476
defined-contribution, 477
discrepancy between will and beneficiary designation, 478
ERISA, 477-479, 485
private sector plans, 485
state or local government plans, 485
survivor benefits, 477
Per capita at each generation, 56, 59-60, 63, 64, 65
Per stirpes
English ("strict"), 56, 57-58, 62-63
modern (per capita with representation), 56, 58-59, 63
Perpetual trusts, 381, 383-384
Personal property
intangible personal property, 200
intestacy, 43
meaning of, 200, 297
tangible personal property, defined, 200
Personal representative
administrator cum testament annexo, 357
administrator for intestate estates, 14, 15, 16
appointment of, 14
bond, 220
defined, 14
executor for estates with will, 14, 15, 16
fiduciary duties of. *See* Fiduciary duties
powers, 219-220
primary duties, 16
Pet trusts, 381, 446

Plain meaning rule, 287
POD. *See* Payable-on-death (POD) accounts
"Poor person's will," 17
Portfolio asset management, 522
Pour-over will, 293, 368-369, 450-452
Powers of appointment, 353
  appointee, 206
  broad in scope, 541
  definitions, 205, 206-211
  disclaimer of, 36
  donee, 206
  donor, 206
  exercise of, 211-214
  general, 206, 211, 563-564, 566
    sample, 540
  limited in scope to donee's issue, 540-541
  nongeneral, 206-207
  objects, 206
  permissible appointees, 206
  residuary clauses, effect of, 211-212
  special, 206-207, 211, 563, 564, 581
    samples, 540-541
  specific reference requirement, 211
  takers in default, 206
  trustee's discretionary power vs., 391
Precatory language, 355-356
Preemption, 422, 477-479
Prerogative court, 14
Pretermitted share, 183
Pretermitted spouses or children. *See* Omission
"Private place," 5, 6-8
Private trusts, 352-384
  alienation of trust interest, 390, 391
  appointment of trustee, 358
  ascertainable beneficiaries, 360, 371
  assignment of trust interest, 390
  attestation not required, 370
  beach-bum trusts, 382
  beneficiaries, 370-371, 389-403
  business trusts, 381
  capacity of settlor, 354-360
  corpus, 361. *See also* Trust property
  creation of, 355
  creditors, rights of. *See* Creditors' rights
  declarations of trust. *See* Declarations of trust
  deeds of trust. *See* Deeds of trust
  descendants' trust, 381
  disabled beneficiaries. *See* Disabled beneficiaries
  discretionary standard, effect of, 392-401, 404-406
  discretionary trust interest, 390-391
  distributions, 389-403
  dry trust, 361, 368
  dynasty trusts, 381, 383-384
  elements of, 352-381
    required elements, 353-354
  exemption trust, 381
  express trust, types of, 352. *See also* Charitable trusts; Private trusts
  fiduciary duties of trustees, 355
  HEMS standard. *See* HEMS (health, education, maintenance, and support) standard
  intent of settlor, 354-360
  inter vivos, 382
  irrevocable, 382-383
  mandatory trust interest, 390
  material trust purposes, 428
  methods of creating, 352-353
  minor as trust beneficiary, 390
  minority trusts. *See* Minors' trusts
  modification of, 427-435. *See also* Modification and termination of trust
  oral, 353, 369-370
  perpetual, 381, 383-384
  pet, 381
  precatory language, 355-356
  purposes, lawful, 381-382
  requirements for creation, 353-354
  res, 361. *See also* Trust property
  revocable, 382-383
  self-settled asset protection trusts, 416-424
  special needs trusts, 382, 424-427
  spendthrift trusts, 381, 392, 406-416
  spray trust, 391
  sprinkle trust, 390-391
  support standard, effect of, 406
  support trust interests, 391-392
  termination of, 427-435. *See also* Modification and termination of trust
  testamentary, 381, 382
  testamentary "marital trust," 381
  transfer of trust interest, 390
  trust property. *See* Trust property
  trustees. *See* Trustees
  types of, 381-384
Privilege, attorney-client, 288
Probate, 14-16
  ancillary administration, 16
  avoidance of, 17-18
  creditor claims, 16
  domiciliary jurisdiction, 16
  formal, 15

informal, 15
intestacies, 15
inventory, 16
jurisdiction, 16
letters of administration, 15
letters testamentary, 15, 217
nonclaim statutes, 16
primary jurisdiction, 16
probate estate, 15
testacies, 15
will contests, 15
Probate courts, 14
Probate judges, 14
Probate property, 16-18
Procrustean standard, 286
Professional responsibility, 40-42. *See also* Model Rules of Professional Conduct (MRPC)
confidentiality of information, 41
conflicts of interest, 41-42
joint representation, 41
malpractice liability, 40-41
Prudence. *See* Duty of prudence
Prudent Investor Rule, 522-525, 533
"Purging" statutes, 122-123

Q

QPRT. *See* Qualified Personal Residence Trust (QPRT)
QTIP. *See* Qualified terminable interest property (QTIP)
Qualified Personal Residence Trust (QPRT), 559-560
sample QPRT with subsequent grantor trust, 603-613
Qualified terminable interest property (QTIP), 543-544
QTIP election, 566-567
QTIP trusts, 570, 571-573
model terms, 572
Quantum meruit, 188
Quasi-community property, 325

R

Reagan, Ronald, 84
Real property
in another state, 43
gift of, 346
intestacy, 43
joint tenancy in, 452-454
Receipts, character of, 532-533
Reciprocal wills, 189, 437
Reformation to correct mistake, 299-305
Relation-back doctrine, 36
Release and Refunding Bond, 568
Remains
disposition of, 18, 25-30
disputes over, 26-30
Renunciation, 36. *See also* Disclaimers
Report, duty to, 533-535. *See also* Fiduciary duties
Republication by codicil, 158, 159, 195
Residuary clause, 304, 450, 483-484
abatement, 279
ambiguities, 288, 289, 291
antilapse, 257, 264-265
class gifts, 266
common law rules of construction, 287
discrepancies between dispositive provisions and probate estate, 271, 273, 274, 276-278, 279, 280, 281
lapse and, 244-249
mistakes, 300-303
negative wills, 239
pour-over wills, 450
power of appointment, exercise of, 211-212, 214
property not disposed of by will, 279
survive, failure to, 244-249
Resignation of trustee, 372
Restatement (Third) of Property: Wills & Other Donative Transfers
ademption, 270
ambiguity
defined, 291
resolution of, in accordance with donor's intention, 292
burden of proof, 85
change-in-form principle, 274
class gifts, 266-267
creation of, 267
defined, 267
common law principles, 344
confidential relationships, 99
dependent relative revocation, 183-184
devises, classification of, 268
dominant-subservient relationship, 99
donative intent, 345, 539
vs. donative motive, 345
donative transfer, 98
duress, 97-98, 104
evidence that may be considered, 286, 288
expectancies, 361
extrinsic evidence, 286, 288
failure of specific devises by extinction, 270
fiduciary relationship, 99

Restatement (Third) of Property (*contd.*)
fraud, 97-98, 110
general power of appointment, 206
gifts of property, requirements for, 346
holographic wills, 138
ineffective revocation, 184
insane delusion, 94
integration of multiple pages or writings into single will, 191
intent theory, 269-270
inter vivos gift by testator to devisee, 276
law reform project, 14
lucid interval, 90
mental capacity
to create trust, 355
to make will, 82
to revoke will, 157
negative wills, 237
nonexistent property interests, 361
"personal usage" exception, 290
post-execution events affecting wills, 276
pour-over devises, 369, 450
power of appointment
defined, 205
requisites for exercise of, 212
probate estate, 15
reformation
limitations on scope of, 484-485
mistakes, correction in donative documents, 299
reliant relationship, 99
republication by codicil, 159
revocation of will, 157
capacity requirement for, 157
ineffective, 184
securities, devise of specific number of, 282
settlor's intent to create trust, 357
stock dividends, effect of, 282
stock splits, effect of, 282
survivorship requirement, 242
suspicious circumstances, 99
undue influence, 97-98, 99, 100
Restatement (Third) of Restitution and Unjust Enrichment
constructive trust, 440, 443
secret and semi-secret trusts, 443
slayer rule, 30
Restatement (Third) of Trusts
any property may be trust property, 361
ascertainable beneficiary, 371
beneficiaries, 371
capacity of settlor to create trust, 355
common law principles, 344
discretionary interests, enforcement and construction of, 391
honorary trusts, 445
impartiality, duty of, 532
income productivity, 532
intention to create trust, 355, 357
law reform project, 14
loyalty, duty of, 496
noncharitable purposes, trusts for, 445
oral inter vivos trusts, validity of, 369
pour-over dispositions by will, 369
prudence, duty of, 512
secret trusts, 444
testamentary trusts, creation of, 382
trust property, 361
Resulting trusts, 344, 435-439, 439-440
Retirement accounts, 16, 17, 476-485
Revenue Act of 1916, 560
Revised Uniform Fiduciary Access to Digital Assets Act (RUFADAA)
consent to allowing access to electronic accounts, 25
transmission of digital assets, 25
user direction for disclosure of digital assets, 24
Revival of revoked will, 185, 186-188
Revocable trusts
pour-over will and, 450-452
as will substitutes, 450-452
Revocation of will, 156-188
cancellation, act of, 176
dependent relative revocation, 183-186
express revocation clause, 160
implied revocation, 160-161
ineffective revocation, doctrine of, 183-186
lost wills. *See* Lost wills
mistaken belief, due to, 184
by operation of law, 181-183
partial revocation by physical act, 176-181
by physical act, 162-172
revival of revoked will, 186-188
by subsequent writing, 160-162
Rhode Island, multiple-party accounts in, 461, 462-468
Rule Against Perpetuities, 3, 343, 371, 381, 383, 384, 386-387, 445, 446, 574, 575, 579
Rules of construction, 286, 287
evidentiary rules from civil litigation, 288
extrinsic evidence, consideration of, 286, 287, 288
"no extrinsic evidence" rule, 287
no reformation rule, 287
plain meaning rule, 287

S

SCA. *See* Stored Communications Act (SCA)
Schiavo litigation, 19
Scrivener's error, 287, 300
Second line collaterals, 50. *See also* Intestacy
Secret trusts, 442-444
Securities, devise of
  corporate merger, 281
  stock dividend, 281
  stock split, 281
  subsidiary spinoff, 281
Self-dealing transactions, 494-495, 497. *See also* Duty of loyalty
Self-proving affidavits, 123-136
Self-settled asset protection trusts, 416-424
Self-settled special needs trusts, 425
Semi-secret trusts, 442-444
Separate property states, 315-316
  community vs. separate property, 324
  spouse, protection of. *See* Elective share
Settlor, 343
  defined, 2
  express trusts, 344
Sexual advance directives, 21
Signature requirements for wills, 81, 97, 115-116, 119, 120, 123, 159
  attesting witnesses, 122-123
  definition of "signature" or "signed," 135
  disabled testator, 120
Simultaneous death, 55, 249-256
Simultaneous Death Act, 250, 255
Simultaneous presence requirement, 116, 146-147
Slayer rule, 18, 30-36
  civil liability in wrongful death action, 31
  felonious and intentional killing, 31
  indirect beneficiaries, 31
  involuntary manslaughter, 31
  negligent homicide, 31
  voluntary manslaughter, 35
Social media accounts
  accessing a decedent's electronic accounts, 23-24, 25
  inheritability of, 2, 18
  "lawful consent" to disclosure of electronic communications, 24
Sources of law, 13
South Carolina
  accession, 282-284
  elective share statute, 320
  intestacy under UPC provisions, 43
  securities, devise of, 282-284
South Dakota
  express trust, 344
  intestacy under UPC provisions, 43
Special needs trusts, 382, 424-427
Specific risk, 527. *See also* Investments
Spendthrift, defined, 407
Spendthrift trusts, 381, 392, 406-416
  self-settled. *See* Self-settled asset protection trusts
Split interest trusts, 384
Spouse omitted from will, 183, 331-337
Spray trust, 391
Sprinkle trust, 390-391
Stale wills, 241, 267
Standing
  charitable trusts, enforcement of, 387-388
  will challenges, 79
Staple rule, 191-192, 193
State death taxes paid, deductibility of, 567. *See also* Estate tax
State law, testamentary freedom, 3-9
State probate courts, 14
Statute of Frauds, 113, 114, 115, 346, 353, 361, 442
Statutes of descent and distribution, 43. *See also* Intestacy
Statutory distribution. *See* Intestacy
Stock certificates, 200
Stock dividend, 281
Stock split, 281
Stored Communications Act (SCA), 24
Strict compliance, doctrine of
  ERISA, 485
  nonprobate transfers, 475
  will formalities, 114, 116, 119, 120, 122, 146, 149, 155, 159, 185, 287, 447-448
Subsidiary spinoff, 281
Substantial compliance, doctrine of, 146-148, 149, 475
Successor trustee, 372
Supernumerary, 123
"Superwills," 491-492
Support standard, effect of, 406
Support theory of marriage, 315, 321
Support trusts, 391-392
Surrogate's court, 14
Survival requirement, intestacy, 55
Survive, failure to. *See* Lapse
Surviving spouse
  antilapse rules, 257
  as executor, 215
  intestacy and, 49, 50-51
  protecting rights of, 3, 9, 77, 182. *See also* Elective share
  remarriage of, 189

Survivorship rights
  disclaimer of, 36
  words of survivorship, 259
Symbolic delivery, 346, 361
Systematic risk, 527. *See also* Investments

T
Takings, 10-13
  just compensation for, 13
Takings Clause, 13
Tangible personal property (TPP)
  defined, 200
  gift of, 346, 348-352
  joint tenancy in, 454-460
  set-aside, 330
  unattested separate writing, 196-200
Taxation, 537-582
  basics, 538-539
  contracts concerning succession, 189
  "death taxes," 539, 582
  estate tax. *See* Estate tax
  gift tax. *See* Gift tax
  GST tax. *See* Generation-skipping transfer (GST) tax
  "inheritance" taxes vs. federal transfer taxes, 539
  unification of gift and estate taxes, 538
  unified credit, 538
Tenants by the entirety, 17
  creditor rights, 458
  death of one spouse, effect of, 459
Tennessee
  affidavits, 135
  definitions, 135
  execution of will, manner of, 135
  exoneration, applicability of doctrine of, 233-235
  just debts, payment of, 233-235
  strict compliance, 136
  witnesses to will, 135
Terminable interests, 565-566
Testamentary capacity
  diminished capacity, 85
  mental capacity, requirement of, 82-89
Testamentary dynasty trusts, 580-581
Testamentary freedom, 2-13, 240
  civil law countries compared, 2-3
  constitutional law, 9-13
  dead hand control, 3
  destruction of asset of estate, 5-9
  high rate of Americans without wills, 44-45
  lapse of, 44-45
  justifications for, 2
  public policy violations, 3
  state law, 3-9
Testamentary intent, 79-82
  donative, 79
  operative, 79
  protection of. *See* Wills
  substantive, 79-80
Testamentary "marital trust," 381
Testator, defined, 2
Texas
  community property, 324
  executor, selection of, 215
  family trust distributions as separate property, 325-328
  testamentary capacity, 85
  undue influence, 98
Text messages, inheritability of, 2. *See also* Digital assets
Theft losses, deductibility of, 565. *See also* Estate tax
Third-party special needs trusts, 425-426
TOD. *See* Transfer-on-death (TOD) deed
Tort creditors, 410-413. *See also* Creditors' rights
Transfer-on-death (TOD) deed, 17, 453
Transfer taxes. *See* Taxation
Transfers, nonprobate. *See* Nonprobate transfers
Trump, Donald, 582
Trust property, 361-369
  declaration of trust, 362
  delivery to trustee, 361-362
  dry inter vivos trust to be funded by pour-over will, 368-369
  ineffective inter vivos transfers, 362
  intangible personal property, 361
  personal property, delivery of, 361
  Statute of Frauds, property subject to, 361
  symbolic delivery, 361
Trustees, 343, 372-381
  abuse of discretion, 405-406
  appointment of, 358, 372
  breach of trust, 389-390
  compensation, 372-379
  corporation as, 372
  failure to distribute trust assets upon beneficiary's entitlement, 389-390
  fiduciary duties, 380-381, 391, 404. *See also* Fiduciary duties
  lack of, 372
  powers of, 379-380
  powers vs. duties, 380
  prudence, 380
  resignation of, 372

responsibilities of, 372
successor, 372
vacancy in position, 372
Trustor, 343
Trusts
beneficiaries, 344
bypass, 570-571
capricious purposes, 445
cestui que trust, 344, 370
charitable. *See* Charitable trusts
constructive. *See* Constructive trust
corpus, 344
Crummey trust, 550-556
declaration of trust, 344, 353, 362, 369-370, 384, 494
deed of trust, 344, 346, 353, 369-370, 384, 494
distributions, 389-446
donor, 343
dry trust, 361, 368-369, 429
elements required, 353-354
equitable title, 343
express, 344
types of, 352. *See also* Charitable trusts; Private trusts
fiduciary duties of trustees. *See* Fiduciary duties
formation and elements, 343-388
future interest (contingent) in remainder, 347
gift tax practice, 549-560
gifts distinguished, 345-352
grandchildren trusts with general power of appointment, 581-582
grantor, 343
Grantor Retained Annuity Trust, 556-559, 596-602
Grantor Retained Income Trust, 556-557, 559
Grantor Retained Unitrust, 557, 558, 559
GST tax. *See* Generation-skipping transfer (GST) tax
honorary, 344, 444-446
implied. *See* Implied trusts
incapacitated person and, 21, 22
income, interest in, 347
inter vivos, 344
dynasty trusts, 579-580
revocable trusts, 344
land, interests in, 13
legal title, 343
life insurance trust, 555-556, 583-595
merger doctrine, 344
methods of creating, 352-353
minors', 573-574, 614-615
non-charitable. *See* Private trusts
"non-trusts," 435-446
oral, 353
overview, 329
pet, 446
private. *See* Private trusts
purchase-money, 436
QTIP, 570, 571-573
Qualified Personal Residence Trust, 559-560, 603-613
remainder, contingent future interest in, 347
requirements for creation, 353-354
res, 344
resulting, 344, 435-439
revocable, 450-452
secret, 442-444
semi-secret, 442-444
settlor, 343
split interest trusts, 384
testamentary dynasty trusts, 580-581
transfer taxes. *See* Taxation
trustees. *See* Trustees
trustor, 343
uneconomic, 433
as will substitute, 329

U
u/d/t (under deed of trust), 362
Undue influence, 97-98, 98-104
Uneconomic trusts, 433
Unified credit, 538
Uniform Disposition of Community Property at Death Act, 325
Uniform Law Commission, 14, 24, 344, 535
Uniform Multiple-Person Accounts Act, 468, 470
Uniform Power of Attorney Act, 22
Uniform Principal and Income Act (UPIA), 532-533
Uniform Probate Code (UPC)
abatement, 279-280
accessions, 281-282
ademption by satisfaction, 276
adoptee and adoptee's adoptive parent or parents, parent-child relationship, 71
adoptee and adoptee's genetic parents, parent-child relationship, 71-72
advancements, 75
age to make a valid will, minimum, 77
annulment of marriage, effect of, 182-183, 308
antilapse provisions, 242-243, 257, 259-260

Uniform Probate Code (UPC) (*contd.*)
- attested will, procedural requirements for, 115
- augmented estate, 317-318, 318-319, 321, 322-323
- bonds, 220
- cause for removal, 216
- change in circumstances relevant to testator's estate, 181, 183
- charging spouse with gifts received, 319
- codicil, holographic, 158
- complete disposition of estate under instrument, 159, 162
- composition of augmented estate, 322-323
- contracts concerning succession, 188-189
- default survivorship rules, 243
- disclaim, power to, 37
- disclaimer barred or limited, 37
- dispositions in favor of relative of former spouse, 308
- distribution, 279-280
- divorce, effect of, 182-183, 308
- divorce, then remarriage, 307
- elective share of surviving spouse
  - amount, 322
  - liability of others for balance of, 319
  - partnership theory of marriage and, 316, 320-321
  - right of, 318
  - sources from which payable, 323-324
- events of independent significance, 137
- exclusionary clause, 236-237
- execution of will, 115
- executor, removal of, 219
- exoneration rule and, 236
- extrinsic evidence, 115, 140, 286
- failure of testamentary provision, 243
- family allowance, 330
- formalities, loosening of, 353
- future interests in trust, 260
- gestation, individual in, 251
- governing instrument, defined, 308, 484
- guardian, appointment of
  - judicial appointment, 227
  - objection by minor or others to parental appointment, 227, 231
  - parental appointment, 226-227
- harmless error rule, 120, 149, 170-171, 205, 299, 353, 475
- holographic codicils, 158
- holographic wills, 115
- homestead allowance, 330
- homicide, effect of, 30-31
- in terrorem clause, 221
- incorporation by reference, 192, 194-195
- intent theory, 269-270
- interested witness, 123
- intestacy, 341
  - intestate estate, defined, 43
  - no taker of intestate estate, 55
  - share of heirs other than surviving spouse, 52-53
  - share of surviving spouse, 50-51
- judicial appointment of guardian, 227
- just debts, payment of, 232, 236
- kindred of half-blood, 66
- lapse, 264
- law reform project, 14
- marital property portion of augmented estate, 322-323
- minimum age to make valid will, 77, 82
- minor children, guardian for, 231
- modern per stirpes, 58, 63
- multiple-party accounts
  - lifetime, ownership in, 469
  - rights on death of party, 468
- negative wills, 236-237
- no contest clause, 221
- no revocation by other changes in circumstances, 183
- no taker of intestate estate, 55
- nonademption of specific devises, 270
- nonexoneration, 232
- nonprobate transfers on death, 448
- notarization as alternative to witness attestation, 115, 118-119
- nuncupative wills, 115
- omitted children, 337, 338-339, 341
- operation of law, revocation by, 182-183
- order in which assets abated, 279-280
- parental appointment of guardian, 226-227
- parent-child relationship, effect of, 71-72
- partial revocation by physical act, 176
- partnership theory of marriage, 316
- penalty clause for contest, 221
- per capita at each generation, 59, 63, 65
- per stirpes, modern, 59, 63
- personal representatives, powers of, 220
- pour-over wills, 450
- premarital will, 331
- pretermitted child statute, 337, 338-339, 341
- real property transfer-on-death deed, 453
- reciprocal wills, 189
- reformation of governing instrument, 484
- reformation to correct mistakes, 299
- remarriage after divorce, 307
- revival if divorce nullified, 307

revival of revoked will, 187-188
revocation by writing or by act, 157
revocation of probate and nonprobate transfers by divorce, 182-183, 308
revocatory act, 162
revocatory intent, 162
securities, increase in, 281-282
self-proved will, 124-125
separate writing identifying tangible personal property, 196, 199, 200
separation, effect of, 308
slayer rule, 30-31
specific devise, sale or mortgage of, by conservator or agent under power of attorney, 275
spouse, entitlement of, 331
strict compliance and, 114
survival by 120 hours, requirement of, 251
survivorship rules, 242-243, 251
tangible property set-aside, 330
termination of appointment by removal, 216
testamentary intent or capacity, 97
Uniform Testamentary Additions to Trusts Act, 451
who may make will, 82
witness competency, 122
witnessed or notarized wills, 115

Uniform Prudent Investor Act (UPIA)
allocation of trust assets between income and principal, 533
diversification of trust assets, 529
Prudent Investor Rule, 522-525, 533

Uniform Real Property Transfer on Death Act (URPTODA), 453

Uniform Testamentary Additions to Trusts Act, 369, 450-451

Uniform Transfers to Minors Act (UTMA)
annual gift tax exclusion, 545, 546
gift tax–filing obligations, 549
grandchildren, gifts to, 581

Uniform Trust Code (UTC)
adoption of, 344
amendment of revocable trust, 383
animal, trust for care of, 446
assignee of beneficiary, rights of, 404
breaching trustee, personal liability of, 501
capacity of settlor of revocable trust, 354
charitable purposes, 386
creation of valid trust, requirements for, 352
creditor of beneficiary, rights of, 404
creditor's claims against settlor, 417
declaration of trust, 353
definitions, 361
discretionary trusts, effect of standard of distribution, 405-406
duty to administer trust, 494
duty to inform and report, 534-535
enforcement of charitable trust, 386
exceptions to spendthrift provision, 414
exculpation of trustee, 536
express trusts, 352
impartiality, 532
inability to administer trust effectively, 433
information and reporting, 534-535
law reform project, 14
lawful purposes, 381
loyalty, duty of, 496
methods for creating trust, 352, 353
modification of noncharitable irrevocable trust by consent, 432
modification of trust, 432, 433
"no further inquiry" rule, 495
notice requirements, 534-535
oral trust, evidence of, 369
pet trusts, 446
property, defined, 361
prudent administration, 512
Prudent Investor Rule, 522-525
remedies for breach of trust, 501, 535
requirements for creating trust, 354
revocation of revocable trust, 383
spendthrift provisions, 408, 414, 432
statutory law, as primary source of, 344
subsidiary duties, 531
termination of noncharitable irrevocable trust by consent, 432
termination of trust, 432, 433
trust purposes, 381
trustees, powers of 493
general powers of, 379-380
specific powers of, 380
unanticipated circumstances, 433
written instrument not required, 369

Uniform Trustees' Powers Act of 1964, 380
United States Virgin Islands, intestacy in, 43
UPC. *See* Uniform Probate Code (UPC)
UPIA. *See* Uniform Principal and Income Act (UPIA); Uniform Prudent Investor Act (UPIA)
URPTODA. *See* Uniform Real Property Transfer on Death Act (URPTODA)
Utah, intestacy in, 43
UTC. *See* Uniform Trust Code (UTC)
UTMA. *See* Uniform Transfers to Minors Act (UTMA)

V

Virginia
  holographic wills, 140-144
  simultaneous presence requirement, 146-147
Voluntary manslaughter, 35. *See also* Slayer rule

W

Washington
  breach of fiduciary duties of personal representative, 216-219
  community property, 324
  executor, removal of, 219
  fiduciaries, appointment of, 216-219
  superwill statute, 491-492
Wealth transfer taxation. *See* Taxation
Will formalities. *See* Wills Act formalities
Will substitutes, 293, 329, 447-452
  imperfect, 449
  POD accounts. *See* Payable-on-death (POD) accounts
  pure, 449
  revocable trusts as, 450-452
Wills
  abatement. *See* Abatement
  accession. *See* Accession
  accidental omission. *See* Omission
  ademption. *See* Ademption
  administrative provisions, 215-220
  age requirement, 77, 82
  ambiguities in. *See* Ambiguity
  amendments, 156-157
  antilapse, 257-265
  capacity. *See* Testamentary capacity
  class gifts. *See* Class gifts
  classification of devises. *See* Devises
  codicils. *See* Codicils
  "common disaster" provisions, 250, 255-256
  components and provisions of, 191-240
  contracts concerning testamentary succession, 188-189
  default rules, 241-305
  destruction of, 172
  discrepancies between dispositive provisions and probate estate, 267-285
  dispositive provisions, 201-240
  drafting principles, 241-305
  duress, 97-98, 104-109
  errors in. *See* Mistakes
  exclusionary clause, 236-240
  executor. *See* Personal representative
  explicit revocation clause, 344
  extrinsic evidence, 286
  failure to survive, 242-249
  family protection. *See* Family protection
  fiduciaries, appointment of. *See* Fiduciaries
  formalities. *See* Wills Act formalities
  fraud, 97-98, 110-111
  high rate of Americans without, 44-45
  holographic, 82, 91-92
  in terrorem clause, 220-226
  incorporation by reference, 192-196
  insane delusion, 92, 93-97
  integration, 191-192, 193
  intent. *See* Testamentary intent
  intestate heirs, right to exclude, 236-240
  "just debts," payment of, 232-236
  lapse, 241, 242-249
  last will and testament, 187
  lost. *See* Lost wills
  lucid intervals, 89-93
  mental capacity. *See* Testamentary capacity
  minor children, guardian for. *See* Guardian for minor children
  mistakes in. *See* Mistakes
  mortgage on property, 232-236
  natural objects of one's bounty, 83
  negative wills, 236-240
  no contest clause, 220-226
  no-residue-of-a-residue rule, 201, 247, 264
  nuncupative, 115
  oral, 115
  personal representative. *See* Personal representative
  pour-over, 293, 368-369, 450-452
  powers of appointment. *See* Powers of appointment
  property not disposed of by, defined, 279
  protective doctrines, 77-111
    external factors, 97-111
    internal factors, 79-97
  reciprocal, 189
  residuary clause. *See* Residuary clause
  revival of revoked will, 185, 186-188
  revocation. *See* Revocation of will
  rules of construction. *See* Rules of construction
  safeguarding the will, 136
  simultaneous death, 249-256
  stale wills, 241, 267
  standing for challenges to, 79
  staple rule, 191-192, 193
  substitutes. *See* Will substitutes
  survivorship, words of, 259
  tangible personal property, unattested separate writing, 196-200

testamentary capacity. *See* Testamentary capacity
testamentary intent, 79-82
transfer taxes. *See* Taxation
undue influence, 97-98, 98-104
Wills Act formalities, 113-189
attested wills, requirements for. *See* Attested wills
codicils, 157
curative doctrines, 146-156
dispensing power, 149
functions of, 114, 146
harmless error, 149-156
holographic wills. *See* Holographic wills
incorporation by reference and, 192
nonprobate transfers and, 447-448
oral expressions of intent, 443
origin of, 113
revocation of will, 160, 170, 171. *See also* Revocation of will
separate writing rule and, 196
strict compliance with, 114, 116, 119, 120, 122, 146, 149, 155, 159, 185, 287, 447-448
substantial compliance, 146-148, 149
vocabulary of, 115-116
Wisconsin, community property in, 324
Witnesses, attesting
competency of, 122-123
interested witnesses, 122-123
World War I, 560
Writing requirement. *See also* Statute of Frauds
trusts, 353, 370
wills, 115

Y

Yahoo!, decedent's electronic account on, 23, 24. *See also* Digital assets